RELATED TITLES FROM BROOKS/COLE

Psychology of Language (2nd ed.), Carroll

Learning and Behavior (3rd ed.), Chance

The Principles of Learning and Behavior (3rd ed.), Domjan & Burkhard, as revised by Domjan

A Primer of Learning, Domjan

Human Motivation (3rd ed.), Franken

Cognitive Psychology: In and Out of the Laboratory, Galotti

Experimenting with the Mind, Komatsu

Sniffy, the Virtual Rat, Version 4.5, Krames, Graham, and Alloway

Learning: Behavior and Cognition (2nd ed.), Lieberman

Learning and Memory, Lutz

Doing Psychology Experiments (4th ed.), Martin

Cognitive Psychology: A Neural-Network Approach, Martindale

Critical Thinking: A Functional Approach, Zechmeister and Johnson

COGNITION

Theory and Applications

Fourth Edition

Stephen K. Reed is currently professor of psychology and a member of the Center for Research in Mathematics and Science Education at San Diego State University. He has also taught at Florida Atlantic University (1980–1988) and at Case Western Reserve University (1971–1980).

After receiving his B.S. in psychology from the University of Wisconsin in 1966 and his Ph.D. in psychology from the University of California, Los Angeles, in 1970, Dr. Reed worked as an NIH postdoctoral fellow at the Laboratory of Experimental Psychology at the University of Sussex, Brighton, England.

His research on problem solving, carried out in part through grants from NIMH, the National Science Foundation, and the Air Force Office of Scientific Research, has been extensively published in numerous journals, including *Cognition and Instruction; Cognitive Psychology; The Journal of Experimental Psychology: Learning, Memory, and Cognition;* and *Memory and Cognition.* He is the author of numerous articles and books, including *Psychological Processes in Pattern Recognition* (Academic Press, 1973).

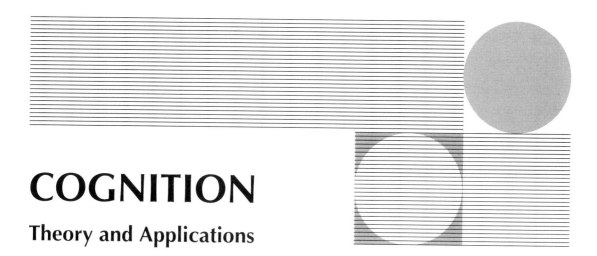

COGNITION

Theory and Applications

Fourth Edition

Stephen K. Reed

San Diego State University

Brooks/Cole Publishing Company

I(T)P™ An International Thomson Publishing Company

Pacific Grove • Albany • Bonn • Boston • Cincinnati • Detroit • London • Madrid • Melbourne
Mexico City • New York • Paris • San Francisco • Singapore • Tokyo • Toronto • Washington

Sponsoring Editor: *Marianne Taflinger*
Marketing Team: *Margaret Parks and Carolyn Crockett*
Editorial Assistant: *Laura Donahue*
Production Coordinator: *Fiorella Ljunggren*
Production: *Scratchgravel Publishing Services*
Manuscript Editor: *Betty Berenson*
Permissions Editor: *Lillian Campobasso*
Interior Design: *Anne Draus, Scratchgravel Publishing Services*

Cover Design: *Roy R. Neuhaus*
Cover Photo: *Courtesy of Marcus E. Raichle, M.D.,*
   Washington University School of Medicine
Interior Illustration: *Greg Draus, Cyndie C. H. Wooley, and*
   Judith L. Macdonald
Typesetting: *Scratchgravel Publishing Services*
Cover Printing: *Phoenix Color Corporation, Inc.*
Printing and Binding: *Quebecor Printing, Fairfield*

The ITP logo is a registered trademark under license.

For more information, contact:

BROOKS/COLE PUBLISHING COMPANY
511 Forest Lodge Road
Pacific Grove, CA 93950
USA

International Thomson Publishing Europe
Berkshire House 168-173
High Holborn
London WC1V 7AA
England

Thomas Nelson Australia
102 Dodds Street
South Melbourne, 3205
Victoria, Australia

Nelson Canada
1120 Birchmount Road
Scarborough, Ontario
Canada M1K 5G4

International Thomson Editores
Campos Eliseos 385, Piso 7
Col. Polanco
11560 México D. F. México

International Thomson Publishing GmbH
Königswinterer Strasse 418
53227 Bonn
Germany

International Thomson Publishing Asia
221 Henderson Road
#05-10 Henderson Building
Singapore 0315

International Thomson Publishing Japan
Hirakawacho Kyowa Building, 3F
2-2-1 Hirakawacho
Chiyoda-ku, Tokyo 102
Japan

Printed in the United States of America

10   9   8   7   6   5   4   3

Library of Congress Cataloging-in-Publication Data
Reed, Stephen K.
   Cognition : theory and applications / Stephen K. Reed. — 4th ed.
      p.   cm.
   Includes bibliographical references and indexes.
   ISBN 0-534-21954-3 (case-bound : alk. paper)
   1. Cognition.   2. Cognitive psychology.   I. Title.
BF311.R357   1996
153—dc20   95-15683
                                                CIP

To my parents,
Anita M. Reed and Kenneth D. Reed

Brief Contents

Contents

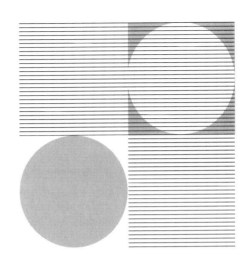

Preface

The most exciting development in the field of cognitive psychology is not a particular theory or experimental finding but a general trend. Cognitive psychologists have demonstrated an increasing interest in studying complex, real-world tasks and are making significant progress in understanding how people perform on these tasks. I hope that one result of this trend will be that undergraduates discover the direct relevance of cognitive psychology to many of their daily activities. A course about cognition should be useful not only to psychology students but also to those who have selected other fields of study.

In this book I have attempted to place a greater emphasis on the application of cognitive psychology than is typically found in an undergraduate text. The study of reading, for example, is discussed in the chapters on pattern recognition, attention, language, and text comprehension. Efficient learning strategies are major topics in the chapters on long-term memory and visual imagery. The chapter on expertise and creativity shows how the study of problem solving is currently being extended to include the kinds of problems students encounter in their courses. The chapter on language discusses how the implications of sentences influence legal testimony and advertising, and the chapter on decision making includes a section on applications to medicine and to emergency situations. In order to help students relate the study of cognition to popular articles they are likely to read, I have included many magazine and newspaper clippings on such contemporary topics as implanting false memories and determining the value of a human life in order to justify life-saving decisions.

The 14 chapters in the book cover a wide range of topics, and instructors should be able to expand on whatever topics interest them. The book is divided into three parts: Information-Processing Stages, Representation and Organization of Knowledge, and Complex Cognitive Skills. Part I consists of an introductory chapter followed by chapters on pattern recognition, attention, short-term memory, and long-term memory. The chapters describe what occurs during the different information-processing stages and how the stages interact. Part II contains chapters on levels of processing, visual images, categorization, and semantic organization. The first two chapters in this part describe qualitatively different memory codes, and the next two chapters discuss the organization of knowledge in long-term memory. Part III consists of chapters on language, comprehension and memory for text, problem solving, expertise and creativity, and decision making. The discussion of these complex cognitive skills is often related to ideas presented earlier in the book.

The organization of a book on cognition should reflect what we actually know about cognition. Research suggests that a hierarchy is a particularly effective way to organize knowledge (see Chapter 9). Recall is facilitated when information is partitioned into categories, which are further partitioned into smaller categories. Hierarchical organization seems to be particularly effective when the number of partitions varies from two to five. I deliberately selected such a structure for this book in the hope that the material would thereby be more accessible to students.

The fourth edition retains the same organization as the previous editions. I had two objectives in revising the book: I wanted to help the reader master the information more easily by putting key terms in bold type, by providing a glossary in the margins as well as an alphabetical glossary at the end of the book, and by adding discussion questions at the end of each chapter. Also, I wanted to report on some of the new research that had been done since the publication of the third edition.

Examples of new material include, in Part I, an expanded discussion of the relation of cognitive psychology to other fields including neuropsychology, neural network models, automatic encoding, working memory models, and very long-term retention. Part II, on the representation and organization of knowledge, now contains additional material on the distinctiveness of memory codes, mood-dependent memory, neuropsychological evidence relating imagery and perception, reinterpretation of images, the power of suggestion on the creation of false memories, effect of expertise on categorization, assumptions of schema theory, and autobiographical memory. Additions to Part III, on complex cognitive skills, include new material on vowel discrimination, speech errors, aphasia, individual differences in comprehension, local and global coherence in text, situation models for text, improving readability, transfer of problem representations, pragmatic reasoning schemata, effect of examples on creativity, inventing products, effect of mood and decision frames on estimated probabilities, and action-based decision making.

Acknowledgments

I wrote the first edition of this book while spending a sabbatical year at the University of California at Berkeley. I am grateful to Case Western Reserve University and the Group in Science and Mathematics Education at Berkeley for providing financial support during that year. The Group in Science and Mathematics Education also furnished me with a stimulating environment, and the Institute of Human Learning provided an excellent library. Shortly after arriving at Berkeley, I had the good fortune to meet C. Deborah Laughton, a psychology editor at Brooks/Cole. She expressed confidence in the book long before it was deserved and, with the assistance of an excellent staff at Brooks/Cole and first-rate reviewers, helped in the development of the text.

I am grateful to Marianne Taflinger, Fiorella Ljunggren, Anne Draus, Betty Berenson, Lillian Campobasso, and all the others who have contributed to this fourth edition. I would also like to thank the following reviewers for their helpful suggestions on this edition: Charles K. Allen, University of Montana; Stephen Christman, University of Toledo; Ira Fischler, University of Florida; Dennis Kerkman, Southwest Texas State University; John Kruschke, Indiana University; Thomas P. Pusateri, Loras College; Laurette Reeves, Rowan College of New Jersey; and Stephen Schmidt, Middle Tennessee State University. The comments of others are always welcome, and I would appreciate receiving suggestions from readers.

Stephen K. Reed

COGNITION

Theory and Applications

Fourth Edition

INFORMATION-PROCESSING STAGES

Introduction

*Cognitive psychology refers to all processes by which
the sensory input is transformed, reduced, elaborated,
stored, recovered, and used.*

ULRIC NEISSER (1967)

COGNITION IS USUALLY defined simply as the acquisition of knowledge. However, both the acquisition and the use of knowledge involve many mental skills. If you glanced at the table of contents at the beginning of this book, you saw a list of some of these skills. Psychologists who study cognition are interested in pattern recognition, attention, memory, visual imagery, language, problem solving, and decision making.

The purpose of this book is to provide an overview of the field of cognitive psychology. The book summarizes experimental research in cognitive psychology, discusses the major theories in the field, and attempts to relate the research and theories to cognitive tasks that people encounter in their daily lives—for example, reading, driving, studying, judging advertising claims, evaluating legal testimony, solving problems in the classroom, and making medical decisions.

Neisser's definition of cognitive psychology quoted on the preceding page reflects how psychologists study cognition. Let me repeat it for emphasis: "**Cognitive psychology** refers to all processes by which the sensory input is transformed, reduced, elaborated, stored, recovered, and used."

Cognitive psychology
The study of the mental operations that support people's acquisition and use of knowledge

This definition has several important implications. The reference to a sensory input implies that cognition begins with our contact with the external world. Transformation of the sensory input means that our representation of the world is not just a passive registration of our physical surroundings but an active construction that may involve both reduction and elaboration. That is, we can attend to only a small part of the physical stimulation that surrounds us, and only a small part of what we attend to can be remembered. Reduction occurs when information is lost. Elaboration occurs when we add to the sensory input. For example, when you meet a friend, you may recall many shared experiences.

The storage and the recovery of information are, of course, what we call memory. The distinction between storage and recovery implies that the storage of information does not guarantee recovery. A good example of this distinction is the "tip of the tongue" phenomenon. Sometimes we can almost, but not quite, retrieve a word to express a particular thought or meaning. Our later recall of the word proves that the earlier failure was one of retrieval rather than one of storage. The word was stored in memory; it was simply hard to get it back out.

The last part of Neisser's definition is perhaps the most important. After information has been perceived, stored, and recovered, it must be put to good use—for example, to make decisions or to solve problems. We will learn more about problem solving and decision making in Part III, after we review the progress that has been made in understanding perception and memory.

THE INFORMATION-PROCESSING APPROACH

The fact that cognitive psychology is often called **human information processing** reflects the predominant approach to the subject used by cognitive psychologists. The acquisition, storage, retrieval, and use of information comprise a number of separate stages, and the information-processing approach attempts to identify what happens during these stages (Haber, 1969).

Figure 1.1 identifies the stages that researchers most commonly include in information-processing models. The stages are arranged in temporal order; however, since information flows in both directions, as indicated by the two-headed arrows, an earlier stage can be influenced by information in a later stage. For example, in order to recognize a pattern in the pattern recognition stage, we need to store information about patterns in long-term memory.

A brief consideration of the model in Figure 1.1 provides a superficial account of the stages, each of which will be elaborated in later chapters. The **sensory store** provides brief storage for information in its original sensory form. Presumably, a sensory store exists for each of the senses, although the visual and auditory stores have been the most widely studied. The sensory store extends the amount of time that a person has to recognize a pattern. If a visual pattern is flashed on a screen for 5 msec (5 milliseconds, or 5/1000 of a second), the observer has more time than 5 msec to identify it if the visual information can be briefly maintained in a sensory store. Although the sensory store for vision lasts only about one-quarter of a sec (250 msec), this is much longer than the 5-msec exposure.

The information in the sensory store is lost at the end of this time unless it can be described during the **pattern recognition** stage. Most of the

Human information processing The psychological approach that attempts to identify what occurs during the various stages (attention, perception, short-term memory) of processing information

Sensory store That part of memory that holds unanalyzed sensory information for a fraction of a second, providing an opportunity for additional analysis following the physical termination of a stimulus

Pattern recognition The stage of perception during which a stimulus is identified

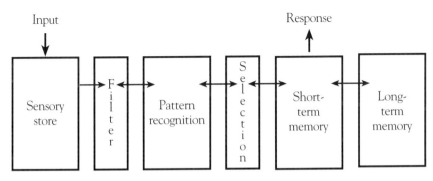

Figure 1.1 *Stages of an information-processing model.*

patterns we encounter are familiar, and recognition consists in classifying a pattern as a cat, the letter *a*, the word *ball*, and so on. When we recognize a familiar pattern, we are using information that we have previously stored in memory. If the description does not match a description of a familiar pattern, the observer may want to store the new description in memory if it is important.

The relation between pattern recognition and attention has been a topic of much debate. Some theorists have claimed that we can recognize only one pattern at a time. They argue that attention acts as a **filter** that determines which patterns will be recognized when many patterns arrive simultaneously. Other theorists have argued that simultaneous patterns can all be recognized but that only some of the recognized patterns will be remembered while others are immediately forgotten. That is, this latter view states that attention selects the patterns that will be remembered. Since the most popular current view is that both theories are correct, depending on the circumstances, attention is represented in Figure 1.1 by both filter and **selection stages.** The filter limits the amount of information that can be recognized at one time, and the selection stage limits the amount of material that can be entered into memory.

Memory is represented in Figure 1.1 by *short-term* and *long-term* memory. We use **short-term memory (STM),** for example, to remember a telephone number as we are dialing it. This form of memory is limited in both the amount of information it can hold (capacity) and the length of time it can hold the information (duration). Most adults can remember a seven-digit number, but they find it very difficult to remember a ten-digit number, such as an unfamiliar area code in addition to the telephone number. The limited duration of STM is illustrated by our quickly forgetting the number if we don't repeat it to ourselves by using verbal rehearsal. **Long-term memory (LTM)** has neither of the two limitations of STM. It has no limitations on the amount of information it can hold, and forgetting occurs relatively slowly, if at all.

The "higher" cognitive skills, such as decision making and problem solving, do not have a stage in our information-processing model. However, they depend greatly on the other stages. For example, pattern recognition skills are important in playing chess, a very demanding intellectual task. The limited capacity of STM is a major determinant of performance on tasks that require complex decision making or problem solving. The role of problem solving in learning new information is receiving increasing emphasis as cognitive psychologists discover more about the active nature of learning. Specifying the interactions among perception, memory, and thought is one of the challenges that confront cognitive psychologists.

Filter That part of attention in which some perceptual information is blocked (filtered) out and not recognized, while other information receives attention and is subsequently recognized

Selection stage The stage that follows pattern recognition and determines which information a person will try to remember

Short-term memory (STM) The part of memory that has limited capacity and that lasts only about 20 to 30 sec in the absence of attending to its content

Long-term memory (LTM) The part of memory that has no capacity limits and lasts from minutes to an entire lifetime

THE GROWTH OF COGNITIVE PSYCHOLOGY

It is difficult to pinpoint the exact beginning of any field of study, and cognitive psychologists would likely offer a wide variety of dates if asked when cognitive psychology began. James's *Principles of Psychology*, published in 1890, included chapters on attention, memory, imagery, and reasoning. Kohler's *The Mentality of Apes*, published in 1925, investigated processes that occur in complex thinking. He and other Gestalt psychologists emphasized structural understanding—the ability to understand how all the parts of a problem fit together (the Gestalt). Bartlett's book *Remembering: A Study in Experimental and Social Psychology*, published in 1932, contained a theory of memory for stories that is very consistent with current views. There are some other important articles or books that seem modern but did not cause a major shift toward the way cognitive psychology is currently studied.

One book that had a major negative impact was *Behaviorism*, published in 1924 by Watson. The book's central theme was that psychologists should study only what they could directly observe in a person's behavior. Watson's argument lent support to a **stimulus-response (S-R)** approach, in which experimenters record how people respond to stimuli without attempting to discover the thought processes that cause the response. The stimulus-response approach is consistent with Watson's view because the stimulus and the response are both observable. The problem with this approach is that it does not reveal exactly what the person does with the information presented in the stimulus. By contrast, the information-processing approach seeks to identify how a person transforms information between the stimulus and the response. Psychologists who follow the latter approach seek to understand what occurs during each of the stages shown in Figure 1.1. Finding out what occurs during each of these stages is particularly important when a person has difficulty performing a task, for the psychologist can then try to identify which stage is the primary source of the difficulty.

Stimulus-response (S-R) The approach that emphasizes the association between a stimulus and a response, without identifying the mental operations that produced the response

Information Processing Gathers Momentum

The change from the S-R to the information-processing approach began to gather momentum in the middle to late 1950s, stimulated by the growing popularity of computers and computer programs that illustrated the different operations in the processing of information. Psychologists became interested in using the computer as an analog of how people process information and tried to identify how different stages of processing influence performance. One stage that can have a dramatic influence on how people perform mental tasks is STM. G. A. Miller argued in a classic paper published in 1956 that STM capacity limited performance on many cognitive tasks. Miller's paper was important in demonstrating how a single stage—STM—can influence performance on a wide variety of tasks.

Two years later Broadbent (1958) proposed one of the first models based on an information-processing analysis—a filter model to account for performance on selective listening tasks. When subjects were asked to listen simultaneously to different messages played in each ear, they found it difficult. Broadbent proposed that many sensory inputs can simultaneously enter the sensory store, but that only a single input can enter the pattern recognition stage. The filter model proposes that the listener can attend to only one message at a time; attention is controlled by the filter. Two simultaneous messages can both be recognized only if the unattended message passes through the filter before it decays from the sensory store. The filter model implies that a perceptual limitation prevents people from comprehending two messages spoken at the same time.

The year after Broadbent's filter model appeared, Sperling completed his doctoral dissertation at Harvard. In one of Sperling's tasks (1960), observers viewed a very brief exposure of an array of letters and were required to report all the letters in one of the rows of the display. The pitch of a tone signaled which row was to be reported. Sperling designed the procedure to determine whether perception or memory limited the number of letters people could report from the brief exposure. His analysis of this task resulted in an information-processing model that proposed how the sensory store, pattern recognition, and short-term memory combined to influence performance on the task (Sperling, 1963).

Both Broadbent's and Sperling's models had an important influence on subsequent information-processing theory, the former on models of auditory attention and the latter on visual recognition.

Higher Cognitive Processes

The information-processing analysis of perceptual tasks was accompanied in the late 1950s by a new approach to more complex tasks. The excitement of this new approach is described by Newell and Simon (1972). The development of digital computers after World War II led to active work in **artificial intelligence**, a field that attempts to program computers to perform intelligent tasks such as playing chess and constructing derivations in logic. A seminar was held at the RAND Corporation in the summer of 1958 with the aim of showing social scientists how computer simulation techniques could be applied to create models of human behavior. The RAND seminar had a major impact on integrating the work on computer simulation with other work on human information processing.

Artificial intelligence
The study of how to produce computer programs that can perform intellectually demanding tasks

One consequence of the RAND seminar was its influence on three psychologists who spent the 1958–1959 academic year at the Center for Advanced Study in the Behavioral Sciences at Stanford University. The three—George Miller, Eugene Galanter, and Karl Pribram—shared a common dissatisfaction with the then-predominant theoretical approach to psychology, which viewed human beings as bundles of stimulus-response reflexes. Miller brought with him a large amount of material from the RAND seminar, and this material, along with other recent work in artificial intelligence, psychology, and linguistics, helped shape the view expressed in their book, *Plans and the Structure of Behavior* (Miller, Galanter, & Pribram, 1960).

The authors argue that much of human behavior is planned. A **plan**, according to their formulation, consists of a list of instructions that can control the order in which a sequence of operations is to be performed. A plan is essentially the same as a program for a computer. Since the authors found it difficult to construct plans from stimulus-response units, they proposed a new unit called TOTE, an abbreviation for Test-Operate-Test-Exit. A plan consists of a hierarchy of TOTE units.

Plan A temporally ordered sequence of operations for carrying out some task

Consider a very simple plan for hammering a nail into a board. The goal is to make the head of the nail flush with the board. At the top of the hierarchy is a test to determine whether the goal has been accomplished. If the nail is flush, one can exit. If the nail sticks up, it is necessary to test the position of the hammer. The position of the hammer determines which of two operations, lifting or striking, should be performed.

The ideas expressed by Miller, Galanter, and Pribram were influenced by earlier work in two areas outside psychology. The work of Newell, Shaw, and Simon (1958a) in the area of artificial intelligence identified strategies that people use to perform complex tasks such as playing chess. A second major influence came from the linguist Noam Chomsky, who argued that a stimulus-response theory of language learning could not account for how people learn to comprehend and generate sentences (Chomsky, 1957). His alternative proposal—that people learn a system of rules (a grammar)—was consistent with Miller, Galanter, and Pribram's emphasis on planning. We will return to both contributions, as well as to the contributions of Miller, Broadbent, and Sperling, in the following chapters.

COGNITION'S RELATION TO OTHER FIELDS

The ideas expressed by these theorists have continued to be developed and refined. Neisser's *Cognitive Psychology* (1967) brought many of these ideas together into a single source; other books on cognition have followed. Cognitive psychology currently has widespread appeal among psychologists. Almost all of the psychologists studying perception, attention, learning, memory, language, reasoning, problem solving, and decision-making refer to themselves as cognitive psychologists even though the methodology and theories vary widely across these topics. In addition, other disciplines, such as educational psychology (Gagne, 1985; Mayer, 1987) and social psychology (Devine, Hamilton, & Ostrom, 1994), have been greatly influenced by the cognitive approach.

Cognitive psychology is also having an increasing impact on applied psychology (Hoffman & Deffenbacher, 1992). Much research funding is now directed toward applied projects, and many recent doctoral graduates are hired for applied positions. The increasing application of cognitive theory is also evident in the emergence of new journals such as *Applied Cognition* and the *Journal of Experimental Psychology: Applied*. The title of this book, *Cognition: Theory and Applications*, indicates that I believe these applications are important. We will look at many applications throughout this book, including facilitating perceptual learning, predicting the accident rate of drivers, improving eyewitness recall, using memory strategies, recognizing the biasing effects of language in advertising and legal testimony, improving the readability of text, and using problem-solving strategies.

The influence of ideas does not move in only one direction. Other fields of study have also influenced cognitive psychology and led to a combined field of study called cognitive science, characterized by its own society, journal, and even major at some universities. **Cognitive science** is the study of intelligence in humans, computer programs, and abstract theories, with an emphasis on intelligent behavior as computation (Simon & Kaplan, 1989). It is also an attempt to unify views of thought developed by studies in psychology, linguistics, anthropology, philosophy, artificial intelligence, and the neurosciences (Hunt, 1989).

Cognitive science The interdisciplinary attempt to study cognition through such fields as psychology, philosophy, artificial intelligence, neuroscience, linguistics, and anthropology

Box 1.1 contains an article on artificial intelligence that appeared in a 1980 issue of *Newsweek* magazine. Computers could already perform many intelligent tasks by this time, and their capabilities have continued to grow. The concepts used in these programs have influenced the construction of models describing human intelligence. For instance, we will see in Chapter 9 that cognitive psychologists borrowed a concept from artificial intelligence (semantic networks) to describe how people organize ideas in long-term memory. Another concept borrowed from artificial intelligence (production systems) explains how we use rules to perform cognitive tasks. We will learn about production systems in Chapter 13.

Cognitive neuroscience The study of the relation between cognitive processes and brain activities

Magnetic resonance imaging A diagnostic technique that uses magnetic fields and computerized images to locate mental operations in the brain

An important field receiving increasing study is that of **cognitive neuroscience.** Advances in technology have made it possible to examine which parts of the brain are used to perform a variety of cognitive tasks. One of these techniques, called **magnetic resonance imaging**, uses magnetic fields and computerized enhancement to produce high-resolution

How smart can computers get?

On a Monday morning at Yale University, Margot Flowers sits down with her friend Abdul for another debate on Mideast politics:

Margot: Who started the 1967 war?
Abdul: The Arabs did, by blockading the Strait of Tiran.
Margot: But Israel attacked first.
Abdul: According to international law, blockades are acts of war.
Margot: Were we supposed to let you import American arms through the strait?
Abdul: Israel was not importing arms through the strait. The reason for the blockade was to keep Israel from importing oil from Iran.

They don't have the finesse of U.N. diplomats, but then Margot Flowers is one of three scientists who created Abdul, a computer program that dips into its memory of data to reason out answers to questions. The dialogue is an exercise in a 25-year-old field called artificial intelligence (AI), and with the remarkable advances in computer technology at their command, hundreds of AI researchers are testing the potential of the new electronic brains. Their goal is as remarkable as their technology: to determine how close a computer can come to simulating the human mind and, perhaps, transcending it.

The results thus far are both tantalizing and reassuring. In scores of AI experiments, well-programmed computers can play chess and backgammon, draw analogies among Shakespearean plays, and understand tales involving friendship and adultery. Computers can use facts to make inferences and draw on experience to reach unprogrammed conclusions. But only up to a point: What AI researchers are learning is that the human brain is even more astonishing than they thought—and that true intelligence involves elements of will, consciousness, and creativity of which today's computers are incapable. "So far, artificial intelligence falls under the definition of problem solving," says AI scientist Terry Winograd of Stanford. "That's the first step."

The first "thinking" problem solver was probably a 1956 computer program called the Logic Theorist, which could choose from a set of facts and use logical operations to prove mathematical statements. Its first triumph was finding a proof of a theorem in mathematical logic that both Bertrand Russell and Alfred North Whitehead had missed.

Today's problem solvers are even more sophisticated. One of the most impressive is the backgammon champ programmed by Hans J. Berliner of Carnegie-Mellon University of Pittsburgh. The program chooses among all possible legal moves by reducing each to a mathematical equation that measures threats and opportunities and then picks the move whose equation has the highest value. BACON, another program developed by Nobel laureate Herbert A. Simon and his colleagues at Carnegie-Mellon, looks for patterns in scientific data. On its own, BACON "discovered" a rule of planetary mechanics first established by Johannes Kepler in 1609. And when it was fed all the facts that were known about chemistry in the year 1800, BACON deduced the principle of atomic weight—a feat that took human scientists another 50 years.

SOURCE: *Newsweek*, June 30, 1980. Copyright 1980, Newsweek, Inc. All rights reserved. Reprinted by permission.

pictures of brain structure. The expense of these machines ($3 million
when introduced in 1988) has limited their availability, but their impact
is already remarkable. Box 1.2 shows how such technology is greatly enhancing our understanding of cognitive problems.

Other imaging techniques, such as **positron emission tomography
(PET),** provide a measure of which parts of the brain people use as they
perform various cognitive tasks. This method measures cerebral blood
flow by injecting a radioactive tracer into the bloodstream. Measuring
this low-level radiation allows cognitive neuroscientists to determine activity levels in various parts of the brain.

A limitation of spatial imaging techniques is that they do not provide
the kind of precise temporal information that is important in analyzing
many cognitive tasks in which fractions of a second are theoretically important. But recording electrical activity from the scalp does provide
more precise temporal information. The use of these **event-related potentials (ERP)** allows scientists to link mental operations recorded in reaction time tasks to brain activity. And by combining PET and ERP studies
it is possible to take advantage of the more precise spatial localization of
imaging techniques and the more precise temporal resolution of electrical
potentials (Posner & Rothbart, 1994).

Figure 1.2 illustrates how the PET and ERP techniques can be combined to help us understand how people process written words (Snyder,
Abdullaev, Posner, & Raichle, 1995). This same illustration has been

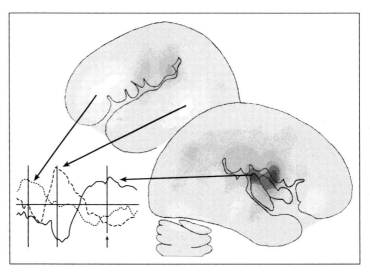

Figure 1.2 *A PET scan showing changes in blood flow in the brain
during a cognitive task.*

Adapted from photo provided by Marcus E. Raichle, M.D., Washington University
School of Medicine.

reproduced on the cover of this book in color. In Figure 1.2 the shaded areas inside the two outlines of the brain show cortical changes in blood flow when the person is asked to generate uses of visually presented nouns (such as *pound* for *hammer*) compared to the changes caused by reading aloud the same nouns. The lightest areas (yellow and red on the cover) show increases in blood flow that are particularly evident in the frontal and temporal areas of the left hemisphere (upper left outline). The darkest areas (blue and green on the cover) show decreases in blood flow relative to the control task of simply reading the words. These decreases are more prominent in the right hemisphere (lower right outline).

The arrows in Figure 1.2 connect PET blood flow changes with the ERP waveforms recorded at the nearest overlying electrode on the scalp. The activation in the frontal part of the left hemisphere—the dotted waveline (yellow on the cover)—leads the activation in the temporal part of the left hemisphere—the dashed waveline (red on the cover)—by several hundred milliseconds. An implication of these findings is that the earlier, frontal activation is important for encoding the meaning of individual words, and the later temporal activation may be more important for the integration of word meanings to obtain the overall meaning of phrases and sentences (Snyder et al., 1995). This hypothesis is consistent with the finding that damage to the temporal area of the left hemisphere often produces a language deficit that leaves the person unable to combine words to produce meaningful ideas. We will later learn more about this deficit in Chapter 10 on language.

Even though cognitive psychology is still a young science, our understanding of cognition has increased greatly over the past 40 years. Aronson, in the introduction to his popular book, *The Social Animal* (1972), explained the major reason he wrote the book: He once told one of his classes that social psychology was a young science, but he then felt like a coward. That is, he came to believe that labeling social psychology as a young science was a gigantic cop-out—a way of pleading with people not to expect too much, a way of avoiding the responsibility for applying findings to the problems of the world we live in. Aronson wrote his book to demonstrate that social psychology does have a lot to contribute. I hope you feel the same way about cognitive psychology after reading this book.

ORGANIZATION OF THIS BOOK

This book is divided into three major parts: The first discusses information-processing stages, the second discusses the representation and organization of knowledge, and the third part discusses complex cognitive skills.

In this chapter I have presented a brief overview of the information-processing approach to the study of cognition. One of the primary objectives of that approach, as was illustrated in Figure 1.1, is to identify the

**BOX
1.2**

Brain images: New windows to illness

BY FLOYD BLOOM AND ROBERT POOL

When Nancy Andreasen reaches into her appointment calendar to pull out a photo, you expect to see a son or daughter, perhaps even a pet, but certainly not this. It is a photo of a living brain, and it is her brain.

The picture is a calling card of sorts. Andreasen, a well-known research psychiatrist, uses pictures like this to study what goes wrong in the brains of people with schizophrenia, manic depression, and other mental illnesses.

Not long ago, the only way to get such detailed images of a brain was to wait until the person died and remove the brain during an autopsy. Now doctors and medical scientists can get pictures of a brain while the person is still very much alive. . . .

Andreasen, for example, has been examining the brains of people with schizophrenia. Using magnetic resonance imaging, or MRI, she and her colleagues have shown that schizophrenics who experience auditory hallucinations tend to have abnormalities in the parts of the brain devoted to hearing. Schizophrenics with disorganized speech often have abnormalities in the parts of the brain devoted to language and memory. . . .

Imaging techniques also are being used to study the normal brain to shed light on brain disorders. With the newest techniques, for example, researchers can watch different parts of the brain in action as they demand more blood flow and oxygen. As people learn a complicated new task, the brain learns to do the job more efficiently, and fewer parts of the brain are required.

This research and other investigations are showing that the brain is much more flexible than was thought just a few years ago. In some cases, adjacent or related parts of the brain can take over functions from parts that are damaged. By studying this rewiring process, researchers hope to mend spinal cord injuries, and perhaps even block the neural degeneration caused by Alzheimer's disease.

The general impression from this work is one of great optimism. Just a few years ago, scientists thought that brain cells formed fixed circuits early in life that remained largely unchanged. Now they have discovered that these cells are constantly forming new connections in response to input from the outside world. If researchers can unravel and eventually learn how to influence this process, powerful new treatments for brain disorders will be possible.

SOURCE: From "Brain Images: New Windows to Illness," by Floyd Bloom and Robert Pool, appearing in the *San Diego Union-Tribune*, May 26, 1994. Reprinted by permission.

major information-processing stages. Part I summarizes our knowledge of what occurs during each of these stages. Chapters 2 and 3, on pattern recognition and attention, are both concerned with perception. Theories of pattern recognition seek to specify how people recognize and store descriptions of patterns in memory. These theories also seek to determine why performance limitations occur, such as when a person cannot report all the letters in an array of letters, and why it is easier to perceive letters when they form a word. Theories of attention are needed to explain performance when too much perceptual information arrives at the same time. Usually a person can respond to only some of the information. Experiments designed to measure how much is processed have led to theories about whether a particular stage causes the limitation or whether the tasks simply require too much mental effort to be performed at the same time.

Chapters 4 and 5 are both concerned with memory, and they discuss STM and LTM, respectively. Short-term memory is a "working memory" that enables us to combine information retrieved from long-term memory with information that arrives from the environment. But the limited capacity and fast decay rate of STM make it necessary for us to enter into LTM any new information we want to remember over a long period. The chapter on LTM discusses the various strategies that we can use when learning new information, including verbal rehearsal. Both chapters distinguish between recall and recognition tests and show how theories of recognition memory differ depending on whether the information is retained in STM or LTM.

The second part of the book is concerned with the representation and organization of knowledge in memory. Chapters 6 and 7 illustrate different kinds of memory codes since our ability to remember depends on the kind of memory code that is constructed. An influential theory of memory has been the levels-of-processing theory proposed by Craik and Lockhart (1972). Their theory was stimulated by research showing that a person's ability to remember a word depended on what characteristics of the word were emphasized in a judgment task. Memory codes can also be distinguished by whether they emphasize verbal information or visual information. The study of visual and verbal codes has important implications for how efficiently people can perform different tasks.

Chapters 8 and 9 emphasize the organization of LTM. Chapter 8 is primarily theoretical; it examines how knowledge is organized into categories and how categories are organized into hierarchies. The ability to categorize is a skill that is frequently used in pattern recognition. Identification usually occurs when an item is classified as a member of a particular category. The organization of knowledge in LTM can also be studied by measuring how quickly people can make classification decisions. Chapter 9 examines how psychologists have used this and other techniques to study relations among concepts in semantic memory, the part of LTM that represents the meaning of words.

The last part of the book contains five chapters on cognitive skills. The section begins with a discussion of language in Chapter 10. Language involves not only the meaning of individual words but the combination of words to form sentences that are grammatically correct and convey intended meanings. Chapter 11, on text comprehension, focuses on our ability to comprehend paragraphs rather than individual sentences. Over the past several years psychologists have made significant progress in identifying factors that influence text comprehension. They have even developed some rather detailed models of how the organization of ideas in a text interacts with STM and LTM to determine what is remembered.

Chapter 12, the first of two chapters on problem solving, shows how cognitive psychologists have studied this area. The chapter describes attempts to identify the skills needed to solve different kinds of problems, identify general strategies used, and examine the role of memory in problem solving. Chapter 13, on expertise and creativity, discusses how people use prior knowledge in reasoning and how they acquire expertise in solving "classroom" problems. The final section of this chapter describes recent theoretical and empirical approaches to the study of creativity.

Chapter 14 discusses decision making. The study of decision making has shown that people often find it difficult to combine information in an optimal way when evaluating alternatives. The term *risky decision making* is used to describe situations in which there is uncertainty regarding possible outcomes. The study of how people make probability estimates, how they revise their estimates when they receive new information, and how they use their estimates to make decisions constitutes most of the research on risky decision making.

STUDY QUESTIONS

Although Chapter 1 is short, it is densely packed. It will repay close attention since it provides a "road map" of where the book is going. Your learning journey will be easier if you know where you're headed and what landmarks to look for along the way.

1. Neisser's definition of cognitive psychology may not fit your notion of what this course would be about. If so, how does it differ?
2. Notice the assumptions of cognitive psychology. How does each jibe with what you imagine a person in the street would assume about the acquisition of knowledge?
3. What are the implications of the terms *information processing,* and *stage model,* taken separately and together? Formulate a tentative idea of what is involved at each stage of processing mentioned.
4. The historical sketch may include many names that are new to you. Which ones are familiar? What do you know about them? Except for James and Watson, don't worry about the names of the other people

now—but do explain the importance of their work for the development of cognitive psychology.

5. What are the higher cognitive processes? Why are they called "higher"? Think of an everyday example of each process, and *write it down*. What did you have to consider in generating your examples?

6. If cognitive psychology is related to other fields, then some of the ideas in this book would appear in other courses. Have you already taken courses where some of these ideas have been discussed? If so, in what courses?

KEY TERMS

The page number in parentheses refers to where the term is discussed in the chapter.

artificial intelligence (8)
cognitive neuroscience (10)
cognitive psychology (4)
cognitive science (10)
event-related potentials (ERP) (12)
filter (6)
human information processing (5)
long-term memory (LTM) (6)
magnetic resonance imaging (10)

pattern recognition (5)
plan (9)
positron emission tomography (PET) (12)
selection stage (6)
sensory store (5)
short-term memory (STM) (6)
stimulus-response (S-R) (7)

RECOMMENDED READING

The first chapter in Eysenck and Keane (1990) provides a more elaborate account of the ideas expressed in this chapter. An early statement of the assumptions of the information-processing approach is given by Haber (1969). Lachman, Lachman, and Butterfield's (1979) book on cognitive psychology contains an excellent discussion of how other disciplines—such as behaviorism, verbal learning, human engineering, information theory, and linguistics—contributed to the information-processing paradigm. A more recent, but advanced, overview of information-processing models is described by Massaro and Cowan (1993). An interesting paper by Roediger (1980) discusses how people have used familiar analogies to help them understand memory. Roediger begins with Aristotle's and Plato's comparison of memory to a wax tablet and ends with the computer analogy that is currently emphasized. Readers interested in how other major theoretical approaches influenced the history of psychology should read Heidbreder (1961). The book contains chapters on prescientific psychology, the beginning of scientific psychology, the psychology of William James, functionalism, behaviorism, dynamic psychology, Gestalt psychology, and psychoanalysis. Gardner (1985) provides a very readable account of the evolution of cognitive psychology. Hoffman and Deffenbacher (1992) give a detailed account of the development of applied cognitive psychology. The articles by Hunt (1989) and Simon and Kaplan (1989) provide excellent overviews of cognitive science. The Simon and Kaplan article is the first chapter in an outstanding book, *Foundations of Cognitive Science* (Posner, 1989).

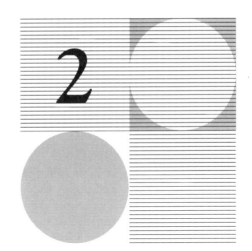

Pattern Recognition

About patterns, philosophers and psychologists have been strangely silent; yet most interesting phenomena are almost certainly patterned. Of course, this silence is really not at all strange, for patterns are amazingly complicated things to come to grips with. Even a consensus of what we mean by the word "pattern" is lacking, but a growing number of people are beginning to feel that many of the central problems of behavior, intelligence, and information processing are problems that involve patterns.

LEONARD UHR (1966)

WE BEGIN OUR STUDY of cognitive psychology by starting with a skill that people use very well—pattern recognition. The study of **pattern recognition** is primarily the study of how people identify the objects in their environment. Our ability to recognize patterns should seem impressive if we stop to consider how much variation there is in different examples of the same pattern. Each letter of the alphabet, for example, is one kind of pattern. Figure 2.1 shows various styles of handwriting. It is obvious that not all people have the same style of writing and that some handwriting styles are much less legible than others. However, unless it is very illegible, we usually are successful in reading it—that is, in recognizing the words.

The ease and accuracy with which we can recognize patterns make it difficult to study this ability. It is not very interesting or revealing if someone easily identifies all of a variety of patterns. In order to make the task more difficult, psychologists often resort to using a **tachistoscope**—a device for presenting patterns very rapidly under controlled conditions. If the patterns are presented for only a few milliseconds, people start to make mistakes, and psychologists start to take notes about the kinds of mistakes they make.

A large part of the literature on pattern recognition is concerned with alternative ways of describing patterns. The first section of this chapter discusses three kinds of descriptions that represent different theories of pattern recognition. The second section is about information-processing models of visual pattern recognition. We will take a more detailed look at Sperling's research and how his results influenced later theories. The third section deals with word recognition and will give us the opportunity to consider some of the factors that influence reading.

DESCRIBING PATTERNS

Consider the following explanation of how we recognize patterns. Our LTM contains descriptions of many kinds of patterns. When we see or hear a pattern, we form a description of it and compare the description against the descriptions stored in our LTM. We are able to recognize the pattern if its description closely matches one of the descriptions stored in LTM. Although this is a plausible explanation, it is rather vague. For example, what form do these descriptions take? Let us consider three explanations that have been suggested: (1) templates, (2) features, and (3) structural descriptions.

Template Theories

Template theories propose that patterns are really not "described" at all. Rather, **templates** are holistic, or unanalyzed, entities that we compare with other patterns by measuring how much two patterns overlap. Imag-

Pattern recognition The stage of perception during which a stimulus is identified

Tachistoscope A box that presents visual stimuli at a specified duration and level of illumination

Template An unanalyzed pattern that is matched against alternative patterns by using the degree of overlap as a measure of similarity

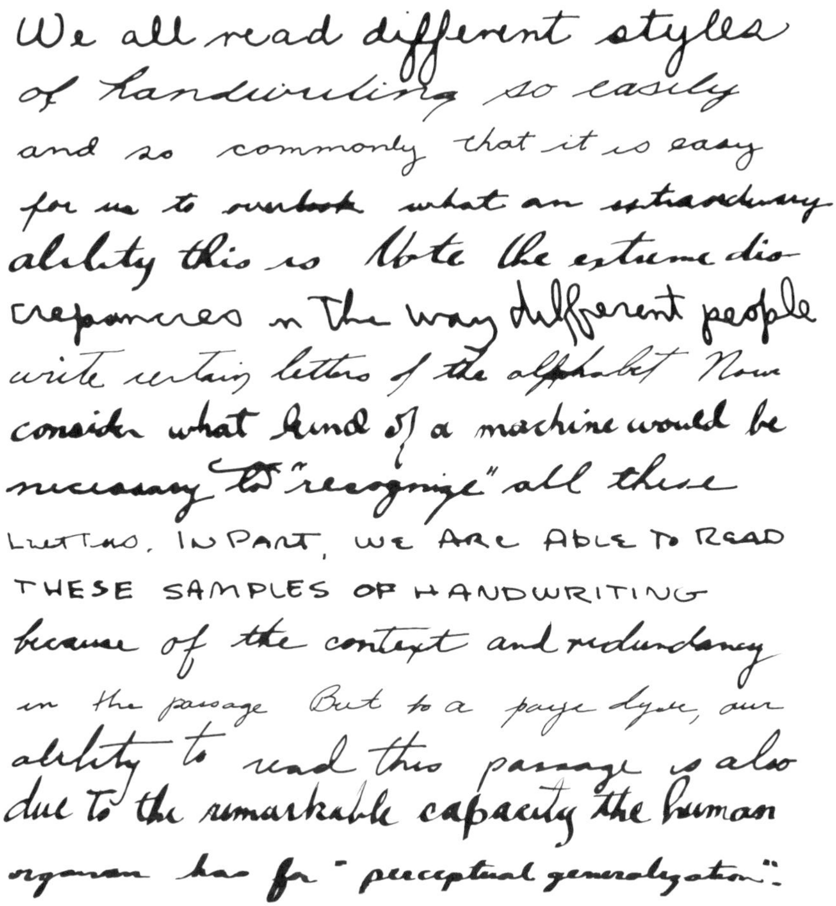

We all read different styles of handwriting so easily and so commonly that it is easy for us to overlook what an extraordinary ability this is Note the extreme discrepancies in the way different people write certain letters of the alphabet Now consider what kind of a machine would be necessary to "recognize" all these LETTERS. IN PART, WE ARE ABLE TO READ THESE SAMPLES OF HANDWRITING because of the context and redundancy in the passage But to a page type, our ability to read this passage is also due to the remarkable capacity the human organism has for "perceptual generalization".

Figure 2.1 *Variations in handwriting.*

From *Man Machine Engineering*, by A. Chapanis. Copyright © 1965 by Wadsworth, Inc. Reprinted by permission of Brooks/Cole Publishing Company, Pacific Grove, California.

ine that you made a set of letters out of cardboard. If you made a cutout to represent each letter of the alphabet, and I gave you a cutout of a letter that I had made, you could measure how my letter overlapped with each of your letters—the templates. The identity of my letter would be determined by which template had the greatest amount of overlap. The same principle would apply if you replaced your cardboard letters with a visual image of each letter and used the images to make mental comparisons.

There are a number of problems with using the degree of overlap as a measure of pattern recognition. First, the comparison requires that the template be in the same position and the same orientation, and be the same size, as the pattern you are trying to identify. Thus the position, orientation, and size of the templates would have to be continuously adjusted to correspond to the position, orientation, and size of each pattern you wanted to recognize. A second problem is the great variability of patterns, as was illustrated in Figure 2.1. It would be difficult to construct a template for each letter that would produce a good match with all the different varieties of that letter. Third, a template theory doesn't reveal how two patterns differ. We could know from a template theory that the capital letters *P* and *R* are similar because one overlaps substantially with the other. But in order to know how the two letters differ, we have to be able to analyze or describe the letters. By contrast, the feature theory, considered in the next section, allows us to analyze patterns into their parts. A fourth problem is that a template theory does not allow for alternative descriptions of a pattern. The pattern in Figure 2.5 (page 29), for example, can be perceived as either a stingray or a full-blown sail, depending on which lines are grouped together. The structural theory, considered later, will allow us to specify the relations of parts of a pattern.

These weaknesses of the template theory make it very unpromising as a general theory of pattern recognition, and it is usually quickly dismissed. There are, however, some situations in which a template theory might provide a useful model. Remember from Chapter 1 that the **sensory store** briefly preserves sensory information to give the observer more time to recognize patterns. But how are the patterns preserved in the sensory store if they are unrecognized? One possibility is that the patterns can be represented as unanalyzed templates, which are analyzed into their features during the pattern recognition stage.

This interpretation of the sensory store is most clearly presented by Phillips (1974). Subjects in Phillips's experiment viewed patterns made by randomly filled cells in a square matrix. The first pattern was presented for 1 sec and was followed after a variable interval by either an identical or a similar pattern. The subject's task was to decide, as quickly as possible, whether the two patterns were the same or different. On half of the trials, the second pattern occurred in exactly the same location as the first. Since the second pattern was exactly superimposed over the sensory image of the first pattern, it might be possible to use the sensory store to make a template match. On the other half of the trials, the second pattern was moved horizontally by the width of one cell. The slight shift in position should prohibit a template match because the two patterns were not correctly aligned.

Figure 2.2 shows the results of Phillips's experiment. The **interstimulus interval**—the time separating the two patterns—was 20, 60, 100, 300, or 600 msec. When the two patterns were presented in identical locations (labeled *still* in Figure 2.2), accuracy declined as the interstimulus interval was lengthened. This finding suggests that the subjects were making use of a sensory store that was rapidly decaying. When the second pattern was moved, subjects could not use the sensory store to make a

Sensory store   That part of memory that holds unanalyzed information for a fraction of a second, providing an opportunity for additional analysis following the physical termination of a stimulus

Interstimulus interval The amount of time between the end of a stimulus and the beginning of another stimulus

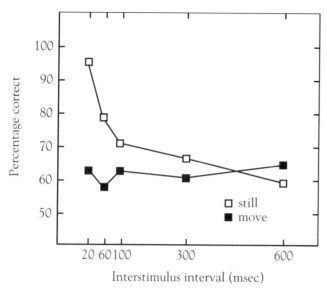

Figure 2.2   *Percentage of correct responses for an 8 x 8 matrix as a function of interstimulus interval and movement.*

From "On the Distinction between Sensory Storage and Short-Term Visual Memory," by W. A. Phillips, 1974, *Perception and Psychophysics, 16,* 283–290. Copyright © 1974 by the Psychonomic Society. Reprinted by permission.

template match, and so accuracy was not influenced by the interval separating the patterns. Note that the use of the sensory store resulted in more accuracy when the interstimulus interval was less than 300 msec. This suggests that the sensory store lasts only about a quarter of a second. When the separation was only 20 msec (the data points on the extreme left of the graph) and the patterns were presented in the same location, performance was almost perfect, even for the most complex pattern.

When the second pattern was moved, subjects had to rely on a description of the first pattern rather than on a sensory image. The description might be in the form of a visual image, but unlike a sensory image, in which the pattern still appears to be physically present, a visual image has to be retrieved from memory. Thus the description was less accurate than the sensory image. Since comparing the descriptions of two patterns takes longer than making a template match, the speed of response was highly correlated with accuracy. The reaction time results would look very much like the accuracy results in Figure 2.2 if we were to replace "Percentage correct" with "Speed of response." Reaction times were very fast for the "still" condition but became slower as the interstimulus interval was increased. Reaction times were slower for the "move" condition and were uninfluenced by the interstimulus interval.

Both the accuracy and reaction time results suggest that the sensory store can be used for a rapid template match if the two patterns are separated by less than 300 msec and are presented in the same location.

Feature Theories

The success of the template theory in accounting for Phillips's results depends on matching the second pattern to a sensory image of the first pattern. The sensory image can be thought of as a kind of afterimage in which the pattern still appears to be physically present until the sensory store decays away. But it is questionable whether the sensory store plays an important role outside the laboratory; even if it did, the information would be quickly lost. Since we usually cannot rely on the sensory store to match patterns, we must compare descriptions of patterns. **Feature theories** allow us to describe a pattern by listing its parts. For example, we might describe a friend as having long blond hair, a short nose, and bushy eyebrows.

Feature theories are convenient for describing perceptual learning, and one of the best discussions of feature theories is contained in Gibson's *Principles of Perceptual Learning and Development* (1969). The theory proposed by Gibson is that perceptual learning occurs through the discovery of features that *distinguish* one pattern from another. Children learn to identify an object by being able to identify differences between it and other objects. For example, when first confronted with the letters *E* and *F*, the child might not be aware of how the two differ. Learning to make this discrimination depends on discovering that a low horizontal line is present in the letter *E* but not in the letter *F*. The low horizontal line is a **distinctive feature** for distinguishing between an *E* and an *F*; that is, it enables us to distinguish one pattern from the other.

Perceptual learning can be facilitated by a learning procedure that highlights distinctive features. An effective method for emphasizing a distinctive feature is to initially make it a different color from the rest of the pattern and then gradually change it back to the original color. Egeland (1975) used this procedure to teach prekindergarten children how to distinguish between the confusable letter pairs *R-P*, *Y-V*, *G-C*, *Q-O*, *M-N*, and *K-X*. One letter of each pair was presented at the top of a card with six letters below it, three of which matched the sample letter and three of which were the comparison letter. The children were asked to select those letters that exactly matched the sample letter.

One group of children received a training procedure in which the distinctive feature of the letter was initially highlighted in red—for example, the diagonal line of the *R* in the *R-P* discrimination. During the training session, the distinctive feature was gradually changed to black to match the rest of the letter. Another group of children viewed only black

Feature theories Theories of pattern recognition that describe patterns in terms of their parts, or features

Distinctive feature A feature present in one pattern, but absent in another, aiding one's discrimination of the two patterns

letters. They received feedback about which of their choices were correct, but they were not told about the distinctive features of the letters. Both groups were given two tests—an immediate test at the end of the training session and a delayed test a week later. The "distinctive features" group made significantly fewer errors on both tests, even though the features were not highlighted during the tests. They also made fewer errors during the training sessions.

Emphasizing the distinctive features produced two benefits. First, it enabled the children to learn the distinctive features so they could continue to differentiate letters after the distinctive features were no longer highlighted. Second, it enabled them to learn the features without making many errors during the training session. The failure and frustration that many children experience in the early stages of reading (letter discrimination) can impair their interest in later classroom learning.

Another example of how distinctive features can be useful concerns face recognition. Distinctive features of faces can be further exaggerated to create **caricatures** by using a computer-implemented caricature generator (Brennan, 1985). The program converts photographs of faces into line drawings that either accurately represent the face or exaggerate the distinctive features. For instance, if a person had large ears and a small nose, the caricature would have even larger ears and an even smaller nose than the accurate drawing. When students were shown line drawings of acquaintances, they identified people faster when shown caricatures than when shown accurate line drawings (Rhodes, Brennan, & Carey, 1987). That is, making distinctive features even more distinctive through exaggeration facilitated recognition.

Caricature An exaggeration of distinctive features to make a pattern more distinctive

Evaluating feature theories.   Part of the evidence for feature theories comes from recording the action potentials of individual cells in the visual cortex. By placing microelectrodes in the visual cortex of animals, Hubel and Wiesel (1962, 1963) discovered that cells respond to only certain kinds of stimuli, such as a line of a certain width, oriented at a correct angle, and located at the correct position in its visual field. Other cells are even concerned about the length of the line. In 1981 Hubel and Wiesel received a Nobel Prize for this work.

Although most pattern recognition theorists make use of the feature concept, it is often a challenging task to find a good set of features. Gibson (1969) proposed the following criteria as a basis for selecting a set of features for uppercase letters:

1. The features should be critical ones, present in some members of the set but not in others, so as to provide a contrast.
2. The identity of the features should remain unchanged under changes in brightness, size, and perspective.

3. The features should yield a unique pattern for each letter.
4. The number of proposed features should be reasonably small.

Gibson used these criteria, empirical data, and intuition to derive the set of features for uppercase letters shown in Figure 2.3. Note that the features primarily consist of different lines and curves but also include some global characteristics of the pattern such as symmetry and closure.

A set of features is usually evaluated by determining how well it can predict **perceptual confusions** since confusable items should have many features in common. For example, Figure 2.3 reveals that the only difference in features for the letters *P* and *R* is the presence of a diagonal line for the letter *R*; therefore, the two should be highly confusable. The letters *R* and *O* differ in five features, and so they should seldom be confused.

There are several experimental procedures for generating perceptual confusions. The feature set shown in Figure 2.3 was initially tested by examining confusion errors made by 4-year-old children (Gibson, Osser, Schiff, & Smith, 1963). Since these children made errors on a perceptual matching task, it was possible to determine which pairs of letters were likely to be confused. One problem with this procedure was that even 4-year-old children made few errors, and many letters were never confused at all.

Perceptual confusion
A measure of the frequency with which two patterns are mistakenly identified as each other

Features	A	E	F	H	I	L	T	K	M	N	V	W	X	Y	Z	B	C	D	G	J	O	P	R	Q	S	U
Straight	●	●	●	●		●	●								●				●							
horizontal		●	●	●	●	●	●	●	●	●					●		●	●				●	●			
vertical	●							●	●		●	●	●	●												
diagonal /	●							●	●	●	●	●	●	●								●	●			
diagonal \																										
Curve																										
closed																●		●			●	●	●	●		
open vertical																				●						●
open horizontal																	●	●	●						●	
Intersection	●	●	●	●		●	●						●			●						●	●	●		
Redundancy																										
cyclic change		●						●		●					●										●	
symmetry	●	●		●	●			●	●	●	●	●	●	●		●	●	●			●					●
Discontinuity																										
vertical	●		●	●	●		●	●	●	●			●									●	●			
horizontal		●	●		●	●									●											

Figure 2.3 *A possible set of features for capital letters.*

From *Principles of Perceptual Learning and Development*, by E. Gibson, p. 88, © 1969 by Prentice-Hall, Inc. Englewood Cliffs, New Jersey. Reprinted by permission.

A second procedure projected a pair of letters on a small screen and required that subjects indicate whether the two letters were the "same" or "different" by pushing one of two buttons as soon as they could make their decision (Gibson, Schapiro, & Yonas, 1968). The subjects were college students and 7-year-old children. Since all the possible combinations of "different" pairs and an equal number (to prevent a response bias toward saying "different") of "same" pairs required too many judgments, two sets of nine letters were used. The assumption was that it should take longer to decide that two rather similar letters were different than to decide about two very dissimilar letters. The results supported the assumption. The average time for adults to decide that G and W were different was 458 msec, compared with 571 msec to decide that P and R were different.

The reaction times were analyzed by **hierarchical cluster analysis** (S. Johnson, 1967). The analysis partitions letters into finer and finer categories on the basis of their perceived similarity. The letters in each category are difficult to distinguish from each other, as revealed by the longer reaction times to discriminate between any pair of letters in a category. An analysis of the children's reaction times revealed that the letters C, G, P, and R belonged to one category and the letters E, F, M, N, and W to another (see Figure 2.4). By looking at the letters in each category, we can infer the features of the letters that were important in determining perceived similarities—all the letters with curves were grouped into one category and the letters composed of straight lines into another. This grouping reveals that people are slower in responding that two letters are

Hierarchical cluster analysis An analysis that separates—clusters— patterns into categories of similar patterns by dividing larger categories into smaller and smaller categories

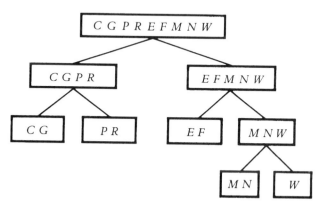

Figure 2.4   *A hierarchical cluster analysis illustrating perceived similarities among letters.*

From "Confusion Matrices for Graphic Patterns Obtained with a Latency Measure," by E. Gibson, R. Shapiro, and A. Yonas, in *The Analysis of Reading Skill: A Program of Basic and Applied Research.* Final report, project no. 5-1213, Cornell University and USOE, 1968. Reprinted by permission of Dr. Eleanor J. Gibson.

different when both letters contain curves or when both letters contain only straight lines.

The cluster analysis next partitioned the curved letters into the two confusable pairs CG and PR, distinguished by the presence of a vertical line. The other branch was then partitioned into EF and MNW, distinguished by the presence of either a horizontal line or a diagonal line. Finally, the pair MN was established as a confusable pair. The analysis of the adult reaction times yielded very similar results. The cluster analysis for both groups showed that the straight/curved contrast was the major determinant of perceived similarity. The presence of a particular line orientation (vertical or diagonal) also influenced reaction times.

A third method for measuring perceived similarity is to ask an observer to identify letters that are presented very rapidly in a tachistoscope (Townsend, 1971). It is often difficult to discriminate physically similar letters under these conditions, and the errors provide a measure of perceived similarity. Holbrook (1975) compared two feature models to determine how successfully each could predict the pattern of errors found by Townsend. One was the Gibson model shown in Figure 2.3 and the other was a modification of the Gibson model proposed by Geyer and De Wald (1973). The major change in the modification was the specification of the number of features in a letter (such as two vertical lines for the letter H) rather than simply listing whether that feature was present. A comparison of the two models revealed that the feature set proposed by Geyer and De Wald was superior in predicting the confusion errors made both by adults (Townsend, 1971) and by 4-year-olds (Gibson et al., 1963). The prediction of both models improved when the features were optimally weighted to allow for the fact that some features are more important than others in accounting for confusions. Since the straight/curved distinction is particularly important, it should be emphasized more than the others.

A potential source of embarrassment for proponents of feature models is that even the best-predicting model did not predict Townsend's data as well as a template model that measured the physical overlap of each pair of letters. The correlation between predicted errors and obtained errors was .70 for the template model and .50 for the Geyer and De Wald model using optimally weighted features. The higher correlation for the template model means that it was more successful than the feature model at predicting correct responses. Why did the template model do better if it is not a very good theory of how people recognize patterns? Perhaps one reason it predicted well in these circumstances is that all the letters came from the same type font and there were no variations of each letter. But a more important reason is that a template preserves the relations among the features. The letters E and F would produce considerable overlap because the vertical line and two horizontal lines in the letter F are connected in the same way as the vertical line and the upper two horizontal lines in the letter E. However, the similarity of two letters is determined not only by what features each contains but also by how the features are joined together. In order for feature theories to predict more accurately, the relations among features would have to be made more explicit. This is the main objective of structural theories.

Structural Theories

The importance of the relations among the features of a pattern is a guiding principle of Gestalt psychology. To Gestalt psychologists a pattern is more than the sum of its parts. Relations among pattern features have been formalized by people working in the field of artificial intelligence who discovered that the interpretation of patterns usually depends on making explicit how the lines of a pattern are joined to other lines. I pointed out previously that a template theory would be unable to distinguish between the two interpretations of Figure 2.5. A feature theory would also have problems because, although it could identify the four sides as features, the features are identical for the two interpretations. **Structural theories**, however, emphasize the relations among the features, and Clowes (1969) used Figure 2.5 as an example of why structural theories are often necessary to produce adequate descriptions of patterns. Perceiving the pattern as a stingray requires grouping adjacent lines: line *a* with line *d* (forming the head) and line *b* with line *c* (forming the tail). Perceiving the pattern as a sail requires grouping opposite lines: line *a* with line *c* (top and bottom) and line *b* with line *d* (the sides of the sail).

Structural theories build upon feature theories. Before we can specify the relation among features, we have to specify the features. A structural theory allows for specification of how the features fit together. For example, the letter *H* consists of two vertical lines and a horizontal line.

Structural theories of pattern recognition Theories that specify how the features of a pattern are joined to other features of the pattern

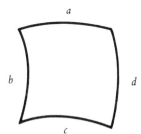

Figure 2.5 *An ambiguous pattern, showing a stingray or a sail.*

From "Transformational Grammars and the Organization of Pictures," by M. Clowes, 1969, in A. Graselli (Ed.), *Automatic Interpretation and the Organization of Pictures*. Copyright 1969 by Academic Press, Inc. Reprinted by permission.

But we could make many different patterns from two vertical lines and a horizontal line. What is required is a precise specification of how the lines should be joined together—the letter *H* consists of two vertical lines connected at their midpoints by a horizontal line.

A simple experiment shows how creating a relation between features can facilitate rapid discrimination between two patterns. The bottom pair of letters in Figure 2.6 differs from the top pair by the addition of a dot. The dot appears in the same physical location for each letter, but it creates a different relation for each letter. It falls inside the curve for the letter *b* and outside the curve for the letter *p*. If people can use this relation, it should be easier to discriminate between the two dotted letters than between the two normal letters.

G. R. Lockhead and W. B. Crist (1980) tested this prediction by asking kindergarten children to sort a deck of cards into two bins. The deck contained either the two normal letters or the two dotted letters, arranged in a random order. The children sorted the dotted letters significantly faster than the normal letters, indicating that the addition of the dot made it easier to discriminate between the *b* and the *p*. The children also made fewer errors on the dotted letters. These results showed that adding the same feature to a pair of patterns made it easier to distinguish the two patterns because of the differing relation between the features.

The features that we have considered thus far are features of two-dimensional shapes such as letters. However, it may be more convenient to describe three-dimensional objects in terms of simple volumes such as cylinders, blocks, wedges, and cones. Like the features of letters, these components can be combined in many different ways to produce a variety

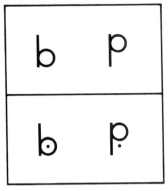

Figure 2.6 *Normal (top) and dotted letters.*

From "Making Letters Distinctive," by G. R. Lockhead and W. B. Crist, 1980, *Journal of Educational Psychology, 72,* 483–493. Copyright 1980 by the American Psychological Association. Reprinted by permission.

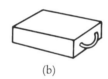

(a)   (b)   (c)   (d)

Figure 2.7   *Different arrangements of the same components can produce different objects.*

From "Human Image Understanding: Recent Research and a Theory," by I. Biederman, *Computer Vision, Graphics and Image Processing,* 1985, 32, 29–73. Copyright 1985 by Academic Press. Reprinted by permission.

of objects. For example, the mug and the pail in Figure 2.7 contain the same two components in a different arrangement.

The advantage of being able to form many different arrangements from a few components is that we may need relatively few components to describe objects. Biederman (1985) has proposed that we need only about 35 simple volumes (which he called **geons**) to describe the objects in the world. If so, then pattern recognition consists mainly in describing the relations among this limited set of components, rather than in discriminating among hundreds of components.

One consequence of Biederman's argument is that deleting information about the relation of features should reduce people's ability to recognize patterns. To test this hypothesis, Biederman removed 65% of the contour from drawings of objects, such as the two cups shown in Figure 2.8. In the cup on the left, the contour was removed from the middles of the segments, allowing observers to see how the segments were related. In the cup on the right, the contour was removed from the vertices so observers

Geons Different three-dimensional shapes that combine to form three-dimensional patterns

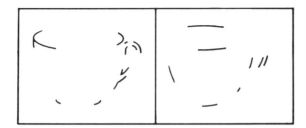

Figure 2.8   *Illustration of 65% contour removal centered at either midsegments (left object) or vertices (right object).*

From "Human Image Understanding: Recent Research and a Theory," by I. Biederman, *Computer Vision, Graphics and Image Processing,* 1985, 32, 29–73. Copyright 1985 by Academic Press. Reprinted by permission.

would have difficulty recognizing how the segments were related. When drawings of different objects were presented for 100 msec, subjects correctly named 70% of the objects if the contours were deleted at midsegments. But if the contours were deleted at the vertices, subjects correctly named fewer than 50% of the objects (Biederman, 1985). As predicted, destroying relational information was particularly detrimental for object recognition.

These results show that the relations among features are important, but they do not directly show that features are grouped together to form larger components (geons). A later study (Biederman & Cooper, 1991) provided a direct test of this assumption and again used the contour deletion method. This time 50% of the contours were deleted to form a pair of complementary images. That is, contours missing from one image are present in its complementary image, as shown by the two pairs of examples in Figure 2.9. Notice that superimposing one complementary image over the other re-creates the entire pattern.

The difference between the top and bottom complementary images in Figure 2.9 is that the geons are preserved in each complementary im-

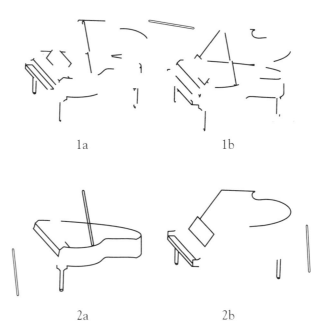

1a   1b

2a   2b

Figure 2.9   *Examples of complementary images that show either the same geons (1a and b) or different geons (2a and b).*
From "Priming Contour-Deleted Images: Evidence for Intermediate Representations in Visual Object Recognition," by I. Biederman & E. E. Cooper, *Cognitive Psychology*, 23, 393–419. Copyright © 1991 by Academic Press. Reprinted by permission.

age for the top pair, but are divided between the two complementary images for the bottom pair. For instance, the contours and vertices of the uplifted cover of the piano are divided in the top pair, but appear entirely in the right image in the bottom pair. Biederman and Cooper (1991) measured how quickly and how accurately participants could name the objects when they had already correctly named the complementary image. Based on their theory, they predicted that correctly naming 1*a* should be particularly helpful for later naming 1*b* because the same geons would be activated for 1*a* and 1*b*. In contrast, correctly naming 2*a* would be less helpful for later naming 2*b* because different geons would be activated in 2*a* and 2*b*. Both the response times and the accuracy levels supported their predictions. People were faster and more accurate when the complementary images had the same geons than when they had different geons. These findings support the theory that relations are important both for grouping features together into larger units (geons) and for showing the relation among geons to form more complex objects.

In conclusion, structural theories extend feature theories by specifying how the features are related. Sutherland (1968) was one of the first to argue that, if we want to account for our very impressive pattern recognition capabilities, we will need the more powerful kind of descriptive language contained in a structural theory. The experiments in this section show that Sutherland was correct. We will now look at how pattern recognition occurs over time.

INFORMATION-PROCESSING STAGES

The Partial-Report Technique

In order to understand how people perform on a pattern recognition task, we have to identify what occurs during each of the information-processing stages discussed in Chapter 1. Sperling (1960) is responsible for the initial construction of an information-processing model of performance on a visual recognition task. Subjects in Sperling's task saw an array of letters presented for a brief period (usually 50 msec) in a tachistoscope and were asked to report all the letters they could remember from the display. Responses were highly accurate if the display contained fewer than 5 letters. But when the number of letters was increased, subjects never reported more than an average of 4.5 letters correctly, regardless of how many letters were in the display.

A general problem in constructing an information-processing model is to identify the cause of a performance limitation. Sperling was interested in measuring the number of letters that could be recognized during a brief exposure, but he was aware that the upper limit of 4.5 might be caused by an inability to remember more than that. In other words, subjects might have recognized most of the letters in the display but then

forgot some before they could report what they had seen. Sperling therefore changed his procedure from a **whole-report procedure** (report all the
letters) to a **partial-report procedure** (report only some of the letters).

In the most typical case, the display consisted of three rows, each
containing 4 letters. Subjects would be unable to remember all 12 letters
in a display, but they should be able to remember 4 letters. The partial-report procedure required that subjects report only one row. The pitch of a
tone signaled which of the three rows to report: the top row for a high
pitch, the middle row for a medium pitch, and the bottom row for a low
pitch. The tone sounded just after the display disappeared, so that subjects would have to view the entire display and could not simply look at
a single row (see Figure 2.10).

Use of the partial-report technique is based on the assumption that
the number of letters reported from the cued row equals the average number of letters perceived in each of the rows since the subjects did not
know in advance which row to look at. The results of this procedure
showed that subjects could correctly report 3 of the 4 letters in a row, implying that they had recognized 9 letters in the entire display.

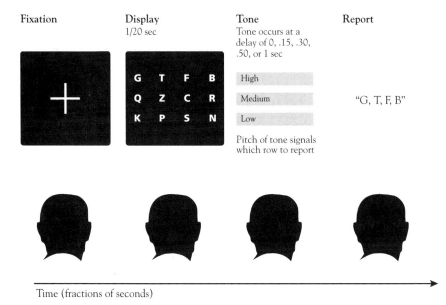

Time (fractions of seconds)

Figure 2.10 *Sperling's (1960) study of sensory memory. After the subjects
had fixated on the cross, the letters were flashed on the screen just long enough to
create a visual afterimage. High, medium, and low tones signaled which row of
letters to report.*

From "The Information Available in Brief Visual Presentations," by G. Sperling, 1960, *Psychological
Monographs, 74,* (Whole No. 498). Copyright 1960 by the American Psychological Association.
Reprinted by permission.

Sperling's Model

It often happens that what is best remembered about a scientist's work is
not what that person originally set out to investigate. Although Sperling
designed the partial-report technique to reduce the memory requirements
of his task and to obtain a "pure" measure of perception, his work is best
remembered for the discovery of the importance of a visual sensory store.
How did this come about? The estimate that subjects had perceived 9 letters was obtained when the tone occurred immediately after the termination of the 50-msec exposure. In this case, subjects could correctly report
about three-quarters of the letters, and three-quarters of 12 is 9. But when
the tone was delayed until 1 sec after the display, performance declined to
only 4.5 letters. That is, there was a gradual decline from 9 letters to 4.5
as the delay of the tone was increased from 0 to 1 sec (Figure 2.11).

The most interesting thing about the number 4.5 is that it is exactly
equal to the upper limit of performance on the whole-report task, as represented by the black bar in Figure 2.11. The partial-report procedure has no
advantage over the whole-report procedure if the tone is delayed by 1 sec

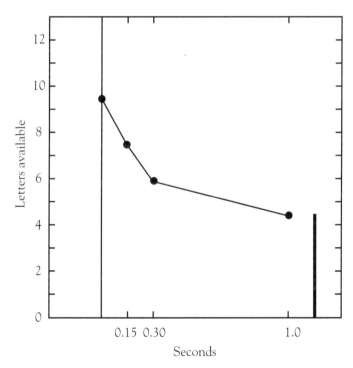

Figure 2.11   *Recalled as a function of delay of a signaling tone.*

From "The Information Available in Brief Visual Presentations," by G. Sperling,
1960, *Psychological Monographs, 74*, (Whole No. 498). Copyright 1960 by the
American Psychological Association. Reprinted by permission.

or more. To explain this gradual decline in performance, Sperling proposed that the subjects were using a visual sensory store to recognize letters in the cued row. When they heard the tone, they selectively attended to the cued row in the store and tried to identify the letters in that row. Their success in making use of the tone depended on the clarity of information in their sensory store. When the tone occurred immediately after termination of the stimulus, the clarity was sufficient for recognizing additional letters in the cued row. But as the clarity of the sensory image faded, it became increasingly difficult to recognize additional letters. When the tone was delayed by 1 sec, the subjects could not use the sensory store at all to focus on the cued row, so their performance was determined by the number of letters they had recognized from the entire display that happened to be in that row. Their performance was therefore equivalent to the whole-report procedure, in which they attended to the entire display.

In 1963 Sperling proposed an information-processing model of performance on his visual report task. The model consisted of a visual information store, scanning, rehearsal, and an auditory information store.

Visual information store (VIS) This is a sensory store that maintains visual information for approximately a quarter of a second

The **visual information store (VIS)** is a sensory store that preserves information for a brief period lasting from a fraction of a second to a second. The decay rate depends on such factors as the intensity, contrast, and duration of the stimulus and also on whether exposure of the stimulus is followed by a second exposure. Visual masking occurs when a second exposure, consisting of a brightly lighted field or a different set of patterns, reduces the effectiveness of the visual information store.

In order for pattern recognition to occur, the information in the sensory store must be scanned. Sperling initially considered scanning to occur for one item at a time, as if each person had a sheet of cardboard with a hole in it just large enough for a single letter to appear.

Rehearsal Repeating verbal information to keep it active in STM or to transfer it into LTM

Auditory information store In Sperling's model this store maintains verbal information in STM through rehearsal

The next two components of the model were **rehearsal** (saying the letters to oneself) and an **auditory information store (AIS)** (remembering the names of the letters). In order to remember the items until recall, subjects usually reported rehearsing the items. Additional evidence for verbal rehearsal was found when recall errors often appeared in the form of auditory confusions—in other words, producing a letter that sounded like the correct letter. The advantage of the auditory store is that subvocalizing the names of the letters keeps them active in memory. Sperling's auditory store is part of short-term memory, a topic we will consider later in the book.

Serial processing When we carry out one operation at a time, such as pronouncing one word at a time

Parallel processing When we carry out more than one operation at a time, such as looking at an art exhibit and carrying on a conversation

Sperling revised his initial model in 1967. By this time evidence had begun to accumulate suggesting that patterns were not scanned one at a time but were analyzed simultaneously. This distinction between performing one cognitive operation at a time (**serial processing**) and performing more than one cognitive operation at a time (**parallel processing**) is a fundamental distinction in cognitive psychology. Sperling therefore modified his idea of the **scan component** to allow for pattern recognition to occur simultaneously over the entire display, although the rate of recognition in a given location depended on where the subject was focusing attention. As I indicated in Chapter 1, this was one of the first models that attempted to indicate how various stages (sensory store, pattern recognition, and STM) combined to influence performance on a visual processing task. It contributed to the construction of the general model illustrated in Figure 1.1 and led to further development of more detailed models of how people recognize letters in visual displays (Rumelhart, 1970).

Scan component   The attention component of Sperling's model that determines what is recognized in the visual information store

Rumelhart's Model

In 1970 Rumelhart proposed a detailed mathematical model of performance on a wide range of information-processing tasks, including the whole-report and partial-report procedures studied by Sperling. Rumelhart's model assumes that recognition occurs by identification of the features of a pattern. Feature recognition occurs simultaneously over the entire display, but it takes time to recognize features; the more time the observer has, the more features the observer can recognize. Imagine that you are looking at the screen of a tachistoscope and the experimenter presents a brief exposure of the letters *F*, *R*, and *Z*. If the exposure is very short, you might see only the vertical line of the letter *F*, the curve of the letter *R*, and the diagonal line of the letter *Z*. If forced to guess at this point, you would most likely use this information. You might guess that the *R* was an *R*, *P*, or *B* because these letters have curved segments at the top. If the exposure is a little longer, you will be able to see more features, and it will be easier to guess or even recognize the entire letter.

Your success in identifying the letters will be determined then not only by the length of the exposure but also by how quickly you can recognize the features. The rate of feature recognition in Rumelhart's model is influenced by both the clarity of the information and the number of items in the display. When the exposure terminates, the clarity declines as the visual information store decays. The number of items in the display affects the rate of feature recognition because the model assumes that people have a limited amount of attention, which is divided across all the items in the display. As the number of items increases, the amount of attention that can be focused on each item declines, and this slows down the rate of recognizing that particular item.

The assumption that the rate of feature recognition depends on both the number of items in the display and the clarity of the information is used by Rumelhart to account for performance on Sperling's task. Rumelhart's model proposed that people can report an average of only 4.5 letters in the whole-report procedure because of a perceptual limitation rather than a memory limitation. As the number of letters is increased up to 12, people continue to try to recognize all the letters simultaneously. But the rate of recognizing each letter slows down as more letters are added to the display. Although there are more letters that could be recognized, the increase is compensated for by the lower probability of recognizing each letter.

Rumelhart's model assumed that in the partial-report procedure the observer tries to recognize letters over the entire display before hearing the tone. Then, on hearing the tone, the observer attends only to the cued row in the visual information store and tries to recognize additional letters in that particular row. The rate of recognition is faster because the observer now has to attend to only 4 letters rather than 12. But as the visual information store decays, not only is there less time to use it, but it becomes harder to use because of decreasing clarity. Success in focusing on the cued row therefore depends very critically on the timing of the tone, as illustrated by Figure 2.11. Rumelhart's assumptions provided adequate and quantitative predictions about performance not only on Sperling's tasks but on a number of other tasks as well.

More recent studies have confirmed many of these assumptions, including the assumption that people switch from looking at the entire display to looking only at the cued row after they know which row to report (Gegenfurtner & Sperling, 1993). However, before receiving the cue, observers attend primarily to the middle row and therefore are more accurate when asked to report letters from this row.

You may have guessed by now that it is difficult to use the partial-report paradigm to answer Sperling's initial question about how many letters people perceive during a brief exposure. Observers begin by trying to perceive letters over the entire display with an emphasis on the middle row; they then hear a tone and decide where to shift their attention; and finally they try to recognize letters in only the cued row.

Detection paradigm
A procedure in which observers have to specify which of two possible target patterns is present in a display

A better procedure for answering this question, called the **detection paradigm**, was designed by Estes and Taylor (1966). This procedure requires that the observer report which one of two target letters is in a display of letters. For instance, the subject might be told that a display will contain either a *B* or an *F*, and the task is to report which letter is present. The memory requirements are minimal because the subject must report only a single letter. By using the percentage of trials on which the observer was right, and correcting for guessing, Estes and Taylor were able to calculate the average number of letters perceived on each trial. The detection procedure has also been analyzed by Rumelhart (1970) as a part of his general model—a model that provided an impressive account of performance on the visual information-processing tasks studied during the 1960s.

WORD RECOGNITION

The Word Superiority Effect

Much of the research on pattern recognition during the 1970s shifted away from how people recognize isolated letters to how people recognize letters in words. This research was stimulated by a finding that has been labeled the *word superiority effect*. Reicher (1969), in his dissertation at the University of Michigan, investigated a possible implication of the scan component in Sperling's 1967 model. If the observer tries to recognize all the letters in an array simultaneously, is it possible to recognize a four-letter unit in the same amount of time as it takes to recognize a single letter? To answer this question, Reicher designed an experiment in which observers were shown a single letter, a four-letter word, or a four-letter nonword. The task was always to identify a single letter by selecting one of two alternatives. The exposure of the stimulus was immediately followed by a visual masking field with the two response alternatives directly above the critical letter. For example, one set of stimuli consisted of the word *WORK*, the letter *K*, and the nonword *OWRK*. The two alternatives in this case were the letters *D* and *K*, which were displayed above the critical *K* (see Figure 2.12). Observers indicated whether they thought the letter in that position had been a *D* or a *K*.

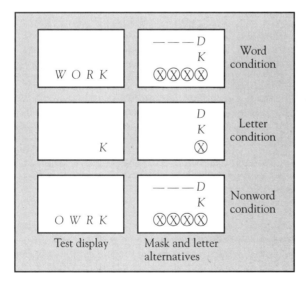

Figure 2.12 *Example of the three experimental conditions in Reicher's (1969) experiment. The mask and response alternatives followed the test display. The task was to decide which of the two alternatives had appeared in the test position.*

This example illustrates several characteristics of Reicher's design. First, the four-letter word has the same letters as the four-letter nonword. Second, the position of the critical letter is the same for the word and the nonword. Third, both of the response alternatives make a word (*WORD* or *WORK*) for the word condition and a nonword for the nonword condition. And, fourth, the memory requirements are minimized by requiring that subjects identify only a single letter, even when four letters are presented.

The results showed that subjects were significantly more accurate in identifying the critical letter when it was part of a word than when it was part of a nonword or when it was presented alone (the **word superiority effect**). Eight of the nine subjects did better on single words than on single letters. The one subject who reversed this trend was the only subject who said that she saw the words as four separate letters, which she made into words; the other subjects said that they experienced a word as a single word, not as four letters making up a word.

A Model of the Word Superiority Effect

One of the great challenges for psychologists interested in word recognition has been to explain the word superiority effect (Pollatsek & Rayner, 1989). A particularly influential model, the **interactive activation model** proposed by McClelland and Rumelhart (1981), contains several basic assumptions that build upon the assumptions of Rumelhart's (1970) earlier model of letter recognition. The first assumption is that visual perception involves parallel processing. There are two different senses in which processing occurs in parallel. Visual processing is spatially parallel, resulting in the simultaneous processing of all four letters in a four-letter word. This assumption is consistent with Sperling's parallel scan and with Rumelhart's model of how people attempt to recognize an array of letters.

Visual processing is also parallel in the sense that recognition occurs simultaneously at three different levels of abstraction. The three levels—the feature level, the letter level, and the word level—are shown in Figure 2.13. A key assumption of the interactive activation model is that the three levels interact to determine what we perceive. Knowledge about the words of a language interacts with incoming feature information to provide evidence about which letters are in the word. This is illustrated by the arrows in Figure 2.13, which show that the letter level receives information from both the feature level and the word level.

There are two kinds of connections between levels: excitatory connections that are illustrated in Figure 2.13 by pointed arrows and inhibitory connections that are illustrated by the filled circles. **Excitatory connections** provide positive evidence and **inhibitory connections** provide negative evidence about the identity of a letter or word. For example, a

Word superiority effect The finding that accuracy in recognizing a letter is higher when the letter is in a word than when it appears alone or is in a nonword

Interactive activation model A theory that proposes that both feature knowledge and word knowledge combine to provide information about the identity of letters in a word

Excitatory connections Reactions to positive evidence for a concept, as when a vertical line provides support for the possibility that a letter is a *K*

Inhibitory connections Reactions to negative evidence for a concept, as when the presence of a vertical line provides negative evidence that a letter is a *C*

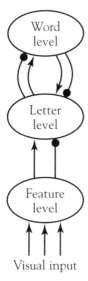

Figure 2.13   *The three levels of the interactive activation model, with arrows indicating the excitatory connections and circles indicating inhibitory connections.*

From "An Interactive-Activation Model of Context Effects in Letter Perception: Part 1. An Account of Basic Findings," by J. L. McClelland and D. E. Rumelhart, 1981, *Psychological Review*, 88, 375–407, Fig. 2. Copyright © 1981 by the American Psychological Association. Reprinted by permission.

diagonal line provides positive evidence for the letter *K* (and all other letters that contain a diagonal line) and negative evidence for the letter *D* (and all other letters that do not contain a diagonal line). Excitatory and inhibitory connections also occur between the letter level and word level depending on whether the letter is part of the word in the appropriate position. Recognizing that the first letter of a word is a *W* increases the activation level of all words that begin with a *W* and decreases the activation level of all other words.

The interactive activation model builds on the assumptions of Rumelhart's (1970) theory of letter recognition, discussed previously. Each feature in the display has some probability of being detected that varies with the visual quality of the display. Features that are detected increase the activation level of letters that contain the feature and decrease the activation level of those letters that do not contain the feature. The excitatory and inhibitory influences combine to determine the total activation of each letter. For instance, detecting a vertical and a diagonal line would strongly activate those letters (such as *K* and *R*) that contain both of these features.

Figure 2.14 illustrates how these assumptions apply to identifying the letter *K* when it appears in the word *WORK*. The bottom graph shows how the activation of letters in the fourth position changes over time and the top graph shows how the activation of words changes over time. Evidence for the letter *K* steadily increases over time as the observer identifies more features of the letter. Activation of the letter *D* does not increase because it receives inhibitory influences from identified features

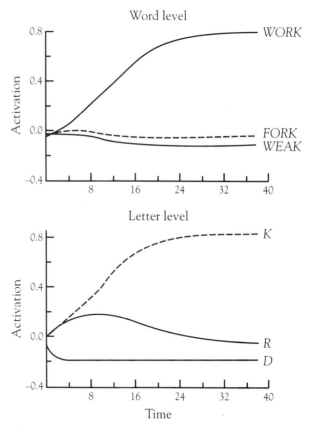

Figure 2.14   *Activation levels for selected letter and word units with increasing duration of the display for the word condition in Figure 2.12.*

From "An Interactive-Activation Model of Context Effects in Letter Perception: Part 1. An Account of Basic Findings," by J. L. McClelland and D. E. Rumelhart, 1981, *Psychological Review*, 88, 375–407, Fig. 2. Copyright © 1981 by the American Psychological Association. Reprinted by permission.

that are not in the letter *D*. The activation of the letter *R* initially increases because it shares two features with the letter *K*, but it receives inhibitory feedback from the word level as it becomes apparent that having an *R* in the fourth position will not make a word. Notice that in the top graph, the activation of the word *WORK* steadily increases over time, relative to other words, as the observer identifies more features.

Not all psychologists believe that the interactive activation model is correct. Massaro and Cohen (1991), in particular, have carefully compared the predictions of the interactive activation model with the predictions of a model that assumes that word and letter information combine independently, rather than interact. Unlike the interactive activation model, illustrated in Figure 2.13, their model does not have connections coming from the word level back down to the letter level. Information about words therefore does not directly influence the activation of letters. Massaro and Cohen's data suggest that assuming independent integration of information from letter and word levels may generate more accurate predictions than assuming that information at the word level interacts with information at the letter level.

I have devoted a considerable amount of space to discussing the interactive activation model and you may be wondering if it is worth your time if some psychologists believe it is wrong. I have two responses. A general response is that there are very few (if any) theories in psychology that have gone unchallenged. Psychologists continually try to formulate better theories and there is often considerable debate about which is the best theory. A more specific response is that the interactive activation model has had a tremendous impact on the formulation of psychological theories because it helped rekindle interest in neural network models of cognition. Although neural network models have been developed for many cognitive tasks, such as storing information in STM (Burgess & Hitch, 1992), selecting an analogous problem in problem solving (Holyoak & Thagard, 1989), and comprehending text (Kintsch, 1988), they have been most widely used to model pattern recognition. Let's now consider the general assumptions of this approach.

Neural Network Models

The interactive activation model was the first step for McClelland and Rumelhart in their development of neural network models of cognition. They referred to such models as **parallel distributed processing (PDP)** models because information is evaluated in parallel and is distributed throughout the network. A **neural network model** consists of a number of components (Rumelhart, Hinton, & McClelland, 1986), some of which we have already considered in the interactive activation model. These include:

Parallel distributed processing When information is simultaneously collected from different sources and combined to reach a decision

Neural network model A theory that uses a neural network as a metaphor in which concepts (nodes) are linked to other concepts through excitatory and inhibitory connections

Nodes   The format for representing concepts in a semantic network

1. A set of processing units called **nodes.** Nodes are represented by features, letters, and words in the interactive activation model. They can acquire different levels of activation.
2. A pattern of *connections* among nodes. Nodes are connected to one another by excitatory and inhibitory connections that differ in strength.
3. *Activation rules* for the nodes. **Activation rules** specify how a node combines its excitatory and inhibitory inputs with its current state of activation.
4. A state of *activation.* Nodes can be activated to various degrees. We become conscious of nodes that are activated above a threshold level of conscious awareness. For instance, we become consciously aware of the letter *K* in the word *WORK* when it receives enough excitatory influences from the feature and word levels.
5. *Output functions* of the nodes. The output functions relate activation levels to outputs; for example, what threshold has to be exceeded for conscious awareness.
6. A *learning rule.* Learning generally occurs by changing the weights of the excitatory and inhibitory connections between the nodes, and the learning rule specifies how to make these changes.

Activation rules   Rules that determine how inhibitory and excitatory connections combine to determine the total activation of a concept

The last component—the learning component—is one of the most important features of a neural network model because it enables the network to improve its performance. An example would be a network model that learns to make better discriminations among letters by increasing the weights of the distinctive features—those features that are most helpful for making the discrimination.

The neural network approach has resulted in thousands of research efforts and an industry that spends several hundred million dollars annually (Schneider & Graham, 1992). The excitement of this approach is illustrated in Box 2.1 and can be attributed to several reasons. First, many psychologists believe that neural network models more accurately portray how the brain works than other, more serial models of behavior. Second, adjusting the excitatory and inhibitory weights that link nodes allows a network to learn and this may capture how people learn. Third, the models allow for a different kind of computing in which many weak constraints (such as evidence from both the feature and word levels) can be simultaneously considered.

However, critics have questioned whether the models are really theories because they primarily involve changing many connection weights (Schneider & Graham, 1992). For instance, a system called NET-TALK (Sejnowski & Rosenberg, 1987) produces words at about the level of a 2-year-old child after 40,000 learning trials. NET-TALK learns by adjusting

BOX 2.1

Computer "learns" from own mistakes

BY DAVID GRAHAM
STAFF WRITER

In a laboratory of the Salk Institute in La Jolla, California, Terry Sejnowski has a computer that "learns" how to speak by reading and rereading simple English sentences—improving from its mistakes.

After 10 hours of sounding out the text, the computer's high-pitched babble becomes an intelligible sentence like "I walk home with friends from school."

Across the road at the University of California, San Diego (UCSD), David Zipser and Jeffrey Elman have a computer that "listens" to spoken words and then, with practice, writes them in symbolic language on a computer screen.

The success of these and other powerful computers that operate in ways similar to the human brain has persuaded scientists from the two institutions to form a program to advance neural network technology.

Called the Neural Computing Project at UCSD, it is intended to be a focus for grants and a clearinghouse for the ideas of 40 faculty members from a variety of disciplines, said Halbert White, a UCSD economics professor and project member.

The approach to computing, called neural computation, seeks to apply to computers the organizational principles the brain uses when it thinks.

Unlike traditional computers—such as word processors—that perform programmed functions step by step, neural network computers usually involve several "processing units." They work together, in parallel, and transfer information among themselves to accomplish complex tasks rapidly.

Neural network computers, the scientists say, could perform many sophisticated tasks by recognizing patterns and variations.

Already sonar systems guided by neural network computers can be used to discriminate among objects, for example, between a rock on the floor of the ocean and an undersea mine waiting to be detonated, White said.

"This is an exciting new approach to a computational alternative to the standard serial computers that have had such an effect on present technology," White said.

SOURCE: From "Computer 'Learns' from Own Mistakes," by David Graham, appearing in the *San Diego Union,* September 25, 1989. Reprinted by permission.

the weights of more than 18,000 connections. McCloskey (1991) has argued that to be a good theory, a neural network model must formulate its assumptions at a more abstract level than the particular network simulation. The theorist needs to make clear which aspects of the network are crucial to the theory and which aspects are incidental. For example, is the particular learning procedure used to train the network and adjust the weights an important part of the theory?

In response to McCloskey's (1991) criticism, Seidenberg (1993) has argued that neural network models provide theoretical contributions at two levels. At the most general level, neural network models propose general principles about the acquisition of knowledge (such as how knowledge is distributed and how learning occurs by weight changes) that are explanatory because they apply to many different situations. For example, Seidenberg used the same principles to formulate neural network models for learning both the pronunciation of words and the past tense of verbs. At a more specific level, neural network models often incorporate theoretical assumptions that are specific to a particular application and differ from other models. The assumption of the interactive activation model that the activation of words influences the activation of letters is an example of a theoretical assumption that differs from the assumption of competing models (Massaro & Cohen, 1991). The inclusion of both general and specific assumptions that are testable will help determine the theoretical usefulness of neural network models.

SUMMARY

Pattern recognition is a skill that people perform very well. Three alternative explanations of pattern recognition are template, feature, and structural theories. A template theory proposes that people compare two patterns by measuring their degree of overlap. A template theory has difficulty accounting for many aspects of pattern recognition, but it is a useful way of representing information in the sensory store before it is analyzed during the pattern recognition stage. The most common theories of pattern recognition assume that patterns are analyzed into features. Feature theories are often tested by determining how well they can account for perceptual confusions. Structural theories state explicitly how the features of a pattern are joined together. They provide a more complete description of a pattern and are particularly useful for describing patterns consisting of intersecting lines.

Sperling's interest in the question of how many letters can be perceived during a brief tachistoscopic exposure resulted in the construction of information-processing models for visual tasks. Sperling proposed that information is preserved very briefly in a visual information store, where all the letters can be simultaneously analyzed. When a letter is recognized, its name can be verbally rehearsed and preserved in an auditory store (short-term memory). Rumelhart's model proposed that we recognize patterns by identifying their features. The rate of feature identification depends on both the clarity of items in the visual information store and the number of letters in a display. The model accounts for performance on Sperling's partial-report task by assuming that the observer focuses attention on the cued row as soon as the tone is heard. The probability of recognizing additional letters in the row depends on the clarity of the visual information store.

Recognition of letters in a word is influenced by perceptual information and the context of the letter. The finding that a letter can be recognized more easily when it is part of a word than when it is part of a nonword or is presented by itself has been called the word superiority effect. An influential model of the word superiority effect is the interactive activation model proposed by McClelland and Rumelhart. Its major assumption is that knowledge about the words of a language interacts with incoming feature information to provide evidence regarding which letters are in the word. This approach has continued under the general label of parallel distributed processing and is inspired by neural network models of the brain.

STUDY QUESTIONS

1. The opening quotation claims there is no definite agreement of what a pattern is. Don't by daunted—write your own definition of pattern. Now look up *pattern* in a good dictionary. Does that help?

2. In what sense can pattern recognition be considered a skill? (In order to answer this question, you must have a usable definition of skill. What is yours?)

3. Distinguish among template, feature, and structure. What is each like, and how do the concepts differ?

4. What does Phillips's 1974 experiment tell us about the presumed characteristics of the sensory store? What is the difference between a sensory image and a visual image?

5. The text tells about an application of feature theory that helps children learn differences between similar letters. What is involved in the search for a "good" set of features—that is, how would you tell whether a suggested set of features is good?

6. What are the various procedures for studying perceived similarity/perceptual confusion?

7. How does structural theory go beyond feature theories? What evidence would you cite to support its claim to be the best description of visual pattern recognition?

8. Why is Sperling's 1960s research still discussed in most introductory psychology texts?

9. How does a visual masking field work? What does it do? Why is this procedure essential to the study of the word superiority effect?

10. Neural network models represent a major theoretical approach in psychology, but are difficult to summarize in simple terms. Explain the major assumptions of these models in your own words.

KEY TERMS

The page number in parentheses refers to where the term is discussed in the chapter.

activation rules (44)
auditory information store
    (AIS) (36)
caricatures (25)
detection paradigm (38)
distinctive feature (24)
excitatory connections (40)
feature theories (24)
geons (31)
hierarchical cluster analysis (27)
inhibitory connections (40)
interactive activation model (40)
interstimulus interval (22)
neural network model (43)
nodes (44)
parallel distributed processing
    (PDP) (43)

parallel processing (36)
partial-report procedure (34)
pattern recognition (20)
perceptual confusions (26)
rehearsal (36)
scan component (37)
sensory store (22)
serial processing (36)
structural theories (29)
tachistoscope (20)
templates (20)
visual information store (VIS) (36)
whole-report procedure (34)
word superiority effect (40)

RECOMMENDED READING

Kolers's (1983) paper provides an overview of issues related to perception and representation. Townsend and his colleagues (Townsend & Ashby, 1982; Townsend, Hu, & Evans, 1984) have evaluated formal models of pattern recognition in which feature detection has a major role. Garner (1974) reviews research on the structural characteristics of patterns. In Garner (1979) he discusses the relationship between his work and Gibson's. Palmer (1977) shows how structural descriptions influence the analysis and synthesis of patterns; Bower and Glass (1976) demonstrate how structural descriptions determine the effectiveness of memory cues; and Marr and Nishihara (1978) propose a structural theory for three-dimensional shapes. Characteristics of the visual information store are described by Long (1980) and Loftus, Shimamura, and Johnson (1985). Models of word recognition have been proposed by McClelland and Rumelhart (1981), Rumelhart and McClelland (1982), Paap, Newsome, McDonald, and Schvaneveldt (1982), Grossberg and Stone (1986), and Richman and Simon (1989). Other areas of research on pattern recognition include the recognition of speech (Massaro, 1989), faces (Pittenger & Shaw, 1975; Bruce, 1994), scenes (Biederman, 1981), and maps (B. Tversky, 1981). Martindale's (1991) book, *Cognitive Psychology: A Neural-Network Approach*, provides a very readable introduction to the influence of neural network theories on cognitive theories.

Attention

Everyone knows what attention is. It is the taking possession by the mind, in clear and vivid form, of one out of what seem several simultaneously possible objects or trains of thought. Focalization, concentration, of consciousness are of its essence.

WILLIAM JAMES (1890)

*T*HE PRECEDING QUOTE from William James's famous *Principles of Psychology*, published in 1890, refers to two characteristics of attention that continue to be studied today—focalization and concentration. Focalization implies **selectivity**. We are usually bombarded by all kinds of perceptual stimuli and must decide which of these are of interest to us. The selective nature of attention is illustrated by the behavior of subjects in Sperling's partial-report task: When a cue signaled which row to report, subjects were able to attend selectively to the cued row and ignore the information in the other two rows.

The selective nature of perception is necessary to keep us from becoming overloaded with information. This is particularly true in large cities. According to Milgram (1970), a well-known social psychologist, in midtown Manhattan it is possible to encounter 220,000 people within a 10-minute radius of one's office. This kind of overload, Milgram argues, can affect our life on several levels, influencing role performance, the evolution of social norms, and cognitive functioning. Adaptive responses to information overload include spending less time on each input, disregarding low-priority inputs, or completely blocking off some sensory inputs. The first part of this chapter is concerned with theories that try to locate the stage at which this selection occurs. Do we block off the sensory input before it reaches the pattern recognition stage, or do we make the selection after recognition? Theories that attempt to answer this question are called **bottleneck theories** because they assume that selection is necessary whenever too much information reaches a bottleneck—a stage that cannot process all of it.

The second aspect of attention is **concentration**. Imagine that you are the first to arrive at a cocktail party, and you carry on a conversation with the hostess. As long as there are no other conversations in the room, it will require little concentration or mental effort to follow what your hostess is saying. If she were not speaking in your native language, however, comprehension would be less automatic and would require more mental effort. You would also have to concentrate more to follow what she was saying if you were surrounded by many other conversations. If you wanted to eavesdrop on one of the other conversations while you were listening to the hostess, still more concentration or mental effort would be required.

The second section of this chapter discusses **capacity theories** of attention, which try to determine how capacity or mental effort is allocated to different activities. Such theories propose that attention is limited in capacity, and when we try to attend to more than one event—studying while watching television, for instance—we pay the price of doing each less efficiently. Rumelhart's model, discussed in Chapter 2, is a theory that assumes a limited capacity. According to his model, feature recognition slows down as the number of items increases because a limited amount of attention must be distributed over more patterns.

An important area of research related to capacity theories is the study of automatic processing. **Automatic processing** occurs when the capacity required for carrying out a task is minimal. If a task requires very little capacity to perform, it should not interfere with other tasks. The third section of this chapter examines the characteristics of automatic processing and illustrates how the concept can be applied to the acquisition of reading skills.

Automatic processing
Performing mental operations that require very little mental effort

The final section presents some research on using selective listening tests to predict success in a pilot training program and to predict the accident rate of commercial drivers. There are other potential applications of research on selective attention. One example is the diagnosis of heart murmurs. Rushmer (1970) pointed out that it is difficult for medical students to learn how to classify heart murmurs. Part of the difficulty results from the demands of selective attention—it is hard to hear the murmur embedded in the sound of a heartbeat. Perhaps we will see still more applications of selective-attention research in the future.

Before I talk about attention in my own course on cognitive psychology, I have the students try to listen to two verbal messages at once. Two volunteers come to the front of the class and read different passages from one of their books. The rest of the class usually find it very difficult to comprehend both of the messages simultaneously. It is easier to try to comprehend only one of the messages, but the difficulty of the task depends on physical characteristics such as pitch and separation. The difficulty increases as the pitch of the two speakers becomes more similar or the two speakers stand closer together. If you have the opportunity, try to participate in such a demonstration and observe some of these effects for yourself. It will give you a better understanding of the listener's task.

BOTTLENECK THEORIES

Broadbent's Filter Model

As you may recall, the discussion of information-processing models in Chapter 1 included a summary of Broadbent's (1958) filter model. That model could account for much of the data on attention that had been collected at that time. One example is an experiment in which enlisted men in England's Royal Navy listened to three pairs of digits (Broadbent, 1954). One member of each pair arrived at one ear at the same time that the other member of the pair arrived at the other ear. For example, if the sequence were 73–42–15, the subject would simultaneously hear 7 and 3, followed by 4 and 2, followed by 1 and 5. That is:

Left ear	Right ear
7	3
4	2
1	5

The pairs were separated by a half-second interval, and the subjects were asked to report the digits in whatever order they chose. They were able to report 65% of the lists correctly, and almost all the correct reports involved recalling all the digits presented to one ear, followed by all the digits presented to the other ear. In other words, if 741 had been presented to the left ear and 325 to the right ear, the subject would recall either in the order 741–325 or in the order 325–741.

Another group of men was instructed to recall the digits in the actual order of their arrival: the first pair of digits, followed by the second pair, followed by the third pair. The time between successive pairs of digits varied from ½ sec to 2 sec. Figure 3.1 shows the percentage of lists correctly recalled as a function of the interval between pairs. Performance was better at the longer intervals; nevertheless, it was much worse than when subjects could recall the digits heard in one ear and then the other ear.

To account for these findings, Broadbent (1957) used the **filter model**, which can be represented by the mechanical model shown in Figure 3.2. The mechanical model consists of a Y-shaped tube and a set of identifiable balls. The tube has a narrow stem that can accept only a single ball at a time (the **limited-capacity perceptual channel**) but upper branches (the *sensory store*) are wider and can accept more than one ball at a time. At the junction of the stem and branches is a hinged flap (the *filter*), which can swing back and forth to allow balls from either branch of the Y to enter the stem.

Filter model The proposition that a bottleneck occurs before pattern recognition and that attention determines what information reaches the pattern recognition stage

Limited-capacity perceptual channel The pattern recognition stage of Broadbent's model, which is protected by the filter (attention) from becoming overloaded with too much perceptual information

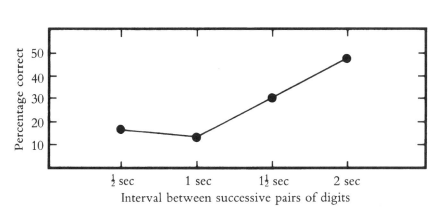

Figure 3.1 *Recall of digit sequences as a function of the interval between pairs.*

From "The Role of Auditory Localization in Attention and Memory Span," by D. E. Broadbent, 1954, *Journal of Experimental Psychology, 47*, 191–196. Copyright 1954 by the American Psychological Association. Reprinted by permission.

and the two branches represent
:ously dropped, one into each
e side to allow one of the balls to
uld be held in a sensory store. If
digits entering one ear, the flap
alls from one branch entered the
or reporting the left ear first. The
side, allowing the three balls from
the observer were forced to report
d have to be shifted back and forth
order in which they arrived.

nce on Broadbent's (1954) task by
assuming that it takes time to switch attention (represented by the flap,
or filter) from ear to ear. If the interval separating the pairs of balls is too
short, the flap will not have time to switch back and forth, and performance will deteriorate as it did when the interval was 1 sec or less (see
Figure 3.1). The easiest case should be when the listener can report all
the digits entering one ear before reporting all the digits entering the
other ear. In this case the listener can recognize all the digits entering
one ear before recognizing the digits entering the other ear, and only a
single shift of attention is required. But the shift has to occur before the
information entering the unattended ear decays from the auditory sensory

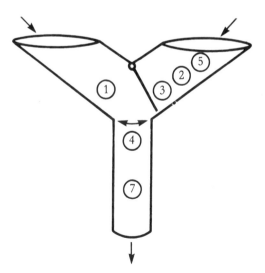

Figure 3.2   *A mechanical model of attention.*

From "A Mechanical Model for Human Attention and
Immediate Memory," by D. E. Broadbent, 1957, *Psychologi-
cal Review, 64*, 205–215. Copyright 1957 by the American
Psychological Association. Reprinted by permission.

store. A limitation of the filter model is that the sensory store would have to last fairly long in order to operate as proposed; otherwise, the information would decay before it could be recognized.

Treisman's Attenuation Model

A common experimental paradigm for testing Broadbent's assumption that the listener can recognize information on only one channel at a time is to present a different, but continuous, message to each ear and ask the listener to **"shadow,"** or repeat aloud, one of the messages. Shadowing a message provides proof that the listener is following instructions and attending to the correct ear. The initial findings from shadowing experiments supported the filter model. As predicted, subjects were almost completely unaware of the content of the message played to the unattended ear (Cherry, 1953).

Shadowing An experimental method that requires people to repeat the attended message out loud

However, later research indicated that listeners occasionally could report information on the unattended channel. Moray (1959) discovered that subjects sometimes heard their own names on this channel. Treisman (1960) found that the **contextual effects** of language would sometimes cause subjects to report words on the unattended channel and therefore shadow inappropriately. Following are two examples of the intrusions that occurred:

Contextual effects The influence of the surrounding context on the recognition of pattterns

1. . . . I SAW THE GIRL / song was WISHING . . .
   . . . me that bird / JUMPING in the street . . .
2. . . . SITTING AT A MAHOGANY / three POSSIBILITIES . . .
   . . . let us look at these / TABLE with her head . . .

The first line in each example is the message that the listener was asked to shadow. The second line is the unattended message. The words in capital letters are the words actually spoken by the subjects. The intrusions from the unattended channel fit the semantic context better than the words on the attended channel. The contextual cues were not sufficient to cause subjects to change permanently to the unattended message in order to follow the meaning of the passage, but the results did raise some questions for the filter theory. If the filter completely blocks out the unattended message, how could subjects report hearing their names or shadow words on the unattended channel?

To answer this question, Treisman (1960) proposed a model consisting of two parts—a *selective filter* and a "dictionary". The filter distinguishes between two messages on the basis of their physical characteristics, such as location, intensity, or pitch. However, the filter in Treisman's model does not completely block out the unattended message but merely attenuates it, making it less likely to be heard. The recognition of a word occurs in the dictionary if the intensity or subjective loudness of the word exceeds its **threshold** (the minimum intensity needed for recognition). The thresholds have two important characteristics. First, they vary across words. Some words have permanently lower thresholds than others and thus are more easily recognized—for example, important words such as a person's own name and perhaps danger signals such as *fire*. Second, the thresholds can be momentarily lowered by the listener's expectations. For instance, if the words *sitting at a mahogany* are heard, the threshold for the word *table* will be momentarily lowered, making recognition of that word more likely.

Threshold The minimal amount of activation required to become consciously aware of a stimulus

The model proposed by Treisman was able to explain why usually very little is heard on the unattended channel, but occasionally some words are recognized. The **attenuation** of words on the unattended channel implies that they will be subjectively less loud than words on the attended channel. They will usually not be loud enough to exceed their threshold unless they have a very low threshold or their threshold is momentarily lowered. Figure 3.3 shows a schematic representation of this effect. The height of the arrows represents the subjective loudness of the two messages, and the height of the thresholds represents the loudness that is necessary for recognition of the word. Since important words have permanently low thresholds, they can occasionally be heard on the unattended channel, as was found by Moray (1959). A word like *table* normally has a high threshold, but its threshold can be momentarily lowered by expectations. This aspect of the model could account for Treisman's (1960) finding that words on the unattended channel were sometimes incorrectly shadowed if they better fit the context of the message on the attended channel.

Attenuation A decrease in the perceived loudness of an unattended message

The Deutsch-Norman Memory Selection Model

The models proposed by Broadbent and Treisman placed the bottleneck at the pattern recognition stage. Attention was represented by a selective filter that completely blocked out the unattended message in Broadbent's model and attenuated it in Treisman's model, with the implication that very few words should be recognized on the unattended channel. An unattended message could be recognized, in Broadbent's model, only if attention switched to that message before it decayed from the sensory store. In Treisman's model, words in the unattended message could be recognized only if their thresholds were low enough to be exceeded by the attenuated message.

We have previously seen that a frequent problem in constructing information-processing models is identification of the stage at which a performance limitation occurs. Constructing models of attention is no exception. According to the models proposed by Deutsch and Deutsch (1963) and Norman (1968), the bottleneck occurs *after* pattern recognition. The

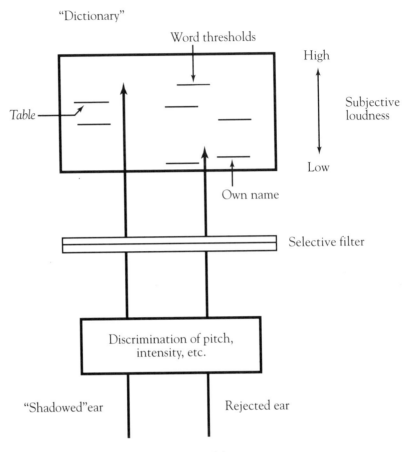

Figure 3.3 *Treisman's attenuation model.*

From "Contextual Cues in Selective Listening," by A. M. Treisman, 1970, *Quarterly Journal of Experimental Psychology, 12,* 242–248. Copyright 1970 by the Experimental Psychology Society. Reprinted by permission.

problem is not one of perception but one of selection after perception occurs. In their models attention is equivalent to the *selection stage* in Figure 1.1 (Chapter 1).

The model proposed by Deutsch and Deutsch involves two different conversations (messages). The model assumes that words in both conversations are recognized but are quickly forgotten unless they are important. Words on the attended channel are important because people have to shadow them. Words on the unattended channel are usually unimportant because the listener is asked to attend to another channel. Although recognized, they are quickly forgotten unless they are important—a person's own name, for instance. The probability that information will enter memory depends on the general level of arousal in addition to the importance of the material. Much more will enter memory when a person is alert than when the person is drowsy.

Norman expanded the Deutsch and Deutsch model in a 1968 paper. Figure 3.4 is a schematic diagram of Norman's model. Three sensory inputs—i, j, and k—are recognized by being matched to their representations in memory. They will be quickly forgotten, however, unless they can be selected for more permanent storage. Selection is determined not only by the strength of the sensory input but also by the pertinence, or importance, of each input. Certain words have a permanently high level of importance, whereas others have low levels but can fluctuate as a result

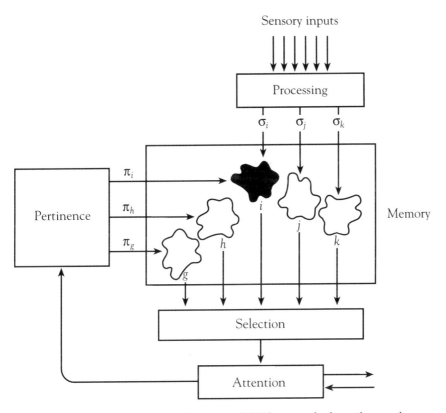

Figure 3.4   *Norman's memory selection model. The example shows five words, represented by the subscripts g, h, i, j, and k. Words g, h, and i are important, and words i, j, and k are consistent with the sensory input. The word selected for further processing—in this case, i—is the one with the greatest combination of pertinence (importance) and sensory activation.*

From "Toward a Theory of Memory and Attention," by D. A. Norman, 1968, *Psychological Review*, 75, 522–536. Copyright 1968 by the American Psychological Association. Reprinted by permission.

of expectations formed from contextual, grammatical, or semantic cues. The input that is acted on or stored more permanently in memory is determined by a combination of sensory activation and importance (labeled σ and π in Figure 3.4). Stimulus *i* has the highest combination in the example, so it is the one selected for further processing. One problem with distinguishing between Treisman's and Norman's models is that they both try to explain the same data, but in different ways. Words that are important or are expected are more easily recognized in Treisman's model because of lower thresholds; they are more likely to be selected in Norman's model because of their importance.

Treisman attempted to determine the location of the bottleneck by asking participants to listen to a different list of words arriving in each ear and to tap whenever they heard an identical target word in either ear. In addition, they had to shadow (repeat out loud) all the words that arrived on the attended ear. She argued that the tapping response was so simple and immediate that people should do equally well in tapping to target words on the attended and unattended ears if the bottleneck occurred at the response selection stage, but they should do much better in tapping to the target words in the attended ear if the bottleneck occurred at the perception stage. The participants detected the target word 87% of the time that it occurred in the attended ear and only 8% of the time that it occurred in the unattended ear (Treisman & Geffen, 1967), supporting the hypothesis that the bottleneck occurred at the perception stage.

However, Deutsch, Deutsch, and Lindsay (1967) did not accept these results as evidence against their theory. They argued that the shadowed words on the attended message are more important because they are shadowed and this added importance increased the probability that they would elicit the tapping response. Furthermore, the fact that people occasionally report hearing their name or an expected word in the unattended message makes it clear that at least some words are heard on the unattended message.

CAPACITY THEORIES

The models proposed by Broadbent, Treisman, Deutsch and Deutsch, and Norman stimulated many experiments and arguments regarding the location of the bottleneck. Some data seemed to support the assertion that the bottleneck was caused by the limitations of perception, whereas other data supported the assertion that the bottleneck occurred after perception (Johnston & Dark, 1986). The failure to agree on the location of the bottleneck has had two consequences.

First, psychologists have become more interested in studying the capacity demands of different tasks than in locating the bottleneck (Kahneman, 1973). Capacity models are based on the assumption that tasks require **mental effort**. Even dreaming, which does not seem to require mental effort, causes a high activity level in some parts of the brain (see Box 3.1). Second, it now seems reasonable to assume that the observer has some control over where the bottleneck occurs depending on what is required in a particular task (Johnston & Heinz, 1978).

We will look first at the capacity model of attention proposed by Kahneman to see how a capacity model differs from a bottleneck model. Then we will review the theory proposed by W. A. Johnston and S. P. Heinz (1978), which suggests that attention is flexible. This theory is particularly interesting because it shows how a bottleneck theory can be related to a capacity theory since the location of the bottleneck determines how much capacity is required to perform a task.

Mental effort The amount of mental capacity required to perform a task

---

The world of dreams is no place for loafers: Pioneer study finds brain hard at work in realm of tall tales

BOX 3.1

SANTA ANA—He was roller-skating on the main floor of Neiman-Marcus when a roaring tiger chased him through the store.

Her boss demanded she paint the office floor several colors. He could not explain what colors he wanted or why, but he wanted the job done right away.

He was in the country, riding a horse that responded to commands to stop by galloping wildly.

Waking up from a technicolor, full-fledged nightmare, who has not wondered what stuff dreams are made of?

A pioneering study of brain metabolism during nighttime dreaming conducted at UC Irvine has found the dreaming brain uses as much energy as when it is awake.

Dreams may germinate in a region of the brain that spawns emotions and probably are spun into narratives by a side of the brain linked to making up tall tales, said Dr. Monte Buchsbaum, a psychiatrist and the director of UCI's Brain Imaging Center.

Buchsbaum said the study of normal volunteers showed that during sleep without dreams brain activity drops steeply, by an average of 23 percent. The drop enforces the common-sense view that sleep allows the brain as well as the body to rest.

But during dreams the brain "lights up" with activity. One region in particular—the cingulate gyrus—works even harder during dreams than when a person is awake and could play a special role in dreams.

SOURCE: From "The World of Dreams Is No Place for Loafers," appearing in the *San Diego Union,* September 25, 1989. Reprinted by permission of Knight-Ridder Newspapers.

Example of a Capacity Model

Capacity theories are concerned with the amount of mental effort required to perform a task. Kahneman's *Attention and Effort* (1973) helped to shift the emphasis from bottleneck theories to capacity theories. Kahneman argued that a capacity theory assumes there is a general limit on a person's capacity to perform mental work. It also assumes that a person has considerable control over how this limited capacity can be allocated to different activities. For example, we can usually drive a car and carry on a conversation at the same time if both activities do not exceed our capacity for attending to two different tasks. But when heavy traffic begins to challenge our skills as a driver, it is better to concentrate only on driving and not try to divide our attention between the two activities.

Allocation of capacity When a limited amount of capacity is distributed to various tasks

A model of the **allocation of capacity** to mental activities is shown in Figure 3.5. Any kind of activity that requires attention would be represented in the model because all such activities compete for the limited capacity. Different mental activities require different amounts of attention; some tasks require little mental effort and others require much effort. When the supply of attention does not meet the demands, the level of performance declines. An activity can fail entirely if there is not enough capacity to meet its demands or if attention is allocated to other activities.

Arousal A physiological state that influences the distribution of mental capacity to various tasks

Kahneman's model assumes that the amount of capacity available varies with the level of **arousal;** more capacity is available when arousal is moderately high than when it is low. However, very high levels of arousal can interfere with performance. This assumption is consistent with Yerkes and Dodson's (1908) law that performance is best at intermediate levels of arousal.

The level of arousal can be controlled by feedback (evaluation) from the attempt to meet the demands of ongoing activities, provided that the total demands do not exceed the capacity limit. The choice of which activities to support is influenced by both enduring dispositions and momentary intentions. **Enduring dispositions** reflect the rules of involuntary attention. A novel event, an object in sudden motion, or the mention of our own name may automatically attract our attention. **Momentary intentions** reflect our specific goals or objectives at a particular time. We may want to listen to a lecturer or scan a crowd at an airport in order to recognize a friend.

Enduring dispositions These automatically influence where people direct their attention

Momentary intentions These are conscious decisions to allocate attention to certain tasks or aspects of the environment

The use of alarm systems to automatically attract attention is one way to help people cope with situations that overload their limited capacity. Recently a Boeing 707 was flying in clouds toward the World Trade Center at an altitude that was 200 feet below the top of the North Tower mast. An alarm system buzzed in the nearby airport control tower to signal that the plane was flying at a dangerously low altitude. Instantly

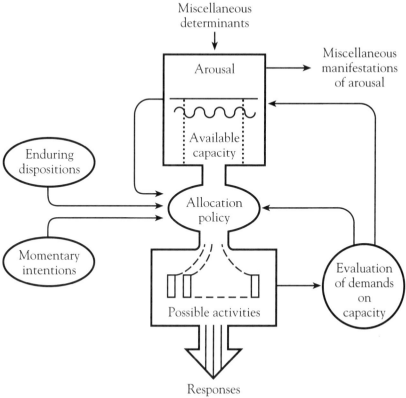

Miscellaneous
determinants

Arousal

Miscellaneous
manifestations
of arousal

Available
capacity

Enduring
dispositions

Allocation
policy

Momentary
intentions

Evaluation
of demands
on
capacity

Possible activities

Responses

Figure 3.5 *A capacity model for attention.*

From Daniel Kahneman, *Attention and Effort,* © 1973, p. 10. Reprinted by permission of
Prentice-Hall, Inc., Englewood Cliffs, New Jersey.

the controller radioed the crew to turn around and climb to 3000 feet. The controller did not initially notice the low altitude because he was responsible for controlling seven other planes at the time of the near accident, a situation that overloaded his limited capacity.

The capacity model proposed by Kahneman was designed to supplement, rather than to replace, the bottleneck models. Both types of theories predict that simultaneous activities are likely to interfere with each other, but they attribute the interference to different causes. A bottleneck theory proposes that interference occurs because the same mechanism is required to carry out two incompatible operations at the same time, whereas a capacity model proposes that interference occurs when the demands of two activities exceed available capacity. Thus a bottleneck model implies that the interference between tasks is specific and depends on the degree to which the tasks use the same mechanisms. A capacity model, in contrast, implies that the interference is nonspecific and depends on the total demands of the task. Both kinds of interference occur, and both kinds of theories are therefore necessary.

Capacity and Stage of Selection

The flexibility of attention and the interaction between a bottleneck and a capacity theory have been demonstrated by Johnston and Heinz (1978). They used selective listening tasks to develop their theory, so a bottleneck would be likely to occur. However, unlike the early bottleneck theories, their theory proposed that the listener has control over the location of the bottleneck. The location can vary along a continuum ranging from an early mode of selection—in other words, before recognition (as represented by Broadbent's theory)—to a late mode of selection—in other words, following a semantic analysis (as represented by Deutsch and Deutsch's theory). Johnston and Heinz call their theory a **multimode theory** because of its flexibility: The observer can adopt any mode of attention demanded by, or best suited to, a particular task.

Multimode theory A theory that proposes that people's intentions and the demands of the task determine the information-processing stage at which information is selected

Although a listener can attempt to understand the meaning of two simultaneous messages by adopting a late mode of selection, the use of a late mode is achieved at a cost. As the perceptual processing system shifts from an early to a late mode of selection, it collects more information about the secondary message, but this reduces the capacity to comprehend the primary message. The predicted result is that comprehension of the primary message will decline as the listener tries to process a secondary message more fully.

Johnston and Heinz tested these predictions in a series of five experiments. A common procedure for measuring the amount of capacity required to perform a task is to determine how quickly a person can respond to a **subsidiary task**. The main task in their research was a selective listening task. A light signal occurred randomly throughout the listening task, and, as the subsidiary task, subjects were instructed to respond to it as quickly as possible by pushing a button. The experimenters assumed that the greater the portion of capacity allocated to selective listening, the less should be available for monitoring the signal light, causing longer reaction times.

Subsidiary task A task that typically measures how quickly people can react to a target stimulus in order to evaluate the capacity demands of the primary task

One of the experiments used a paradigm in which subjects heard pairs of words presented simultaneously to both ears. Undergraduates at the University of Utah were asked to shadow words defined either by the pitch of a voice or by a semantic category. One set of stimuli used a male and a female voice, and the undergraduates were asked to shadow the words spoken by either the male or the female. These subjects could use an early, sensory mode of selection because the two messages were physically different. Another group of undergraduates heard two messages spoken by the same voice. One message consisted of words from a category,

such as names of cities, and the other message consisted of words from a
different category, such as names of occupations. Subjects were asked to
report the words from one of the categories and ignore the words from
the other category. These subjects had to use a late, semantic mode of selection because it was necessary to know the meaning of the words in order to categorize them.

The multimode theory predicts that more capacity is required to perform at a late mode of selection. Use of the semantic mode should therefore cause slower reaction times to the light signal and more errors on the
selective listening task. The theory also predicts that listening to two lists
should require more capacity than listening to and shadowing one list,
which should require more capacity than listening to no lists. Reaction
times for the subsidiary task supported the predictions. The average time
to respond to the light signal was 310 msec for no lists, 370 msec for one
list, 433 msec for two lists that could be distinguished by using sensory
cues (pitch), and 482 msec for two lists that could be distinguished by using only semantic cues (categories). These results were accompanied by
different levels of performance on the shadowing task. The percentage of
errors was 1.4 for a single list, 5.3 for the two lists that could be separated
using sensory cues, and 20.5 for the two lists that could be separated using
only semantic cues.

Johnston and Heinz interpreted the results as supporting their view
that selective attention requires capacity and that the amount of capacity
required increases from early to late modes of selection. The first assumption received support from the consistent finding across experiments that
reaction times were slower when the listener had to listen to two lists
rather than only one. The second assumption received support from the
consistent finding that reaction times were slower when the listener had
to attend on the basis of semantic cues rather than sensory cues. This latter finding, when combined with the performance results on the selective
listening task, suggests that a person can increase breadth of attention,
but only at a cost in capacity expenditure and selection accuracy. But
there are two silver linings to this otherwise dark cloud. First, if attention
is as flexible as suggested by the multimode theory, a person at least has
the choice of how best to use it. And, second, psychologists have demonstrated that, with sufficient practice, some tasks can become so automatic
that they do not appear to require any of the precious capacity postulated
by a capacity theory.

AUTOMATIC PROCESSING

The work of Johnston and Heinz and other cognitive psychologists has
shown that tasks vary considerably in the amount of mental effort required to perform them. Some skills become so well practiced and routine

that they require very minimal capacity. Psychologists have used the term *automatic processing* to refer to such skills.

Acquisition of automatic processing is often an advantage. It allows us to perform routine activities without much concentration or mental effort. However, automatic processing can also be a disadvantage. We may put so little thought into what we are doing that we make a silly mistake or fail to remember what we did.

We will begin by examining criteria that people can apply to determine whether they are using automatic processing. We will then see how automatic processing is useful in performing complex tasks such as reading.

When Is a Skill Automatic?

Posner and Snyder (1975) have proposed three criteria to determine whether a skill is automatic. A skill is automatic if it (1) occurs without intention, (2) does not give rise to conscious awareness, and (3) does not interfere with other mental activities.

Learning to ride a bicycle is a familiar example that we can evaluate by using these criteria. Most of us have learned how to ride a bicycle, and perhaps we can still remember the early experience of wobbling back and forth for a few feet before stopping and having to start over. Balancing the bicycle initially required intention, conscious awareness of what we were trying to do, and mental effort that could interfere with our concentration on other activities. Once we learned how to balance, it became hard to imagine why we had had so much trouble initially. We could then ride a bicycle without consciously intending to balance, we had little conscious awareness of the movements we used to achieve balance, and we became more able to attend to the scenery or our thoughts because we no longer had to concentrate on balancing.

Another task that initially requires a lot of mental effort or capacity is reading a word. But, like riding a bicycle, reading a word eventually becomes a fairly automatic skill. In fact, it becomes so automatic that it is difficult to stop, even when reading would be a disadvantage. Consider a task in which you are shown words that are printed in red, green, or blue ink and your objective is simply to name the color of the ink. If the words are names of colors that cause a competing response (such as the word *red* printed in blue ink), it is better to avoid reading the words because it makes the task much harder. However, people cannot completely avoid reading the words, as is revealed by the fact that they perform the task more slowly when there are competing responses. This finding is called the **Stroop effect** after its discoverer (Stroop, 1935).

The Stroop effect provides a partial answer to the question asked by Posner and Snyder (1975) at the beginning of their article: To what extent are our conscious intentions and strategies in control of the way in-

Stroop effect The finding that it takes longer to name the color of the ink a word is printed in when the word is the name of a competing color (for example, the word *red* printed in blue ink)

Sleepwalker's acquittal upheld

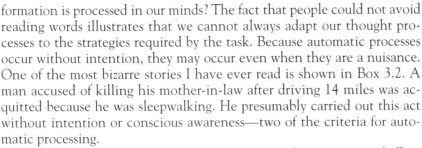

OTTAWA—A man acquitted of killing his mother-in-law while sleepwalking had the verdict upheld by Canada's highest court yesterday.

The Supreme Court said a lower court was right in saying the sleepwalker was legally sane but suffered from a sleep disorder. Early one morning in May 1987, Kenneth James Parks, then 23, of Pickering, Ontario, drove his car 14 miles and stabbed his wife's parents while they were asleep.

The court heard that the man, under financial stress after betting on horse races, was being supported by his parents-in-law.

SOURCE: From "Sleepwalker's Acquittal Upheld," appearing in the *San Diego Union*, August 28, 1992. Reprinted by permission of Reuters News Desk.

formation is processed in our minds? The fact that people could not avoid reading words illustrates that we cannot always adapt our thought processes to the strategies required by the task. Because automatic processes occur without intention, they may occur even when they are a nuisance. One of the most bizarre stories I have ever read is shown in Box 3.2. A man accused of killing his mother-in-law after driving 14 miles was acquitted because he was sleepwalking. He presumably carried out this act without intention or conscious awareness—two of the criteria for automatic processing.

Fortunately, automatic processes usually are advantageous and allow us to perform complex skills that would otherwise overload our limited capacity. Two of these skills are encoding information into memory and reading.

Automatic Encoding

You may be asked over the dinner table at the end of the day how your day went. You would find it fairly easy to recall the events that occurred even though you did not make a conscious effort to learn that information. It is likely that you automatically encoded that information into memory.

In 1979 Hasher and Zacks proposed a theory of *automatic encoding* that distinguished between two kinds of memory activities—those that require considerable effort, or capacity, and those that require very little or none. The former, or effortful processes, include various strategies to improve memory, such as visual imagery, elaboration, organization, and verbal rehearsal. The latter, or automatic processes, support **incidental learning** when we are not consciously trying to learn. Hasher and Zacks proposed that we can automatically record frequency, spatial, and temporal information without consciously intending to keep track of this information.

Incidental learning
Learning that occurs when we do not make a conscious effort to learn

Frequency information is information about how frequently different stimuli occur. An experimenter might vary the number of times people see different pictures during an experiment and then ask them to estimate how many times each picture appeared. *Spatial information* is information about where objects occur in the environment. The experimenter could present pictures in different locations and then ask people to recall the locations. *Temporal information* is information about when or for how long events occur. The experimenter might ask people about the relative recency or the relative duration of events that occurred during the experiment.

The claim that all three kinds of information can be automatically recorded in memory cannot be tested unless we specify the implications of automatic processing. Hasher and Zacks proposed five criteria that distinguish between automatic and effortful processing. Table 3.1 summarizes the criteria and their predicted effects. The predictions are:

1. *Intentional versus incidental learning:* Intentional learning occurs when we are deliberately trying to learn; incidental learning occurs when we are not. Incidental learning is as effective as intentional learning for automatic processes but is less effective for effortful processing. People have knowledge of frequency, spatial, and temporal information even when they are not trying to learn this information. (For example, we know that a word is more likely to begin with the letter *t* than with the letter *z* without trying to learn this information.)

2. *Effect of instructions and practice:* Instructions on how to perform a task and practice on the task should not affect automatic processes because they can already be carried out very efficiently. Both instructions and practice should, however, improve performance on effortful processes.

3. *Task interference:* Automatic processes should not interfere with each other because they require little or no capacity. Effortful processes require considerable capacity and should interfere with each other when they exceed the amount of available capacity.

4. *Depression or high arousal:* Emotional states such as depression or high arousal can reduce the effectiveness of effortful processes. Automatic processes should not be affected by emotional states.

5. *Developmental trends:* Automatic processes show little change with age. They are acquired early and do not decline in old age. Effortful processes show developmental changes; they are not performed as well by young children or the elderly.

If Hasher and Zacks (1979) are correct, then memory for frequency, temporal, and spatial information should not be affected by intentional versus incidental learning, practice, task interference, depression or high arousal, and developmental trends. The greatest amount of empirical sup-

Table 3.1 *Predicted effects for automatic and effortful processing*

	Automatic Processing	Effortful Processing
Intentional versus incidental learning	No difference	Intentional better
Effect of instructions and practice	No effects	Both improve performance
Task interference	No interference	Interference
Depression or high arousal	No effects	Decreased performance
Developmental trends	None	Decreased performance in young children or elderly

port for these predictions has been for frequency information (Hasher & Zacks, 1984). Neither practice nor individual differences, including changes in development, have much influence on people's ability to judge the relative frequency of events. There is also considerable incidental learning of event frequencies. People were very good at judging the relative frequency of events, even when they did not know they would be tested on their knowledge of frequencies. The automatic encoding of this information is useful because knowledge of frequencies allows us to develop expectancies about the world. We will see specific examples of how people make use of this information in the chapters on categorization (Chapter 8) and decision making (Chapter 14).

Evidence for automatic encoding of spatial and temporal information has been more mixed and is influenced by such variables as the complexity of the task. Imagine that you are shown 20 drawings of common objects that occupy 20 of the cells in a 6 × 6 matrix. Later you see the same matrix but the experimenter has switched the location of 10 of the objects. Could you identify the 10 objects that had not been moved?

If you had automatically encoded spatial location, this should be a relatively easy task, and it should not be influenced by the variables listed by Hasher and Zacks (1979). But each of the variables investigated by Naveh-Benjamin (1988) influenced people's ability to identify which objects had not changed locations. Intentional learning was better than incidental learning, the simultaneous performance of another task disrupted spatial encoding, younger participants did better than older participants, and memory for locations improved with practice.

Naveh-Benjamin argued that for fairly complex tasks, the criteria suggested by Hasher and Zacks might still hold, but in a weaker sense. Those encoding processes showing less noticeable change as a function of age, practice, simultaneous processing, and incidental learning could be considered as more automatic than others. Another theoretical approach is to allow for the possibility that automatic processing is usually achieved only after extensive practice. For instance, reading a word requires little effort for skilled readers, but achieving automatic processing could require extensive practice. In the next section we consider the important role that automatic processing plays in reading.

Automatic Processing and Reading

One of the most demanding cognitive skills that face the young child is learning how to read. Learning to read requires many component skills, some of which we considered in the previous chapter. The child must analyze the features of letters, combine the features to identify the letters, convert the letters into sounds for pronouncing words, understand the meanings of individual words, and combine the meaning of the words to comprehend the text. According to a theory proposed by LaBerge and Samuels (1974), the ability to acquire complex, multicomponent skills such as reading depends on the capability of automatic processing. Their criterion for deciding when a skill or subskill is automatic is that it can be completed while attention is directed elsewhere. The rationale behind this argument is that, unless at least some of the component skills can be completed without requiring capacity, the total demands of all the component skills will be simply too great for the individual to perform the task.

As we saw in the previous chapter, an initial component skill for successful reading is the ability to identify the features of a letter. The features must then be organized or combined to form a letter, a process that initially requires attention, according to LaBerge and Samuels. However, after sufficient practice in recognizing letters, the features can be combined automatically to form a letter, freeing some capacity for the other necessary component skills. Learning to read depends not only on learning the component skills but on learning them so well that they make very little demand on the limited capacity of attention.

LaBerge and Samuels used a letter-matching task to illustrate the acquisition of the automatic processing of letters. They studied how quickly people could decide whether two mirror-image letters were the same (such as *bb*) or different (such as *bd*). The pairs were either familiar letters or artificial letters (such as *b √*). When subjects were shown only mirror-image letters, they could match the artificial letters as quickly as they could match the familiar letters; familiarity didn't make any difference. However, when subjects matched other letters and were only occasionally shown mirror-image pairs, they matched a familiar pair faster than an artificial pair. The time to match the artificial pairs declined with practice, however, and after 5 days of practice the subjects could match artificial pairs as quickly as familiar pairs (Figure 3.6).

The researchers interpreted these results as demonstrating the acquisition of automatic processing. When subjects were expecting a different group of letters, they had to switch their attention to the appropriate set

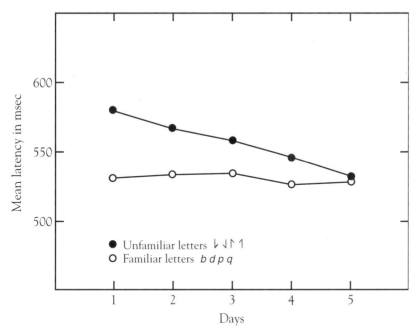

Figure 3.6 *Average response times for matching familiar and unfamiliar letters when subjects were expecting a different letter set.*

From "Toward a Theory of Automatic Information Processing in Reading," by D. LaBerge and S. J. Samuels, 1974, *Cognitive Psychology*, 6, 293–323. Copyright 1974 by Academic Press, Inc. Reprinted by permission.

when artificial letters were presented. This would require additional time and delay their response. But a switch of attention was not required for the familiar letters because these letters could be identified automatically, without attention. The finding that artificial letters eventually were compared as quickly as familiar letters suggested that something was being learned about the unfamiliar letters over the 5 days of practice. Since there was no difference in matching pairs when subjects were expecting the correct set of letters, LaBerge and Samuels proposed that subjects were learning to automatically process the artificial pairs when their attention was directed elsewhere. The theorists suggested that acquiring the ability to carry out a component skill automatically is an important part of learning that should be tested in addition to accuracy. Accurate performance of a component skill (such as recognizing letters) could nonetheless hinder the acquisition of a new component skill (such as pronouncing words) if the performance required so much capacity that little was left for learning the new component.

   LaBerge and Samuels argued that the automatic processing of letters became possible when people could recognize a letter as a unit rather than attend to its individual features. As an extension of their argument, words should require less capacity to recognize if we can recognize the word as a unit rather than as a string of individual letters. You may recall that almost all the people who participated in Reicher's (1969) experiment reported that they perceived a four-letter word as a unit rather than as four separate letters.

One consequence of perceiving a word as a unit is that it should cause us to attend less to the individual letters in the word. You can test your own ability to perceive individual letters in words by reading the following sentence. Read it once and then read it again, counting the *f*'s.

FINISHED FILES ARE THE RESULT OF YEARS OF SCIENTIFIC STUDY COMBINED WITH THE EXPERIENCE OF MANY YEARS.

There are six *f*'s in the sentence. If you counted fewer than six, please try again.

Most people find this a difficult task because they fail to detect the *f* in one of the words (*of*) even though it occurs three times in the sentence. One explanation of why we overlook this particular *f* is that it is pronounced like the letter *v*. Although this is a contributing factor, unitization also plays an important role (Schneider, Healy, & Gesi, 1991). Results obtained by Healy (1980) indicate that we often recognize frequently occurring words as units and therefore find it difficult to focus on their individual letters. Healy asked people to read a prose passage at normal reading speed but to circle the letter *t* whenever it occurred in the passage. She found that people were more likely to miss the letter when it occurred in common words than when it occurred in unusual words. In particular, they often missed the letter *t* in the word *the*, which is the most common word in the English language.

Healy's results are consistent with the theory advocated by LaBerge and Samuels. Since people encounter frequent words more often than unusual ones, they should be better able to recognize a frequent word as a unit. This explanation is analogous to the explanation that familiar letters are more likely than unfamiliar letters to be recognized as units. Less capacity should be required to recognize a frequent word because the reader does not have to pay as much attention to the individual letters. If less capacity is required to recognize a familiar word, the reader should have more capacity available for comprehending the meaning of the sentence.

INDIVIDUAL DIFFERENCES AND APPLICATIONS

The preceding section showed how a capacity theory can help us understand complex skills such as reading. Research on the selective nature of attention also has potential applications. Effective design of emergency instructions, for example, depends on making certain that people attend to the instructions. When the emergency could create a panic, this re-

Emergency instructions

Our May colloquium speaker, Dr. Elizabeth Loftus, spoke at the Document Design Center about her pioneering work on the design and testing of emergency instructions for public places. Dr. Loftus, a cognitive psychologist at the University of Washington, began working in the field of public messages in 1973, when she and a colleague, Dr. Jack Keating, were asked by the Government Services Administration to develop emergency evacuation messages for a 37-story federal building. They extracted what they could from the published psychological literature on perception, attention, memory, and crowd behavior and began to answer questions about the design of messages: Should there be a warning tone? Should a male or a female voice speak the message? How should the message be logically constructed? What types of sentences should be used? What words should be included or avoided?

Their initial success with applying psychological principles to the design of emergency messages led the National Bureau of Standards to request Loftus to extend her findings to hospital situations, where the words of emergency messages must be carefully chosen to avoid panic among patients. Loftus found still another way to develop and apply cognitive principles when San Francisco's subway system, BART, asked her to redesign their evacuation instructions following a disastrous fire. Three recommendations that emerged from that project were: parts of the message must be repeated, since there is no assurance that people are attending to the message the first time it is uttered; the message should be prerecorded, since a conductor's accent or emotional state can interfere with intelligibility; the structure and timing of the message need to be coordinated with the movement of people as they are obeying the instructions—too much information given too soon can prevent people from carrying out the instructions. In most of these emergency situations, designers must also carefully coordinate vocal and written instructions to make them most effective.

SOURCE: From "Emergency Instructions," appearing in the May 1980 issue of *Fine Print* (now called *Simply Stated*). Reprinted with permission from the Document Design Center, American Institutes for Research.

---

quirement is not trivial (see Box 3.3). Another application is the evaluation of individual differences in order to select people who will perform well in occupations that require selective attention. We will now look at studies that have successfully applied the selective listening task to predict flight performance and road accidents.

Predicting Flight Performance

The ability to attend selectively is important in many activities outside the laboratory. For example, Gopher and Kahneman (1971) found that flight instructors frequently emphasized the importance of selective attention in learning to fly high-performance aircraft. Flight cadets often failed because they could not appropriately divide their attention among simultaneous activities or were slow to recognize crucial signals that arrived on unattended channels. Although the selective listening paradigm was a popular laboratory task, psychologists had not developed it to study individual differences or to predict performance outside the laboratory. Gopher and Kahneman tried to remedy this situation by determining whether a test of selective listening would help them predict progress in a flight-training program.

The subjects were 100 cadets in the Israeli air force. The test consisted of a series of messages that simultaneously presented different information to the two ears. Each message contained two parts that were preceded by a tone that signaled which ear was relevant. The task was to report every digit on the relevant ear as soon as it was heard.

The 100 cadets were divided into three groups according to how far they had progressed during flight school: (1) 17 cadets had been rejected during initial training on light aircraft; (2) 41 cadets had been rejected early in training on jet aircraft; and (3) 42 cadets had reached advanced training on jet aircraft. The cadets' performance on the second part of the selective listening task, in which they had to decide whether to switch attention to the other ear, was the best predictor of their progress in flight school. Cadets who made three or more errors on this part of the test included 76% of those rejected during training on light aircraft, 56% of those rejected early in jet training, and 24% of those who had progressed to advanced training. The findings indicate that selective listening tasks have promise as a test, particularly since these results were obtained from a select group of people who probably all possessed good attentive skills relative to the general population.

Predicting Road Accidents

Kahneman, Ben-Ishai, and Lotan (1973) evaluated the generality of these findings by testing the validity of the task as a predictor of the accident rate of bus drivers. The study involved three groups of drivers. The accident-prone drivers had had at least two moderately severe accidents during a single year; the accident-free drivers had had no accidents during the same time period; the intermediate group fell between these two extremes. The drivers from the three groups took the selective listening test, and their performance was correlated with their driving records. Performance on the second part of the test again produced the highest correlation with the accident rate. Kahneman and his coinvestigators concluded that the test should enable a company to reject from 15 to 25% of the accident-prone drivers with a relatively negligible cost in rejecting potentially safe drivers.

The potential usefulness of the test was confirmed by Mihal and Barett (1976), who included a slightly modified version in a battery of seven tests. The test that best predicted the accident involvement of 75 commercial drivers was the selective listening test. Mihal and Barett's findings are interesting because we might think that some other test, such as a visual test of selective attention, would have produced the highest correlation, as driving would seem to emphasize visual skills over auditory skills. However, an embedded-figures test was not as good a predictor; nor was a simple reaction-time test. The selective listening test was likely a good predictor in this case because it measures general attention skills. People who are good at switching attention during an auditory task are also good at switching attention during a visual task (Hunt, Pellegrino, & Yee, 1989).

Thought Suppression

I would like to conclude this chapter by considering that aspect of attention that is concerned with **internal**, rather than **external**, sources of **information**. William James, whose quote began this chapter, was interested in attention to both internal and external events, but most contemporary research has studied only external events (Johnston & Dark, 1986). And yet the ability to control our attention may be as important for internal events as it is for external events. For example:

Internal information Information generated by a person's thoughts, as opposed to **external information** in the environment

> It is sometimes tempting to wish one's thoughts away. Unpleasant thoughts, ideas that are inappropriate to the moment, or images that may instigate unwanted behavior each can become the focus of a desire for avoidance. Whether one is trying not to think of a traumatic event, however, or is merely attempting to avoid the thought of food while on a diet, it seems that thought suppression is not easy. It is said, for instance, that when the young Dostoyevski challenged his brother not to think of a white bear, the child was perplexed for a long while. Contemporary psychology has not focused much inquiry on such puzzling yet important phenomena, and our research was designed to initiate such investigation. (Wegner, Schneider, Carter, & White, 1987, p. 5)

You can try Dostoyevski's challenge for yourself. For the next few minutes try not to think of a white bear. When you have finished this exercise, reflect on how successful you were and what you did to carry out the task.

If you behave like most people who are given this assignment, you probably generated distracting thoughts so you would have something else to think about. You probably also discovered that thought suppression is difficult and that the thought of a white bear kept reentering your stream of consciousness.

Suppression task
A task that instructs people not to think specified thoughts, whereas an **expression task** instructs people to think about specified thoughts

In order to study how effectively people can either avoid or continuously generate a thought, Wegner and his colleagues asked one group of students to not think of a white bear during a 5-min interval (**suppression**) and then asked them to think of a white bear during another 5-min interval (**expression**). A second group of students received the same instructions but in the reverse order. All students were told to ring a bell whenever they did think of a white bear.

Figure 3.7 shows how many bell rings occurred throughout the 5-min interval. The two lower curves indicate that people initially found it difficult to suppress their thoughts but became better as the interval lengthened. When instructed to think about a white bear, appropriate thoughts also decreased over the 5 min unless subjects had just finished the sup-

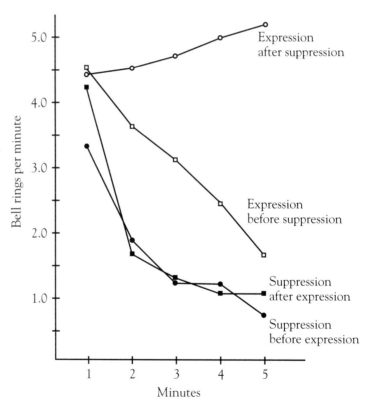

Figure 3.7   *Bell rings per min in response to thoughts of a white bear over 5-min periods*

From "Paradoxical Effects of Thought Suppression," by D. M. Wegner, K. F. Schneider, S. R. Carter, and T. L. White, 1987, *Journal of Personality and Social Psychology, 53,* 5–13, Figure 1. Copyright 1987 by the American Psychological Association. Reprinted by permission.

pression task. Those students who were now allowed to think about a white bear maintained a high rate of responding throughout the entire 5 min (upper curve).

The paradoxical effect of thought suppression is that it later produces a preoccupation with the suppressed thought. A promising explanation suggests that this finding is partly caused by attending to environmental cues to avoid attending to the inappropriate thought. People can avoid inappropriate thoughts by thinking about the objects that surround them, but these objects now become associated with the inappropriate thoughts, helping the subjects to think about such thoughts during the expression phase of the experiment. This explanation suggests several remedies for the large rebound effect following suppression. First, people could be given a single competing thought to reduce their attention to environmental cues. Instructions to think about a red Volkswagen instead of a white bear reduced white-bear thoughts during a subsequent expression task, presumably because there were fewer environmental cues associated with the task (Wegner et al., 1987). Second, subjects who changed their surroundings had fewer white-bear thoughts than subjects who performed the suppression and expression tasks in the same surroundings (Wegner & Schneider, 1989).

Wegner and Schneider conclude that it is better to work on suppression in an environment that differs from the one a person will later inhabit. This should reduce the possibility that suppressed thoughts will be cued by the very context in which they were suppressed. If the environment cannot be changed, it is better to focus on a limited number of distracters to reduce the number of cues associated with the suppression.

SUMMARY

Two characteristics of attention are selectivity and mental effort. Selectivity is necessary to keep us from becoming overloaded with too much information. The initial theories developed within the information-processing approach proposed that selectivity occurred at a bottleneck—a stage that could process only one message at a time. Broadbent's filter theory specified that the bottleneck occurred at the perception or pattern recognition stage, and attention was represented by a filter that preceded this stage. Treisman modified the filter theory to allow for occasional recognition of words on an unattended channel. She proposed that the filter attenuated the unattended message but did not completely block it out. Important words or expected words could be recognized on the unattended channel if their thresholds were low enough to be exceeded by the attenuated message. Unlike Broadbent and Treisman, Deutsch and Deutsch suggested that the bottleneck occurs after perception and determines what is selected into memory. Norman further developed the latter theory and argued that the quality of the sensory information is combined with importance to determine what enters memory.

The results of many experiments on selective listening failed to agree on the location of the bottleneck. The effect was to shift emphasis to capacity theories of attention and to encourage a more flexible view of the stage at which selection occurs. Capacity theories emphasize the amount of mental effort that is required to perform tasks and are concerned with how effort is allocated to different activities. Capacity theory supplements bottleneck theory by proposing that the ability to perform simultaneous activities is limited when the activities require more mental effort than is available. The interaction between a capacity theory and a bottleneck theory is illustrated by results obtained by Johnston and Heinz. They effectively argue that a person has control over the stage at which selection occurs, but late modes of selection (following recognition) require more capacity than early modes. The attempt to comprehend two messages therefore results in a decline in accuracy on the primary message and slower responses to a subsidiary task designed to measure capacity.

Automatic processing occurs when a task requires very little capacity to perform. Posner and Snyder proposed three criteria to determine whether a skill is automatic: (1) it occurs without intention, (2) it does not give rise to conscious awareness, and (3) it does not interfere with other mental activities.

The work on selective attention has implications for performance outside the laboratory. LaBerge and Samuels suggested that the acquisition of complex, multicomponent skills such as reading depends on the ability to carry out some of the skills automatically, without attention. But ability to perform some components correctly does not necessarily mean that a person is ready to acquire new components if all the available capacity must be used to perform already learned components. The performance of flight cadets and commercial drivers on selective listening tasks is one of the best predictors of success in flight school and of accident rates. It is not entirely clear, however, what the tests measure; further research linking theory and applications may prove beneficial to both areas. And, finally, attention to our own thoughts can be a nuisance if the thoughts are ones we wish to avoid. Thinking of distracting thoughts may help, if the distractions do not later serve as retrieval cues for the suppressed thoughts.

STUDY QUESTIONS

More than usual, this chapter will necessitate learning several names—there is unfortunately no handier way to refer to the theories. Practice may foster automaticity.

1. Try to think of some common sayings or expressions that refer to attention. Do they relate to selectivity or mental effort (capacity)?
2. As you read, notice the paradigms or tasks used to study attention. Cognitive psychologists who attempt to deal with complex behaviors such as reading perform a task analysis to determine what component skills are required. Think of some everyday activities you engage in and try to identify how attention enters into the performance of each.
3. What is the essential difference between the filter models of Broadbent and of Treisman?
4. Since the Deutsch-Norman model is said to involve a stage after pattern recognition but before STM why is it called a "memory selection model"? What are some examples of specific factors that would increase sensory activation?—or pertinence (importance)?
5. How persuasive do you find the explanation of the shift in interest from selection to the capacity aspect of attention?
6. It would be worthwhile to work through Kahneman's capacity model using a couple of the examples you generated in question 2. How about shaving, or putting on makeup, in different situations? Choose one and write it out.
7. How does one get a measure of capacity?
8. In what sense is Johnston and Heinz's multimode theory of attention interactive? What is the basis for their prediction that "more capacity is required to perform at a late mode of selection"? What task did they use to test this prediction?
9. Can you think of some skills that are automatic for you? What criteria did you use to decide?
10. How might reported individual differences of pilots and drivers on the selective listening task have come about? Can you think of some other real-world applications of either selection or capacity theories?

KEY TERMS

The page number in parentheses refers to where the term is discussed in the chapter.

allocation of capacity (60)	expression task (74)
arousal (60)	external information (73)
attenuation (55)	filter model (52)
automatic processing (51)	incidental learning (65)
bottleneck theories (50)	internal information (73)
capacity theories (50)	limited-capacity perceptual
concentration (50)	channel (52)
contextual effects (54)	mental effort (59)
enduring dispositions (60)	momentary intentions (60)

multimode theory (62)   subsidiary task (62)
selectivity (50)   suppression task (74)
shadow (54)   threshold (55)
Stroop effect (64)

RECOMMENDED READING

Kahneman's *Attention and Effort* (1973) provides a comprehensive discussion of attention in addition to presenting a capacity theory. A more recent, brief survey by LaBerge (1990) summarizes current issues about attention, relating them to the ideas expressed by William James. Chapters by Johnston and Dark (1986), Shiffrin (1988), and C. D. Wickens and A. Kramer (1985) also summarize much of the work on attention. Neisser and Becklen (1975) studied selective attention by using a visual task that was somewhat analogous to the selective listening tasks we have looked at. Schneider and Shiffrin (1977; Shiffrin & Schneider, 1977) describe their research on the acquisition of automatic processing through extensive practice and present a general theoretical framework for integrating a large number of experimental findings. More recent work on this topic is reported by Logan (1988). Hirst, Spelke, Reaves, Caharack, and Neisser (1980) evaluate different theoretical explanations of how people can perform two complex tasks (dictation and reading) at the same time. Navon and Gopher (1979) propose a general theory of how people allocate their attention when the demands of a task exceed their capacity. The role of conscious awareness during perceptual processing is discussed by Marcel (1983) and Klatzky (1984). Treisman's work (Treisman & Gelade, 1980; Treisman & Schmidt, 1982) on the importance of attention for integrating the features of a pattern is related to the theory proposed by LaBerge and Samuels (1974). See Stanovich (1990) for an evaluation of LaBerge and Samuel's theory regarding the role of automaticity in reading.

Short-Term Memory

My problem is that I have been persecuted by an integer. For seven years this number has followed me around, has intruded in my most private data, and has assaulted me from the pages of our most public journals. This number assumes a variety of disguises, being sometimes a little larger and sometimes a little smaller than usual, but never changing so much as to be unrecognizable. The persistence with which this number plagues me is far more than a random accident. There is, to quote a famous senator, a design behind it, some pattern governing its appearances. Either there really is something unusual about the number or else I am suffering from delusions of persecution.

GEORGE A. MILLER (1956)

*T*HE PRECEDING QUOTATION is the first paragraph of Miller's famous paper "The Magical Number Seven, Plus or Minus Two: Some Limits on Our Capacity for Processing Information." Miller found that people are limited in the number of items they can keep active in memory and that this limited capacity influences their performance on a variety of tasks. The previous chapter, on attention, also dealt with a capacity limitation, but our concern there was with simultaneously arriving information. The capacity model of attention proposed that our ability to carry on several activities at the same time is restricted by the total amount of mental effort that is available for distributing to these activities.

The tasks in this chapter do not require that people recognize simultaneously arriving information. There is no perceptual overload, and there is enough time to recognize each item and enter it into short-term memory (STM). The problem is that STM can hold only a limited number of items, which has a profound effect on the many tasks that require using it. The implications of this limitation are evident throughout this book—not only in this chapter but in later chapters on text comprehension, problem solving, and decision making.

Figure 4.1 shows a theory of memory proposed by Atkinson and Shiffrin (1968, 1971) that emphasizes the interaction among the sensory store, short-term memory, and long-term memory. We saw in Chapter 2 that the sensory store preserves information for a few hundred milliseconds; its characteristics were identified by Sperling (1960) for the storage of visual information. Short-term memory, the second basic component of Atkinson and Shiffrin's system, is limited in both capacity and duration. Information is lost within 20 to 30 sec if it is not rehearsed. Long-term memory is unlimited in capacity and holds information over a much longer interval, but it often takes a fair amount of effort to get information into it.

The fact that STM is needed when we perform most cognitive tasks reflects its important role as a **working memory** that maintains and manipulates information. Figure 4.1 shows that STM can combine information from both the environment and LTM whenever a person tries to learn new information, make decisions, or solve problems. When you add the numbers in your checking account, you are receiving some information from the environment (the numbers in your account) and other information from LTM (the rules of addition). Getting a correct answer depends on using both sources of information appropriately.

The goal of this chapter is to summarize the major characteristics of STM. We begin by examining both the rate and the cause of forgetting. The emphasis will be on interference as the primary cause. The second section discusses the capacity of STM. After looking at Miller's (1956) insights about capacity, we will learn how the formation of groups of

Working memory Use of STM as a temporary store for information needed to accomplish a particular task

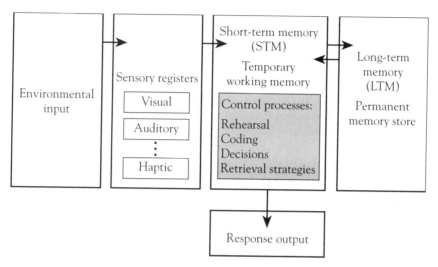

Figure 4.1   *Flow of information through the memory system.*

items in LTM can partly compensate for limited capacity. The third section deals with memory codes and emphasizes acoustic codes because they are used to maintain verbal information in STM, including information obtained from reading. However, a more complete model of working memory requires the storage of both visual and verbal codes in STM and the control of their use in manipulating information. The final section presents a model of how people recognize whether an item is in STM. In particular, we will consider how quickly people can examine the contents of their STM.

FORGETTING

Rate of Forgetting

The label *short-term memory* indicates that information in STM is lost rapidly unless it is preserved through rehearsal. The rapid rate of forgetting from STM was established by Peterson and Peterson (1959) at Indiana University. They tested undergraduates on their ability to remember three consonants over a short retention interval. To prevent subjects from rehearsing the letters, Peterson and Peterson required them to count backward by 3s, starting with a number that occurred after the consonants. For example, a subject might hear the letters *CHJ* followed by the number 506. She would then count backward until she saw a light, which

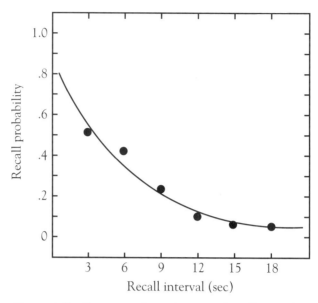

Figure 4.2   *Correct recall as a function of recall interval.*
From "Short-Term Retention of Individual Verbal Items," by L. R.
Peterson and M. J. Peterson, 1959, *Journal of Experimental Psychology,*
58, 193–198. Copyright 1959 by the American Psychological
Association. Reprinted by permission.

was a signal for recalling the three consonants. The light went on 3, 6, 9,
12, 15, or 18 sec after the subjects began counting.

Figure 4.2 shows the results of the experiment. The probability of a
correct recall declined rapidly over the 18-sec retention interval. The
rapid forgetting rate implies that we must rehearse verbal information to
keep it available in STM. It also shows why it is very likely that, if we are
momentarily distracted after looking up a telephone number, we will
have to look it up again before dialing.

This rapid rate of forgetting can be very frustrating when we are trying to learn new information, but it can also be beneficial. There are
many occasions when we need to remember something only briefly.
Think of all the phone numbers you have dialed. Most of these you dialed
only once or twice and will never need again. If all these numbers were
permanently stored in LTM, it could be very difficult to retrieve the few
numbers that you constantly use.

Decay versus Interference

One question raised by Peterson and Peterson's findings is whether the
loss of information from STM is caused by decay or by interference. Try
to remember the consonants *RQW* over a short interval without thinking

about them. Since it's difficult not to think about them if you have nothing else to do, subjects in memory experiments are asked to perform some other task. An **interference theory** proposes that memory for other material or the performance of another task interferes with memory and causes forgetting. A **decay theory** proposes that forgetting should still occur even if the subject is told not to do anything over the retention interval, as long as the subject does not rehearse the material.

The decay theory and interference theory make different predictions about whether the passage of time or the number of interfering items is the primary cause of forgetting. If memory simply decays over time, then the amount of recall should be determined by the length of the retention interval. If memory is disrupted by interference, then recall should be determined by the number of interfering items.

Waugh and Norman (1965) tested whether the loss of information from STM is caused mainly by decay or by interference. They presented lists of 16 single digits. The last digit in every list (a probe digit) occurred exactly once earlier in the list. The task was to report the digit that had followed the probe digit. For example, if the list were 5 1 9 6 3 5 1 4 2 8 6 2 7 3 9 4, the probe digit would be 4, and the correct answer (the test item) would be 2. For this particular example, there are 7 digits that occur after the test item. The number of interfering items is therefore 7. Waugh and Norman varied the number of interfering items by varying the location of the test digit in the list. There were many interfering items if the test item occurred early in the list and only a few if the test item occurred late in the list.

The experimenters also varied the rate of presentation in order to determine whether the probability of recalling the test digit would be influenced by the length of the retention interval. They presented the 16 digits in a list at a rate of either 1 digit or 4 digits per sec. Decay theory predicts that performance should be better for the fast rate of presentation because there would be less time for the information to decay from memory. Figure 4.3 shows the results. The rate of presentation had very little effect on the probability of recalling the test digit. Consider the case in which there are 12 interfering items. The retention interval would be 12 sec for the 1-per-sec rate and 3 sec for the 4-per-sec rate. Memory is only slightly (and insignificantly) better for the shorter retention interval. In contrast, the number of interfering items has a dramatic effect on retention. The probability of recall declines rapidly as the number of interfering items increases.

Waugh and Norman's findings support the contention that interference, rather than decay, is the primary cause of forgetting. Although some decay may occur (see Reitman, 1974), the amount of forgetting caused by decay is substantially less than the amount caused by interference. As Reitman and many others have shown, the extent of forgetting is determined not only by the number of interfering items but also by the

Interference theory
Proposal that forgetting occurs because other material interferes with the information in memory

Decay theory Proposal that information is spontaneously lost over time, even when there is no interference from other material

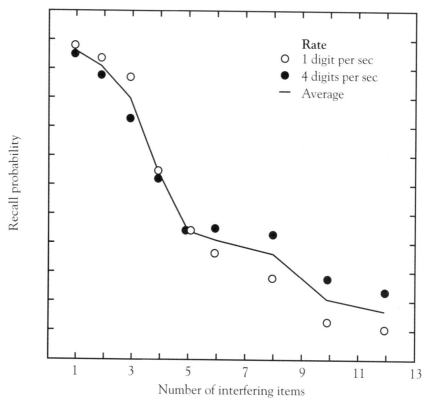

Figure 4.3   *Effect of rate of presentation and number of interfering items on recall probability.*

From "Primary Memory," by N. C. Waugh and D. A. Norman, 1965, *Psychological Review, 72,* 89–104. Copyright 1965 by the American Psychological Association. Reprinted by permission.

degree of similarity between the interfering and test items. Increasing the similarity makes it harder to recall the test items.

The finding that interference is the chief cause of forgetting is good news. If information spontaneously decayed from memory, we would be unable to prevent its loss. If information is lost through interference, we can improve retention by structuring learning so as to minimize interference. A phenomenon called "release from proactive interference" illustrates how interference can be reduced by decreasing the similarity among items.

Release from Proactive Interference

Retroactive interference   Forgetting that occurs because of interference from material encountered after learning

Psychologists have distinguished between two kinds of interference—proactive interference and retroactive interference. **Retroactive interference** is caused by information that occurs after an event. The Waugh and

Norman (1965) study demonstrated the effect of retroactive interference—the number of digits that followed the probe digit influenced how well it could be recalled. **Proactive interference**, in contrast, is caused by events that occurred before the event that someone attempts to recall.

Keppel and Underwood (1962) had previously demonstrated the effect of proactive interference in the Peterson and Peterson STM task. They found that people initially performed very well in recalling three consonants after a short retention interval, but their performance deteriorated over subsequent trials. The reason is that the consonants they had tried to remember during the initial trials began to interfere with their memory for consonants during the later trials. People found it increasingly difficult to distinguish between consonants that were presented on the current trial and consonants that had been presented on earlier trials.

Reduction of this interference is called the **release from proactive interference** (Wickens, Born, & Allen, 1963). The study by Wickens and his colleagues was the first of many studies to show that the recall of later items can be improved by making them distinctive from early items. Figure 4.4 shows a clear illustration of release from proactive interference. Students in this particular experiment were required to remember either three numbers or three common words over a 20-sec interval, during which time they performed another task to keep from rehearsing. The control group received items from the same class (either numbers or words) on each of four trials. The interference effect is evident from the decline in performance over trials. The experimental group received items from the same class over the first three trials but on the fourth trial received items from the other class. If they had been remembering words, they now remembered three numbers; if they had been remembering numbers, they now remembered three words. The shift in categories caused a dramatic improvement in performance, as Figure 4.4 illustrates. The interference effect was specific to the class of material being presented and was greatly reduced when the distinctive items occurred.

Release from proactive interference also occurs when people are asked to remember more complex events (Gunter, Clifford, & Berry, 1980). The events consisted of television news items that people heard while they viewed a videotape of the same events. People heard three items during each trial and attempted to recall them after a 1-min delay. The control group received items from the same class (either politics or sports) over a series of four trials. The experimental group received items from the same class over the first three trials, but on the fourth trial they received items from the other class. If they had been recalling sports events, they now recalled political events, and vice versa. The results were very similar to the results shown in Figure 4.4. The proportion of correct responses declined for the control group over the four trials—87% on the first trial, 67% on the second, 55% on the third, and 43% on the fourth trial. The recall of the experimental group showed a similar

Proactive interference
Forgetting that occurs because of interference from material encountered before learning

Release from proactive interference Reducing proactive interference by having information be dissimilar from earlier material

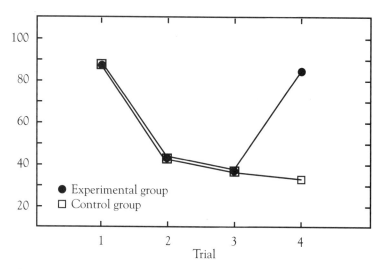

Figure 4.4   *Release from proactive interference is demonstrated on Trial 4 for experimental group.*

From "Characteristics of Word Encoding," by D. D. Wickens. In A. W. Melton and E. Martin (Eds.), *Coding Processes in Human Memory.* Copyright 1972 by V. H. Winston & Sons. Reproduced with permission from Hemisphere Publishing Corporation, Washington, D. C.

decline over the first three trials but improved dramatically on the fourth trial, when they heard items from the different category. The experimental group recalled 82% of the items on the first trial, 67% on the second, 55% on the third, and 74% on the fourth.

The practical implications of these results are simply that, whenever possible, we should try to reduce interference by ordering material in an appropriate sequence. Items that are likely to interfere with each other should be studied at different times rather than during a single session. Reduction of interference through appropriate sequencing can partly compensate for the rapid forgetting from STM. Let us now look at how we can partly compensate for the limited capacity of this store.

CAPACITY

The Magic Number 7

Memory span The number of correct items that people can immediately recall from a sequence of items

A second limitation of STM is that it can hold only about seven items. The limited capacity of STM is demonstrated by a task that is often used as a measure of its capacity. It is called a *digit span* or, more generally, a *memory span task.* The task requires that a person recall a sequence of items in their correct order. **Memory span** is the longest sequence that a person can typically recall. An example of a memory span task is shown below. Read each row of letters once; then shut your eyes and try to recall these letters in the correct order.

T M F J R L B
H Q C N W Y P K V
S B M G X R D L T
J Z N Q K Y C

If you are like most other adults, you could probably easily recall a string of seven letters (rows 1 and 4) but not a string of nine letters (rows 2 and 3). It was this number 7 that plagued Miller. The "magic number 7" kept appearing in two different kinds of studies: experiments on absolute judgment and those on memory span. In the **absolute judgment task,** an experimenter presents stimuli that vary along a sensory continuum, such as loudness. The experimenter selects different levels of loudness that are easy to discriminate and assigns a label to each. The labels are usually numbers that increase as the values on the continuum increase: If there were seven stimuli, the softest stimuli would be labeled 1, the loudest 7. The subject's task is to learn to identify each stimulus by assigning the correct label. The experimenter presents the stimuli in a random order and corrects mistakes by providing the correct answer.

Absolute judgment task
Identifying stimuli that vary along a single, sensory continuum

The experimenter is interested mainly in how many stimuli the subject can label correctly before the task becomes too difficult. The results vary depending on the sensory continuum, but Miller was impressed with the finding that the upper limit for a single dimension was usually around 7, plus or minus 2. The upper limit was about 5 for loudness, 6 for pitch, 5 for the size of squares, and 5 for brightness. The average across a wide variety of sensory tasks was 6.5, and most of the upper limits were between 5 and 9.

It is important to point out that these results were not caused by an inability to discriminate adjacent values of the stimuli. All the stimuli would be easy to discriminate if the subject had to judge which one of two adjacent stimuli was louder, larger, brighter, or higher in pitch. The limitation was caused by the inability to keep more than about seven sensory values available in STM because of its limited capacity. The results represent performance during the early stages of learning, before the different sensory stimuli are stored in LTM. With sufficient experience, the upper limits can be increased, as is illustrated by a musically sophisticated person who can accurately identify any one of 50 or 60 pitches. However, that person is using LTM, which is not limited in capacity.

The upper limit found in the absolute judgment experiments corresponds very well with the upper limit found in memory span tasks. Miller cited the results found by Hayes (1952), which indicated that the memory span ranged from five items for English words (*lake, jump, pen, road, sing*) to nine items for binary digits (0 0 1 0 1 1 1 0 1). The memory span for numbers or letters fell in about the middle of this range.

Miller's paper was important for drawing attention to how little the upper limit varies in performance on absolute judgment and memory span tasks. His paper was also important for suggesting that recoding the information to form chunks can help one overcome the limited capacity of STM. **Chunks** consist of individual items that have been learned and stored as a group in LTM. You can demonstrate for yourself how chunking can increase the number of letters that can be recalled from STM. Tell someone that you will read 12 letters to him and that you would like him to repeat them back in the correct order. Then read the 12 letters grouped in the following way: *FB–ITW–AC–IAIB–M*. Next read to another person the same 12 letters grouped in a different way: *FBI–TWA–CIA–IBM*. You will likely find that the second person can recall more letters (of course the groups are now familiar abbreviations). The first person has to recall 12 separate letters, but the second person can recall 4 chunks, each containing 3 letters. Miller argued that the capacity of STM should be measured in chunks rather than in individual items. The 12 letters should be easy for the second person to recall because they take up only 4 "slots" in STM rather than 12.

Chunks Clusters of items that have been stored as a unit in long-term memory

Individual Differences in Chunking

There is increasing evidence that a major determinant of individual differences in memory is how effectively people can group material into familiar chunks. The initial evidence for this conclusion came from the study of how chess players reproduce the pieces on a chessboard. The classic study of this task was begun by de Groot, a Dutch psychologist, during the 1940s and was later published in his book *Thought and Choice in Chess* (1965). The main conclusion of his study was that the difference in skill between chess masters and lesser players results more from differences in perception and memory than from differences in the quality of their operational thinking.

Empirical support for de Groot's conclusion came from a series of clever experiments that required players of different abilities to reproduce a chessboard as it might appear 20 moves into a game (de Groot, 1966). Figure 4.5 shows two of the board configurations that were used in the study. The subjects were given 5 sec to view the board. The pieces were then removed, and the subjects were asked to place the pieces back on the board to reproduce what they had just seen. When the subject was finished, the experimenter removed the pieces that were incorrectly placed and asked the subject to try again. The subjects continued to try to replace the incorrect pieces until they correctly reproduced the board or until 12 trials were completed.

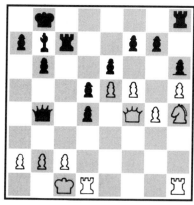 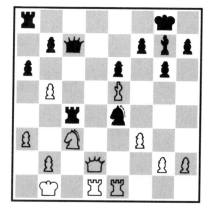

From: Janosevic-Krisnik;   From: Bannik-Geller
Zenica 1964   Moskou 1961

Figure 4.5   *Examples of experimental positions used in the guessing and reproduction experiments.*

From "Perception and Memory Versus Thought: Some Old Ideas and Recent Findings," by A. D. de Groot. In B. Kleinmuntz (Ed.), *Problem Solving: Research, Method and Theory.* Copyright 1966 by John Wiley & Sons, Inc. Reprinted by permission.

The average performance of five master players and five weaker players is shown in Figure 4.6. The master players correctly reproduced about 90% of the pieces on their first attempt, compared with only 40% for the weaker players. To determine whether the results were caused by the masters' ability simply to guess where the pieces should be located, de Groot chose other board configurations and asked the players to guess where the pieces were located, without ever seeing the board or receiving any clues. Figure 4.6 shows that the master players were only slightly better at guessing where the pieces were located. The weaker players, in fact, did about as well guessing as when they actually saw the board. De Groot argued that the master players depended on their ability to code the pieces into familiar groups. When the players viewed pieces that were placed randomly on the board, the master players no longer had an advantage over the weaker players, and the two groups performed about the same.

Chase and Simon (1973) extended de Groot's paradigm in order to identify the groups of pieces (chunks) that presumably produced the superior coding ability of master chess players. A master chess player, a Class-A player, and a beginner were tested on de Groot's reproduction task. Chase and Simon assumed that pieces belonging to the same chunk would be placed on the board as a group. They measured the time between successive pieces and classified pauses greater than 2 sec as indicating chunk boundaries. The latencies suggested that, for middle-game positions, the average number of chunks per trial was 7.7 for the master

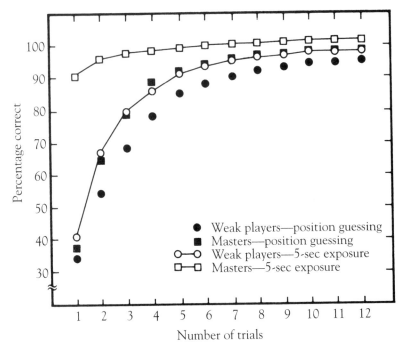

Figure 4.6 *Percentage of correctly located chess pieces.*

From "Perception and Memory Versus Thought: Some Old Ideas and Recent Findings," by
A. D. de Groot. In B. Kleinmuntz (Ed.), *Problem Solving: Research, Method and Theory.*
Copyright 1966 by John Wiley & Sons, Inc. Reprinted by permission.

player, 5.7 for the Class-A player, and 5.3 for the beginner; the number of
pieces per chunk averaged 2.5, 2.1, and 1.9, respectively. There was some
tendency for more skilled players to use more chunks, particularly for
end-game positions, in which the average number of chunks per trial was
7.6, 6.4, and 4.2, respectively.

A simulation program (Memory-Aided Pattern Perceiver, or MAPP)
of the chess reproduction task was developed by Simon and Gilmartin
(1973) to gain further insight into the kinds of chunks stored in LTM.
The memory of the program contained 572 chunks, with two to seven
chess pieces in each. The simulation program was somewhat more effective than the Class-A player in coding the configurations but less effective than the master player. There was, however, a substantial correlation
between the pieces that MAPP remembered and those the master player
remembered, even though the patterns stored by MAPP were selected independently of a detailed knowledge of the master's performance. Ex-
trapolating from the performance of the simulation model, Simon and
Gilmartin estimated that master players have between 10,000 and
100,000 chunks stored in LTM. Their estimate implies that there is no
shortcut to becoming a chess master.

Recall of Circuit Diagrams

Skill in reading nonverbal symbolic drawings is important for a wide range of occupations, including electronics, engineering, chemistry, and architecture. A skilled electronics technician, for example, must be able to understand circuit diagrams and relate the symbols to hardware in need of repair or to circuit design problems. Egan and Schwartz (1979) conducted a study to determine what differences distinguish the novice and the skilled technician in the ability to reproduce a circuit diagram. Discovering what the skilled technician actually knows should be useful for assessing skill levels, developing job aids for skilled performance, or improving training in such skills.

The earlier work of de Groot, Chase, Simon, and Gilmartin on chess influenced the design of the experiments. Chunks were determined by asking an expert (a skilled electronics technician at Bell Laboratories who had over 25 years of experience working with electronic circuits) to mark off meaningful groups of symbols in circuit drawings by circling symbols that served a common function. Figure 4.7 shows an example of a circuit drawing. The enclosed groups and verbal labels indicate how the technician organized the diagram.

The subjects in one of Egan and Schwartz's experiments were six skilled electronics technicians and six novices. The technicians had been employed at Bell Laboratories for at least 6 years. The novice subjects

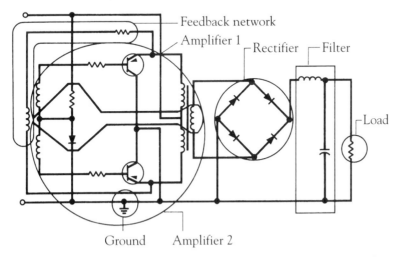

Figure 4.7 *An example of a circuit drawing. Enclosed groups and verbal labels indicate the organizational description provided by a skilled technician.*

From "Chunking in Recall of Symbolic Drawings," by D. E. Egan and B. J. Schwartz, 1979, *Memory & Cognition, 7,* 149–158. Copyright 1979 by the Psychonomic Society, Inc. Reprinted by permission.

were college students who had little knowledge of electronics. Each subject participated in 12 meaningful recall tasks, 12 random recall tasks, and 12 construction tasks, all involving different circuit diagrams. The meaningful recall tasks used actual circuit diagrams copied from texts. The random recall tasks used drawings that had the same wiring pattern and circuit symbols as the meaningful diagrams but with the symbols positioned randomly in the spaces. After viewing the diagrams for either 5 or 10 sec, subjects tried to reconstruct the drawings from memory by placing magnetized circuit symbols on the blank spaces of the answer sheet. The construction task required that subjects guess the location of the symbols on the answer sheet without having seen the diagrams.

Figure 4.8 shows how well the two groups of subjects did on each of the three tasks. The technicians did significantly better than the novices at reproducing a meaningful configuration but did no better at reproducing a random configuration. Both these findings replicate the results obtained for chess (de Groot, 1965; Chase & Simon, 1973). Although an expert's opinion, rather than latencies, was used to determine chunk boundaries, the time between replacing successive symbols was significantly shorter for pieces belonging to the same chunk. This finding is

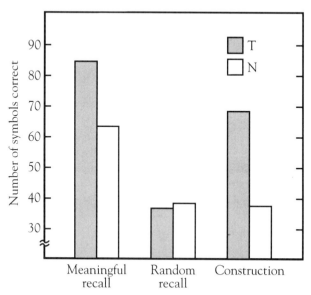

Figure 4.8 *Performance by technicians (T) and novices (N) on meaningful recall, random recall, and construction tasks.*

From "Chunking in Recall of Symbolic Drawings," by D. E. Egan and B. J. Schwartz, 1979, *Memory & Cognition, 7,* 149–158. Copyright 1979 by the Psychonomic Society, Inc. Reprinted by permission.

consistent with the research on chess, as is the finding that the recall of circuit diagrams by skilled technicians (whether measured by number correct, chunk size, or number of chunks) was very similar to the recall of chess positions by chess players in the Class-A to master range (Chase & Simon, 1973). One difference between the results obtained by de Groot (1966) and those obtained by Egan and Schwartz (1979) is that the skilled technicians, but not the master chess players, did significantly better on the construction task. This finding raises the question whether the superior performance of the skilled technicians was caused by more sophisticated guessing rather than by encoding more information into memory. Egan and Schwartz present several arguments against the guessing interpretation; more research might prove beneficial in answering this question.

MEMORY CODES

Rapid forgetting rate and limited capacity are the two most important characteristics that distinguish STM from LTM. Psychologists once emphasized a third distinction based on differences in memory codes. They argued that **acoustic** (speech-based) **codes** are the predominant memory codes in STM, and **semantic** (meaning-based) **codes** are the predominant codes in LTM. The emphasis on acoustic codes occurred because of the nature of the material used to study STM and because of the usefulness of verbal rehearsal for retaining information. The material usually consisted of sequences of letters, numbers, or nonsense syllables, all of which could be labeled but were not very meaningful. It is therefore not surprising that a person would use acoustic codes rather than visual or semantic codes to maintain such information in STM.

Acoustic codes
Memory codes based on the sound of the stimulus

Semantic codes
Memory codes based on the meaning of the stimulus

The emphasis on acoustic codes declined when psychologists used material that would activate other kinds of codes. Release from proactive interference, for example, is often cited as evidence that semantic codes influence STM because recall improves greatly when the material changes to a different semantic category. There is also evidence that people can use visual images to maintain information in STM, particularly when trying to remember the details of visual patterns.

Although the acoustic code is no longer considered the only code that influences STM, it continues to be studied extensively. This code is important because verbal rehearsal is an effective way of retaining information in STM. We will begin by looking at how acoustic codes are used to represent verbal rehearsal and how they can account for the errors that result from rehearsal (acoustic confusions). We will then examine the importance of acoustic codes in reading. Finally, we will see how recent work on maintaining and manipulating information in STM has been greatly influenced by the working memory model proposed by Baddeley (1992; Baddeley & Hitch, 1974). Baddeley partitioned short-term working memory into three components: one for retaining and manipulating acoustic codes, one for maintaining and manipulating visual/spatial codes, and one for managing the maintenance and manipulation of this information.

Acoustic Codes and Rehearsal

Psychologists' interest in acoustic codes has been motivated by people's reliance on verbal rehearsal as a means of preserving information in STM. We saw in Chapter 2 that one of the early information-processing models provided for the translation of visual information into acoustic information so that people could verbally rehearse the names of the letters (Sperling, 1963). Evidence for this translation included Sperling's finding that subjects made **acoustic confusions**—errors that sounded like the correct response. The subsequent work of Conrad (1964) also established that acoustic confusions occur in STM. Conrad selected two groups of letters that had high within-group confusability but low between-group confusability: *BCPTV* and *FMNSX*. Conrad used a film projector to visually present six-letter sequences consisting of letters from both sets. After each sequence subjects had to write the six letters in their correct order.

Acoustic confusions Errors that sound like the correct answer

If acoustic confusions occur, an error would be more likely to involve substitution of a letter from the same group than substitution of a letter from a different group. Conrad found that 75% of the errors involved one of the other four letters belonging to the same acoustic group, and 25% of the errors involved one of the five letters in the other acoustic group. It is particularly easy for acoustic confusions to occur when all the letters in a sequence sound alike. Try to recall the letters in each of the two following rows. You should find that the letters in the second row are easier to recall than the letters in the first row (Schweickert, Guentert, & Hersberger, 1990).

G Z D B P V C T
M J Y F H R K Q

The finding that acoustic confusions occur in an STM task shows that acoustic codes are important, but it does not reveal how the errors occur. One way of accounting for the errors is to use auditory components to represent the names of items. For example, the name of the letter C ("sē") has two components—namely, the s and ē sounds. The components—called **phonemes**—are the basic sounds of the English language.

Phonemes The basic sounds of a language that are combined to form speech

Table 4.1 lists the phonemes used in English. Note that some letters are represented by several phonemes because they can be pronounced in

Table 4.1   *Phonemes of general American English*

Vowels	Consonants	
ee as in h*ea*t	*t* as in *t*ee	*s* as in *s*ee
I as in h*i*t	*p* as in *p*ea	*sh* as in *sh*ell
e as in h*ea*d	*k* as in *k*ey	*h* as in *h*e
ae as in h*a*d	*b* as in *b*ee	*v* as in *v*iew
ah as in f*a*ther	*d* as in *d*awn	*th* as in *th*en
aw as in c*a*ll	*g* as in *g*o	*z* as in *z*oo
u as in p*u*t	*m* as in *m*e	*zh* as in ga*r*a*g*e
oo as in c*oo*l	*n* as in *n*o	*l* as in *l*aw
Λ as in t*o*n	*ng* as in si*ng*	*r* as in *r*ed
uh as in th*e*	*f* as in *f*ee	*y* as in *y*ou
er as in b*ir*d	θ as in *th*in	*w* as in *w*e
oi as in t*oi*l		
au as in sh*ou*t		
ei as in t*a*ke		
ou as in t*o*ne		
ai as in m*igh*t		

different ways. For example, the letter *a* is pronounced differently in the words *father, had, call,* and *take;* each pronunciation is represented by a different phoneme. The letter *e* has two pronunciations: the long-*e* sound in *heat* and the short-*e* sound in *head.* It is also possible for two letters to combine to form a phoneme—for example, *ch* and *th.*

It is convenient to use phonemes to account for acoustic confusions because words that sound alike usually have some phonemes in common. Let's look again at the two sets of letters in Conrad's experiment. The names of the letters in the set *FMNSX* have the same initial phoneme— the short-*e* sound—but their second phoneme differs. The letters in the set *BCPTV* (b*ē*, s*ē*, p*ē*, t*ē*, v*ē*) all share a common phoneme—the long-*e* sound—but have different first phonemes.

The major assumption of a model proposed by Laughery (1969) is that each of the auditory components representing an item can be independently forgotten. In other words, if a name consists of two phonemes, a person might remember one phoneme but not the other. The model also assumes that the auditory components can be forgotten at different rates; the decay rates were determined from experimental results (Wickelgren, 1965). Laughery makes the reasonable assumption that a person who cannot recall all the auditory components of a letter uses whatever is recalled to limit the number of possible responses. It is therefore easy for the model to account for acoustic confusions. Whenever only the $\bar{e}$ phoneme is recalled, the subject will guess one of the letters in the *BCPTV* set. If only the $\grave{e}$ phoneme is recalled, the subject will guess one of the letters in the *FMNSX* set. An incorrect guess in either case will result in an acoustic confusion.

Although acoustic confusions occasionally occur, it is usually advantageous to use verbal rehearsal when we want to maintain information in STM. Translation of visual material into an acoustic code is not limited to remembering strings of letters or digits. The most common example of converting visual material into acoustic codes occurs when we read.

Acoustic Codes in Reading

Subvocalization
Silently speaking to oneself

Most of us read by **subvocalizing** (saying to ourselves) the words in the text. Although subvocalizing can help us remember what we read, it limits how fast we can read. Since covert speech is not much faster than overt speech, subvocalization limits reading speed to the rate of speaking; we could read faster if we didn't translate printed words into a speech-based code (see Box 4.1).

When I was a graduate student, I attempted to improve my reading rate by enrolling in a speed-reading course. A prerequisite for increasing my speed was that I learn to eliminate subvocalization. The trick is to go directly from the printed word to its meaning without covertly pronouncing the word. I was successful at increasing my reading rate while maintaining comprehension when the material was fairly simple. However, I found it quite difficult to read more complex or technical material without using subvocalization. I soon returned to my slower rate. I don't know how representative my experience was or what percentage of graduates from speed-reading courses successfully eliminate subvocalization. However, the experimental analysis of speech processing during reading has produced results that seem consistent with my own experience. The results suggest that, although we can comprehend the meaning of words without subvocalization, subvocalization is useful in facilitating the detailed recall of a text (Levy, 1978).

Levy attempted in her own experiments to suppress subvocalization by requiring that subjects repeatedly count from one to ten as they read a short paragraph. They were told to count quickly and continuously in a soft voice while reading the sentences and to try to remember all the sentences in the paragraph. (You may want to try this as you read the two paragraphs in Table 4.2.) When they finished reading the paragraph, the subjects were shown one of the sentences in the paragraph or a slight

Table 4.2 *Examples of lexical, semantic, and paraphrase tests*

1. An emergency
The hospital staff paged the busy doctor.
The solemn physician distressed the anxious mother.
The sobbing woman held her unconscious son.
A speeding truck had crossed the mid-line.
Her oncoming car was hit and damaged.
Her child had plunged through the windshield.
The medical team strove to save him.

The solemn physician distressed the anxious *woman*. (lexical)

The solemn *mother* distressed the anxious *physician*. (semantic)

The solemn *doctor upset* the anxious mother. (paraphrase—yes)

The solemn *officer helped* the anxious mother. (paraphrase—no)

2. A lost boy
The lost boy searched the crowded street.
His careless mother had forgotten about him.
The concerned policeman approached the worried child.
The kindly man dried the boy's tears.
The young lad gave his home address.
And the police cruiser escorted him home.
In future his mother was more careful.

The concerned policeman approached the worried *youngster*. (lexical)

The concerned *child* approached the worried *policeman*. (semantic)

The concerned *officer* approached the *upset* child. (paraphrase—yes)

The concerned *woman* approached the *carefree* child. (paraphrase—no)

SOURCE: From "Speech Processing During Reading," by B. A. Levy, 1978, in A. M. Lesgold, J. W. Pellegrino, S. D. Fokkema, and R. Glaser (Eds.), *Cognitive Psychology and Instruction*, New York: Plenum. Copyright 1978 by Plenum Publishing Corporation. Reprinted by permission.

variation and were asked to judge whether the test sentence was identical to the one presented earlier.

Since the altered sentences were only slightly changed, the subjects had to remember the details to do well on this task. The first two sentences following each paragraph in Table 4.2 are examples of altered sentences. The **lexical alteration** changes a single word but preserves the meaning of the sentence—the word *mother* is changed to *woman* for the first paragraph and the word *child* to *youngster* for the second paragraph. The **semantic alteration** changes the meaning of the sentence by switching the order of

Lexical alteration
Substituting a word with similar meaning for one of the words in a sentence

Semantic alteration
Changing the order of words in a sentence to change the meaning of the sentence

**BOX
4.1**

Does speed reading really exist?

ALEXANDRA D. KORRY

Begin reading now.
Use your hand to guide your eyes.
Don't regress.
Stop subvocalizing.
Faster.

This is the message of Evelyn Wood Reading Dynamics, the California company that has made millions teaching Americans how to glide through that pile of best-sellers sitting on the shelf.

Evelyn Wood claims it will have you reading at up to 5000 words a minute at the conclusion of a seven-session course. They'll triple your reading, they say, or your money back.

More than one million speed-reading aspirants, including President Carter, John F. Kennedy's military advisers, actor Charlton Heston, and a host of members of Congress, have enrolled in the courses since they were first offered in 1959.

But now a growing number of reading specialists are raising serious questions about speed reading. They dispute the value of the $395 Evelyn Wood course and others like it, saying simply that no one—regardless of training—can read that fast.

"They have the illusion of improving their reading when in fact they are skimming," charged John Guthrie, director of research for the 70,000-member International Reading Association. To Evelyn Wood officials, those are fighting words.

"Skimming is a nasty word in our business," said M. Donald Wood, husband of the woman who founded the system and helped organize a national franchise system that teaches speed reading in 26 cities around the country. "It works. We know that."

"I think it's the greatest invention since the printing press," said Evelyn Wood, now 72, and recovering from a stroke in her native Salt Lake City. She was a graduate student at the University of Utah when she discovered the technique after years of observing naturally fast readers.

Many reading experts challenge the system. Although they differ as to what is the proper upper limit for reading speed, most agree that anyone who claims to be reading more than 900 words a minute is, in fact, skimming.

"I can't imagine that someone reading 4000 words a minute is reading," said Keith Rayner, a professor of psychology at the University of Massachusetts in Amherst. "Given the anatomy of the eye . . . I have a hard time believing that people can read beyond 900 words per minute."

Ronald Carver, an education professor at the University of Missouri, says tests he gave students there tend to support that notion. When the students were tested at 600 words a minute, they were "simply getting an idea of what they were reading," in effect, skimming.

Evelyn Wood officials, who regularly claim to have students reading at 2000 words a minute, said such studies ignore a basic premise of their approach. At Evelyn Wood, people learn a new way to read—one that teaches readers to take in whole ideas rather than single words, they said.

"It's a visual form of reading," said Verla Nielson, director of the program's Salt Lake City operations. "It's seeing words in chunks—reading as the author thought it. It's like learning to read music—you can see many notes at the same time."

To prove that the method works, the company cites the results of comprehension tests given to their students at the beginning and end of the course. Some reading specialists take issue with those multiple-choice quizzes.

Carver, a reading specialist for 13 years, told a group of college students to imagine they were reading material from the Wood course and then gave them the Wood tests. The students averaged a 60% comprehension level without ever reading the material, a reflection of what Carver says is the tests' shortcomings.

"They claim you can increase your perception of the number of words taken at once. That's absurd," said the Reading Association's Guthrie. "There's a lot of scientific evidence that shows you can only take in 20 characters at a time."

Carlos Garcia Tunon, a Washington marketing consultant and an Evelyn Wood alumnus who reportedly went from 362.5 to 5024 words per minute with a 20% increase in comprehension, said he didn't feel he was seeing every word he was supposed to be reading at the faster speeds. What you get from the speed reading, he said, is the basic theme, the characters, and the plot of a book.

Tunon was one of thousands of people who have been drawn to the reading system's free mini-lessons by advertising that features students flipping through texts as if they were looking through picture books.

Once at the mini-session, an instructor tells the students that anyone can learn the necessary skills, that all it takes is practice, that if you break the bad habits you learned as a child, you'll be reading six times faster. It's a 15-minute buildup that ends with a passing reference to the $395 price tag ($295 if another member of your family enrolls).

The students are told if they stop subvocalizing—reading the individual words to yourself—and regressing—rereading a line—they'll save 40% of reading time.

They also show a 15-minute film on the reading method. The highlight is a 1975 "Tonight Show" segment of an interview with Elizabeth Jaffee, then a 13-year-old wunderkind of speed reading, who reads 30 pages of a highly technical book in one minute.

What they don't tell you is that Jaffee, now a college freshman, isn't really a speed reader anymore. That the Evelyn Wood alumna sued and received a $25,000 out-of-court settlement because she claimed that the technique works only for certain kinds of reading.

two nouns—for the first paragraph, the order of *mother* and *physician*. The results of this study revealed that subjects performed more poorly when they had to count while reading. They were not as accurate in identifying when changes occurred, regardless of whether there were lexical changes or semantic changes.

Suppressing subvocalization did not interfere with performance when the subjects listened to the sentence, however. The fact that counting while listening did not affect performance shows that suppression interfered specifically with reading, not with language comprehension in general. The difference between listening and reading is that the listener receives an acoustic code rather than a visual code. The fact that counting interfered only with recall following reading suggests that translating visual material into an acoustic code helps preserve detailed information in the text.

Although the acoustic code improved recall of detailed information, it was not necessary to preserve the gist of the paragraph (Levy, 1978). Support for this claim comes from a second experiment, in which subjects made paraphrase judgments. These subjects were not encouraged to maintain the exact wording of sentences because word changes occurred in all the test sentences. However, positive examples preserved the general meaning of an original sentence and negative examples altered the meaning. In the **paraphrase** changes, unlike the semantic changes, the meaning was altered by replacing two words in the sentences rather than by changing the order of words (see Table 4.2). Therefore, less information was required to distinguish between positive and negative examples in the paraphrase task than to judge correctly in the lexical or semantic task. People could do well on the paraphrase if they remembered the general ideas expressed in the paragraph. Since the counting task did not interfere with performance, Levy concluded that acoustic coding was not required to remember the more important ideas.

Levy's findings are consistent with my own experiences in preventing subvocalization. When the material is relatively simple and detailed recall is not required, people can recall the major ideas without subvocalization. However, subvocalization did facilitate the detection of more subtle changes, such as changing the order of two words or replacing a word with a semantically similar word. Additional evidence also supports this conclusion. Hardyck and Petrinovich (1970) measured subvocalization by recording the muscle activity of the larynx. Subjects in the experimental group were trained to keep their muscle activity at nonreading relaxation levels. Any increases in activity during reading activated an audio signal to remind them to suppress subvocalization. A control group read the same material but were allowed to subvocalize as they read. A comprehension test revealed that the two groups did not differ in

Paraphrase   Using different words to express the same ideas in a sentence

recall of easy material, but the subvocalization group recalled more of the difficult material than the suppression group.

The studies on speech processing during reading suggest that, although subvocalization is not necessary for comprehension, it does facilitate retention of detailed or complex information. A popular explanation of these findings is that subvocalization makes it easier to retain words in STM until they can be integrated with other words in the sentence or paragraph (Conrad, 1972; Kleiman, 1975). We would be able to evaluate this suggestion more accurately if we had a better understanding of the role of STM in reading. Fortunately, considerable progress has been made over the past several years in understanding the psychological processes involved in text comprehension. Chapter 11 summarizes this progress and indicates how STM is used in reading.

Baddeley's Working Memory Model

The previous section on the role of acoustic codes in reading illustrates one example of how we use STM to perform daily activities. I mentioned at the beginning of this chapter that STM is often referred to as a working memory because of its use in numerous mental activities such as text comprehension, reasoning, and problem solving. Over 20 years ago Baddeley and Hitch (1974) began constructing a working memory model that is still evolving. Recently, Baddeley (1992) gave the Bartlett Memorial Address at the University of Cambridge, which gave him the opportunity to evaluate the current status of the model.

The model consists of three components: (1) a **phonological loop** responsible for maintaining and manipulating speech-based information, (2) a **visuospatial sketchpad** responsible for maintaining and manipulating visual or spatial information, and (3) a **central executive** responsible for selecting strategies and integrating information. Psychologists know most about the operation of the phonological loop, perhaps because most of the early research on STM used verbal material, as was illustrated in the previous sections of this chapter.

However, as psychologists began to include more visual or spatial material in their study of STM, it became apparent that not all material is translated into a speech-based code. Let's take another look at the task of reproducing a chessboard in which chess players group the pieces into familiar chunks. We might speculate that chunks are based more on visual/spatial information than on speech-based information. Certainly, de Groot (1966) believed that perception played an important role in distinguishing good chess players from weaker players.

Baddeley (1992) reports a study on reproducing a chessboard that examined the relative contributions of the three components of his working

Phonological loop
A component of Baddeley's working memory model that maintains and manipulates acoustic information

Visuospatial sketchpad
A component of Baddeley's working memory model that maintains and manipulates visual/spatial information

Central executive
A component of Baddeley's working memory model that manages the use of working memory

memory model. As chess players of various abilities attempted to reproduce the board, they performed a secondary task that was designed to limit the use of a particular component. Levy's attempt to prevent subvocalization by asking people to count while reading is an example of this procedure. In fact, the experimenters used a similar procedure to prevent people from subvocalizing—that is, using the phonological loop component of Baddeley's model. To prevent the use of the visuospatial sketchpad, people were asked to tap a series of keys in a predetermined pattern. To prevent the use of the central executive, people were asked to produce a string of random letters at a rate of one letter per second. The rationale was that producing random letters requires people to make decisions about which letter to produce next and this requirement will restrict their ability to make decisions about performing the primary task (how to code the chess pieces into memory).

The results of the study showed that suppressing speech had no effect on people's ability to reproduce a chessboard, but suppressing visual/spatial processing, and requiring people to generate random numbers caused a marked impairment in their ability to correctly place the pieces on the board. These findings suggest that verbal coding does not play an important role in this task, but both the visuospatial sketchpad and the central executive are needed to have good memory for the chess pieces (which is a visual task). Other research has confirmed that simply counting the number of pieces on the board, or making decisions about moves, is affected by secondary tasks that interfere with visual/spatial processing but is unaffected by secondary tasks that prevent subvocalization (Saariluoma, 1992).

Although the results of both studies show that the visuospatial sketchpad is an important component in playing chess, Baddeley (1992) admits that its operation is still not well understood. One problem is that although it is clear that we can rehearse verbal information by subvocalization, it is not clear how we rehearse visual images. Another problem is that it may be difficult to separate maintaining visual information from maintaining spatial information. The secondary task of tapping keys in a set pattern primarily produces spatial interference because it is possible to tap the keys without looking at them. Some recent research suggests that active spatial attention is required for maintaining visual/spatial information in STM, and this information is interfered with by any task (visual, auditory, perceptual, motor) that also makes demands on spatial attention (Smyth & Scholey, 1994).

Another component of Baddeley's model that requires further research is the central executive. This is the decision-making component of working memory and it also played a role in reproducing the chessboard. A possible reason is that although chunking is important in this task, pieces on the board do not come "prepackaged" into chunks; the chess player has to decide how to partition the pieces to form chunks. The central executive also plays a predominant role when people have to reach conclusions in a logical-reasoning task (Gilhooly, Logie, Wetherick, & Wynn, 1993). A secondary task that interfered with the central executive (generating random numbers) significantly impaired logical reasoning, but tasks that interfered with subvocalization or visual/spatial processing did not impair logical reasoning.

In conclusion, Baddeley's working memory model shows that more is involved in using STM than simply maintaining and operating on phonological codes. And although psychologists still have more to learn about the working of the three components, Baddeley and others have made significant progress in advancing our understanding of how we use STM as a working memory.

RECOGNITION OF ITEMS IN SHORT-TERM MEMORY

Our discussion of STM up to this point has emphasized the recall of material, as shown in the experiments asking for recall of three consonants, a string of letters or digits, a chessboard, or a circuit diagram after a short delay. Psychologists have also been interested in how people try to "recognize" whether a given item is contained in STM. Imagine that I show you four randomly chosen digits, perhaps 3, 8, 6, and 2. Then I show you a test digit and ask you to decide as quickly as possible whether the test digit was one of the four digits that I showed you previously. To perform this task you would need to store the initial set of digits in STM and then compare the test digit to the digits stored in STM to determine if there is a match.

Perhaps you can think of instances in which you have to carry out this kind of comparison. Such an instance occurs for me whenever I finish recording test scores for an exam. I always discover when I am finished that there are several students on my class list that don't have a test score. This usually means that they didn't take the test, but I am always concerned that they may have taken the test and I failed to record the score. I therefore place their names in my STM and again read the name on each test to see whether it matches one of the names in my STM. You may follow a similar procedure when you go shopping by comparing items on the shelves to the names of items you want to purchase and have stored in your STM. People are fairly accurate at performing this kind of task, so psychologists have focused on response time as a measure of performance. We will now look at what determines response time and what this tells us about how we search STM.

Searching Short-Term Memory

The digit-example task that I just described was invented by S. Sternberg at Bell Laboratories in order to study how people encode a pattern and compare it with other patterns stored in STM. Sternberg first showed a sequence of digits (the **memory set**), which the subject stored in STM. Then he presented a test digit, and the subject had to quickly decide whether the test digit was a member of the memory set. When Sternberg (1966) varied the size of the memory set from one to six digits, he discovered that the time required to make the decision increased as a linear function of the number of digits in STM. Whenever the size of the memory set was increased by one additional digit, the response time was lengthened by 38 msec. Sternberg proposed that the test digit was sequentially compared with each item stored in STM and that it required about 38 msec to make each comparison.

One important issue concerning the scanning process is whether it continues after a match is found. Imagine that I showed you the digits 5, 3, 7, and 1 and then gave you the test digit 3. Would you respond yes after matching the 3 in the memory set (a **self-terminating search**), or would you respond yes only after comparing the test digit to all the digits in the memory set (an **exhaustive search**)? Most of us would probably say that we would respond yes as soon as we found a match. But Sternberg claimed that we scan the entire memory set before responding. This seems counterintuitive, so let's take a close look at the evidence.

Two aspects of Sternberg's data suggested that people were making an exhaustive search. First, response times for positive and negative responses were approximately the same. We would expect this finding if people always scanned the entire memory set. But if they responded as soon as they found a match, positive responses should be faster than negative responses because people would not always have to scan the entire memory set. Second, Sternberg found that response times were not influenced by the location of the matching digit in the memory set. We would expect this finding if people scanned the entire memory set, but not if they responded as soon as they found a match.

The trouble with an exhaustive search is that it would seem to be a very inefficient strategy to use. Why should comparisons continue once a match has been found? Sternberg's answer was that scanning occurs very rapidly but checking for a match takes considerably longer (Sternberg, 1967a). If we had to check for a match following each comparison, searching STM would be less efficient. But if we waited until after scanning the entire memory set to check whether a match occurred, we would have to perform the slower checking process only a single time.

Memory set   A set of items in STM that can be compared against a test item to determine if the test item is stored there

Self-terminating search   A search that stops as soon as the test item is successfully matched to an item in the memory set

Exhaustive search   A search that continues until the test item is compared to all items in the memory set

Degraded Patterns

In one of the early applications of this paradigm, Sternberg (1967b) varied the quality of the test digit in addition to the size of the memory set. The memory set consisted of one, two, or four digits, and the test digit was either intact or degraded to make it difficult to recognize. The degraded test digit looked like the degraded letters in Figure 5.8 (p. 137). Sternberg suggested that two operations were needed to perform the task. First, the observer had to **encode** the test digit in order to compare it with other digits stored in STM. The subject then had to **scan** the memory set to determine whether any of the digits matched the test digit.

Sternberg showed how it would be possible to determine whether a degraded pattern would influence the encoding time or the memory scan time. The **slope** of the function relating reaction time (RT) to memory-set size indicates the amount of time needed to compare the test digit with a digit stored in STM; that is, it is the amount of additional time needed whenever another digit is added to the memory set. If a degraded digit slows down the rate of comparison, the slope should increase. Figure 4.9a shows this prediction. Note that the more items in the memory set,

Encoding Creating a visual or verbal code for a test item so it can be compared with the memory codes of items stored in STM

Scanning Sequentially comparing a test item with items in STM to determine if there's a match

Slope A measure of how much response time changes for each unit of change along the x-axis (memory set size)

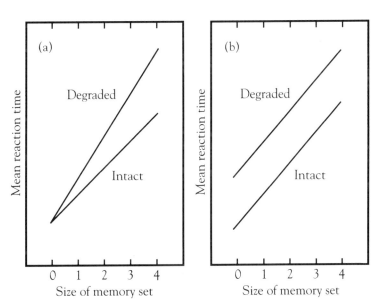

Figure 4.9 *Predicted reaction time functions if degrading affects the memory comparison time (a) or the encoding time (b).*

From "Two Operations in Character Recognition: Some Evidence from Reaction Time Measurements," by S. Sternberg, 1967, *Perception & Psychophysics, 2,* 45–53. Copyright 1967 by the Psychonomic Society, Inc. Reprinted by permission.

the greater the difference in RT. The encoding of the test digit occurs only once, however, and should be independent of the number of items in the memory set. If the degraded digit lengthens the encoding time, the reaction time should increase by a constant amount (the additional time needed for encoding), which is independent of the number of items in the memory set. Figure 4.9b shows this prediction.

Figure 4.10 shows the results Sternberg actually obtained over two sessions. Degradation greatly affected the encoding time in both sessions. The data for degraded and intact digits form nearly parallel lines, similar to those shown in Figure 4.9b. The effect on the memory comparison time (as measured by differences in the slopes) was minimal. Degrading the test digit primarily affected the time needed to encode the pattern and had little effect on the time required to compare the test digit with other digits stored in STM. This finding implies that the visually degraded digit was not directly compared with the other digits since this would have slowed down the comparisons. The longer encoding time suggests that the effect of degradation was compensated for during the encoding stage. The subject might have changed the degraded image into a normal image and matched the normal image against the visual images stored in STM. Or the subject might have named the test digit and com-

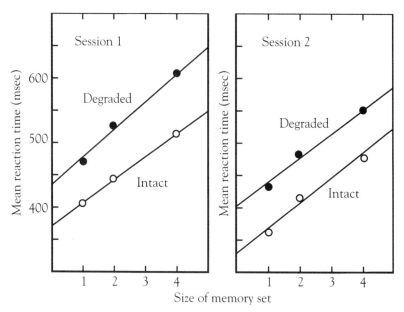

Figure 4.10 *Mean reaction time for intact and degraded test stimuli.*

From "Two Operations in Character Recognition: Some Evidence from Reaction Time Measurements," by S. Sternberg, 1967, *Perception & Psychophysics, 2*, 45–53. Copyright 1967 by the Psychonomic Society, Inc. Reprinted by permission.

pared it with the names of digits stored in STM. The latter explanation is particularly attractive because acoustic codes are usually used to maintain information in STM. It should take longer to name a degraded digit, and hence the encoding time would be slowed down. However, once named, the degraded image would no longer be used, so the rate of comparison would be relatively unaffected.

Some Determinants of the Memory Comparison Rate

Although degradation of the test digit had very little effect on the comparison rate, use of qualitatively different kinds of stimuli does influence the comparison rate. Furthermore, there is a very orderly relation between the memory span and the rate of searching STM. Cavanagh (1972) found seven classes of stimuli in which measures were available for both the number of stimuli that could be recalled in a memory span test and the comparison rate of stimuli in a Sternberg task. Both measures were available for the digits 0 through 9; colors; the letters of the alphabet; familiar words; geometrical shapes such as squares, circles, and triangles; random forms; and nonsense syllables composed of a vowel between two consonants.

The average comparison rate ranged from 33 msec for digits to 73 msec for nonsense syllables. The average memory span ranged from 3.4 items for nonsense syllables to 7.7 items for digits. Figure 4.11 shows the almost perfect inverse relation between the two measures—the greater the memory span for a particular item, the less the comparison rate. An interesting implication of the results shown in Figure 4.11 is that the same amount of time is always required to search STM when it is filled to its capacity. The average capacity of STM is 3.4 nonsense syllables, 3.8 random forms, 5.3 geometrical shapes, 5.5 words, 6.4 letters, 7.1 colors, and 7.7 digits. It takes about 0.25 sec to search STM in each of these cases. When there are more items to search, the rate of search is faster, so the total search time remains constant.

We still don't know the cause of this inverse relation, but Cavanagh suggests several possible explanations. One of the simplest is that the items are represented in memory by a list of features. Short-term memory has a constant, limited amount of "space," which can hold only a fixed number of features. Since nonsense syllables, random forms, and geometrical shapes are more complex than letters, colors, and digits, they would have more features, and each item would take up more space in STM. The feature explanation of the comparison rate would assume that the time it takes to compare a test item with an item in the memory set is determined by how many features have to be compared. The complexity of the stimulus, as defined by its number of features, would therefore affect both how many items could be stored in STM and how much time is

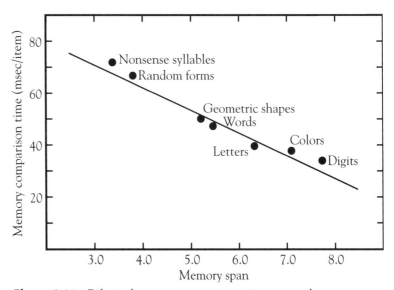

Figure 4.11   *Relation between memory comparison rate and memory span.*
From "Relation between the Immediate Memory Span and the Memory Search Rate," by
J. P. Cavanagh, 1972, *Psychological Review, 79*, 525–530. Copyright 1972 by the American
Psychological Association. Reprinted by permission.

required to compare two items. The feature explanation is consistent
with many of the ideas about pattern recognition discussed in Chapter 2;
however, further research is necessary in order to determine whether it is
the best explanation.

Although the stimuli studied by Cavanagh had different rates of
comparison, they all caused the typical increase in response time as the
size of the memory set increased. Is it possible to find cases in which the
size of the memory set does not influence response time? There are a few
such interesting cases, one of which was revealed by DeRosa and Tkacz
(1976). The subjects in their experiment were shown a series of three,
four, or five pictures. The pictures were part of the ordered sequence of
pictures shown in Figure 4.12. If the pictures were randomly selected
from the sequence, response time increased as a linear function of the
number of items in the memory set. For example, if people were shown
the five birds numbered 3, 7, 6, 9, and 1 in Figure 4.12, it would take
them longer to search STM than if they were shown only birds 3, 7, and
9. However, the size of the memory set did not make any difference when
they were shown sequences of adjacent items. They could search memory
as fast for the sequence 3, 4, 5, 6, and 7 as they could for the sequence 3,
4, and 5. Furthermore, the sequence did not have to be presented in an
ascending order to obtain this result. People who were shown items 3 to

Stimulus type   Ordinal position

Figure 4.12   *Five organized sequences of visual stimuli.*

From "Memory Scanning of Organized Visual Material," by D. V. DeRosa and D. Tkacz, 1976,
Journal of Experimental Psychology: Human Learning and Memory, 2, 688–694. Copyright 1976
by the American Psychological Association. Reprinted by permission.

7 in order 5, 3, 7, 4, 6 could also search a five-item sequence as fast as
they could search a three-item sequence.

The results indicate that people can represent a sequence of adjacent
items as a single, unified whole rather than as separate items. The finding
that the order of presentation within the sequence did not make a difference suggests that we are able to rapidly reorganize items to make a unified whole. Perhaps we quickly establish the two boundaries of the sequence and examine whether the test item falls within the boundaries.
This interpretation is supported by the fact that the speed of negative responses is determined by how far the test item is from the nearest boundary of the sequence. If the memory set consisted of items 2, 3, 4, and 5, it
would take much longer to reject the sixth item than the ninth item in
the sequence. The finding that organization facilitates the search of information in STM is but one example of how organization can improve performance.

I have attempted in this chapter to discuss some of the major characteristics of STM. We use STM in so many different cognitive tasks that it
would be impossible to confine this discussion to a single chapter. The
next chapter focuses on LTM but also emphasizes the interaction between STM and LTM. If we are interested in learning information, rather
than simply maintaining it over a short period of time, we must attempt

to enter that information into a more permanent store. We will begin our study of learning by looking at a model that represents learning as the transfer of information from STM into LTM.

SUMMARY

Short-term memory has several limitations that distinguish it from long-term memory. First of all, STM results in rapid forgetting. Items that are not actively rehearsed can be lost in 20 to 30 sec. Evidence suggests that interference, rather than decay, is the primary cause of forgetting. Interference can result from items presented either before (proactive interference) or after (retroactive interference) the tested item. Release from proactive interference illustrates how the reduction of interference improves memory.

Another limitation of STM is its capacity. After reviewing a large number of findings on absolute judgment and memory span, Miller identified the capacity limitation as consisting of about seven chunks. A chunk is a group of items stored as a unit in LTM. For instance, the sequence *FBITWACIAIBM* is easy to recall when grouped as *FBI-TWA-CIA-IBM* because the 12 letters have been grouped as four chunks—as familiar abbreviations. De Groot argued that the superior ability of a master player to reproduce a chessboard is a result of the ability to group the pieces into familiar configurations. Using pauses as a measure of chunk boundaries, Chase and Simon concluded that master chess players have both more chunks and larger chunks stored in LTM than less experienced players. Success in reproducing other configurations, such as circuit diagrams, also depends on the availability of chunks.

The use of verbal rehearsal to maintain information in STM is confirmed by acoustic confusions—errors that sound like the correct response. Laughery's simulation model accounts for acoustic confusions by assuming that acoustic codes consist of phonemes, which can be independently forgotten. Although we usually rely on an acoustic code when we read, we can remember the general ideas from our reading without subvocalizing. However, subvocalization improves our ability to recall details and complex material. Baddeley's working memory model provides a more complete account of STM by proposing an articulatory loop for maintaining and manipulating acoustic information, a visuospatial sketchpad for maintaining and manipulating visual/spatial information, and a central executive for making decisions. Much of the current work on STM is directed at determining how each of these three components is used across a variety of tasks.

A recognition task consists of showing an item and asking the subject to verify whether the item is contained in a set of items stored in STM.

The finding that the time required to make this decision increases as a linear function of the number of items stored in STM suggests that people search the items one at a time. Degrading the test item has relatively little effect on the rate of search, but it does lengthen the time needed to encode the test item before comparing it with the other items in STM. However, the comparison rate is influenced by whether the items are simple, such as letters or digits, or more complex, such as random forms or nonsense syllables. There is an inverse relation between search rate and memory span—the faster the search rate, the greater the number of items that can be stored in STM. A possible explanation is that both findings are influenced by the number of features composing each item. There are a few cases in which time is uninfluenced by the number of items in STM, one example being items that can be sequentially organized.

STUDY QUESTIONS

1. What is Miller's magic number? What is magical about it? Why is his 1956 paper famous?
2. The study by Peterson and Peterson is another "golden oldie." Why do you think it is still cited in virtually every introductory text? Why did they have their subjects count backward?
3. What different predictions do decay theory and interference theory make? How have these been tested?
4. What factors produce greater or lesser interference? Can you see how the findings on proactive and retroactive interference could be applied to your own study strategies?
5. Does your experience bear out the claim that chunking can partially overcome the limited capacity of STM? (Think of an area in which you are an expert rather than a novice.) Is there research evidence that chunking works?
6. A college student is ideally an expert reader. Before you read Box 4.1, write your answer to the question posed—does speed reading really exist?—with a sentence or two stating the reasons for your answer.
7. What is "acoustic coding"? Why is acoustic coding at issue in studies of reading comprehension? Does it help you remember what you read?
8. Review the methods used by Levy and by Hardyck and Petrinovich to suppress subvocalization by their subjects. Which do you think was most effective? Why?
9. What is at issue in Sternberg's studies of recognition of items in STM? Why did he need to invent a paradigm to investigate the problem? What did he discover about how we search for items in STM?

10. What is the implication of Cavanagh's (1972) findings on memory span and memory comparison rate for qualitatively different types of stimuli?

KEY TERMS

The page number in parentheses refers to where the term is discussed in the chapter.

absolute judgment task (87)
acoustic codes (93)
acoustic confusions (94)
central executive (101)
chunks (88)
decay theory (83)
encode (105)
exhaustive search (104)
interference theory (83)
lexical alteration (97)
memory set (104)
memory span (86)
paraphrase (100)
phonemes (94)

phonological loop (101)
proactive interference (85)
release from proactive
   interference (85)
retroactive interference (84)
scan (105)
self-terminating search (104)
semantic alteration (97)
semantic codes (93)
slope (105)
subvocalizing (96)
visuospatial sketchpad (101)
working memory (80)

RECOMMENDED READING

Reviews of memory research frequently appear in the *Annual Review of Psychology* (for example, Johnson & Hasher, 1987; Hintzman, 1990, Squire, Knowlton, & Musen, 1993) and provide a summary of research over the past several years. The book edited by Gruneberg, Morris, and Sykes (1978) contains articles on the practical aspects of memory. Slowiaczek and Clifton (1980) investigated the role of subvocalization in reading and found that subvocalization is useful when people have to combine ideas expressed in different sentences. There have been occasional critics of STM as a theoretical construct. Crowder (1982) has argued against the importance of STM, and Klapp, Marshburn, and Lester (1983) have argued against equating STM and working memory.

Long-Term Memory

Memory is that part of the brain that reminds us on Friday what we should have done the previous Monday.

POPULAR SAYING

Most of us at one time or another have envied someone who has a very good memory and wished that we could improve our own memory. For students, this is particularly true at exam time. If only we could remember everything that we studied, we would do so much better. The need to remember the material after the exam may seem less pressing, but even in this case a good memory may be quite beneficial.

One question students often ask before I give my first cognition exam each semester regards the importance of remembering names. Students believe that names are particularly challenging to remember, and there is some evidence that this is correct. Students who completed a cognitive psychology course at the Open University in England were tested on their ability to recall names and general concepts following a retention interval that ranged from 3 months to 125 months (Conway, Cohen, & Stanhope, 1991). The questions were fill-in-the-blank questions in which the missing name or concept was represented only by its initial letter. For example: E——— *was an early German psychologist who studied the learning of nonsense syllables. In p——— inhibition forgetting is caused by interference from prior learning.*

Figure 5.1 shows the results. Names were forgotten more rapidly than concepts over the initial 3 years, but between 3 and 10 years, recall leveled off at about the same level for both kinds of knowledge. Particularly encouraging is the finding that even after 10 years people were still recalling more than 25% of the material.

One of the best ways to remember material over a life span is simply to spend considerable time studying it (Bahrick & Hall, 1991). Students who took college-level mathematics courses at or above the level of calculus had excellent retention of high school algebra for nearly 50 years. The performance of students who did equally well in a high school algebra course, but took no college-level mathematics courses, declined to near chance levels over the same period. Surprisingly, academic measures such as Scholastic Aptitude Test (SAT) scores and grades have little impact on retention (Bahrick & Hall, 1991; Semb & Ellis, 1994).

In order to retain information over a long time span, we have to get it out of short-term memory and enter it into a more permanent store called **long-term memory (LTM)**. This chapter summarizes some of the research on LTM—such as how we enter information into LTM and how it is tested. The first section of this chapter describes some ways in which information can be transferred from a temporary to a more permanent store. We start by considering the basic characteristics of LTM, including learning strategies. Much of what was known about this topic was summarized in an important paper by Atkinson and Shiffrin, published in 1968. The authors discussed several strategies that could facilitate learn-

Long-term memory
Memory that has no capacity limits and holds information from minutes to an entire lifetime

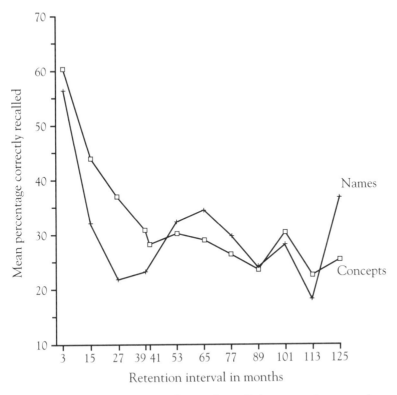

Figure 5.1   *Mean percentage of correctly recalled names and concepts for different retention intervals.*

From "On the Very Long-Term Knowledge Acquired Through Formal Education: Twelve Years of Cognitive Psychology" by M. A. Conway, G. Cohen, and N. Stanhope, 1991, *Journal of Experimental Psychology: General, 120,* 395–409. Copyright 1991 by the American Psychological Association. Reprinted by permission.

ing, but they primarily studied verbal rehearsal. They assumed that each time an item was rehearsed, information about that item was entered into LTM. Another strategy that influences learning is the allocation of study time, which requires judging when an item is learned well enough that it does not need additional study.

Psychologists have also been interested in discovering how people retrieve information after it is stored in LTM. An initial step is to decide whether the information is in LTM. If we decide that it is, our next step is to select a plan for retrieving the information if we cannot immediately recall it. Recalling relevant information is usually important, even in recognition tasks, because recognizing an event or a person as familiar is often insufficient—we usually need to know additional information. After discussing some theoretical aspects of recall and recognition, I will conclude the section with an example of how the two combine to determine the accuracy of eyewitness identification.

Recall and recognition tests are both direct tests of memory in which the instructions specifically refer to previously presented material. In contrast, indirect tests of memory determine whether previously presented material helps people perform better on tasks that do not refer to the previous material, such as identifying degraded words. Patients with memory disorders often do as well as people with normal memories on indirect tests. We will examine some theories of this effect in the last section, but first let us return to the basics, as represented by the Atkinson-Shiffrin model that was shown in Figure 4.1 (page 81).

THE ATKINSON-SHIFFRIN MODEL

Transferring Information from Short-Term Memory to Long-Term Memory

The theory proposed by Atkinson and Shiffrin (1968, 1971) emphasized the interaction between STM and LTM. They were particularly interested in how people could transfer information from STM to LTM. Long-term memory has two crucial advantages. First, as we have already seen, the rate of forgetting is much slower for LTM. Some psychologists have even suggested that information is never lost from LTM, although we lose the ability to retrieve it. Whether information is lost or impossible to recover may not be of much practical significance, but, if we knew that it was still in memory, we might hope to recover it eventually. Another difference between STM and LTM is that LTM is unlimited in its capacity. Although we saw in the previous chapter that there is a limit to the amount of information that we can maintain in STM, we will never reach the point were we cannot learn new information because the LTM is filled.

Nevertheless, it is not always easy to enter new information into LTM. Atkinson and Shiffrin proposed several control processes that could be used in an attempt to learn new information. The **control processes** are strategies that a person uses to facilitate the acquisition of knowledge. They include the *acquisition strategies* of rehearsal, coding, and imaging.

Rehearsal is the repetition of information—either aloud or silently—over and over until it is learned.

Coding attempts to place the information to be remembered in the context of additional, easily retrievable information, such as a mnemonic phrase or sentence. For example, many of us learned that the lines of a

Control processes Strategies that determine how information is processed

Rehearsal Verbal repetition of information in an attempt to learn it

Coding Semantic elaboration of information to make it easier to remember

treble clef are E, G, B, D, F by remembering the sentence "Every good boy does fine."

Imaging involves creating visual images to remember verbal information. This is an old memory trick—it was even recommended by Cicero for learning long lists or speeches.

The list could be further expanded, but rehearsal, coding, and imaging are three of the primary ways of learning. Because there are so many control processes to study, Atkinson and Shiffrin (1968) decided to focus their research on only one—verbal rehearsal.

Imaging Creating visual images to make material easier to remember

Verbal Rehearsal and Learning

Verbal rehearsal is usually considered a form of **rote learning** because it involves simply repeating information over and over until we think we have learned it. It can be useful when the material seems rather abstract, which makes it difficult to use strategies such as coding or imaging. The task designed by Atkinson and Shiffrin (1968) required the learning of abstract, meaningless material and therefore encouraged the use of rehearsal.

Rote learning Learning by repetition rather than through understanding

The undergraduates in the experiment tried to learn associations between a two-digit number (the stimulus) and a letter (the response). The paired associates included items such as 31-Q, 42-B, and 53-A. Each pair was shown for 3 sec, followed by 3 sec before the next trial. Interspersed throughout these study trials were test trials, in which only the two-digit number was presented and the subject was asked to supply the letter that had accompanied it earlier. One of the variables in the experiment was the number of trials that occurred between the study and test trials. Some associates were tested on the very next trial and others after a delay that could last as long as 17 trials.

Atkinson and Shiffrin interpreted the data from this experiment by proposing a model in which verbal rehearsal was used to learn the associates. They assumed that the students maintained a fixed number of items in STM and that these items were rehearsed whenever the student was not viewing a new item or responding during a test trial. The effect of rehearsal was to transfer information about that item into LTM. The extent of learning depended on how long a particular pair was maintained in the rehearsal set. Atkinson and Shiffrin proposed that learning increased as a function of the number of trials over which the item was rehearsed. Once the item was no longer rehearsed, information about that particular item decreased as each succeeding item was presented for study. The predicted probability of a correct response therefore depended on both the number of trials in which the item was rehearsed and the number of intervening trials that occurred between the time the item left the rehearsal set and the test trial.

In the preceding example, an item has been rehearsed but is not in STM at the time of the test. If the item has been rehearsed but is no longer in STM, the answer has to be retrieved from LTM. A second possibility is that the item is rehearsed and is still active in STM. A third possibility exists when an item is not rehearsed at all. Since the model assumes that only a limited number of items can be maintained in the rehearsal set, rehearsing a new item will be done at the expense of eliminating one of the items already in the set. Atkinson and Shiffrin proposed that an item that is not rehearsed can be responded to correctly only if it is tested on the trial immediately following its presentation.

Rehearsal and the Serial Position Effect

An easy way to test the proposal that verbal rehearsal results in learning is to ask someone to rehearse out loud. The experimenter can then count the times each item is rehearsed and determine whether the probability of recalling an item is related to the number of rehearsals. A task designed by Rundus (1971) was exactly of this type. He presented lists of 20 nouns to undergraduates at Stanford. The words were presented one at a time for a period of 5 sec each. Rundus instructed the students to study by repeating aloud words on the list during each 5-sec interval. They were free to rehearse any word on the list as long as their rehearsal filled the intervals. After presentation of the list, the students tried to recall the words in any order.

Figure 5.2 shows the results of the experiment. The probability of recalling a word depended on its position in the list. Words at the beginning and words at the end were easier to recall than words in the middle of the list. The U shape of the recall curve, which is called a **serial position effect**, is often obtained in recall experiments. The better recall of words at the beginning of the list is called a **primacy effect**, and the better recall of words at the end of the list is called a **recency effect**.

The curve showing the number of times each word was rehearsed illustrates that words at the beginning of the list were rehearsed more often than the other words. This is also illustrated in Table 5.1. The relation between the rehearsal and recall curves reveals that the primacy effect can be explained by Atkinson and Shiffrin's theory. Since early words were rehearsed more often than the other words, they should have a higher probability of being retrieved from LTM. This explanation implies that the primacy effect should be eliminated if all the words on the list are rehearsed equally often. In fact, when subjects were instructed to rehearse each word equally often by rehearsing only the displayed word, the primacy effect disappeared (Fischler, Rundus, & Atkinson, 1970).

Although the number of rehearsals can predict the primacy effect, it does not predict the recency effect. People were very good at recalling the words at the end of the list even though they did not rehearse them

Serial position effect The ability to recall words at the beginning and end of a list better than words in the middle of the list

Primacy effect The better recall of words at the beginning of a list

Recency effect The better recall of words at the end of a list

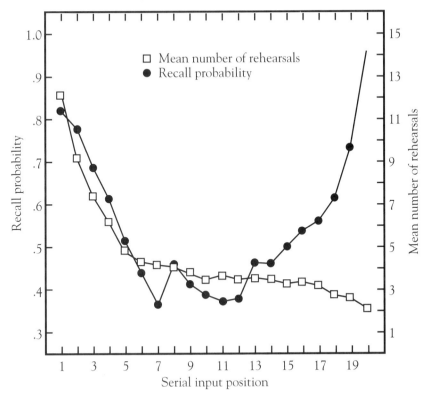

Figure 5.2   *Relation between the average probability of recall and the average number of rehearsals as a function of a word's serial position.*

From "Analysis of Rehearsal Processes in Free Recall," by D. Rundus, 1971, *Journal of Experimental Psychology*, 89, 63–77. Copyright 1971 by the American Psychological Association. Reprinted by permission.

any more than the words in the middle of the list. The recency effect is often explained by the proposal that the words at the end of the list are still in STM when a person begins the recall. The students in Rundus's experiment recalled the words immediately after the last item was presented; it is therefore reasonable to assume that the words they had just seen were still available in STM.

We learned from the Peterson and Peterson experiment discussed in Chapter 4 that information is rapidly lost from STM if people have to perform another task. If the recency effect is caused by retrieving the most recent items from STM, it should be eliminated if a person has to perform another task before recalling the items. Subjects in an experiment designed by Postman and Phillips (1965) had to perform an arithmetic task for 30 sec before they tried to recall a list of words. The arithmetic task was successful in eliminating the recency effect, implying that the words at the end of the list had decayed from STM.

Table 5.1   *A partial listing of items rehearsed by a subject in the Atkinson-Shiffrin experiment*

Item Presented	Items Rehearsed (Rehearsal Set)
1. Reaction	Reaction, reaction, reaction, reaction
2. Hoof	Hoof, reaction, hoof, reaction
3. Blessing	Blessing, hoof, reaction
4. Research	Research, reaction, hoof, research
5. Candy	Candy, hoof, research, reaction
6. Hardship	Hardship, hoof, hardship, hoof
7. Kindness	Kindness, candy, hardship, hoof
8. Nonsense	Nonsense, kindness, candy, hardship
20. Cellar	Cellar, alcohol, misery, cellar

Another piece of evidence for the proposal that the primacy effect is caused by retrieval from LTM and the recency effect is caused by retrieval from STM comes from patients who suffer from amnesia. These people have difficulty in retrieving information from LTM, but often have a normal STM as measured by the typical memory span test discussed in the previous chapter. This suggests that they should do much worse than control subjects on recalling the initial words on a list, but should do as well as control subjects on recalling the most recent words on the list. In fact, these results were obtained (Baddeley & Warrington, 1970).

It is only fair to point out that there have been other explanations of the recency effect, reviewed by Greene (1986). One such explanation is that the recency effect occurs because the positions at the end of the list are more distinctive than those in the middle. In the next chapter we will see that distinctive items are easier to recall, but I would now like to return to the topic of how people can use control strategies to learn new information.

CONTROL PROCESSES

Control processes determine how we use our memory to learn information. We have examined a particular control process—verbal rehearsal—but this is only a single example of the kinds of strategies that we use to learn and retrieve information. Imagine that you have to learn the English translations of a list of German vocabulary words. Figure 5.3 shows other examples of control processes that you might use to carry out the

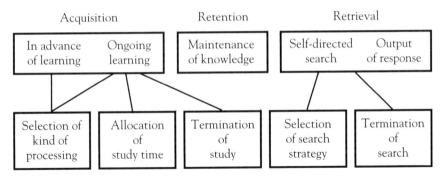

Figure 5.3 *Examples of control strategies that influence the acquisition and retrieval of knowledge.*

From "Metamemory: A Theoretical Framework and Some New Findings," by T. O. Nelson and L. Narens. In G. Bower (Ed.), *The Psychology of Learning and Motivation*, Figure 2, Copyright 1990 by the Academic Press. Reprinted by permission.

task (Nelson & Narens, 1990). First, you need to decide what kind of processing to use. Would you use rehearsal, coding, or imaging? If you could think of ways to make the material more meaningful (coding) or could easily generate visual images (imaging), you might want to use either of these more elaborative strategies. Second, you need to decide how to allocate study time among the items (Nelson, Dunlosky, Graf, & Narens, 1994). You will probably need more time to learn the translation of *der Gipfel* than to learn the translation of *die Kamera*. Third, you need to decide when to terminate study based (hopefully) on how well you know the material.

All of these decisions depend upon our ability to accurately judge when learning has occurred. For example, deciding which processing strategy to use depends on our ability to judge that one strategy is more effective than another. But judgments of learning can be inaccurate if they are made shortly after studying an item because learning may only be temporary. We may be very confident that we have learned some material immediately after studying it, only to discover that we can't later recall it. For this reason, it is best to delay judgments of learning until we are more certain that learning is relatively permanent.

These points are nicely illustrated in a study by Dunlosky and Nelson (1994). They designed a paired associates task in which students studied half of the associates by using a rehearsal strategy and studied the remainder by using an imagery strategy. The imagery strategy was much more effective—it resulted in 59% correct recall, compared to only 25% correct recall for the rehearsal strategy. Students were more accurate in judging the differential effectiveness of the two strategies when they made delayed judgments (at least 30 sec later) than when they made a judgment immediately after studying each item. They were also more accurate in identifying which individual items they had learned when they made delayed judgments.

Knowledge acquisition
Storage of information
in LTM

Retrieval strategies
Strategies for recalling
information from LTM

Control strategies such as selecting a good learning strategy and evaluating the learning of specific items are concerned with the **acquisition of knowledge**—getting information into LTM. Other strategies are concerned with retrieval—getting information back out of LTM. **Retrieval strategies**, shown on the right side of Figure 5.3, involve searching LTM to find an answer. If you retrieve an answer you think is correct, you terminate the search. Otherwise, you continue searching or give up if you think the situation is hopeless.

This section looks at control strategies that involve the allocation of study time and the search for information in LTM. In both cases we will look at these strategies from an applied point of view. Can psychologists improve acquisition by controlling the distribution of study time over items and improve retrieval by questioning people in a way that will improve their recall? Fortunately, the answer is yes for both acquisition and retrieval.

Allocating Study Time

Let's return to the task of learning English translations of German words. You would want to be able to recall the translations not only during the time you study the words but also on subsequent days. To succeed, you must be able to tell when you have really learned the translation and are not simply retrieving it from STM. My own experience has been that I sometimes find it difficult to judge when I have really learned what I was studying. Although the information appeared easy to recall shortly after I read or heard about it, it was gone the next day.

There are many tasks that a computer can do much better than people can, so why not let the computer decide when we have really learned an item? Since a computer can only follow the instructions of a programmer, it must be given instructions derived from a good model of learning. The advantage of using a formal model of learning and a computer to improve recall was demonstrated in a study by Atkinson (1972a, 1972b). The task required that undergraduates learn the English translations of 84 German words. The words were divided into seven lists, each containing 12 words. One of the lists was displayed on each trial of an instructional session, and either the student or the computer selected one of the items for test and study. After the student attempted to provide the English translation, the correct translation was presented. The computer then displayed the next list, and the procedure was repeated for a total of 336 trials. Figure 5.4 shows a typical list and the design of the instructional session.

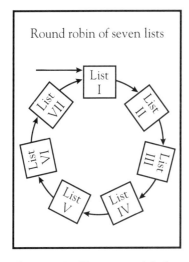

Round robin of seven lists

List I
List II
List III
List IV
List V
List VI
List VII

Typical list

1. *das Rad*
2. *die Seite*
3. *das Kino*
4. *die Gans*
5. *der Fluss*
6. *die Gegend*
7. *die Kamera*
8. *der Anzug*
9. *das Geld*
10. *der Gipfel*
11. *das Bein*
12. *die Ecke*

Figure 5.4   *Illustration of the language-learning task designed by Atkinson.*
From "Ingredients for a Theory of Instruction," by R. C. Atkinson, 1972, *American Psychologist, 27,* 921–931. Copyright 1972 by the American Psychological Association. Reprinted by permission.

Atkinson designed the experiment to compare the learning of three groups of students. Students in one group were allowed to pick which words they wanted to study. They were told that they should try to learn all the vocabulary words and that the best way to proceed was to test and study words that they did not already know. Students in a second group received items to study that were selected according to a learning model. Atkinson formulated the model in an attempt to optimize learning by presenting those words that the students most needed to study. The words were selected on the basis of a response-sensitive strategy that carefully kept track of a student's previous responses. Students in a third group received words that were randomly selected. Random selection, of course, is not a very good procedure because it might include words that a student had already learned. The performance of this third group is of interest because it provides a standard against which to compare the other two groups.

The learning model assumes that an item can be in one of three states:

1. *An unlearned state.* Items in this state have not yet been learned, so the learner will respond incorrectly.
2. *A temporary state.* Items in this state have been temporarily learned. The learner will initially give the correct answer but will forget the translation as she attempts to learn other items. We might think of these items as being stored in STM.

3. A *permanent state*. The translations of items in this state are relatively permanent in the sense that the learning of other vocabulary items will not interfere with them. We might think of these items as being stored in LTM.

The goal of the learning model is to select for study those items that are not yet in LTM in order to maximize the number of items in LTM at the end of the session. Items in the unlearned state are easy to identify because the student will be unable to provide the correct translation. Clearly, these items need further study, and on the basis of the research discussed previously we might expect that students would study them. Items in the temporary state are more difficult to identify because the student will be able to provide the correct answer on some of the trials. Let's consider the case in which a student receives two tests on the same item and responds correctly on both occasions. Is that item in a permanent state, implying that it wouldn't have to be presented again? We don't know for certain, but our decision should be influenced by the number of trials that occurred between the two tests. The greater the number of intervening trials, the greater the probability that the item is in the permanent state because studying other items should cause the student to forget the translation if it had been only temporarily learned.

The advantage of a computer is that it can record and remember exactly how a student responded on each of the items. When this information is used in a model that attempts to optimize learning, it is possible that the model could select items for study better than the student could. The results of Atkinson's experiment demonstrated that this possibility can be realized. Figure 5.5 shows the performance of each of the three groups during a delayed test given 1 week later. It is apparent that, the worse the students did during instruction, the better they did on the test. The reason is that successful instruction requires identifying and presenting the unlearned words, resulting in many errors during the instruction. The **response-sensitive strategy** based on the learning model was the most successful in identifying unlearned items. Those students who could select their own items for study (the **learner-controlled strategy**) did much better on the test than when the items were randomly selected, but they did much worse than the model. Performance on the test indicated that the learner-controlled strategy yielded a gain of 53% over the random procedure, but the computer-controlled strategy yielded a gain of 108%.

The results provide a clear demonstration of the usefulness of a good learning model that can be carried out by a computer. Although learner-controlled instruction was better than random selection, it was worse than selection of items by the learning model. It seems clear that serious consideration should be given to using the model on a wide scale. The declining cost of computers should make instructional programs like that developed by Atkinson a possibility in more situations.

Response-sensitive strategy   A computer-implemented strategy that uses the learner's previous responses to decide what items to present during learning trials

Learner-controlled strategy   A strategy in which the learner decides which items to study during learning trials

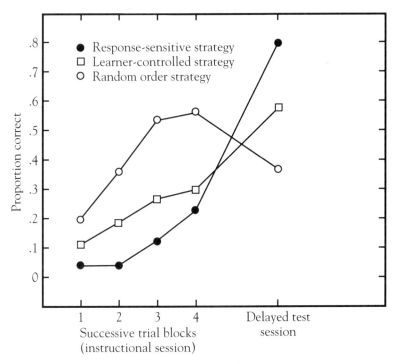

Figure 5.5   *Proportion of correct responses during the instructional session and during the delayed test given 1 week later.*

From "Ingredients for a Theory of Instruction," by R. C. Atkinson, 1972, *American Psychologist, 27*, 921–931. Copyright 1972 by the American Psychological Association. Reprinted by permission.

Retrieval Strategies

Effective learning depends not only on getting information into LTM but also on getting it back out through the use of effective retrieval strategies. If asked a difficult question, you may have to initially decide whether you have the relevant information in memory. Glucksberg and McCloskey (1981) proposed that people first conduct a preliminary search of memory to decide whether they have stored any information that is relevant to the question. Most people would not find any relevant information if asked "Does President Clinton use an electric toothbrush?" so they could quickly respond that they didn't know. If potentially relevant facts were retrieved, however (as could occur for a question such as "Is Kiev in the Ukraine?"), a person should then search LTM for confirming or discon-firming evidence.

After deciding that it is worthwhile to search LTM, you must decide how to conduct the search. Atkinson and Shiffrin (1968) proposed that people develop plans for searching LTM. For example, if asked to recall the names of all 50 states, you could organize your search by either alphabetical order or geographical location.

Recalling information from LTM sometimes occurs so rapidly that psychologists have little opportunity to study how people retrieve the information. However, occasionally retrieval succeeds only after a slow search of LTM, such as occurs in the **"tip of the tongue" (TOT)** phenomenon. A word is on the tip of your tongue when you know it is stored in LTM but are momentarily blocked from retrieving it. Successful retrieval is often helped by using partial information, such as the length of the word or its initial letter, to limit the search of LTM (R. Brown & D. McNeill, 1966).

There are two general experimental methods for studying the TOT state. The laboratory approach requires bringing people into the laboratory and asking them to recall words that might elicit the TOT state. The diary approach requires that people keep detailed records of what happens when faced with memory blocks in their daily lives.

The first systematic laboratory study was conducted by R. Brown and D. McNeill (1966) who gave people definitions of infrequent words and asked them to try to recall the words. For example, "What is the name of the instrument that uses the position of the sun and stars to navigate?" Some of the words produced the TOT state; that is, people were unable to immediately think of the word but were confident that they would soon recall it. Successful retrieval was often helped by using partial information related to the spelling of the word, such as its length or its initial letter. When attempting to answer the previous question, people may recall that the word starts with the letter *s* and has two syllables (sextant).

Another study found similar results using pictures and verbal descriptions of entertainers (Read & Bruce, 1982). For example, the verbal description of Ray Bolger was "On Broadway he created the role of Charley in *Charley's Aunt*, but he is perhaps best remembered as the scarecrow in the Judy Garland movie *The Wizard of Oz*." The most frequently reported strategy for recalling names was to make use of partial information, as reported initially by Brown and McNeill (1966). Partial information includes information about the length of a name or letters or sounds within a name. Two other popular strategies were to generate plausible names and to use contextual information. The generation of plausible names was often guided by partial information to limit the search. Contextual information is information associated with the person, such as movie and television roles or ethnic origin. Only infrequently did subjects report that they spontaneously recalled the name without thinking about the target person. Successful retrievals, therefore, usually occurred as a result of a planned search of memory.

Tip of the tongue (TOT)
A retrieval state in which a person feels he or she knows the information but cannot immediately retrieve it

In **naturalistic studies** of TOTs subjects carry a diary to document TOT states as they occur. They are asked to record what information they could retrieve as they searched for the word and how the memory block was resolved. A review of this literature (A. S. Brown, 1991) reported a number of consistent findings. For example:

Naturalistic studies
Studies of the tip-of-the-tongue state in which people record these events as they occur outside the laboratory

1. TOTs are reported to occur in daily life about once a week and to increase with age. Most are triggered by the names of personal acquaintances.
2. Words related both to the meaning and the spelling of the target word are retrieved but spelling predominates. People can guess the first letter about 50% of the time.
3. Approximately half of the TOT states are resolved within a minute.

The finding that the predominant retrieval strategy involves the partial recall of spelling information is consistent across both laboratory and naturalistic studies, but there are also some differences in the findings. Naturally occurring TOTs yield a moderate number (ranging from 17 to 41%) of **spontaneous retrievals** in which the word suddenly "pops into mind" without a conscious effort to retrieve it. In contrast, spontaneous retrievals seldom occur (5% or less) in laboratory studies, perhaps because people are kept busy actively searching for the words. For those of you who want to design your own experiment to study the TOT condition, you will be happy to learn that not all the issues have been resolved. For example, it is still not clear whether retrieval of related words facilitates eventual retrieval of the target word or helps maintain the blockage (Brown, 1991).

Spontaneous retrievals
Retrievals that occur without making a conscious effort to recall information

Improving Eyewitness Recall

These findings raise the issue of whether psychologists can provide techniques to help people search LTM for important information. Consider the example of a person who has observed a crime and is later questioned by law-enforcement personnel. Hypnosis has been extensively used in such cases to improve the witness' ability to retrieve information about the crime. This use of hypnosis is based on a model of memory in which the witness tries to "replay a videotape" of the event. An important component of this technique is that the hypnotist attempts to reinstate the context by telling the witness to imagine that he is once again at the scene of the crime.

Although there have been many reports of cases in which hypnosis helped witnesses recall additional details about a crime, there are problems associated with its use (M. E. Smith, 1983). A major concern is that encouragement by the hypnotist may induce witnesses to report inaccurately. For example, in one study 90% of the hypnotized witnesses tried to recall the number on a shirt in a simulated crime, compared with only 20% of the subjects in a control group (Buckhout, Eugenio, Licitra, Oliver, & Kramer, 1981). None of the witnesses was able to recall the number correctly. The possibility that recall may be inaccurate has caused the courts to question the reliability of recall during hypnosis.

Another problem with evaluating the effectiveness of hypnosis is that successful recall during hypnosis may not have been caused by the hypnosis. M. E. Smith (1983) identifies other possible causes, such as repeated testing and the reinstatement of context. As indicated by the findings of Read and Bruce (1982), repeated testing can cause additional recall. That is, improved recall attributed to hypnosis may simply result from the fact that witnesses are attempting a second or a third recall, which would have resulted in retrieval of more details without hypnosis. Or improved recall could result from some aspect of the procedure such as encouraging witnesses to try to reinstate the context of the crime.

To determine whether encouraging nonhypnotized subjects to reinstate the context would improve recall, Malpass and Devine (1981) asked an actor to vandalize some equipment during a demonstration before a large class of unsuspecting students. Five months after the staged vandalism, witnesses viewed a lineup of five individuals and were asked to identify the vandal if he was in the lineup. Half the witnesses were to reinstate the context of the crime before they made their choice. The interviewer asked them to try to visualize the events of that evening, including the lecture room, the equipment, the vandal, and their own feelings.

Witnesses who were told to reinstate the context before making a decision were correct 60% of the time. Those who did not receive special instruction were correct 40% of the time. Thus, guided retrieval that emphasizes the reinstatement of context can lead to improved recall. But how does guided retrieval without hypnosis compare with guided retrieval with hypnosis?

To answer this question, Geiselman, Fisher, MacKinnon, and Holland (1985) asked both hypnotized and nonhypnotized subjects to recall information about a simulated crime. Subjects saw a 4-min film of a violent crime and were interviewed 2 days later by law-enforcement personnel. The subjects were randomly assigned to one of three interview conditions. The standard interview followed questioning procedures that law-enforcement personnel would normally use. The hypnosis interview involved asking hypnotized subjects to restate what they remembered from the film. The **cognitive interview** involved the use of four memory retrieval techniques that encouraged subjects to reinstate the context of the incident, report everything, recall the events in different orders, and recall the incidents from different perspectives.

Cognitive interview
The use of cognitively based retrieval techniques to improve recall

Both the cognitive and hypnosis procedures resulted in the recall of a significantly greater number of correct items of information than did the standard interview. The investigators attributed this finding to the memory guidance techniques that are common to these two procedures. Although the cognitive interview did not result in better recall than the use of hypnosis, it is easier to learn and to administer.

The application of the cognitive interview procedure to real crimes has also produced encouraging results (Fisher, Geiselman, & Amador, 1989). Seven experienced detectives in Dade County (Miami), Florida, were trained in the procedure. Both before and after training, the experimenters tape-recorded interviews with victims and witnesses of crimes. The detectives obtained 47% more information from the interviews following the training. In many cases there was more than one victim or witness, so it was possible to determine whether the obtained information was consistent across the people interviewed. A high rate of consistency suggested that the obtained information was accurate. These positive results indicate that we may see more widespread use of these techniques (see Box 5.1).

RECOGNITION MEMORY

Retrieval strategies are obviously important when people have to recall information, but what happens when they must make a recognition judgment, such as looking at mug shots of criminals to determine whether they recognize a suspect? Current theories of **recognition memory** emphasize that there are two components of recognition, one based on judging the familiarity of the item and one based on recalling information about the item (G. Mandler, 1980; Humphreys & Bain, 1983).

Recognition memory
Deciding whether an item had previously occurred in a specified context

Part of the problem in deciding whether we recognize someone or something is to recall the context in which a previous encounter might have occurred. G. Mandler (1980) gives an example of a person who sees a familiar-looking person on a bus but is unsure why the person looks familiar. It is only after a suitable context is recalled—the person works in the supermarket—that recognition seems complete. Thus the recall of contextual information is valuable in both recall and recognition experiments.

The next section of this chapter is concerned with an important application of how both judged familiarity and the recall of contextual information are needed for eyewitness identification. But before considering this application, I want to show you how familiarity is modeled by cognitive psychologists. The model was borrowed from psychologists who were interested in a seemingly simple act of perception.

A Signal Detection Theory of Recognition

The theory we're about to consider was originally developed to describe performance in signal detection experiments. The **signal detection task** requires that an observer report whether a signal occurred—for instance,

Signal detection task
A task that requires observers to report whether a signal occurred

**BOX
5.1**

Making the eye a better witness

EDWIN CHEN
TIMES STAFF WRITER

One intruder had on a blue backpack. The other was wearing tan slacks. Or was it a green backpack and brown slacks?

It happened so quickly—less than a minute—that 42 witnesses could not agree on such vital details when asked about the robbery two days later through conventional police interview techniques. The witnesses had been assembled by UCLA psychologists ostensibly to view a slide show. But during the viewing, two participants in the experiment barged into the room, turned on the lights and made off with the projector.

Then the interviewers changed tactics, with remarkable results. They didn't just ask "What happened?" Rather, they told the witnesses to first recall the physical setting and their own frame of mind at the time of the robbery. They told the witnesses to omit no detail no matter how trivial. They told them to reconstruct the crime in a variety of orders, not just from start to finish. Finally, they told the witnesses to recreate the incident not only from their own perspective but also from that of the robbers.

"Cognitive interview"

This "cognitive interview" technique, pioneered by UCLA psychologist R. Edward Geiselman, elicited up to 35% more details about the crime—all of them accurate and many of them crucial, according to the researchers.

With little notice, psychologists have been developing new and relatively simple ways to jog the human memory, raising the potential of making eyewitness testimony far more reliable than previously thought possible.

These advances may also prove useful well beyond the world of criminal justice, they say. For instance, such memory-enhancing tools can aid public health officials in tracing partners of people with venereal diseases, said Ronald Fisher, a psy-

---

whether a tone occurred in a background of noise. The listener can make two kinds of errors. First, he can respond negatively when a signal did occur. This kind of error is called a miss because the subject failed to detect the signal. Second, the listener can respond positively when a signal did not occur. This kind of error is called a false alarm.

J. P. Egan (1958) showed that the theory developed to describe performance on a signal detection task could also be used to describe performance on a recognition memory test. There are two kinds of items on such a memory test—old items that occurred before in the experiment and new items that did not occur. Although the task requires distinguishing between old and new items rather than between signals and noise, the same kinds of errors can occur when people try to identify old items. A person can respond negatively to an old item by failing to remember

chologist at Florida International University. The techniques can even help a person locate a missing wallet or keys, he said.

"Enhance recall"

"We've known for a long time how to increase learning, but until now little has been known about how to enhance recall," Fisher said.

The cognitive interview, in particular, has been adopted by many law-enforcement agencies, including the FBI, the U.S. Secret Service and the Metro-Dade Police Department in Florida.

"I really believe in this technique," said John S. Farrell, chief of detectives at the Metro-Dade Police Department. "This is a whole different ballgame."

Researchers in Florida and Minnesota have also found that false identifications at police lineups can be reduced by as much as half when witnesses view suspects one at a time instead of six simultaneously, which is the prevalent practice.

Scientists elsewhere have shown that memory can be significantly affected—for better and worse—simply by the way a witness is asked about crime details.

These emerging insights are timely because many scientists now believe that hypnosis is far less reliable than most people assume. And courts across the country, including in California, are placing severe restrictions on its use in criminal cases.

New ways to increase eyewitness reliability are especially important because juries tend to give great weight to eyewitness testimony—sometimes without realizing how unreliable such witnesses can be.

"The confidence of the eyewitness is the most powerful predictor of verdicts," said Brian L. Cutler, a Florida International University psychologist. Yet research shows that confidence is "only weakly correlated with identification accuracy," he said.

SOURCE: From "Making the Eye a Better Witness," by Edwin Chen appearing in the *Los Angeles Times*, March 3, 1989. Copyright 1989, *Los Angeles Times*. Reprinted by permission.

---

that it occurred before. This error is called a **miss**, as when a person misses a signal. Or a person can respond positively to a new item that hadn't occurred before. This error is called a **false alarm**, as when a person incorrectly states that a signal occurred.

Signal detection theory assumes that items vary along a continuous dimension, which is labeled *memory strength* or *familiarity*. The effect of presenting an item during the experiment is to increase its familiarity in the experiment. Since old items were previously presented in the experiment, they will generally have higher familiarity values than new items. This situation is represented in Figure 5.6 by the placement of the two distributions (representing new items and old items) along the continuum. The height of the distribution on the left shows how many new items have that particular familiarity value. The average value for new

Miss When an observer fails to report a signal in a signal detection task or a previously presented item in a recognition memory task

False alarm When an observer incorrectly reports a signal in a signal detection task or an item that was not previously presented in a recognition memory task

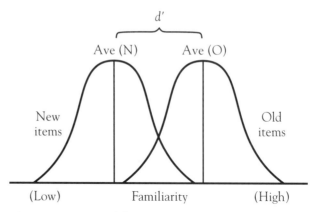

Figure 5.6   *A signal detection representation of old and new items along a familiarity continuum. Ave(N) is the average familiarity value for new items, and Ave(O) is the average familiarity for old items.*

items is represented by the vertical line labeled Ave(N). The height of the distribution on the right shows how many old items have that particular familiarity value. The average value for old items is represented by the vertical line labeled Ave(O).

Notice that the two distributions overlap and that some new items actually have higher familiarity values than old items. Why should this be? First, we must remember that the term ***familiarity*** is being used to define how familiar an item seems to be within the context of the experiment. You are very familiar with your name, but, if it didn't occur in the experiment, it would have a low familiarity value. Since the familiarity values reflect how confident you are that an item occurred in the experiment, your name should have a very low familiarity value because you should be very confident that it was not one of the old items. Other new items, however, would be more difficult to judge. For example, if the word *boat* were presented and you were later tested on the word *ship,* you might respond positively because the two words have similar meanings. The word *ship* would seem familiar even though it did not occur.

A measure called ***d' (d prime)*** is used to represent how much the two distributions overlap or how well a person performs on a recognition test. It is a measure of the difference in the means of the two distributions—that is, $\text{Ave}(O) - \text{Ave}(N)$—relative to the variance of the new-item distribution. A low value of d' implies that there is a considerable overlap of the two distributions because a person makes many mistakes. The extreme case is $d' = 0$, which indicates that the average familiarity value is the same for old and new items. A d' of 0 would occur if a person couldn't

Familiarity A judgment of how familiar an item is with respect to a particular context

***d* prime (*d'*)** A measure of accuracy in a recognition memory test based on the ability to discriminate between old items and new items

remember any of the items in the experiment and simply guessed when given the memory test.

Since d' is a measure of how well a person performs on a recognition memory test, it reflects the probability of making an error on the test. It does not, however, tell us the kinds of errors that occur. In order to know the kinds of errors, we have to know how a person distinguishes new items from old items. Since old items generally have higher values on the continuum than new items, a person should respond that familiar items were previously presented and unfamiliar items were not previously presented. This sounds simple enough, but exactly where should the cutoff be placed separating familiar from unfamiliar items if familiarity varies along a continuum? The placement of the dividing line differs across people and tasks, so it is necessary to calculate the location of the boundary. The vertical line labeled ß **(beta)** in Figure 5.7 shows two possible locations. Signal detection theory assumes that people respond that an item was not previously presented if its familiarity value is less than ß and that it was previously presented if its familiarity value is greater than ß.

The location of ß determines how a person's errors are divided into misses and false alarms. Notice in Figure 5.7 that part of each distribution is on the wrong side of the dividing line. The familiarity values of most new items are less than ß, so they will be correctly labeled as new items. But a few new items have familiarity values greater than ß, so they will be incorrectly identified as having previously occurred, resulting in a false alarm. The probability of a false alarm is represented by the proportion of new items that have familiarity values greater than ß, the areas of vertical lines in Figure 5.7. The probability of a miss is represented by the proportion of old items that have familarity values less than ß, the areas shaded with horizontal lines. Since the latter do not seem very familiar, they will be classified as new items.

Beta (ß) The location of the response criterion in a recognition memory test that determines whether an item is judged as old or new

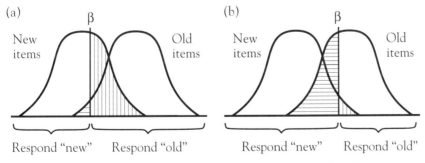

Figure 5.7 *Influence of the response criterion (ß) on the probability of a miss (horizontal lines) and a false alarm (vertical lines).*

Notice in Figure 5.7 that there is a tradeoff between misses and false alarms as the criterion is moved either to the left or to the right. Moving the criterion to the left (Figure 5.7a) implies that a person responds positively more often. This causes a decline in the number of misses but an increase in the number of false alarms. Moving the criterion to the right (Figure 5.7b) implies that a person responds positively less often. This causes an increase in the number of misses but a decline in the number of false alarms. The exact placement of the criterion can be calculated by making use of this tradeoff in proportion between false alarms and misses.

The application of signal detection theory to recognition memory therefore provides two measures of performance. The first measure—d'—is a measure of accuracy. It indicates how well a person can distinguish between old items and new items. Accuracy is determined by such factors as individual differences in memory, length of the retention interval, and degree of similarity between old and new items. The second measure—ß—indicates the response criterion selected by an individual. It is a value on the familiarity continuum that the individual uses for deciding whether an item was presented before. Items with familiarity values greater than the criterion are classified as old, and items with familiarity values less than the criterion are classified as new. The location of the criterion determines whether the errors are primarily misses or false alarms.

Eyewitness Identification

Recognition memory has been discussed only abstractly so far. Let's see how it is used in a particular task. We previously looked at techniques that could be used to help eyewitnesses *recall* more details about a crime. We will now look at how laboratory tests of recognition memory are related to the ability to *recognize* whether a person was involved in a crime.

Recognition memory is studied in the laboratory by showing people a sequence of items and then asking them whether a test item was a member of the sequence. The subjects have to remember not only that they saw that item before but that they saw it during the experiment. In other words, they have to remember the context in which they saw the item. Recalling the correct context is often useful in everyday situations. For instance, you may recognize someone as a person you met before but may not be able to remember where the meeting took place. Remembering the appropriate context might help you recall additional information about that person, as was shown by the use of the cognitive interview procedure.

Eyewitness identification is a situation in which recalling the context of information is particularly important. Accurate identification depends not only on being able to recognize a face as someone familiar but on recalling that the person was seen performing a crime rather than seen in a newspaper, on television, or in police mug shots. The possibility that the witness might be able to recognize a face without being able to recall the correct context was addressed by the U.S. Supreme Court in *Simmons v. United States* (390 U.S. 377, 1968) (cited in E. Brown, K. Deffenbacher, & W. Sturgill, 1977). The Court noted the potential biasing effect caused by showing a witness a single mug shot or by showing mug shots that emphasized a particular suspect. The ruling held that the biasing effects would be particularly misleading if the witness originally had only a brief glimpse of the suspect or saw the suspect under poor conditions (Buckhout, 1974).

The possible biasing effects that can occur during eyewitness identification were investigated in two experiments by E. Brown, K. Deffenbacher, and W. Sturgill (1977). In one experiment students in a large introductory psychology class were asked to view ten "criminals" (graduate and upperclass undergraduate white males) for 25 sec each. The experimenter told the class to observe them carefully because the students would have to pick the "criminals" out from mug shots later that evening and from a lineup the following week. An hour and a half later, the students looked at 15 mug shots consisting of color slides showing a front and a side view. The students were asked to indicate, for each mug shot, whether that person had appeared earlier in front of the class. Of the 15 mug shots, 5 were of people who had actually appeared. The five "criminals" were correctly identified as criminals 72% of the time; however, the ten noncriminals were also identified as criminals 45% of the time. The value of d' calculated from these percentages is significantly above 0, but it is not very large. This finding implies that, although the accuracy of identification was significantly above chance, it was not very good. Furthermore, the high false alarm rate (45%) indicates that many people in the mug shots were falsely accused.

A major goal of this experiment was to determine whether presenting a mug shot would cause a bias toward identifying the person in the photograph as a criminal. Notice that the students saw the mug shots of only five of the ten "criminals." Would they be more likely later to identify these five as criminals than the five whose mug shots were not presented? One week later students saw a lineup and were asked to indicate whether each person in the lineup was one of the original "criminals" who had appeared in front of the class. The "criminals" whose mug shots had been shown were identified on 65% of the occasions, compared with 51% for "criminals" whose mug shots had not been shown. Showing a mug shot made it significantly more likely that a person would be identified as a criminal, perhaps because the "witnesses" could not recall whether they had previously seen the person or the photograph.

At this point we might say "So what? They were all guilty anyway." But what about innocent people? Would showing their mug shots make it more likely that they would be identified as criminals during a lineup? This was the issue that concerned the Supreme Court in the *Simmons v. United States* decision. In the Brown, Deffenbacher, and Sturgill experiment, nine of the persons included in the lineup had not initially appeared in front of the class, but pictures of four of the nine were included among the mug shots. If showing a mug shot of an innocent person biases the witnesses to label that person as a criminal, these four should be identified as criminals more often than the other five. The results support this hypothesis. The four persons whose pictures had been included in the mug shot session were incorrectly identified as criminals on 20% of the occasions, compared with 8% for persons whose pictures had not appeared. The greater tendency to identify a person as a criminal after seeing a mug shot affected the "innocent" as well as the "guilty."

One objection to this experiment is that students were initially asked to remember what ten persons looked like rather than only one or two, a more typical situation in a real crime. Brown and his colleagues eliminated this objection in a second experiment, in which a different class of students was asked to identify only two persons. Two males handed out the first midterm exam in the class; members of the class were not told that they would later be asked to identify the two individuals. The design of the experiment was similar to the one described above except that the mug shots were shown 2 or 3 days after the exam and the lineup occurred 4 or 5 days after the students viewed the mug shots. The same pattern of results occurred as in the previous experiment: presenting a mug shot of a person made it more likely that the person would be identified as a criminal in the lineup.

The false identification occurred because the person identified looked very familiar as a result of having his picture included among the mug shots. However, as stated earlier, successful recognition often depends on the recall of a specific context in addition to a judgment of familiarity. Although these experiments do not pretend to duplicate what an actual witness is confronted with during a crime, they do raise serious questions about our ability to identify the context in which a person is perceived. The findings suggest that great care should be taken in what material is shown to a witness who must make the final identification of a suspected criminal.

INDIRECT TESTS OF MEMORY

Traditional tests, such as recognition and recall, are not the only way to evaluate a person's memory. Look for a moment at the word fragment in Figure 5.8. Can you identify the word? People are more successful at identifying difficult word fragments if they are previously shown a

Figure 5.8 *Example of a word fragment.*
From "Amnesic Syndrome: Consolidation or Retrieval?" by E. K.
Warrington and L. Weiskrantz, 1970, *Nature*, *228*, 628–630. Copyright
© 1970 Macmillan Magazines Ltd. Reprinted by permission.

list of words that includes the answers to the fragments (such as the word
METAL for this example). The fact that the list is helpful suggests that
people remember some of the words on the list, indicating that this task
could be used as a test for memory.

You may feel that this memory test is less direct than the recall and
recognition tests discussed in the previous section. Recall and recognition
tests are called **direct tests of memory** because they refer to a particular
event in a person's past. The directions ask people to recall or recognize
events that occurred earlier and are therefore measures of **explicit
memory**. In contrast, instructions for **indirect tests of memory** refer only
to the current task and do not refer to prior events (Richardson-Klavehn
& Bjork, 1988). People performing the word-fragment task only have to
identify the word, not judge whether they had previously seen the word
during the experiment. Indirect tests are therefore measures of **implicit
memory**.

One reason for distinguishing between these two types of tests is that
what we learn about a person's memory depends on how we test it. This
point was strikingly illustrated in a study by Warrington and Weiskrantz
(1970) at the National Hospital in London. They compared patients
with severe amnesia with control patients who were closely matched for
age and intelligence. The comparison involved four tests of memory for
word lists. The recall test required a verbal recall of the words. The recognition
memory test required a yes or no decision regarding whether a test
word was on the list. The word-fragment test required the identification
of a word fragment. The correct word appeared on the list, and the fragments
were difficult to identify if subjects had not previously seen the list.
The initial-letters test contained the first three letters of a word that had
appeared on the list, and the subjects had to generate a word that began
with those three letters.

The amnesic subjects did significantly worse than the controls on
both the recognition and recall tests. However, they did not differ from
the controls on the word-fragment or initial-letters tests. They were just
as likely as the controls to successfully use the words that they had seen

Direct memory tests
Tests that ask people to
recall or recognize past
events

Explicit memory
Memory evaluated by
direct memory tests (see
above)

Indirect memory tests
Tests that do not explicitly
ask about past
events but are influenced
by memory of
past events

Implicit memory
Memory evaluated by
indirect memory tests
(see above)

on the word list. The lack of difference on these two tests occurred even though the amnesic patients often did not remember that they had seen the word list and approached the tests as a kind of guessing game (Warrington & Weiskrantz, 1968). But the influence of the word list on their answers indicates that they still remembered many of the words.

Processing Theories

Performance differences between direct and indirect tests of memory have encouraged many studies of how the tests differ (see Table 5.2). One theoretical approach has emphasized the *different processing requirements* of the tests. An example of this approach (Jacoby & Dallas, 1981) builds on Mandler's (1980) two-process theory of recognition memory that I briefly discussed previously. According to this theory, recognition memory requires both a judgment of familiarity and an attempt to retrieve the context in which the item occurred. L. L. Jacoby and M. Dallas proposed that the familiarity component of this theory also applies to indirect tests that typically require perceptual identification. Prior experience with the material makes it more familiar and easier to identify in a perceptually difficult situation. However, the second basis for recognition memory—retrieval of when and where an item occurred—is not necessary to do well on indirect tests because such tests do not require memory for a particular context.

This formulation implies that changing the familiarity of the items should influence performance on tests of both recognition memory and perceptual identification task. Jacoby and Dallas manipulated familiarity by presenting the study material either in the same modality (visual presentation) or in a different modality (auditory presentation) than the test material. As predicted, changing the modality made the test material less familiar and lowered performance on both the recognition-memory and perceptual- identification tasks.

Table 5.2   *Differences between direct and indirect tests of memory*

	Direct tests	Indirect tests
Examples	Recall Recognition	Word fragment Initial letters
Process theories	Conceptually driven Retrieval strategies	Data driven Familiarity
Multimemory theories	Episodic memory	Semantic memory Procedural memory

In contrast, variables that help subjects determine in what context they saw a word should only enhance performance on recognition-memory tasks. This prediction was tested by manipulating whether subjects read a list of words (such as *METAL*) or solved the words from anagrams (*EMTLA*). Prior research has shown that it is easier to remember which words occur in an experiment if subjects generate the words from anagrams rather than simply read them. As predicted, generating the words improved performance on a recognition-memory task but did not improve performance on a perceptual-identification task that did not require memory for the context of the presented words.

Jacoby and Dallas's explanation is an example of how direct and indirect measures of memory can be compared on the basis of what processes are required to perform the task. Elaboration of the material through generating the words from anagrams helps people on recall and recognition tests, whereas increasing the familiarity of the material influences performance on recognition-memory and perceptual-identification tasks.

A more general formulation of this approach claims that direct tests of memory are primarily conceptually driven and indirect tests of memory are primarily data driven (Schacter, 1987; Richardson-Klavehn & Bjork, 1988). **Conceptually driven processes** reflect subject-initiated activities such as elaborating and organizing information. Such processes help people on recall and recognition tests. **Data-driven processes** are initiated and guided by the perceptual information in the material, such as its familiarity. However, this distinction is not mutually exclusive. As we have just seen, recognition-memory tests are influenced by both kinds of processing, but data-driven processing is more predominant in indirect tests than in recognition-memory tests. Modality shifts therefore cause greater disruption in indirect tests such as word-fragment identification than in direct tests such as recognition memory (Schacter, 1987).

> **Conceptually driven processes** Processes that are influenced by a person's strategies
>
> **Data-driven processes** Processes that are influenced by the stimulus material

Multiple Memories

An alternative to arguing that memory tests measure different processes is to argue that memory tests measure different memories (Schacter, 1987). This view claims that LTM is not a single unitary system but consists of several different subsystems. One distinction is between episodic and semantic memory (Tulving, 1972, 1985). **Episodic memory** contains temporally dated recollections of personal experiences. It provides a record of what people have done; for example, I had chicken for dinner last night, received my Ph.D. in 1970, and saw a particular person's face as I was looking at mug shots. **Semantic memory** contains general knowledge that is not associated with a particular time and context. For instance, I know that a canary is a bird, Chicago is in Illinois, and the sum of 7 and 8 is 15. Episodic memory is therefore more autobiographical; it contains the kind

> **Episodic memory** Memory of specific events, including when and where they occurred
>
> **Semantic memory** Memory of general knowledge not associated with a particular context

of information I would record in a detailed diary. Semantic information is more general and contains the kind of information I would record in an encyclopedia.

According to this distinction, direct tests of memory, which require recall or recognition of material that occurred earlier in the experiment, measure episodic memory. Subjects are asked to recall items (such as a list of words) from a particular time and place. Indirect tests of memory, such as word identification or word completion, measure semantic memory. These tests depend only on our general knowledge of words and do not require that we associate the words with a particular time and place.

The finding that patients with amnesia do much better on indirect tests than on direct tests has been used as evidence for the distinction between episodic and semantic memory. According to this argument, amnesia affects episodic memory but not semantic memory. However, critics of the episodic/semantic distinction argue that this explanation is less popular than the position that indirect tests differ from direct tests because they depend more on procedural memory (McKoon, Ratcliff, & Dell, 1986). **Procedural memory** is memory for actions, skills, and operations, whereas both episodic and semantic memory are concerned with factual information. Factual information seems more susceptible to forgetting than procedural information, as evidenced by amnesic patients who have difficulty recalling facts but do well at learning and retaining motor skills (Warrington & Weiskrantz, 1970).

Procedural memory
Memory for actions, skills, and operations

Although I don't recall ever suffering from amnesia, I do recall an incident in which my procedural memory was left more intact than my memory for facts. I learned how to type in high school and did some typing in college, but I relied entirely on secretaries when I became a faculty member. When I later decided to try a word-processing program, I began by attempting to recall where the keys were on the keyboard but discovered that I could recall almost nothing. However, when I attempted to use the keyboard, I remembered how to correctly move my fingers. I remembered the correct procedure for typing even though I couldn't recall the location of the keys.

In conclusion, both process theories and multimemory theories offer suggestions for how direct tests of memory differ from indirect tests of memory (Roediger, 1990). Direct tests, such as recall and recognition, are conceptually driven and are influenced by subject-initiated strategies that facilitate retrieval, such as actively generating the items during the study phase. In contrast, indirect tests, such as the word-fragment and initial-letters tests, are data driven. They are influenced by the familiarity of the material, including changes in its modality. Direct tests measure episodic memory in which people recall information about particular events in their past. Indirect tests measure semantic or procedural memory in which people are not instructed to refer back to past events.

SUMMARY

Learning can be represented as the transfer of information from STM to LTM. The decay rate for information in LTM is slow compared with the rapid decay rate from STM. Furthermore, LTM does not suffer from a capacity limitation; that is, it is not limited in the amount of information it can store. The distinction between STM and LTM, as well as the role of rehearsal in transferring information into LTM, was emphasized in a model proposed by Atkinson and Shiffrin. One of the findings that their model accounts for is the serial position effect: the better recall of words at the beginning of a list can be explained by their storage in LTM, and the better recall of words at the end of the list can be explained by their storage in STM. In other situations it may be difficult to decide whether successfully retrieved new information came from STM or LTM. The ability to make this distinction is useful because the student should concentrate on items that are not yet stored in LTM. A learning model used this distinction to determine which items should be presented during an instructional session in order for students to recall them during a test given one week later.

In order to retrieve information from LTM, we must initially decide whether the information is stored in LTM. The tip-of-the-tongue phenomenon occurs when a person knows information is stored in LTM but cannot immediately retrieve it. Strategies for searching LTM include using partial information such as word length or sounds, generating plausible names, and using contextual information associated with a name. The cognitive interview technique successfully encourages eyewitnesses to carefully search memory in order to recall details about a crime.

A recognition task differs from a recall task in that it tests judgment of whether an item was previously presented, usually within a specified context. A model of recognition memory derived from signal detection theory assumes that items vary in familiarity along a continuum. Items that were presented before (old items) generally have higher familiarity values than items that were not presented before (new items), but the two distributions overlap. A person must select a criterion value along this continuum in order to decide whether an item is old or new. The location of the criterion determines whether the errors are primarily misses or false alarms. False alarms in eyewitness identification are increased by showing mug shots to a witness. The witness may falsely identify a person because of a failure to recall the context in which that person was previously seen.

Indirect tests of LTM typically determine whether memory for a list of words helps people to identify word fragments or to generate a word from initial letters. Patients with memory disorders usually perform better on these tests than on direct tests of memory such as recognition or recall.

Process theories attribute this difference to the conceptually driven nature of direct tests and the data-driven nature of indirect tests. In contrast, multimemory theories propose that direct tests evaluate episodic memory whereas indirect tests evaluate either semantic or procedural memory.

STUDY QUESTIONS

1. Long-term memory (LTM) is what most of us mean when we speak of memory. What do we mean when we say a person has a "good memory"? What are the assumed characteristics of LTM?

2. As you think about your own attempts to learn new material, can you identify different instances in which you have used each of the control processes discussed in the book?

3. Notice that the task chosen for the study of verbal rehearsal was a "stupid" task. Why was that desirable?

4. Do the assumptions of the Atkinson-Shiffrin model seem intuitively compelling to you? (Does it matter?) How well do the data fit the predictions generated by the model—for example, the primacy effect?

5. How can the recency effect be explained? How was the most popular theory tested?

6. Atkinson's subsequent work was an impressive extension of his model to a more realistic set of materials. What are the assumptions of his model?

7. What role did the computer play in Atkinson's experiment? Would you like a personal computer to help you learn? Could you, instead, program yourself to do the same things?

8. Be sure you understand the specific uses of the term *context* in studies of recognition and recall. Are recognition and recall different kinds of memory?

9. Signal detection theory tends to scare people, but don't let a few symbols throw you. Realize (a) the special, restricted meaning of "familiarity" used here; (b) that ß, the response criterion, is a construct, the value of which is empirically determined by examining an individual subject's performance on a given set of items; (c) that the distance (d') between the means of the curves for new and old items would vary depending on several factors. Play around with these ideas until you can invent alternate scenarios that would produce differences in d' and ß. *Write* your scenarios.

10. Were you surprised by any of the results of the application of recognition theory to eyewitness identification? Would you recommend any changes in criminal justice procedures on the basis of these experiments? Why or why not?

11. What techniques have been used to test memory indirectly? How do the tasks called for in direct and indirect tests differ? One explanation of the differences shown in performance on direct and indirect tests points to differential processing demands. What sorts of empirical evidence lead to this view?

KEY TERMS

The page number in parentheses refers to where the term is discussed in the chapter.

beta (ß) (133)
coding (116)
cognitive interview (128)
conceptually driven processes (139)
control processes (116)
d prime (*d'*) (132)
data-driven processes (139)
direct memory tests (137)
episodic memory (139)
explicit memory (137)
false alarm (131)
familiarity (132)
imaging (117)
implicit memory (137)
indirect memory tests (137)
knowledge acquisition (122)
learner-controlled strategy (124)

long-term memory (LTM) (114)
miss (131)
naturalistic studies (127)
primacy effect (118)
procedural memory (140)
recency effect (118)
recognition memory (129)
rehearsal (116)
response-sensitive strategy (124)
retrieval strategies (122)
rote learning (117)
semantic memory (139)
serial position effect (118)
signal detection task (129)
spontaneous retrievals (127)
tip of the tongue (TOT) (126)

RECOMMENDED READING

The general references on memory cited at the end of Chapter 4 discuss LTM as well as STM. Schacter (1989) summarizes the major assumptions and some of the research findings from four different approaches to studying memory: experimental cognitive psychology, neuropsychology, ecological psychology, and artificial intelligence. Bahrick (1979) studied very-long-term memory by asking alumni to recall various kinds of information (such as street and building names) about their college town. A thorough review of the literature on long-term retention was conducted by Semb and Ellis (1994). Herrmann and Neisser (1978) designed an Inventory of Everyday Memory Experiences that contained 48 questions about everyday forgetting and 24 questions about memory for events from early childhood. Berkerian and Dennett (1993) review the research literature on the cognitive interview technique. Hasher and Zacks (1979,

1984) discuss how the concept of automatic processing applies to memory. Articles by Burke and Light (1981), Craik and Rabinowitz (1983), and Guttentag (1985) discuss how memory is affected by aging. The distinction between direct and indirect tests of memory continues to be a hot topic that is attracting considerable theoretical interest (Humphreys, Bain, & Pike, 1989; Roediger, 1990; Toth, Reingold, & Jacoby, 1994).

REPRESENTATION
AND ORGANIZATION
OF KNOWLEDGE

Levels of Processing

It is abundantly clear that what determines the level of recall or recognition of a word event is not intention to learn, the amount of effort involved, the difficulty of the orienting task, the amount of time spent making judgments about the items, or even the amount of rehearsal the items receive; rather it is the qualitative nature of the task, the kind of operations carried out on the items, that determines retention.

F. I. M. CRAIK AND ENDEL TULVING (1975)

*T*HE PRECEDING TWO chapters developed a theory of memory as consisting of a short-term store and a long-term store. This theory provides a beginning, but it leaves us with many questions. For example: Why are there many different decay rates in LTM? Does verbal rehearsal always cause learning? What other control processes can we use to enter information into LTM? How is memory organized? And what about visual knowledge?

In the next four chapters I will try to provide some answers to these questions about the representation and organization of knowledge. Our immediate objective is to learn how memory codes differ and what the implications of these differences are for learning and retrieval. A **memory code** is the representation used to store an item in memory. Consider what memory codes might be involved if you were learning to associate pairs of words in a paired-associates task. If the words were presented visually, you might form a visual image of the words. You would also probably rehearse the words and create an acoustic (phonemic) code. If the words were meaningful, you might create meaningful associations to help you learn.

Memory code   The format (physical, phonemic, semantic) of information encoded into memory

The option of creating different memory codes is particularly advantageous when a memory deficit limits the kind of memory codes that a person can create. This is illustrated by a woman (P. V.) who had a selectively impaired **auditory memory span**, being unable to repeat back auditory sequences longer than two or three words. In order to determine how this impairment would influence long-term learning, a group of psychologists varied the characteristics of a paired-associates task (Baddeley, Papagno, & Vallar, 1988). The most challenging task required P. V. to listen to eight pairs in which the stimuli were words and the responses were pronounceable nonwords, such as *svieti*. The dramatic results of this task are shown in Figure 6.1a. Most of the control subjects, matched with P. V. for age and education, had learned the list by ten trials, but P. V. failed to recall even a single item on any of the ten learning trials.

Auditory memory span   Number of items recalled from STM following an auditory presentation of the items

Of course, the difficulty of this task might depend on the material—the auditory presentation made it difficult to use visual coding, and the nonword responses made it difficult to use semantic codes.

So, what would happen if P. V. were asked to learn eight visually presented word-nonword pairs? Figure 6.1b shows the answer. Her performance is still impaired but is markedly improved when compared to the auditory presentation. It looks like the possibility to visually encode the material partially compensates for her impaired auditory memory span. But the big gain occurs when the material is meaningful, consisting of word-word pairs. The opportunity to use meaningful associations between words (semantic codes) resulted in a normal performance (Figure 6.1c).

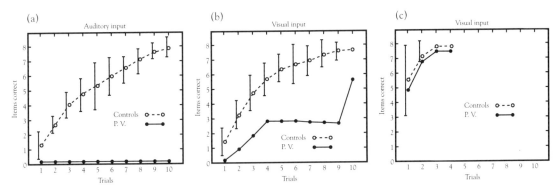

Figure 6.1   *Comparison between P. V. and control subjects for learning (a) auditory input of word-nonword pairs, (b) visual input of word-nonword pairs, and (c) visual input of word pairs.*
From "When Long-Term Learning Depends on Short-Term Storage," by A. Baddeley, C. Papagno, and G. Vallar, 1988, *Journal of Memory and Language, 27*, 586–595. Copyright 1988 by Academic Press, Inc. Reprinted by permission.

This study illustrates how varying the material influences the kind of memory codes that people can create. Another approach to influencing memory codes is to maintain the same material but vary questions about the material in order to direct people's attention to a particular aspect of the stimuli. When people try to learn, they most likely form several kinds of memory codes, and psychologists have little control over what people do. So, instead of asking people to learn, we often ask them to make judgments about words without telling them that they will have to recall the words after the judgment task. The purpose of the judgment task (often called an **orienting task**) is to try to control the kind of memory code formed by requesting that a person make decisions about a particular aspect of the word, such as its pronunciation or its meaning. We can then examine how well that person can recall the word as a function of the aspect emphasized.

The first section of this chapter examines a theory of memory called **levels of processing**, proposed by Craik and Lockhart (1972), which holds that success in recalling a word depends on the kinds of operations carried out while encoding the word. That is, retention is determined by the characteristics that are emphasized during initial perception or rehearsal. Evidence supporting the theory is reviewed in the second section. The third section seeks to explain why semantic codes are particularly effective for increasing retention. The argument that memory for an event is improved by making the code more elaborate and distinctive is used to explain how coding influences retention. The final section considers the principle of encoding specificity, which states that the effectiveness of a retrieval cue depends on how well its characteristics correspond to the characteristics of the stored event.

Orienting task   Instructions to focus on a particular aspect (physical, phonemic, semantic) of a stimulus

Levels of processing
A theory that proposes that "deeper" (semantic) levels of processing enhance memory

THE LEVELS-OF-PROCESSING THEORY

Emphasis on Coding Strategies

The paper by Craik and Lockhart (1972) had three objectives: to examine the reasons for proposing multistore models, to question the adequacy of such models, and to propose an alternative framework in terms of levels of processing. We have already considered some of the major characteristics of the three memory stores (sensory store, STM, and LTM) in the previous chapters. Craik and Lockhart summarized the commonly accepted differences among these stores (see Table 6.1).

The sensory store is preattentive in the sense that it occurs before perceptual recognition. Attention influences what observers recognize, as when they attend to a particular row of letters after hearing a tone. The sensory store provides a literal copy of the stimulus input but rapidly decays away. It isn't possible to use a control process or strategy to maintain the store, so information must be read out using pattern recognition in order to preserve it in a more permanent store.

In order to enter STM, the information must be attended to and described. It can be maintained in STM by continued attendance to it or by use of verbal rehearsal. Since verbal rehearsal is often used, the format is primarily phonemic, but it can also be visual or semantic. Short-term

Table 6.1   *Commonly accepted differences among the three stages of verbal memory*

Feature	Sensory Store	Short-Term Memory	Long-Term Memory
Entry of information	Preattentive	Requires attention	Rehearsal
Maintenance of information	Not possible	Continued attention Rehearsal	Repetition Organization
Format of information	Literal copy of input	Phonemic Probably visual Probably semantic	Largely semantic Some auditory and visual
Capacity	Large	Small	No known limit
Information loss	Decay	Displacement Possibly decay	Possibly no loss Loss of accessibility or discriminability by interference
Trace duration	$\frac{1}{4}$–2 sec	Up to 30 sec	Minutes to years
Retrieval	Readout	Probably automatic Items in consciousness Temporal/phonemic cues	Retrieval cues Possibly search process

SOURCE: From "Levels of Processing: A Framework for Memory Research," by F. I. M. Craik and R. S. Lockhart, 1972, *Journal of Verbal Learning and Verbal Behavior, 11*, 671–684. Copyright 1972 by Academic Press, Inc. Reprinted by permission.

memory is limited by its small capacity and fast decay rate, but retrieval is easy because so few items have to be searched.

Information is entered into LTM mainly through verbal rehearsal. Long-term memory is largely semantic; that is, it is organized according to meaning. It has no known limits in capacity, and its contents, if lost at all, are lost through interference. The ability to retrieve information from LTM can last from minutes to years. Cues are very useful in retrieving information from LTM, as we will see later in this chapter, but retrieval may require a lengthy search and a considerable amount of time.

Although most psychologists had accepted the characterization of memory represented in Table 6.1, Craik and Lockhart believed that the evidence for a distinction between STM and LTM was not as clear as it should be. They argued, first, that the capacity of STM was really more variable than Miller's estimate of from five to nine chunks. For example, people can reproduce strings of up to 20 words if the words form a sentence. One might reasonably argue that the words in a sentence form chunks and that it should be easy to recall 20 words from STM if there are about 3 words in each chunk. But this argument requires objective evidence that such chunks exist. Second, although the format is mainly phonemic in STM and semantic in LTM, there is evidence for visual and semantic codes in STM (see Shulman, 1971) and for visual and phonemic codes in LTM. Third, as we have already seen, decay rates vary considerably depending on the material being learned. Ideally, we would like to see a single, fast rate of decay for STM and a single, slow rate of decay for LTM.

The distinction among the three memory stores summarized in Table 6.1 is therefore an idealized view of how the stores differ. Although I believe there is much experimental support for this view, we must remember that most theories, including the theory that proposes three separate memory stores, are oversimplified. The part of the theory that seems the weakest to me is the variety of decay rates. Where do all these decay rates come from? The strength of the levels-of-processing theory is its attempt to answer this question.

The levels-of-processing theory proposes that there are different ways to code material and that memory codes are qualitatively different. Preliminary processing is concerned with the analysis of physical features such as lines, angles, brightness, pitch, and loudness. Later stages of analysis are concerned with pattern recognition and identification of meaning. After the stimulus is recognized, it may be further elaborated—a word, sight, or smell may trigger associations, images, or stories on the basis of the individual's past experience with that particular stimulus. The levels-of-processing theory claims that analysis proceeds through a series of sensory states to levels associated with pattern recognition to semantic-associative stages.

Each level of analysis results in a different memory code—but a memory code that varies in its decay rate. The memory code and its persistence are therefore both by-products of perceptual processing. When only the physical features of a stimulus have been analyzed, the memory code is fragile and quickly decays. When the stimulus has been identified and named, the memory code is stronger and can be represented by an intermediate decay rate. Memory is best when a person elaborates the meaning of the stimulus.

The levels-of-processing theory is a theory of how we analyze a stimulus and what memory codes result from different levels of analysis. Unlike the Atkinson-Shiffrin (1968) theory, it is not concerned with the structural components or stages of memory; the two theories, therefore, can coexist. Craik (1979b) more recently stated that the point of most levels-of-processing studies has been to gain a fuller understanding of memory codes operating in LTM, not to deny the distinction between STM and LTM. When viewed from this perspective, the work on levels of processing extends rather than replaces a stage analysis by showing how control processes can influence the retention of material.

Implications for Verbal Rehearsal

We saw in the previous chapter that the Atkinson-Shiffrin model emphasized verbal rehearsal as a means of transferring information from STM to LTM. Since most of us have used this method to learn material, the role of rehearsal in learning seems intuitively attractive. But rehearsal does not automatically result in learning, according to Craik and Lockhart. The effectiveness of rehearsal, like that of other methods of study, depends on the level at which material is processed. The reason rehearsal often results in learning is that people usually attend to the meaning of the material during rehearsal.

Nor is rehearsal always used for learning. Sometimes it is used to maintain information in STM, as when we dial a telephone number. Would rehearsal result in learning if people used it simply to maintain items in STM? Does rehearsal automatically result in learning, or are there different kinds of rehearsal, only some of which promote learning? To answer these questions, Craik and Watkins (1973) asked people to perform a fairly simple task. Students were told to listen to a series of word lists and, at the end of each list, to report the last word beginning with a particular letter. The experimenter told them the critical letter before each list and assumed that they would maintain a word starting with that letter in STM until they heard another word beginning with that letter or until the list ended. The task was quite easy, and students almost always gave the correct answer at the end of the list.

The purpose of the experiment was to vary the length of time a word would have to be maintained in STM. For example, if *g* were the critical letter and the list contained, in order, the words *daughter, oil, rifle, garden, grain, table, football, anchor,* and *giraffe,* the word *garden* would be immediately replaced by *grain,* which would eventually be replaced by *giraffe.* Since there are no intervening words between *garden* and *grain* while there are three intervening words between *grain* and *giraffe, grain* would have to be maintained in STM for a longer time than *garden.* The word *grain* should therefore be rehearsed more often than *garden.* Craik and Watkins controlled the amount of time a word would have to be maintained in STM by varying the number of intervening (noncritical) words from 0 to 12. If **maintenance rehearsal** results in learning, the probability of recalling a word at the end of the experiment should be a function of the length of time it was maintained in STM.

Maintenance rehearsal
Rehearsal that keeps information active in STM

After hearing 27 lists of words, the students were asked to recall as many words as they could from all the lists. Craik and Watkins found that the probability of recalling a word was independent of the length of time it was maintained in STM. To consider the two extreme cases, students recalled 12% of the words that were immediately replaced in STM by the next word on the list and 15% of the words that were maintained over 12 intervening words.

The small difference between 12 and 15% shows that rehearsal does not automatically cause learning. According to the levels-of-processing view of memory, the students did not try to form a lasting memory code because they thought they would have to remember the word for only a very short time. In particular, they did not emphasize the meaning of the words. A good analog might be reading the words in a book without thinking about what you are reading. You would be rehearsing the words in the sense that you would be covertly pronouncing them, but your thoughts might be on yesterday's football game or tonight's party. Suddenly you might realize that you can't remember what you just read because you weren't thinking about what it meant.

Another example of how thought processes influence what people remember comes from the study of how professional actors learn their lines. Analysis of recall protocols following the study of a six-page script revealed that actors learn their lines through an elaborative process that emphasizes how their character affects, or is affected by, the other characters in the script (Noice, 1991). When forced to learn their lines through rote rehearsal, they recalled significantly less than when studying by their usual, more elaborative process. Noice concludes that "actors are expert analyzers, not expert memorizers, and one result of this in-depth analysis is that by struggling to uncover the underlying meaning of each line, the actual words are also retained without much deliberate effort to commit them to memory" (Noice, 1991, p. 456).

Let's look now at additional evidence that the way material is processed determines what kind of memory code is formed, which, in turn, determines how well the material is remembered.

SUPPORTING EVIDENCE OF THE LEVELS-OF-PROCESSING THEORY

The Hyde-Jenkins Experiment

The influence of levels of processing on retention was nicely demonstrated in a study by Hyde and Jenkins (1969) at the University of Minnesota. Their results were published several years before Craik and Lockhart's theory and most likely influenced its development. Like most of the studies used later to test the levels-of-processing theory, Hyde and Jenkins's study used an incidental learning paradigm. In an **incidental learning task** people are given some material but are not told that they have to learn it. The experimenter then later gives them a recall or recognition test on the items presented during the experiment. In an intentional learning task, by contrast, the subjects are explicitly told to learn the material.

The first experiment in Hyde and Jenkins's study compared seven groups of subjects, but we will consider only four to simplify the discussion. One of the four groups was given an intentional learning task in which the subjects were asked to try to remember 24 words. The words consisted of 12 pairs of **primary associates**—words that are highly associated. For example, the word *red* is highly associated with the word *green*, and *table* is highly associated with *chair*. The 24 words were presented in a random order, with the restriction that primary associates could not occur together in the list. After the subjects in the "intentional" group had listened to a tape recording of the 24 words, they tried to recall as many as they could, in any order.

The other three groups were incidental learning groups who were not informed that they should try to remember the words. They heard the same recording of 24 words but were asked to make a judgment about each item on the list. One group simply rated the words as pleasant or unpleasant, another group judged whether each word contained the letter *e*, and a third group estimated the number of letters in each word. The purpose of using three judgment groups was to try to create different levels of processing. The first group would have to consider the meaning of the words. The latter two groups would have to consider the spelling of the words; the meaning of the words would be irrelevant to them. Since, according to the levels-of-processing theory, semantic processing should result in better recall than nonsemantic processing, the undergraduates who rated the pleasantness of the words should show better recall than those who considered the spelling of the words.

The results supported the prediction. The average number of words recalled was 16.3 for those students who rated pleasantness, 9.9 for those who estimated the number of letters, and 9.4 for those who judged the presence of the letter *e*. The most striking aspect of the results is that stu-

Incidental learning task A task that requires people to make judgments about stimuli without knowing that they will later be tested on their recall of the stimuli

Primary associates Words that are strongly associated with each other, as typically measured by asking people to provide associations to words

dents in the pleasant/unpleasant group recalled virtually as many words as those who were told to try to learn the words (16.3 versus 16.1). In other words, incidental learning was as effective as intentional learning when the students considered the meaning of the words.

We have been assuming, along with Hyde and Jenkins, that differences in recall among the three incidental groups were caused by the possibility that the students in the pleasant/unpleasant group were more likely to attend to the meaning of the words than the students in the other two groups. Do we have any direct evidence for this assumption? The fact that the list consisted of pairs of words that are semantically related provides a clue. Recognizing that words are related in meaning can make it easier to recall them. For example, the recall of *green* may remind a person that *red* was also on the list. One indication that people were attending to the meaning of the words would be if they recalled the primary associates together—*red* followed by *green* or vice versa.

Hyde and Jenkins defined the percentage of **clustering** as the number of associated pairs recalled together, divided by the total number of words recalled. The amount of clustering was 26% for the group that made judgments about the letter *e*, 31% for the group that estimated the number of letters, 64% for the group that was told to study the words, and 68% for the group that judged the pleasantness of the words. These results support the assumption that the groups differed in how much they used meaning to aid recall. Those groups that were the most sensitive to the meaning recalled the most words.

Clustering Percent of occasions in which a word is followed by its primary associate during the free recall of words

Structural, Phonemic, and Semantic Processing

Tests of the levels-of-processing theory have generally focused on three levels, in which the depth of processing increases from structural to phonemic to semantic coding. Table 6.2 shows examples of questions that were asked in order to emphasize different levels of coding. The **structural** question asks whether the word is in capital letters. Coding at the **phonemic** level is encouraged by asking whether a word rhymes with another word—the question emphasizes pronunciation. Questions about whether a word is a member of a certain category or whether it fits into a sentence encourage coding at the **semantic** level—a person must evaluate the meaning in order to answer correctly.

In a series of experiments conducted by Craik and Tulving (1975), one of the questions preceded each brief exposure of a word. Participants were informed that the experiment concerned perception and speed of reaction. After a series of question-and-answer trials based on the kinds of questions shown in Table 6.2, the subject was unexpectedly given a retention test for the exposed words. Craik and Tulving expected that memory would vary systematically with depth of processing.

Structural coding A memory code that emphasizes the physical structure of the stimulus

Phonemic coding A memory code that emphasizes the pronunciation of the stimulus

Semantic coding A memory code that emphasizes the meaning of the stimulus

Table 6.2   *Typical questions used in levels-of-processing studies*

Level of Processing	Question	Yes	No
Structural	Is the word in capital letters?	*TABLE*	*table*
Phonemic	Does the word rhyme with *WEIGHT*?	*crate*	*MARKET*
Sentence	Would the word fit the sentence "He met a ——— in the street"?	*FRIEND*	*cloud*

SOURCE: From "Depth of Processing and the Retention of Words in Episodic Memory," by F. I. M. Craik and E. Tulving, 1975, *Journal of Experimental Psychology: General, 104,* 268–294. Copyright 1975 by the American Psychological Association. Reprinted by permission.

Figure 6.2 shows the results from one of Craik and Tulving's experiments that used a recognition test. When students were asked which words had been presented during the initial judgment task, they recognized the most words when they had initially judged whether the word fit into a sentence and the fewest words when they had initially judged whether the letters were upper or lowercase. Recognition accuracy was at an intermediate level when the students had been asked whether one word rhymed with another. The findings supported the prediction that retention would increase as processing proceeded from the structural to the phonemic to the semantic level. The same pattern of results occurred when Craik and Tulving used a recall, rather than a recognition, test. Questions about a word's meaning resulted in better memory than those about a word's sound or the physical characteristics of its letters.

The left half of Figure 6.2 shows the average response time required to answer the three kinds of questions. The case questions could be answered most quickly, followed by the rhyme questions, followed by the sentence questions. Although the recognition results on the right can be predicted from the response times on the left, it is not always true that slower responses lead to better memory. It is possible to design a structural decision task that results in slow responses and poor retention.

Imagine that an experimenter shows you a card with a five-letter word such as *stoop* or *black*. Your task is to respond positively if the word consists of two consonants followed by two vowels followed by a consonant and negatively for any other sequence of consonants and vowels. As you might guess, your response times would be relatively slow. In fact, it takes about twice as long to make this kind of structural decision as to make a semantic decision about whether a word fits into a sentence. If good retention is caused by long response times, the structural processing should now result in better retention than the semantic processing. How-

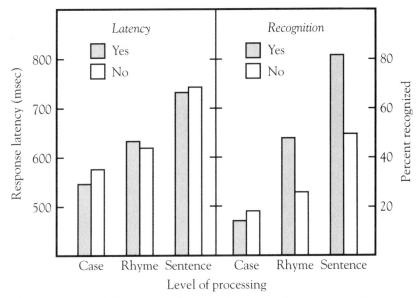

Figure 6.2   *Initial decision time (response latency) and recognition performance for words as a function of the initial task.*

From "Depth of Processing and the Retention of Words in Episodic Memory," by F. I. M. Craik and E. Tulving, 1975, *Journal of Experimental Psychology: General, 104,* 268–294. Copyright 1975 by the American Psychological Association. Reprinted by permission.

ever, recognition is still much better after semantic processing, proving that the level of processing, not the time spent processing, is the best determinant of retention.

CRITICISMS AND MODIFICATIONS OF THE THEORY

Criticisms

The levels-of-processing theory has had a major impact on memory research—many investigators designed studies to explicitly test its implications; others found it a convenient framework in which to discuss their results. Because much of this research was quite supportive of the theory, it wasn't until about 5 years after the Craik and Lockhart paper that psychologists began to seriously question the usefulness of the theory (Nelson, 1977; Baddeley, 1978; Eysenck, 1978). One of the main criticisms was that it was too easy to account for differential rates of forgetting by appealing to the theory. An investigator might claim that differences in rates of forgetting were caused by differences in levels of processing, without measuring the levels of processing.

In order to avoid this criticism, it is necessary to be able to measure depth of processing independently of retention. The argument that depth increases from structural to phonemic to semantic processing appealed to most psychologists because it is consistent with the ordering of the information-processing stages shown in Figure 1.1 (Chapter 1). Analyzing the physical structure of a pattern leads to retrieving its name, which in turn leads to considering its meaning by retrieving stored associations from LTM. One problem with this assumption is that, although this sequence provides a reasonable account of how information is analyzed, it is not a *necessary* sequence (Baddeley, 1978; Craik, 1979b). Although Craik and Lockhart originally hoped that encoding time would provide an independent measure of depth of processing, we have seen that this measure has its limitations (Craik & Tulving, 1975).

Another difficulty with the concept of depth of processing is that, even if we had an objective ordering of the "depth" of different memory codes, it still would not tell us why some codes are more effective than others. Why are semantic codes better than phonemic codes and phonemic codes better than structural codes? Psychologists have suggested two possible answers. One is that memory codes differ in how elaborate they are, and more elaborate codes result in better memory. The other is that memory codes differ in distinctiveness, and more distinctive codes result in better memory.

Elaboration of Memory Codes

One explanation of how memory codes differ proposes that they differ in the number and types of elaborations stored in memory (J. R. Anderson & L. M. Reder, 1979). This view assumes that people store much more than simply the items presented to them—they also store additional associations that help them remember the items. Anderson and Reder have proposed that, although it is very easy to elaborate material at the semantic level, it is difficult to construct elaborations at the structural or phonemic level. Most of the associations we have are concerned with meaning rather than with the physical structure of letters, spelling, or pronunciation. Anderson and Reder suggest that the reason for this difference is that people usually try to remember the meaning of what they read rather than such details as what the letters looked like. As a consequence, people have learned to elaborate on the semantic content because doing so is generally more useful than elaborating on nonsemantic content.

One virtue of the elaboration hypothesis is that it provides a possible explanation of how differences can occur within a particular level of processing (Craik, 1979b). Although the original levels-of-processing proposal predicted that semantic processing should be superior to nonsemantic processing, it could not account for differences in retention for two different semantic tasks. The elaboration hypothesis predicts that such differences should occur if the two tasks differ in the extent of semantic elaboration.

One method for increasing semantic elaboration is to provide a richer, more elaborate context. This approach is illustrated by one of the experiments in the Craik and Tulving (1975) study. The experiment tested for the recall of words after a semantic judgment task in which people determined whether a word would fit into a sentence frame. There were three levels of sentence complexity—simple, medium, and complex. For example:

Simple: She cooked the _____.
Medium: The ripe _____ tasted delicious.
Complex: The small lady angrily picked up the red _____.

After completing 60 judgments, subjects were asked to recall as many words as they could from the initial phase of the experiment. They were then shown the original sentence frames and asked to recall the word associated with each sentence. The first part of the recall task is called **noncued recall**, and the second part is called **cued recall** because students could use the sentence frames as retrieval cues. Figure 6.3 shows the proportion of words recalled as a function of sentence complexity. Sentence complexity had a significant effect on recalling words that did fit the sentence. This was true for both cued recall (CR–yes) and noncued recall (NCR–yes), although the effect was greater for cued recall. The effect of sentence complexity supported Craik and Tulving's hypothesis that more complex sentence frames would produce a more elaborate memory code and would improve recall.

Noncued recall Recall that occurs without hints or cues provided by the experimenter

Cued recall Recall that occurs with hints or cues, such as providing the questions asked during the judgment phase of a task

The more elaborate code was ineffective, however, if the word did not fit the sentence. This finding suggests that the elaboration must be consistent with the meaning of the word in order to be effective. Even when elaboration is generally consistent with the meaning of a word, it can vary in effectiveness depending on how precisely it relates to the word's meaning. Imagine that you read the sentence *The fat man read the sign.* Some time later someone shows you the same sentence with the word *fat* replaced by a blank and asks you to recall the missing word. If elaboration is effective, you might do better if you read an elaborated sentence such as

1. The fat man read the sign that was 2 feet high.
    or
2. The fat man read the sign warning about thin ice.

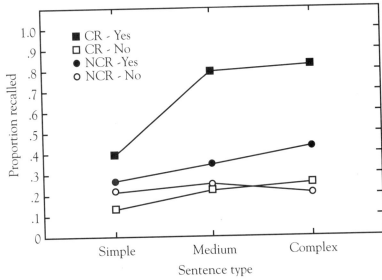

Figure 6.3   *Proportion of words recalled as a function of sentence complexity:* CR = *cued recall;* NCR = *noncued recall.*

From "Depth of Processing and the Retention of Words in Episodic Memory," by F. I. M. Craik and E. Tulving, 1975, *Journal of Experimental Psychology: General, 104,* 268–294. Copyright 1975 by the American Psychological Association. Reprinted by permission.

Imprecise elaboration
Provision or generation of additional material unrelated to remembered material

Precise elaboration
Provision or generation of additional material closely related to remembered material

Although both sentences provide additional information, there is an important distinction between the two elaborations. The first is an **imprecise elaboration** because there is no apparent relation between the adjective *fat* and the height of the sign. The second is a **precise elaboration** because the degree of danger of thin ice depends on a person's weight.

B. S. Stein and J. D. Bransford (1979) tested the effectiveness of precise and imprecise elaboration by comparing four groups of students in an incidental learning task. Students in the control group read ten short sentences and were told that the purpose of the experiment was to measure sentence comprehensibility. The second and third groups of students were told the same thing. They read the same ten sentences elaborated by an additional phrase that was either precisely or imprecisely related to a target word in the sentence. A fourth group of students were told to generate their own elaborations so the experimenters could measure the probability that certain phrases would be generated. At the end of the experiment everyone was shown the unelaborated sentences and asked to recall a missing target word.

Students in the control group recalled an average of 4.2 words, compared with 2.2 words for the imprecise elaboration group, 7.4 words for the precise elaboration group, and 5.8 words for the self-generation group. The results show that elaboration is not always effective in recall, since imprecise elaboration actually caused a decline in performance relative to the control group. In order to be effective, the elaboration should clarify the significance or relevance of a concept (such as *fat man*) relative to the context (*thin ice*) in which it occurs.

The fact that recall following **self-generation** was intermediate between that for precise and imprecise elaboration suggests that the students' elaborations contained a mixture of the two types. Two judges therefore divided the subject-generated elaborations into two groups (precise and imprecise), depending on whether the information clarified the relevance of the target words in the sentence. Students were able to recall 91% of the target words in the cases where they had generated precise elaborations and 49% in the cases where they had generated imprecise elaborations. A second experiment revealed that instructions were effective in encouraging subjects to generate precise elaborations. Subjects in the imprecise elaboration group were asked to elaborate with the question "What else might happen in this context?" Subjects in the precise elaboration group were prompted to elaborate with the question "Why might this man be engaged in this particular type of activity?" Students in the latter group recalled significantly more target words, indicating that elaboration is particularly effective when it is directed toward understanding the potential relevance of the information presented.

Self-generation Generation of items by participants in an experiment, rather than the provision of these items by the experimenter

Distinctiveness of Memory Codes

Memory codes can differ in distinctiveness as well as in the extent of elaboration. The term **distinctive** refers to how easy it is to distinguish one item from another. In order to remember something, we would like to make it really stand out from other items that could interfere with our memory. There are several different ways in which an item can be distinctive and I will follow a classification proposed by Schmidt (1991) that distinguishes among four different kinds of distinctiveness.

Distinctive item   An item different in appearance or meaning from other items

One kind of distinctiveness is called **primary distinctiveness** in which distinctiveness is defined relative to the immediate context. Imagine that you are shown a list of common words and all the words are printed in red ink, except for one word that is printed in black ink. Later you are asked to recall the words on the list. Which word do you think you would have the best chance of recalling? The results of past research indicate that you would more likely recall the word in black ink than the words in red ink. Note that the word in black ink is distinctive only because the color differs from the color of other words on the list. In general, a common word in black ink is not particularly distinctive.

Primary distinctiveness An item distinct from other items in the immediate context

Release from proactive interference (discussed in Chapter 4) is an example of improving recall by making items distinct from other items in the immediate context. People recalled more items when the material changed from words to numbers or from numbers to words than when the material stayed the same. Recall also improved when the items changed from sports events to political events or from political events to sports events. All the changes made these items more distinct from the preceding items.

In contrast, **secondary distinctiveness** is defined relative to information in our LTM rather than to information in the immediate context. One example is a characteristic of a word's spelling, called **orthographic distinctiveness**. A word is orthographically distinctive when it has an unusual shape, as determined by the sequencing of short and tall letters in the word. Orthographically distinctive words include *lymph*, *khaki*, and *afghan*. Examples of orthographically common words are *leaky*, *kennel*, and *airway*. The first three words have unusual shapes, and the last three have more typical shapes. Notice that a shape is unusual (distinctive) relative to all other words, not just to words in the immediate context of the experiment.

When people are asked to recall a list of words, half of which are orthographically distinctive and half of which are orthographically common, they recall significantly more of the distinctive words (R. R. Hunt & J. M. Elliott, 1980). It is clear that the shape of the words, rather than some other factor, causes the results. When the same list is presented orally, rather than visually, there is no difference in recall. There is also no difference in recall when the words are typed in capital letters; people do not recall LYMPH, KHAKI, and AFGHAN any better than LEAKY, KENNEL, and AIRWAY. Apparently the different heights of lowercase letters contribute to the effect since all letters are the same height when capitalized.

A third kind of distinctiveness is called **emotional distinctiveness** and is motivated by the finding that events that produce strong emotional responses are sometimes remembered well. These events include **flashbulb memories**—the vivid recollections that most people have of the circumstances surrounding their discovery of a shocking piece of news (R. Brown & J. Kulik, 1977). Events such as the assassination of President Kennedy or the explosion of the space shuttle *Challenger* (Winograd & Neisser, 1992) have been studied as examples of people's flashbulb memories. I don't remember how I first learned about the *Challenger*, but I'm certain my brother will never forget his experience. He was driving in the direction of the Kennedy Space Center during a business trip to Orlando when he noticed that the vapor trail from the rocket's engine suddenly stopped. Suspecting that something had gone wrong, he turned on his car radio, which confirmed the failure of the launch. Although Schmidt (1991) includes emotional distinctiveness in his taxonomy, he

Secondary distinctiveness An item distinct from items stored in LTM

Orthographic distinctiveness Lowercase words that have an unusual shape

Emotional distinctiveness Items that produce an intense emotional reaction

Flashbulb memories Memories of important events that caused an emotional reaction

admits that it is not always clear which aspects of an emotional memory are enhanced, or even whether the concept of "distinctiveness" provides an adequate explanation of the impact of emotion on memory.

A fourth kind of distinctiveness is called **processing distinctiveness**. Processing distinctiveness depends on how we process the stimulus—it is therefore the result of the memory code that we create for an item rather than the characteristics of the item itself. For instance, even if an item is not very distinctive you may think of a distinctive way of remembering it. If it is distinctive, you may think of a way of processing it to make it even more distinctive. Elaboration is one possible strategy to make an item more distinctive, but the elaboration should emphasize characteristics that differentiate that item from other items (Eysenck, 1979).

An example of processing distinctiveness is that people apparently remember faces as caricatures by exaggerating the distinctive features to make the faces even more distinct. When discussing distinctive features in Chapter 2, I gave an example of a study in which people more quickly identified line drawings of their friends when the line drawings were caricatures rather than accurate (Rhodes, Brennan, & Carey, 1987). Caricatures of unfamiliar faces are also better recognized in a standard recognition memory test than the faces that were actually shown (Mauro & Kubovy, 1992). Undergraduates viewed 100 slides of faces constructed from an Identi-Kit, as illustrated by the two right faces in Figure 6.4. They later were shown 300 test faces and asked to indicate if each test face was exactly the same as one shown in the first series of slides. The test faces included some faces that were new, some faces that were old, and some faces that were caricatures of the old faces.

The caricatures are shown on the left side of Figure 6.4 and were created by making a distinctive feature even more distinct. The high forehead in the top face is made even higher and the long chin of the bottom face is made even longer. The interesting finding is that the caricatures were recognized significantly better than the original (old) faces. This finding is consistent with the processing distinctiveness concept—people encoded the faces into memory in a manner that made each face even more distinct than the original face.

Because both processing distinctiveness and the levels-of-processing theory emphasize the importance of creating good memory codes, it is perhaps not surprising that some psychologists have proposed that the levels-of-processing effect is caused by differences in distinctiveness. In order to demonstrate that distinctiveness can account for the levels-of-processing effect, it would be necessary to show that semantic codes are more distinct than phonemic codes and that phonemic codes are more distinct than physical codes. Some research has already been directed toward the first comparison. Several psychologists (Moscovitch & Craik,

Processing distinctiveness Creation of a memory code that makes that memory distinct from other memories

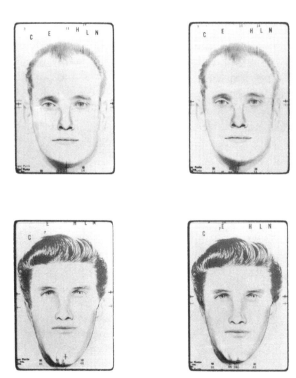

Figure 6.4   *Two Identi-Kit faces (right) and their caricatures (left): top, high forehead; bottom, long chin.*

From "Caricature and Face Recognition," by R. Mauro and M. Kubovy, 1992, *Memory & Cognition, 20*, 433–440. Copyright 1992 by the Psychonomic Society, Inc. Reprinted by permission.

1976; Eysenck, 1979) have argued that semantic codes result in better retention than do phonemic codes because semantic codes are much more distinctive than phonemic codes. They base their argument on the fact that there is a relatively small number of phonemes; thus, phonemic codes necessarily overlap with each other, whereas the domain of possible meanings is essentially limitless.

The experimental study of elaboration and distinctiveness has modified the original conception of levels of processing (Craik, 1979b). Some of the original ideas have survived, however. The central idea that there are qualitative differences in memory codes, that different orienting tasks can determine which codes are emphasized, and that memory codes differ in their decay rate remains a useful conception of memory. The major shift in emphasis has been the attempt to provide a theoretical basis for these findings by determining how structural, phonemic, and semantic codes can differ in distinctiveness and elaboration.

ENCODING SPECIFICITY AND RETRIEVAL

The Encoding Specificity Principle

The change in emphasis from "levels" to "elaboration" and "distinctiveness" was accompanied by another refinement in the theory. The original theory (Craik & Lockhart, 1972) had much to say about how words were coded but little to say about how they were retrieved. Yet we saw in the previous chapter that appropriate retrieval cues, such as encouraging eyewitnesses to reconstruct the context of the crime, can enhance recall. The usefulness of providing an appropriate context for facilitating retrieval is illustrated by the difference between positive and negative responses in Figure 6.2. Words that resulted in positive responses, because they either formed a rhyme or fit the context of a sentence, were recalled more often than words that resulted in negative responses. We have also seen that the use of more complex, elaborate sentence frames facilitated recall for positive responses but not for negative responses (Figure 6.3). This effect was particularly evident when the context was provided as a retrieval cue. Craik and Tulving (1975) interpreted this finding as support for their view that a more elaborate context is beneficial only when the test word is compatible with the context and forms an integrated unit. A complex sentence like *The small lady angrily picked up the red* ———— makes it easier to retrieve a positive response (*tomato*) but does not make it easier to retrieve a negative response (*walking*).

These results show that, under certain conditions, some retrieval cues are more effective than others. A general answer to the question of what makes a retrieval cue effective is provided by the **encoding specificity principle**, which has been stated as follows: "Specific encoding operations performed on what is perceived determine what is stored, and what is stored determines what retrieval cues are effective in providing access to what is stored" (Tulving & Thomson, 1973, p. 369).

Let's dissect this definition into two parts. The first part states that memory traces differ not only in their durability but also in the kind of information they contain. The second part states that the information that memory traces contain determines what kind of retrieval information should facilitate their recovery. The first part is essentially equivalent to the levels-of-processing framework; the second part forces us to take a closer look at retrieval. The second part implies that it is possible to hold constant the encoding conditions of an item and still observe large differences in its recall, depending on the retrieval conditions. The encoding and retrieval conditions can interact in the sense that a cue that is effective in one situation may or may not be effective in another.

The encoding specificity principle has usually been applied to studying how the retrieval cue relates to the memory code for the stimulus. However, the encoding and retrieval conditions can apply to a broader

Encoding specificity principle A theory that states that the effectiveness of a retrieval cue depends on how well it relates to the initial encoding of an item

context such as the location in which learning occurred or even the mood of the learner. The study of **mood dependent memory** tests the hypothesis that we are better able to recall information if our mood during retrieval matches our mood during learning. Although the evidence has generally been supportive of this hypothesis, the degree of support may depend on the particular paradigm used to test the hypothesis; for instance, strongest support may come from situations in which people recall information that they generated themselves. A recent study found strong support for mood dependent memory when people had to recall autobiographical events that they had generated several days earlier (Eich, Macaulay, & Ryan, 1994). Subjects who were in the same (pleasant or unpleasant) mood during both encoding and retrieval recalled significantly more events than people who were in different moods. Tests of the encoding specificity principle have generally focused on the material that people have to recall rather than on where learning occurred or on the mood of the learner. We will now look at this research.

Interaction between Encoding and Retrieval Operations

A study by Thomson and Tulving (1970) provided some initial support for the encoding specificity principle. It seems intuitively obvious that the effectiveness of a retrieval cue should depend on how closely the cue is associated with a test item. The following are good retrieval cues: *white* for BLACK, *meat* for STEAK, *dumb* for STUPID, *woman* for MAN, *ice* for COLD, and *dark* for LIGHT. People who are asked to remember BLACK, STEAK, STUPID, MAN, COLD, and LIGHT can recall more of these words if they are given the retrieval cues during the recall test. It is also intuitively obvious that weakly associated words do not make good retrieval cues—for example, *train* for BLACK, *knife* for STEAK, *lamb* for STUPID, *hand* for MAN, *blow* for COLD, and *head* for LIGHT. When people were given the weakly associated cues during the recall test, they recalled fewer words than subjects who were given no retrieval cues.

Thomson and Tulving demonstrated, however, that even ineffective retrieval cues can become effective if they are presented with the test words during the study session. When a weak associate was paired with a test word, it became a more effective retrieval cue than a strong associate. If people studied *train* and BLACK together, then the presentation of *train* during the recall test would more likely lead to the recall of BLACK than would the presentation of *white*. The effectiveness of a retrieval cue therefore depends on what occurs during the initial encoding of a word, as the encoding specificity hypothesis predicts.

A somewhat similar finding was reported by Light and Carter-Sobell (1970), using a recognition test. Subjects in their experiment were shown sentences that contained an adjective and a noun printed in capital letters. For example, subjects might see the sentence *The CHIP DIP tasted delicious*. They were informed that there would be a memory test on the adjective-noun phrases after they had read all the sentences. The recognition test required that they decide whether a noun had appeared in the previous sentences. Some nouns on the recognition test were preceded by the same adjective (*CHIP DIP*), some were preceded by a different adjective (*SKINNY DIP*), and some were preceded by no adjective (*DIP*). Presenting the same adjective resulted in better recognition of the noun than presenting no adjective, but presenting a different adjective resulted in worse recognition.

Perhaps one reason why a different adjective produces a decline in performance is that the different adjective was consistent with an alternative meaning of the noun—*skinny dip* as opposed to *chip dip*. The experimenters argued that the adjective determines which semantic features of a noun are stored in memory. If their hypothesis is correct, then a different adjective that is consistent with the encoded meaning should be a more effective retrieval cue than a different adjective that is inconsistent with the encoded meaning. *Raspberry jam* should be a more effective retrieval cue than *traffic jam* if the original phrase were *strawberry jam*. The results supported the hypothesis, although the most accurate performance was still the condition in which the same adjective occurred during the study and test sessions.

The studies by Thomson and Tulving (1970) and by Light and Carter-Sobell (1970) investigated encoding specificity within the semantic domain. The first study showed that an ineffective retrieval cue—a weak semantic associate—can become an effective retrieval cue when it is associated with a test item during the study session. The second study showed that an adjective that preserved the semantic encoding of a word is more effective than an adjective that changes the semantic encoding.

Let us now consider how the encoding specificity principle applies when there are two different processing levels—semantic and phonemic. Imagine that you are in an experiment and have to answer yes or no to the question *associated with sleet?* You then see the word *hail* and answer yes. After making a series of judgments about rhymes and associations, you are given one of the following retrieval cues:

1. Associated with *sleet*
2. Associated with *snow*
3. Rhymes with *bail*

Which of the three retrieval cues do you think would be most helpful for retrieving the word *hail*?

You would probably agree that the first cue would be most effective because it is identical to the question asked during the encoding trials. But what about cues 2 and 3? The second cue is similar to the original context in that, like the initial question, it emphasizes semantic associations. The third cue, by contrast, emphasizes the phonemic code and is therefore different from the original context. The encoding specificity principle predicts that the original context is the best retrieval cue, a similar context is the next best cue, and a different context is the least effective cue. The results shown in Table 6.3 support this prediction (R. P. Fisher & F. I. M. Craik, 1977).

Now consider what might have happened if the word *hail* had been preceded by the question *Rhymes with pail?* The same principle applies. Reproducing the exact context is the best cue, and providing a different context—a semantic association in this case—is the worst cue (see Table 6.3). The interaction between encoding and retrieval is illustrated by the fact that the effectiveness of a retrieval cue depends on how a word was coded. When its semantic characteristics were emphasized, a semantic cue was more effective than a phonemic cue. When its phonemic characteristics were emphasized, a phonemic cue was more effective than a semantic cue. In other words, the specific encoding of an item determines which retrieval cues are most effective for gaining access to what is stored—the encoding specificity principle.

A more recent study (Hertel, Anooshian, & Ashbrook, 1986) found that people were unable to accurately predict the relative effectiveness of retrieval cues. Subjects rated the pleasantness of 40 words in a semantic-orienting task, predicted the number of words they could recall, and then tried to recall the words. One group received semantic retrieval cues, another group received phonemic retrieval cues, and a control group received no retrieval cues. We would expect from Fisher and Craik's findings that the semantic retrieval cues would be more effective than phonemic cues—an expectation that was confirmed. Only those subjects who received semantic cues recalled significantly more words than the control group.

Table 6.3   *Proportions of words recalled as a function of similarity between encoding context and retrieval cue*

	Rhyme	Proportion	Associate	Proportion
Encoding context Example: *hail*	Rhymes with *pail*		Associated with *sleet*	
Retrieval context Identical Similar Different	Rhymes with *pail* Rhymes with *bail* Associated with *sleet*	.24 .18 .16	Associated with *sleet* Associated with *snow* Rhymes with *bail*	.54 .36 .22

SOURCE: From "Interaction between Encoding and Retrieval Operations in Cued Recall," by R. P. Fisher and F. I. M. Craik, 1977, *Journal of Experimental Psychology: Human Learning and Memory, 3*, 701–711. Copyright 1977 by the American Psychological Association. Reprinted by permission.

But the superiority of the semantic cues was not anticipated by subjects in the experiment, who predicted that the semantic and phonemic cues would be equally effective. The faulty predictions seemed to be based on overgeneralization from past experiences in which phonemic cues had been effective. For example, when our search has already been limited to a particular category, such as the names of songs, phonemic information is likely to be helpful. What subjects failed to realize was that the effectiveness of a retrieval cue depends on how the word was coded. The memory code, in this case, emphasized the semantic characteristics of the words.

Transfer-Appropriate Processing

A general implication of the encoding specificity principle is the use of **transfer-appropriate processing**, which emphasizes that the value of a particular learning strategy is relative to a particular goal. Transfer-appropriate processing implies that the effectiveness of learning can only be determined relative to the testing situation. For example, if the test emphasizes phonemic information and you had been concentrating on semantic information, you could be in trouble.

Transfer-appropriate processing Encoding material in a manner related to how the material will be used later

A situation from my own undergraduate education provides a good example of transfer-appropriate processing. I had taken three semesters of German in which there was very little emphasis on pronunciation, although we occasionally were asked to read aloud. I therefore did not attend very closely to the phonemic code but concentrated on the meaning of the passage so I could provide a correct translation. After three semesters I enrolled in a conversation course in which the emphasis was on correct pronunciation. I quickly learned how poorly I pronounced German words.

It is relatively rare, however, that we must emphasize the phonemic code since we are generally required to recall or recognize semantic information. Transfer-appropriate processing therefore usually means semantic processing. There are different ways to process material semantically, and knowledge of the test format should help you decide how to study. If the test is a multiple-choice test, it is likely that knowledge of details will be more useful than knowledge about the general organization of the material. If the test is an essay test, it is likely that careful organization of the material will be more useful than knowledge of many details.

There is evidence to support the claim that students' performance on a test is influenced by the kind of test they expect. Half of the subjects in an experiment by d'Ydewalle and Rosselle (1978) expected a multiple-choice test and half expected a series of open questions. Only some of the subjects in each group received the expected test, and those subjects did better than the subjects who received the unexpected test. Apparently each group used different learning strategies—ones that were appropriate for the expected test.

Another distinction between test questions is whether they emphasize factual recall or problem solving. Sometimes an instructor asks students to recall information; at other times students must apply the information to solve problems. The hypothesis about transfer-appropriate processing predicts that **problem-oriented acquisition** of the material is better than **fact-oriented acquisition** when people must solve problems.

Consider the following two problems:

- Uriah Fuller, the famous Israeli superpsychic, can tell you the score of any baseball game before the game starts. What is his secret?
- A man living in a small town in the United States married 20 different women in the same town. All are still living, and he has never divorced one of them. Yet he has broken no law. Can you explain?

Now imagine that you had rated a number of statements for general truthfulness earlier in an experiment. Among the statements were answers to the problems:

- Before it starts, the score of any baseball game is 0 to 0.
- A minister marries several people each week.

Somewhat surprisingly, receiving the answers in this incidental rating task was not very helpful for later solving the problems (Perfetto, Bransford, & Franks, 1983).

One interpretation of these findings is that people acquired the statements in a fact-oriented manner and therefore failed to perceive their relevance for the problem-solving task (Adams, Kasserman, Yearwood, Perfetto, Bransford, & Franks, 1988). Now suppose the statements were modified to encourage problem-oriented acquisition; would people be more likely to perceive their relevance? To induce problem-oriented processing, the experimenters changed the statement *A minister marries several people each week* to *It is possible to marry several people each week* (pause) *if one is a minister*. The pause lasted approximately 2 sec and gave people a brief chance to reflect on the problem-oriented content of the statement. There were corresponding changes for nine other statements that provided answers to problems. People who received problem-oriented statements later solved 56% of the problems, compared to 36% for people who received fact-oriented statements.

In conclusion, transfer-appropriate processing could be considered an application of the encoding specificity principle. If the effectiveness of retrieval cues depends on how well they correspond to the encoding of the material, then we should try to encode material in a way that will take advantage of the retrieval cues. If retrieval occurs during problem solving, then emphasizing the problem-oriented nature of the material should enhance the retrieval of helpful information.

Problem-oriented acquisition Encoding material in a manner that is helpful for its later use in solving problems

Fact-oriented acquisition Encoding material in a manner that emphasizes factual knowledge without emphasizing its application

SUMMARY

The levels-of-processing theory proposes that how an item is encoded determines how long it can be remembered. Qualitatively different memory codes were established by asking people in an incidental learning task to make decisions about a word's physical structure, pronunciation, or meaning. When people are unexpectedly asked to recall the words, they recall the most words following semantic processing and the fewest words following structural processing. Further support for the theory comes from the finding that rehearsal does not necessarily result in learning, presumably because subjects do not attend to the meaning of words they want to keep active only in STM.

Although the levels-of-processing theory originally proposed that retention is determined by the depth of processing (with physical, phonemic, and semantic processing, respectively, representing increasing depth), the failure to find an independent measure of depth resulted in an increasing emphasis on the elaborateness and distinctiveness of memory codes. The elaboration hypothesis claims that it is easier to retrieve more elaborate codes and easier to provide associations at the semantic level. The distinctiveness hypothesis claims that it is easier to retrieve distinctive codes and that semantic codes are more distinctive than phonemic codes. Studies of elaborateness and distinctiveness using semantic material have found that increasing either one will improve recall. Making the semantic context more elaborate (by using complex sentences) or making words more distinctive (by shifting to a new semantic category) increases the number of words recalled.

The encoding specificity principle states that the effectiveness of a retrieval cue is determined by how well it corresponds to the characteristics of the memory trace. Although some studies have focused on the broader context of encoding, such as a person's mood during encoding and retrieval, most studies have focused on the encoding of the stimulus. When the memory trace emphasizes semantic characteristics, a semantic cue is the most effective; when the memory trace emphasizes phonemic information, a phonemic cue is most effective. The best retrieval cue is one that exactly duplicates the original context, and, for the cue to be at all effective, the item should fit the context. Transfer-appropriate processing suggests that people should create memory codes that will correspond to how they will eventually use the material, such as in a multiple-choice, essay, or problem-solving test.

STUDY QUESTIONS

This chapter and the next focus primarily on the representation of information. Representation implies that some sort of mental activity transforms physical stimuli into what are usually called *codes*. This reminds us that we construct reality—it is not somehow dropped into our heads like a slide into a projector.

In order to understand the levels-of-processing approach, it is essential to appreciate what qualitative differences are. If you're not sure, look it up.

1. As you proceed, ask yourself whether the levels-of-processing theory (hereafter LOP for short) necessarily conflicts with the STM/LTM separate store theory. (Remember, you don't have to take anybody's word for it.)
2. Since memory is at issue, what is the LOP rationale for using judgmental orienting tasks rather than learning tasks?
3. Don't skip Table 6.1. Much information has been condensed in this valuable summary. Is the summary of STM and LTM consistent with what you read in the previous two chapters?
4. What were Craik and Lockhart's objections to the Atkinson-Shiffrin picture of the memory system represented in Figure 4.1? How persuasive do you find them to be?
5. Why is the assumption that the different memory traces vary in their decay rate essential to the LOP position?
6. If you had a friend who firmly believed that rehearsal automatically results in learning, which of Craik's studies would you describe to your friend? What makes it so conclusive at this point?
7. Why did Hyde and Jenkins (pre-LOP) use an incidental learning paradigm? How did their clever choice of materials allow inferences about what their subjects were doing?
8. To make sure you understand the distinctions, make up a new question, with new yes/no instances, for each of the levels of processing in Table 6.2. Write out your questions.
9. Why was it essential to basic LOP theory that one must be able to measure depth of processing independently of retention? How do the notions of elaboration and distinctiveness get around this problem?
10. What does it mean to say that there is an interaction between encoding and retrieval operations? Generate examples of different types of memory traces and retrieval cues and test your understanding by making predictions congruent with the encoding specificity principle.

KEY TERMS

The page number in parentheses refers to where the term is discussed in the chapter.

auditory memory span (148)   distinctive item (161)
clustering (155)   emotional distinctiveness (162)
cued recall (159)   encoding specificity principle (165)

fact-oriented acquisition (170)
flashbulb memories (162)
imprecise elaboration (160)
incidental learning task (154)
levels of processing (149)
maintenance rehearsal (153)
memory code (148)
mood dependent memory (166)
noncued recall (159)
orienting task (149)
orthographic distinctiveness (162)

phonemic coding (155)
precise elaboration (160)
primary associates (154)
primary distinctiveness (161)
problem-oriented acquisition (170)
processing distinctiveness (163)
secondary distinctiveness (162)
self-generation (161)
semantic coding (155)
structural coding (155)
transfer-appropriate processing (169)

RECOMMENDED READING

A book edited by Cermak and Craik (1979) contains many excellent chapters on how the levels-of-processing concept evolved during the 1970s. Eich (1985) has developed a holographic recall model to account for many of these findings. Although elaborative rehearsal is clearly more effective than maintenance rehearsal, students are not always aware of this difference and may therefore not learn as much as they should (Shaughnessy, 1981). Other applied areas that can be related to the concepts of levels of processing and encoding specificity are context-dependent memory of deep-sea divers, enhancement of face recognition, and attempts to understand certain aspects of amnesia and aphasia (Baddeley, 1982). Johnson (1983) has proposed a memory model in which events can create multiple entries in a sensory, perceptual, and reflection system. The similarities—and differences—between her theory and the levels-of-processing theory are evident in her chapter. Brewer and Pani's (1983) chapter in the same book contains a more complex taxonomy of memory. Blaney's (1986) review of research on affect and memory includes a discussion of issues on encoding specificity, and the book edited by Winograd and Neisser (1992) contains chapters on affect and flashbulb memories. Lundeberg and Fox's (1991) review of the literature on test expectancy shows how the test format and our expectations about it influence our scores.

Visual Images

Mental imagery has long played a central role in psychologists' and philosophers' accounts of cognitive processes and the representation of knowledge in the mind. The construct of the image, however, has never been operationalized well enough to satisfy most psychologists, and so it is not surprising that imagery has disappeared periodically from the mainstream of Western psychology. Nevertheless, the concept has such magnetism that it has never stayed away for long, and it is currently enjoying remarkable popularity.

STEPHEN KOSSLYN AND JAMES POMERANTZ (1977)

*T*HE DISCUSSION IN the preceding chapters emphasized verbal knowledge. The stimuli studied usually consisted of items that could be easily assigned a verbal label, such as words, letters, digits, or even nonsense syllables. We may question, however, whether we assign verbal labels to everything we perceive. Some events may be hard to describe verbally, and others may simply be easier to remember as an image. Although images can exist for each of the sensory modalities, psychologists have been interested mainly in visual images. This chapter considers how visual images contribute to knowledge.

Verbal knowledge
Knowledge expressed in language

Spatial knowledge
Knowledge of spatial relations that may be stored as images

A distinction between verbal knowledge and visual or spatial knowledge is often made on intelligence tests. **Verbal knowledge** is usually measured by vocabulary questions or questions that test comprehension of written material. **Spatial knowledge** is usually measured by performance of such operations as mentally folding connected squares into a cube or mentally rotating an object to determine whether it matches another object. Although most tests place a much greater emphasis on verbal knowledge than on spatial knowledge, some specialized tests contain rather difficult questions on spatial transformations. One example is the Dental Admissions Test, used to help select applicants to dental schools. Since spatial skills are very useful in dentistry, the test includes some challenging problems on spatial relations. People would presumably answer the question illustrated in Figure 7.1 by forming a visual image of the object and rotating the image to align it with the openings.

The study of visual imagery has been one of the main contributions of cognitive psychology. However, psychologists ignored imagery for many years because of the influence of Watson's *Behaviorism* (1924), which was dedicated to wiping out the study of mental events. Watson argued that only behavior could be objectively studied, an argument that certainly had some merit but almost completely eliminated the study of mental processes such as visual imagery. It wasn't until the 1960s that psychologists once again began to try to understand the role of visual images in the acquisition of knowledge. Visual imagery is still difficult to study because it cannot be directly observed, but research over the past

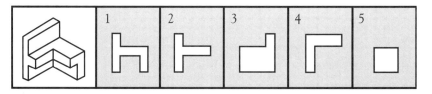

Figure 7.1   *A sample question from the Dental Admissions Test. Students must select the opening through which the object at the far left could pass.*
Reproduced with permission from the American Dental Association.

two decades has provided strong evidence that visual images are used in performing many tasks.

The first section of this chapter argues that forming visual images is an effective method for remembering information. However, formation of a visual image is much easier for concrete material than for abstract material, and we will examine the implications of this finding. For many centuries people have recognized the usefulness of imagery in aiding memory, and many mnemonic strategies are based on visual imagery. The second section describes several memory strategies and shows how they can be used to learn names of people, foreign languages, and lists of items. The third section presents some evidence that visual images are used in performing most spatial reasoning tasks. The results of the experiments would be difficult to explain if we believed that all knowledge was verbal. The final section shows that even visual images have limitations. Fortunately, their lack of detail usually doesn't restrict their usefulness.

VISUAL IMAGERY AND LEARNING

You may be able to recall times when you relied on visual imagery to learn material. When I moved to Cleveland some years ago to begin my academic career at Case Western Reserve University, my home telephone number was 283-9157. I decided to learn the number by verbal rehearsal. I wrote it down and rehearsed it several times before I was confident that I had learned it. After 2 days of unsuccessful practice, however, I decided to look for a different learning strategy.

My choice was influenced by the old "Sing along with Mitch" routine, in which a bouncing ball appears over the words of a song. Where would the ball go if I pictured it bouncing over a sequence of numbers— 1 2 4 5 6 7 8 9? If you try it for the sequence 283-9157, you will see that it has a rather nice pendulum motion, swinging back and forth and ending up in the middle. Once I discovered this relationship, I immediately learned the number, and I have been able to reconstruct it even though it ceased being my number quite a few years ago.

This may be an unusual example of how creation of an image can facilitate learning. But there are many other ways that imagery is used in learning, as we will see in the next two sections. The most obvious example is when we try to remember pictures without having to translate the entire picture into words.

Memory for Pictures

One indication that visual imagery might provide an effective memory code is that people usually find it easier to recognize pictures than to recognize words. Shepard (1967) was one of the first to show that recognition accuracy for visual material is very high. Subjects in his experiment viewed 612 pictures at a self-paced rate and were later given a recognition memory test on pairs of pictures. Each pair consisted of a picture they had previously seen and a novel picture. When they were tested 2 hours later, the participants were virtually perfect in identifying which member of the pair they had seen. Another group of participants, tested 1 week later, was still able to identify the correct picture in 87% of the pairs.

One reason they did so well is that the test was easy. We could remember very little about a picture itself and still be able to tell which of two possibilities had been presented. But when the same test was repeated using words instead of pictures, recognition accuracy wasn't as high. Subjects tested immediately after seeing the words could identify which of two words had been presented in only 88% of the pairs (Shepard, 1967). Their performance was about the same as when pictures were tested after a week's delay.

An experiment by Standing (1973) provided further evidence that it is easier to remember pictures than words. One group of dedicated subjects viewed 10,000 pictures over a 5-day period. Immediately after the learning session on the fifth day, the participants were given a recognition memory test similar to the one designed by Shepard. Standing estimated the number of items they must have retained in memory in order to reach the level of performance they attained on the test (taking into account the probability of guessing correctly). His estimate was that the participants must have remembered 6600 pictures. This estimate does not imply that the participants remembered all the details of a picture—but they did remember enough details to distinguish that picture from a novel picture.

Subjects in Standing's experiment were not shown 10,000 words for comparison, but other groups were shown 1000 words, 1000 ordinary pictures (such as a dog), or 1000 vivid pictures (such as a dog holding a pipe in its mouth). Two days later subjects were asked which of two possibilities had occurred in the experiment. Standing estimated that the participants had retained enough information about 880 vivid pictures, 770 ordinary pictures, and 615 words to make the correct choice without guessing. The finding that recognition memory is better for pictures than for words replicates Shepard's results.

Images and Advertising

The finding that people are better at recognizing pictures than words should have important implications for a number of applied fields. Let's consider advertising as an example. Advertisers often spend a lot of money trying to convince people that they should buy a product. Part of their task, particularly for a new or little-known product, is to help people remember the product's name. An ad may seem very interesting and even enjoyable, but it would not be effective if the potential buyer couldn't remember the name of the product being advertised.

When I was a graduate student in Los Angeles, I participated in a marketing study that tested an audience's response to two new television shows scheduled to appear the following September. We were asked to rate the shows and a series of commercials that occurred between them. When the second show finished, the staff asked us to recall the names of the products advertised 30 min earlier. This was a surprisingly difficult task.

Lutz and Lutz (1977) studied the role that imagery can play in advertising. Learning the names of products is an example of paired-associate learning, in which the advertiser wants us to associate the brand name with the product being advertised. Research on memory for pictures suggests that combining the product and brand name into a single interactive picture should facilitate recall of the brand. When people shop for that particular product, they may remember the picture of the product and the associated brand name.

Lutz and Lutz searched the Yellow Pages of a telephone directory to collect samples of two kinds of pictures: (1) an **interactive illustration**, which integrated the brand and product into a single illustration, and (2) a **noninteractive illustration**, which showed either the brand or the product by itself. The second type of illustration is more common and usually includes a picture of the product with the brand name next to it. Figure 7.2 shows two examples of interactive illustrations and two examples of noninteractive illustrations. Interactive illustrations combine the brand and product into a single picture, either by including an illustration of each (picture interaction) or by combining the illustration of a product and a letter of the brand name (letter accentuation). Noninteractive pictures contain either an illustration of the brand name or an illustration of the product.

Interactive illustration Illustration in which key concepts interact

Noninteractive illustration Illustration in which key concepts do not interact

The students' task was to learn to associate the company's brand name with its product or service. Each student was assigned to one of four groups, consisting of two imagery groups (interactive and noninteractive) and their corresponding control groups. Students in each group studied 24 brand/product pairs for 10 sec each. Members of the interactive imagery group were shown pictures like the ones at the top of Figure 7.2. The control group had to learn the same pairs (such as Rocket Messenger Service or Dixon Crane Co.) but saw only the words without the pictures. The noninteractive group saw a picture of either the product or the brand name, but the pictures were not shown to its control group.

In the recall test, participants were given a list of the 24 products and asked to supply the appropriate brand name for each. The results indicated that only the interactive pictures facilitated recall of the brand

Interactive imagery

Picture interaction

Rocket Messenger Service

Letter accentuation

Dixon Crane Co.

Noninteractive imagery

Name

OBear Abrasive Saws

Product or service

Jack Fair Guard Dogs

Figure 7.2   *Interactive and noninteractive advertisements.*
From "Effects of Interactive Imagery on Learning: Applications to Advertising," by K. A. Lutz and R. J. Lutz, 1977, *Journal of Applied Psychology, 62,* 493–498. Copyright © 1977 by the American Psychological Association. Reprinted by permission.

names. People in the interactive group recalled significantly more names than people who had tried to learn the same pairs without the pictures. However, this finding was based almost entirely on the picture interaction condition; the letter accentuation condition was much less effective. People in the noninteractive group did not learn more pairs than the people in their control group.

The experimenters interpreted the results as supporting the use of pictures in ads—if the pictures form interactive images. Picture interaction is the most effective type of imagery, but it requires that both the product and the brand name be portrayable as pictures. This constraint is usually easy to satisfy for products but is more difficult for brand names unless the company has a name like Lincoln National Life or Bell Telephone. The fact that words vary in how easy they are to translate into images implies that the successful use of imagery depends on the nature of the material to be learned.

Effect of Material on Image Formation

The work of Paivio at the University of Western Ontario established that the effectiveness of visual and verbal codes is influenced by the abstractness of material. After an extensive series of studies, Paivio (1969) argued that there were two major ways a person could elaborate on material in a learning experiment. One form of elaboration emphasizes verbal associations. A word like *poetry* may result in many associations that could help you distinguish it from other words. You might think of different styles of poetry, particular poems, or experiences in an English class. We saw in the previous chapter that verbal associations helped people recall words in the Hyde and Jenkins (1969) experiment. People who considered the meaning of the words recalled primary associates together, because recalling one word reminded them of its associate.

The other form of elaboration is creation of a visual image to represent a word. If I asked you to remember the word *juggler*, you might form an image of a person juggling three balls. If I asked you to remember the word *truth*, however, you would probably have difficulty forming an image. The first word refers to a concrete object, the second to an abstract concept. It is easy to form an image to represent a concrete object but difficult to form an image for an abstract concept. Paivio (1969) argued that the **concrete/abstract dimension** is the most important determinant of ease in forming an image. At the concrete end of the continuum are pictures, because the picture itself can be remembered as a visual image and the person doesn't have to create an image. Pictures often result in better memory than do concrete words, which usually result in better memory than abstract words.

Concrete/abstract dimension Extent to which a concept can be represented by a picture

If visual images and verbal associations are the two major forms of elaboration, is one more effective than the other? To answer this question, we have to know how easy it is to form either an image or a verbal association of a word. The **imagery potential** of words is usually measured by asking people to rate on a scale how easy it is to form an image for a given word. As we might expect, concrete words are rated high on imagery and abstract words are rated low. The **association value** of a word is usually measured by asking people to give as many associations as they can over a 1-min interval. Paivio and his colleagues have found that the imagery potential of words is a more reliable predictor of learning than the association potential of words. High-imagery words are easier to learn than low-imagery words, but high-association words are not necessarily easier to learn than low-association words (Paivio, 1969).

Imagery potential Ease with which a concept can be imaged

Association value The number of verbal associations generated for a concept

A study by Paivio, Smythe, and Yuille (1968) reveals the beneficial effect of imagery on learning. Students at the University of Western Ontario were asked to learn a list of paired associates consisting of 16 pairs of words. The words were equally divided between high-imagery (H) words, such as *juggler, dress, letter,* and *hotel,* and low-imagery (L) words, such as *effort, duty, quality,* and *necessity.* The list contained four pairs each that were high-high, high-low, low-high, and low-low, where the first term refers to the imagery value of the stimulus and the second term refers to the imagery value of the response. Examples include *juggler–dress* (H-H), *letter–effort* (H-L), *duty–hotel* (L-H), and *quality–necessity* (L-L).

Figure 7.3 shows how well the students could recall the response when given the stimulus. The powerful effect of imagery is quite evident. The H-H pairs resulted in the best recall and the L-L pairs the worst. When only one member of the pair had a high-imagery value, recall was better when that word was used as the stimulus (H-L). The fact that H-H pairs were easiest to learn is consistent with the previously mentioned finding that interactive pictures improve the recall of brand names. When images can be created for both members of a word pair, the images can be combined to form an interactive image. For example, one can associate the word *dress* with *juggler* by forming an image of a juggler wearing a dress.

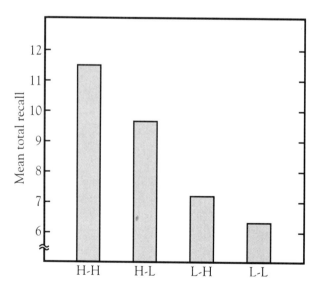

Figure 7.3 *Mean total recall over four trials as a function of high (H) and low (L) imagery values.*

From "Imagery versus Meaningfulness of Nouns in Paired-Associate Learning," by A. Paivio, P. E. Smythe, and J. C. Yuille, 1968, *Canadian Journal of Psychology, 22,* 427–441. Copyright © 1968 by the Canadian Psychological Association. Reprinted by permission.

It is interesting to note that high-imagery words were easier to recall than low-imagery words even though the learners were not told to use visual imagery. Perhaps the participants spontaneously generated images whenever they could. Support for this hypothesis was obtained in a questionnaire completed after the learning task. The students indicated, for each of the 16 pairs on the list, which one of five strategies they had used in trying to learn that pair. Their options were *none, repetition* (rehearsal), *verbal* (a phrase or rhyme connecting two words), *imagery* (mental pictures that include the items), and *other*. The *none* and *other* options were reported infrequently. The distribution of the other three responses depended on whether the pairs consisted of high- or low-imagery words (see Figure 7.4). The reported use of imagery was highest for the H-H pairs and lowest for the L-L pairs. The striking resemblance between learning (Figure 7.3) and the reported use of imagery (Figure 7.4) suggests that imagery is an effective learning strategy.

The reason images are effective, according to Paivio (1975), is that an image provides a second kind of memory code that is independent of the verbal code. Paivio's theory is called a **dual-coding theory** because it proposes two independent memory codes, either of which can result in recall. A person who has stored both the word *cat* and an image of a cat

Dual-coding theory
A theory that memory is improved when items can be represented by both verbal and visual memory codes

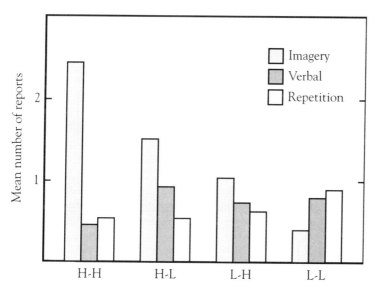

Figure 7.4 *Mean number of pairs for which imagery, verbal, and repetition strategies were reported as a function of high (H) and low (L) imagery values.*

From "Imagery versus Meaningfulness of Nouns in Paired-Associate Learning," by A. Paivio, P. C. Smythe, and J. C. Yuille, 1968, *Canadian Journal of Psychology, 22,* 427–441. Copyright © 1968 by the Canadian Psychological Association. Reprinted by permission.

can remember the item if she retrieves either the image or the word. Evidence suggests that the two memory codes are independent in the sense that a person can forget one code without forgetting the other (Paivio, 1975). Having two memory codes to represent an item therefore provides a better chance of remembering that item than does having only a single code.

A criticism of dual-coding theory is that it works only in situations in which people focus on **relational information**, such as the associations between items in a paired-associates task (Marschark & Hunt, 1989). Subjects in Marschark and Hunt's experiment initially rated 12 concrete and 12 abstract word pairs in an orienting task. One group rated how easily the two words of each pair could be combined into an integrated unit. When they were later asked to recall the words, they recalled significantly more concrete than abstract words. Another group was told to ignore the fact that the words were presented in pairs and to rate the words individually on the ease with which each evoked a mental image. This group did not recall any more concrete words than abstract words, as would be expected from dual-coding theory. The emphasis on relational coding is also consistent with the finding that improving the recall of brand names depended on forming an *interactive* picture that combined the product and brand name.

If Marschark and Hunt are correct—that relational processing is necessary to achieve the benefits of concreteness—then dual-coding theory has a restricted range of application. But the restricted range is still fairly large because many learning activities require that we learn associations between items. Since images facilitate recall in these situations, it is only natural that they should play a key role in suggestions for improving memory.

Relational information
Information specifying how concepts are related

MNEMONIC STRATEGIES

Every so often a book appears on how to improve memory. Such a book is usually written by a person who not only has practiced **mnemonic** (memory) **techniques** but can successfully apply them to demonstrate rather remarkable acts of recall. One example, *The Memory Book*, by Lorayne and Lucas (1974), was on the bestseller list for weeks.

Although memory books always discuss several techniques for improving memory, they usually emphasize visual imagery. The author presents a mnemonic strategy, in which imagery usually plays a key role, and claims that use of the strategy will improve recall. The claim, however, is seldom supported by experimental data. Is there proof that the proposed strategy works? Fortunately, supportive data exist in the psychology journals. We will now consider some of those data.

Mnemonic techniques
Strategies that improve memory

Comparison of Association Learning Strategies

The results obtained by Paivio et al. (1968) suggested that visual imagery is a particularly good strategy to use when images can be generated to represent words. Their study, however, was not designed to teach people to use a particular strategy, unlike an experiment conducted by Bower and Winzenz (1970). Subjects in the latter experiment were asked to learn paired associates consisting of concrete nouns. Each participant was assigned to one of four groups given different instructions on how to learn the associations. Students in the *repetition condition* were asked to rehearse each pair silently. Students in the *sentence-reading condition* read aloud a sentence in which the two words of a pair were capitalized as the subject and object of the sentence. The experimenters told the members of this group to use the sentence to associate the two critical nouns. Students in the *sentence-generation condition* made up their own sentence to relate the two words in a sensible way. Students in the *imagery condition* formed a mental image that combined the two words in a vivid interaction. They were encouraged to make their image as elaborate or as bizarre as they wished.

After a single study trial on each of 30 word pairs, the students were given a recall test on 15 pairs and a recognition test on the other 15. Recognition of the correct response was easy, and all four study strategies resulted in a high level of performance. Recall of the correct response was more difficult, however, and here the differential effectiveness of the strategies was apparent. The average number of correct recalls was 5.6 for the repetition group, 8.2 for the sentence-reading group, 11.5 for the sentence-generation group, and 13.1 for the imagery group. The data dramatically illustrate that, although verbal rehearsal does result in some learning, it is less effective than the elaboration strategies. Comparison of the imagery and sentence-generation conditions shows that visual elaboration was more effective than semantic elaboration. Although the use of concrete nouns made visual elaboration possible, the fact that sentence generation was also an effective strategy suggests that this technique could be used when it is necessary to learn abstract words.

A specific application of the imagery strategy in paired-associate learning is learning to associate a name to a face. I would guess that just about everyone has had difficulty learning names at one time or another. Many authors of memory books can perform a very impressive demonstration in which they repeat back the names of all the members of an audience after hearing them only once. The method used by Lorayne involves first converting the name into a visual image and then linking the image to a prominent feature of the person's face. For example, if Mr. Gordon has a large nose, the image might be a garden (*garden* sounds like *Gordon*) growing out of his nose. Although the method may seem rather bizarre, it has experimental support.

A group of British psychologists found that people who were taught this strategy learned significantly more names than a control group that was not taught the strategy (P. E. Morris, S. Jones, & P. Hampson, 1978). The learning task required associating a different name (randomly selected from a telephone directory) to each of 13 photographs of male adults. After a study period of 10 sec for each item, the imagery group could correctly name ten of the photographs, compared with five for the control group. The authors admit that the use of mnemonic strategies requires some effort, and not everyone will be willing to make that effort to learn names. However, their results should provide encouragement to those who wonder whether the effort will be worthwhile.

Bizarre images Fantastic or unusual images

Although research has shown that the use of visual imagery is effective for learning associations, it has also shown that **bizarre images** are not always more effective than plausible images. Rather, the degree of interaction in the image is a better predictor of its effectiveness (Kroll, Schepeler, & Angin, 1986). Bizarre imagery is more effective than plausible imagery only in limited situations, such as when the greater distinctiveness of bizarre images can enhance memory (McDaniel & Einstein, 1986).

The Mnemonic Keyword Method and Vocabulary Learning

The use of imagery to remember names obviously depends on how easy it is to form an image from a name. Some names should be fairly easy, such as Smith (form an image of a blacksmith) or Green (form an image of the color). Other names, such as Gordon or Detterman, may require associating a concrete word to the name and then forming an image of the associated word. The associated word, called a **keyword**, should sound like the name that is being learned. The association of *garden* with *Gordon* is an example of the keyword method. *Garden* is a keyword that can be used to form an image. The words *debtor–man* might be a good keyword for Detterman if one formed an image of Mr. Detterman dressed in ragged clothes.

Keyword A concrete word that sounds like an abstract word so it can be substituted for the abstract word in an interactive image

You may have some reservations at this point about the keyword method. It is certainly more complicated than simply forming an image because you have to remember not only the image but also the association between the keyword and the name in order to remember the original name correctly. Mr. Gordon might not appreciate being called Mr. Garden, and Mr. Detterman would certainly not like being called Mr. Debtorman.

Keyword method A mnemonic strategy using keywords to improve paired-associate learning

Even though the **keyword method** requires two stages—learning the association between the name and the keyword and forming an image of the keyword—the method is still very effective. A striking demonstration of its effectiveness is illustrated in a study by Atkinson and Raugh (1975)

on the acquisition of Russian vocabulary. The keyword method divides the study of a vocabulary word into two stages. The first stage is to associate the foreign word with an English word, the keyword, which sounds approximately like some part of the foreign word. The second stage is to form a mental image of the keyword interacting with the English translation. For example, the Russian word for *building* (*zdanie*) is pronounced somewhat like *zdawn-yeh*, with the emphasis on the first syllable. Using *dawn* as the keyword, one could imagine the pink light of dawn being reflected in the windows of a building.

   Appropriate selection of keywords is an important aspect of the method. A good keyword should satisfy the following criteria: it should (1) sound as much as possible like a part of the foreign word, (2) be different from the other keywords, and (3) easily form an interactive image with the English translation. Table 7.1 shows a sample of 20 Russian words and their associated keywords. As an exercise in using the method, you can try to create an image linking the first pair of words.

Table 7.1   *A sample of 20 Russian words with related keywords*

Russian	Keyword	Translation
VNIMÁNIE	[pneumonia]	ATTENTION
DÉLO	[jello]	AFFAIR
ZÁPAD	[zap it]	WEST
STRANÁ	[straw man]	COUNTRY
TOLPÁ	[tell pa]	CROWD
LINKÓR	[Lincoln]	BATTLESHIP
ROT	[rut]	MOUTH
GORÁ	[garage]	MOUNTAIN
DURÁK	[two rocks]	FOOL
ÓSEN	[ocean]	AUTUMN
SÉVER	[saviour]	NORTH
DYM	[dim]	SMOKE
SELÓ	[seal law]	VILLAGE
GOLOVÁ	[Gulliver]	HEAD
USLÓVIE	[Yugoslavia]	CONDITION
DÉVUSHKA	[dear vooshka]	GIRL
TJÓTJA	[Churchill]	AUNT
PÓEZD	[poised]	TRAIN
KROVÁT	[cravat]	BED
CHELOVÉK	[chilly back]	PERSON

SOURCE: From "An Application of the Mnemonic Keyword Method to the Acquisition of a Russian Vocabulary," by R. C. Atkinson and M. R. Raugh, 1975, *Journal of Experimental Psychology: Human Learning and Memory, 104,* pp. 126–133. Copyright 1975 by the American Psychological Association. Reprinted by permission.

Students in Atkinson and Raugh's study tried to learn the English translations of 120 Russian words over a 3-day period. The students were divided into two groups—the "keyword" group and a control group. Subjects in the keyword group were taught how to use the keyword method. After the pronunciation of each Russian word, they were shown both a keyword and the English translation. The instructions said that the students should try to picture an interactive image linking the keyword and the English translation or should generate a sentence incorporating both words if they could not form an image. The keywords were not shown to students in the control group, who were told to learn the translations in whatever manner they wished. The control group did not receive instructions on the use of keywords or mental imagery.

On the day after the three study sessions, students in both groups were tested on the entire 120-word vocabulary. Students in the keyword group provided the correct translations for 72% of the Russian words; students in the control group did so for 46% of the words. This difference is particularly impressive considering that Russian was selected as a special challenge to the keyword method because the pronunciation of most Russian words is quite different from English pronunciation. Since many people find Russian vocabulary harder to learn than the vocabularies of other foreign languages, it is valuable to have a method that can facilitate learning. Atkinson and Raugh planned to use the keyword method in a computerized vocabulary-learning program designed to supplement a college course in Russian. Students would be free to study the words in any way they wished but would have the option of requesting a keyword by pressing an appropriate button on the terminal.

The Method of Loci

Serial learning Learning items in a specified order

The mnemonic methods we have reviewed so far have been applied to paired-associate learning such as associating a name with a face or an English word with a Russian word. Another kind of memory task is **serial learning**, which means memorizing a sequence of items in their correct order. For example, if you are going shopping, you may want to remember a list of items in the order in which you plan to purchase them.

Method of loci A mnemonic technique for learning the order of objects by imaging them in specific locations

A long list of items can be memorized by using the **method of loci**, a technique invented many centuries ago. The need for a good memory was particularly important in the ancient world, which lacked printing and even paper for notes. The classical art of memory was taught mainly as a technique for delivering long speeches (Yates, 1966). An unknown teacher of rhetoric recorded the principles in *Ad Herennium*, a book written in about 86–82 B.C. The first step was to commit to memory a series of loci, or places—usually parts of a building, such as the forecourt, living room, bedrooms, and parlors, including statues and other ornaments in the rooms. The topics of the speech were then translated into images that were placed at the various locations in the order in which they would be discussed. The orator imagined walking through the building in a specified order, retrieving each image as he came to the next location. The method assures that the topics are remembered in their correct order since the order is determined by the sequence of locations in the building.

The memory section of *Ad Herennium* did more than simply describe the method of loci; it gave a detailed set of rules for how the method should be used. For instance, there were rules for selecting locations:

> Memory loci should not be too much like one another, for instance too many intercolumnar spaces are not good, for their resemblance will be confusing. They should be of moderate size, not too large, for that renders the images placed on them vague, and not too small for then an arrangement of images will be overcrowded. They must not be too brightly lighted for then the images placed on them will glitter and dazzle; nor must they be too dark or the shadows will obscure the images. (Yates, 1966, p. 23)*

And rules for creating images:

> We ought, then, to set up images of a kind that can adhere longest in memory. And we shall do so if we establish similitudes as striking as possible; if we set up images that are not many or vague but active; if we assign to them exceptional beauty or singular ugliness; if we ornament some of them, as with crowns or purple cloaks, so that the similitude may be more distinct to us; or if we somehow disfigure them, as by introducing one stained with blood or soiled with mud or smeared with red paint, so that its form is more striking, or by assigning certain comic effects to our images, for that, too, will ensure our remembering them more readily. (Yates, 1966, p. 25)

Two aspects of these rules are rather striking. The first is the concern with the visual precision of images. The recommendation that images be of a certain size to be most effective is consistent with current research on imagery (Kosslyn, 1975; Kosslyn, Ball, & Reiser, 1978). However, the recommendation that the loci not be too bright or too dark seems unusual to me. Do our images so closely reflect reality that we have to be concerned about lighting? Perhaps people who relied extensively on imagery had images that were so detailed and accurate that lighting was a concern. My own belief is that the images of most people are highly schematic and not very detailed, a belief I will try to support in the next section.

The second significant aspect of the rules is their attempt to reduce interference by creating loci and images that are highly distinctive. The

---

*Quotes from *The Art of Memory*, by Dame Frances Yates. Copyright © 1966 by Frances A. Yates. Reprinted by permission of The University of Chicago Press and Routledge.

importance of distinctiveness is still emphasized in current theories of memory, as we saw in the previous chapter. The author of *Ad Herennium* recommended that the loci should be different enough from one another that they would not be confused. One implication of this rule is that storing more than one image in a single location interferes with retrieval.

Crovitz (1971) tested this implication by asking undergraduates at Duke University to learn a set of 32 English words. Another set of 32 items (such as *pet store, zoo, fire station, hospital*) represented memory loci. The locations were typed individually on cards, which were placed on the experimenter's table. The number of cards or locations varied across groups. The control group was given no memory instructions and no cards. Six other groups received 1, 2, 4, 8, 16, or 32 locations, along with instructions to picture each word on the list vividly at the successive locations. The instructions indicated that the subjects would hear 32 words and would have to store more than 1 word at a location if there were fewer than 32 cards.

Figure 7.5 shows the percent of words that were recalled in their correct order as a function of the number of locations. The group that was asked to associate all the words with a single location did not do significantly better than the control group (0 locations), which tried to learn the words without using the method of loci. However, performance im-

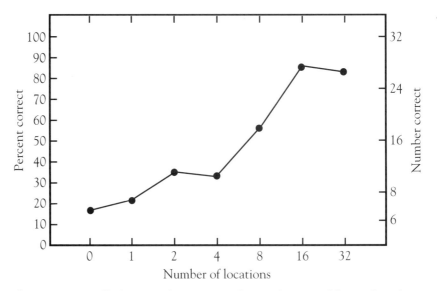

Figure 7.5   *Recall of items in their correct order as a function of the number of locations.*

From "The Capacity of Memory Loci in Artificial Memory," by H. F. Crovitz, 1971, *Psychonomic Science, 24,* 187–188. Copyright © 1971 by the Psychonomic Society, Inc. Reprinted by permission.

proved rapidly as the number of locations increased to 16, suggesting that two images could be stored at each location without producing interference. Storing more than two images at a location made it hard to remember the words, particularly in their correct order. It is important to note, however, that even a few locations led to better recall than the control group produced, and using many locations produced a substantial improvement in recall.

The research on the helpful role of images in learning, particularly Paivio's work in the 1960s, revitalized psychologists' interest in the study of visual imagery. It also attracted the attention of cognitive psychologists who became interested in the cognitive operations that people perform on their images. Can we scan images the same way that we can scan pictures? Can we manipulate images, such as mentally rotating a piece of furniture to see whether we can move it through a door? This application of the imagery construct to a broader range of tasks initiated a debate between those psychologists who believed that imagery should have a major theoretical role in psychological theories and those psychologists who believed that imagery is not an important theoretical construct. In the next section we examine the evidence for the importance of imagery as a theoretical construct in explaining how people perform many tasks that require spatial reasoning.

EVIDENCE FOR IMAGES IN PERFORMING COGNITIVE TASKS

Although psychologists have seldom questioned that images exist, some have questioned the usefulness of images as explanatory constructs. The most influential paper challenging the usefulness of images in psychological theories was written by Pylyshyn (1973). Pylyshyn argued that it was misleading to think of images as uninterpreted photographs, analogous to pictures in the head. He supported the alternative view that an image is much closer to being a description of a scene than a picture of it. The emphasis on the descriptive characteristics of images, rather than their sensory characteristics, is the central theme of a **propositional theory**.

Kosslyn and Pomerantz (1977) agreed with Pylyshyn that images are interpreted and organized, but they argued that we often process images in the same way that we process perceptual information. In response to Pylyshyn's paper, they summarized five experimental findings that they thought could be better explained on the basis of imagery than by nonsensory information. Two of the five findings were concerned with scanning visual images, a task studied by Kosslyn and his associates. We will look first at one variable influencing scanning time—the effect of distance between objects. We will then examine the other three findings, on visual matching, mental rotation, and selective interference.

Propositional theory
A theory that all knowledge, including spatial knowledge, can be expressed in semantic-based propositions

Scanning Visual Images

Visual scanning A shift
of attention across a
visual display or image

Many explanations of performance based on visual imagery assume that an image is a spatial representation analogous to the experience of seeing an object during visual perception. Furthermore, many of the operations that are used in analyzing visual patterns are also used to analyze visual images (Kosslyn & Pomerantz, 1977). One such operation is **visual scanning**. The analogy between pictures and images suggests that the time it takes to scan between two objects in an image should be a function of their distance from each other. Evidence obtained by Kosslyn, Ball, and Reiser (1978) supports this prediction.

One of their experiments required that undergraduates at Johns Hopkins University learn the exact locations of the objects shown in Figure 7.6. The map was then removed, and the students were given a series of trials that began with the name of an object. The task required that they form a mental image of the entire map and focus on the named ob-

Figure 7.6   *A fictional map used to study the effect of distances on mental scanning time.*

From "Visual Images Preserve Metric Spatial Information: Evidence from Studies of Image Scanning," by S. M. Kosslyn, T. M. Ball, and B. J. Reiser, 1978, *Journal of Experimental Psychology: Human Perception and Performance, 4*, 47–60. Copyright © 1978 by the American Psychological Association. Reprinted by permission.

ject. Subjects then heard the name of a second object and scanned the map in the way they had been instructed—by imagining a black speck moving in a straight line from the first object to the second. When they reached the second object, they pushed a button that stopped a clock. There are 21 possible distances among the seven objects, and the longest distance is nine times as great as the shortest distance. If distance determines the scanning time, as predicted, reaction time should be a linear function of the distance between two locations. Figure 7.7 shows how closely the prediction was supported.

These results suggest that we can mentally scan visual images in the same way that we can scan pictures. But an alternative view is that subjects in imagery tasks may be able to respond appropriately without actually using visual images (Pylyshyn, 1981; Intons-Peterson, 1983). According to this view, subjects may guess what the experimenter expects and respond so as to please the experimenter. A study by D. B. Mitchell and C. L. Richman (1980) showed that people can accurately predict how distance should influence scanning time. When the experimenters asked subjects to predict their scanning time for the different pairs of objects in

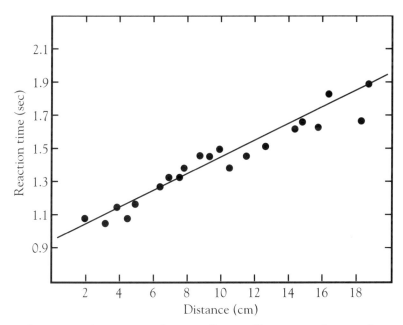

Figure 7.7   *Scanning time between all pairs of locations on the imaged map.*

From "Visual Images Preserve Metric Spatial Information: Evidence from Studies of Image Scanning," by S. M. Kosslyn, T. M. Ball, and B. J. Reiser, 1978, *Journal of Experimental Psychology: Human Perception and Performance, 4,* 47–60. Copyright © 1978 by the American Psychological Association. Reprinted by permission.

Figure 7.6, predicted scanning times also increased as a linear function of distance. It is therefore possible that subjects did not actually mentally scan their visual images but simply waited longer before pushing the button as the distance increased between two objects.

This criticism can be avoided if the outcome of the experiment cannot be predicted. Reed, Hock, and Lockhead (1983) hypothesized that people may not be able to predict how the shape of patterns will influence their scanning time. For example, one of these researchers' patterns was a straight line and another was a spiral. The rate at which people scanned a visual image of the pattern depended on its shape. An image of a straight line was scanned more quickly than an image of a spiral. However, people were unsuccessful in predicting how the different shapes would influence their scanning time. Because they couldn't predict the outcome of the experiment, their scanning times must have been produced by their actually scanning the different patterns rather than by their predictions.

Although the data of some imagery experiments may have been generated without subjects' using imagery, it is highly unlikely that people could perform many spatial tasks without using imagery. Finke (1980) cites specific examples of tasks in which the expected outcome would not be obvious to subjects, usually because they were doing the task for the first time. Let us now consider some other tasks that allow us to distinguish between visual and verbal memory codes.

Sequential versus Parallel Processing

One difference between information maintained in a visual image and information maintained as a verbal code is that a visual image makes it possible to match information in parallel. When you look at the schematic faces in Figure 7.8, you can perceive many features of the faces simultaneously. However, when you describe these same features verbally, you do not have access to all the features at the same time, because language is sequential. You would have to decide the order in which to describe the features if you were to describe someone's face over the phone.

Parallel representation
Representation of knowledge in which more than one item at a time can be processed

Sequential representation Representation of knowledge in which only one item at a time can be processed

The **parallel representation** of spatial information and the **sequential representation** of verbal information influence how quickly a person can determine whether a perceived pattern matches a memorized pattern. If the memorized pattern is stored as a visual image, the match should occur quickly and should be relatively uninfluenced by the number of features that have to be matched. If a pattern is stored as a verbal description, the match should occur more slowly and should be influenced by the number of features that have to be compared.

Nielsen and Smith (1973) tested these predictions by showing students either a picture of a schematic face or its verbal description. There

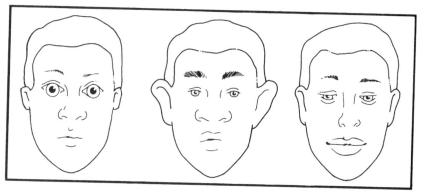

Figure 7.8   *Three sample faces illustrating size differences of feature values.*
From "Representation and Retrieval Processes in Short-Term Memory: Recognition and Recall of
Faces," by E. E. Smith and G. D. Nielsen, 1970, *Journal of Experimental Psychology, 85,* 397–405.
Copyright © 1970 by the American Psychological Association. Reprinted by permission.

were five features of the face—ears, eyebrows, eyes, nose, and mouth—
which varied in size. Each of the features could assume one of three values—large, medium, or small (see Figure 7.8 for an example). After students studied either the description or the picture for 4 sec, the stimulus
was removed. After a retention interval that lasted either 4 or 10 sec, the
experimenters presented a test face, and the students had to decide
whether it matched the face or description presented earlier.

In order to test the prediction that the number of features would influence reaction time only when people compared the test face with a
verbal description, Nielsen and Smith varied the number of relevant features from three to five. The students knew that they could ignore the
ears and eyebrows when there were three relevant features because these
features never changed, and they could ignore the ears when there were
four relevant features. But they had to compare all five features when all
five were relevant. Figure 7.9 shows the amount of time needed to respond that either the initial face (FF task) or the description (DF task)
matched the test face. The data are from the 4-sec delay, but the same
pattern of results occurred for the 10-sec delay. The response times indicate that matching was relatively fast and independent of the number of
relevant features only when the initial item was a visual pattern.

The results imply that, when a person can maintain a visual image of
a pattern in STM, a second visual pattern can be compared with it very
quickly. It's almost as if the person were superimposing the two patterns
and comparing all the features simultaneously. When the features are
described verbally, a match requires sequentially retrieving information from the description, such as large ears, small eyebrows, small eyes,

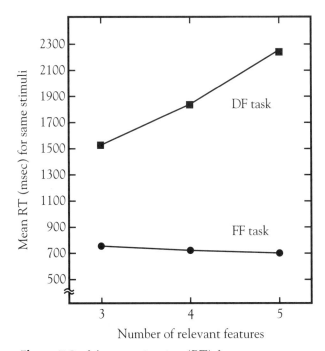

Figure 7.9 *Mean reaction time (RT) for correct responses when stimuli were the same, as a function of the task and number of relevant features.*

From "Imaginal and Verbal Representations in Short-Term Recognition of Visual Forms," by G. D. Nielsen and E. E. Smith, 1973, *Journal of Experimental Psychology, 101*, 375–378. Copyright © 1973 by the American Psychological Association. Reprinted by permission.

medium nose, and large mouth. Each feature on the list is individually compared with the corresponding feature on the test face. The response time therefore increases as a function of the number of relevant features on the list. The reaction time functions for the DF task in Figure 7.9 may remind you of the reaction time functions found in the Sternberg (1967b) memory scanning task (Figure 4.10, Chapter 4). The similarity is not surprising, since both tasks require that people sequentially scan a list of items in STM. Maintaining an image in the FF task avoids a list of separate items by combining the individual features on the list into a single integrated pattern. The efficiency with which this integrated pattern can be compared with other visual patterns is an important difference between a visual image and a verbal description.

Mental Rotation

Deciding whether two patterns match is considerably more difficult if they differ in orientation. The task shown in Figure 7.10 requires judging whether the two patterns in each pair are the same object (Shepard & Metzler, 1971). Pairs A and B are different orientations of the same pattern, but pair C consists of two different patterns. One method for determining whether two patterns are identical is to rotate one pattern mentally until it has the same orientation as the other pattern. When the patterns have the same orientation, it is easier to determine whether they match.

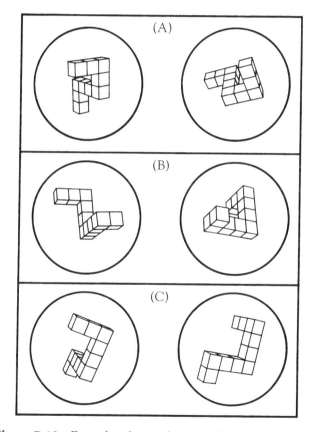

Figure 7.10 *Examples of pairs of patterns differing in orientation.*

From "Mental Rotation of Three-Dimensional Objects," by R. N. Shepard and J. Metzler, 1971, *Science, 171,* 701–703. Copyright © 1971 by the American Association for the Advancement of Science. Reprinted by permission.

The pairs used by Shepard and Metzler differed in orientation from 0 degrees to 180 degrees in 20-degree steps. Half of the pairs could be rotated to match each other, and half were mirror images that did not match. Figure 7.11 shows that the time required to decide that two patterns were identical increased linearly with an increase in the number of degrees they differed in orientation, suggesting that the subjects were rotating a visual image of one of the forms until it had the same orientation as the other form. Self-reports were consistent with this interpretation—subjects reported that they imagined one object rotating until it had the same orientation as the other and that they could rotate an image only up to a certain speed without losing its structure.

Similar results occur when people have to make judgments about familiar patterns. Cooper and Shepard (1973) showed subjects letters of the alphabet and asked them to indicate whether the pattern was a normal letter (R) or its mirror image (Я). Response times depended on how much the pattern was rotated from its normal upright position. Response times were shortest when the pattern was upright and longest when the pattern was upside down (rotated 180 degrees). However, response times were not a linear function of the angle of rotation, as they were for the

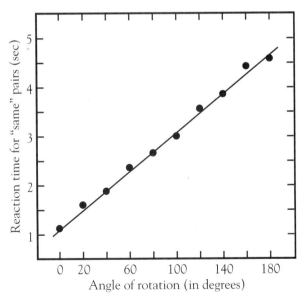

Figure 7.11   *Reaction time to judge whether two patterns have the same three-dimensional shape.*

From "Mental Rotation of Three-Dimensional Objects," by R. N. Shepard and J. Metzler, 1971, *Science, 171,* 701–703. Copyright © 1971 by the American Association for the Advancement of Science. Reprinted by permission.

block patterns. A 60-degree increase in rotation increased the response time more between 120 and 180 degrees than between 0 and 60 degrees.

A plausible explanation of why letters are less affected by small degrees of rotation than block patterns are is that letters may appear to be upright even when they are slightly rotated (Hock & Tromley, 1978). Some letters (such as *F*) can be rotated more than others (such as *G*) and still appear upright. Hock and Tromley used the physical characteristics of letters to classify them into sets that should appear either tilted or upright when slightly rotated. The "tilted" letters produced results that were similar to those obtained for block patterns. Since these letters are very sensitive to orientation, the response time to decide whether the letter was normal or reversed increased as a linear function of its rotation. The "upright" letters produced results similar to those obtained by Cooper and Shepard. Since these letters were less affected by small changes in orientation, decision times changed very little for small angles of rotation.

The ability to imagine movement is valued in sports training programs that use mental rehearsal as a training technique. Box 7.1 describes some of these programs. A key feature of mental rehearsal is the transformation of a list of instructions into an image of continuous movement. There is a need, however, for additional research to evaluate the success of this technique. Suinn (1983) provides a good summary of the experimental study of imagery in sports.

Interference

We have seen in earlier discussions that a major cause of forgetting is interference. Research on release from proactive interference (D. D. Wickens, 1972) has demonstrated that interference can be reduced by shifting semantic categories. Interference can also be reduced by shifting between visual and verbal material, as shown in a study by Brooks (1968).

In the visual task in this study, subjects were shown a block diagram of a letter (see Figure 7.12). The letter was then removed, and the subjects had to use their memory of the letter to respond yes to each corner that was on the extreme top or bottom and no to each corner that was in between. The correct answers for the example, starting at the asterisk at the lower left and proceeding in the direction of the arrow, are yes, yes, yes, no, no, no, no, no, no, yes.

The verbal task in Brooks's experiment required that people respond positively to each word in a sentence that was a noun. For example, people listened to the sentence *"A bird in the hand is not in the bush"* and then had to classify each word as a noun or nonnoun. The correct answers for the example are no, yes, no, no, yes, no, no, no, no, yes.

Brooks assumed that his subjects would rely on a verbal code to maintain the sentence in memory and a visual image to maintain the

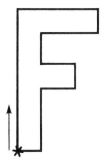

Figure 7.12   *Block diagram of a letter.*
From "Spatial and Verbal Components of the Act
of Recall," by L. R. Brooks, 1968, *Canadian
Journal of Psychology, 22*, 349–368. Copyright ©
1968 by the Canadian Psychological Association.
Reprinted by permission.

block diagram in memory. If his assumption is correct, it should be possible to *interfere selectively* with performance by using two different methods of responding. One method required that the answers be given verbally, by overtly responding yes or no. A verbal response should cause a
greater conflict when classifying the words of a sentence than when classifying the corners of a block diagram. Another method required that a
subject point to a Y for each positive response and an N for each negative
response, using a diagram like the one in Figure 7.13. The diagram shows
the correct answers for classifying the words in the sample sentence.
Pointing to the correct letter requires close visual monitoring and should
interfere more with the block task than with the sentence task.

The selective nature of interference is revealed by the average response time required to complete each task. Classifying the words in a
sentence took longer when people gave a verbal response; classifying the
corners of a letter took longer when people pointed to the correct response. In other words, giving a verbal response interfered more with
memory for verbal material (a sentence) than with memory for visual material (a block diagram), and vice versa.

The selective nature of interference within a modality has implications for the number of items that can be maintained in STM. When we
reviewed the evidence on STM capacity in Chapter 4, we looked at research that presented items from the same modality, such as a string of
letters in a memory span task or different levels of brightness in an absolute judgment task. What would happen if we designed a memory span
task in which some items could be retained by using a verbal code and
other items could be retained by using a visual code? According to

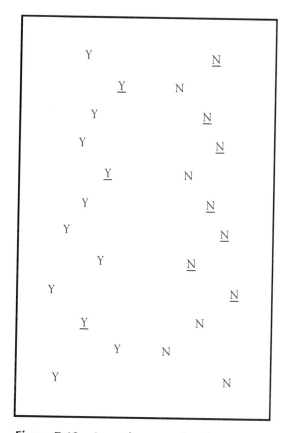

Figure 7.13 *A sample answer sheet for responding yes or no in classifying words in a sample
sentence. Correct responses are underscored.*
From "Spatial and Verbal Components of the Act of Recall,"
by L. R. Brooks, 1968, *Canadian Journal of Psychology, 22,*
349–368. Copyright © 1968 by the Canadian Psychological
Association. Reprinted by permission.

Baddeley's (1992) working memory model, verbal information should be
maintained in the articulatory loop and visual information should be
maintained in the visuospatial sketchpad (see pages 101–102). If such variety reduces interference, people should be able to recall more items.

An experiment by two Dutch psychologists (Sanders & Schroots,
1969) revealed that a person's memory span can, in fact, be increased by
using material from two different modalities. One modality was the typical verbal modality, created by showing a string of consonants. The other
modality was a visual or spatial modality, created by showing a random

Mental images help athletes train their bodies

CHARLES GARFIELD

"I never hit a shot, not even in practice, without having a very sharp, in-focus picture of it in my head."—golfer Jack Nicklaus

If you learn mental rehearsal techniques by using your imagination to create mental images of yourself performing, you can perform at optimal levels. This technique is the single most powerful tool in the Soviet mental training arsenal. It enables you to build confidence, accelerate reaction times and improve physical coordination and accuracy, and it allows you to work out complex strategies before executing them.

Mental rehearsal is by no means unknown to most athletes. But the formalization of the technique and its systematic use in athletic training programs, as has been done in the Soviet Union, are quite new to us [article written in 1984]. And whereas the Russians and East Germans use the technique in routine "mental workouts" as a way to perform their best, mental rehearsal has been applied in the United States largely to correct, rather than prevent, problems.

What exactly is mental rehearsal? Soviet psychologist Gregory Raiport, who worked with Russian national teams from 1972 to 1976, has explained how mental rehearsal is used to help train athletes at the National Research Institute of Physical Culture in Moscow: In their mental rehearsal sessions, the Russian athletes are taught to "imagine or visualize themselves performing the different stages of the event," and by doing so they actually provide themselves with invaluable neuromuscular practice.

In mental rehearsal, the mental images must include movement.

In his study on the effects of mental rehearsal on 53 Alpine skiers, Swedish sports psychologist Lars-Eric Unestahl found the most positive results were obtained when athletes created mental images of actions rather than of static postures.

The temptation for many people just starting out with mental rehearsal is to create "still shots" of positions that they know, in principle, are correct. This has the effect of freezing the mental image, a little like what happens when film gets stuck in a motion picture projector. But because motion is the essence of sports, movement and one's response to the changing circumstances created by movement must be included in the rehearsal.

---

sequence of lights on a two-dimensional lightboard. In the second condition subjects responded by pointing to the lights on the board in the correct order of their appearance.

The lack of interference between modalities suggests that people should be able to increase their memory span by storing the consonants as a verbal code and the light sequence as a visual code. Recall was, in fact, better when a sequence consisted of both visual and verbal items. For example, when people were asked to recall a string of 11 consonants, they correctly recalled an average of 5.4 items. When they were asked to

Thus, Unestahl instructed his athletes: "Tell your body what to do by thinking through the run—that is, imagining yourself skiing down. Then start your body and let it do the rest. The task while you are skiing down will be to sing, hum or whistle a melody."

According to Unestahl, the highest number of negative results came when athletes created mental images that focused on specific postures, and so subconsciously directed their bodies to remain set in particular positions—even when they were performing complex actions that required constant change in response to changing circumstances.

The mental images that athletes create are what Stanford University researcher Karl Pribram has called mental holograms, three-dimensional mental images that direct nerve impulses to all the muscles of the body that will be involved in executing a task. As long as we allow these holograms to direct our movements—and the word "movements" is the key here—those moves in real life will be smooth, confident and precise.

The following is the example Unestahl presents of a mental rehearsal that hurts performance: "Concentrate on the following things while you are skiing down: (a) arms forward, easily bent, the underarms parallel to the ground; (b) initiate the turn: sink down and put your poles down during the raising up; (c) the vertical work: turn the skis when you are in the highest position; (d) the turn: bring your hip in toward the hill and compensate with your upper body down while sinking down."

Unestahl's point is subtle, but if you imagine how you would feel if you were to ski while trying to remember this long list of static instructions, you will probably clutch up just thinking about it.

With movement and change programmed into the mental image, athletes can then let the mind and body take over. Once the action begins, the athletes turn their attention away from deliberate mental activity by whistling or humming. Conscious, deliberate thought ceases and the images of action take over automatically.

SOURCE: From "Mental Images Help Athletes Train Their Bodies," by Charles Garfield, appearing in the *Sun-Sentinel,* Fort Lauderdale, July 23, 1984. Copyright © 1984 Charles Garfield. Reprinted by permission.

recall a string of 6 consonants followed by a string of 5 spatial positions, they correctly recalled an average of 8.3 items. The improvement in recall was not due to the possibility that spatial positions were easier to recall than consonants because previous research had shown that recalling spatial positions was actually more difficult. Rather, the findings were caused by the relative lack of interference between the visual and verbal codes. These results, along with those obtained by Brooks and many other psychologists, show that using two different modalities can reduce interference and improve performance.

This research illustrates how visual images can be used to improve performance on many cognitive tasks, including preserving the spatial relations among different parts of a picture, lowering reaction times for processing spatial information, and reducing interference between visual and verbal codes. We will now look at an additional source of evidence about the use of visual imagery.

Evidence from Neuropsychology

More recently, evidence from neuropsychology is increasingly playing an important role in informing us about which tasks involve visual imagery. Farah (1988) was one of the first psychologists to gather together the evidence that linked visual imagery with visual perception. She argued that supporting evidence from neuropsychology could be grouped into two broad categories: (1) results showing that visual imagery uses the same brain areas as vision and (2) results showing that selective damage to the brain impairs visual imagery in the same manner that it impairs vision.

Evidence that visual perception and visual imagery use the same areas of the brain comes from two different methods of measuring brain activity, based on either cerebral blood flow or electrophysiological activity. **Cerebral blood flow** provides a precise measure of brain activity, with increased blood flow indicating increased activity in that part of the brain. **Event-related potentials** measure electrical activity of the brain that is synchronized with (and presumably related to) the processing of a stimulus. Both measures indicate that many tasks in which we would expect visual imagery to be involved show increased activity in that part of the brain used for visual perception—the occipital lobes, which contain the primary and secondary visual cortex (Farah, 1988).

Roland and Friberg (1985) measured cerebral blood flow while subjects performed one of three cognitive tasks: mental arithmetic, memory scanning of a musical jingle, or visually imaging a walk through one's neighborhood. They found increased activity in the visual cortex for the visual imagery task, but not for the mental arithmetic or the memory scanning task. A similar finding occurred for a simpler imagery task (Goldenberg, Podreka, Steiner, & Willmes, 1987). Different groups of subjects listened to lists of concrete words under instructions to try to learn the words either by simply listening to them or by forming visual images to represent them. Recall was better for the imagery group, as would be expected from Paivio's dual-coding theory, and there was more blood flow to the occipital lobes for the imagery group. There were also differences in the distribution of event-related brain potentials for concrete and abstract words, which is consistent with the dual-coding theory (Kounios & Holcomb, 1994).

Cerebral blood flow
Measurement of blood flow to localize where cognitive operations occur in the brain

Event-related potentials
Recording brain waves to measure the timing of cognitive operations

Besides studying brain activation in normal people, psychologists have learned much about visual images by studying the behavior of people who have suffered brain damage (Farah, 1988). As one example, we have learned from patients with brain damage that there is a dissociation between knowing what an object is and knowing where the object is located. Damage to one part of the visual cortex results in an impairment of the ability to recognize visual stimuli, whereas damage to another part of the visual cortex results in an impairment of the ability to indicate the spatial location of visual stimuli. These preserved and impaired aspects of vision are similarly preserved and impaired in visual imagery (Levine, Warach, & Farah, 1985). A patient with object identification difficulties was unable to draw or describe the appearance of familiar objects from memory, despite being able to draw and describe in great detail the relative locations of landmarks in his neighborhood, cities in the United States, and furniture in his hospital room. A patient with object localization difficulties was unable to use his memory to perform well on the spatial localization tasks, but was able to provide detailed descriptions of the appearance of a variety of objects.

Another very striking example of the parallel loss in visual perception and visual imagery comes from the study of **visual neglect**. Patients with right-parietal-lobe damage often fail to perceive stimuli presented in the left half of the visual field and they have the same problem when viewing visual images. Two patients suffering from visual neglect were asked to imagine viewing a famous square in Milan, Italy, from a particular vantage point and to describe the view. Both patients failed to describe the landmarks that would have fallen on the left side of the scene. They were then asked to imagine the scene from a vantage point that was on the opposite side of the square. The left- and right-half of the visual scene was therefore reversed to see if the patients would now see landmarks they did not see in their previous imaging. And, indeed, the patients' descriptions now included landmarks that they had previously omitted and failed to include landmarks that they had previously described.

The major consequence of the neurological studies of imagery is that the results of these studies are having an increasing impact on the construction of cognitive models. This is particularly true for Kosslyn, a leader in the empirical and theoretical study of imagery. Kosslyn's (1991) goal was to explain how each of a number of different subsystems interacted to determine performance across various imagery tasks. His key assumption was that visual mental imagery shares processing subsystems with visual perception. For example, he proposed that an image is generated and then maintained in a **visual buffer** by retrieving information from LTM. Because the visual buffer typically contains more information

Visual neglect Failure to respond to visual simulation on the side of the visual field that is opposite a brain lesion

Visual buffer A component of Kosslyn's model in which a generated visual image is maintained in STM

Attention window
The attended part of
the visual buffer in
Kosslyn's model

than can be processed, the **attention window** selects a region within the visual buffer for further detailed processing. That is, participants in Kosslyn, Ball, and Reiser's (1978) experiment could maintain the image of an island in the visual buffer and use the attention window to focus on a particular object on the island. The proposed operation of these, and other, subsystems is closely linked to both behavioral and neurological findings in Kosslyn's (1991) model.

LIMITATIONS OF IMAGES

The emphasis throughout this chapter has been on the usefulness of visual images for learning and for performing many spatial reasoning tasks. Perhaps you find this surprising. If you are like me, you may feel that you cannot create very vivid images and perhaps even question whether you use any images at all. Let me give you a chance to form an image by asking: "Does the Star of David contain a parallelogram (a four-sided figure whose opposite sides are parallel)?" Try to form an image of the Star of David and examine it to answer the question. Many people have difficulty using images to identify the parts of a pattern, even after they have just seen the pattern (Reed & Johnsen, 1975). Since we have seen many results that show the usefulness of images, it is only fair to discuss a few limitations of images before leaving the topic.

Memory for Details

Our discussion so far has focused on the successful use of visual images. We learned that memory for pictures is better than memory for words and memory for concrete words is better than memory for abstract words. Both of these findings are related to the ease with which an image can be created to represent a concrete word or picture. We also saw how instructions to form interactive images facilitated the learning of people's names, vocabulary words, and lists of items. If images can do all this, in what ways are they limited?

One answer is that the tests that showed good memory for visual material were not very challenging. For example, the experiments by Shepard (1967) and Standing (1973) used a recognition memory test in which a person decided which one of two pictures had occurred in the experiment. Although the results of these studies suggest that visual memory contains an abundance of information, in reality the results do not allow us to conclude how much information is stored. All we know is that people retained enough information to distinguish the "old" picture from the new one.

Nickerson and Adams (1979) investigated how completely and accurately people remember visual details by asking them to recognize a very common object, a U.S. penny. Figure 7.14 shows 15 drawings of a penny, only one of which is correct. If you can identify the correct choice, you did better than the majority of subjects in the experiment, who selected incorrectly. Although we have seen a penny many times, most of us have never learned its details, probably because they are not very useful in everyday life. Attributes such as color and size allow us to distinguish quickly between a penny and other coins, making the learning of additional details unnecessary. If a new coin is introduced (such as the Susan B. Anthony dollar) that requires more attention to details to distinguish it from another coin, there is considerable resistance to its acceptance.

Evidence from imagery studies shows that people are quite selective in which details they maintain in their images. Let's begin with another demonstration of your ability to manipulate a visual image. Form a visual image of the animal in Figure 7.15a. Now examine your image, without looking at the drawing in the book, and see if you can reinterpret the figure to perceive it as a different animal. Were you successful? If not, try to

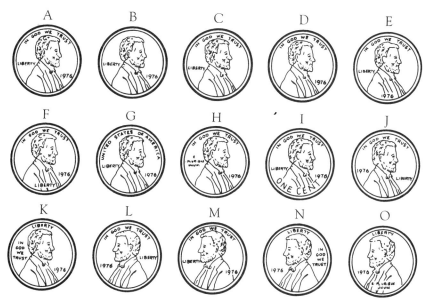

Figure 7.14   *Fifteen drawings of a penny that were used in a recognition memory test.*

From "Long-Term Memory for a Common Object," by R. S. Nickerson and M. J. Adams, 1979, *Cognitive Psychology, 11*, 287–307. Copyright © 1979 by Academic Press, Inc. Reprinted by permission.

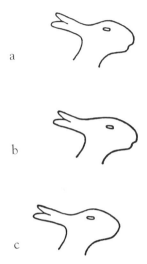

Figure 7.15 *(a) Duck/rabbit ambiguous figure. (b) Modification of the duck's bill. (c) Modification of the rabbit's nose.*

From "What an Image Depicts on What an Image Means," by D. Chambers and D. Reisberg, 1992, *Cognitive Psychology, 24,* 145–174. Copyright © 1992 by Academic Press, Inc. Reprinted by permission.

reinterpret the figure in the book. If your experience was similar to the students studied by Chambers and Reisberg (1985), you should have found it much easier to reinterpret the drawing in the book than to reinterpret your image of the drawing. In fact, in one of their studies they found that none of the 15 students in the experiment could reinterpret their image of the figure but all 15 could reinterpret a drawing of the figure.

In a subsequent study Chambers and Reisberg (1992) examined why people had difficulty reinterpreting their image. They hypothesized that people maintain only the more important aspects of the image; in this case, the face of the animal (that is, the front side of the head). People who perceive the pattern in Figure 7.15a as a duck should therefore have a detailed image of the left side of the pattern and people who perceive the pattern as a rabbit should have a detailed image of the right side of the pattern. The results from a recognition memory test confirmed this hypothesis. In one test people were asked to indicate whether they were shown pattern 7.15a (the correct choice) or pattern 7.15b, which changed the front part (the bill) of the duck's face. People who had perceived the pattern as a duck did significantly better than chance on this test, but people who had perceived the pattern as a rabbit performed at chance level. The opposite results occurred when the participants had to choose between the original pattern and a pattern that modified the front part (the nose) of the rabbit's face, shown in Figure 7.15c. People who had perceived the pattern as a duck now performed at a chance level, while people who had perceived the pattern as a rabbit performed significantly better than chance. People therefore have difficulty reinterpreting the pattern because they are missing those details that are important for the new interpretation.

The fact that we lose some of the details in our images is partly the result of our failing to maintain a detailed image once we have a verbal code. People are more successful in reinterpreting an image of the duck/rabbit ambiguous figure if they are discouraged from forming a verbal code during the initial encoding of the figure. Brandimonte and Gerbino (1993) had one group of subjects perform an articulatory suppression task (repeatedly say la-la-la) while viewing the ambiguous figure. These subjects were more successful in later reversing their image of the pattern than those subjects who did not have to perform an articulatory suppression task as they viewed the figure. The authors concluded that people are better at maintaining details in an image when forced to rely solely on the image.

Fortunately, images can be useful in many tasks even when we do not have a detailed memory of an object. For instance, the retention of details is usually unnecessary when we use images to remember words. Your image of a penny would not have to be detailed or accurate to help you remember the word *penny*; it would only have to be detailed enough to allow you to recall the correct word when you retrieved your image. Experimental results have shown that people who were good at recalling the names of pictures they had seen 2 weeks earlier did not have more detailed images than people who could not recall as many names (Bahrick & Boucher, 1968). For example, people who could recall that they had seen a cup did not necessarily remember many details of the cup in a recognition test similar to the one illustrated by Figure 7.14. The evidence suggested that people were using visual images to aid their recall, but it was necessary to remember only enough details about an object to recall its name. Visual images can therefore be incomplete if the task does not require memory for details.

Studies showing the limitations of visual images provide both good news and bad news. The bad news is that using visual images is not a universal solution for improving memory performance. The good news is that, even if people believe they have poor images, their images may still be sufficient for performing the many tasks that do not require great detail.

Reality Monitoring

If our images of objects or events were as accurate and detailed as the actual events, then our ability to distinguish between actual and imagined events would be impaired. People can remember information from two basic sources: external sources, derived from perception, and internal sources, derived from imagination or thought. The ability to distinguish between external and internal sources has been called **reality monitoring** by Johnson and Raye (1981).

Reality monitoring
Discriminating between actual and imagined events

In order to study how well people can distinguish between actual and imagined events, Johnson, Raye, Wang, and Taylor (1979) showed subjects pictures of common objects. Subjects saw the picture of each object either two, five, or eight times and the name of each object either two, five, or eight times. They were instructed to generate an image of an object each time its name occurred. At the end of the session they received an unexpected test in which they had to estimate how often they had seen each of the pictures.

If people are very good at discriminating between seeing and imagining pictures, then their estimates of seeing should not be influenced by the number of times they imagined each picture. Note that, although the ability to form accurate images is an asset for performing most spatial tasks, good imagery would be a liability for this particular discrimination task. Because people with good imagery might find it hard to discriminate between what they imagined and what they saw, the experimenters also gave subjects an imagery test to measure their imagery ability.

Figure 7.16 shows the results. The left panel contains the average estimates of the good imagers, and the right panel contains the average estimates of the poor imagers. The labels 8, 5, and 2 on the lines that show the estimates refer to the number of times the pictures had been shown. Notice that subjects were quite good at estimating how many times they had seen each picture, even when they had to distinguish between seeing and imagining the pictures. But the image trials did influence their judgments—the estimates of presentation frequency increased as the number of image trials increased. A comparison of the left and right panels of Figure 7.16 reveals that the number of image trials had a greater effect on the good imagers than on the poor imagers. As expected, people with good imagery distinguished less accurately between seeing and imagining.

Johnson and her colleagues' findings show that, although the number of image trials did influence subjects' judgments of presentation frequency, their judgments were nonetheless fairly accurate. In general, people are able to remember the origin of information (internal versus external) remarkably well. What kind of cues help us make this distinction?

Johnson and Raye (1981) have proposed that several kinds of cues are helpful. First, there is *sensory information*. Perceptual events have

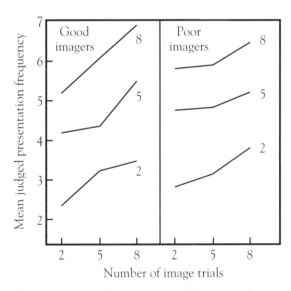

Figure 7.16 *Judged presentation frequency of pictures as a function of the number of image trials. The number next to each line indicates whether a picture was presented two, five, or eight times.*

From "Fact and Fantasy: The Roles of Accuracy and Variability in Confusing Imaginations with Perceptual Experience," by M. K. Johnson, C. L. Raye, A. Y. Wang, and T. T. Taylor, 1979, *Journal of Experimental Psychology: Human Learning and Memory*, 5, 229–240. Copyright © 1979 by the American Psychological Association. Reprinted by permission.

more spatial detail than imagined events, although the amount of sensory information varies among individuals, as shown by the difference between good and poor imagers. Second, there is *contextual information*. Perceptual events occur in an external context that contains other information. We have seen in previous chapters that contextual information is important in recalling material, and it is also important in helping us distinguish whether an event was internally or externally generated.

A third cue for making this distinction is memory for the *cognitive operations* that are required to generate the image. If we can generate an image automatically without much conscious awareness, we will have poor memory of the cognitive operations used to generate the image. Dreams that occur during sleep are of this type. They often seem very real because we are not aware of generating them. In contrast, daydreams seem much less real because they are more influenced by our conscious control.

Breakdown of Reality Monitoring

Although people are normally fairly good at reality monitoring, there are cases where judging between reality and imagination breaks down. One aspect that has attracted much recent attention concerns whether a traumatic event, such as childhood sexual abuse, actually occurred or was imagined, perhaps because a therapist or other authoritative person suggested that it occurred (see Box 7.2). The importance of this topic resulted in an entire issue of the journal *Applied Cognitive Psychology* being devoted to articles discussing it.

The lead article set the stage with these opening comments:

> There is no doubt that many children are sexually abused, and that this is a tragedy. Furthermore, survivors of childhood sexual abuse often suffer long-lasting harm, and may be helped by competent therapists. Although cognitive researchers have differing views about the mechanisms underly-

**BOX
7.2**

Miscoding is seen as the root of false memories

DANIEL GOLEMAN

In a scientific nod to the frailty of memory, neurologists and cognitive scientists are coming to consensus on the mental mechanisms that can foster false memories.

The leading candidate is "source amnesia," the inability to recall the origin of the memory of a given event. Once the source of a memory is forgotten, scientists say, people can confuse an event that was only imagined or suggested with a true one. The result is a memory that though it fades, carries the feeling of authenticity.

May was an epic month for false memory—three new books were published that investigated the phenomenon and its mirror opposite, repressed memory.

In mid-May, a Napa, California, court awarded $500,000 to the father of a woman who had accused him of sexual abuse after supposedly recovering memories of childhood incest during therapy.

The plaintiff, Gary Ramon, had asked for $8 million in damages against his daughter's therapists and the medical center where they worked.

Earlier in the month new scientific agreement on the most likely neurological and cognitive bases of false memory emerged during a conference on the issue at Harvard Medical School.

Part of the fragility of memory is due to the way the mind encodes a memory, distributing aspects of the experience over far-flung parts of the brain, various researchers said at the meeting . . .

This means the source of a memory may fade even as the rest of memory can be retrieved, said Stephen Ceci, a psychologist at Cornell University . . .

Part of the new scientific evidence for the vulnerability of memory to suggestion comes from studies in which false memories are implanted through experimental manipulations.

ing loss of memory (e.g., repression, dissociation, or normal forgetting; see
Loftus, 1993; Singer, 1990), all would agree that it is possible that some
adult survivors of childhood abuse would not remember the abusive events,
and that memories might be recovered given appropriate cues. Thus we
accept that some clients may recover accurate memories of childhood
sexual abuse during careful, non-leading, non-suggestive therapies. But
there is no doubt in our minds that extensive use of techniques such as
hypnosis, dream interpretation, and guided imagery (which are advocated
in some self-help books and by some clinical psychologists, psychiatrists,
clinical social workers, therapists, and counselors) can create compelling
illusory memories of childhood sexual abuse among people who were not
abused. This too is a tragedy. (Lindsay & Read, 1994, pp. 281–282)

Lindsay and Read (1994) indicate that memory research has identified a number of factors that increase the possibility of creating false

---

Many of these studies have involved young children, who are particularly susceptible to false memories. At the Harvard meeting, Ceci reported a series of recent
experiments, none of which have been published, showing the surprising ease with
which children can become convinced that something they only imagined or was
suggested to them really happened.

In an earlier study involving 96 preschool children reported last year, Ceci
showed that with repeated questioning about events that had never occurred, many
children gradually came to believe that the events happened. The false memories
were so elaborate and detailed that psychologists who specialize in interviewing
children about abuse were unable to determine which memories were true, Ceci
said.

At the Harvard meeting, Ceci reported on five more studies with a total of 574
preschool children, all of which confirm his earlier results. After 10 weeks, 58 percent of the children in those studies had made up a false account for at least one fictitious event repeatedly suggested to them, and a quarter of them had concocted
false stories for most of the phony events. Three of the studies are scheduled for publication next year, one in *The Journal of Child Development*.

"Each time you encourage a person to create a mental image, it becomes familiar," said Ceci. "Finally they see the imagined image as an actual memory, with
same feel of authenticity. In our studies there are about a quarter of the children we
can't talk out of the fact the memory we implanted was real, even though we explain their parents helped us concoct the false memory."

SOURCE: From "Miscoding Is Seen As the Root of False Memories," by Daniel Goleman, appearing in
The New York Times, May 31, 1994. Copyright © 1994 by The New York Times Company.
Reprinted by permission.

memories. These include long delays between the event and the attempt to remember, repeated suggestions that the event occurred, the perceived authority of the source of the suggestions, the perceived plausibility of the suggestions, mental rehearsal of the imagined event, and the use of hypnosis or guided imagery. Because some of these factors are necessarily part of therapy, practitioners need to be particularly concerned about the use of techniques that may increase the risk of creating illusory memories.

Creating illusory memories can be especially damaging because there are no guaranteed techniques that experts can use to discriminate between real and false memories. Lindsay and Read argue that the overriding theme of their literature review is that illusory memories can look, feel, and sound like real memories and include the strong affect that accompanies real memories of abuse. The experience of coming to believe that abusive events occurred would be tremendously traumatic regardless of whether the remembered event actually occurred.

Hallucinations
Imagined events or images believed to be real

Another example of the breakdown in reality monitoring is the **hallucinations** of psychiatric patients. Available data suggest that hallucinations result from an impairment of skills in discrimination between real and imaginary events (Bentall, 1990). The analysis of reality discrimination of normal people should therefore provide a valuable source of information for psychopathologists interested in hallucinations. But it is important to recognize that hallucinators do not hallucinate random events. The content of the hallucinations is presumably related to the personalities and to the stresses of the patients. Different kinds of hallucinations almost certainly reflect different causes of defective reality discrimination, and the challenge is to find which type of reality discrimination errors are linked to the different kinds of hallucinatory experiences (Bentall, 1990). Continuation of the theoretical and empirical work reported by Johnson and Raye should therefore provide a bridge between clinical and cognitive psychology in their study of imagery.

SUMMARY

The usefulness of visual images in learning is supported by research showing that people usually remember pictures better than concrete words and concrete words better than abstract ones. These results correspond to the fact that images are easiest to form from pictures and hardest to form from abstract words. Learning pairs of items is facilitated by forming an interactive image that combines the members of the pair. For example, recall of advertisements was best when people saw an illustration that combined a picture of the brand name with a picture of the product. The dual-coding theory explains the usefulness of visual imagery in recall by proposing that a visual image provides an extra memory code that is independent of the verbal code. A person therefore has two chances to recall the item rather than only one.

The knowledge that visual imagery improves memory has existed for centuries and has resulted in the use of imagery in many mnemonic strategies. A study that compared four strategies—verbal rehearsal, sentence reading, sentence generation, and imagery—found that people who used the imagery strategy recalled the most words. However, the two sentence-elaboration strategies produced much better recall than simple rehearsal, suggesting that the former strategies could facilitate learning abstract words. Visual images can also be used to learn people's names and a foreign vocabulary, although it is often necessary to translate a name or foreign word into a similar-sounding concrete keyword first. An interactive image is then formed to link the keyword with a face or with the English translation of the foreign word. The method of loci is a mnemonic strategy that can be used to learn a sequence of items, such as the major topics in a speech. A person selects a familiar physical structure, such as a building, and produces an interactive image linking a word or topic with each location in the building. The order of the topics is preserved by locating the topics in the order in which one would encounter them while walking through the building. Experiments evaluating the effectiveness of mnemonic strategies have usually found a dramatic improvement in performance.

A variety of evidence suggests that visual images are important to our ability to perform many spatial reasoning tasks. Visual images preserve the spatial relations among the objects of a scene or the features of a pattern. The time it takes to mentally scan between two objects in an image is therefore a function of the distance between them. Visual images also make it possible to compare all the features of two patterns simultaneously when we try to match a visual pattern with an image of another pattern. In contrast, features described verbally must be compared one at a time because of the sequential nature of language. When we are comparing two patterns that are in different orientations, a visual image makes it possible to rotate one of them mentally until the two patterns have the same orientation. The distinction between visual and verbal codes is also suggested by selective interference between the two codes. In addition, neurological studies provide evidence for when people use imagery. Electrophysiological and blood-flow measures of brain activity show that the same areas of the brain are used in visual perception and visual imagery. Studies of brain-damaged patients with visual deficits reveal that the same deficits occur during imagery tasks.

Although visual images are often helpful in many learning and spatial reasoning tasks, the images of most people seem to be limited in clarity and detail. An experiment that asked people to select the correct drawing of a penny from a set of similar alternatives found that most people made the wrong choice. The lack of memory for details is caused by focusing on only the most important details, but encouraging people to rely on images increases their ability to use them. Fortunately, detailed images are not always necessary. In fact, for images used to represent words in a memory task, it is only necessary to remember enough about the image to recall the word. An advantage of the lack of detailed sensory information in images is that it helps us distinguish between perceived and imagined events (reality monitoring). Research on reality monitoring should contribute to our understanding of hallucinations and illusory memories created through the suggestions of an authority figure.

STUDY QUESTIONS

1. The beginning quotation talks about the problem of operationalizing the construct of the image. Is the image construct any more difficult to observe directly than any other supposed mental event? Explain your answer.
2. What are the operations or processes that have been used to study images?
3. Critics pointed out that Kosslyn's mental scanning results could be explained by demand characteristics. Do you think Reed et al. succeeded in eliminating this possibility? How?
4. Be sure you know what parallel processing means. Why would it confer an advantage in matching tasks? In what sensory modalities besides vision is parallel processing possible?
5. Have you ever used mental rehearsal for athletic or other physical activities, or heard others say they were using it? When can it hinder rather than help performance? (*Hint:* why were skiers told to sing, hum, or whistle a tune on their runs?)
6. How does Paivio explain the fact that using more than one code/modality usually improves learning? What is the best way to associate words and images? Words and words?
7. If formal mnemonic strategies produce such wonderful results why don't more people use them more of the time? Do you use any of them at all?
8. What makes a keyword "good"? Take three words in a language you have studied, or some unfamiliar technical terms, and generate a list of good keywords for each. Write each word, keyword, and English translation.

9. Has modern cognitive psychology advanced knowledge beyond the first century B.C. in regard to the method of loci? How good was each specific piece of advice of the author of *Ad Herennium*, in light of pertinent modern research?
10. Is there no limit to the usefulness of images to represent things in memory?

KEY TERMS

The page number in parentheses refers to where the term is discussed in the chapter.

association value (181)
attention window (206)
bizarre images (186)
cerebral blood flow (204)
concrete/abstract dimension (181)
dual-coding theory (183)
event-related potentials (204)
hallucinations (214)
imagery potential (181)
interactive illustration (179)
keyword (186)
keyword method (186)
method of loci (188)

mnemonic techniques (184)
noninteractive illustration (179)
parallel representation (194)
propositional theory (191)
reality monitoring (210)
relational information (184)
sequential representation (194)
serial learning (188)
spatial knowledge (176)
verbal knowledge (176)
visual buffer (205)
visual neglect (205)
visual scanning (192)

RECOMMENDED READING

Paivio (1971) discusses the experimental work during the 1960s that helped restore imagery as a major topic in experimental psychology. Kosslyn (1983) provides a very readable introduction to the research on creating and using images. The work edited by Sheikh (1983) contains chapters on a wide variety of topics, including the clinical implications of imagery. Individual differences in the use of imagery have been studied by MacLeod, Hunt, and Mathews (1978). Articles by J. R. Anderson (1978), Finke (1985), Kosslyn (1981), Pylyshyn (1981), and Shepard and Podgorny (1978) discuss the representation of information in images and the relation between imagery and perception. Recent work has linked this research to the specialization of functions in the left or right hemispheres of the brain (Kosslyn, 1987, 1991; Hellige, 1990). Research by Posner, Boies, Eichelman, and Taylor (1969) provided evidence on the maintenance of visual codes in STM. However, their conclusion that visual codes are quickly replaced by verbal codes has been challenged by

Kroll and Parks (1978). Psychologists continue to study the practical implications of imagery, including its use as a mnemonic (Bellezza, 1987; McCarty, 1980; Pressley, Levin, Hall, Miller, & Berry, 1980) and its role in the acquisition of spatial knowledge (Thorndyke & Stasz, 1980) and problem solving (Hegarty, 1992). In addition, research continues on issues related to reality monitoring (R. E. Anderson, 1984; Bentall, 1990; Johnson, Hashtroudi, & Lindsay, 1993).

Categorization

We begin with what seems to be a paradox. The world of experience of any normal man is composed of a tremendous array of discriminably different objects, events, people, impressions. But were we to utilize fully our capacity for registering the differences in things and to respond to each event encountered as unique, we would soon be overwhelmed by the complexity of our environment. The resolution of this seeming paradox—the existence of discrimination capacities which, if fully used, would make us slaves to the particular—is achieved by man's capacity to categorize. To categorize is to render discriminably different things equivalent, to group the objects and events around us into classes, and to respond to them in terms of their class membership rather than their uniqueness.*

J. S. BRUNER, J. J. GOODNOW, AND G. A. AUSTIN (1956)

*T*HIS CHAPTER AND the next discuss ways in which people organize knowledge. One way to organize knowledge is to form categories. Categories consist of objects or events that we have grouped together because we feel they are somehow related. The ability to categorize enables us to interact with our environment without becoming overwhelmed by its complexity. Bruner, Goodnow, and Austin, in their influential book, *A Study of Thinking* (1956), listed five benefits of forming categories.

1. Categorizing objects "reduces the complexity of the environment." Scientists have estimated that there are more than 7 million discriminable colors. If we responded to all of these as unique, we could spend our entire lifetime just trying to learn the names of colors. When we classify discriminably different objects as being equivalent, we respond to them in terms of their class membership rather than as unique items.

2. Categorizing is "the means by which objects of the world are identified." We usually feel that we have recognized a pattern when we can classify it into a familiar category such as *dog, chair,* or the letter A.

3. The third achievement is a consequence of the first two—the establishment of categories "reduces the need for constant learning." We do not have to be taught about novel objects if we can classify them; we can use our knowledge of items in the category to respond to the novel object.

4. Categorizing allows us to "decide what constitutes an appropriate action." A person who eats wild mushrooms must be able to distinguish between poisonous and nonpoisonous varieties. Eating a poisonous variety is clearly not an appropriate action.

5. Categorizing "enables us to order and relate classes of objects and events." Although classification is by itself a useful way to organize knowledge, classes can be further organized into subordinate and superordinate relations. The category *chair,* for example, has *high chair* as a subordinate class and *furniture* as a superordinate class. The three categories form a hierarchy in which *furniture* contains *chair* as a member and *chair* contains *high chair* as a member.

Psychologists have used several experimental procedures to study how people make classifications. The first section of this chapter describes a procedure called **concept identification**. The categories in concept identification tasks typically contain geometric patterns that vary along several obvious dimensions—for example, shape, size, and color. The experimenter selects a rule to define the concept, and the task requires discovering the rule through learning which patterns are examples of the concept. The rule might be relatively simple, such as "All red pat-

Concept identification
A task that requires deciding whether an item is an example of a concept, where concepts are typically defined by logical rules

terns are examples," or it might be more complex, such as "Either red patterns or small patterns are examples."

One limitation of this approach is that many categories cannot be distinguished on the basis of a simple rule. We can usually distinguish a dog from a cat, but it is questionable whether we use a simple rule to make this distinction. The second section discusses some characteristics of natural, or real-world, categories and emphasizes how we use these characteristics to organize knowledge. In order to recognize objects and reduce the need for constant learning, we have to be able to classify novel objects into a familiar category. The final section discusses how people do this.

CONCEPT IDENTIFICATION
Discovering Logical Rules

The most basic distinction between two categories occurs when they can be distinguished by the values of a single dimension. For example, a rule for sorting objects could state that large objects belong to one category and small objects belong to another category. Experimenters do not always use such simple concepts, however, and they have often studied how people learn concepts defined by **logical rules** typically requiring two dimensions, such as shape and color. Figure 8.1 shows how four logical rules divide stimuli into two categories. Note that each dimension has three attributes—*red* (cross-hatched), *black*, and *white* for color; and *square*, *triangle*, and *circle* for shape. The attributes *red* and *square* specify the concept in the example.

The rule that is usually the easiest to learn is the **conjunctive rule**. Since the conjunctive rule uses the logical relation *and*, the concept in this case is *red and square*. A stimulus is a member of the category only if both attributes are present. The red square is the only stimulus that satisfies this criterion.

The **disjunctive rule** uses the logical relation *or*. A stimulus is an example of the concept if it is red or if it is a square. The three red stimuli and the three squares are now all examples of this concept.

The **conditional rule** makes use of the *if, then* relation—for example, if the stimulus is red, then it must be a square to be an example. One characteristic of the conditional rule that may seem strange is that all stimuli that are not red are positive examples. An analog would be if you worked in a fancy restaurant and had to enforce the rule that, if a person is a man, he must wear a tie. All people who were not men would be admitted under this restriction.

Logical rules Rules based on logical relations, such as conjunctive, disjunctive, conditional, and biconditional rules

Conjunctive rule A rule that uses the logical relation *and* to relate stimulus attributes, such as *small and square*

Disjunctive rule A rule that uses the logical relation *or* to relate stimulus attributes, such as *small or square*

Conditional rule A rule that uses the logical relation *if, then* to relate stimulus attributes, such as *if small, then square*

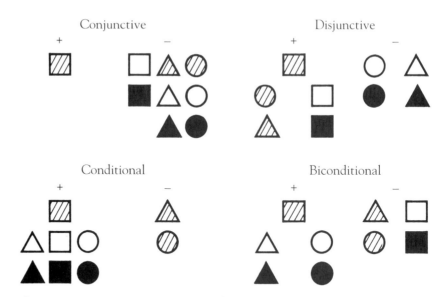

Figure 8.1   *Positive and negative examples for four logical rules—conjunctive, disjunctive, conditional, and biconditional. The relevant attributes are red and square.*
From "Knowing and Using Concepts," by L. E. Bourne, Jr., 1970, *Psychological Review, 77*, 546–556. Copyright © 1970 by the American Psychological Association. Reprinted by permission.

Biconditional rule
A rule that uses the logical relation *if, then* to relate stimulus attributes in both orders, such as (1) *if small, then square* and (2) *if square, then small*

The **biconditional rule** is so called because the conditional rule applies in both directions. The biconditional rule includes the previous rule—if a stimulus is red, then it must be a square to be an example. But it also applies in the reverse direction—if a stimulus is a square, then it must be red. You should notice in Figure 8.1 that the biconditional rule excludes two squares from the positive category that were not excluded by the conditional rule. Since the biconditional rule applies in both directions, a square is not an example of the category unless it is red. The greater exclusiveness of the biconditional rule is also illustrated by the previous analog. In addition to excluding men who were not wearing ties, the biconditional rule would exclude women who were wearing ties. The reverse of the *if man, then tie* rule is *if wearing a tie, then man*.

As you can imagine, learning the correct conceptual rule can be difficult. One way to simplify the task would be to tell subjects the relevant attributes. This task is called **rule learning** because people have to learn only the correct logical rule when they are told the relevant attributes (Haygood & Bourne, 1965).

Rule learning   A concept identification task in which people are told the relevant attributes (such as *small, square*) but have to discover the logical rule

Bourne (1970) tested the comparative difficulty of the four rules by designing an experiment in which subjects solved a series of nine successive rule-learning problems. The stimuli varied on four dimensions—color, shape, number, and size—but the experimenter always specified the two relevant attributes before each problem. Each problem required that a person learn to classify the stimuli as either positive or negative examples of the concept. Subjects received one stimulus at a time, made their classification, and were told whether they were correct. They were considered to have solved a problem when they could state the rule or make a certain number of correct responses in a row.

Figure 8.2 shows the results. There are large initial differences in the difficulty of the four rules. The conditional rule requires more than twice as many trials to learn on the first problem as the conjunctive and disjunctive rules, and the biconditional rule requires more than three times as many trials to learn. However, with practice people become very good at applying the biconditional and conditional rules and eventually perform as well on these problems as on the conjunctive and disjunctive

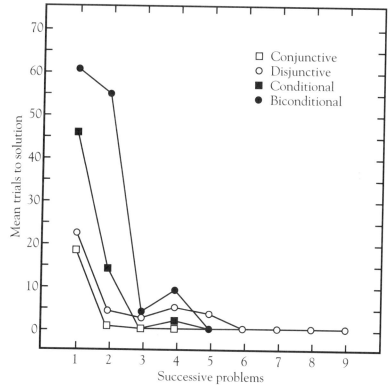

Figure 8.2   *Average number of trials to solution for four logical rules—conjunctive, disjunctive, conditional, biconditional.*

From "Knowing and Using Concepts," by L. E. Bourne, Jr., 1970, *Psychological Review, 77*, 546–556. Copyright © 1970 by the American Psychological Association. Reprinted by permission.

problems. After solving six problems using the same rule, all subjects solved the remaining problems without errors, no matter how difficult the rule was at the outset.

Discovering Relevant Attributes

In the rule-learning problems, the experimenter told the subjects what the two relevant attributes were but did not tell them the appropriate rule. A variation of the procedure—called **attribute learning**—is to tell people the rule and let them discover the appropriate attributes (Haygood & Bourne, 1965). The problem is solved when people can consistently identify stimuli as either positive or negative instances of the concept.

Studies of attribute learning generally reveal that efficiency in identifying the relevant attributes depends on which rule specifies the concept. The order of difficulty of the four rules is the same as in rule-learning tasks: Attribute problems based on the conjunctive rule are the easiest, followed by the disjunctive rule, the conditional rule, and the biconditional rule (Bourne, Ekstrand, Lovallo, Kellogg, Hiew, & Yaroush, 1976).

Why should the choice of rule influence the difficulty of the task when participants are told the rule before each problem? Bourne and his colleagues proposed a **frequency theory** to account for these results. The frequency theory can apply to stimuli in both positive and negative categories, but the results indicate that the positive category is more important (Bourne et al., 1976). Let's return to the categories shown in Figure 8.1 to see how the frequency theory works when applied to stimuli in the positive category.

It is easy to identify the relevant attributes for a conjunctive rule because irrelevant attributes (*black* and *white* or *circle* and *triangle*) never appear in the positive category. The relevant attributes therefore appear 100% of the time because all positive stimuli are red and square. It is not quite so easy for the disjunctive rule. Figure 8.1 shows that three of the five positive stimuli are red and three of the five positive stimuli are square. The relevant attributes therefore appear 60% of the time in the positive category. For the conditional rule, only one of the seven positive stimuli is red, and three of the seven are square. The two relevant attributes therefore occur 29% of the time (the average of 1/7 and 3/7). The lowest percentage occurs for the biconditional rule. Only one of the five positive stimuli is red, and only one is square. The two relevant attributes therefore occur only 20% of the time.

You should notice that the ordering of these percents corresponds to the ordering of the difficulty of attribute identification tasks. The results suggest that people form frequency differences among the values of each dimension. When the relevant values (such as *red* and *square*) occur fre-

---

Attribute learning
A concept identification task in which people are told the logical rule (such as conjunctive) but have to discover the relevant attributes

Frequency theory
A theory that explains the ease of attribute learning by the relative frequency with which the attributes appear in positive and negative examples of the concept

quently in the positive category, it is fairly easy to identify these values as relevant. When the relevant values seldom occur in the positive category, it is much harder to identify them as relevant. The attribute frequency theory is consistent with several other findings in the concept identification literature. We will return to one of these findings later in the chapter when we discuss a feature frequency theory of categorization.

Critique of the Concept Identification Paradigm

Not all cognitive psychologists are satisfied with the concept identification task; some have criticized it as highly artificial and unrelated to the cognitive tasks we usually encounter in the real world. This criticism does not mean that we are unable to draw any analogy between the skills needed in concept identification tasks and skills needed in other tasks. For example, to learn the correct rule in a concept identification task, subjects must evaluate a number of hypotheses. Our inability to evaluate a large number of hypotheses simultaneously is found not only in concept identification tasks (Levine, 1966) but also in real-world tasks such as medical diagnosis (Elstein, Shulman, & Sprafka, 1978). Yet real-world tasks are often different enough from concept identification tasks that we must be very careful in making generalizations.

The predominant criticism of the concept identification paradigm is that real-world categories are unlike the categories studied in the laboratory. This is not a new argument. The philosopher Wittgenstein (1953) argued that category members do not have to share identical attributes. Rather, they may have a family resemblance in which category members share some attributes with other members but there are no or few attributes that are common to all members of the category.

Bruner, Goodnow, and Austin (1956) also recognized that most real-world categories cannot be distinguished by logical rules that apply to all members of the category. One of the chapters in their book discussed categorizing with probabilistic cues in which the values of a dimension did not uniquely specify a category. For example, 67% of the airplanes in one category may have a straight tail, and 67% of the planes in another category may have a curved tail. The tail is a probabilistic cue because it tells us only the most likely category of a plane, not its definite category.

Although Bruner, Goodnow, and Austin reported some experiments on categorizing with probabilistic cues, their work is remembered mainly for research using the standard concept identification paradigm. A dramatic change in how psychologists viewed real-world categories had to wait until the 1970s, when Rosch and her students at the University of California, Berkeley, began to study the characteristics of natural categories (Rosch, 1973). One of the characteristics of concept identification tasks that bothered Rosch is that all members of the concept are equally good members. Consider the five examples in Figure 8.1 that satisfy the disjunctive rule *red or square*. All of the five positive instances are equally good members because they all satisfy the rule. In contrast, natural categories are not composed of equally good members. If we gave people different variations of the color *red*, they would agree that some variations were more representative of the color than others (a "good" red versus an "off" red).

Representativeness A measure of how typical an item is as a category member

Even mathematical categories that can be defined on the basis of rules contain examples that differ in the **representativeness** of their members. For example, a rule can be used to determine whether a number is even or odd. People are therefore likely to agree that even numbers can be decided by definition (Malt, 1990). They also agree that it does not make sense to rate even numbers for degree of membership (Armstrong, Gleitman, & Gleitman, 1983). Nonetheless, people rate some even numbers (such as 4) as better members than others (such as 106).

Continuous dimensions Attributes that can take on any value along a dimension

Hierarchically organized An organizing strategy in which larger categories are partitioned into smaller categories

Another characteristic of natural categories is that they may be composed of **continuous dimensions** rather than discrete dimensions (Rosch, 1973). Colors, for example, vary along a continuum in which red gradually becomes orange and orange gradually becomes yellow. Natural categories are also **hierarchically organized**—larger categories often contain smaller categories. These characteristics of natural categories have important implications for how we use categories to organize knowledge. The next section discusses these implications.

NATURAL CATEGORIES

As we saw, one characteristic of real-world, or natural, categories is that they are hierarchical—some categories contain other categories. For example, the category *furniture* contains chairs, and the category *chairs* contains *living-room chairs*. Each of these levels contains a variety of objects, but the variety decreases as the category becomes smaller. There are many kinds of furniture (beds, sofas, tables, chairs), fewer kinds of chairs (living-room chairs, dining-room chairs, high chairs), and still fewer kinds of living-room chairs. The first part of this section looks at how the hierarchical organization of categories influences our behavior.

Another characteristic of natural categories is that some members seem to be better representatives of the category than others. We could all agree that chairs are furniture, but what about a piano? Shirts are certainly a good example of clothing, but what about a necklace? The second part of this section examines the implications of the fact that the members of categories are not all equally good members.

The Hierarchical Organization of Categories

Rosch and her colleagues studied the hierarchical organization of categories by using the three levels shown in Table 8.1 (Rosch, Mervis, Gray, Johnsen, & Boyes-Braem, 1976). The largest categories are the **super-ordinate categories**, such as *musical instruments*. They contain the **basic-level categories** (such as *drum*), which in turn contain the **subordinate categories** (such as *bass drum*). The most important of the three levels, according to Rosch, is the basic level, because basic-level categories are the most differentiated from one another, and they are therefore the first categories we learn and the most important in language.

The differentiation of categories can be measured by determining how much the members of a category share attributes with one another but have different attributes than the members of other categories have. At the superordinate level, the difficulty is that members share few attributes. Examples of furniture—such as *table*, *lamp*, and *chair*—have few

Superordinate categories Large categories at the top of a hierarchy, such as furniture, tools, and vehicles

Basic-level categories Intermediate categories in the middle of a hierarchy, such as table, saw, and truck

Subordinate categories Small categories at the bottom of a hierarchy, such as lamp table, jigsaw, and pickup truck

Table 8.1 *Examples of subordinate, basic, and superordinate categories*

Superordinate	Basic Level	Subordinates	
Musical instruments	Guitar Piano Drum	Folk guitar Grand piano Kettle drum	Classical guitar Upright piano Bass drum
Fruit	Apple Peach Grapes	Delicious apple Freestone peach Concord grapes	Mackintosh apple Cling peach Green seedless grapes
Tools	Hammer Saw Screwdriver	Ball-peen hammer Hack handsaw Phillips screwdriver	Claw hammer Cross-cutting handsaw Regular screwdriver
Clothing	Pants Socks Shirt	Levi's Knee socks Dress shirt	Double-knit pants Ankle socks Knit shirt
Furniture	Table Lamp Chair	Kitchen table Floor lamp Kitchen chair	Dining-room table Desk lamp Living-room chair
Vehicles	Car Bus Truck	Sports car City bus Pickup truck	Four-door sedan car Cross-country bus Tractor-trailor truck

SOURCE: From "Basic Objects in Natural Categories," by E. Rosch, C. B. Mervis, W. D. Gray, D. M. Johnsen, and P. Boyes-Braem, 1976, *Cognitive Psychology*, 8, 382–440. Copyright © 1976 by Academic Press, Inc. Reprinted by permission.

attributes in common. At the subordinate level, the difficulty is that the members share many attributes with members of similar subordinate categories. For example, a kitchen table has many of the same attributes as a dining-room table. The intermediate level of categorization—the basic level—avoids the two extremes. Members of a basic-level category, such as *chair*, not only share many attributes but have attributes that differ from those of items in other basic-level categories, such as *lamp* and *table*.

Evidence for the differentiation of categories comes from a study in which people were asked to list the attributes of objects at different levels in the hierarchy (Rosch et al., 1976). Some people listed the attributes of superordinate objects (such as musical instruments, fruit, tools, clothing); others listed the attributes of basic-level objects (guitar, apple, hammer, pants); still others listed the attributes of subordinate objects (classical guitar, Mackintosh apple, claw hammer, Levi's).

The experimenters analyzed the data by identifying attributes that people seemed to agree were associated with the specified category. Table 8.2 shows the average number of shared attributes at each level in the hierarchy. The number of shared attributes increases from the superordinate to the subordinate level. The members of a superordinate category have very few attributes compared with those at the basic level. However, the increase in shared attributes from the basic level to the subordinate level is very small. The differences between levels can be illustrated by the three examples shown in Table 8.3. Only two attributes were listed for the superordinate category *clothing*—*you wear it* and *keeps you warm*.

Table 8.2   *Number of attributes in common at each hierarchical level*

Category	Raw Tallies			Judge-Amended Tallies		
	Super-ordinate	Basic Level	Sub-ordinate	Super-ordinate	Basic Level	Sub-ordinate
Musical instruments	1	6.0	8.5	1	8.3	8.7
Fruit	7	12.3	14.7	3	8.3	9.5
Tools	3	8.3	9.7	3	8.7	9.2
Clothing	3	10.0	12.0	2	8.3	9.7
Furniture	3	9.0	10.3	0	7.0	7.8
Vehicles	4	8.7	11.2	1	11.7	16.8

SOURCE: From "Basic Objects in Natural Categories," by E. Rosch, C. B. Mervis, W. D. Gray, D. M. Johnsen, and P. Boyes-Braem, 1976, *Cognitive Psychology, 8,* 382–440. Copyright © 1976 by Academic Press, Inc. Reprinted by permission.
Note: Raw tallies are attributes listed by subjects. These were modified if all seven judges thought another hierarchial level was more appropriate (judge-amended columns).

Table 8.3 *Examples of shared attributes at different hierarchical levels*

Tools	Clothing	Furniture
make things	you wear it	no attributes
fix things	keeps you warm	**Chair**
metal	**Pants**	legs
Saw	legs	seat
handle	buttons	back
teeth	belt loops	arms
blade	pockets	comfortable
sharp	cloth	four legs
cuts	two legs	wood
edge	**Levi's**	holds people—you sit
wooden handle	blue	on it
Cross-cutting handsaw	**Double-knit pants**	**Kitchen chair**
used in construction	comfortable	no additional
Hack handsaw	stretchy	**Living-room chair**
no additional		large
		soft
		cushion

SOURCE: From "Basic Objects in Natural Categories," by E. Rosch, C. B. Mervis, W. D. Gray, D. M. Johnsen, and P. Boyes-Braem, 1976, *Cognitive Psychology*, 8, 382–440. Copyright © 1976 by Academic Press, Inc. Reprinted by permission.

These same two attributes plus an additional six were listed for the basic-level category *pants*. Pants have *legs*, *buttons*, *belt loops*, *pockets*, and *two legs* and are made of *cloth*. One additional attribute was listed for the subordinate category *Levi's—blue—*and two additional attributes were listed for *double-knit pants—comfortable* and *stretchy*. Notice that, although the items in subordinate categories share slightly more attributes than those in basic-level categories, there is a considerable overlap of attributes for subordinate categories. Although Levi's and double-knit pants differ on a few attributes, they also share many attributes, which makes it easier to distinguish between pants and shirts than to distinguish between Levi's and double-knit pants.

Rosch tested her claim that categorization is fastest at the basic level by asking people to verify the identity of an object at each of the three levels in the hierarchy. For instance, before being shown a picture of a living-room chair, people given superordinate terms were asked whether the object was a piece of furniture, people given basic terms were asked whether the object was a chair, and people given subordinate terms were asked whether the object was a living-room chair. The fastest verification times occurred for the group that verified objects at the basic level

(Rosch et al., 1976). Rosch proposed that people initially identify objects at the basic level, and then classify them at the superordinate level by making an inference (a chair is a piece of furniture), or classify them at the subordinate level by looking for distinguishing features (in this case, features that distinguish a living-room chair from other chairs).

But Rosch discussed the possibility that experts might be very quick in making subordinate classifications in their area of expertise. For instance, a furniture salesperson might be able to classify a living-room chair as a *living-room chair* as quickly as he or she could classify it as a *chair*. Some recent work has confirmed this hypothesis (Tanaka & Taylor, 1991). Dog experts and bird experts, recruited from local organizations, were asked to identify colored pictures of dogs and birds at either the superordinate (*animal*), basic (*dog* or *bird*), or subordinate (such as *beagle* or *sparrow*) level. The results replicated Rosch and her colleagues' (1976) findings when dog experts classified birds and bird experts classified dogs. Classification was fastest at the basic level. However, the results were different when dog experts classified dogs and bird experts classified birds. Their subordinate-level classifications were as fast as their basic-level classifications. The experts were so good at distinguishing between different kinds of dogs, or different kinds of birds, that they could identify the type of dog, or type of bird, as quickly as they could recognize that the picture was a dog or a bird.

Another characteristic of categories is particularly important for prototype theories—the shape of objects within the category. The **prototype** of a category is usually defined as the "average" of the patterns in the category. It represents the central tendency of the category. But is it meaningful to talk about the average shape of real-world categories? The answer depends on which hierarchical level we are talking about.

The objects in Figure 8.3 represent basic-level categories, and the four objects in each row belong to the same superordinate category. Rosch and her colleagues found that people were not very good at identifying the average shape of two different basic-level objects belonging to the same superordinate category. For example, the average shape of a table and a chair together would look like neither a table nor a chair but something in between that would be difficult to identify. These results are not surprising if we try to think of what an "average" object would look like for superordinate categories such as *furniture, clothing, vehicles,* and *animals*. We can think of good examples of each category, but this is not the same as forming an average of all the examples.

The concept of an average example becomes meaningful if we think of objects from the same basic level. Although the average shape of furniture is unreasonable, the average shape of a chair is a more plausible concept. In fact, people were quite accurate in identifying the average shape of two objects from the same basic-level category—for example, the aver-

Prototype An item that typifies the members in a category and is used to represent the category

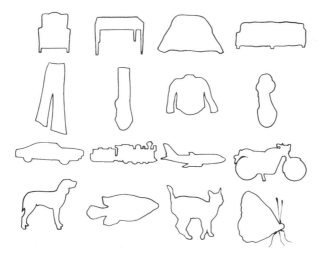

Figure 8.3   *Examples of outlines of pictures representing basic-level categories. The pictures in each row belong to the same superordinate category.*

From "Basic Objects in Natural Categories," by E. Rosch, C. B. Mervis. W. D. Gray, D. M. Johnsen, and P. Boyes-Braem, 1976, *Cognitive Psychology, 8,* 382–440. Copyright © 1976 by Academic Press, Inc. Reprinted by permission.

age of two chairs still looks reasonably like a chair, and the average of two shirts still looks reasonably like a shirt. Basic-level objects are sufficiently similar to each other that the average shape is identifiable. Creation of an average pattern to represent a category is therefore possible at the basic level (and at the subordinate level, where the shapes of objects in the same category are even more similar) but is not possible at the superordinate level.

Typicality and Family Resemblances

So far we have emphasized comparing categories at different levels of generality. Rosch and her colleagues argued that the intermediate level of generality—the basic level—is the most important. It is the most general level at which a prototype, or concrete image, can be formed to represent the category as a whole. It is also the level at which categories are the most differentiated from one another because the members of basic-level categories share many attributes with one another but do not share many attributes with members of other categories.

We will now shift our emphasis to comparing members within a category. Psychologists use the term **typicality** to refer to differences in how

Typicality A measure of how well a category member represents that category

well members of a category represent that category. For instance, people agree that chairs, sofas, and tables are good examples of furniture; cars, trucks, and buses are good examples of vehicles; and oranges, apples, and bananas are good examples of fruit. Table 8.4 lists 20 members for each of six superordinate categories, ranked from the most typical to the least typical, based on people's ratings.

Although the rank order may seem fairly obvious to us, it isn't obvious why the order exists. Why is a car a good example and an elevator a poor example of a vehicle? Both can transport people and materials. Rosch and Mervis (1975) hypothesized that good members will share many attributes with other members of the category and few attributes with members of other categories. Notice that Rosch is applying the same hypothesis she used to compare superordinate, basic, and subordinate categories to compare the typicality of members within a category.

Rosch and Mervis tested their hypothesis by asking people to list the attributes of each of the category members shown in Table 8.4. For example, for a bicycle, people might list that it has two wheels, pedals, and handlebars; you ride on it; and it doesn't use fuel. To test the hypothesis that the good examples of categories should share many attributes with other members of the category, it is necessary to calculate a measure of **family resemblance** for each item by considering how many other members share each attribute of the item. Let's take a specific example. Since a car has wheels as one of its attributes, we would count the vehicles that also have wheels. Since a car has a windshield, we would count the members that have a windshield. The numerical score for each attribute can vary from 1 to 20, depending on how many of the 20 members in Table 8.4 possess that attribute. The family resemblance score for each member is obtained by adding together the numerical scores of all attributes possessed by that member. If 14 members of the category have wheels and 11 have windshields, the family resemblance score would be 25 for a car if it had only those two attributes. The actual score, of course, is much higher, since we also have to add the numerical scores for all the other attributes listed for a car. The results revealed that good representatives of a category had high family resemblance scores. The correlations between the two variables were between .84 (for *vegetable*) and .94 (for *weapon*) for the six superordinate categories listed in Table 8.4.

Another way of viewing these results is to compare how many attributes are shared by the five most typical and five least typical examples in each category. The five most typical vehicles are *car, truck, bus, motorcycle,* and *train*. The five share many attributes since they possess many common parts; the subjects in the experiment were able to identify 36 attributes that belonged to all five members. The five least typical examples are *horse, blimp, skates, wheelbarrow,* and *elevator*—subjects identified only two attributes that belong to all five of the least typical members

Family resemblance
A measure of how frequently the attributes of a category member are shared by other members of the category

Table 8.4 *Typicality of members in six superordinate categories*

			Category			
Item	Furniture	Vehicles	Fruit	Weapons	Vegetables	Clothing
1	Chair	Car	Orange	Gun	Peas	Pants
2	Sofa	Truck	Apple	Knife	Carrots	Shirt
3	Table	Bus	Banana	Sword	String beans	Dress
4	Dresser	Motorcycle	Peach	Bomb	Spinach	Skirt
5	Desk	Train	Pear	Hand grenade	Broccoli	Jacket
6	Bed	Trolley car	Apricot	Spear	Asparagus	Coat
7	Bookcase	Bicycle	Plum	Cannon	Corn	Sweater
8	Footstool	Airplane	Grape	Bow and arrow	Cauliflower	Underpants
9	Lamp	Boat	Strawberry	Club	Brussels sprouts	Socks
10	Piano	Tractor	Grapefruit	Tank	Lettuce	Pajamas
11	Cushion	Cart	Pineapple	Tear gas	Beets	Bathing suit
12	Mirror	Wheelchair	Blueberry	Whip	Tomato	Shoes
13	Rug	Tank	Lemon	Ice pick	Lima beans	Vest
14	Radio	Raft	Watermelon	Fists	Eggplant	Tie
15	Stove	Sled	Honeydew	Rocket	Onion	Mittens
16	Clock	Horse	Pomegranate	Poison	Potato	Hat
17	Picture	Blimp	Date	Scissors	Yam	Apron
18	Closet	Skates	Coconut	Words	Mushroom	Purse
19	Vase	Wheelbarrow	Tomato	Foot	Pumpkin	Wristwatch
20	Telephone	Elevator	Olive	Screwdriver	Rice	Necklace

SOURCE: From "Family Resemblances: Studies in the Internal Structure of Categories," by E. Rosch and C. B. Mervis, 1975, *Cognitive Psychology 7*, 573–605. Copyright © 1975 by Academic Press, Inc. Reprinted by permission.

(perhaps that they carry people and move). The results were similar for the other five superordinate categories.

The fact that typical members of categories tend to share attributes with other members is also true for basic-level categories. You may have noticed that the examples of the superordinate categories shown in Table 8.4 are basic-level categories. Rosch and Mervis (1975) selected six of these examples (*car, truck, airplane, chair, table, lamp*) to test the same hypothesis—that the most typical members of basic-level categories should share more attributes with other members than the least typical members. For each of the six categories the experimenters selected 15 pictures, varying from good to poor examples. They then asked groups of undergraduates to rate how well each picture represented their idea of the category. As was found for the members of superordinate categories, there was a high correlation between the typicality of a member and the number of shared attributes.

Although family resemblance scores are useful for predicting the typicality of members in common taxonomic categories like those listed in Table 8.4, they are not useful in predicting typicality for goal-derived categories (Barsalou, 1985). **Goal-derived categories** consist of examples that satisfy a goal, such as "make people happy when you give a birthday present." According to subjects' ratings, good examples of birthday presents include clothing, a party, jewelry, dinner, a watch, a cake, and a card. Notice that these examples are dissimilar to one another and do not share many attributes. Barsalou calculated family resemblance scores for members of goal-derived categories and found that family resemblance scores did not predict the typicality of the examples.

The explanation for this finding is that members of goal-derived categories are selected on the basis of some underlying principle, rather than on the basis of shared attributes (Murphy & Medin, 1985). Thus, when we select weekend activities, we consider events that we enjoy; when we select things we would take from our home during a fire, we consider things that are valuable and irreplaceable, such as children and important papers. Although similarity of attributes determines how we form many categories and judge the typicality of category members, Murphy and Medin argue that we will need to learn more about underlying principles in order to have a more complete understanding of categorization.

For goal-derived categories, an underlying principle is the extent to which members satisfy the goal. Barsalou (1991) has shown that goal-derived categories are organized around **ideals**, and the more typical members of the category are those members that best satisfy the goal. For the category *foods to eat on a diet*, the ideal number of calories is zero, so the fewer calories a food has, the better it satisfies the goal of losing weight. Those of us who have attempted to diet probably realize that we often like to satisfy more than one goal. We may therefore try to select foods

Goal-derived categories Categories whose members are selected to satisfy a specified goal

Ideals Attribute values that relate to the goal of a goal-derived category

that have minimal calories, maximal nutrition, and maximal taste in order to satisfy the multiple goals of losing weight, staying healthy, and enjoying food.

Person Perception

The structure of natural categories, such as hierarchical organization and typicality, is also relevant for how we classify people (Cantor & Mischel, 1979). An example of a superordinate category might be people who have a strong commitment to a particular belief or cause. This category can be subdivided into religious devotees and social activists. Religious devotees can be further classified according to their particular religions, and social activists can be classified according to their particular causes. Cantor and Mischel's work parallels that of Rosch and her colleagues by examining such issues as the number of shared attributes at different levels in the person hierarchy.

As we saw at the beginning of this chapter, categorization allows us to create a manageable view of the world, but it also has disadvantages that can be particularly troublesome when the category members are people. Exaggerating within-group similarity by creating **stereotypes** might not only result in erroneous assumptions about others but also make it more difficult for people to remember impressions that disconfirm their stereotypes (Cantor & Genero, 1986). In the process of organizing the world into social categories, people may perceive members of the same social category as remarkably similar and different from members of other social categories. It is maladaptive, once having categorized a person, to exaggerate the similarity among people in the category, discount disconfirming evidence, and focus on stereotypic examples of the category.

Stereotypes Attribute values believed to be representative of social categories

The need to distinguish among individuals is particularly important when the categories are created through clinical diagnosis. Examples of diagnostic categories include functional psychosis, paranoid schizophrenia, and affective disorder. Attributes associated with each of these categories are used in diagnosis. For example, attributes that characterize paranoid schizophrenia include delusions of persecution, hostility, suspicion, associative disturbance, delusions of grandeur, hallucinations, autism, affective disturbance, projection, and rigidity in coping with stress. Differences in typicality occur because more typical patients have most of the attributes associated with a particular diagnostic category, whereas less typical patients have only some of those attributes (Cantor, Smith, French, & Mezzich, 1980).

The diagnostic manual of the American Psychiatric Association distinguishes among different categories by listing a large number of features, some of which appear in more than one category (Cantor et al., 1980). This approach to classification has several implications. In contrast to the approach in which each category is defined by several unique features, the recommended approach allows treatment of the patient to take into account the overlap in symptoms across disorders. It also encourages clinicians to expect diversity among patients who have the same diagnosis and to react appropriately to individual differences.

Loss of Categorical Knowledge

Another source of evidence for how categories influence semantic organization in LTM is the selective loss of knowledge following brain damage. In most cases, such losses appear to be linked to specific modalities such as impaired recognition of visual or auditory patterns. In some cases, however, brain damage causes category-specific losses of knowledge, as in people who have lost their knowledge of living things, or people who have lost their knowledge of nonliving things.

In the first report of this type of loss, Warrington and Shallice (1984) described four patients who were much worse at identifying living things (animals or plants) than nonliving things (inanimate objects). All four of the patients had recovered from herpes encephalitis and had sustained bilateral damage to their temporal lobes. Table 8.5 shows the results for two patients who were studied in detail. The top part of the table shows the results from a picture identification task in which they were asked to identify by name or description an object shown in a colored picture. They were able to identify most of the nonliving objects, but almost none of the living objects.

The same pattern occurred when they were asked to provide definitions when the names of these same items were presented auditorily (spoken word identification). Examples of their definitions are shown at the bottom of the table.

The most straightforward interpretation of these findings is that living and nonliving things represent two different categories in semantic memory. But Warrington and Shallice offered a different interpretation. If living things are primarily distinguished by visual features and nonliving things by functional features, then the selective loss may be a visual-functional distinction rather than a living-nonliving distinction. The inability to identify and define living things, as illustrated in Table 8.5, may therefore be caused by the selective loss of the visual attributes of objects. Patients may recall what a desk is used for (a functional feature), but forget what a leopard looks like.

The hypothesis that visual features play a predominate role in our knowledge of living objects and functional features play a predominant role in our knowledge of nonliving objects was directly tested in an experiment by Farah and McClelland (1991). They compiled a list of living and nonliving things that were used in the Warrington and Shallice

Table 8.5 *Performance of two patients with impaired knowledge of living things on various semantic memory tasks*

Case	Living Thing		Nonliving Thing
		Picture identification	
JBR	6%		90%
SBY	0%		75%
		Spoken word definition	
JBR	8%		79%
SBY	0%		52%
		Examples of definitions	
JBR	Parrot: don't know		Tent: temporary outhouse, living home
	Daffodil: plant		Briefcase: small case used by students to carry papers
	Snail: an insect animal		Compass: tools for telling direction you are going
	Eel: not well		Torch: hand-held light
	Ostrich: unusual		
SBY	Duck: an animal		Wheelbarrow: object used by people to take material about
	Wasp: bird that flies		Towel: material used to dry people
	Crocus: rubbish material		Submarine: ship that goes underneath the sea
	Holly: what you drink		Umbrella: object used to protect you from water that comes
	Spider: a person looking for things, he was a spider for his nation or country		

SOURCE: From "A Computational Model of Semantic Memory Impairment: Modality Specificity and Emergent Category Specificity," by M. J. Farah and J. L. McClelland, 1991, *Journal of Experimental Psychology: General, 120*, 339–357. Copyright © 1991 by the American Psychological Association. Reprinted by permission.

(1984) experiment and asked subjects to underline visual and functional features that described each of the objects. Although visual features were selected more often than functional features for both living and nonliving objects, visual features were emphasized much more for living objects. This finding would suggest that the loss of visual features should impair the identification of living objects much more than the identification of nonliving objects.

Farah and McClelland tested this hypothesis by building a neural network model based on the general principles of neural networks that we discussed at the end of Chapter 2. Living things were represented in their network by an average of 16.1 visual features and 2.1 functional features. Nonliving things were represented by an average of 9.4 visual and 6.7 functional features. The ratio of visual features to functional features for both living and nonliving things is based on the relative frequency with which subjects selected visual and functional features in the experiment. The next step was to train the model to associate the correct names with objects by adjusting the weights in the neural network after corrective feedback was given on each learning trial.

After training the network to respond perfectly, it was "damaged" by eliminating either 0, 20, 40, 60, 80, or 100% of the visual features. Figure 8.4 shows the resulting ability of the network to correctly associate names and pictures as a result of the amount of damage to the visual features in its memory. As expected, the loss of visual information from the network severely limited the model's ability to identify living things, without producing a large deficit in its ability to identify nonliving things. It should be noted that a complete (100%) loss of visual information produces results that are very similar to the problems the two patients had in Table

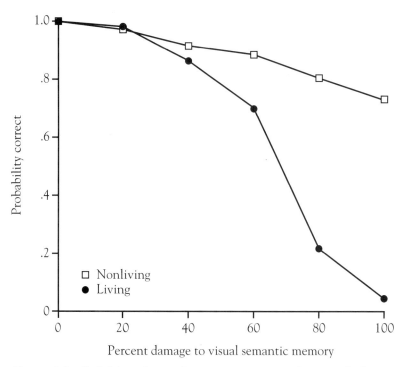

Figure 8.4   *Probability of correctly associating names and pictures for living and nonliving things after different amounts of damage to visual features in a neural network.*

From "A Computational Model of Semantic Memory Impairment: Modality Specificity and Emergent Category Specificity," by M. J. Farah and J. L. McClelland, 1991, *Journal of Experimental Psychology: General, 120*, 339–357. Copyright © 1991 by the American Psychological Association. Reprinted by permission.

8.5. The network can still identify 73% of nonliving things, but only 5% of living things.

Farah and McClelland also used their network to produce the opposite result by randomly eliminating functional features. The elimination of functional features produced a deficit in the network's ability to identify nonliving things, but did not cause a deficit in the network's ability to identify living things. The network could still identify all of the living things (by using visual features) even when the functional features were completely eliminated. Although this result obviously does not simulate the performance of the two patients shown in Table 8.5, it does simulate the performance of patients who have an impaired knowledge of nonliving things.

The strategies that people use to classify objects constitute a pervasive topic in cognitive psychology. The young child or brain-damaged adult who is trying to decide whether an animal is a dog or a cat and a trained clinician who is trying to decide whether a patient is a paranoid schizophrenic or a chronic undifferentiated schizophrenic are both faced with categorization problems. In the next section we will examine different models of how people make these decisions. It should not surprise you by now that features play an important role in all of these models. We will first consider perceptual patterns such as schematic faces and will later consider person perception in which the features (such as educational level or marital status) are more abstract .

CATEGORIZING NOVEL PATTERNS

At the beginning of this chapter we learned that one advantage of categories is that they enable us to recognize novel objects. A young child who encounters a new dog for the first time can use previous knowledge of dogs to recognize the new dog. Lacking this ability to classify novel objects, the child would have to be told the identity of every new object.

People are quite good at making perceptual classifications, and psychologists are naturally interested in how they do it. The characteristics of natural categories may provide a clue. One characteristic is that some category members are more prototypical, or better representatives, of the category than other members. People might therefore create a pattern, or prototype, which they feel is a very good representative of the category and use it to classify other patterns. A model based on this strategy is called a *prototype model*. Another characteristic of category members is that they share features, or attributes. People might therefore classify a novel pattern by determining how many of its feature values match the feature values of category patterns. A model based on this strategy is called a *feature frequency model*.

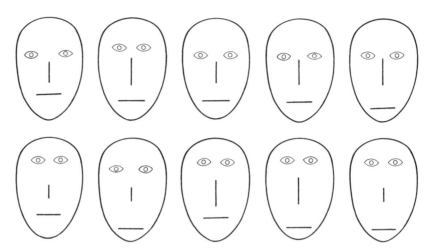

Figure 8.5   *Example of a perceptual categorization task. The upper five faces represent Category 1, and the lower five faces represent Category 2.*

From "Perceptual vs. Conceptual Categorization," by S. K. Reed and M. P. Friedman, 1973, *Memory & Cognition, 1,* 157–163. Copyright © 1973 by the Psychonomic Society, Inc. Reprinted by permission.

The two models can be illustrated by referring to the examples in Figure 8.5, taken from one of my experiments (Reed, 1972). If you were a subject in this experiment, I would first tell you that the upper row of faces represents one category and the bottom row represents another category. I would then ask you to study the two categories because you would have to classify novel faces as members of one of the two categories. Students in my experiments classified from 20 to 25 novel faces (faces that didn't match any of the faces shown in Figure 8.5). Figure 8.6 shows three novel faces.

The feature frequency model proposes that people match the feature values of the novel pattern to the feature values of the patterns in the two categories. For example, the four features of each novel face (forehead, eyes, nose, and mouth) would be compared with the features of the five faces in each category. The novel pattern is then classified into the category that results in the most feature matches.

The prototype model proposes that people create a pattern that best represents each category. This prototype is usually a pattern that is the average of all the other patterns in the category. The prototype for either row of faces in Figure 8.5 is the pattern that is created by finding the average feature values of the five patterns in that category. It has the average forehead height, average eye separation, average nose length, and average mouth height. The middle pattern in Figure 8.6 is the prototype for

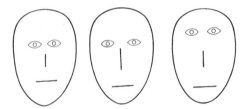

Figure 8.6   *Examples of novel faces for Figure 8.5.
The middle face is the Category 1 prototype, and the
right face is the Category 2 prototype.*

From "Pattern Recognition and Categorization," by S. K. Reed,
1972, *Cognitive Psychology, 3*, 382–407. Copyright © 1972 by
Academic Press, Inc. Reprinted by permission.

the top row of faces, and the right pattern is the prototype for the bottom
row of faces. We will now review evidence that supports each of these
two models, beginning with the prototype model.

The Prototype Model

The prototype model proposes that the perceiver creates a prototype to
represent each category and classifies a novel pattern by comparing it
with the category prototypes, finding which prototype it most closely resembles, and selecting that category. For example, if the novel pattern is
more similar to the Category 1 prototype than to the prototype for any
other category, it will be classified into Category 1.

The prototype rule has the advantage that it doesn't require many
comparisons in order to classify a pattern. Instead of comparing a novel
pattern with every pattern in the category, a person has to compare a
novel pattern with only a single pattern in each category—the pattern
that is the best representative of that category. As we encounter more
patterns in a category, it would become harder to compare a novel pattern with all of them. The prototype strategy is therefore an economical
strategy because only a single comparison is required for each category regardless of how many patterns are in it.

Initial support for the use of a prototype strategy in classifying patterns came from a study by Posner and Keele (1968). The investigators
created four prototype patterns—a triangle, the letter M, the letter F, and
a random pattern. Each prototype was made up of nine dots and could be
distorted by varying the dots. Figure 8.7 shows different amounts of distortion for one of the prototypes. The numbers show how much the dots
were allowed to vary, with larger numbers implying greater distortions.

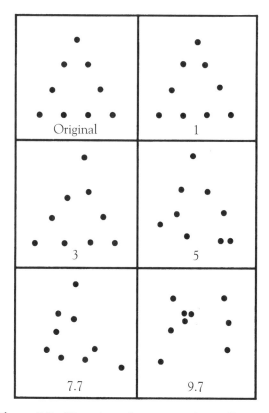

Figure 8.7   *Distortions of a prototype (original) pattern at different levels of variability.*

From "Perceived Distance and the Classification of Distorted Patterns," by M. I. Posner, R. Goldsmith, and K. E. Welton, 1967, *Journal of Experimental Psychology, 73*, 28–38. Copyright © 1967 by the American Psychological Association. Reprinted by permission.

Posner and Keele constructed distortions of each prototype at three levels of variability: low variability (Level 1), moderate variability (Level 5), and high variability (Level 7.7). Undergraduates at the University of Oregon learned a list of 12 patterns, 3 from each prototype (triangle, M, F, and random). Group 1 subjects learned to classify three low-variability distortions of each prototype, and Group 5 subjects learned to classify three moderate-variability distortions of each prototype. Note in Figure 8.7 that the prototype is fairly obvious for Level 1 distortions but not so obvious for Level 5 distortions. Group 1 subjects should therefore have a much better idea than Group 5 subjects of what the prototype looks like.

After the undergraduates could correctly classify all 12 patterns into the four categories, they were asked to classify high-variability patterns they had never seen before. The crucial comparison in this experiment is whether Group 1 subjects or Group 5 subjects would be better at classifying the novel patterns. Group 1 subjects should have a better idea of what the prototype looked like, but Group 5 subjects should have a better idea of how patterns could vary within a category since they had trained on more variable patterns. It turned out that Group 5 subjects were significantly better than Group 1 subjects in classifying the highly distorted, novel patterns. In other words, subjects were more able to recognize highly distorted patterns when they had trained on moderately distorted patterns than when they had trained on slightly distorted patterns. The implication is that making the prototype very obvious by using low-distortion patterns is not sufficient when people have to classify highly distorted patterns; it is also necessary to learn how patterns can vary within a category.

Although the superiority of the Group 5 subjects suggested that learning about category variability might be more important than learning the category prototypes, Posner and Keele also obtained results that supported the use of a prototype strategy. First, they found that the ability to correctly classify a novel pattern depended on the degree of similarity between the novel pattern and the category prototype. The more similar a novel pattern was to one of the category prototypes, the easier it was to classify correctly. This result would be expected if people had created a prototype to represent each category. Second, undergraduates who had trained on the moderately distorted patterns could later classify the category prototypes as well as they could classify the patterns they had studied during the training session. Remember that they had not seen the prototypes previously, because all the training patterns were distortions of the prototype. This finding suggests that even Group 5 subjects could create a prototype from the training patterns.

The results of this study suggested that people could create prototypes to represent categories and use them to classify novel patterns. However, there was also evidence that people learned more than just the category prototypes since the variability of the patterns within a category also influenced their performance on classifying novel patterns. Posner and Keele's findings were an important contribution to the study of how people classify patterns. Subsequent research by other investigators has mainly focused on directly comparing the prototype model with other categorization models.

Comparing Alternative Models

The results obtained by Posner and Keele (1968) were certainly consistent with a prototype model, but how would a prototype model compare with alternative models? I became interested in this question as a graduate

Nearest-neighbor rule
A classification strategy that selects the category containing an item that is most similar to the classified item

Average distance rule
A classification strategy that selects the category containing items that have the greatest average similarity to the classified item

Prototype rule   A classification strategy that selects the category whose prototype is the most similar to the classified item

Feature frequency rule
A classification strategy that selects the category that has the most feature matches with the classified item

student and decided to devote my dissertation to it. It seemed to me that people classify a pattern into a category because that pattern is similar to other patterns in the category. One method of measuring similarity is simply to show people pairs of patterns and ask them to rate the similarity of the two patterns in each pair. The use of similarity to categorize patterns can be illustrated by considering a simple classification rule called the **nearest-neighbor rule**. The nearest-neighbor rule states that a person should classify a novel pattern by comparing it with all the patterns in each category in order to find the single category pattern that is most similar to the novel pattern. The novel pattern is then classified into the category that produces the best match. The problem with the nearest-neighbor rule is that it requires a person to compare the test pattern with all category patterns but uses only a single pattern (the one most similar to the test pattern) as the basis for decision. If the most similar pattern is not very representative of its category, the decision could easily be wrong. For example, a young child who had a Pekingese dog as a pet might classify a long-haired cat as a dog because the cat looks more like the Pekingese than like other cats. The error would occur because, although a Pekingese is a dog, it is not a very good representative of the category.

A better rule, called the **average distance rule**, states that a person should compare the novel pattern with all the patterns in each category in order to determine the average similarity between the novel pattern and the patterns in each category. If the average similarity is greater for Category 1 patterns, Category 1 should be selected; otherwise, Category 2 should be selected. The average distance rule has an advantage over the nearest-neighbor rule in that it uses all category patterns as the basis for the decision instead of only one pattern. It has the disadvantage that a person must compute average similarity in addition to comparing the novel pattern to all category patterns.

Both of these disadvantages are eliminated by the **prototype rule**. If a person can create a prototype to represent each category, a novel pattern has to be compared only with this single pattern. According to the prototype rule, a person should select Category 1 whenever a novel pattern is more similar to the Category 1 prototype and Category 2 whenever a novel pattern is more similar to the Category 2 prototype.

The final model we will consider is different from the first three in that it uses features in making predictions. The **feature frequency rule** is concerned with matching features rather than measuring the similarity between patterns. It looks at the features of the novel pattern and compares how many times they exactly match features of the category patterns. Consider the left pattern shown in Figure 8.6. It has a large forehead, closely spaced eyes, a short nose, and a high mouth. Inspection of the two categories in Figure 8.5 reveals that four faces in Category 1 have a large forehead, one has closely spaced eyes, and one has a high mouth. Therefore the total number of feature matches with the novel face is six.

By contrast, four faces in Category 2 have closely spaced eyes, three have short noses, and two have high mouths. Since the number of matches is higher for Category 2, the pattern should be classified into Category 2, according to the feature frequency rule.

You may have noticed that each of the four models—nearest neighbor, average distance, prototype, and feature frequency—states how a pattern should be classified. Since the models use different information, they sometimes differ in their selection of categories. Therefore the models could be used to make predictions about how people would classify the patterns. If the prototype model, for example, were more successful than the other models in predicting how people classified novel patterns, this would imply that they used a prototype strategy. In fact, the results of my studies did support the prototype model.

The results do not prove that everyone used the prototype strategy, but they suggest that it was the predominant strategy used. This suggestion was confirmed by asking people which strategy of the four listed in Table 8.6 they had used. The majority selected the prototype strategy, and very few selected the two strategies that required comparing the novel patterns (projected faces) with all the category patterns. These

Table 8.6   *Percent of subjects who reported using each classification strategy after learning the category patterns*

Strategy	Percent
1. Prototype I formed an abstract image of what a face in Category 1 should look like and an abstract image of what a face in Category 2 should look like. I then compared the projected face with the two abstract images and chose the category that gave the closest match.	58
2. Nearest neighbor I compared the projected face with all the faces in the two categories, looking for a single face that best matched the projected face. I then chose the category in which that face appeared.	10
3. Feature frequency I looked at each feature on the projected face and compared how many times it exactly matched a feature in each of the two categories. I then chose the category that gave the highest number of matches.	28
4. Average distance I compared the projected face with each of the five faces in Category 1 and with each of the five faces in Category 2. I then chose the category in which the faces were more like the projected face, basing my decision on all faces in the two categories.	4

SOURCE: From "Pattern Recognition and Categorization," by S. K. Reed, 1972, *Cognitive Psychology, 3,* 382–407. Copyright © 1972 by Academic Press, Inc. Reprinted by permission.

particular results are from an experiment in which University of California, Los Angeles, undergraduates had to classify novel patterns after learning the two categories shown in Figure 8.5. Comparing a novel pattern with all the category patterns should be particularly difficult when the category patterns are stored in memory rather than physically present. However, the data supported the prototype model even when all the patterns were simultaneously present, as they are in Figure 8.5 (Reed, 1972).

One qualification of these results is necessary before we consider other research. The best-predicting model was a prototype model in which the dimensions were differentially weighted, or emphasized, to account for the fact that some dimensions were more useful than others in distinguishing between categories. For the two categories shown in Figure 8.5, the weights calculated to reflect the usefulness of the dimensions were .46 for forehead (eye height), .24 for eye separation, .24 for nose length, and .06 for mouth height. The weights indicate that the forehead is a good dimension for distinguishing between the two categories and the mouth is a poor dimension. The results suggest that the most popular strategy was to compare the similarity of the novel pattern to the two category prototypes but to emphasize some dimensions more than others when making the comparison. The finding that people emphasized some dimensions more than others is consistent with our discussion of pattern recognition (Chapter 2), in which we saw that difficulty in discriminating pairs of letters could be analyzed in terms of the relative importance of feature dimensions.

Limitations of Prototype Models

One of the limitations of prototype models is that they are difficult to apply to patterns that cannot be represented along continuous dimensions. Schematic faces consist of features that vary along continuous dimensions such as eye separation or mouth height, so it is possible to create an average pattern, or prototype, to represent the category. Not all items consist of features that vary along a continuous dimension, however. Consider the following task, designed by Hayes-Roth and Hayes-Roth (1977).

The task was to classify people as belonging to Club 1, Club 2, or neither club. The variation of three features affected the classification: age, education, and marital status. Each feature had one of four values. The age of a person was 30, 40, 50, or 60; the educational level was junior high, high school, trade school, or college; and the marital status was single, married, divorced, or widowed. People would have considerable difficulty creating an average person to represent each of the two clubs. It would be easy to compute the average age, but computing an average for education or marital status is more problematic. We might translate educational level into years of education, but this would blur the distinction between trade school and college. Forming an average marital status is even more difficult.

The point of this example is simply that the kind of stimuli being classified places constraints on which strategies are the easiest to use. Hayes-Roth and Hayes-Roth found that a version of the feature frequency model was a good predictor of how students would classify people into clubs. The most successful model compared combinations of features in addition to individual features. For example, if a person were 30 years old and divorced, the model would examine how many people in each club were both 30 and divorced in addition to matching the two individual features. Neumann (1974) also tested a feature frequency model that matched both individual features and combinations of features. Once again, the model was successful in predicting how people would classify patterns that did not consist of continuous dimensions.

Some patterns consist of both continuous and discrete dimensions. Box 8.1 shows how both feature frequencies and category averages were used to predict the composite Miss America. The average values of previous winners were used to determine height, weight, and measurements. Other data—such as the fact that winners typically have green eyes, major

BOX 8.1

Computer didn't miss in selecting Miss Mississippi

SEATTLE—A retired statistics professor said Sunday he never doubted Susan Akin of Mississippi would walk down the runway as Miss America.

"No one in all my eight years of forecasting Miss America has ever come so close to the composite Miss America," George Miller said. "She deviated the least."

Akin's only possible drawbacks to winning the crown were her blue eyes, which over the years have been less popular than green or brown, said Miller, who taught statistics and forecasting at Northern Illinois University before moving to the Northwest where last year he taught at Seattle University.

Miller, 62, has correctly picked the winner ahead of the judges four times out of seven—beginning with the 1979 pageant when he chose another Miss Mississippi. He also accurately forecast the 1980 and 1983 winners.

Miller doesn't compute hair color or the contestants' overall appearance into his statistical study. What he uses are facts and figures that can be correlated—such as talent, weight, height, education level and major, and physical measurements.

"I don't consider hair color because one-third of the contestants are blondes and one-third of the winners over the years have been blonde," he said. "And I don't look at their pictures because a photographer can pose them or doctor the photos."

Miller said the "ideal Miss America" would be 5 feet 7 inches tall, weigh 115 pounds, have measurements of 35-23-35, be 21 years old, have green eyes, be a college junior majoring in communications, and sing classical music.

SOURCE: From "Computer Didn't Miss in Selecting Miss Mississippi," appearing in the *Sun-Sentinel,* Fort Lauderdale, September 16, 1985. Reprinted by permission of Associated Press.

in communications, and sing classical music—were determined by how frequently previous winners possessed these particular characteristics. By using a combination of category averages and feature frequencies, a statistical analyst successfully predicted the winner of the pageant.

Another problem for a prototype theory is that people often have knowledge about individual examples in a category (Medin, 1989). For instance, in the Posner and Keele (1968) experiment on dot patterns, subjects were influenced by the variability of the examples. According to an influential model proposed by Medin and Schaffer (1978), people store examples of category patterns in memory and classify new patterns by comparing them with retrieved examples. The greater the similarity of the new pattern to an example stored in memory, the greater the probability that the example will be retrieved. But, unlike the nearest-neighbor and average distance models, Medin and Schaffer's model uses combinations of features to measure similarity. In a test of how subjects would use symptoms to diagnose fictitious diseases, Medin and his colleagues found that subjects' decisions were influenced by feature combinations (Medin, Altom, Edelson, & Freko, 1982).

Additional theories that assume that people store individual examples in memory have been successful in predicting subjects' classifications. Nosofsky (1991) had subjects learn the schematic faces shown in Figure 8.5 and found support for the view that they classified test faces by comparing them to the individual examples. His findings differ from those obtained by Reed (1972) because a model based on memory for examples predicted better than a prototype model how subjects would classify the faces. However, the results were similar to Reed's in supporting the view that people emphasize those features that are most helpful in discriminating between categories.

In conclusion, there is still controversy regarding which models provide the best explanation of how people classify novel patterns. Prototype theories are not sensitive enough to people's memory for individual examples. For instance, our prototype for a spoon likely consists of a small metallic spoon, but this doesn't account for our knowledge of large wooden spoons. On the other hand, it seems unrealistic that people would remember all the examples of a category, such as all the spoons that they have encountered. One could propose that there are distinct subtypes for concepts such as *spoon*, but current prototype models do not describe how and when subtypes are created (Medin, 1989). This could be a promising area for future research.

SUMMARY

One way we organize knowledge is through categories and hierarchies made up of categories. Categories reduce the complexity of the environment and the need for constant learning and enable us to recognize objects, respond appropriately, and order and relate classes of events.

The concept identification paradigm is one approach to the study of categorization. People try to learn a conceptual rule by receiving feedback on positive and negative instances of the concept. Concepts that are defined by logical rules are easiest to learn for a conjunctive rule, followed by the disjunctive, conditional, and biconditional rules. The same order of difficulty occurs when people are told the rule and have to identify the relevant attributes.

Real-world, or natural, categories generally cannot be distinguished by a simple rule. Frequently they are hierarchically organized—for example, double-knit pants are included in the category *pants*, and pants are included in the category *clothes*. Rosch has argued that most classifications are made at the intermediate or basic level—the most general level at which a prototype can be constructed and the level at which categories are most differentiated. The members of natural categories vary in how well they represent the category. Oranges and apples are considered good examples of *fruit*; coconuts and olives are considered poor examples. The attributes of good members are shared with other members of the category, except for goal-derived categories in which the typicality of members is determined by how well they satisfy the goal. The concepts of hierarchical organization and category typicality also apply to person perception.

Two theories that assume people use abstracted information to classify novel patterns are the prototype model and the feature frequency model. The prototype model proposes that people create patterns that best represent the categories and then classify novel patterns by comparing them with the category prototypes. The prototype is usually the central tendency of the category, formed by calculating the average of all the patterns in the category. Prototype theories have been most successful in predicting how people will classify perceptual patterns consisting of feature values that vary continuously along a dimension. By contrast, the feature frequency model proposes that people classify patterns by comparing how frequently their feature values match those of the category patterns and then selecting the category that results in the greatest number of feature matches. Predictions are often improved by considering feature combinations. The feature frequency theory has been most successful in predicting how people classify patterns consisting of feature values that do not vary continuously along a dimension. Other theories propose that people remember specific examples rather than abstract information.

STUDY QUESTIONS

1. Bruner was one of the early group of U.S. psychologists who attempted study of the "higher mental processes." Among other things

he has been interested in both education and creativity. Can you account for the fact that he and his colleagues chose to use such an apparently arid and mind-numbing procedure as concept identification in their research?

2. Much of the vocabulary here may be new, and it is certainly abstract. Don't panic. In concept identification, the task is something like the game of Twenty Questions. The subject is shown patterns and is told that they *are* (positive) or *are not* (negative) instances of the to-be-identified concept. Rule learning and attribute learning are variants of what the subject must "guess." How do they differ?

3. Be sure you can give specific examples of the following terms, and understand their relationship: *dimension, attribute, feature, class, category, subordinate, superordinate, hierarchy, conjunctive, disjunctive, conditional, biconditional, probabilistic, continuous, discrete.*

4. How does attribute frequency theory account for the findings on task difficulty in various concept identification tasks?

5. What makes a basic category basic, according to Rosch? To put it another way, what are the characteristics of a basic category? How would you know whether a given category is basic or not?

6. How does expertise change people's ability to quickly identify objects at the different hierarchical levels? Do you have an area of expertise where you can make rapid identifications?

7. What makes an object a "good" member of a category? What is a family resemblance score? How do taxonomic and goal-derived categories differ?

8. For most of us, other people are the most important and interesting "objects" in our world. We say that each human being is unique, yet we constantly classify people. Is that good? or bad? or both? Why?

9. When we meet up with an object we have never encountered before, how do we decide what it is (to which class it belongs)? The prototype and feature frequency models both attempt to answer this question. Does either succeed, in your judgment?

10. Do you think that a knowledgeable person could produce a computer program to predict the winner of, say, the Heismann trophy, or similar award? (Your pick.) How would one go about it; what data would you use? Write out your answer.

KEY TERMS

The page number in parentheses refers to where the term is discussed in the chapter.

attribute learning (224)
average distance rule (244)
basic-level categories (227)

biconditional rule (222)
concept identification (220)
conditional rule (221)

conjunctive rule (221)
continuous dimensions (226)
disjunctive rule (221)
family resemblance (232)
feature frequency rule (244)
frequency theory (224)
goal-derived categories (234)
hierarchically organized (226)
ideals (234)
logical rules (221)

nearest-neighbor rule (244)
prototype (230)
prototype rule (244)
representativeness (226)
rule learning (222)
stereotypes (235)
subordinate categories (227)
superordinate categories (227)
typicality (231)

RECOMMENDED READING

Komatsu (1992) and Medin (1989) provide recent overviews of the literature on categorization, supplementing earlier reviews by Mervis and Rosch (1981) and Medin and Smith (1984). Taylor and Crocker (1981) discuss the role of categorization in social information processing and Widiger and Trull (1991) discuss the role of categorization in clinical assessment. Martin and Caramazza (1980) investigated whether subjects would use logical rules or similarity relations to classify schematic faces. Kemler-Nelson (1984) found that the incidental learning of categories favors learning based on overall similarity, whereas intentional learning favors the learning of criterial attributes. Some limitations of similarity-based models are discussed by Murphy and Medin (1985). Homa (1984) also reviews categorization models and discusses how variables such as category size, distortion, and feedback influence classification. J. M. Mandler and P. J. Bauer (1988) argue that basic-level categories are not as developmentally important as Rosch's theory implies. Strauss (1979) studied prototype abstraction in infants and adults to determine whether the prototype or the feature frequency theory could best account for the findings. Although both theories seek to explain how people abstract information, some investigators (Brooks, 1978; Jacoby & Brooks, 1984; Medin & Ross, 1989) have argued that people use specific examples rather than abstracted information.

Semantic
Organization

A scientist must organize. One makes a science with facts in the same way that one makes a house with stones; but an accumulation of facts is no more a science than a pile of stones is a house.

Henri Poincaré

T HE NEED TO organize knowledge is universal—it applies as much to the arts and humanities as to the sciences. Imagine that you wrote every fact you knew on a separate card and someone shuffled all the cards and dropped them in a gigantic pile. Now imagine that someone asked you in which city the Declaration of Independence was signed and you had to retrieve the right card in order to answer the question. How would you find the card? Even worse, what if you had to write an essay on the Declaration of Independence? Since all the cards are mixed up, finding one card would provide no clues about the location of other cards on the same topic.

In order to retrieve related information from LTM, we must be able to organize our memory. Much of this organization is semantic—that is, it is based on the meaning of the information. Ericsson (1985) has argued that people who have exceptional memories are not genetically endowed with a superior memory. Rather, they have acquired very efficient encoding and retrieval skills through extensive practice. A particularly effective way to organize information is to form hierarchies. An illustration of how reorganizing information into a hierarchy can be very effective is Ericsson and Polson's (1988) analysis of how a waiter could recall up to 20 complete dinner orders without taking notes. We will see other examples of how hierarchical organization facilitates recall in the first section of this chapter.

A popular procedure for studying the organization of semantic memory is to ask people to respond true or false to statements such as "A robin is a bird" or "A canary is a building." In order to answer the question "Is a robin a bird?" we have to consider the meaning of both *robin* and *bird*. The time needed to respond provides psychologists with a clue about the organization of semantic information in LTM. The second section of this chapter describes how psychologists have followed this approach to construct models of semantic memory. Two major classes of models are used. One model assumes that people compare the features of two categories to determine their relationship. For example, we could decide whether a robin is a bird by determining whether a robin possesses the features of a bird. This model is somewhat similar to the categorization models discussed in the previous chapter. The other model assumes that the relation between two categories is stored directly in memory in a **semantic network,** which consists of concepts joined to other concepts by links that specify the relation between them.

The third section of this chapter illustrates how semantic networks can be applied to tasks that require the integration of ideas. A key assumption here is the idea of spreading activation. **Spreading activation** means that the activation of a concept can lead to the activation of related concepts as the activation spreads along the paths of the network.

Semantic network
A theory proposing that semantic information is organized in LTM by linking concepts to related concepts

Spreading activation
A theoretical construct proposing that activation spreads from a concept in a semantic network to activate related concepts

The number and organization of paths are therefore important variables in determining how rapidly people can retrieve information from LTM.

The fourth section discusses organized clusters of knowledge called *schemata*. When I briefly reviewed the history of cognitive psychology in Chapter 1, I mentioned that behaviorism had less of a hold on psychology in Europe than it did in the United States. Two psychologists in particular, Bartlett in England and Piaget in Switzerland, rejected the idea that knowledge consists of learning many stimulus-response associations in favor of the idea that knowledge consists of larger, schematic structures. These ideas eventually spread to the United States and have greatly influenced much of the research in cognitive psychology. We will begin examining schema theories in this chapter and then apply them to theories of comprehension, reasoning, and problem solving in later chapters.

HIERARCHICAL ORGANIZATION

We have seen examples in the previous chapter of how some information is hierarchically organized and how a hierarchical organization can influence our performance on cognitive tasks such as classifying visual patterns. Hierarchical organization can also influence performance by facilitating the recall of semantic information.

Recall of Hierarchical Information

One advantage of a well-organized memory is that it helps us to retrieve information in a systematic way. I began this chapter by asking you to imagine that you had to retrieve information by searching a gigantic pile of cards. If the information on the cards were organized in some systematic way, this would be a manageable task. If the information were not systematically organized, the task would be very difficult and your level of achievement would not be very impressive.

An experimental analog of this task was created to study the effects of hierarchical organization on recall (Bower, Clark, Winzenz, & Lesgold, 1969). The material consisted of conceptual hierarchies of words like the one shown in Figure 9.1. Participants in the experiment saw four different hierarchies, each containing 28 words. One group of subjects, in the "organized" condition, studied the four hierarchies for approximately 1 min each. They then tried to recall all 112 words in whatever order they wished. The study and recall trial was repeated three more times. The upper curve in Figure 9.2 shows how well this group performed—they recalled 73 words after the first study trial and all 112 words after three study trials.

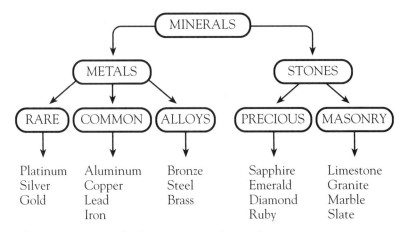

Figure 9.1 *Hierarchical organization of minerals.*

From "Organizational Factors in Memory," by G. H. Bower, 1970, *Cognitive Psychology, 1,* 18–46. Copyright © 1970 by Academic Press, Inc. Reprinted by permission.

Another group of subjects, in the "random" condition, saw the same 112 words inserted randomly in the four hierarchies. For example, if the four hierarchies consisted of plants, instruments, body parts, and minerals, each set of 28 words would contain words from all four hierarchies inserted randomly into a spatial tree like the one shown in Figure 9.1. The

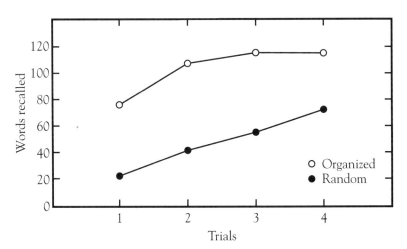

Figure 9.2 *Average number of words recalled by subjects in "organized" and "random" conditions.*

From "Organizational Factors in Memory," by G. H. Bower, 1970, *Cognitive Psychology, 1,* 18–46. Copyright © 1970 by Academic Press, Inc. Reprinted by permission.

high level of performance of subjects in the organized condition is particularly impressive when compared with performance in the random condition. After four study trials the random group was still recalling fewer words than the organized group recalled on the very first trial (see Figure 9.2).

Of course, the effects of organization are not limited to hierarchical organization. In another experiment Bower and colleagues (1969) presented people with associated words linked together. For example, the words *bread, mouse,* and *yellow* were linked to *cheese*; the words *cat* and *trap* were linked to *mouse*; and *sun* and *butterfly* were linked to *yellow.* When the associated words were linked together, people recalled many more words than when the same words were randomly linked together (for example, when *cat* and *bread* were linked to *yellow*). Semantic organization of the material improved recall, even though the organization did not consist of a hierarchy. The difference between the organized and random conditions was more striking for hierarchical organization, however, suggesting that hierarchical organization is particularly effective.

Category Size

Figure 9.1 shows that each category in the hierarchy is divided into several smaller categories. The division of a category into subcategories raises the question of how big the groups should be. The advantage of grouping items might be reduced if the groups were too small. However, information might be difficult to remember or retrieve if the groups were too large.

In Chapter 4 we learned that the capacity of STM can be increased by forming chunks consisting of several items stored as a group in LTM. The grouping of chess pieces (Chase & Simon, 1973) is an example of how chunking improves recall in an STM task—the average size of a chunk for an expert chess player was 2.5 pieces. We know from both research (Charness, 1976) and demonstrations (Box 9.1) that chess experts also have a very good LTM for chess positions. In order for such a good LTM to exist, it is likely that the smaller chunks are part of a very large hierarchy of board positions.

Psychologists have used several techniques to study how people group information. The estimated size of the groups depends on the experimental procedure, but it generally ranges from two to five items. Chase and Ericsson (1979) demonstrated how groupings can improve recall by testing a single subject over a 1-year period. The subject began with a typical digit span of 7 digits. After 1 year of practice he could recall a string of 70 digits. Pauses in his recall indicated that he organized the digits into groups of 3 or 4 and never formed groups larger than 5 digits. Since the subject was a long-distance runner, he initially tried to encode many of

BOX 9.1

At age 75, chess master is still blindfolded whiz

Chess master George Koltanowski set a world's record Saturday in San Francisco—at age 75—by playing and beating four opponents at once without looking at the boards.

Koltanowski, the chess editor of the *Chronicle,* thus became the oldest player to hold what chess players call a blindfold simultaneous exhibition.

His four opponents had full use of chessmen and boards as they called their moves out in turn to the master, who sat in a corner of his apartment with his eyes shut and his arm propped on a television.

The first player was checkmated in 13 moves and the other three resigned shortly thereafter. Mike Duncan of San Mateo lasted 26 moves before moving his rook to the wrong square and falling into a trap.

"I knew I'd lose," said Duncan, "but it's fascinating to find out just when the blow is going to come."

Koltanowski said he was nervous before the exhibition began, but, as his opponents began to slip up, he sat back, cracked an occasional joke and nibbled cookies.

"It was just like the good old days," said the master, who, in 1937, took on 34 opponents in a simultaneous blindfold exhibition in Scotland, winning 24 games and drawing 10.

"I'm back on the warpath," he added. "Next month I'm going to play six at once."

His wife, Leah, who witnessed the exhibition but who does not know how to play chess, smiled when asked if Koltanowski remembers such things as bringing home items from the market.

"George remembers what he wants to remember," she said.

SOURCE: From "At Age 75, Chess Master Is Still a Blindfold Whiz," appearing in the *San Francisco Chronicle,* February 26, 1979. Copyright © 1979 by the San Francisco Chronicle. Reprinted by permission.

the groups as running times. For instance, he encoded 3492 as 3.492, a near-world-record time for running a mile. He also showed evidence of using hierarchical organization—he combined digits into larger groups that usually consisted of three smaller groups. After recalling the first three groups of 4 digits each, he would pause longer before recalling the next three groups of 4 digits each. One interesting finding is that the subject's ability to recall groups of digits didn't generalize to letters. When he was tested on recalling letters, his memory span immediately fell back to about six consonants.

Broadbent (1975) also studied pauses in recall to determine how people store categorized information in LTM. He asked people to name television programs, the countries of Europe, the seven dwarfs, and the colors of the rainbow. On the basis of pauses in their recall and other experimental findings, he argued that people usually form groups consisting of about three items. One of the experiments he cited was a study by Wickelgren (1964) that investigated the size of rehearsal groups. Wickelgren asked people to rehearse a string of digits and instructed them on how to group the digits in the string. The instructions varied both the number and the size of the groups. Recall was best when the digits were divided into groups consisting of either three or four digits. Telephone numbers, of course, are grouped in this way, which presumably makes them easier to rehearse. And we use commas to divide long strings of digits into three-digit groups.

A good example of how small groups can be formed into a very large hierarchy is the organization of information contained in a book or newspaper. Detterman and Ramig (1978) collected paragraphs from a wide variety of newspapers, novels, and upper-division textbooks. They found that the average number of sentences in a paragraph was about two for newspapers, three for novels, and five for textbooks. They then gave people examples of the sentences and asked them to divide each sentence into its major parts. The instructions did not specify the meaning of "major parts," nor did they suggest how many major parts should be in a sentence. People identified an average of 2.4 parts per sentence. They were then instructed to break the major parts into smaller parts if they could. They divided the major parts into an average of 3.6 smaller parts, each containing an average of 2.2 words. Each of the words contained an average of 2.3 syllables, and each syllable contained an average of 2.6 phonemes. The data illustrate how a paragraph can be partitioned into smaller and smaller categories, each consisting of 2 to 4 items.

The paragraph hierarchy contained a mixture of subjective and objective units. The objective units—sentences, words, syllables, and phonemes—are well defined and can be measured simply by counting how frequently they occur. The other two levels—the parts and subparts of sentences—were measured by asking people to break up a sentence into its parts. Of course, it is likely that objective grammatical units—noun phrases, verb phrases, and prepositional phrases—influenced the way people partitioned a sentence. We will encounter some of these units in the next chapter, on language, when we learn how the rules of a grammar can provide a hierarchical description of sentences.

Hierarchical organization could be extended even further if we had started with an entire book rather than a single paragraph. For example, I wrote this book on a hierarchical plan. The book is divided into three major parts: (1) information-processing stages, (2) the representation and organization of knowledge, and (3) complex cognitive skills. Each part contains four or five chapters, and each chapter contains three or four sections, each divided into two to four subsections. I'm not certain whether this kind of organization is beneficial to readers, but it is consistent with experimental findings on hierarchical organization and category size. It also makes a very large hierarchy if we connect it to the paragraph hierarchy investigated by Detterman and Ramig.

Building Semantic Networks

The finding that organization aids recall raises the issue of how to teach people to improve their recall by using effective organizational strategies. One way to organize information is to construct a semantic network. Semantic networks show how concepts are related to each other. Networks are typically represented by diagrams in which the concepts are called **nodes** and the lines showing the relationship between two concepts are called **links**.

Figure 9.1, showing the hierarchical organization of minerals, is an example of a semantic network in which the links have not been labeled. The links in this diagram show only a single relation—that one mineral is a type of another mineral, which represents a larger category. Thus bronze is a type of alloy, alloys are a type of metal, and metals are a type of mineral. This is a good start, but most knowledge is too complex to be represented by a single relation.

Figure 9.3 shows several different kinds of relations among concepts. Notice that this information is also hierarchical. There are two kinds of hierarchical relations, *part* (indicated by a *p*) and *type* (indicated by a *t*). *Part* indicates that a concept in a lower node is part of a concept in a higher node. The discussion of wounds is divided into two parts: the types of wounds and the process of healing. *Type* indicates that a concept in a lower node is an example of a category in a higher node. Open and closed wounds are examples of different types of wounds. This categorical relation is the same one that relates the mineral concepts in Figure 9.1.

In addition, the information on wounds contains two nonhierarchical relations: *characteristics* (indicated by a *c*) and *leads to* (represented by an *l*). *Characteristics* are the features or properties of a concept. A characteristic of an open wound is that there is a break in the skin. The relation *leads to* specifies that one concept leads to or causes another concept. This relation is particularly useful for describing sequential processes, such as the three phases of healing.

The effectiveness of semantic networks has been extensively investigated at Texas Christian University. In a study described by Holley and Dansereau (1984), students received training on constructing semantic networks for material in their regular courses. These students and a control group of students then studied and were later tested on a 3000-word passage from a basic science textbook. Students who constructed semantic networks of this material did significantly better than the control group on short-answer and essay questions but did not do significantly better on multiple-choice questions.

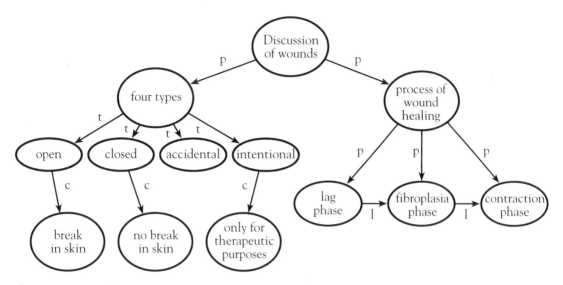

Figure 9.3   *Part of a semantic network that represents information in a nursing text.*
From "Evaluation of a Hierarchical Mapping Technique as an Aid to Prose Processing," by C. D. Holley, D. F. Dansereau, B. A. McDonald, J. C. Garland, and K. W. Collins, 1979, *Contemporary Educational Psychology, 4,* 227–237. Copyright © 1979 by Academic Press, Inc. Reprinted by permission.

This finding is consistent with the results mentioned at the end of Chapter 6 on transfer-appropriate processing. As you may recall, students who expected open questions did better on these questions than students who expected multiple-choice questions. Students who expected open questions apparently placed more emphasis on organizing their knowledge. Constructing semantic networks is a good method for organizing knowledge, as indicated by the resulting higher test scores on the open questions in the essay and short-answer tests.

In order to make the construction of semantic networks an effective learning strategy, we need more data on when they are effective and we need good software to allow us to construct very large networks. The first of these needs is being addressed by continued research at Texas Christian University (Lambiotte, Dansereau, Cross, & Reynolds, 1989). This group has shifted their emphasis from student-generated networks to expert-generated networks that vary along a number of dimensions, such as amount of material, type of material, and level of abstraction. Once investigators achieve a better understanding of what makes an effective network, they will be more able to explore the educational potential of this method.

The second need, effective computer software, allows the construction of very large networks that would be impractical on paper. An example is the *SemNet* software, which allows users to construct very large semantic networks as a means of learning about and organizing their knowledge of a domain (Fisher, Faletti, Patterson, Thornton, Lipson, & Spring, 1990). The largest network constructed to date consists of approximately 2500 concepts from an introductory biology course. The SemNet program allows the user to view a small piece of the network on the computer screen. If I wanted to review information about the nucleus of a cell, I would type *nucleus* to see its relation to other concepts. The computer would then display the part of the network in which *nucleus* was the central concept linked to related concepts.

VERIFICATION OF SEMANTIC STATEMENTS

The first part of this chapter emphasized how effective organization, particularly hierarchical organization, increased the *amount* of information that we can retrieve from LTM. Hierarchical organization also influences the *time* required to retrieve information. A popular procedure for studying the organization of semantic knowledge is to ask people to quickly verify semantic statements. The experimenter might present a statement such as "A bird is an animal" and ask the subject to respond true or false as quickly as possible. The time it takes to respond to different kinds of statements provides some clues about the organization of semantic memory. As you might expect, hierarchical organization influences the time required to verify semantic statements.

Figure 9.4 shows a three-level hierarchy in which the most general category, *animal*, is divided into two subcategories—*bird* and *fish*. At the bottom of the hierarchy are specific instances of birds and fish, such as *canary* and *shark*. The hierarchical organization influences classification time in that people can generally verify that an instance is a member of a basic-level category faster than they can verify that it is a member of a superordinate category. For instance, they can more quickly determine that a canary is a bird than that a canary is an animal. People can also classify more typical instances faster than less typical instances. It is easier to verify that a canary is a bird than that an ostrich is a bird.

A number of theories have been proposed to account for these findings. The two most popular are the hierarchical network model of Collins and Quillian (1969, 1970) and the feature comparison model of Smith, Shoben, and Rips (1974). The distinction between the two models can be summarized briefly with the aid of the diagram in Figure 9.5. The **feature comparison model** assumes that instances are classified by comparing the features, or attributes, of the two nouns representing the member and the category. To verify that a robin is a bird, a person would compare the features of *robin* with the features of *bird*. In contrast, the **hierarchical network model** assumes that category information is stored directly in memory by means of associations. The right half of Figure 9.5 shows that

Feature comparison model A model proposing that items are categorized by matching the item's features to category features

Hierarchical network model A model proposing that items are categorized by using the hierarchical relations specified in a semantic network

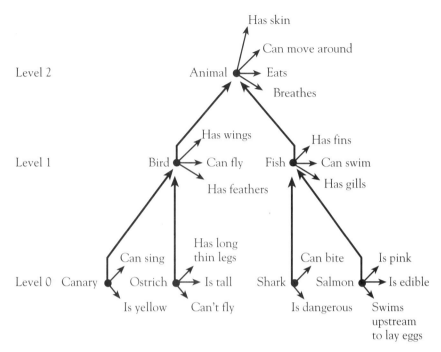

Figure 9.4   *Example of a hierarchically organized memory structure.*

From "Retrieval Time from Semantic Memory," by A. M. Collins and M. R. Quillian, 1969, *Journal of Verbal Learning and Verbal Behavior, 8,* 240–248. Copyright © 1969 by Academic Press, Inc. Reprinted by permission.

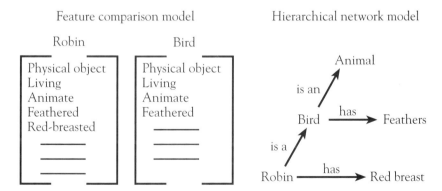

Figure 9.5   *Distinction between the feature comparison model and the hierarchical network model.*

From "Theories of Semantic Memory," by E. E. Smith, 1978, in *Handbook of Learning and Cognitive Processes,* Volume 6, edited by W. K. Estes. Copyright © 1978 by Lawrence Erlbaum Associates, Inc. Reprinted by permission.

robin is associated with *bird* and *bird* is associated with *animal*. In order to make predictions, both theories require more specific assumptions. We will now examine the strengths and weaknesses of these assumptions.

The Hierarchical Network Model

Figure 9.4 shows how information is stored in the hierarchical network model. Each word in the network is stored with pointers (arrows) showing how it is related to other words in the network. By following the pointers, we know that *ostrich* and *canary* are examples of birds and that *bird* and *fish* are examples of animals. We also know that a canary, an ostrich, a shark, and a salmon are animals because the pointers connect these instances with the superordinate category *animal*.

The pointers also show how features are stored at different levels in the hierarchy. Features that are true of all animals—such as eating and breathing—are stored at the highest level. Features that apply to basic-level categories—such as that birds have wings, can fly, and have feathers—are stored at an intermediate level. Properties stored at the lowest level are true for that particular member but not for all members of the category. It is at this level that we know that a canary is yellow and can sing.

One advantage of this kind of network is that it provides an economical way to store information because the information does not have to be repeated at each of the three levels. It isn't necessary to specify that eating and breathing are features of birds, fish, canaries, ostriches, sharks, and salmon, because the network tells us that all are examples of *animals*, which eat and breathe. This economy of storage comes at a cost, however: retrieval of the fact that a canary eats requires two inferences—first, that a canary is a bird and, second, that a bird is an animal. In other words, it is necessary to go to the appropriate level in the hierarchy before retrieving the features stored at that level.

Although the network model was originally developed as an efficient means of storing information in a computer, it provides a number of interesting predictions if we use it as a model of human memory. Collins and Quillian (1969), in fact, used the model for that purpose by making two primary assumptions—that it takes time to move from one level in the hierarchy to another and that additional time is required if it is necessary to retrieve the features stored at one of the levels. Collins and Quillian tested the model by asking people to respond true or false as quickly as they could to sentences like "An elm is a plant" or "A spruce has branches." The first sentence is an example of a question about set relations—it asks whether one category is a member of another. The second question is a question about properties—it asks about the features of a category member.

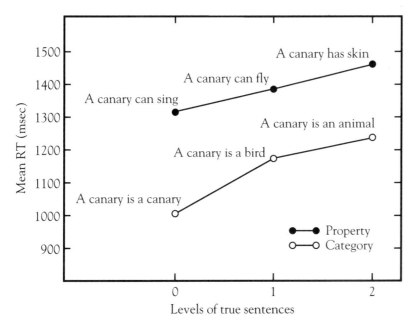

Figure 9.6   *Reaction time (RT) to verify statements about feature attributes and category membership.*

From "Retrieval Time from Semantic Memory," by A. M. Collins and M. R. Quillian, 1969, *Journal of Verbal Learning and Verbal Behavior, 8,* 240–248. Copyright © 1969 by Academic Press, Inc. Reprinted by permission.

The average reaction times to six kinds of true sentences are shown in Figure 9.6. A specific example illustrates the different points on the graph. The three lower points—the response times to questions about set relations—support the prediction that it takes time to move between levels in the network. To verify that "A canary is a canary" requires no change in level; "A canary is a bird" requires a one-level change; and "A canary is an animal" requires a two-level change. The graph shows that response times depend on the number of changes.

The upper three points show that it takes longer to respond to property questions. This finding is consistent with the assumption that response time should increase if it is necessary to retrieve the features stored at one of the levels in the hierarchy. Furthermore, the level in the network where the properties are stored influences response times. The network model proposes that information about singing is stored at the lowest level, information about flying is stored at the intermediate level, and information about skin is stored at the highest level. The data support this assumption and suggest that this is how property information is stored in human memory.

Another interesting prediction based on the network model concerns facilitating retrieval from memory (Collins & Quillian, 1970). Facilitation occurs when the retrieval of information is made easier because the previous question required retrieval of similar information. For example, it should be easier to verify a property of a canary if the previous question was also about a canary. The network model, however, allows us to make a more specific prediction. Collins and Quillian proposed that the degree of facilitation should depend on whether one follows the same path in the network to answer the two questions. This concept can be illustrated by considering whether it would be easier to verify that "A canary is a bird" after "A canary can fly" or after "A canary can sing." The answer isn't intuitively obvious, but the network model predicts that "A canary can fly" should cause greater facilitation because the property *fly* is stored at the bird level and *sing* is stored at the canary level. The same path is followed only when both questions require retrieving information from the bird level. The data were quite supportive of the prediction that the extent of semantic facilitation depends on using the same path as the previous question (Collins & Quillian, 1970).

The successful predictions of the reaction time data in Figure 9.6 and the predictions about semantic facilitation are impressive accomplishments of the network model. There are two findings, however, that the model does not account for without additional assumptions. The first is that it is possible to find instances in which verification time is not a function of levels in the hierarchy. For example, it takes longer to verify that a chimpanzee is a primate than that a chimpanzee is an animal. The network model should predict the opposite because *primate*, like *bird* and *fish*, is at a lower level in the hierarchy than *animal*. The second finding is that the network model does not account for the **typicality effect**—the fact that more typical members of categories are easier to classify than less typical ones. It is easier to verify that a canary is a bird than that an ostrich is a bird. However, since both are one level from *bird*, as is illustrated in Figure 9.4, the model does not predict the differences in response time. The feature comparison model attempted to correct these deficiencies by offering an alternative formulation.

The Feature Comparison Model

The feature comparison model proposed by Smith, Shoben, and Rips (1974) seeks to account for classification times in somewhat the same way that the prototype model accounts for classifications. This model assumes that the meaning of words can be represented in memory by a list of features and that classifications are made by comparing features rather than

Typicality effect The finding that the more typical members of a category are classified more quickly than the less typical category members

by examining links in a network (see Figure 9.5). The features can be used to define categories, but they vary in the extent to which they are associated with a category. Smith and colleagues considered the most essential features to be defining features and the remainder to be characteristic features. **Defining features** are features that an entity must have in order to be a member of a category, whereas **characteristic features** are usually possessed by category members but are not necessary. The defining features for birds might include being alive and having feathers and wings; the characteristic features might include being able to fly and being within a certain size range. Since the defining features are more essential, they should play a more important role in how people make classifications.

The feature comparison model has two stages. The first stage compares all the features of two concepts to determine how similar one concept is to the other. For example, to determine whether a robin is a bird, we would compare the features of *robin* with the features of *bird*. If the comparison reveals that the two concepts are either very similar or very dissimilar, we can respond true or false immediately. The second stage is necessary when the degree of similarity is between the two extremes. The answer isn't obvious in this case, so the model proposes that we examine only the defining features to determine whether the example has the necessary features of the category. The distinction between the two stages corresponds to our experience that sometimes we make classifications very quickly on the basis of the close similarity between two concepts, and sometimes we make classifications more slowly after we evaluate the criteria for category membership.

Examples that are similar to the concept should usually be classified immediately, without consideration of their defining features during the second stage. The probability that the second stage is necessary increases as the similarity between the category concept and the example decreases. The model therefore predicts that the more typical members of a category (such as *robin, sparrow, bluejay*) should be classified more rapidly than the less typical members (*chicken, goose, duck*) because evaluating the defining features during the second stage slows down the classification. Smith and colleagues (1974) found that people could, in fact, classify instances that are typical of the category faster than they could classify instances that are not typical of the category.

The reverse argument applies to false statements such as "A bat is a bird." High similarity between a negative example and a category concept makes it more difficult to reject the example. Because a bat and a bird share many features, it is difficult to reach a conclusion during the initial feature comparison stage. This increases the probability that a person will evaluate the defining features during the second stage. In contrast, two dissimilar noun pairs ("A pencil is a bird") share so few features that an immediate decision can be made during the first stage. The

Defining features
Features that are necessary to be a member of that category

Characteristic features
The features that are usually present in members of that category, but are not necessary

feature comparison model, unlike the hierarchical network model, provides an explanation of why some false statements are evaluated more quickly than others.

Another advantage of the feature comparison model is that, unlike the network model, it can account for the reversal of the category size effect. The **category size effect** refers to the fact that people are usually able to classify a member into a smaller category faster than into a larger category—for example, verifying that a collie is a dog more quickly than that a collie is an animal. The network model is consistent with the category size effect because the smaller category (*dog*) requires fewer inferences than the larger category (*animal*). Since the smaller category is a part of the larger category, it appears lower in the hierarchy and will therefore be reached sooner. There are cases, however, which violate the category size effect because the classification times are faster for the larger category. For example, people were able to verify more quickly that Scotch is a drink than that Scotch is a liquor, even though *drink* is a larger category than *liquor*.

The feature comparison model can account for violations of the category size effect because its predictions are based on similarity rather than category size. The reason it is usually easier to verify that an example belongs to a smaller category is that the similarity between the example and one's concept of the smaller category is greater than the similarity between the example and the larger category. However, there are exceptions to this rule. Sometimes—as Smith, Shoben, and Rips showed—there is a greater similarity between the example and a larger category. The feature comparison model predicts that in this case people should be able to classify into the larger category more quickly than into the smaller category. Experimental results support this prediction (Smith et al., 1974).

Although the feature comparison model accounts for both typicality and category size effects, the model has some weaknesses. Let's now listen to what the critics have to say about its limitations.

Limitations of the feature comparison model.   One of the problems with the feature comparison model, as one of its developers pointed out (Smith, 1978), is that it relies on ratings to make most of its predictions. It's not very surprising that, if people rate an example as highly similar to their concept of a category, they will be fast to verify that it belongs to that category. The predictions about both typicality and category size reflect the degree of similarity between a member and its category. The predictions made by the feature comparison model are therefore rather weak predictions. Its principal asset is that the major alternative—the network model—does not make even these predictions unless it uses so many additional assumptions that it can predict almost anything.

Category size effect
The finding that members of smaller categories are classified more quickly than members of larger categories

A second criticism of the feature comparison model is its proposal that all our classifications require computations—that we use the features of concepts to compute their degree of similarity. Computation is an essential part of the categorization models discussed in the previous chapter, where the emphasis was on classifying novel patterns. But once we have learned to associate examples with categories, is it still necessary to use features to compare the similarity of two concepts? Couldn't we use the associations among concepts, as suggested by the proponents of the network model (Collins & Loftus, 1975)? If we have learned that a robin is a bird, it would seem easier to use this information directly rather than computing the similarity between *robin* and *bird*. What information is stored directly in memory and what is computed is a very important issue that is discussed by Smith (1978).

A third criticism of the feature comparison model is the argument against necessary, or defining, features (Collins & Loftus, 1975; Rosch & Mervis, 1975; McCloskey & Glucksberg, 1979). The feature comparison model avoids this criticism to some extent by proposing that features are more or less defining and that only the more defining features are evaluated during the second stage. This implies, however, that people can identify the more defining features of categories, and we have little direct support for this assumption. Rosch and Mervis's (1975) results, in fact, suggest the opposite—that the structure of categories is based not on defining features possessed by all members of the category but on a large number of features that are true of only some category members.

Although it may be difficult to specify defining features for some concepts, such as *fruit*, the distinction between characteristic and defining features may be helpful for explaining how children learn other concepts, such as *robber*. Consider the following two descriptions:

> This smelly, mean old man with a gun in his pocket came to your house one day and took your color television set because your parents didn't want it anymore and told him that he could have it. Could he be a robber?

> This very friendly and cheerful woman came up to you and gave you a hug, but then she disconnected your toilet bowl and took it away without permission and never returned it. Could she be a robber?

The first description contains characteristic features of a robber, but not the defining features. The second description contains the defining features of a robber, but not the characteristic features. A study of children in kindergarten, second, and fourth grades found that children become more sensitive to defining features as they grow older (Keil & Batterman, 1984). They become more likely to correctly respond that the mean old man is not a robber but the friendly, cheerful woman is a robber.

One interpretation of this finding is that characteristic features are more salient and directly observable than defining features (McNamara & Miller, 1989). Characteristic features such as *mean* and *gun* are observable, whereas defining features such as *taking without permission* are more conceptual. Young children initially emphasize the directly observable features and have to learn to shift their emphasis to the more conceptual features.

In conclusion, the feature comparison model has some advantages over the hierarchical network model, but it also has some limitations. It is more promising for those concepts that we believe have defining features (Malt, 1990) and for those situations in which we use features to make a decision (Keil & Batterman, 1984; McNamara & Miller, 1989). A compromise is that at different times we use either direct associations—links in a semantic network—or features to evaluate a concept. This flexibility is part of the theory discussed in the next section.

The Spreading Activation Model

The preceding discussion reflected both the strengths and the weaknesses of the hierarchical network model and the feature comparison model. Each provided an explanation for some aspects of the data but could not explain other aspects. In an attempt to account for a greater number of findings than either of these two models, Collins and Loftus borrowed assumptions from each of the models to build a model that had greater flexibility.

Spreading activation model A model that accounts for response times by formulating assumptions about how activation spreads in a semantic network

Their **spreading activation model** (Collins & Loftus, 1975) is representative of semantic network models in its emphasis on concepts joined together by links that show relationships between concepts. Figure 9.7 shows how a part of human memory can be represented in a network that is somewhat analogous to the neural networks that were discussed in Chapters 2 and 8. A change from the hierarchical network model is that the length of each link represents the degree of semantic relatedness between two concepts. Thus the concept *red* is closely related to other colors and less closely related to red objects. Notice that the model can now account for the typicality effect because the links represent different degrees of semantic relatedness. The shorter links reveal that the more typical examples *car* and *bus* are more closely related to *vehicle* than are *ambulance* and *fire engine*.

The spreading activation model assumes that, when a concept is processed, activation spreads out along the paths of a network, but its effectiveness is decreased as it travels outward. For example, presentation of the word *red* should strongly activate closely related concepts such as *orange* and *fire* and should cause less activation of concepts such as *sunsets* and *roses*. The model therefore predicts the typicality effect because more

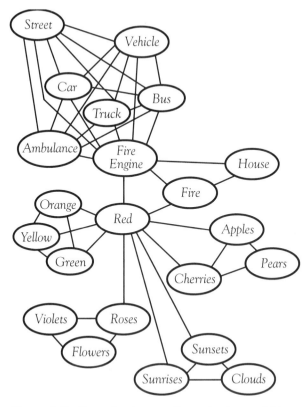

Figure 9.7   *Example of a spreading activation model in which the length of each line (link) represents the degree of association between two concepts.*

From "A Spreading Activation Theory of Semantic Processing," by A. M. Collins and E. F. Loftus, 1975, *Psychological Review, 82,* 407–428. Copyright © 1975 by the American Psychological Association. Reprinted by permission.

typical members will activate the superordinate category sooner than less typical members—for instance, *car* and *bus* will activate *vehicle* sooner than *fire engine* or *ambulance* will.

The idea of activation spreading throughout a semantic network of interconnected concepts provides a clear picture of the semantic relations among concepts. It is easy to imagine activation decreasing in strength as it travels outward. The model also assumes that activation decreases over time or intervening activity. This assumption places a constraint on the amount of activation that can occur because the activation of a second concept will decrease the activation of the first concept.

Priming Reduction of
time processing a con-
cept caused by prior
presentation of related
information

Although the model provides a convenient metaphor, its success
depends on how well it can account for experimental results. One such
result is the effect of *semantic priming*. **Priming** occurs when a decision
about one concept makes it easier to decide about another concept. An
example of priming can be found in the lexical decision task studied by
Meyer and Schvaneveldt (1976), which required that people judge
whether a string of letters formed a word. Some of the letters did (*BUT-
TER*), and some did not (*NART*). Each trial consisted of a pair of strings,
and the second string was presented immediately after subjects made
their decision about the first string. The most interesting results occurred
when both strings were words. If the two words were semantically related,
people were faster in verifying that the second string was a word than if
the two words were unrelated. For example, people verified faster that the
string *BUTTER* was a word when it was preceded by *BREAD* than when
it was preceded by *NURSE*.

The spreading activation model can account for these results because
it proposes that the presentation of a word activates related words. *BUT-
TER* will be activated by *BREAD* but will not be activated by *NURSE*.
The activation of the word makes it easier to identify, resulting in faster
response times.

One controversy regarding the spreading activation model (Ratcliff
& McKoon, 1988) is whether activation spreads beyond a single node as
predicted by the model. Although *BREAD* activates the word *BUTTER*,
would it activate a word like *POPCORN* that is associated with *BUT-
TER*, but not with *BREAD*? According to the model, activation should
spread from *BREAD* to *BUTTER* to *POPCORN*, but *POPCORN* should
be less activated than *BUTTER* because activation decreases in strength
as it spreads outward. Recent research supports the assumption that
spreading activation facilitates identification of words that are two links
away from the activated word, but the facilitation is weaker than for
words directly linked to the activated word (McNamara, 1992).

In addition to the direct representation of semantic relations in a
network, the spreading activation model allows for the use of feature
matching to verify semantic statements. It therefore includes the assumptions of both the hierarchical network model and the feature comparison
model. One way we can decide that a mallard is a bird is to find superordinate links between *mallard* and *duck* and between *duck* and *bird*. Another way is to find that there are common properties in our concept of
mallard and our concept of *bird*. Collins and Loftus suggest that we consider the evidence obtained from both feature comparisons and superordinate links when we make a decision.

An advantage of semantic network models is that they are extremely
flexible. It is very easy to introduce many assumptions into a model to
make it consistent with many kinds of data. However, the price of this
advantage is that it is very hard to test the model. If a model becomes so

flexible that it is consistent with almost any experimental finding, it loses its predictive power. A model has predictive power only if it predicts that certain events should not occur. One can then evaluate the model by determining which events do in fact occur.

The challenge for the developers of semantic network models is not only to take advantage of their flexibility but also to place some constraints on the models in order to make some interesting predictions. Now when a network model fails to make a correct prediction, the developers usually create additional assumptions to give the model greater flexibility. Consequently, the revised model usually succeeds where the original failed, but many psychologists find the revision less satisfactory. Collins and Loftus's (1975) revision of the hierarchical network model corrected the limitations of the former but sacrificed the precise predictions that made the hierarchical network model one of the more interesting semantic network theories.

Thus their model has considerable flexibility, but predictions can only be made with difficulty. Critics of the model (for instance, Smith, 1978; McCloskey & Glucksberg, 1979) have argued that, with so many assumptions, it is not surprising that the model accounts for many empirical findings. They find the model's main weaknesses to be both the number of assumptions made and the failure to make many clear-cut predictions based on it. In fact, the model was developed primarily to show how its assumptions are consistent with existing data rather than to make interesting new predictions. It remains to be seen whether psychologists can design experiments to seriously test the model.

INTEGRATION OF KNOWLEDGE

In spite of their limitations, semantic network models appeal to many people because they are sufficiently general to provide a common framework for many of the issues studied by cognitive psychologists. One of these issues involves the integration of knowledge from stories. We will first look at how a semantic network model called ACT was used to explain the slow retrieval of events that are very difficult to integrate. We will then see how the model was modified to account for the faster retrieval of information that was easier to integrate. And, in Chapter 11, we will see what happens when the integration is particularly easy because the information provides explanations for why the events occurred.

ACT Model

The generality of semantic network models is nicely illustrated by ACT. Anderson (1976) designed ACT to apply to a wide variety of cognitive tasks, ranging from scanning STM to making complex inferences. The basic assumptions of ACT are similar to those of the spreading activation model—knowledge is stored in a semantic network consisting of inter-connected nodes, and activation can spread down network paths from active nodes to activate new nodes and paths. Although the basic assumptions of the two models are the same, Anderson applies ACT to many tasks not considered by Collins and Loftus (1975).

Many aspects of ACT are too technical to discuss in an introductory book, but we will consider how Anderson applied the model to predict how quickly people can retrieve stored knowledge. The stored knowledge in this case was information that people learned in a fact-retrieval experiment. The purpose of asking them to learn information was to control experimentally the number of relations among the concepts. The experimental material consisted of 26 sentences of the form "A [person] is in the [location]" (see Table 9.1 for some examples). A particular individual and a particular location occurred in 1, 2, or 3 sentences; for example, a hippie occurred in 3 sentences, and a debutante occurred in 1 sentence. After the subjects had learned all the information in the sentences, they were given test sentences and instructed to respond true to sentences that they had previously learned and false to any other sentences. Anderson was interested in how quickly people could respond true or false to each test sentence.

Table 9.1 shows examples of the test sentences, each preceded by a two-digit number. The first digit shows the number of times the person

Table 9.1 *Sample sentences used in Anderson's (1976) fact-retrieval study*

Subject Studies

	True Test Sentences
1. A hippie is in the park.	3–3 A hippie is in the park.
2. A hippie is in the church.	1–1 A lawyer is in the cave.
3. A hippie is in the bank.	1–2 A debutante is in the bank.
4. A captain is in the park.	.
5. A captain is in the church.	.
6. A debutante is in the bank.	.
7. A fireman is in the park.	False Test Sentences
.	3–1 A hippie is in the cave.
.	1–2 A lawyer is in the park.
.	1–1 A debutante is in the cave.
26. A lawyer is in the cave.	2–2 A captain is in the bank.
	.
	.
	.

SOURCE: From *Language, Memory, and Thought*, by J. R. Anderson. Copyright © 1976 by Lawrence Erlbaum Associates, Inc. Reprinted by permission.

appeared in the study material, and the second digit shows the number of times the location appeared in the study material. Thus the sentence "A hippie is in the park" is marked 3–3 because *hippie* is associated with three different locations and *park* is associated with three different people. Anderson found that reaction times increased as a function of the number of links to each person node or location node in the network. Subjects were relatively slow in verifying a sentence like "A hippie is in the park" because *hippie* and *park* are both linked to three nodes. In contrast, they were relatively fast in verifying a sentence like "A lawyer is in the cave" because both *lawyer* and *cave* are only linked to each other.

In order to verify "A hippie is in the park," it is necessary to find a **path** in the network that joins *hippie* and *park*. Since the experiment measured response times, the theoretical question is how quickly the path can be found. Presentation of the test sentence "A hippie is in the park" causes the activation of both *hippie* and *park*. The time it takes to find the path that links *hippie* and *park* depends on (1) the rate at which activation spreads from the two concepts, (2) the length of the path joining the two concepts, and (3) the possible alternative paths the activation can take.

When a concept is activated, the rate of spread down the appropriate path (the link joining *hippie* and *park*) is determined by the strength of the appropriate link relative to the strength of the other links that join the concepts. Since the word *hippie* occurred three times in the study material, it is linked to three locations (*park*, *church*, and *bank*). The word *park* is linked to three persons (*hippie*, *captain*, and *fireman*). Increasing the number of links increases the time to find an intersecting path joining two concepts because the spread of activation is slowed along the appropriate path. ACT therefore predicts that verification time should increase with an increase in the number of links to either the person or the location. The general finding that increasing the number of links slows down the spread of activation along any one link is called the **fan effect** because activation is divided (fans out) among all the links.

In conclusion, ACT is an example of a spreading activation model in which the activation spreads throughout a semantic network. At each point in the network, the activation is divided among alternative links according to their relative strengths. Increasing the number of links therefore slows down the spread of activation.

Path   Links in a semantic network that join two concepts

Fan effect   The finding that increasing the number of links to a concept increases the time to verify one of the links

Modification of ACT

The sample sentences shown in Table 9.1 are not easy to integrate. They do not make a story; they merely show arbitrary relations between people and locations. Perhaps this is why retrieval is so slow and depends on the number of links joining the concepts.

Let's again consider ACT's prediction that increasing the number of links to a concept will slow down retrieval time because the spreading activation will be divided among the alternative paths. Smith, Adams, and Schorr (1978) argued that this assumption implies that increased knowledge about a topic should always lead to increased difficulty in answering questions about it. In order to resolve this counterintuitive prediction, they investigated whether the integration of new knowledge could reduce the interference caused by additional links.

Their procedure was similar to Anderson's. Subjects learned either two or three facts about a person—for example, that "Marty broke a bottle" and "Marty did not delay the trip." The third fact either provided a common theme for the first two facts or was unrelated. "Marty was chosen to christen the ship" provides a theme for "Marty broke the bottle" and "Marty did not delay the trip," whereas "Marty was asked to address the crowd" is not obviously related to the first two facts. The test required that people then make rapid judgments about whether test sentences had appeared in the study set. When the facts were unrelated, people required more time to recognize a statement if they had learned three facts than if they had learned two. This finding replicated Anderson's results and is consistent with the predictions of ACT. When the third fact integrated the first two, people could recognize any one of the three facts as quickly as they could when there were only two facts. In other words, integration allows one to overcome the potential interference of learning new information.

This experiment shows that increasing the number of links at a concept node does not necessarily slow down recognition time. Does this result seriously challenge ACT? In the final chapter of *Language, Memory, and Thought* (1976), Anderson provides the following answer:

> Another remark that needs to be made about the empirical accountability of ACT is that one cannot seriously expect to perform a single experiment and slay ACT. If ACT makes a prediction that proves wrong, that exact version of ACT will have to be abandoned but I am obviously going to propose a slight variant of the theory with slightly changed assumptions that is compatible with those data. It would be nice if the theory could be reduced to a few critical assumptions that could be subject to simple experimental tests. However, things just do not work that way. ACT is only going to be rejected by repeated attacks that keep forcing reformulations until the point comes when the theory becomes unmanageable with its patches and bandages. (p. 532)

Anderson has kept his promise by formulating a slight variation of the theory to meet the challenge raised by Smith, Adams, and Schorr. His modified version of ACT uses **subnodes** to integrate related material (Reder & Anderson, 1980). In Figure 9.8a, the original ACT representa-

Subnodes Nodes that link together related ideas in a semantic network

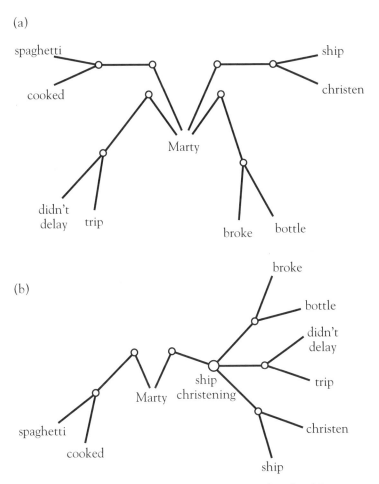

Figure 9.8 *Two possible memory representations for related facts about Marty: (a) ACT representation; (b) modified ACT representation using subnodes.*

From "Partial Resolution of the Paradox of Interference: The Role of Integrating Knowledge," by L. Reder and J. R. Anderson, 1980, *Cognitive Psychology, 12,* 447–472. Copyright © 1980 by Academic Press, Inc. Reprinted by permission.

tion, all four facts are linked directly to Marty. In Figure 9.8b, the modified ACT representation using subnodes, only two facts are linked directly to Marty—that he cooked spaghetti and that he participated in a ship christening. The three facts about the ship christening are all linked to the same subnode.

Reder and Anderson propose that, under certain conditions, people can evaluate a fact by making a consistency judgment rather than by trying to retrieve the fact. When given the test statement "Marty broke the bottle," people respond positively because this information is consistent with the theme that Marty christened the ship. In this case they would respond as soon as activation reached the ship-christening subnode and then would not attempt to retrieve the facts connected to the subnode. Response times would therefore not be influenced by the number of facts connected to the subnode, as Smith et al. (1978) found.

However, the integration of facts at a common subnode does not always eliminate interference. The number of facts influences response time when a person must examine the specific facts at that subnode. Imagine that you read statements about a ship christening, but some of the statements described Marty's activities and other statements described James's activities. If you now had to evaluate the statement "Marty broke the bottle," you might have difficulty, since both were involved in the christening. Evaluating the statement therefore requires retrieving the specific facts associated with Marty. The data collected by Reder and Anderson revealed that even integrated facts can interfere with each other when the subject is forced to examine the specific facts and cannot make a general consistency judgment.

Their findings suggest that integration results in faster decisions when examining only the subnode is sufficient for making the decision. This conclusion is also supported by the influence of irrelevant information on response times. The fact "Marty cooked spaghetti" is irrelevant to his activities associated with ship christening. Inclusion of this statement delays the evaluation of statements about ship christening because activation also spreads down irrelevant paths. However, additional statements about cooking spaghetti do not further delay decisions about ship christening because these statements can be integrated at a *cooking spaghetti* subnode and activation will stop once this irrelevant subnode is reached.

The subnode model is an example of a successful revision of ACT to incorporate new findings. The basic assumption of ACT remains the same—activation spreads along the paths of a semantic network. The revision is simply that activation can stop at a subnode rather than spread to the integrated facts linked to that subnode.

Schema Theory

Semantic networks provide a convenient way of organizing knowledge, but the emphasis is on showing how two nodes are related, and not on showing how ideas are grouped together to form larger clusters of knowledge. The advantage of the subnode model is that it offers a way of forming larger clusters by grouping related ideas around subnodes. However, there is a much older, and more fully developed, theory for representing

clusters of knowledge, called *schema theory*. A **schema** is a cluster of knowledge that represents a general procedure, object, precept, event, sequence
of events, or social situation (Thorndyke, 1984). Schema theory refers to a
collection of models that presume that we encode such knowledge clusters
into memory and use them to comprehend and store our experiences.

Schema A general
knowledge structure
that provides a frame-
work for organizing
clusters of knowledge

I mentioned during the brief historical overview in Chapter 1 that
during the time period that U.S. psychologists were predominantly influenced by stimulus-response theories, psychologists such as Bartlett in England and Piaget in Switzerland were arguing that behavior is influenced
by large units of knowledge organized into schema. We will begin by
looking at Bartlett's theory, as analyzed by Brewer and Nakamura (1984).

Bartlett's schema theory.   The schema theory that Bartlett (1932) developed in his book *Remembering* has inspired many of the modern versions
of schema theory. He defined a schema as an active organization of past
experiences in which the mind abstracts a general cognitive structure to
represent many particular instances of those experiences. Bartlett's book
consists of an elaboration of schema theory and shows its application to
experimental results that he had collected on memory for figures, pictures, and stories.

A fundamental assumption of Bartlett's schema theory is that all new
information interacts with old information represented in the schema.
This interaction was noticed by Bartlett in the errors people made in recall. Many of the errors were more regular, more meaningful, and more
conventional than the original material, suggesting that the material had
been integrated with prior knowledge structures.

Brewer and Nakamura (1984) point out that there are a number of
fundamental differences between schema theory and the stimulus-response approach to psychology. These include:

1. *Atomistic versus molar*. A stimulus-response theory is atomistic and is
   based on small units of knowledge (a single stimulus). A schema is a
   much larger unit, showing how knowledge is combined into clusters.
2. *Associationistic versus nonassociationistic*. A stimulus-response theory
   requires learning an association between a stimulus and a response. A
   schema provides a knowledge structure for interpreting and encoding
   aspects of a particular experience.
3. *Particularistic versus generic*. A stimulus-response theory shows the association between a particular stimulus and a particular response. A
   schema is more general and represents a variety of particular instances, much like a prototype represents the particular instances of a
   category.
4. *Passive versus active*. The association between a stimulus and a response can be learned in a passive manner. Invoking a schema is a

more active process in which a particular experience is matched to the schema that best fits that experience.

Bartlett's ideas had little theoretical impact during his lifetime. In the United States behaviorism and stimulus-response psychology had a strong hold on theory construction. In England his theory was taken more seriously, but by the early 1970s even his own students thought the theory a failure. A dramatic turn of events occurred in 1975 when a number of prominent U.S. cognitive scientists argued that schema are needed to organize knowledge in artificial intelligence, cognitive psychology, linguistics, and motor performance. These theorists adopted the major assumptions of Bartlett's theory, but were more specific about what these knowledge structures looked like. We will now examine some of the contributions of these later theories.

Modern schema theory.   Two of the strongest advocates for the importance of schema were Minsky (1975) for representing knowledge in artificial intelligence programs and Rumelhart (1980) for representing knowledge in cognitive psychology. Rumelhart argued that schema are the building blocks of cognition. According to Rumelhart, a schema theory is basically a theory about how knowledge is represented and about how that representation facilitates the use of knowledge in various ways. Schema are used to interpret sensory data, retrieve information from memory, organize action, and solve problems.

One of the main contributions from artificial intelligence has been that programming languages allow more detailed specification of schema organization than was possible in earlier formulations (Thorndyke, 1984). Although Bartlett emphasized that schema were organized, he was not always very specific about what the organization was. We now think of a schema as providing a skeleton structure, which can be filled out with the detailed properties of a particular instance.

Let's take a familiar routine for students: registering for courses. What kinds of knowledge would you like to have before signing up for a course? You would probably want to know what the prerequisites are, whether it meets some requirement, how many credits you will receive, when and where it meets, and perhaps who is teaching it. An advantage of having schematic knowledge is that we can sometimes rely on **default knowledge**—that is, likely values that enable us to make intelligent guesses in the absence of specific knowledge. For instance, most lecture courses offer the same number of credits, so you could probably guess how many credits you would receive for a cognitive psychology course before looking it up. You might also have guessed that the prerequisite was introductory psychology and might even have guessed the name of the instructor if the same person usually teaches this course.

Default knowledge
Knowledge about the most likely values for the attributes of a schema

I indicated at the beginning of this section that a schema can represent a variety of knowledge structures: procedures, objects, percepts, events, sequences of events, or social situations. We have schemas for solving different kinds of problems, for recognizing faces, for going shopping for groceries, and for forming social stereotypes. Schemas are particularly important for text comprehension and problem solving and we will later examine their influence on these cognitive skills. For now, we want to examine the organization of a particular type of schematic structure—our knowledge about a sequence of events. This will enable us to move from this rather abstract overview to see how cognitive psychologists do research on schematic organization.

Scripts: Representing sequences of events.   Part of our schematic knowledge is organized around routine activities—for example, going to a restaurant, visiting a dentist, changing a flat tire, or riding a bus. Schank and Abelson (1977) used the term ***script*** to refer to what we know about the sequence of events that make up such routine activities. For example, a restaurant script would specify what we know about going to a restaurant. At a very general level, a restaurant script consists of standard roles, props or objects, conditions, and results. The conditions for going to a restaurant are that a customer is hungry and is able to pay for the meal. The props are tables and chairs, a menu, food, a bill, and money or a credit card. Supporting actors include waiters or waitresses and sometimes other personnel such as bartenders or busboys. The results are that the customer has less money but is no longer hungry, whereas the owner has more money. Between the times that a customer enters and leaves, there is a fairly standard sequence of events that includes selecting a table, looking at the menu, ordering the food, eating, and paying the bill.

Script   Knowledge about what occurs during routine activities

Since the sequence of events is quite standard, a natural way of organizing scripts is according to the temporal order in which the events occur. Imagine that you have a flat tire and need to put on the spare. Your memory might consist of an organized sequence of actions, beginning with what you do first and ending with what you do last. Alternatively, your memory might be organized according to the centrality or importance of the events, in which you think of the more important events before you think of the less important events. Figure 9.9 shows these two contrasting memory structures.

Figure 9.9a shows an organization in which some activities (such as removing the bad tire) are more central than others (such as putting away the jack). The more central activities are those that are particularly important in accomplishing the goal. If activities are organized according to their centrality, then people should be faster in verifying that the more central activities are included in a script. You may have noticed that the representation in Figure 9.9a is analogous to the semantic

(a)

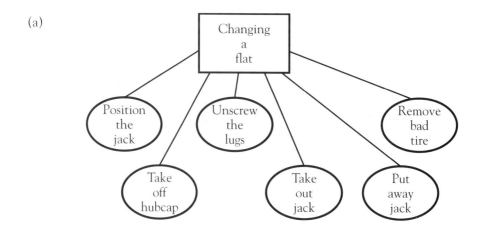

(b)

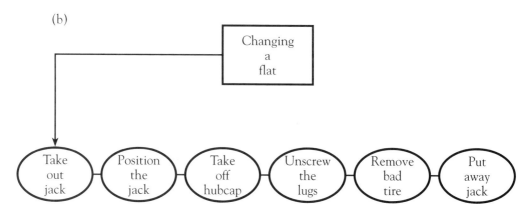

Figure 9.9   *Two representations of a routine: (a) according to the centrality of component activities and (b) according to their sequential order.*

From "Memory for Routines," by J. A. Galambas and L. J. Rips, 1982, *Journal of Verbal Learning and Verbal Behavior, 21*, 260–281. Copyright © 1982 by Academic Press.

network proposed by Collins and Loftus (see Figure 9.6), but the shorter links represent a strong association between an activity and a script instead of a strong association between an exemplar and its category. An alternative representation, shown in Figure 9.9b, consists of activities organized according to their sequential order. If activities are reconstructed in the order in which they are performed, people should be faster in verifying that earlier activities are included in the script.

Galambos and Rips (1982) tested which theory was more appropriate by asking students to rank-order the activities of different scripts according to both their temporal order and their centrality. They then showed another group of subjects pairs of items that consisted of the name of a script (changing a flat) and an activity (take out jack). Students were asked to respond as quickly as possible whether the activity was included in the script. More central events were verified more quickly than less central events, but earlier events were not verified more quickly than later events. The results therefore supported the organization shown in Figure 9.9a.

However, this conclusion was challenged by Barsalou and Sewell (1985) who believed that the temporal order of events is very important in how people organize their experiences. They thought that the results would be different if they used a different experimental procedure. Instead of asking people to verify that a particular activity was part of a script, they gave people 20 sec to name as many activities as they could that belonged to a particular script, such as doing the dishes. One group of subjects was asked "to generate actions from the most central action to the least central action," where centrality was defined in terms of the importance of the action. Another group of subjects was asked "to generate actions from the first action to the last action."

The researchers hypothesized that if the events are temporally organized in memory, then it should be easier to name events in their temporal order than to name events in decreasing importance. Their findings supported this hypothesis. The average number of actions generated in 20 sec was 8.17 when actions were listed in a temporal order, and 6.10 when actions were listed according to importance. One interpretation of these conflicting findings is that both the centrality and the temporal order of events influence how we use our memory. The more central events provide the quickest access to a script, but the temporal order of events is useful for retrieving all the events that are in the script.

Research on **autobiographical memory**—memory for our personal experiences—supports this interpretation. In an experiment by S. J. Anderson and M. A. Conway (1993), subjects verbally indicated the first autobiographical memory that came to mind for a specified time period. They were then asked to list details about the event such as activities, feeling, locations, people, and so forth. Some people were instructed to list the events in a forward, temporal order, and other people were instructed to list the events in the order of their centrality or importance. Significantly more events were recalled for the forward order than for the central order, replicating the findings of Barsalou and Sewell (1985).

However, the centrality of events was the most important factor in determining how quickly people could access their memories. One of the

Autobiographical memory Memory about our personal experiences

autobiographical details listed previously was displayed on a computer screen and the subject responded as soon as she or he knew what the autobiographical event was. Response times following a more central detail were significantly faster than response times following a beginning or ending detail, which did not differ from each other.

These findings support the Galambos and Rips (1982) conclusion that the more central details provide the fastest access to knowledge in LTM. However, once the memory (set of specific details) is located, the remaining details can be most effectively retrieved by a temporally-ordered search strategy. Figure 9.10 shows an example in which one young man recalled his experience of meeting Angela. The events are listed in a forward chronological order, which aids in retrieving specific

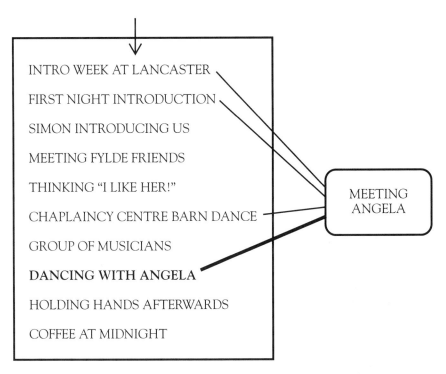

Figure 9.10 *Organization of knowledge in a specific autobiographical memory. Items are listed in chronological order and are initially accessed through the thematic links.*

From "Investigating the Structure of Autobiographical Memories," by S. J. Anderson and M. A. Conway, 1993, *Journal of Experimental Psychology: Learning, Memory, and Cognition*, *19*, 1178–1196. Copyright © 1993 by the American Psychological Association. Reprinted by permission.

details, but the connecting lines show the most central events (such as dancing with Angela), which provided the fastest access to this particular experience.

SUMMARY

Psychologists have studied semantic memory to learn how people use meaning to organize information in LTM. One effective way to organize material is to use hierarchical organization by partitioning a large category into smaller and smaller categories. Experiments have shown that people can learn hierarchical information quickly, but they have considerable difficulty learning the same information when it is presented randomly. The study of how people retrieve information reveals that they typically group from two to five items together. Groups of this size can form the basis for a large hierarchy—for instance, a paragraph: the paragraph can be divided into sentences, sentences into major ideas, major ideas into smaller word groups, word groups into words, words into syllables, and syllables into phonemes. Research on the learning of information in a text has found that creating a semantic network to represent the relations among concepts improves performance on essay and short-answer tests.

The hierarchical organization of categories influences the amount of time it takes to verify sentences about the members of categories. It usually takes less time to verify category membership at the basic level than at the superordinate level. For example, it is easier to verify that a canary is a bird than that a canary is an animal. The hierarchical network model predicts this result by assuming that semantic information is organized in a hierarchy and that it takes time to change levels in the hierarchy. The network model also predicts that the time it takes to verify a property of an object will depend on the level in the hierarchy where the property is stored. This assumption implies that it should take longer to verify that a canary eats than that a canary can fly, because eating is stored at the animal level and flying is stored at the bird level. In contrast, the feature comparison model assumes that statements are verified by using features to compute the similarity of two concepts. When there is an intermediate amount of similarity, people must evaluate only the most necessary, or defining, features of the category. The feature comparison model correctly predicts that classification time depends more on similarity than on category size and also depends on whether the example is a typical member of its category. Critics of the feature comparison model question its reliance on ratings to make predictions, its failure to make direct use of learned associations in memory, and its somewhat artificial distinction between characteristic and defining features.

The hierarchical network model is an example of a semantic network model in which concepts are represented by nodes in a network and relations are represented by links joining the concepts. The spreading activation model was proposed to correct some limitations of the hierarchical network model. Its main assumption is that activation of a concept results in activation of related concepts spreading along the paths of the network. Another network model, ACT, uses the same assumption to provide a theoretical account of many experimental findings, including the differences in reaction time for retrieving facts. The typical increase in reaction time caused by increasing the number of unrelated facts (the fan effect) can be avoided if the facts are well integrated. The advantage of semantic network models is that they are general enough to provide a broad theoretical framework for incorporating a large variety of findings. Their major disadvantage is that so many assumptions are made that the models cannot be used to make predictions.

The integration of knowledge into larger clusters is the primary assumption of schema theory. Emphasis on schematic structures began with the work of Bartlett and Piaget and started to have a major impact on cognitive science in the mid 1970s. In contrast to stimulus-response associations, schematic structures are molar, nonassociationistic, generic, and active. They provide a skeleton structure that can be filled out with the detailed properties of a particular instance, using default knowledge when information is missing. Scripts are one type of schema, consisting of sequences of events that make up routine activities. The temporal order of the events is useful for organizing recall, but the centrality of events determines how quickly people can access the script.

STUDY QUESTIONS

Be prepared for some tough going in this chapter. Since much of it deals with alternative theories or models, the abstraction level is necessarily high. Consult the illustrations of specific examples early and often for visual aids.

1. What does *semantic* mean? *Hierarchy?*
2. What is the evidence that hierarchical organization allows one to recall more material and/or recall it faster? Are you impressed by the evidence?
3. Does the information on category size given here take the magic out of Miller's number? What is the category size effect?
4. Can you state the advantages and disadvantages of Collins and Quillian's network model?
5. Does the feature comparison model seem more useful to you? Or are you persuaded by its critics?

6. In what ways are the semantic network models (spreading activation and ACT) more general than the two models already considered? Write your answer.
7. How does spreading activation theory account for semantic priming and the typicality effect?
8. So far as you can figure it out, does Anderson's later modification of ACT strengthen the theory? Can it better deal with the "fan effect"?
9. What do you make of the statement that "a model has predictive power only if it predicts that certain events should not occur. One can then evaluate the model by determining which events do in fact occur"?
10. Think of an autobiographical memory of your own. Order the specific events according to their temporal order and their order of importance. How do you think each of these two characteristics would influence your recall?

KEY TERMS

The page number in parentheses refers to where the term is discussed in the chapter.

autobiographical memory (283)
category size effect (268)
characteristic features (267)
default knowledge (280)
defining features (267)
fan effect (275)
feature comparison model (262)
hierarchical network model (262)
links (260)
nodes (260)

path (275)
priming (272)
schema (279)
script (281)
semantic network (254)
spreading activation (254)
spreading activation model (270)
subnodes (276)
typicality effect (266)

RECOMMENDED READING

Bower (1970) reviewed research on organizational factors in memory in the first issue of *Cognitive Psychology*. Mandler (1967), one of the first psychologists to study the hierarchical organization of memory, proposed that each level in the hierarchy contained about five categories. Nelson and Smith (1972) studied the acquisition and forgetting of hierarchically organized information, whereas Goldberg (1986) used rating procedures to measure hierarchical levels. Stevens and Coupe (1978) argued that spatial knowledge is also hierarchically organized; for example, most people wrongly infer that San Diego, California, is west of Reno, Nevada, because most of California is of Nevada. Rosch (1975) used the priming technique to investigate the organization of semantic categories.

Ratcliff and McKoon (1988) and Neely and Keefe (1989) have each proposed alternative theories of priming to account for findings that are usually attributed to spreading activation. Additional research on semantic integration is reported by Reder and Ross (1983). J. R. Anderson (1983) describes ACT, and an article by Chang (1986) evaluates alternative models of semantic memory. Recent discussions of the semantic feature approach to describe the meaning of concepts are provided by McNamara and Miller (1989) and Malt (1990). The integration of objects into spatial scenes is another form of integration that enables quick verification times (Radransky & Zacks, 1991).

COMPLEX
COGNITIVE SKILLS

Language

Words differently arranged have a different meaning, and meanings differently arranged have different effects.

PASCAL

Grammar A set of rules for producing correct sentences in a language

Language A collection of symbols, and rules for combining symbols, which can express an infinite variety of messages

Symbolic The use of symbols, such as spoken or written words, to represent ideas

Generative The capability to produce many different messages by combining symbols in different ways

Structured The organization imposed on a language by its grammatical rules

Morphemes The smallest units of meaning in a language

*T*HE DISCUSSION OF semantic memory in the previous chapter emphasized associations among words. We are now ready to consider how words can be combined to form sentences. One possible theory is that this combination occurs by associations. We could argue that, just as *robin* is associated with *bird*, the words in a sentence can be associated with each other. The problem with this view of language is that there are so many ways words can be combined that we would have to learn an infinite number of associations in order to form sentences. An alternative theory is that we learn a **grammar**—a system of rules that is capable of producing sentences. Ideally, the rules of a grammar should generate all the sentences of a language without generating any strings of words that are not sentences.

This brings us to a definition of language. A **language** is a collection of symbols, and rules for combining those symbols, which can be used to create an infinite variety of messages. There are three critical aspects of this definition. First, language is **symbolic**: We use spoken sounds and written words to represent and communicate about the world around us. The symbols are arbitrary—there is no built-in relation between the look or sound of the words and the objects they represent. Second, language is **generative**: A limited number of words can be combined in an endless variety of ways to generate an infinite number of sentences. Third, language is **structured**: By following grammatical rules, we can produce grammatical sentences.

Figure 10.1 shows the hierarchical structure of sentences. At the top of the hierarchy is a sentence that can be broken down into phrases based on the grammatical rules. The grammatical rules partition the sentence in Figure 10.1 into a *noun phrase* (*The strangers*) and a *verb phrase* (*talked to the players*). The phrases are composed of words, which can be partitioned into **morphemes**—the smallest unit of meaning in a language. For spoken sentences, the morphemes can be further partitioned into *phonemes*—the basic sounds of a language.

The next section provides a brief overview of these three aspects of comprehending and producing sentences: grammar, meaning, and sound.

THREE ASPECTS OF LANGUAGE

Grammar

One of the important influences on the development of cognitive psychology during the 1960s was the work of linguist Noam Chomsky. Prior to Chomsky's influence on psycholinguistics (the psychological study of language), psychologists had explored the possibility that people could learn a language by learning the associations between adjacent words in a

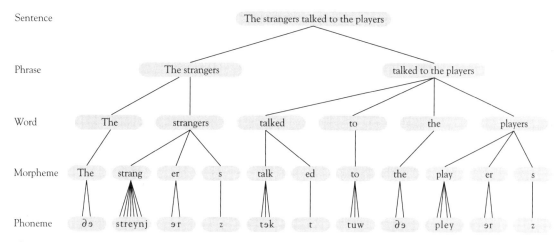

Figure 10.1   *An example of a sentence partitioned into phrases, words, morphemes, and phonemes.*
From *Child Development: A Topical Approach,* by A. Clarke-Stewart, S. Friedman, and J. Koch, p. 417. Copyright © 1985 by
John Wiley & Sons. Reprinted by permission.

sentence. According to this view, we learn to speak correctly through paired-associate learning—each word in a sentence serves as a stimulus for the word that follows it. In the sentence *The boy hit the ball*, the word *the* is a stimulus for the word *boy*, and the word *boy* is a stimulus for the word *hit*. The speaker of a language would therefore have to learn which words could follow any other word in a sentence.

Chomsky (1957) argued that there are several problems with the association view of language. First of all, there are an infinite number of sentences in a language. It is therefore unreasonable to expect that people could learn a language by learning associations between all adjacent words. Consider simply a word like *the*. There are many, many words that could follow *the*, and a person might never learn all of them. When you consider all the possible words that can occur in a sentence and all the words that could possibly follow each word, you can see that this would be a very inefficient way to learn a language. Another problem with the association view is that it does not account for the relations among nonadjacent words. For example, in the sentence *Anyone who says that is lying*, the pronoun *anyone* is grammatically related to the verb *is lying*, but this relation is not revealed if we consider only the relation between adjacent words. The association view, in fact, ignores the hierarchical structure of sentences in proposing how people learn to speak grammatically correct sentences.

The hierarchical structure of sentences is revealed in the diagrams that you may have constructed in school. Many of us were taught how to break down a sentence into parts. We might begin by dividing a sentence into a noun phrase and a verb phrase, as shown in Figure 10.1, and then divide the noun phrase and verb phrase into smaller units that reveal the grammar of the sentence. After this brief overview, let's take a closer look at these grammatical rules and their relation to the hierarchy in Figure 10.1.

Meaning

Although I have been emphasizing the grammatical aspects of language, a sentence that is grammatically correct isn't necessarily meaningful. Chomsky's famous example is the sentence *Colorless green ideas sleep furiously*. Notice that this is a grammatically correct sentence even though it doesn't make sense. The opposite effect also occurs; we can make ourselves understood to a reasonable extent without producing grammatically correct sentences. I spent the summer before my junior year in college working in Germany with a student from Sweden. We managed to communicate with each other fairly well in German while violating many rules of German grammar.

This distinction between syntax (grammar) and semantics (meaning) is also evident in language disorders that are caused by brain damage (Carroll, 1986). A disorder known as **Broca's aphasia** was discovered by and named after a French surgeon who noticed that some patients spoke in halting, ungrammatical speech following a stroke or accident (Broca, 1865). These patients were typically limited to expressing themselves by stringing together single words, as illustrated in the following excerpt from a patient who had come to the hospital for dental surgery:

> Yes . . . ah . . . Monday er . . . Dad and Peter H . . . , and Dad . . . er . . . hospital . . . and ah . . . Wednesday . . . Wednesday, nine o'clock . . . and oh . . . Thursday . . . ten o'clock, ah doctors . . . two . . . an' doctors . . . and er . . . teeth . . . yah. (Goodglass & Geschwind, 1976, p. 408)

This inability to express grammatical relationships is typically found in individuals who have suffered damage to the frontal regions of the left hemisphere of the brain (an area called *Broca's area*, shown in Figure 10.2).

A few years after Broca's discovery, another surgeon, named Carl Wernicke, discovered a different kind of aphasia (Wernicke, 1874), resulting from damage to the temporal lobe of the left hemisphere (see Figure 10.2). The speech associated with **Wernicke's aphasia** is more fluent and grammatical but doesn't convey much semantic content:

> Well this is . . . mother is away her working her work out o'here to get her better, but when she's looking in the other part. One their small tile into her time here. She's working another time because she's getting, too . . . (Goodglass & Geschwind, 1976, p. 410)

Broca's aphasia
A language disorder attributed to damage in the frontal lobe of the brain

Wernicke's aphasia
A language disorder attributed to damage in the temporal lobe of the brain

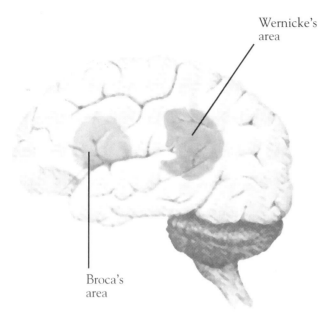

Figure 10.2   *A view of the left hemisphere showing the location of two language centers in the brain.*

From *Psychology: Themes and Variations* by Wayne Weiten. Copyright © 1995, 1992, 1989 by Brooks/Cole Publishing Company, a division of International Thomson Publishing Inc., Pacific Grove, CA 93950. Reprinted by permission of the publisher.

This difficulty with the semantic content of words was confirmed by direct tests of semantic relations (Zurif, Caramazza, Meyerson, & Galvin, 1974). When given three words (such as *husband, mother, shark*) and asked to indicate which two were most similar, Wernicke's aphasics did poorly on the test, in contrast to Broca's aphasics.

We can represent meaning by breaking words into morphemes, the smallest units of meaning. Morphemes include stem words, prefixes, and suffixes. The word *unfriendly* consists of the stem word *friend*, the prefix *un*, and the suffix *ly*. Notice that each of these morphemes produces a change in meaning. Adding *ly* to *friend* changes a noun into an adjective. Adding *un* to *friendly* changes the meaning of the adjective.

Other examples are shown in Figure 10.1. The word *strangers* consists of the stem word *strange* and the suffixes *er* and *s*. The first suffix (*er*) converts an adjective into a noun, and the second suffix (*s*) changes the noun from singular to plural. The verb *talked* contains the stem word *talk* and the suffix *ed*, which changes the tense of the verb. Each of these morphemes contributes to the meaning of the entire word.

One advantage of morphemes is that they allow us to generate novel words. A young child who did not know the plural of *stranger*, but knew that plurals are often formed by adding an *s* to the end of a noun, could generate the word *strangers*. If she did not know the past tense of *talk*, but knew that the past tense is often formed by adding *ed* to the end of a verb, she could generate the word *talked*. These rules do not always work (the plural of *deer* is not *deers* and the past tense of *speak* is not *speaked*), but children eventually learn the exceptions.

Sound

The symbols of a language consist of both written and spoken words. However, as we saw in Chapter 4 when discussing acoustic coding in STM, written words are typically converted into spoken words through subvocalization. Thus the acoustic aspects of language are important even when we encounter written words.

Before children can understand written sentences by learning to read, they must understand spoken sentences. The first step toward understanding spoken sentences is to be able to discriminate among the basic sounds (phonemes) of a language. This ability is excellent in newborns who are able to discriminate among phonemes in many different languages of the world (Kuhl, 1993). But infants also need to respond to similarity among sounds and to categorize sounds into the phonemic categories that make up their particular language. This presents the same pattern recognition problem that we discussed in Chapter 2, where we emphasized visual patterns. Just as there are variations in people's handwriting that can make visual pattern recognition difficult, there are variations in people's speech that can make speech recognition difficult.

We saw in Chapter 8 that a prototype theory of categorization argues that people classify patterns by comparing them to category prototypes. Recent work by Kuhl (1993) indicates that prototypes are important in speech recognition and that infants as young as 6 months old have formed prototypes to represent the phonemes in their language. Evidence for prototype formation comes from Kuhl's (1991) research demonstrating that the ability to discriminate sounds within a phonemic category (as if different people pronounced the long-*e* sound) is worse if the category prototype is involved in the discrimination. Adults and 6-month-old infants can more easily discriminate between two nonprototypical sounds than between a prototypical and a nonprototypical sound. Kuhl (1991) uses the metaphor of a "perceptual magnet" to describe the effect. The prototypic long-*e* sound draws similar long-*e* sounds closer to it, making these variations sound more like the prototype.

This magnet effect has several interesting implications. First, we might expect that infants become better at discriminating sounds as they grow older. Wrong—if the sounds belong to the same phonemic category. Forming prototypes of the various phonemes reduces discrimination within a phonemic category because variations of the prototype begin to sound more like the prototype. Notice, however, that this should make it easier to recognize the phonemes.

We might also expect that infants could better discriminate among familiar sounds in their own language than among unfamiliar sounds from a different language. Wrong again—if the sounds belong to the same phonemic category. For example, 6-month-old Swedish infants were better than U.S. infants at discriminating between a prototypic long-*e* sound and other long-*e* sounds, even though this was an unfamiliar sound to them (Kuhl, Williams, Lacerda, Stevens, & Lindblom, 1992). The reason is that the U.S. infants had formed a prototypic long-*e* sound and were therefore victims of the magnet effect, whereas the Swedish infants had not formed a prototypic long-*e* sound because this sound did not occur in their language. The opposite result occurred for a vowel that occurred in Swedish, but not in U.S. English. American infants were now better in discriminating variations of this vowel from the category prototype.

In conclusion, infants are born with the ability to discriminate among phonemes in many different languages but learn the prototypic speech sounds in their own language. Once the prototypic speech sounds are acquired, it becomes more difficult to discriminate between the prototype and variations of the prototype. In other words, variations of a phoneme caused by differences in pronunciation sound more alike. This makes us look bad on discrimination tests but presumably makes it easier to recognize speech because phonemes sound more like their category prototypes.

Speech Errors

As children grow older, they not only recognize speech but learn to produce speech of their own. However, even adults can make errors when speaking. Now that we have reviewed the grammatical, semantic, and phonemic aspects of sentences we can see how these three aspects of language can give rise to the kind of errors that occur when we produce spoken sentences. These speech errors, or **slips of the tongue**, are unintended deviations from a speech plan (Dell, 1986). Most of what we know about these slips come from analyses of errors that were personally heard and noted by investigators. Although such methods may be subject to sampling biases, there are so many regularities in these collections of speech errors that it is unlikely that there are systematic biases in the data.

The usefulness of the hierarchical organization shown in Figure 10.1 for representing speech errors is that the errors typically occur within, but not across, levels in the hierarchy (Dell, 1986). Errors can therefore be divided into *word errors, morpheme errors,* and *phoneme errors* depending on

Slips of the tongue
Speech errors

Exchange errors Errors in which two linguistic units are substituted for each other during sentence production

Word exchanges Errors in which two words are substituted for each other during sentence production

Morpheme exchanges Errors in which two morphemes are substituted for each other during sentence production

Phoneme exchanges Errors in which two phonemes are substituted for each other during sentence production

the size of the linguistic unit involved in the error. Occurrence of errors within these linguistic units is most easily seen in **exchange errors** in which two linguistic units are substituted for each other in the sentence. That is, **word exchanges** are illustrated by the speaker saying "writing a mother to my letter" rather than "writing a letter to my mother." The exchanged words are typically members of the same syntactic category, demonstrating the constraints of grammar on speech. In this case, both *mother* and *letter* are nouns. **Morpheme exchanges** are illustrated by the speaker saying "slicely thinned" rather than "thinly sliced." There are also categorical constraints on morpheme errors; in this case the two stems *slice* and *thin* are interchanged while the suffixes *ly* and *ed* remain in their original position. Just as nouns are interchanged with other nouns or verbs interchanged with other verbs at the word level, stems are interchanged with other stems or suffixes interchanged with other suffixes at the morpheme level. **Phoneme exchanges** are illustrated by the speaker saying "lork yibrary" for "York library." Once again, there are category constraints on the exchanges. In phoneme errors, initial consonants are exchanged with other initial consonants, final consonants are exchanged with other final consonants, and vowels are exchanged with other vowels.

The rest of this chapter focuses on the syntactic and semantic aspects of language. The first section provides a brief description of two kinds of grammatical rules—phrase structure rules and transformation rules. The second section deals with the effect of context on the comprehension of sentences. The comprehension of ambiguous sentences is a particularly interesting area of study because we must resolve the ambiguity in order to understand the sentences. The final section considers the distinction between asserted and implied statements. Findings on how well people can make this distinction offer some applications of research on the understanding of language, particularly in relation to the evaluation of courtroom testimony and advertising claims.

PSYCHOLOGY AND GRAMMAR

Phrase Structure Grammar

We have seen that an alternative to representing language as a string of words is representing it as a rule system. For example, we saw in Figure 10.1 that we could divide the sentence into a noun phrase and a verb phrase. We could further subdivide the verb phrase *talked to the players* into the verb *talked* and the prepositional phrase *to the players*. The rules that we use to divide a sentence into its grammatical parts form a **phrase structure grammar** because they reveal how we can partition a sentence into phrases consisting of groups of words.

Phrase structure grammar A set of rules for partitioning a sentence into its grammatical units

This approach can be illustrated by considering a very simple set of rules taken from a phrase structure grammar (Table 10.1). The rules are

Table 10.1   *Examples of phrase structure rules*

1. S → NP + VP	4. Det → *a, the*
2. NP → Det + Noun	5. Noun → *boy, ball, stick*
3. VP → Verb + NP	6. Verb → *hit*

expressed by using an arrow that means *can be rewritten as*. The symbols refer to sentences (S), noun phrases (NP), verb phrases (VP), and determiners (Det). The first rule states that a sentence can be rewritten as a noun phrase followed by a verb phrase. The second rule states that a noun phrase can be rewritten as a determiner followed by a noun. The third rule states that a verb phrase can be rewritten as a verb followed by a noun phrase. The last three rules give examples of words that can be substituted for a determiner, a noun, and a verb.

The rules may seem more familiar to you if they are expressed visually. Figure 10.3 shows how they can be used to reveal the grammatical structure of a sentence. The sentence is first rewritten as a noun phrase followed by a verb phrase (Rule 1). Rule 2 then allows us to rewrite the noun phrase, and Rule 3 allows us to rewrite the verb phrase. Since the application of Rule 3 produces another noun phrase, it is necessary to apply Rule 2 again to rewrite the second noun phrase. Using the vocabulary rules to substitute words for the determiners, nouns, and verbs, we can now produce a small number of sentences. For instance:

The boy hit a ball.
The stick hit the boy.
A ball hit a ball.

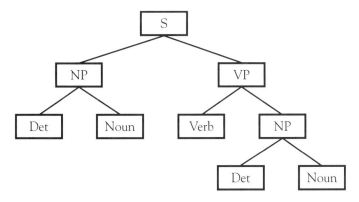

Figure 10.3   *A sentence diagram based on the phrase structure rules in Table 10.1.*

Although the number of sentences we can produce using this particular grammar is quite limited, the grammar illustrates how sentences can be produced through the application of rules. Creation of additional rules, such as including adjectives in a noun phrase, would allow us to generate a greater variety of sentences.

Transformational Grammar

Chomsky (1957) argued that one limitation of a phrase structure grammar is that it does not reveal how a sentence can be modified to form a similar sentence. For example, how can we change (1) an active statement into a passive statement, (2) a positive statement into a negative statement, or (3) an assertion into a question? Given the sentence *The boy hit the ball*, the first change produces *The ball was hit by the boy*; the second change produces *The boy did not hit the ball*; and the third change produces *Did the boy hit the ball?* The modification in each case *transforms* an entire sentence into a closely related sentence. Transformation rules therefore serve a different function than phrase structure rules, which reveal the grammatical structure of a sentence. Chomsky, however, used phrase structure rules in developing his transformational grammar because the transformations are based on the grammatical structure of a sentence.

Consider the transformation of *The boy hit the ball* into *The ball was hit by the boy*. The transformation rule in this case is

$$\text{NP1} + \text{Verb} + \text{NP2} \rightarrow \text{NP2} + was + \text{Verb} + by + \text{NP1}$$

The transformation changes the position of the two noun phrases and inserts additional words into the passive sentence. The passive sentence begins with the second noun phrase (*the ball*) and ends with the first noun phrase (*the boy*). It is also necessary to add the words *was* and *by*. Notice that the transformation rule shows how a phrase structure description of a passive sentence can be formed from a phrase structure description of an active sentence.

The **transformational grammar** proposed by Chomsky in 1957 was an advance over a phrase structure grammar because, in addition to revealing grammatical structure, it showed how sentences could be transformed. Chomsky was not entirely satisfied with the transformational grammar, however, and in 1965 he wrote a second book to correct some of its limitations. The changes that he made were concerned mainly with allowing meaning to play a more important role in the grammar.

One problem with the 1957 grammar was that it could generate sentences that seemed grammatical but did not express meaningful ideas. This point can be illustrated by adding another verb—*took*—to the rules shown in Figure 10.3. This addition allows us to produce new sentences

Transformational grammar   A set of rules for transforming a sentence into a closely related sentence

like *The boy took the ball* and *The ball took the boy*. Although both sentences appear to be grammatical, the second sentence doesn't make much sense. The reason is that the verb *took* usually requires an animate subject—someone who is alive and therefore capable of taking something. Chomsky tried to correct this deficiency by placing constraints on which words could be substituted into a sentence. Instead of treating all verbs the same, he argued that some verbs require animate subjects. This restriction is based on the meaning of words.

Another problem with the earlier version of the transformational grammar was that it could not always distinguish between different meanings of an **ambiguous sentence**, although it was sometimes successful because some ambiguous sentences can be distinguished by the use of phrase structure rules. Consider the sentence *They are flying planes*. One interpretation considers *flying* to be part of the verb phrase *are flying*, whereas the other interpretation considers *flying* to be an adjective in the noun phrase *flying planes*. In the first interpretation *they* refers to someone who is flying planes; in the second interpretation *they* refers to the planes. A phrase structure grammar can make this distinction because each interpretation has a different derivation (see Figure 10.4).

There are other ambiguous sentences, however, that cannot be distinguished by phrase structure rules because both interpretations of the sentence produce the same derivation. Consider the sentence *Flying planes can be dangerous*. The sentence has the same ambiguity as the previous sentence. The two interpretations can be revealed by rephrasing the sentence as either *Flying planes is dangerous* or *Flying planes are dangerous*. The first interpretation means that flying is dangerous to the pilot; the second

Ambiguous sentences
Sentences that have more than one meaning

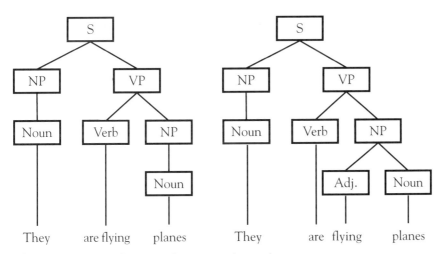

Figure 10.4   *Two alternative derivations of an ambiguous sentence.*

means that the planes themselves are dangerous. In both interpretations, however, *flying planes* is the subject of the sentence, so the ambiguity cannot be resolved by appealing to different phrase structure rules.

Chomsky (1965) proposed that, in order to resolve the ambiguity, it is necessary to postulate a level of analysis that directly represents the meaning of a sentence. He therefore modified the transformational grammar to consist of two levels: the **surface structure**, directly related to the sentence as it is heard, and the **deep structure**, directly related to the meaning of the sentence. The only way to resolve the ambiguity of a sentence such as *Flying planes can be dangerous* is to know which of the two deep levels is intended—flying is dangerous to the pilot or the planes themselves are dangerous.

The concepts Chomsky introduced had a major impact on the emerging field of psycholinguistics. Psychologists who were interested in language studied the implications of a transformational grammar for theories of how people comprehend and remember sentences. The following study of ambiguous sentences illustrates the kind of research that resulted from Chomsky's ideas.

Ambiguous Sentences

Comprehension of sentences, like recognition of patterns, is a complex skill that we perform very well. Ambiguous sentences afford us some insight into how difficulties in comprehension might arise. One technique for studying comprehension is to measure how quickly people can complete a sentence. Try to finish the following three sentences as quickly as you can.

1. Although he was continually bothered by the cold . . .
2. Although Hannibal sent troops over a week ago . . .
3. Knowing that visiting relatives could be bothersome . . .

Each of the three sentences represents a different kind of ambiguity studied by MacKay (1966). The first example represents **lexical (word) ambiguity** because the word *cold* can refer either to the temperature of the environment or to an illness. The second example represents **surface ambiguity** because it concerns the grouping of words. The word *over* can be either part of the verb phrase (*sent troops over*) or part of the prepositional phrase (*over a week ago*). Linguistically, this distinction can be represented by phrase structure rules because each interpretation has a different derivation. The third example represents an **underlying ambiguity** because the ambiguity can be resolved only if we know the underlying meaning (deep structure) of the sentence. Notice that the phrase *visiting relatives* is ambiguous in the same sense that *flying planes* was ambiguous in the example given earlier. It is unclear who are the visitors—and this ambiguity cannot be resolved at the phrase structure level.

Surface structure The structure of a spoken sentence

Deep structure The underlying meaning of a sentence

Lexical ambiguity A word that has more than one meaning

Surface ambiguity Alternative meanings of a sentence that can be differentiated by different phrase structure rules

Underlying ambiguity Alternative meanings of a sentence that cannot be differentiated by different phrase structure rules

It is possible, of course, that people might never notice these ambiguities and therefore find it as easy to complete these sentences as to complete closely related unambiguous sentences. The following three sentences show unambiguous variations of each of the three examples. The italicized word is the only change.

4. Although he was continually bothered by the *headache* . . .
5. Although Hannibal sent troops *almost* a week ago . . .
6. Knowing that visiting *some* relatives could be bothersome . . .

MacKay studied the effect of ambiguity on sentence completion times by giving people either ambiguous sentences or unambiguous variations of the same sentences. The subjects' task was to finish each sentence as quickly as possible. The completions had to be short, grammatical, and related to the beginning of the sentence.

Figure 10.5 shows the average amount of time required to complete each class of sentences. There was no difference among the unambiguous control sentences, but there were differences among the three kinds of ambiguous sentences—all of which took more time to complete than the

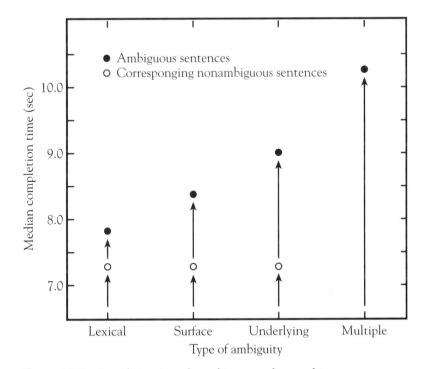

Figure 10.5 *Completion times for ambiguous and nonambiguous sentences.*
From "To End Ambiguous Sentences," by D. G. MacKay, 1966, *Perception & Psychophysics, 1,*
426–435. Copyright © 1966 by the Psychonomic Society. Reprinted by permission.

control sentences. Subjects had the least difficulty with lexical ambiguities, more difficulty with surface ambiguities, and still more difficulty with underlying ambiguities. Sentences that contained more than one ambiguity (multiple ambiguities) were the most difficult to complete. Interestingly, very few of the subjects reported that they noticed the ambiguities, although they took significantly longer to complete the ambiguous sentences.

Although Chomsky's ideas had a major impact on the emerging field of psycholinguistics, current research on language is more concerned with meaning than with grammar (see Lachman, Lachman, & Butterfield, 1979, for a detailed account of this shift in emphasis). For example, ambiguous words and noun phrases often do not seem ambiguous to us when we read them in a sentence because their meaning is made clear by the meaning of the words that preceded them. The sentence provides a context for interpreting words. In the next section we will learn how this context influences comprehension.

EFFECT OF CONTEXT ON COMPREHENSION

There are a variety of ways in which the context of the material we are reading can influence comprehension. The first is simply its influence on word recognition. We have all experienced difficulty in recognizing a word when reading illegible handwriting and having to rely on the surrounding words and sentences to help us identify the illegible word. A second way in which context can influence comprehension is by helping us identify the appropriate meaning of an ambiguous word. You may have noticed in the previous section that MacKay (1966) carefully designed his ambiguous sentences so context would not be helpful. When his subjects read the partial sentence, *Although he was continually bothered by the cold*, it is not yet clear whether *cold* refers to the person's health or to the temperature of the environment, but usually either the words preceding or following an ambiguous word inform us of the intended meaning. A third way in which context influences comprehension concerns how we combine the meaning of individual words to form larger units. If we read about a burning house, do we independently combine the meanings of the adjective (*burning*) and noun (*house*) to form an image of a burning house, or does the adjective directly modify the meaning of the noun? We will search for the answer to this, and other questions, in this section.

Context and Word Recognition

Although I discussed word recognition in the chapter on pattern recognition, I focused on the word superiority effect. We learned that a letter is easier to recognize in the context of a word than when it appears by itself. Similarly, a word is often easier to recognize when it appears in the context of a sentence than when it appears by itself. An example of how context can influence word recognition is shown in Figure 10.6. The two sentences contain a physically identical word, yet we have little difficulty identifying the word as *went* in the upper sentence, and as *event* in the lower sentence.

Although the effect of context is most obvious to us when we have to struggle to identify a word, it also influences recognition time when we identify words relatively quickly. Usually context is helpful and makes word recognition faster, but it can also slow us down, as is illustrated in the following two sentences: (1) *John kept his gym clothes in a locker.* (2) *John kept his gym clothes in a closet.* The words *locker* and *closet* are both preceded by a suitable context, but the context creates a strong expectation for the word *locker*. Sentences that create a high expectation for a particular word are called **high-constraint sentences**.

Schwanenflugel and Shoben (1985) studied the effect of high-constraint sentences on the processing of expected words (*locker*) and unexpected words (*closet*) by using the **lexical decision task** that we discussed in the previous chapter. After reading either a high-constraint context or a neutral context, readers had to decide whether a string of letters was a word. The high-constraint context facilitated recognition of the expected word but interfered with recognition of the unexpected word. People were faster at deciding that *locker* was a word when they received the high-constraint context but were faster in deciding that *closet* was a word when they received the neutral context, consisting of a string of Xs.

The high-constraint sentence caused interference in the latter case because people were expecting a particular word, which did not occur. What would happen if our expectations for a particular word were not as strong? Schwanenflugel and Shoben tried to answer this question by

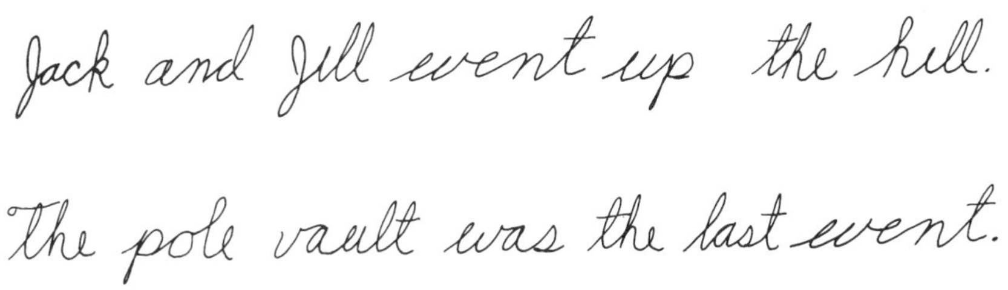

High-constraint sentences   Sentences that produce a high expectation for a particular word

Lexical decision task   A task that requires people to decide whether a string of letters is a word

Jack and Jill event up the hill.

The pole vault was the last event.

Figure 10.6   *Dependence of letter perception on context.*
From "Toward an Interactive Model of Reading," by D. E. Rumelhart, 1977, in *Attention and Performance*, Volume 6, edited by S. Dornic. Copyright © 1977 by Lawrence Erlbaum Associates, Inc. Reprinted by permission.

Low-constraint sentences   Sentences that produce an expectation for a broader range of words

Semantic features   Attributes that represent the meaning of a concept

including **low-constraint sentences** in their study. The following two sentences are examples: (1) *The lady was a competent cook.* (2) *The lady was a competent chef.* The sentences are low-constraint because a lady could be competent in performing many different tasks. However, the first sentence contains an expected word and the second sentence contains an unexpected word because a lady is more likely to be called a cook than a chef. The results of several experiments indicated that the low-constraint context caused facilitation for both the expected and unexpected words. In contrast to the high-constraint sentences, in which a large facilitation effect occurred for the expected word and a large interference effect occurred for the unexpected word, the low-constraint sentences caused a moderate amount of facilitation for both words.

Schwanenflugel and Shoben account for this finding by proposing an explanation based on **semantic features**. They argue that changes in the scope of facilitation due to sentence constraint may occur because subjects generate fewer and more general features for low-constraint than for high-constraint sentences. For the low-constraint example, *The lady was a competent* ———, the missing word is constrained only by features such as [skilled activity] and [something humans can be]. Facilitation could occur for any concepts that possess these two features. In contrast, high-constraint sentences may cause an expectation for concepts that satisfy a more detailed set of features. The sentence *John kept his gym clothes in a* ——— may cause readers to generate nearly the complete set of features for *locker*, such as [small], [rectangular], [associated with gyms], [holds clothes], and [shuttable]. If facilitation is restricted to those concepts that completely match the feature description, low-constraint sentences will facilitate recognition of many more words than high-constraint sentences. Thus the word *chef* would satisfy the two semantic features generated from the low-constraint sentence, but the word *closet* would not satisfy the more extensive set of specific features generated from the high-constraint sentence.

The study by Schwanenflugel and Shoben (1985) shows that contexts may occasionally have negative, as well as positive, effects. A high-constraint context can slow down lexical decisions for unexpected words. One caution, however, in evaluating such studies is the finding that contextual interference is affected by the research methodology used to study contextual effects. Another frequently used procedure, instead of lexical decision, is to measure how quickly subjects can name a word that follows a context. Studies that have used both procedures have revealed that interference effects are more likely to be found in lexical decision tasks than in naming tasks (Stanovich & West, 1983). An important challenge for cognitive psychologists is therefore to show how performance on such tasks as naming and lexical decision is related to the comprehension that occurs during normal reading (Seidenberg, Waters, Sanders, & Langer, 1984).

Context and Ambiguous Meanings

After readers or listeners identify words they still must select the appropriate meaning if the word has multiple meanings. We have previously seen that psychologists like to study comprehension by including ambiguous words in their sentences. It is important to realize, however, that ambiguous sentences are not simply invented by psychologists to study language comprehension. They also frequently occur outside the laboratory, such as in newspaper headlines. Comprehending newspaper headlines is more challenging than comprehending ordinary sentences because space constraints sometimes make it necessary to delete helpful words. Examples of ambiguous headlines include Teacher Strikes Idle Kids, Pentagon Plans Swell Deficit, Department Heads Store Clerk, and Executive Secretaries Touch Typists. Each of these headlines has more than one meaning. For instance, the headline Executive Secretaries Touch Typists could mean that (1) executive secretaries are touch typists or that (2) executive secretaries touch the typists. Most people agree which interpretation of these statements is the intended meaning, but the ambiguity nonetheless slows down their comprehension. It takes longer to comprehend an ambiguous headline than to comprehend one of the unambiguous interpretations (Perfetti, Beverly, Bell, Rodgers, & Faux, 1987).

The ambiguity of some newspaper headlines is particularly troublesome because we often lack a context to interpret the headline. The headline is the first sentence we read to find out what the article is about. The reason many potentially ambiguous sentences do not seem ambiguous is that the intended meaning is usually clear from the preceding sentences. If I say that I am bothered by the cold, the preceding sentences should reveal the intended meaning. We might therefore expect that a clarifying context should make it as easy to comprehend ambiguous sentences as unambiguous sentences. An experiment by Swinney and Hakes (1976) supports this hypothesis.

The subjects in their experiment performed two tasks simultaneously while they listened to pairs of sentences. One task asked them to judge how closely they felt the two sentences of each pair were related. This task required comprehension of the sentences. The second task required that they press a button as soon as they heard a word beginning with a specified sound (phoneme). The rationale of this experiment is that people should be slower in responding to the phoneme whenever they are having difficulty in comprehending the sentence. The following pair of sentences is a typical example:

> Rumor had it that, for years, the government building had been plagued with problems. The man was not surprised when he found several "bugs" in the corner of his room. (Swinney & Hakes, 1976, p. 686)

The target phoneme in this example occurs at the beginning of the word *corner*, shortly after the ambiguous word *bugs*. To determine whether the ambiguous word would delay comprehension and therefore detection of the phoneme, Swinney and Hakes compared performance on the ambiguous sentences with performance on unambiguous control sentences. The unambiguous version of the example contained the word *insects* in place of the word *bugs*. Swinney and Hakes found that subjects took significantly more time to detect the phoneme when it followed an ambiguous word than when it followed an unambiguous word. The findings were consistent with MacKay's (1966) results in suggesting that an ambiguity can delay comprehension.

However, sometimes the ambiguous word occurred in a context that made it clear which meaning of the word was intended. For example:

> Rumor had it that, for years, the government building had been plagued with problems. The man was not surprised when he found several spiders, roaches, and other "bugs" in the corner of his room. (Swinney & Hakes, 1976, p. 686)

When the context clarified the meaning of the ambiguous word, people could comprehend the ambiguous word *bug* as quickly as they could comprehend the unambiguous word *insect*. There was no longer any difference in response times to the target phoneme.

We could interpret these results by arguing that only a single meaning of the ambiguous word is activated when the context indicates the intended meaning. This argument has considerable intuitive appeal, but recent findings suggest that it is wrong. In the previous chapter we saw that, when people are asked to decide whether a string of letters is a word, their decision is faster when a word is preceded by a semantically related word, such as *bread* preceded by *butter*. If people consider only a single meaning of an ambiguous word, a word such as *bug* should facilitate the recognition of either *ant* or *spy*, depending on which meaning is activated.

Swinney (1979) tested this prediction by replacing the phoneme-monitoring task with a lexical decision task. He explained to the subjects that a string of letters would appear on a screen as they listened to some sentences, and they were to decide as quickly as possible whether or not each letter string formed a word. He did not mention that some of the sentences and words were related. The letter string, which appeared on the screen immediately after subjects heard the ambiguous word, was contextually appropriate, contextually inappropriate, or unrelated to the meaning of the ambiguous word. A contextually appropriate word appearing on the screen, such as *ant*, was consistent with the meaning of the ambiguous word that was suggested by the context. A contextually inappropriate word, such as *spy*, was consistent with the meaning that was not suggested by the context. An unrelated word, such as *sew*, was consistent with neither of the two meanings.

If the context causes the activation of only a single meaning, it should be easier to recognize only the contextually appropriate word (*ant*). But if both meanings of the ambiguous word are activated, the contextually inappropriate word (*spy*) should also be easier to recognize than the unrelated word (*sew*). The results showed that, when the visual test word immediately followed the ambiguous word, both the contextually appropriate and the contextually inappropriate words were easier to recognize than the unrelated words. But when the test word occurred four syllables (about 750 to 1,000 msec) after the ambiguous word, recognition of only the contextually appropriate word was facilitated.

Swinney's findings suggest that more than one meaning of an ambiguous word is activated even when a prior context indicates which meaning is appropriate. If only one meaning of *bugs* were activated by the phrase *He found several spiders, roaches, and other bugs*, it is not clear why it would be as easy to respond to *spy* as to *ant*. However, when the test word occurred four syllables after the ambiguous word, recognition of only the word *ant* was facilitated. It therefore appears that, although both meanings of an ambiguous word are momentarily activated, the context allows the listener to select the appropriate meaning quickly. Selection of the appropriate meaning occurred quickly enough to prevent interference in the phoneme detection task. As you may recall, there was a slight delay between the ambiguous word and the target phoneme. This was sufficient time to resolve the ambiguity when there was an appropriate context. An appropriate context therefore seems to allow the listener to select the appropriate meaning of a word quickly rather than to prevent more than one meaning from being activated.

Individual Differences in Resolving Ambiguities

Some people are better at resolving ambiguities than others. In fact, the picture we have painted so far is for how good readers resolve ambiguities. Before looking at what happens for less skilled readers, let us elaborate on what we have already learned by looking at a model of how context influences the interpretation of a word. Figure 10.7 shows a model proposed by Carpenter and Daneman (1981).

The first step is to fixate on and encode each word in the sentence. The encoding of a word will activate one or more concepts, which are retrieved into STM if the activation reaches some threshold level. When at least one concept reaches threshold, the reader tries to integrate it with the previous text. If the concept is compatible with the context, such as the interpretation of *bug* as an insect, it will be used in further processing. If the concept is not compatible with the context, such as the interpretation of *bug* as a monitoring device, its activation level will quickly decay.

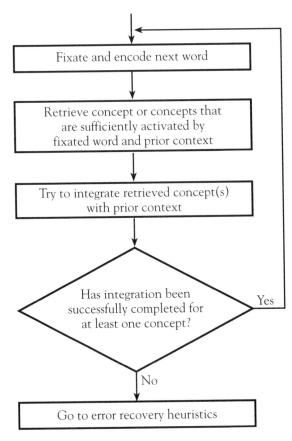

Figure 10.7   *A flowchart showing the encoding, activation, integration, and error recovery stages of reading.*

From "Lexical Retrieval and Error Recovery in Reading: A Model Based on Eye Fixations," by P. A. Carpenter and M. Daneman, 1981, *Journal of Verbal Learning and Verbal Behavior*, 20, 137–160. Copyright © 1981 by Academic Press, Inc. Reprinted by permission.

Although this is a description of what happens for skilled readers, it is not a good description of what happens for less skilled readers (Gernsbacher, 1993). The problem for less skilled readers is that they do not quickly resolve which of the activated meanings is the correct one. Like the good readers, both meanings of an ambiguous word are initially activated, but unlike the good readers, both meanings are still active 1 sec after encountering the ambiguous word. Less skilled readers are simply less able to **suppress** the inappropriate meaning.

Suppress Eliminating inappropriate meanings in a sentence

It would be simpler for everyone if only a single meaning (the correct one, of course) were initially activated. Although this might seem beneficial when the correct meaning is obvious, an advantage of activating multiple meanings is that the clarifying context occasionally does not occur until *after* the ambiguous word. In this case, it would be advantageous to try to keep both meanings active in STM until we gain enough information to select the appropriate one.

See if you can find the ambiguous word in the following partial sentence: *Since Ken really liked the boxer, he took a bus to the nearest.* . . . . If you found the ambiguous word, can you resolve the ambiguity by using the sentence context? The ambiguous word is *boxer,* and at this point we don't have enough information to know whether Ken is interested in a fighter or a dog. The remainder of the sentence resolves the ambiguity by informing us that Ken took the bus to the nearest pet store to buy the animal. Notice, however, that unlike the previous examples in which the clarifying context preceded the ambiguous word, in this case we had to read considerably more of the sentence following the ambiguous word before the meaning became clear.

People's ability to excel in these situations is influenced by the capacity of their working memory (Miyake, Just, & Carpenter, 1994). We saw in Chapter 4 that STM is often used as a working memory in which people both store and process material in STM. In this example we would like to keep active in working memory both interpretations of the word *boxer* until we later encounter information that would enable us to select the correct one. People who have a large **working memory capacity** are able to keep both interpretations active over a longer span than people who have a smaller working memory capacity. The latter group is able to maintain only the more likely (dominant) interpretation and therefore has difficulty resolving the ambiguity when the less likely interpretation proves to be the correct one.

Working memory capacity The amount of information that can be kept active in working memory

Because the word *boxer* is more likely to refer to a fighter than to a dog, people with a small working memory capacity would have difficulty comprehending a sentence in which they later learned that the sentence was about a dog. In this case their integration would be unsuccessful and they would have to use the **error recovery heuristics** in Figure 10.7. Examples include trying to reinterpret the inconsistent word, checking previous words that might have caused the difficulty, reading on for further information, and elaborating the apparent inconsistency to make it consistent (perhaps Ken was buying a dog at the pet store to give to the fighter).

Error recovery heuristics Strategies for correcting comprehension errors

In conclusion, good readers are those readers who are able to initially keep active in working memory both interpretations of an ambiguous word and then quickly select the appropriate meaning as soon as they receive a clarifying context. We have seen two ways in which reading can be impaired. Readers with limited working memory capacity are less able to maintain both meanings in working memory when the clarifying context occurs later, and less skilled readers are less able to quickly suppress the inappropriate meaning when they encounter the clarifying context.

Understanding Noun Phrases

The preceding discussion emphasized how context influences the understanding of a single word. Let us now consider a larger unit, such as a noun phrase consisting of an adjective and a noun. An important issue in studying how people understand groups of words such as noun phrases is whether the meaning of the noun is influenced by the meaning of the adjective. When we hear a noun phrase such as the *burning house*, do we select the meaning of *burning* and the meaning of *house* independently and then combine the two meanings? Or is the meaning of *house* directly influenced by the adjective that precedes it? Comprehension would be facilitated if the meaning of an adjective directly influenced the meaning of the noun. The evidence suggests that there is a direct influence for noun phrases such as the *burning house*.

Potter and Faulconer (1979) used a picture probe task to investigate how people understand noun phrases. (Figure 10.8 shows examples of sentences and pictures used in the experiment.) Subjects listened to sentences such as *It was already getting late when the man first saw the burning house ahead of him.* Immediately after the noun *house*, a picture appeared illustrating either the noun alone (*house*) or the noun phrase (*burning house*). The subject's task was to decide whether the pictured object had been named in the sentence. When the adjective was not included in the noun phrase, subjects were faster in verifying the more typical pictures shown on the left in Figure 10.8. For example, when the subjects heard the sentence *It was already getting late when the man first saw the house*, they could verify the picture of a typical house faster than a picture of a burning house. This finding is analogous to the typicality effects discussed in the chapter on categorization (Chapter 8). Since the typical pictures are more representative of their category than the modified pictures, they can be verified more quickly.

A more interesting question is what happens when the noun is preceded by the adjective. If the meaning of the noun is selected independently of the meaning of the adjective, then we would expect that the more typical picture should still be verified more rapidly. However, if the meaning of the noun is influenced by the adjective, the modified picture should be verified more quickly. The results supported the second of the two alternatives—the subjects verified the modified picture more quickly than the typical picture when the noun was preceded by the adjective. These results occurred even though the task required only verification of

It was already $\begin{Bmatrix} \text{burning} \\ \text{getting late} \end{Bmatrix}$ when the man first saw the {burning}
house ahead of him.

"It's {dripping} on the table," Sally said, gesturing at the
{dripping} candle that she had made.

Seeing it {drooping} in the yard, the Boy Scout wondered how many
years the {drooping} flag had been used.

Although it was $\begin{Bmatrix} \text{low} \\ \text{borrowed} \end{Bmatrix}$, Jill thought that the {low} table
would be adequate.

Figure 10.8   *Examples of sentences and typical versus modified picture probes.*
From "Understanding Noun Phrases," by M. C. Potter and B. A. Faulconer, 1979, *Journal of Verbal Learning and Verbal Behavior, 18,* 509–521. Copyright © 1979 by Academic Press, Inc. Reprinted by permission.

the noun, so participants could have ignored the meaning of the adjective when they made their decisions.

In another version of this experiment, the information conveyed by the adjective came at the beginning of the sentence rather than just before the noun. For example, people heard the sentence *It was already burning when the man first saw the house ahead of him.* People's verification times for this condition were similar to their verification times when the adjective was not presented—they were faster at verifying the typical picture than the modified picture. The results imply that selecting the meaning of a noun can be influenced by an immediately preceding adjective but selection is not likely to be influenced when the same information occurs earlier in a sentence.

Although Potter and Faulconer found that an immediately preceding adjective modified the meaning of the noun, the magnitude of the effect was related to the familiarity of the noun phrase. The modified picture was verified faster for familiar noun phrases, such as *roasted turkey*, than for unfamiliar noun phrases, such as *broken screwdriver*. More recent findings have shown that both the typicality and the relevance of the adjective contribute to this familiarity effect (Murphy, 1990). **Typicality** is illustrated by the distinction between *cold beer* and *hot beer*. *Cold* is a typical adjective for *beer*, and *hot* is an atypical adjective. **Relevancy** is illustrated by comparing the temperature of *beer* with the temperature of *garbage*. Although *cold garbage* is more typical than *hot garbage*, the temperature of garbage is usually irrelevant.

Murphy found that relevancy had a large, significant effect on how long subjects took to decide whether a noun phrase made sense. Response times were much faster for relevant phrases (such as the temperature of *beer*) than for irrelevant phrases (such as the temperature of *garbage*). Typical adjectives resulted in faster judgments than atypical adjectives, although the difference was not significant.

In conclusion, these studies show various ways in which context influences comprehension. Although the context usually facilitates word recognition, it can interfere with word recognition if it creates an expectation for a particular word that does not occur. It can also help people select the appropriate meaning of an ambiguous word, although good reading skills require maintaining multiple meanings in STM and then quickly suppressing the unintended meaning after encountering a clarifying context. An adjective can have an immediate impact on the interpretation of the noun that follows it, although this result depends on the familiarity of the adjective-noun combination.

Typicality The extent to which a particular value (such as large, medium, or small) is expected when an adjective modifies a particular noun

Relevancy The extent to which an adjective (such as size) is a meaningful modifier of a particular noun

IMPLICATIONS OF SENTENCES

Our study of comprehension has thus far been limited to considering how people understand sentences in which information is directly asserted. However, we can also use language to imply something without directly asserting it. It is often sufficient for a message simply to imply an action to convince a listener that the action actually occurred. For example, the sentence *The hungry python caught the mouse* may convince the listener that the python ate the mouse, even though that action is not explicitly stated.

Psychologists have demonstrated that people are influenced by the implications of sentences by showing that subjects falsely recognize implied statements (Bransford, Barclay, & Franks, 1972). Consider how the following two sentences are related.

1a. Three turtles rested on a floating log, and a fish swam beneath them.
1b. Three turtles rested on a floating log, and a fish swam beneath it.

The second sentence is implied by the first sentence because the fish swam beneath the turtles who were on the log. People therefore often falsely recognize the second sentence when they had actually seen the first sentence.

False recognitions are not a problem when the presented sentence does not imply the test sentence, as in the following example:

2a. Three turtles rested beside a floating log, and a fish swam beneath them.
2b. Three turtles rested beside a floating log, and a fish swam beneath it.

This pair of sentences is identical to the first pair except that the word *beside* replaces the word *on*. Because the first sentence no longer implies that the fish swam beneath the log, people are less likely to falsely recognize the second sentence.

The finding that people may not distinguish implications from direct statements can have important consequences. For example, a consumer could be misled by the implications of an advertisement, or a jury could be misled by the implications of testimony. We will first consider the effect of implications on courtroom testimony.

Courtroom Testimony

Asking leading questions is one way implications can influence a person's responses. Loftus designed a procedure to simulate what might occur during eyewitness testimony (for example, Loftus, 1975). The procedure consists in showing people a short film of a car accident and, immediately afterward, asking them questions about what occurred in the film. One experimental variation involved phrasing a question as either "Did you see a broken headlight?" or "Did you see the broken headlight?" The word *the* implies that there was a broken headlight, whereas the word *a* does not. The results showed that people who were asked questions containing the word *the* were more likely to report having seen something, whether or not it had actually appeared in the film, than those who were asked questions containing the word *a*.

Another experiment revealed that the wording of a question can affect a numerical estimate. The question "About how fast were the two cars going when they smashed into each other?" consistently yielded a higher estimate of speed than when *smashed* (*into*) was replaced by *collided, bumped, contacted,* or *hit.* These results, when combined with similar findings from other experiments conducted by Loftus and her associates, show that leading questions can influence eyewitness testimony.

Implications can influence not only how a witness responds to questions but what a jury remembers about the testimony of a witness. In another experiment (Harris, 1978) subjects listened to simulated courtroom testimony and then rated statements about information in the testimony as true, false, or of indeterminate truth value. Half of the test statements were directly asserted (for instance, "The intruder walked away without taking any money"), and half were only implied ("The intruder was able to walk away without taking any money"). The test item that the intruder did not take any money would be true for the asserted statement but of indeterminate truth value for the implied statement.

Harris found that people were more likely to indicate that asserted statements were true than that implied statements were true. There was, however, a disturbing tendency to accept implied statements—subjects responded true to 64% of the statements that were only implied. Furthermore, instructions warning people to be careful to distinguish between asserted and implied statements did not significantly reduce the acceptance of implied statements.

The work of Loftus and Harris should be of interest to people in the legal professions. A judge can immediately rule a leading question out of order, but not before the members of the jury have heard the question. Instructions from the judge to disregard certain evidence may not prevent the jurors from considering that evidence when making their decision. More subtle uses of language, such as use of the word *crash* rather than the word *hit,* may not even be identified as potentially misleading.

Harris has speculated that the distinction between asserted and implied statements may be even harder to make in a real courtroom than in an experimental situation. People in his experiment made their judgments immediately after hearing a 5-min segment of simulated trial testimony. Members of a jury make their final decision after a much longer delay and after they have heard much more information. It is therefore important to clarify immediately any courtroom statements that are ambiguous regarding whether information was asserted or implied. If the witness is unwilling to assert the information directly—and thus become liable to charges of perjury—the jury should be made aware of the questionable value of that information.

Advertising Claims

The acceptance of implied statements is as important an issue in advertising as it is in courtroom testimony. The Federal Trade Commission makes decisions about deceptive advertising, but deciding what constitutes deceptive advertising is a complex question. The decision may be particularly difficult if a claim is merely implied. Consider the following commercial:

> Aren't you tired of sniffles and runny noses all winter? Tired of always feeling less than your best? Get through the whole winter without colds. Take Eradicold Pills as directed.

Note that the commercial does not directly assert that Eradicold Pills will get you through the whole winter without colds—that is only implied. To test whether people can distinguish between asserted and implied claims, Harris (1977) presented subjects with a series of 20 fictitious commercials, half of which asserted claims and half of which implied claims. The subjects were instructed to rate the claims as true, false, or of indeterminate truth value on the basis of the information presented. Some of the people made their judgments immediately after hearing each commercial, and others made their judgments after hearing all 20 commercials. In addition, half the people were given instructions that warned them not to interpret implied claims as asserted and were shown an example of a commercial that made an implied claim.

The results showed that subjects responded true significantly more often to assertions than to implications. Furthermore, instructions were helpful in reducing the number of implications accepted as true. Although these results are encouraging, however, they are not unqualifiedly positive. First, even in the condition that was most favorable to rejecting implications—the group that had been warned and that gave an immediate judgment after hearing each commercial—people accepted about half the implied statements as true. When the judgments were delayed until all 20 commercials were presented, people accepted as true about as many implied statements as direct statements—even when they had been explicitly warned about implied statements.

Acceptance of implied statements is a problem that exists outside the psychology laboratory. In fact, one of the most frequently accepted implied statements in Harris's (1977) study was a verbatim statement from a real commercial. Another real commercial, created after Harris's study, was changed because competitors complained that it made unfair implications about their product (see Box 10.1). These complaints resulted in a modification of the commercial.

American Express ads challenged

NEW YORK—Those "Don't-leave-home-without-them" television commercials for American Express Travelers Cheques are under attack, and American Express reportedly plans to re-do them.

Competitors say the ads unfairly imply that people who lose travelers checks may not be able to get a refund unless the checks were issued by American Express.

NBC News reported that American Express has agreed to change its commercials. Actor Karl Malden will reshoot the endings, NBC said, and make it clear that all travelers checks are refundable, not just American Express checks.

Collot Guerard of the division of advertising practices in the Federal Trade Commission's Bureau of Consumer Protection said the agency "probably will take a look at the American Express ad."

Deciding whether it is deceptive, she said, will depend on the answers to a number of questions, including: "How easy is it to get refunds for the other companies' travelers checks?"

The American Express TV campaign introduced in June shows people in a variety of situations. They lose their travelers checks. Panic. A plea for help. But the checks were not American Express. What is to be done? The question is unanswered. At the end, comes the voice of Malden: "American Express Travelers Cheques. Don't leave home without them."

SOURCE: From "American Express Ads Challenged," appearing in the *San Francisco Chronicle*, August 17, 1979. Copyright © 1979 by the Associated Press. Reprinted by permission of Associated Press Newsfeatures.

In the next chapter, on text comprehension, we will continue to study language, but at a larger unit of analysis. We will focus less on individual sentences and more on how information is combined across sentences. We will try to determine which variables influence people's ability to comprehend paragraphs and remember what they read.

SUMMARY

One of the major questions that have fascinated psychologists interested in language is how people learn to speak in grammatically correct sentences. An early view suggested that children learn to associate the adjacent words in a sentence. According to this view, each word serves as a stimulus for the word that follows it. There are several problems with this theory, the major one being that a person would have to learn an infinite number of associations. The alternative view is that a child learns a grammar consisting of rules for generating sentences. The transformational grammar proposed by Chomsky stimulated much research as psychologists investigated how well it could account for the results of language experiments. The grammar consisted of both phrase structure rules for describing the parts of a sentence (such as noun phrase and verb phrase) and transformation rules for changing a sentence into a closely related sentence (such as an active sentence into a passive sentence).

Psychologists have occasionally used ambiguous sentences to study comprehension and have found that it takes longer to complete an ambiguous sentence than an unambiguous one. A clarifying context apparently allows the listener to quickly select the appropriate meaning of an ambiguous word, although both meanings have been activated. However, a context can also cause interference if it is misleading or if a strongly expected word does not occur. Individual differences in resolving ambiguities are caused by differences in the ability of readers to keep multiple meanings active in STM until encountering a clarifying context, and then quickly suppressing the inappropriate meaning. The study of how people comprehend noun phrases indicates that the meaning of a noun is immediately influenced by the adjective that precedes it. The research on comprehension seeks to identify how context influences the meaning of words and raises the question of how different experimental tasks relate to the comprehension that occurs during ordinary reading.

An aspect of language that has direct practical applications is the distinction between assertions and implications. A sentence that only implies some event may have as great an impact as a sentence that directly asserts this event. Making people aware of the distinction between an asserted and an implied statement is particularly important in courtroom testimony. Research using simulated testimony has found that people often do not distinguish or do not remember what information was only implied and what was asserted. Similar results have been found for advertising claims.

STUDY QUESTIONS

By the time we are college students we are such skilled users of language that we don't usually think about it at all. If you haven't thought about the "parts of speech" lately (or ever), you may need to look them up before you get into this chapter.

1. Make sure you understand the term *morpheme* by thinking of several stem words that you can change the meaning of by adding a prefix and a suffix.
2. What is a grammar? In what sense do all of us "know" English grammar?
3. What are the respective domains of phrase structure grammar and

transformational grammar? Or are the two fighting over the same turf?

4. There are three possible types of ambiguous sentences. Can you think of a new example of each type?

5. Note the various experimental tasks that have been used to study language comprehension. Have you run into any of them before in this course?

6. Many of the words we use can take on separate meanings, but most of the time we don't experience ambiguity. Why, then, is it important to determine how we "disambiguate" words in a sentence?

7. It is intuitively obvious that context facilitates word interpretation, but how may it interfere with interpretation? How has the influence of context been studied experimentally?

8. Form images for the following adjective-noun pairs: yellow submarine, green whale, white cloud, blue house. Which pairs seemed to result in an image in which the adjective immediately influenced your image of the noun? Why?

9. Be sure you understand the meaning of *imply* and *implication* versus *assertion*. Test yourself by inventing a sentence that asserts an event or state of affairs and then change it so it merely implies the same thing. Write out the sentences.

10. Since the interpretation of both courtroom testimony and advertising copy may be manipulated misleadingly, should educators specifically warn students to be aware of implied statements? What else could be done about the problem?

KEY TERMS

The page number in parentheses refers to where the term is discussed in the chapter.

ambiguous sentence (301)
Broca's aphasia (294)
deep structure (302)
error recovery heuristics (311)
exchange errors (298)
generative (292)
grammar (292)
high-constraint sentences (305)
language (292)
lexical ambiguity (302)
lexical decision task (305)
low-constraint sentences (306)
morpheme exchanges (298)
morphemes (292)
phoneme exchanges (298)

phrase structure grammar (298)
relevancy (314)
semantic features (306)
slips of the tongue (297)
structured (292)
suppress (310)
surface ambiguity (302)
surface structure (302)
symbolic (292)
transformational grammar (300)
typicality (314)
underlying ambiguity (302)
Wernicke's aphasia (294)
word exchange (298)
working memory capacity (311)

RECOMMENDED READING

An easy introduction to the theoretical contributions of Chomsky is a book by Lyons (1970). Jenkins (1969) discusses the influence of grammatical theories on the way psychologists have thought about language acquisition. Lachman, Lachman, and Butterfield (1979) review the shift in psycholinguistics from a preoccupation with syntax to a preoccupation with semantics. The consistent use of either syntactic or semantic information creates parallel structure and facilitates comprehension (Frazier, Taft, Roeper, Clifton, & Ehrlich, 1984). Schvaneveldt, Meyer, and Becker (1976) used their lexical decision task to study the effect of semantic context on visual word recognition. Blank and Foss (1978) studied how an appropriate semantic context facilitates comprehension of sentences. Gernsbacher and Faust (1991) show that the ability to quickly suppress inappropriate meanings is an important skill in a variety of comprehension tasks. Examples of how knowledge sources interact to determine comprehension are discussed by Bock (1982) and Salasoo and Pisoni (1985).

There have been many studies on memory for sentences. Jarvella (1979) reviewed studies on immediate memory for the exact words of a sentence. Bransford and Franks (1971) performed a classic study on the integration of ideas in sentences, in which they showed that people have difficulty recognizing the exact words in a sentence because they combine the ideas in related sentences. Kintsch and Bates (1977) studied recognition memory outside the laboratory by testing students' memory for statements made during a classroom lecture. Keenan, MacWhinney, and Mayhew (1977) found that their colleagues often could remember the exact words of statements that had high emotional content, although usually only the general meaning of sentences was remembered (Sachs, 1967). Foss's (1988) chapter in the *Annual Review of Psychology* contains an overview of studies on language.

Comprehension and Memory for Text

Reading a book should be a conversation between you and the author.

MORTIMER ADLER AND CHARLES VAN DOREN

*I*T MAY BE difficult to single out any one cognitive skill as most important, but, if we had to make a choice, *comprehension* would be a prime contender for the honor. Much of what we learn depends on our ability to understand written material. Thus the comprehension of written material has attracted considerable attention.

One application of this interest in comprehension has been rewriting regulations and instructions to make them easier to understand. An example of an attempt to improve instructions is the study conducted by Charrow and Charrow (1979). The goal of the study was to make it easier to understand jury instructions by identifying difficulties in comprehension. Box 11.1 shows two versions of instructions to a jury. The first version is the original; the second version is a modification designed to be easier to understand.

Charrow and Charrow tested the success of their modifications by asking prospective jury members to paraphrase the instructions. After the members heard the instructions, they tried to recall them in their own words. The jury members who listened to the modified instructions were more successful than the members who listened to the original instructions. For the example shown in Box 11.1, ability to recall the instructions improved by about 50%.

Psychologists have primarily used two measures of comprehension, and we will encounter examples of each in this chapter. One is a subjective measure. Psychologists ask people to rate on a scale how easy various texts are to understand, or they might ask people to press a button as soon as they think they understand a sentence. The second measure is the number of ideas that people can recall from a text. This measure assumes that someone who has really understood the text should be able to recall more ideas than someone who didn't understand it.

Two important components influence comprehension—the reader and the text. The reader comes equipped with prior knowledge that can help her understand the text by relating what she reads to what she already knows. The quotation at the beginning of this chapter—"Reading a book should be a conversation between you and the author"—reflects this interaction between the reader and the author. But, unlike a real conversation, the conversation proceeds in only one direction. This places an added burden on the author to anticipate how the reader might respond—to foresee difficulties and answer questions that the reader might have.

The three sections of this chapter emphasize the reader, the text, and the interaction between the reader and the text. The first section looks at how the reader's knowledge influences the comprehension and recall of ideas in a text. The second section is about how the organization of ideas in a text affects comprehension. The final section discusses a specific

Making legal language understandable

BOX 11.1

Original

You must not consider as evidence any statement of counsel made during the trial; however, if counsel for the parties have stipulated to any fact, or any fact has been admitted by counsel, you will regard that fact as being conclusively proved as to the party or parties making the stipulation or admission.

As to any question to which an objection was sustained, you must not speculate as to what the answer might have been or as to the reason for the objection.

You must not consider for any purpose any offer of evidence that was rejected, or any evidence that was stricken out by the court; such matter is to be treated as though you had never known of it.

You must never speculate to be true any insinuation suggested by a question asked a witness. A question is not evidence and may be considered only as it supplies meaning to the answer.

Modified

As I mentioned earlier, it is your job to decide from the evidence what the facts are. Here are five rules that will help you decide what is, and what is not, evidence.

1. *Lawyers' statements.* Ordinarily, any statement made by the lawyers in this case is not evidence. However, if all the lawyers agree that some particular thing is true, you must accept it as the truth.
2. *Rejected evidence.* At times during this trial, items of testimony were offered as evidence, but I did not allow them to become evidence. Since they never became evidence, you must not consider them.
3. *Stricken evidence.* At times, I ordered some piece of evidence to be stricken, or thrown out. Since that is no longer evidence, you must ignore it, also.
4. *Questions to a witness.* By itself, a question is not evidence. A question can only be used to give meaning to a witness's answer. Furthermore, if a lawyer's question to a witness contained any insinuations, you must ignore those insinuations.
5. *Objections to questions.* If a lawyer objected to a question, and I did not allow the witness to answer the question, you must not try to guess what the answer might have been. You must also not try to guess the reason why the lawyer objected to the question.

SOURCE: From "Making Legal Language Understandable: A Psycholinguistic Study of Jury Instructions," by R. P. Charrow and V. R. Charrow, 1979, *Columbia Law Review, 79,* 1306–1374. Reprinted by permission of the authors.

model of how comprehension occurs. In addition to its theoretical success, the model has increased our ability to measure and improve the readability of texts.

PRIOR KNOWLEDGE OF THE READER

Effect of Prior Knowledge on Comprehension

A central issue for psychologists interested in studying comprehension is specifying how people use their knowledge to understand new or abstract ideas. The influence of prior knowledge on the comprehension and recall of ideas was dramatically illustrated in a study by Bransford and Johnson (1973). They asked people to listen to a paragraph and to try to comprehend and remember it. After listening to the paragraph, subjects rated how easy it was to comprehend and then tried to recall as many ideas as they could. You can get some feeling for the task by reading the following passage once and then trying to recall as much as you can.

> If the balloons popped, the sound wouldn't be able to carry, since everything would be too far away from the correct floor. A closed window would also prevent the sound from carrying, since most buildings tend to be well insulated. Since the whole operation depends on a steady flow of electricity, a break in the middle of the wire would also cause problems. Of course, the fellow could shout, but the human voice is not loud enough to carry that far. An additional problem is that a string could break on the instrument. Then there could be no accompaniment to the message. It is clear that the best situation would involve less distance. Then there would be fewer potential problems. With face to face contact, the least number of things could go wrong. (p. 392)

Bransford and Johnson (1973) intentionally designed the passage to consist of abstract, unfamiliar statements. If you found it difficult to recall the ideas, your experience was similar to the experience of the people who participated in the experiment. They recalled only 3.6 ideas from a maximum of 14. The ideas can be made less abstract by showing people an appropriate context, as is illustrated in Figure 11.1. Does the picture help you recall any more ideas?

Bransford and Johnson (1973) tested the effect of context by comparing a *no-context* group with two other groups. The *context-before* group saw the picture before they read the passage. They recalled an average of 8.0 ideas, a substantial improvement over the no-context group. The *context-after* group saw the picture immediately after reading the passage. They recalled only 3.6 ideas—the same number as the no-context group. The effect of context was useful, but only if people were aware of the context before reading the passage.

The results suggest that context does much more than simply provide hints about what might have occurred in the passage. If the picture provided useful retrieval cues, the people who saw the picture after reading the passage should have recalled more ideas than the group who didn't see the picture. Since recall was improved only when people saw the pic-

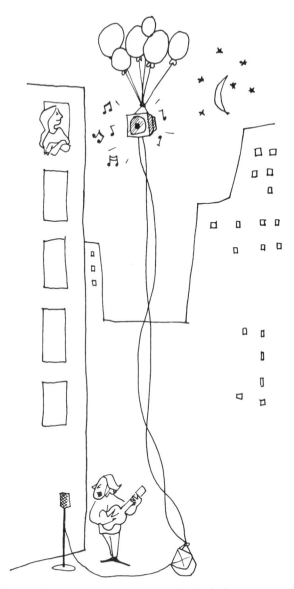

Figure 11.1   *Appropriate context for the balloon passage.*

From "Considerations of Some Problems of Comprehension," by J. D.
Bransford and M. K. Johnson, 1973, in *Visual Information Processing,*
edited by W. G. Chase. Copyright © 1973 by Academic Press, Inc.
Reprinted by permission.

ture before reading the passage, the experiment suggests that the context
improved comprehension, which in turn improved recall. People in the
context-before group rated the passage as easy to comprehend, in contrast

to the context-after group. When the abstract ideas were difficult to comprehend, they were quickly forgotten, and providing the context after the passage had no effect on recall.

The balloon passage is an example of a novel context since most of us have never encountered this particular situation. What would happen if readers saw a passage about a familiar event that could activate the kind of schematic structures that we discussed in Chapter 9? But even reading about a familiar event is helpful only when we can recognize it. Consider the following passage:

> The procedure is actually quite simple. First you arrange things into different groups. Of course, one pile may be sufficient depending on how much there is to do. If you have to go somewhere else due to lack of facilities, that is the next step; otherwise you are pretty well set. It is important not to overdo things. That is, it is better to do too few things at once than too many. In the short run this may not seem important, but complications can easily arise. A mistake can be expensive as well. At first the whole procedure will seem complicated. Soon, however, it will become just another facet of life. It is difficult to foresee any end to the necessity for this task in the immediate future, but then one never can tell. After the procedure is completed, one arranges the materials into different groups again. Then they can be put into their appropriate places. Eventually they will be used once more, and the whole cycle will then have to be repeated. However, that is part of life. (p. 400)*

The paragraph actually describes a very familiar procedure, but the ideas are presented so abstractly that the procedure is difficult to recognize. People who read the passage had as much trouble recalling ideas as the people who read the balloon passage—they recalled only 2.8 ideas from a maximum of 18. A different group of subjects, who were informed after reading the passage that it referred to washing clothes, didn't do any better; they recalled only 2.7 ideas. But subjects who were told before they read the passage that it described washing clothes recalled 5.8 ideas. The results are consistent with the results on the balloon passage and indicate that background knowledge isn't sufficient if people don't recognize the appropriate context. Although everyone is familiar with the procedure used to wash clothes, people didn't recognize the procedure because the passage was so abstract. Providing the appropriate context before the passage therefore increased both comprehension and recall, as it did for the balloon passage.

---

*From "Considerations of Some Problems of Comprehension," by J. D. Bransford and M. K. Johnson, 1973, in *Visual Information Processing*, edited by W. G. Chase. Copyright © 1973 by Academic Press, Inc. Reprinted by permission.

Effect of Prior Knowledge on Retrieval

The failure of the context-after group to recall more ideas than the no-context group was caused by the difficulty in comprehending material when there was not an obvious context. The results might have been different, however, if the material had been easier to understand as presented. Bransford and Johnson (1973) suggest that, if people initially understand a text and are then encouraged to think of the ideas in a new perspective, they might recall additional ideas that they failed to recall under the old perspective.

A study by R. C. Anderson and J. W. Pichert (1978) supports the hypothesis that a shift in perspective may result in the recall of additional ideas. The participants in their study read about two boys who played hooky from school. The story told that they went to one of the boys' homes because no one was there on Thursdays. It was a very nice home on attractive grounds, set back from the road. But because it was an older home, it had some defects—a leaky roof and a damp basement. The family was quite wealthy and owned a lot of valuable possessions, such as ten-speed bikes, a color television, and a rare coin collection. The entire story contained 72 ideas, which had previously been rated for their importance to a prospective burglar or to a prospective home buyer. For example, a leaky roof and damp basement would be important to a home buyer, whereas valuable possessions and the fact that no one was usually home on Thursday would be important to a burglar.

The subjects read the story from one of the two perspectives and, after a short delay, were asked to write down as much of the exact story as they could remember. After another short delay they again attempted to recall ideas from the story. Half did so from the same **perspective** and half from a new perspective. The experimenters told the subjects in the same-perspective condition that the purpose of the study was to determine whether people could remember things they thought they had forgotten if they were given a second chance. Subjects in the new-perspective condition were told that the purpose of the study was to determine whether people could remember things they thought they had forgotten if they were given a new perspective.

Perspective A particular point of view

As might be expected, the perspective influenced the kind of information people recalled during the first recall period. The group that had the burglar perspective recalled more burglar information, and the group that had the home-buyer perspective recalled more home-buyer information. The results during the second recall attempt supported the hypothesis that a change in perspective can result in recall of additional information. The group that shifted perspectives recalled additional ideas that were important to the new perspective—7% more ideas in one experiment and 10% more in another. In contrast, the group that did not shift perspective recalled slightly less information on its second attempt than on its first attempt.

Notice that these findings differ from the findings of Bransford and Johnson (1973) in that the shift to a new perspective aided the retrieval, rather than the comprehension, of ideas. Since the story was easy to comprehend, comprehension wasn't a problem; the problem was being able to recall all the ideas. Anderson and Pichert proposed three possible explanations for why changing perspectives aided recall. One possibility is that people simply guessed ideas that they didn't really remember but that were consistent with the new perspective. The chance of guessing correctly, however, is rather low. A second alternative is that people did not recall all they could remember because they thought it was not important to the original perspective. The instructions, however, were to recall all the information. The third possibility was the one favored by Anderson and Pichert because it was the most consistent with what the participants reported during interviews that followed their recall. Many subjects reported that the new perspective provided them with a plan for searching memory. They used their knowledge about what would interest a home buyer or a burglar to retrieve new information that was not suggested by the original perspective.

Effect of Prior Knowledge on False Recognition and Recall

The previous studies support the idea that prior knowledge influences either the comprehension or the retrieval of information in a text. People who could interpret abstract ideas as related to a serenade or to the washing of clothes had an advantage in comprehending and recalling the ideas. In addition, adopting a particular perspective enabled people to retrieve more concrete ideas than they had initially been able to comprehend.

Although background knowledge usually makes comprehension and recall easier, it can also be the source of errors. When we already know something about the given topic and then read more about it, we may have difficulty distinguishing between what we read and what we already know. This can create a problem if we are asked to recall the source of the information. Consider the following biographical passage:

> Gerald Martin strove to undermine the existing government to satisfy his political ambitions. Many of the people of his country supported his efforts. Current political problems made it relatively easy for Martin to take over. Certain groups remained loyal to the old government and caused Martin trouble. He confronted these groups directly and so silenced them. He became a ruthless, uncontrollable dictator. The ultimate effect of his rule was the downfall of his country. (Sulin & Dooling, 1974, p. 256)

People who read this passage should not associate it with their knowledge of famous people since Gerald Martin is a fictitious person. It would be easy, however, to modify the passage by changing the name of the dictator. In an experiment designed by Sulin and Dooling (1974), half the subjects read the Gerald Martin passage, and half the subjects read the same passage with the name changed to Adolf Hitler. Either 5 minutes or 1 week after reading the passage, the subjects were given a recognition memory test consisting of seven sentences from the passage randomly mixed with seven sentences that were not in the passage. Subjects were asked to identify the sentences that occurred in the passage.

Four of the sentences not in the passage were completely unrelated (neutral), and the other three varied in their relatedness to the Hitler theme. The low-related sentence was *He was an intelligent man but had no sense of human kindness.* The medium-related sentence was *He was obsessed by the desire to conquer the world.* The high-related sentence was *He hated the Jews particularly and so persecuted them.* Figure 11.2 shows the recognition of sentences for the two retention intervals. At the short retention interval there were few false recognitions, and the results were uninfluenced by whether the passage was about a famous person (Hitler) or a fictitious person (Martin). After 1 week, however, it was more difficult for people who had read the Hitler passage to distinguish between what was in the passage and what they knew about Hitler. People were likely to recognize a sentence incorrectly as having occurred in the passage if it described Hitler. False recognitions also increased with the retention interval for people who read the Gerald Martin (fictitious) passage, but to a lesser degree.

Information can also be falsely recognized or recalled when it matches our knowledge of scripts. As we saw in Chapter 9, a script represents our memory for an organized sequence of events, such as what typically occurs during a crime. The false recall of such information can be a serious problem if members of a jury incorrectly remember events that they associate with a crime, but which did not actually occur in this case. Holst and Pezdek (1992) asked people to list all of the events that occur in a typical robbery of a convenience store, a bank, and a mugging. Some of these events were then included in a tape-recorded transcript of a mock trial in which the prosecutor questions an eyewitness to a robbery. Four of the events associated with a robbery (act like a shopper, go to the cash register, demand money, threaten people) were stated by the eyewitness, but four other robbery events were unstated (case the store, pull out a gun, take the money, drive away in a getaway car).

The participants in the experiment then returned a week later and were asked to recall as many actions as they could from the witness's testimony. They recalled 31% of the stated events and falsely recalled 15% of the unstated events, indicating that their prior knowledge of what

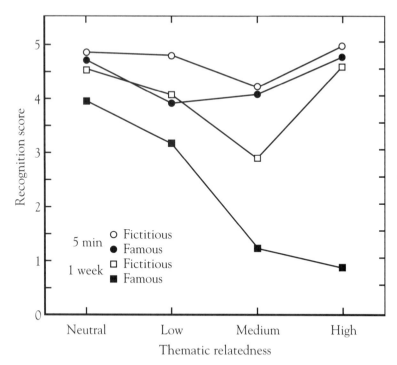

Figure 11.2   *Recognition performance (high score = high performance) on new information as a function of main character, retention interval, and thematic relatedness.*

From "Intrusion of a Thematic Idea in Retention of Prose" by R. A. Sulin and D. J. Dooling, 1974, *Journal of Experimental Psychology, 103,* 255–262. Copyright © 1974 by the American Psychological Association. Reprinted by permission.

might occur in a robbery (such as pulling out a gun) influenced their recall. When misleading information was introduced by an attorney, the incorrect recall of unstated events increased to 25%. Thus, if an attorney implied that the robber had a gun, participants were more likely to recall that the robber had a gun even though they were instructed to recall only events mentioned by the eyewitness.

In conclusion, prior knowledge can influence the comprehension and recall of text in a variety of ways. Prior knowledge can make abstract ideas seem less abstract and easier to comprehend. It can also determine what we emphasize in a text and can provide a framework for recalling ideas. The price we pay for these benefits is that it may be more difficult to locate the source of our knowledge if what we read is integrated with what we know. In most cases the price is fairly small relative to the benefits, but can have serious consequences in some instances.

ORGANIZATION OF TEXT

I mentioned at the beginning of this chapter that both the prior knowledge of the reader and the organization of ideas in the text influence comprehension. A large component of the research on text comprehension is concerned with reading stories that describe a sequence of events. In order to understand the story, we need to organize information at two levels (Graesser, Singer, & Trabasso, 1994). At one level we need to establish a **global coherence** about the main events that occur throughout the story. We need to keep track of what is happening to the major characters (Albrecht & O'Brien, 1993) and to the events related to achieving goals (Dopkins, Klin, & Myers, 1993). At a more detailed level we need to establish a **local coherence** about the most recent events in the story. We need to integrate the ideas that we are reading to the ideas that immediately preceded those ideas. Our ability to integrate ideas at both the local and global levels will be greatly influenced by how well the author has organized the text.

Global coherence
Integration of major ideas that occur throughout a text

Local coherence
Integration of ideas within an immediate context in a text

We will begin by looking at the different parts of a story and the important role that goals play in organizing the major events in a story—global coherence. We will then see how causal relations provide a means of organizing events around these goals. And, finally, we will look at how readers integrate the details of a story to establish local coherence by constructing a semantic network much like the semantic networks discussed in Chapter 9.

Story Structure

One characteristic of simple narrative stories is that the structure determines how the events in the story are organized. We can study this structure at a very general level by representing a story as consisting of a setting, a theme, a plot, and a resolution (Thorndyke, 1977). The **setting** describes time, location, and major characters. The **theme** provides the general focus of the story, often a goal that the main character is trying to achieve. The **plot** consists of a series of actions the main character takes to try and achieve the goal. There may be several subgoals or intermediate goals that have to be accomplished before the main goal is reached. The **resolution**—the final outcome of the story—often describes whether the main character was successful in achieving the goal. Each of the components is evident in the following story. (Statements are numbered for the purpose of the discussion that follows.)

Setting   The time and place in which narrative events occur

Theme   The main goals of characters in a narrative

Plot   The sequence of events related to achieving goals in a narrative

Resolution   The outcome of events in the plot

(1) Circle Island is located in the middle of the Atlantic Ocean (2) north of Ronald Island. (3) The main occupations on the island are farming and ranching. (4) Circle Island has good soil but (5) few rivers and (6) hence a shortage of water. (7) The island is run democratically. (8) All issues are

decided by a majority vote of the islanders. (9) The governing body is a senate (10) whose job is to carry out the will of the majority. (11) Recently, an island scientist discovered a cheap method (12) of converting salt water into fresh water. (13) As a result, the island farmers wanted (14) to build a canal across the island, (15) so that they could use water from the canal (16) to cultivate the island's central region. (17) Therefore, the farmers formed a procanal association (18) and persuaded a few senators (19) to join. (20) The procanal association brought the construction idea to a vote. (21) All the islanders voted. (22) The majority voted in favor of construction. (23) The senate, however, decided that (24) the farmers' proposed canal was ecologically unsound. (25) The senators agreed (26) to build a smaller canal (27) that was 2 feet wide and 1 foot deep. (28) After starting construction on the smaller canal, (29) the islanders discovered that (30) no water would flow into it. (31) Thus the project was abandoned. (32) The farmers were angry (33) because of the failure of the canal project. (34) Civil war appeared inevitable. (Thorndyke, 1977, p. 80)*

The setting is described in the first ten statements, which inform us about the location and central characters. The next six statements establish the theme and introduce the goal of building a canal across the island. Statements 17 through 31 contain the plot, which describes how the islanders attempted to accomplish the goal but were overruled by the senate. The last three statements describe the final resolution, or outcome.

The structure of this simple narrative is very apparent. It proceeds from the setting to the theme, plot, and resolution. To evaluate how useful the goal structure of a story is in facilitating comprehension, Thorndyke modified the story to make the structure less apparent. One modification placed the theme at the end of the story, so people would not encounter the goal until after they had read the plot and the resolution. People read or heard the story only once, so, when they finally reached the information about the goal, they had to use it to interpret what they had previously read about the plot. A more extreme modification was to delete the goal statement entirely. People recalled less information when the goal statement occurred at the end of the story and still less information when the goal was deleted.

The importance that people place on goals is directly illustrated in a study on scripts. We saw in Chapter 9 that one facet of our organized knowledge is our knowledge of common activities (scripts). Bower, Black, and Turner (1979) performed one of the first investigations of how people's knowledge of such routine activities helps them understand and

---

*From "Cognitive Structures in Comprehension and Memory of Narrative Discourse," by P. W. Thorndyke, 1977, *Cognitive Psychology, 9*, 77–110. Copyright 1977 by Academic Press, Inc. Reprinted by permission.

remember information in a text. The researchers first measured the extent to which people agree about the events that occur in standard activities such as going to a restaurant, attending a lecture, getting up in the morning, going grocery shopping, or visiting a doctor. They asked people to list about 20 actions or events that occur during each of these activities. Table 11.1 presents the lists in the order in which the events were usually mentioned. All the events listed in Table 11.1 were mentioned by at least 25% of the subjects. The lists show that there is considerable agreement on the actions that occur during routine activities.

The typical events in a script provide a framework for comprehension but are themselves uninteresting because we already know about them. What is usually interesting is the occurrence of an event that is related to the script but unexpected. For example, a customer may need help translating a menu because it is in French, or the waiter may spill soup on the customer. Schank and Abelson (1977) refer to such events as **obstacles** because they interrupt the major goals of the script, such as ordering and eating in this case.

Obstacles Events that delay or prevent the attainment of a goal

Bower and his colleagues (1979) hypothesized that such interruptions should be remembered better than the routine events in the scripts listed in Table 11.1. From the viewpoint of the reader, they are the only "point" of the story. The researchers also hypothesized that events that are irrelevant to the goals of the script should be remembered less well than the routine events in the script. For example, the type of print on the menu or the color of the waitress's hair is irrelevant to the goals of the ordering and eating a meal.

Bower and his colleagues tested this hypothesis by asking subjects to read six script-based stories about making coffee, attending a lecture, getting up in the morning, attending a movie, visiting a doctor, and dining at a restaurant. After reading all six stories and then completing an intervening task for 10 min, subjects attempted to recall the stories in writing. The results supported the predictions—subjects recalled 53% of the interruptions, 38% of the script actions, and 32% of the irrelevant information. The interuptions either prevented or delayed the main character from accomplishing a goal, and this aspect of the story was well remembered.

Causal Connections

When a goal is included in a story, people use the goal to help themselves organize the actions described in the story. A character's attempts to achieve a goal result in the establishment of causal relations among many of the statements in a text. Work by Trabasso and his students at the University of Chicago (Trabasso & Sperry, 1985; Trabasso & van den Broek, 1985) indicates that it is these causal relations that underlie what

Table 11.1 *Actions associated with different events*

Going to a Restaurant	Attending a Lecture	Getting Up	Grocery Shopping	Visiting a Doctor
Open door	ENTER DOOR	*Wake up*	ENTER STORE	*Enter office*
Enter	*Look for friends*	Turn off alarm	GET CART	CHECK IN WITH RECEPTIONIST
Give reservation name	FIND SEAT	Lie in bed	Take out list	SIT DOWN
Wait to be seated	SIT DOWN	Stretch	Look at list	Wait
Got to table	Settle belongings	GET UP	Go to first aisle	Look at other people
BE SEATED	TAKE OUT NOTEBOOK	Make bed	*Go up and down aisles*	READ MAGAZINE
Order drinks	*Look at other students*	Go to bathroom	PICK OUT ITEMS	*Name called*
Put napkins on lap	Talk	Use toilet	Compare prices	Follow nurse
LOOK AT MENU	Look at professor	*Take shower*	Put items in cart	Enter exam room
Discuss menu	LISTEN TO PROFESSOR	Wash face	Get meat	Undress
ORDER MEAL	TAKE NOTES	Shave	Look for items forgotten	*Sit on table*
Talk	CHECK TIME	DRESS	Talk to other shoppers	Talk to nurse
Drink water	Ask questions	Go to kitchen	Go to checkout counters	NURSE TESTS
Eat salad or soup	Change position in seat	Fix breakfast	*Find fastest line*	Wait
Meal arrives	Daydream	EAT BREAKFAST	WAIT IN LINE	Doctor enters
EAT FOOD	Look at other students	BRUSH TEETH	*Put food on belt*	Doctor greets
Finish meal	Take more notes	Read paper	Read magazines	Talk to doctor about problem
Order dessert	Close notebook	Comb hair	WATCH CASHIER RING UP	Doctor asks questions
Eat dessert	Gather belongings	Get books	PAY CASHIER	DOCTOR EXAMINES
Ask for bill	Stand up	Look in mirror	*Watch bag boy*	Get dressed
Bill arrives	Talk	Get coat	Cart bags out	Get medicine
PAY BILL	LEAVE	LEAVE HOUSE	Load bags into car	Make another appointment
Leave tip			LEAVE STORE	LEAVE OFFICE
Get coats				
LEAVE				

SOURCE: From "Scripts in Memory for Text," by G. H. Bower, J. B. Black, and T. J. Turner, 1979, *Cognitive Psychology, 11*, 177–220. Copyright © 1979 by Academic Press, Inc. Reprinted by permission.

NOTE: Items in all capital letters were mentioned by most subjects, items in italics by fewer subjects, and items in lowercase letters were mentioned by the fewest subjects.

a reader judges to be important in a text. A formal statement of a **causal relation** is that one event, A, is judged to be the cause of another event, B, if the absence of A implies the absence of B. In other words, you cannot accomplish your goal if someone eliminates the events that are necessary for achieving that goal. Consider the goal of walking into your house. You couldn't walk into your house unless you opened the door, which you couldn't do unless you unlocked the door, which you couldn't do unless you took out your keys. Thus all three actions are causally related (necessary) for accomplishing the goal of walking into your house.

Causal relation   An event that results in the occurrence of another event

An important variable in determining the judged importance of statements in a story is the number of causal connections linked to the statement. In the previous example, walking into your house has three causal connections (taking out the keys, unlocking the door, and opening the door), and unlocking the door has one causal connection (taking out the keys). Trabasso and Sperry (1985) found that, when subjects rated the importance of events in stories, the judged importance of an action was directly related to the number of causal connections associated with that action. The number of causal connections was also important in determining what people could recall from a story and what they would include in a summary of the story (Trabasso & van den Broek, 1985).

Causal connections also determine how quickly people can retrieve text information. When we considered spreading activation models in Chapter 9, we learned that adding more links to a node in the network slows down retrieval time (the fan effect found by J. R. Anderson, 1976), unless the information could be integrated around a subnode (the high-integrated condition of Reder & Anderson, 1980). The integration prevented the slower retrieval times of the added information. What is remarkable about adding causal connections is that the added information actually speeded up decisions about information in the text (Myers, O'Brien, Balota, & Toyofuku, 1984).

These psychologists followed the general procedure used by Reder and Anderson (1980) but, in a high-integration condition, used facts that were causally linked. The facts were presented in four pairs of stories. Each pair of stories shared a common theme—going to a baseball game, a restaurant, a saloon, or a racetrack.

Each story had three variations, as shown in Table 11.2 for the baseball pair. Notice that, although the Fan-3 condition contained three facts and the Fan-6 condition contained six facts, the two test sentences (marked by asterisks) were identical for each condition. For the high-integration condition, the two test sentences were preceded by statements that were causally related. For example, the banker had to wait in line *because* he found a crowd buying tickets, and he cheered loudly *because* his team scored. In the low-integration condition, the additional facts were not causally related to the test statements.

Table 11.2   *Sample sentences used in integration study*

Fan 3

The banker	The actor
arrived at the ball park.	went to the ball game.
waited in line.*	saw the start of the ball game.*
cheered loudly.*	went home early.*

Fan 6: High integration

The banker	The actor
decided to see a baseball game.	had a ticket for a Red Sox game.
arrived at the ball park.	went to the ball game.
found a crowd buying tickets.	sat down as the umpire yelled play ball.
waited in line.*	saw the start of the game.*
entered to see his team score.	found the first few innings boring.
cheered loudly.*	went home early.*

Fan 6: Low integration

The banker	The actor
decided to see a baseball game.	had a ticket for a Red Sox game.
arrived at the ball park.	went to the ball game.
bought a souvenir pennant.	bought a hot dog from a vendor.
waited in line.*	saw the start of the ball game.*
sat near the first-base dugout.	looked at his program.
cheered loudly.*	went home early.*

SOURCE: From "Memory Search without Interference: The Role of Integration," by J. L. Myers, E. J. O'Brien, D. A. Balota, and M. L. Toyofuku, 1984, *Cognitive Psychology, 16,* 217–242. Copyright © 1984 by Academic Press, Inc. Reprinted by permission.
NOTE: The Fan-3 examples contain three facts and the Fan-6 examples contain six facts. The test sentences are marked by asterisks.

Myers and his colleagues found that students were usually faster in deciding whether test sentences were true or false if they had studied six highly integrated statements than if they had studied three statements. Providing the additional causal statements therefore facilitated memory retrieval. However, the fan effect usually occurred for the six low-integrated statements; that is, in the low-integration condition, students responded more slowly if they had learned six facts than if they had learned three.

The experiments that show the importance of goals and causal connections in texts demonstrate that both contribute to the global coherence of the text. However, readers also need to understand the details and establish local coherence by relating the ideas in a sentence to the immediately preceding ideas. Before considering a model of comprehension, we need to find out how the organization of ideas in a text determines how well readers can integrate these ideas. The answers to the following three questions generally determines the ease of integration.

1. Can a current idea be related to previously expressed ideas?
2. Are related ideas still available in STM?
3. Is it necessary to make an inference to establish the relation?

Integration of Details

Establishing local coherence by integrating the details of a sentence is very challenging when the ideas in a sentence are not related to ideas expressed in previous sentences. An important determinant of comprehension difficulty is whether the ideas in a sentence were given in a previous sentence or whether they are new. The ease with which new ideas can be related to old ideas is illustrated by the two sequences of sentences in Table 11.3 (Kieras, 1978). The two examples contain the same seven sentences presented in a different order. The letter preceding each sentence indicates whether the information in the sentence is given (g) or new (n). The sentence is classified as *given* if it contains at least one noun that appeared in the preceding sentences. The first example contains only one new sentence; all sentences but the first refer to information that preceded them. The second example contains four new sentences that do not refer to preceding information. Kieras predicted that the ideas in the first example should be easier to integrate and recall than the ideas in the second example, and the results supported his prediction.

A second determinant of comprehension difficulty is whether the integration uses ideas that are active in STM. You may have noticed that all but one of the given sentences in Example 1 repeat a noun from the

Table 11.3   *Examples of presentation orders, showing the given (g) or new (n) status of each sentence*

Example 1	Example 2
n—The ants ate the jelly.	n—The kitchen was spotless.
g—The ants were hungry.	n—The table was wooden.
g—The ants were in the kitchen.	n—The ants were hungry.
g—The kitchen was spotless.	g—The ants were in the kitchen.
g—The jelly was grape.	n—The jelly was grape.
g—The jelly was on the table.	g—The jelly was on the table.
g—The table was wooden.	g—The ants ate the jelly.

SOURCE: From "Good and Bad Structure in Simple Paragraphs: Effects on Apparent Theme, Reading Time, and Recall," by D. E. Kieras, 1978, *Journal of Verbal Learning and Verbal Behavior, 17*, 13–28. Copyright © 1978 by Academic Press, Inc. Reprinted by permission.

immediately preceding sentence. The one exception—*The jelly was grape*—repeats a noun (*jelly*) from a sentence that occurred four sentences earlier. This sentence may be more difficult to integrate with the preceding sentences because the given information may no longer be in STM, a situation requiring a search of LTM to retrieve the first sentence. Evidence, in fact, suggests that comprehension is influenced by whether the preceding relevant information is still active in STM or whether it must be retrieved from LTM (Lesgold, Roth, & Curtis, 1979).

The following sentences (from Lesgold, Roth, & Curtis, 1979) should be easy to integrate because the first sentence contains relevant information that should still be available in STM when the reader encounters the second sentence.

> 1. A thick cloud of smoke hung over the forest. The forest was on fire. (p. 294)

Now let's insert two sentences that change the topic and make it less likely that the information about the smoke over the forest is still in STM when the reader learns about the fire.

> 2. A thick cloud of black smoke hung over the forest. Glancing to one side, Carol could see a bee flying around the back seat. Both of the kids were jumping around but made no attempt to free the insect. The forest was on fire. (p. 295)

The inserted information is irrelevant to the fire in the forest and should make it more difficult to comprehend the final sentence than in Case 1. Now consider the insertion of two sentences that are consistent with the initial topic.

> 3. A thick cloud of smoke hung over the forest. The smoke was thick and black, and began to fill the clear sky. Up ahead Carol could see a ranger directing traffic to slow down. The forest was on fire. (p. 295)

The two inserted sentences continue the initial topic, making it easier for the reader to keep active in STM information about the cloud of black smoke. Lesgold and his colleagues predicted that less time should be required to comprehend the final sentence in Case 3 than in Case 2. Their results supported their predictions.

A less direct way of keeping information active in STM is to associate it with other information that continues to be emphasized in the text (Glenberg, Meyer, & Lindem, 1987). This is illustrated by the sentences in Table 11.4. The first sentence in the paragraph describes the setting and is followed by one of two critical sentences. Some subjects read that Warren picked up his bag (the associated condition), and other subjects read that Warren set down his bag (the dissociated condition). The filler sentence refers only to Warren, but the test sentence contains a pronoun

Table 11.4   *Examples of associated and dissociated information*

Setting sentence	Warren spent the afternoon shopping at the store.
Critical (associated)	He picked up his *bag* and went over to look at some scarves.
Critical (dissociated)	He set down his *bag* and went over to look at some scarves.
Filler	He had been shopping all day.
Test sentence	He thought it was getting too heavy to carry.

SOURCE: From "Mental Models Contribute to Foregrounding during Text Comprehension, " by A. M. Glenberg, M. Meyer, and K. Lindem, 1987, *Journal of Memory and Language, 26*, 69–83, Table 4. Copyright © 1987 by Academic Press, Inc. Reprinted by permission.

(*it*) that refers back to the bag. Subjects, who were instructed to read the materials carefully for comprehension, took significantly less time to read the test sentence in the associated condition.

Glenberg and his colleagues argue that readers constructed a **mental model** of the situation described in the text that maintains information about the main actor. The mental model includes those objects that are spatially associated with the main actor—for example, a mental picture of Warren carrying his bag. If the text continues to refer to this person, then objects associated with the person are also kept active in STM, even if they are not mentioned. Subjects were therefore faster to interpret the test sentence when the bag was spatially associated with Warren than when the bag was dissociated from Warren.

Mental model A person's mental representation of a situation

A third determinant of comprehension difficulty is whether the ideas can be directly linked to each other or must be linked by making an **inference** (Haviland & Clark, 1974). This distinction can be illustrated by the following pairs of sentences:

Inference The use of reasoning to establish relations in a text when the relations are not directly stated

1. Ed was given an alligator for his birthday. The alligator was his favorite present.
2. Ed was given lots of things for his birthday. The alligator was his favorite present.

In both cases the first sentence provides an appropriate context for the second sentence, but the first case makes it clear that Ed received an alligator for his birthday. The second requires an inference that one of the things Ed received was an alligator.

Participants in Haviland and Clark's experiment saw pairs of sentences in a tachistoscope. After reading the first sentence, they pressed a button to see the second sentence. When they thought they understood the second sentence, they pushed another button, which stopped a clock that measured how long the second sentence had been displayed. As predicted by Haviland and Clark, it took significantly less time to comprehend the second sentence when the same idea (such as an alligator) was mentioned in both sentences than when the relation between the two sentences had to be inferred.

In conclusion, a number of variables influence comprehension, according to these studies. All the variables reflect how easy it is to integrate what a person is reading with what that person has already read. One variable is whether the reader can relate newly acquired information to ideas that were already expressed in the text. Kieras's (1978) research indicated that it was easier to recall ideas in the text if the sentences referred to previous information than if they contained only new information. A second variable is whether previously expressed ideas are still active in STM or whether they must be retrieved from LTM. Comprehension is easier when related ideas are still active in STM (Lesgold et al., 1979; Glenberg et al., 1987). A third variable is whether newly acquired information can be related directly to previous information or whether the reader must infer the relation. Inferences slow down comprehension (Haviland & Clark, 1974). A theory of comprehension should incorporate each of these three variables.

KINTSCH'S MODEL OF COMPREHENSION

The first two sections of this chapter reviewed research on two very important components of comprehension: the prior knowledge of the reader and the organization of ideas in the text. This final section describes psychologists' attempts to develop detailed models of text comprehension. Because text comprehension requires the integration of ideas in the text, a model of text comprehension requires assumptions about how this integration occurs.

Processing Assumptions

A model developed over nearly two decades by Kintsch (1979, 1994) at the University of Colorado has given us the most comprehensive theory of text comprehension. Because the model is fairly complex, I will give only a brief summary of its major assumptions, emphasizing those that are related to the previous studies. There are two inputs in the model, the reader and the text, both of which are necessary to understand comprehension. The knowledge and goals of the reader influence how the reader determines what is relevant, establishes expectations, and infers facts that are not directly stated in the text. The text itself is represented in the model by propositions. The **propositions** divide the text into meaningful units, which are then arranged in a network that is similar to the semantic networks discussed in Chapter 9.

Propositions Meaningful ideas that typically consist of several words

The general characteristics of the model can be illustrated with a simple example (Kintsch, 1979). Consider the following text:

> The Swazi tribe was at war with a neighboring tribe because of a dispute over cattle. Among the warriors were two unmarried men, Kakra and his younger brother Gum. Kakra was killed in a battle. (p. 6)

The model specifies rules for dividing the text into propositions, but we will not be concerned with the details of these rules. We will consider word groups that correspond approximately to the underlying propositions. Figure 11.3 shows how the first sentence is divided into word groups and how the groups are related in a network. The proposition *was at war with* is the most important proposition, and the others are joined to it. An important parameter in the model is the number of propositions that can be kept active in STM. Since STM is limited in capacity, only a few propositions can be kept active; our example assumes that the capacity limit is three propositions, as indicated by the enclosed propositions in the figure. Propositions describing the plans and goals of the characters are particularly likely to be selected (Fletcher, 1986).

Figure 11.4 shows the propositions of the second sentence and the propositions from the first sentence that are still active in STM. The reader first tries to connect the new propositions with the old ones in STM, but the words in the second sentence don't match any of the words in STM. The reader next determines whether the new propositions can be related to any propositions in LTM. Kintsch proposes that the search of LTM, which he calls a **reinstatement search**, is one of the factors that make a text difficult to read. If information in the text can be related to ideas that are still active in STM, comprehension is easier than if the reader must first search LTM in order to reinstate old information in STM so it can be integrated with the new information. This assumption

Reinstatement search
The search of LTM to place words in STM where they can be used to integrate a text

Coherence analysis: Cycle I

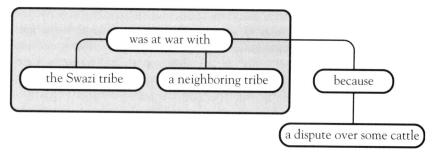

Figure 11.3 *Analysis of the first sentence in the Swazi example.*

From "On Modeling Comprehension," by W. Kintsch, 1979, *Educational Psychologist, 14*, 3–14. Copyright © 1979 by Lawrence Erlbaum Associates, Inc. Reprinted by permission.

Coherence analysis: Cycle II

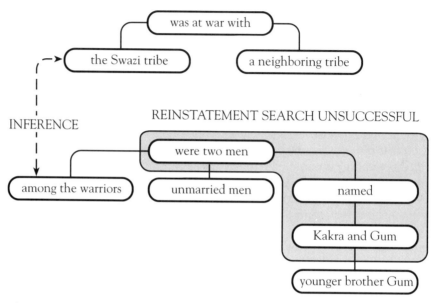

Figure 11.4   *Analysis of the second sentence in the Swazi example.*

From "On Modeling Comprehension," by W. Kintsch, 1979, *Educational Psychologist, 14,* 3–14. Copyright © 1979 by Lawrence Erlbaum Associates, Inc. Reprinted by permission.

is consistent with the findings of Lesgold and colleagues (1979) and of Glenberg and his colleagues (1987).

The reinstatement search also fails for the example because there are no concepts that are common to the first two sentences. The model must therefore construct a new network rather than add on to the old one. It may also make an inference at this point to interrelate the two networks. The inference is that the warriors mentioned in the second sentence were members of the Swazi tribe. This seems like a reasonable inference, but it is not stated directly. Kintsch's model assumes that inferences, like reinstatement searches, slow down the reader and make comprehension more difficult. The evidence supports this assumption (for example, Haviland & Clark, 1974).

The model once again selects three propositions from the second sentence to keep active in STM. Figure 11.4 shows that the three selected specify the names of the two men. The third sentence—*Kakra was killed in a battle*—is easy to relate to previous information because information about Kakra is still available in STM. The new information can therefore be added directly to the network without having to search LTM or make an inference.

This example should give you an approximate idea of how the model works. The major theme of the model is that incoming information can be understood more easily when it can be integrated with information that the reader has already encountered. The easiest case is when the new information can be related to information that is still active in STM. If it cannot be related, a reinstatement search attempts to relate the new information to propositions stored in LTM. If the reinstatement search fails, a new network must be started, resulting in a memory for ideas that are not very well integrated. The result should be poorer recall, as was found by Kieras (1978) when the new sentences could not be related to previous sentences. Integration of ideas can sometimes be achieved by inference, but the need for inferences also contributes to the difficulty of the text.

Predicting Readability

One attractive aspect of Kintsch's model is that it is complete enough to allow predictions about the ease of reading different kinds of text. Predicting readability is an important applied problem. The developers of educational materials want to be assured that their materials can be understood by the students who read them. A former professor of mine once wrote a chapter for *The Mind*, a book in one of the Time-Life series. His chapter required nine revisions before it satisfied the editors of Time-Life. Although he was a good writer and was familiar with the topic, he was inexperienced at writing for students in junior high school—the reading level selected for the series.

There have been many attempts to predict readability. According to Kintsch and Vipond (1979), the earliest formulas appeared in the 1920s. There are now about 50 **readability formulas**, most containing word and sentence variables (unfamiliar words and long sentences generally make a text harder to read). What the formulas lack, however, is a good way of measuring text organization. If someone placed all the words in a sentence in a scrambled order, the sentence would be very difficult to comprehend, but the predictions of most formulas would be unchanged because they don't consider the order of words in a sentence or the order of sentences in a paragraph. The formulas are thus limited because they are not based on a theory of text comprehension.

Readability formulas Formulas that use variables such as word frequency and sentence length to predict the readability of text

The theory developed by Kintsch has already contributed to overcoming many of these limitations by providing an account of how the reader's information-processing capabilities interact with the organization of the text. Kintsch defined **readability** as the number of propositions recalled divided by the reading time. The measure takes into account both recall and reading time, because it is easy to improve either measure at the expense of the other.

Readability The number of recalled propositions divided by reading time

Kintsch used his model, along with more traditional measures, to predict the readability of paragraphs. The two best predictors of readability were word frequency and the number of reinstatement searches. The first measure is contained in most readability formulas. As we might expect, the use of common words, those that occur frequently in the language, improves comprehension. The second measure—the number of reinstatement searches—is calculated from Kintsch's model. Application of the model determines how often a person must search LTM to relate new information to previous information. A reinstatement search is required only when the new information cannot be related to the propositions in STM. Another theoretical measure that improves the readability predictions is the number of inferences that are required. An inference is required whenever a concept is not directly repeated—for example, when *war* was mentioned in the first sentence and *warriors* in the second sentence. Kintsch found that the number of inferences influenced readability, although not as much as word frequency and the number of reinstatement searches. The required inferences were fairly easy, however; their influence might increase if they were more difficult.

More difficult inferences are often required for reading academic material, such as history passages on the Korean and Vietnam wars. Studies using this material showed that, the more inferences were required to link ideas, the worse the ideas were recalled (Britton, Van Dusen, Glynn, & Hemphill, 1990). Historical events are less likely to fit the standard framework of fictional stories, making the inferences more challenging. Other research programs are also collecting data to distinguish between inferences that are immediate and automatic and inferences that require specialized knowledge by the reader (McKoon & Ratcliff, 1990; Swinney & Osterhout, 1990).

In conclusion, the results show that a theory of comprehension can contribute to predicting readability. The theoretical measures—the number of reinstatement searches and the number of inferences—are determined by how well the ideas in the text relate to other ideas in the text. These measures were not included in the traditional measures of readability. Kintsch's model also provides a framework for considering the interaction between the reader and the text. The model implies that readability is determined not only by the text; it is also the result of the interaction between a particular reader and a particular text (Kintsch & Vipond, 1979). For example, a reinstatement search is required only when new information cannot be related to information in STM. A person who can retain many propositions in STM therefore has an advantage in having to make fewer reinstatement searches than a person with a more limited STM. There are several ways in which the facilitating effect of prior knowledge could be incorporated into the model. Prior knowledge might increase the number of propositions held in STM because of their greater familiarity. Prior knowledge might also make it easier to make inferences in order to relate different concepts in the text. We explore this possibility in the next section.

Incorporating Prior Knowledge

We began this chapter by looking at how a person's prior knowledge influences text comprehension. Can we "capture" this prior knowledge and incorporate it into Kintsch's model of comprehension? In his Distinguished Scientific Award address to the annual meeting of the American Psychological Association, Kintsch (1994) had the opportunity to describe his most recent research, much of it focusing on the role that prior knowledge plays in learning from a text.

Our emphasis thus far has been on representing the semantic relations in the text through integrating the propositions in a semantic network. But there is also another, deeper level of understanding that Kintsch calls a *situation model*. The **situation model** is constructed by combining prior knowledge and information in the text to produce a more elaborate understanding of the situation described in the text.

Figure 11.5 shows an example for a two-sentence text fragment: *When a baby has a septal defect, the blood cannot get rid of enough carbon dioxide through the lungs. Therefore, it looks purple.* The situation model in

Situation model
Integration of prior knowledge and text information to construct an understanding of the situation described in a text

TEXT:
When a baby has a septal defect, the blood cannot get rid of enough carbon dioxide through the lungs. Therefore, it looks purple.

SITUATION MODEL:

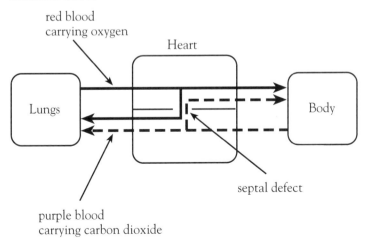

Figure 11.5 *A diagramatic situation model for the text fragment.*
From "Text Comprehension, Memory, and Learning," by W. Kintsch, 1994, *American Psychologist, 49*, 294–303. Copyright © 1994 by the American Psychological Association. Reprinted by permission.

this case is represented as a diagram. It shows that, because of the septal defect, red blood carrying oxygen is mixed together with purple blood carrying carbon dioxide. Some of the purple blood is therefore recirculated back into the body without picking up oxygen in the lungs. Notice that much of the information in the situation model is derived from the reader's knowledge of the circulatory system, rather than derived directly from the text.

The deeper level of understanding represented by the situation model can also be represented in the semantic networks that we discussed previously. In this case, the semantic network model would contain propositions that are derived both from the text and from the reader's prior knowledge. The propositions about the septal defect, color of the blood, and excess carbon dioxide come from the text, but other propositions such as the mixing of the blood depend on inferences based on prior knowledge.

In the previous section we discussed the possibility that inferences will have a greater effect on the readability of academic material than on the readability of stories because academic material is more difficult. A study by Britton and Gulgoz (1991) provides a demonstration of how one can apply Kintsch's model to improve readability by rewriting academic material to reduce the need to make inferences. They used the model to identify where inferences were required in a passage on the air war in North Vietnam. They found 40 such locations and then revised the text by inserting the inferences into the passage so readers would not have to make the inferences. For instance, the information in parentheses was inserted into the original passage so the reader would not have to infer the relation between the title and the first sentence.

Air War in North (Vietnam)

By the Fall of 1964, Americans in both Saigon and Washington had begun to focus on Hanoi (capital of North Vietnam) as the source of the continuing problem in the South.

The insertion prevents an inference because the revision allows a direct link between the title and the first sentence. Both now contain the term *North Vietnam*.

Britton and Gulgoz used the same readability measure as Kintsch, and found that their revised passage had a much higher readability score than the original. People who read the original version recalled 3.44 propositions per minute of reading time, and people who read the revision recalled 5.24 propositions per minute of reading time. The investigators suggested that writers typically do not include this additional material because their extensive knowledge about the topic makes the inferences easy for them.

There is, however, an interesting qualification to the statement that a good text shouldn't require any inferences. Kintsch (1994) describes a study in which the investigators rewrote the passage about the faulty heart by adding explanations and elaborations at both the local and global levels. As was found by Britton and Gulgoz (1991), those people who read the revised text recalled more propositions than those people who read the original text. However, for problem-solving questions, performance interacted with the knowledge of the reader. Low-knowledge readers did better with the elaborated text, but high-knowledge readers did better with the original text.

It is clear why low-knowledge students performed better with the elaborated text. They lacked the knowledge to make the inferences in the original text and so didn't understand it as well. But why were the high-knowledge readers better at solving problems when they received the original text? It is likely that this text challenged them more, requiring them to think more deeply and make inferences—which they could make because of their prior knowledge. Notice that this explanation is consistent with the fact-oriented versus problem-oriented processing of riddles, discussed in the section on transfer-appropriate processing in Chapter 6. Problem-oriented processing produced greater reflection and prepared people better to later answer the riddles.

As stated earlier, interaction between the fields of psychology and education was very apparent in the early part of this century but diminished during the following decades as psychologists began to study simple and somewhat artificial materials. The amount of current research activity on complex skills such as comprehension suggests that the interaction between the two fields is increasing. In the next two chapters we will study another complex skill that has attracted the interest of both psychologists and educators—problem solving.

SUMMARY

Psychologists study comprehension by investigating how people's prior knowledge and information-processing characteristics interact with the organization of ideas in a text. The importance of prior knowledge is evident when people have to comprehend very abstract ideas. A meaningful context improves recall if the context is given before people read the abstract material. It is necessary to improve comprehension in order to improve recall. Recall of more concrete ideas may be improved by providing a context after people have read the text if the context causes a change in perspective. People's knowledge about everyday activities can be represented by scripts that describe the most common events associated with the activities. Scripts influence what a person emphasizes when reading a text. One disadvantage of prior knowledge is that it sometimes makes it hard to distinguish between recently read material and prior knowledge about the topic.

Comprehension is determined not only by what a person already knows but also by the organization of ideas in a text. The global structure of narrative stories includes setting, theme, plot, and resolution. The theme provides the general focus of the story and often consists of a goal that the main character tries to achieve. Comprehension is best when the theme precedes the plot; it deteriorates when the theme follows the plot and deteriorates even more when the theme is left out. Statements that have either a positive or a negative impact on the attainment of a goal are judged most important and are best remembered. Causal relations are also helpful in facilitating the quick retrieval of information.

A model of text comprehension must account for how the reader attempts to relate the ideas in the text to ideas already read. Comprehension is easiest when the ideas can be related to ideas that are still available in STM. If no relations are found, the reader can search LTM to look for a relation. If no relations are found in LTM, the new material must be stored separately rather than integrated with old material. Relations can sometimes be found by making inferences, but inferences slow down comprehension compared with direct repetition of the same concepts.

A model of comprehension proposed by Kintsch has been quite successful in predicting and improving readability. The model can account for the organization of a text by considering how many LTM searches and inferences are required. Its parameters include the number of propositions that are processed at one time, the probability of storing a proposition in LTM, and the number of propositions that can be kept active in STM. In addition to improving previous readability formulas, the model provides a theoretical framework for investigating how a person's information-processing characteristics interact with the organization of the text to influence comprehension. In particular, the prior knowledge of the reader determines the ease of making inferences, and the subsequent success in recalling and using text information to solve problems.

STUDY QUESTIONS

1. What is a paraphrase? If a person can produce a paraphrase of something she has read, what does that tell us?
2. Why is the reader's prior knowledge of context especially important in trying to understand abstract ideas?
3. Anderson and Pichert list three possible explanations for the evidence that changing perspectives aids recall of a story. Can you think of any way to rule out those not favored by Anderson and Pichert?

4. How often does it make a difference if you can recall where you read something (the source of information)? Can you think of any real-life situation in which it could matter?

5. Using all the described components of "scripts," write a brief script for a common activity not mentioned in the book. Did you have any trouble doing so, once you decided on the activity?

6. What sort of departures from a standard script are especially likely to be remembered? Think of weddings you attended, for example. Does what you remember most vividly agree with what Bower and others hypothesize would be the types of information recalled?

7. Consider the basic elements of story structure. Have you ever heard a young child retell a story? What is usually missing in young children's accounts that often make them difficult to follow?

8. The various studies on integration of ideas that led to Kintsch's model of comprehension used carefully contrived materials. What variables were the researchers attempting to manipulate? Did those variables actually influence text comprehension? Why or why not?

9. The exposition of Kintsch's model is necessarily abstract and therefore difficult to comprehend. Persevere in your reinstatement searches! See if you can use it to deal with a new example of text selected from another course. What factors are included in Kintsch's model? How does the *reader* enter into this model?

10. Why did Kintsch's definition of readability include two factors? What did he find to be the best predictors of readability? How would you use the ideas in his model to improve your writing?

KEY TERMS

The page number in parentheses refers to where the term is discussed in the chapter.

causal relation (337)
global coherence (333)
inference (341)
local coherence (333)
mental model (341)
obstacles (335)
perspective (329)
plot (333)

propositions (342)
readability (345)
readability formulas (345)
reinstatement search (343)
resolution (333)
setting (333)
situation model (347)
theme (333)

RECOMMENDED READING

Reder (1980) and N. L. Stein and T. Trabasso (1982) summarize research on the comprehension and retention of prose. Just and Carpenter (1980), Kieras (1983), and Haberlandt and Graesser (1985) have proposed detailed models to predict processing times for the different components of reading. Others have studied the effect of the reader's prior knowledge on learning information in a text (Chiesi, Spilich, & Voss, 1979; Spilich, Vesonder, Chiesi, & Voss, 1979). Alba and Hasher (1983), Brewer and Nakamura (1984), and Graesser and Nakamura (1982) discuss the impact of schemata on comprehension and memory; Sharkey and Mitchell (1985) and Walker and Yekovich (1987) describe how scripts are used in reading. Recent work on inferences and text comprehension is summarized in a collection of chapters in a book edited by Graesser and Bower (1990) and in an article by Graesser, Singer, and Trabasso (1994). The model developed by Kintsch and his associates is discussed in papers by Kintsch and Van Dijk (1978), J. R. Miller and W. Kintsch (1980), Van Dijk and Kintsch (1983), Keenan, Baillet, and Brown (1984), and Kintsch (1994). The psychology of reading is discussed in a book by Just and Carpenter (1987).

Problem Solving

Solving a problem means finding a way out of a difficulty, a way around an obstacle, attaining an aim that was not immediately understandable. Solving problems is the specific achievement of intelligence, and intelligence is the specific gift of mankind: Solving problems can be regarded as the most characteristically human activity.

GEORGE POLYA (1962)

HUMANS ARE NOT the only creatures who can solve problems, yet identifying problem solving as the most characteristically human activity, as Polya has done in our chapter-opening quotation, emphasizes its importance in the development of civilization. This and the next chapter discuss problem solving and emphasize recent progress in our attempt to understand how people solve problems. This chapter establishes the basic components of a theory of problem solving. The first section contains examples of different kinds of problems. A question that has interested psychologists is how general problem-solving skills are. At one extreme the answer is that the skills are very general, and a person who is good at solving one type of problem will also be very good at solving other types. At the other extreme is the claim that skills are very specific, and a person who is good at solving one type of problem may be poor at solving other types. The claim made in the first section falls between these two extremes. The proposed classification identifies three general kinds of problems on the basis of the skills required to solve them.

The second section describes the general characteristics of a theory of problem solving proposed by Newell and Simon (1972). The theory describes how problem solving is influenced by (1) people's information-processing capabilities as determined by STM and LTM, (2) the structure of the problem and its effect on the search for a solution, and (3) the effectiveness of different strategies and sources of information. The third section discusses general strategies such as the use of subgoals, analogy, and diagrams.

The problems discussed in this chapter are mainly puzzles. You may wonder why psychologists are interested in puzzles—wouldn't it be more appropriate to study the kinds of problems people encounter in school or work? One reason for studying problems like the anagram and series completion problems shown in Table 12.1 is that they often appear on intelligence tests. If we want to understand what intelligence tests really measure, we must take a closer look at the specific skills required to answer the questions (Carpenter, Just, & Shell, 1990). Another reason is that, when studying puzzles, psychologists can be less concerned about differences in people's education; everyone should have more of an "equal chance" on puzzles than on problems taken from a textbook. However, psychologists have also become more interested in classroom problems, as we will see in the next chapter. Fortunately, most of the issues discussed in this chapter will still be relevant when we later discuss how prior knowledge and expertise influence problem solving.

CLASSIFYING PROBLEMS

Any attempt to improve problem-solving skills raises the question of what skills are needed for different kinds of problems. Students are taught

Table 12.1   *Examples of problems*

A.   **Analogy**
       What word completes the analogy?
           Merchant : Sell :: Customer : _____
           Lawyer : Client :: Doctor : _____

B.   **String problem**
       Two strings hang from a ceiling but are too far apart to allow a person to
       hold one and walk to the other. On the floor are a book of matches, a screw-
       driver, and a few pieces of cotton. How could the strings be tied together?

C.   **Missionaries and cannibals**
       Five missionaries and five cannibals who have to cross a river find a boat,
       but the boat is so small that it can hold no more than three persons. If the
       missionaries on either bank of the river or in the boat are outnumbered at
       any time by cannibals, they will be eaten. Find the simplest schedule of
       crossings that will allow everyone to cross safely. At least one person must
       be in the boat at each crossing.

D.   **Water jar**
       You have an 8-gallon pail and a 5-gallon pail. How could you obtain 2 gal-
       lons of water?

E.   **Anagram**
       Rearrange the letters in each row to make an English word.
           RWAET
           KEROJ

F.   **Series completion**
       What number or letter continues each series?
           1 2 8 3 4 6 5 6_____
           A B M C D M _____

how to solve statistics problems in a statistics class and chemistry problems in a chemistry class. Have they learned any general skills in a statistics class that can make them better problem solvers in a chemistry class,
or do the problems in each class require a different set of skills? The question would be easier to answer if we could classify problems according to
the skills needed to solve them.

   Table 12.1 shows examples of problems that have been studied by
psychologists. You will better understand this chapter if you try to solve
these problems before reading further. When you have finished working
on the problems, try to classify them according to the skills needed to
solve them. We will examine one method of classification that proposes
that the six problems can be divided into three categories.

   The proposed classification is based on the general kinds of psychological skills and knowledge needed to solve different problems (Greeno,

1978). Greeno suggested that there are three types of problems: *arrangement, inducing structure*, and *transformation*. The classification does not imply that we will be able to classify every problem into one of the three categories. Rather, it provides three ideal types in order to determine whether a given problem requires primarily rearrangement, inducing structure, transformation, or some combination of the three skills. We will now consider examples of each type in order to see how the types differ.

Arrangement

Arrangement problem
A problem that requires rearranging its parts to satisfy a specified criterion

Anagram A problem that requires rearranging a string of letters to form a word

Arrangement problems present some objects and require the problem solver to arrange them in a way that satisfies some criterion. The objects usually can be arranged in many different ways, but only one or a few of the arrangements form a solution. An excellent example is the rearrangement of the letters of an **anagram** to form a word, such as rearranging the letters *KEROJ* to spell *JOKER* and *RWAET* to spell *WATER*. Solving an arrangement problem often involves much trial and error, during which partial solutions are formed and evaluated. Greeno argued that the skills needed to solve arrangement problems include the following:

1. *Fluency in generating possibilities.* Flexibility is needed to generate many partial solutions and discard those that appear unpromising.
2. *Retrieval of solution patterns.* Ability to retrieve words from memory should be related to ability in solving anagrams.
3. *Knowledge of principles that constrain the search.* Knowing the relative frequency with which various letters occur together should help guide the search. Since the pair *JR* is an unlikely combination, for instance, it should be avoided when forming partial solutions.

Gestalt psychologists were particularly interested in how people solve arrangement problems. Gestalt psychology, which began as the study of perception, emphasized the structure of patterns, and consequently it analyzed problem solving from this perspective. Many Gestalt tasks required the rearrangement of objects in order to find the correct relation among the parts.

A well-known example is the problem described by Kohler (1925) in his book *The Mentality of Apes*. Kohler hung some fruit from the top of a cage to investigate whether a chimpanzee or other ape could discover how to reach it. The cage contained several sticks and crates. The solution depended on finding a correct way to rearrange the objects—for example, standing on a crate and using a stick to knock down the fruit. According to the Gestalt analysis, solving the problem required the reorganization of the objects into a new structure.

Insight The sudden discovery of a solution following unsuccessful attempts to solve a problem

Gestalt psychologists argued that discovering the correct organization usually occurred as a flash of insight. **Insight** is the sudden discovery of the correct solution following a period of incorrect attempts based primarily on trial and error. The key factor distinguishing insight from other forms of discovery is the suddenness of the solution. In contrast to solutions that are achieved through careful planning or through a series of small steps, solutions based on insight seem to occur "in a flash."

Evidence supports the Gestalt argument that the correct arrangement of parts often occurs quite suddenly (Metcalfe, 1986b). Metcalfe gave her subjects anagrams to solve, such as *ssoia*, *pmuoi*, and *ttnua*. They were asked to assess how close they were to solving the problem, on a scale from 1 to 10, during the course of solving the anagrams. Every 10 sec a tap occurred and subjects recorded their ratings. The ratings remained very low until the discovery of the solution, implying that the correct answer suddenly appeared. In contrast, transformation problems are usually solved through an ordered sequence of correct steps in which people gradually progress toward the solution (Metcalfe, 1986b).

One factor that makes it difficult to find a correct arrangement is **functional fixedness**—the tendency to perceive an object only in terms of its most common use. The candle problem, studied by Duncker (1945), illustrates how functional fixedness can influence performance. The goal is to place three small candles at eye level on a door. Among other objects on a nearby table are a few tacks and three small boxes about the size of matchboxes. In one condition the boxes were filled with candles, tacks, and matches. In another condition the boxes were empty. The solution requires tacking the boxes to the door so they can serve as platforms for the candles (Figure 12.1). More subjects solved the problem when the boxes were empty (Duncker, 1945; Adamson, 1952). The use

Functional fixedness
The tendency to use an object in a typical way

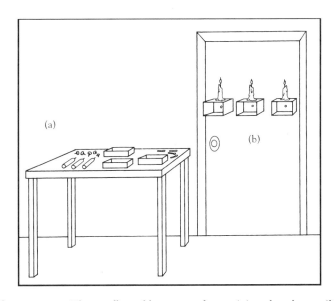

Figure 12.1   *The candle problem—initial state (a) and goal state (b).*

BOX 12.1

Pair of crafty inmates melt way out of jail

SALINAS (AP)—Two crafty inmates used a length of shower pipe, a sheet, and a wall socket to melt an unbreakable plastic window and escape from Monterey County's new jail, officials said Wednesday.

A sheriff's deputy said the pair escaped Tuesday night after using a makeshift cutting torch to reduce part of the cell window to mushy goo.

Lieutenant Ted Brown said the inmates wrapped a sheet around a piece of flattened shower pipe, wired the contraption and plugged it into a wall socket.

The gizmo heated up and the inmates pressed it against the window until its edge had melted away, Brown said.

Then they snapped a leg off the cell bed, placed it into the newly burned hole, pried out the entire window, and skipped to freedom, Brown said.

SOURCE: From "Pair of Crafty Inmates Melt Way Out of Jail," appearing in the *Los Angeles Times*, January 6, 1978. Copyright © 1978 by the Associated Press. Reprinted by permission of Associated Press Newsfeatures.

---

of boxes as containers, rather than as platforms, was emphasized when they contained objects, and so it was more difficult to recognize their novel function.

The string problem in Table 12.1 requires finding a novel use for a tool. The screwdriver is tied to one string to create a pendulum that can be swung to the other string. One of the best examples of overcoming functional fixedness outside the laboratory is the attempt of prisoners to break out of jail. Since tools are not readily available in prison, prisoners have to use items that are available. Box 12.1 describes the ingenuity of two prisoners in finding novel uses for common objects.

Inducing Structure

Inducing-structure problem A problem that requires finding a pattern among a fixed set of relations

Series extrapolation A problem that requires finding a pattern among a sequence of items in order to continue the sequence in the same pattern

Analogy problem A four-term problem that requires finding the answer that completes the relation: *A* is to *B* as *C* is to *D*

Arrangement problems require the rearrangement of objects to form a new relation among them. In problems of **inducing structure**, by contrast, the relation is fixed and the problem is to discover it. Some objects are given, and the task is to discover how they are related. For example, **series extrapolation** problems consist of a series such as 1 2 8 3 4 6 5 6 ———. The task is to find the next element of the series. Notice that there are two series in the example. One is the ascending series 1 2, 3 4, 5 6; the other is the descending series 8, 6, ———. So the correct answer is 4. Similarly, the answer to the letter series in Table 12.1 is E.

Another example of inducing structure is **analogy problems** like Merchant : Sell : : Customer : Buy. The instructions might indicate that the analogy should be labeled true or false, or the last word could be replaced by a blank, with instructions to fill in the word that best completes the analogy. Analogical reasoning is of particular interest because of its use in intelligence tests. The Miller Analogies Test, which is widely used for admission to graduate school, is composed exclusively of verbal analogies. Other ability tests, such as the Graduate Record Exam (GRE) and the Scholastic Aptitude Test (SAT), include analogies among the test items.

The psychological processes used in solving an analogy or series extrapolation problem involve identifying relations among the components and fitting the relations together in a pattern (Greeno, 1978). The importance of discovering relations among the terms of an analogy is illustrated in a model proposed by R. J. Sternberg (1977). There are four processes in Sternberg's model: *encoding, inference, mapping,* and *application.* Consider the problem *Washington is to 1 as Lincoln is to 10 or 5.* The task is to choose either 10 or 5 to complete the analogy. The *encoding* process identifies attributes of the words that could be important in establishing relations. The first term, *Washington,* might be identified as a president, a portrait on a $1 bill, or a war hero. The *inference* process establishes valid relations between the first two terms. Washington was the first president of the United States, and his portrait appears on a $1 bill—two possible relations between Washington and 1. The *mapping* process establishes relations between the first and third terms. Both Washington and Lincoln were presidents, and portraits of both appear on bills, so both possibilities remain as the basis for the analogy. The *application* process attempts to establish a relation between Lincoln and 10 or 5 that is analogous to the one between Washington and 1. Since Lincoln was the 16th president of the United States, neither answer fits the presidential relation. However, Lincoln's portrait appears on a $5 bill, so the choice of 5 is consistent with the currency relation. This example reveals the importance of discovering relations. Suppose we had considered only the presidential relation. If we did not know that Lincoln was the 16th president, we would be more likely to guess that he was the 10th president than the 5th, and so we would have chosen the wrong answer.

Sternberg measured how quickly students were able to answer different kinds of problems in order to estimate how much time was needed to complete each of the four processes—encoding, inference, mapping, and application. One goal of his research was to study how these times vary across individuals and to correlate the times with other measures of intellectual performance.

Sternberg and Gardner (1983) examined whether common components are involved in three different reasoning tasks that required inducing structure (series completion, analogy, and classification). They combined the three central reasoning components—inference, mapping, and application—to form a single reasoning variable, which correlated significantly across the different tasks. In other words, students who were rapid in reasoning in one kind of induction task were also rapid in reasoning during other induction tasks. The results indicate that some common skills are involved in inducing structure across different tasks, as implied by Greeno's (1978) taxonomy.

A particularly challenging test that requires the induction of abstract relations is the *Raven Progressive Matrices Test* (Raven, 1962). Each problem consists of a 3×3 matrix in which the bottom-right entry is missing. The instructions are to look across the rows and then down the columns to determine the rules that can be used to generate the missing pattern. You can try to solve one of these problems by determining which of the eight alternatives in Figure 12.2 is the missing pattern.

People initially try to match the rectangles, curves, and lines across rows, but exact matches do not exist. For instance, the two curved vertical lines in the first row do not occur in the second and third rows. Number and shape are both relevant, however, because each row contains one, two, and three vertical shapes, representing each of the three shapes, and one, two, and three horizontal shapes, representing each of

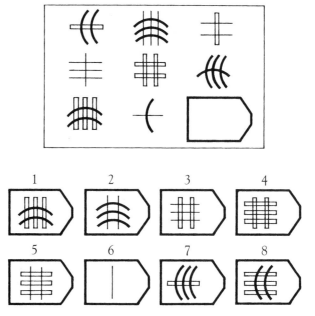

Figure 12.2   *A test question based on Raven's Progressive Matrices Test.*

From "What One Intelligence Test Measures: A Theoretical Account of the Processing in the Raven Progressive Matrices Test," by P. A. Carpenter, M. A. Just, and P. Shell, 1990, *Psychological Review, 97,* 404–431. Copyright © 1990 by the American Psychological Association. Reprinted by permission.

the three shapes. The missing number in the bottom row is three for the horizontal shape, and the missing horizontal shape is the open rectangles. The missing number is two for the vertical shape, and the missing vertical shape is the lines. The correct alternative is 5. A high score on this test depends primarily on the ability to induce abstract relations and the ability to manage many comparisons in working memory (Carpenter et al., 1990).

Transformation Problems

Transformation problems consist of an initial state, a goal state, and a sequence of operations for changing the initial state into the goal state. Transformation problems differ from problems of inducing structure and arrangement by providing the goal state rather than requiring solvers to produce it. An anagram problem requires finding the word that solves the anagram, and Duncker's candle problem requires finding the correct arrangement of parts that supports the candle. In contrast, a transformation problem like the missionaries-and-cannibals problem provides the goal state.

Transformation problem A problem that requires changing the initial state through a sequence of operations until it matches the goal state

The *missionaries-and-cannibals problem* requires transporting missionaries and cannibals across a river under the constraint that cannibals can never outnumber missionaries, in the boat or on either side of the river. In one version of this problem, the initial state consists of five missionaries, five cannibals, and a boat that can hold three persons, all starting on the left bank of the river. The goal state consists of the ten persons and the boat, all on the right bank of the river. The operations consist of moving from one to three persons in the boat back and forth across the river. The problem can be solved in 11 moves, but people usually require about 20 to 30 moves to reach a solution.

According to Greeno (1978), solving transformation problems primarily requires skills in planning based on a method called *means/end analysis*. Since a definite goal state is given in transformation problems, the problem solver can compare the current problem state with the goal state. **Means/end analysis** requires identifying differences that exist between the current state and the goal state and selecting operations that will reduce these differences.

Means/end analysis A strategy that can be used to solve transformation problems by eliminating differences between the initial and goal states

The problems that we will consider in the rest of this chapter are mostly transformation problems. This focus will provide us the opportunity to study means/end analysis and alternative planning strategies. Much of what psychologists know about how people solve these problems is the result of the pioneering work of Newell and Simon at Carnegie-Mellon University. We will review the major aspects of their theory of human problem solving before looking at the applications of their ideas to particular problems.

NEWELL AND SIMON'S THEORY

Objectives and Method

The initial development of Newell and Simon's theory was described in a paper titled "Elements of a Theory of Human Problem Solving" (Newell, Shaw, & Simon, 1958b), which, as we saw earlier, had an important influence on the development of information-processing theory. The paper described the first 2 years of a project that involved programming a digital computer to solve problems. One objective of the project, in fact, was to consider how programming a computer could contribute to a theory of human problem solving. The first step was to use all available evidence about human problem solving to program processes resembling those used by humans. The second step was to collect detailed data on how humans solve the same problems as those solved by the computer. The program could then be modified to provide a closer approximation of human behavior. Once success was achieved in simulating performance on a particular task, the investigators could examine a broader range of tasks, attempting to use the same set of elementary information processes and program organization in all the **simulation programs**. A long-term goal would be to draw implications from the theories for improving human performance.

Why does the computer play a central role in theory construction? Simon and Newell's (1971) answer is that much of our thinking is not directly observable. The covert nature of thought can make it seem magical or mysterious, leading to vague theories that obscure more than they clarify. The advantage of computer programs is that terms like *memory* and *strategy* can be defined in precisely stated instructions for a computer. Furthermore, the requirement that the programs must work—that is, must be able to solve the problem—provides a guarantee that no steps have been left unspecified. A successful program provides a **measure of sufficiency**—a test that the steps in the program are sufficient for solving the problem. However, a successful program does not guarantee that a person would solve the problem the same way; it is still necessary to make detailed observations on how people solve problems and modify the program to simulate their behavior.

To obtain details about how people solve problems, Newell and Simon (1972) usually collected **verbal protocols** from their subjects. They told the subjects to report verbally everything they thought about as they worked on the problem. The verbal statements often provided enough details to build a computer simulation program that would solve the problem in the same way that people solved it.

The method of collecting verbal protocols and constructing a simulation program has not been widely adopted by other investigators, although the approach is slowly gaining more appeal. One deterrent is simply that this method requires a lot of work for the investigator. The investigator therefore usually studies only a few subjects and assumes that

Simulation programs
Computer programs that attempt to reproduce the operations used by people to carry out various tasks

Measure of sufficiency
A demonstration that the instructions in a computer program are capable of solving a problem

Verbal protocols
Records of verbalized thought processes

they are fairly typical in the way they solve problems. Another limitation is that the method yields many details, and it is not always clear how to summarize the results in order to emphasize what is most important. Failure to collect verbal protocols, however, can result in the loss of valuable information because a subject's behavior may reveal little about what he or she is thinking.

Although the particular method used by Newell and Simon has not been widely adopted, their theory of problem solving has been very influential in determining how psychologists think about human information processing in general and problem solving in particular. The theory provides a general framework for specifying how information-processing characteristics, the structure of the problem, and different sources of knowledge interact to influence behavior.

Theoretical Assumptions

An important component of Newell and Simon's theory is the identification of the basic characteristics of human information processing that influence problem solving. These characteristics are the same ones that we discussed in earlier chapters—performance on a problem-solving task is influenced by the capacity, storage time, and retrieval time of STM and LTM. The limited capacity of STM places a constraint on the number of sequential operations that can be carried out mentally. Although most people can multiply 17×8 without using paper and pencil, multiplying 17×58 is much more difficult because the number of required operations (multiplying 17×8 and 17×5, storing the products, aligning, and adding) can exceed the limit of STM. Long-term memory does not have these capacity limitations, but it takes time to enter new information into LTM. This can make it difficult to remember the steps that were used to solve a problem, causing us to repeat incorrect steps. Thus both the limited capacity of STM and the time required to store new information in LTM can greatly influence the efficiency of a human problem solver. The simulation model proposed by Atwood and Polson (1976) nicely demonstrates this point; we will return to this model later.

Simon and Newell's (1971) theory is concerned not only with the person but also with the task. The sequential nature of many problems raises the question of what options are available at each point in solving the problem. If there are many choices available, only a few of which lead to a solution, the problem can be very difficult. However, if one has a good plan for solving the problem and can therefore ignore unpromising paths, the number of unpromising paths will have little effect on performance. Simon and Newell illustrate this point by referring to the problem DONALD + GERALD = ROBERT.

The problem is to substitute a digit 0 to 9 for each of the ten letters in order to satisfy the constraint that the substitution obeys the rules of addition. The hint is $D = 5$. Therefore, $T = 0$, and a 1 has to be carried into the next column to the left. Although the number of possible choices is very large (there are 362,880 ways of assigning nine digits to nine letters), by following the rules of arithmetic and using accumulated information (such as that R must be odd), it is possible to explore relatively few promising choices. You can observe this for yourself by trying to solve the problem. What is important, therefore, is not the number of incorrect paths but how effectively one can discover a plan that avoids the incorrect paths. To use Newell and Simon's analogy, we need not be concerned how large the haystack is if we can identify a small part of it in which we are quite sure to find the needle.

The number of available choices for solving the cryptarithmetic problem does not look very large when compared to the number of available choices during a game of chess. Box 12.2 describes a computer program

**BOX
12.2**

Computer chess champ no match for human's best, grandmaster Kasparov

ASSOCIATED PRESS

NEW YORK—It was a battle of two chess champions—one active and outspoken, known to sip tonic water during matches, the other sitting quietly on a desk, taking in a different kind of juice.

World chess champion Garri Kasparov, who hasn't lost a tournament since 1981, met Deep Thought, the winner of this year's World Computer Chess Championship, for two games yesterday.

The human won the first game after 2 hours when the computer retired from the game after Kasparov's 52nd move. He won the second match after 2 hours when the computer surrendered after 37 moves.

"I expected it," Kasparov said. "It's a good player, but without position and experience."

Kasparov said after the first game he realized early on that he would win when the computer missed some tactical opportunities and was not able to analyze all of the champion's decisions.

"I don't mind who's sitting opposite me," said Kasparov, who lives in the Soviet city of Baku, in Azerbaijan. "If a computer should win, of course, I would have to challenge it to protect the human race."

Murray Campbell, who helped create the computer at Carnegie-Mellon University in Pittsburgh, said it appeared there was a bug in the computer during the first game.

"It wasn't looking at the right moves," he said after the first match. "It wasn't given a chance to show its best style of play."

Commentator Shelby Lyman, who helped arrange the match, said before the games that Deep Thought was "clearly the first chess computer with the potential to draw blood and defeat the world champion."

called Deep Thought that can analyze 700,000 possible positions per second and plan 5 to 20 moves ahead. Even this amount of computing power was unable to defeat world chess champion Garri Kasparov. Kasparov's expertise enabled him to evaluate a limited number of very promising moves.

Newell and Simon use the term **problem space** to refer to the choices that the problem solver evaluates while solving a problem. The problem itself determines the number of possible choices and paths that could be followed in searching for a solution, but the problem solver determines which of these to actually explore. Among the sources of information that influence how a person constructs a problem space are the following:

Problem space The set of choices confronted by a problem solver at each step in solving a problem

1. The task instructions that give a description of the problem and may contain helpful information.
2. Previous experience with the same task or a nearly identical one.
3. Previous experience with analogous tasks.

Deep Thought, created by five graduate students at Carnegie-Mellon, can analyze 700,000 possible positions on the chessboard per second and 5 to 20 moves ahead by each side, as well as discern each move's implications.

Deep Thought evaluates the millions of possible board positions created by each sequence of five moves it imagines.

The computer didn't even have to travel for the match; it remained in Pittsburgh with a telephone line to relay its moves to a terminal in New York.

Feng-Hsiung Hsu, who designed the computer's silicon guts, said he wouldn't call it intelligent. "It's just mathematical applications," he said. "When humans play chess, they use their intelligence. When machines play chess, they do calculations."

Last November, Deep Thought beat Denmark's Bent Larsen—the first time a computer had defeated a grandmaster in tournament play. Larsen is the world's 96th-ranked player, with an International Chess Federation rating of 2580 based on his tournament performances.

In comparison, the computer's rating from the United States chess Federation is 2250; the International Chess Federation put Kasparov at 2775. A beginner typically would rank about 1200.

Kasparov said the computer was "fully aggressive" but that its "mind was too straight and too primitive."

"Chess is much wider than just calculations. It's even wider than logic. You have to use fantasy, intuition and some kind of prediction," Kasparov said.

But he said the computer does have some advantages: "We can lose hope. A computer can't lose hope."

---

4. Plans stored in LTM that generalize over a range of tasks.
5. Information accumulated while solving a problem.

Let us now take a closer look at how these sources of information influence problem solving. We will begin by showing how means/end analysis can be used to solve transformation problems.

Means/End Analysis

The use of means/end analysis is illustrated by a computer program called the General Problem Solver (Ernst & Newell, 1969). The program consists of general procedures that should apply across a variety of problems. A *general procedure* for solving transformation problems is to select operators that result in a problem state that is closer to the goal state. **Operators** are the allowed changes that can be made to solve the problem, such as moving missionaries and cannibals in the boat. Getting close to the goal is accomplished by trying to reduce the differences between the current problem state and the goal state. In order to follow this procedure, the General Problem Solver (GPS) must be given the differences that exist between problem states and the operators that are capable of eliminating these differences. A **table of connections** combines these two sets of information by showing which differences can be eliminated by each of the operators. The particular operators and differences will, of course, vary across problems, but the general strategy of consulting a table of connections in order to determine which operators are useful for reducing differences should remain the same across problems.

In most cases the principles used to construct GPS form a reasonable model of how people attempt to solve transformation problems. In fact, GPS was specifically used as a model of human performance on a symbol transformation task studied by Newell and Simon (1972). The problems were similar to the kind of derivations that students encounter in an introductory logic course. Students were given some initial statements, a set of 12 transformation rules, and a goal statement. The task was to use the rules to transform the initial statements in order to produce the goal statement. Newell and Simon identified six differences that distinguish logic statements. The table of connections specified which of these differences could be changed by each of the 12 transformation rules.

For example, a student might be asked to prove that, if A implies B ($A \supset B$), then the absence of B implies the absence of A ($-B \supset -A$). Notice that there are two kinds of differences that distinguish the initial state ($A \supset B$) from the goal state ($-B \supset -A$). First, the two expressions differ in sign—there are negation signs before the A and the B in the goal state. Second, the positions of the A and the B have changed in the goal state. Students could use means/end analysis to solve this problem by ap-

Operators   Actions that are selected to solve problems

Table of connections
A table that links differences between problem states with operators for eliminating those differences

plying transformation rules that changed either the sign or the position of the symbols. Newell and Simon (1972) asked their subjects to verbalize their strategies as they attempted to solve the symbol transformation problems. Students' solutions and verbal protocols revealed that many aspects of their thinking were similar to aspects of the means/end analysis used in the General Problem Solver.

Memory and Problem Solving

Computer programs such as the General Problem Solver provide a good source of ideas for how people might solve problems. However, we must be careful when we make use of a program that was not originally designed to simulate human thinking. As mentioned earlier, an important component of Newell and Simon's theory is the identification of basic characteristics of human memory that influence problem solving. Although the limited capacity of STM and the time required to store new information in LTM are not problems for a large computer, they can limit our progress toward becoming expert problem solvers.

The use of memory while solving problems is nicely illustrated in a model of an attempt to solve the water-jar problem (Atwood & Polson, 1976). The water-jar problem (see Table 12.1) has a relatively small and well-defined search space, making it feasible to predict in detail how people will search for a solution. In one version of this problem, there are three pails, and the goal is to distribute the water equally between the two largest pails. Initially the largest pail is full and the other two pails are empty. For example, in the (8, 5, 3) problem, the pails can hold 8, 5, or 3 gallons of water. The goal is to divide the 8 gallons of water in the largest pail equally between the 8- and 5-gallon pails.

The Atwood and Polson model assumes that people will try to solve the problem by using a means/end heuristic. However, means/end analysis doesn't always work very well for the water-jar problem; in fact, the solution of the (8, 5, 3) problem requires several violations of the means/end strategy. Another problem—one in which the pails hold 24, 21, or 3 gallons—has a similar search space but can be solved without violating the means/end strategy. If people use a means/end strategy, they should find the latter problem easier than the former. Atwood and Polson's results supported this prediction. People required more than twice as many moves to solve the (8, 5, 3) problem even though it is possible to solve both problems in the same number of moves.

The optimal way of using the means/end strategy would be to evaluate all possible moves and select the one that minimizes the discrepancy between the resulting state and the goal state. However, the limited capacity of STM places a constraint on the number of possible moves that can be evaluated and compared simultaneously. The model therefore assumes that people will simply look for a good move rather than always trying to find the best move. If the discrepancy between the resulting state and the goal state is not too large, the probability of making the evaluated move depends on whether the problem solver recognizes the resulting problem state. It is generally helpful to remember previously reached problem states in order not to return to them. Returning to old states generally implies that one is backing up and moving away from the goal state. Backing up is particularly detrimental in the problems studied by Atwood and Polson because it is possible to return all the way to the beginning states by making the wrong move.

To account for how people progress through the search space, Atwood and Polson estimated the probability of making a move to an old problem state as .20, the probability of making a move to a new state as .60, the probability of remembering previously visited states as .90, and the number of moves that can be evaluated in STM as three. These values reveal that people do in fact prefer to move to new states rather than return to old states. They also reveal that people are able to recognize old states with fairly high accuracy. The estimate that only three moves can be compared in STM is consistent with previous estimates of STM capacity because, for each move, the problem solver has to remember not only the move but how much the resulting state differs from the goal state.

If the problem solver does not select a move during the first stage described above, the model specifies other criteria for move selection. The essential characteristics of the model are evident in this brief summary, however: First, there is the use of a means/end strategy to evaluate progress toward the goal. If the problem can be solved by gradually reducing the difference between the current state and the goal state, people solve it in fewer moves than if they are forced to make moves that violate the means/end strategy. Second, the limited capacity of STM places a constraint on the number of moves that can be evaluated. Even if you had a perfect strategy that enabled you always to select the best move at each point, you would not necessarily find the shortest solution if you could not evaluate all the moves at each decision point. For example, if there were four possible moves but you could evaluate only three because of the limitations of STM, the best move might be the one you did not evaluate.

Atwood and Polson's finding that people are much more likely to make a move if it leads to a new problem state is consistent with the idea that it is generally better to move to new states than to return to old states. However, an old state will appear to be a new state if the problem solver does not remember being there. It is therefore useful to remember what states you visited when solving a problem by storing this information in LTM. Atwood and Polson report that people were quite successful at storing such information as they solved the water-jar problem.

GENERAL STRATEGIES

Means/end analysis is an example of a general strategy. A knowledge of general problem-solving strategies can be particularly useful because general strategies apply to many kinds of problems. For this reason books like Wickelgren's (1974) on how to solve problems emphasize general strategies such as forming subgoals or working backward.

Strategies such as using means/end analysis, forming subgoals, and working backward are called **heuristics** because they are often successful but do not guarantee success. In contrast, an **algorithm** is a procedure of steps that does guarantee a solution if one follows the steps correctly. The rules for multiplication constitute an algorithm because a correct answer is guaranteed if a person correctly follows the rules. We will first consider three general heuristics—forming subgoals, using analogy, and constructing diagrams—and then evaluate both their potential usefulness and their limitations as general strategies.

Heuristics Strategies that are often, but not always, helpful in solving problems

Algorithm A set of rules that will solve a problem if correctly followed

Subgoals

A commonly suggested heuristic for solving problems is to divide the problem into parts—that is, to formulate subgoals. **Subgoals** are problem states intermediate between the initial state and the goal state; ideally they are on the solution path. Some problems have fairly obvious subgoals, and research has shown that people take advantage of them. Consider the puzzle called the Tower of Hanoi (see Figure 12.3). This puzzle consists of three pegs and a set of rings that vary in size. The initial state has all the rings stacked on peg A in order of decreasing size. The goal is to move the stack, one ring at a time, to peg C, under the constraint that a larger ring can never be placed on a smaller ring. A reasonable subgoal is to move the largest ring to peg C. But how does one begin in order to achieve this subgoal? The answer is not obvious, and people often make the wrong choice. But as they make other moves and come closer to achieving the subgoal, the correct moves become more obvious and errors decline (Egan & Greeno, 1974).

Using subgoals can make solving a problem easier because knowing that an intermediate problem state is on the solution path makes it possible to avoid searching many unpromising paths. Figure 12.4 shows a search space that contains 16 paths, each four steps in length. Only one path ends in the goal state. If we are given a subgoal state that we know can be reached in two steps, then we can reach the subgoal by searching only four paths, each two steps long. From the subgoal state there are another four paths, each two steps long. The search space has been reduced from 16 four-step paths to the 8 two-step paths represented by the shaded area in Figure 12.4.

Subgoal A goal that solves part of the problem

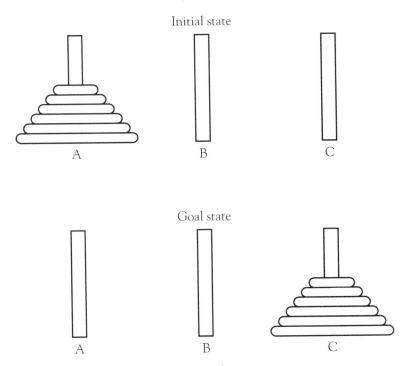

Figure 12.3   *The Tower of Hanoi puzzle.*

Forming subgoals is often helpful, but it does not guarantee an easier solution. There are several limitations to keep in mind when using this method. First, it is not always obvious what are helpful intermediate problem states because some problems do not have obvious subgoals. Second, reaching a subgoal may create confusion about what to do next. Hayes (1966) found that giving people a subgoal helped them solve the part of the problem that came before the subgoal. However, some problems actually took longer to solve with a subgoal because it took a long time to figure out what to do after reaching the subgoal.

An example of a problem in which a subgoal improved performance is the missionaries-and-cannibals problem (described in Table 12.1) requiring the transportation of five missionaries and five cannibals across a river using a boat that can only hold three persons. One group of students, the control group, was simply asked to solve the problem. Another group, the "subgoal" group, was told that, in order to solve the problem, they would have to reach a state in which there were three cannibals across the river by themselves and without the boat. Students in the control group required an average of 30 moves to solve the problem, compared with an average of only 20 moves for students in the subgoal group.

Given

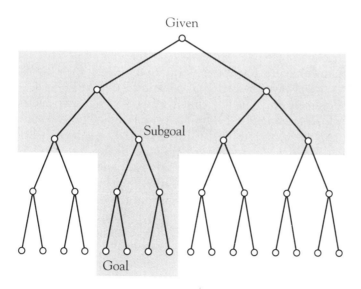

Subgoal

Goal

Figure 12.4   *Search space. Knowledge of a subgoal limits search to the shaded area.*

From *How to Solve Problems*, by W. A. Wicklegren. Copyright © 1974 by W. H. Freeman and Company. Reprinted by permission.

In order to try to understand why the subgoal was so effective, Simon and I developed a simulation model of the way students in the two groups explored the search space. The goal of the model was to predict, for each of the possible legal moves, the average number of times students in each group would make that particular move. We thought students would follow a *means/end strategy* in which they would move as many people across the river as possible and bring as few back as possible. A model based on the means/end strategy was fairly successful in predicting their choices, but some of their moves did not follow this strategy. Violations of the means/end strategy could be accounted for by proposing that people follow a *balance strategy*, which attempts to create equal numbers of missionaries and cannibals on each side of the river. The balance strategy makes it easy to avoid illegal moves because cannibals will never outnumber missionaries as long as the numbers of missionaries and cannibals are equal on both sides. The trouble with the balance strategy is that it tends to lead people away from the solution path and toward unpromising paths. After analyzing the moves made by both groups, we proposed that the subgoal group was more likely to follow the means/end strategy and the control group was more likely to follow the less effective balance strategy. The fact that the subgoal—three cannibals and no missionaries—is an unbalanced state also makes it intuitively likely that students in the subgoal group would not persist in following the balance strategy.

As mentioned previously, one limitation of using the subgoal strategy is that it is not always obvious what constitutes a good subgoal. Educators can therefore help students by explicitly pointing out subgoals, as demonstrated by Catrambone (1995). Students were shown how to solve a probability problem that required finding total frequency as one of the subgoals. When this step was explicitly labeled as *Total Frequency*, students did better in transferring what they had learned to other probability problems that required finding the total frequency. The transfer problems required a different method for calculating total frequency, so it was insufficient to apply by rote the same steps shown in the example problem. Learning required understanding the example, and explicitly labeling a subgoal enhanced understanding.

Analogy

Analogy Solving a problem by using a solution to a related problem

Analogy is another of the major heuristics for solving problems. **Analogy** requires that the problem solver use the solution of a similar problem to solve a current problem. Success in using analogy depends on both recognizing the similarity between the two problems and recalling the solution of the analogous problem. Since the recall of a solution is required, analogy depends more on LTM than do means/end analysis and subgoals.

Let us look now at another version of the missionaries-and-cannibals problem, called the jealous-husbands problem:

> Three jealous husbands and their wives, having to cross a river, find a boat. However, the boat is so small that it can hold no more than two persons. Find the simplest schedule of crossings that will permit all six persons to cross the river so that no woman is left in the company of any other woman's husband unless her own husband is present. It is assumed that all passengers on the boat debark before the next trip and that at least one person has to be in the boat for each crossing.

The jealous-husbands and the missionaries-and-cannibals problems are similar because the solution of one problem can be used to solve the other. Someone who knows the solution to the missionaries-and-cannibals problem can solve the jealous-husbands problem by (1) substituting husbands for missionaries, (2) substituting wives for cannibals, and (3) pairing the couples when men and women are on the same bank of the river. If people can make use of analogy to solve the problems, then it should be easier to solve either problem if a person first solved the analogous problem. However, experimental results indicated that people were in fact not better at solving one problem if they had first solved the other problem (Reed, Ernst, & Banerji, 1974). Why not?

One reason may be that people did not know the relation between the two problems. In a second experiment the experimenter encouraged subjects to use their solution of the first problem to solve the second problem, informing them that *husbands* corresponded to *missionaries* and *wives* corresponded to *cannibals*. The information about how the problems were related helped subjects solve the missionaries-and-cannibals problem but did not help them solve the jealous-husbands problem.

These results show that successful use of analogy does not occur as readily as we might expect. Even when the instructions reveal the exact relation between two problems, the solution of one does not guarantee that it will be easier to solve the other. One explanation of this finding is that it is difficult to remember the correct solution when it consists of a long sequence of moves. This hypothesis suggests that the use of analogy should be more effective when the solution is easier to remember.

The problems studied by Gestalt psychologists typically were problems that could be solved in a few steps. Examples include the crate-and-stick (Kohler, 1925) and candle (Duncker, 1945) problems that we looked at earlier. Another problem studied by Duncker (1945) was the tumor, or radiation, problem. Table 12.2 describes this problem and a solution. The dispersion solution involves dividing the rays so that they will have high intensity only when they converge on the tumor. Although this is a clever solution, Duncker found that very few people solved the problem in this way.

Gick and Holyoak (1980) investigated whether more people would discover the dispersion solution if they were first exposed to an analogous solution. Their subjects read the attack-dispersion story before trying to solve the radiation problem. The attack-dispersion story described a solution to a military problem in which the army had to be divided in order to converge on a fortress. The instructions indicated that the first story might give subjects some hints for solving the radiation problem. The results showed that most people made use of the analogy. Over half of those who read the story included the dispersion solution among their proposed solutions, compared with only 8% of those who did not read the story before solving the radiation problem. But when Gick and Holyoak omitted the hint to use the story, the number of dispersion solutions greatly decreased. Their findings thus demonstrated that people could generate an analogous solution when prompted but that they did not spontaneously recognize the similarity between the two problems.

People's inability to spontaneously notice the relation between analogous problems poses a challenge for psychologists to make analogies more obvious. One reason that analogies are often not obvious is that, although

Table 12.2   *A summary of the attack-dispersion story and of a corresponding solution to the radiation problem*

Attack-dispersion story
A fortress was located in the center of the country.
Many roads radiated out from the fortress.
A general wanted to capture the fortress with his army.
The general wanted to prevent mines on the roads from destroying his army and
   neighboring villages.
As a result the entire army could not attack the fortress along one road.
However, the entire army was needed to capture the fortress.
So an attack by one small group would not succeed.
The general therefore divided his army into several small groups.
He positioned the small groups at the heads of different roads.
The small groups simultaneously converged on the fortress.
In this way the army captured the fortress.

Radiation problem and dispersion solution[a]
A tumor was located in the interior of a patient's body.
A doctor wanted to destroy the tumor with rays.
The doctor wanted to prevent the rays from destroying the healthy tissue.
As a result the high-intensity rays could not be applied to the tumor along one
   path.
However, high-intensity rays were needed to destroy the tumor.
So applying one low-intensity ray would not succeed.
The doctor therefore divided the rays into several low-intensity rays.
He positioned the low-intensity rays at multiple locations around the patient's body.
The low-intensity rays simultaneously converged on the tumor.
In this way the rays destroyed the tumor.

SOURCE: From "Analogical Problem Solving," by M. L. Gick and K. Holyoak, 1980, *Cognitive Psychology*,
12, 306–355. Copyright © 1980 by Academic Press, Inc. Reprinted by permission.
[a]Italicized propositions summarize the target dispersion solution.

the analogy preserves relations among the concepts in a problem, the concepts themselves differ (Gentner, 1983). This point is illustrated in Table
12.3 for the military and radiation problems. Although the concepts
(army and fortress; rays and tumor) differ in the two problems, the solutions preserve the relations of breaking up and converging. The similarity
of the two solutions is represented at the bottom of the table by the convergence schema, in which the concepts are described more generally.
The solutions to both problems require breaking up a large force so that
weak forces can be simultaneously applied along multiple paths.

   Gick and Holyoak (1983) discovered that people were likely to form
this more general schema if they read and compared two analogous stories before trying to solve the radiation problem. For example, some students read the military story and a story about forming a circle around an

Table 12.3 *Correspondences among the military problem, the radiation problem, and the convergence schema*

Military problem
  Initial state
      Goal: Use army to capture fortress.
      Resources: Sufficiently large army.
      Constraint: Unable to send entire army along one road.
  Solution plan: Send small groups along multiple roads simultaneously.
  Outcome: Fortress captured by army.

Radiation problem
  Initial state
      Goal: Use rays to destroy tumor.
      Resources: Sufficiently powerful rays.
      Constraint: Unable to administer high-intensity rays from one direction.
  Solution plan: Administer low-intensity rays from multiple directions simultaneously.
  Outcome: Tumor destroyed by rays.

Convergence schema
  Initial state
      Goal: Use force to overcome a central target.
      Resources: Sufficiently great force.
      Constraints: Unable to apply full force along one path.
  Solution plan: Apply weak forces along multiple paths simultaneously.
  Outcome: Central target overcome by force.

SOURCE: From "Schema Induction and Analogical Transfer," by M. L. Gick and K. Holyoak, 1983, *Cognitive Psychology, 15*, 1–38. Copyright © 1983 by Academic Press, Inc. Reprinted by permission.

oil fire in order to use many small hoses to spray foam on the fire. Students who described the relation between these two stories were much more likely to think of the convergence solution to the radiation problem than were students who read only a single analogous story. Creating the *convergence schema* requires that people compare two analogous stories, which makes them think about the solution in general terms. Reading the two analogous stories without comparing them is not very helpful (Catrambone & Holyoak, 1989).

The advantage of creating a general schema, such as the convergence schema, is that it should be easier for subjects to recognize that the radiation problem is an example of a general schema than to recognize how it relates to a particular problem. But psychologists are still investigating the extent to which people create general schema, as opposed to recalling a particular problem (Ross, 1984) as a basis for analogy. After an extensive review of the literature on analogy, Reeves and Weisberg (1994) concluded that there is sufficient evidence to show that we use both specific problems and more abstract schemata in analogical reasoning. One promising theory is that we begin by using the solution of specific problems, but as we apply a specific solution to other problems, we begin to form more abstract schemata (Ross & Kennedy, 1990). We will see in the next chapter that forming these more abstract schemata is an important part of acquiring expertise.

Diagrams

Problem isomorphs
Problems that have different story contents but identical solutions

Our final example of a general strategy for solving problems is the construction of diagrams. Diagrams can help us represent problems in a way that allows us to search efficiently for a solution. The importance of representation is illustrated by the fact that two problems with identical solutions but different story contents (**problem isomorphs**) may differ greatly in how easy they are to solve. One story may cause the solver to represent the problem in a way that leads to an easy solution, and another story may cause a representation that impedes finding the solution. Furthermore, a person who solves both of the problems may not recognize any similarity between them (Hayes & Simon, 1977).

Carroll, Thomas, and Malhotra (1980) studied the role of representation in design by creating two problem isomorphs. The *spatial version* involved designing a business office for seven employees. Each employee was to be assigned to a corridor a certain number of offices down from a central hallway containing a reception area at one end and accounting records at the other end. Subjects were told to try to assign compatible employees to the same corridor, assigning those with higher prestige nearer to the central hallway. A goal of the problem is to minimize the number of corridors.

Problems of this kind are usually easier to solve by using a diagram such as Figure 12.5. The top of the diagram shows the central hallway connecting the reception and accounting areas. The columns represent corridors. Examples of constraints that are satisfied by the arrangement in Figure 12.5 are that A uses the accounting records less than C, B and C are compatible, and C has more prestige than B.

The *temporal version* of the isomorph had equivalent constraints, but the constraints were placed on a manufacturing process that consisted of seven stages. The columns in Figure 12.5 can now be used to represent work shifts rather than corridors. The horizontal dimension represents time, and the vertical dimension represents priority. Subjects were instructed to assign stages to the same work shift if the stages used the same resources. Some stages had to be assigned to earlier work shifts than others, and some stages had priority over others that belonged to the same work shift. Examples of constraints that are satisfied by the arrangement

Reception   Accounting

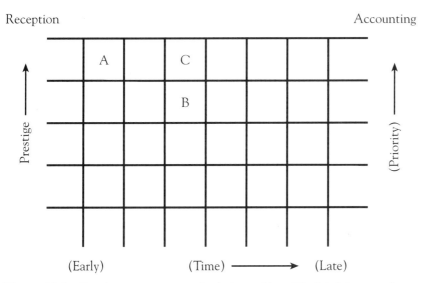

Figure 12.5   *Graphic representation of a design problem. The labels in parentheses accompanied the temporal version.*

From "Presentation and Representation in Design Problem Solving," by J. M. Carroll, J. C. Thomas, and A. Malhotra, 1980, *British Journal of Psychology, 71*, 143–153. Copyright © 1980 by the British Psychological Society. Reprinted by permission.

in Figure 12.5 are that stage A occurs before stage C, stages B and C use the same resources, and stage C has greater priority than stage B. Notice that distance from the accounting area in the spatial version corresponds to time in the temporal version, compatibility corresponds to use of the same resources, and prestige corresponds to priority.

Subjects who worked on the temporal version received 19 constraints that corresponded to the 19 constraints given to subjects who worked on the spatial version. Subjects were not instructed to use a diagram; they were able to select their own method for solving the problem. Performance was measured by how many constraints were satisfied in the design. The importance of representation is illustrated by the finding that subjects did significantly better on the spatial isomorph even though the two problems had equivalent constraints. Subjects given the spatial isomorph not only satisfied more of the constraints but completed their design faster. All 17 subjects in the spatial task used a sketch of the business office to formulate their design, but only 2 of the 18 subjects in the temporal task used a graphic representation.

To determine whether graphic representation made the problem easier for the spatial group, the experimenters conducted a second experiment, in which both groups were instructed to use the matrix shown in Figure 12.5. This time there were no significant differences between the two groups, either in performance scores or in solution times. The differences in the first experiment therefore appear to have been caused by the facilitating effects of a graphic representation of the problem. The usefulness of the graphic representation was obvious in the spatial task, and students spontaneously adopted it. It was not obvious in the temporal task. Performance on the two tasks became equivalent only when both groups were required to use a graphic representation.

An interesting question raised by these findings is whether students could use analogy to improve their performance on the temporal task if they had first worked on the spatial task. Spontaneous use of a graphic procedure to solve the spatial task might then transfer to the temporal task. If students recognized the analogy between the two tasks, the experimenter would not have to tell them to use the graphic procedure on the temporal task. Unfortunately, the initial research on this question indicates that the spontaneous transfer of general methods for solving problems is as difficult as the spontaneous transfer of specific solutions for solving problems.

Representational Transfer

Analogical transfer
Use of the same solution in solving two problems

Representational transfer Use of the same format (such as a matrix) in solving two problems

Novick (1990) refers to the transfer of general methods for solving problems as *representational transfer* to distinguish it from the *analogical transfer* of specific solutions. In **analogical transfer** we were concerned with the transfer of a specific solution, such as using the solution of the military problem to solve the radiation problem. In **representational transfer** we are concerned with the transfer of a general method, such as using a *matrix diagram*, like the one in Figure 12.5, to solve a transfer problem after being shown how to use it to solve an example problem.

Novick became interested in studying representational transfer after noticing that although many psychologists were studying the transfer of specific solutions, no one seemed to be studying the transfer of representations. Diagrammatic representations, in particular, help us represent the underlying structure of many problems. Because problem solvers often do not construct appropriate diagrams to represent problems, Novick and Hmelo (1994) examined whether students would transfer the use of an appropriate diagram from one problem to another problem that had a different solution, but could be solved by using the same diagram.

Figure 12.6 shows three different kinds of diagrams. The first two should be familiar to you if you have read previous chapters in this book. A *network* consists of nodes joined by links. In the example problem, a couple had to plan a trip that involved visiting islands (nodes) joined by bridges (links). The test problem required figuring out which pairs of people (nodes) at a cocktail party shook hands (links) with each other. The example for the *hierarchy* was a categorization problem in which a

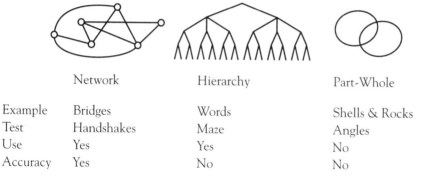

	Network	Hierarchy	Part-Whole
Example	Bridges	Words	Shells & Rocks
Test	Handshakes	Maze	Angles
Use	Yes	Yes	No
Accuracy	Yes	No	No

Figure 12.6 *Representational transfer of network, hierarchical, and part-whole representations.*

From "Transferring Symbolic Representations across Non-isomorphic Problems" by L. R. Novick and C. E. Hmelo, 1994, *Journal of Experimental Psychology: Learning, Memory, and Cognition, 20*, 1296–1321. Reprinted by permission.

mother was trying to group the words her young child knew into categories (zoo animals, farm animals, pets), like the semantic hierarchy shown in Figure 9.1 (page 256). The test problem involved representing different paths that a rat could take through a maze, like the search space hierarchy shown in Figure 12.4. The example for the *part-whole representation* consisted of a set membership problem in which the solver had to determine the number of children who collected only rocks, the number who collected only shells, and the number who collected both. These problems can be represented by the **Venn diagrams** shown in Figure 12.6. The test problem was a geometry problem in which the angles of two intersecting lines could be represented as either parts or wholes.

    Novick and Hmelo (1994) compared students' ability to solve test problems under three conditions: Subjects did not previously see any examples in the control condition, saw a relevant example in the no-hint condition but were not told of its relevance, and saw and were informed about the relevant example in the hint condition. The complete lack of spontaneous transfer was shown by the lack of difference between the control and no-hint groups. When not informed that a previously studied example would be helpful, subjects did not change their representations and improve their performance.

    The results for the hint group varied across the three representations. The network representation was the most successful. Students who were told to use the relevant example (bridge problem) were more likely to use a network representation to solve the handshake problem and were more successful. The results were mixed for the hierarchical representation—more people used a hierarchy to solve the maze problem, but they were

Venn diagram A diagram that shows the set relations (such as overlap) among categories

not more successful. A possible reason is that people who didn't draw a hierarchy typically drew the maze, and drawing the maze was as helpful as drawing a hierarchy to represent the maze. The part-whole problem was the least successful—neither the frequency of use nor the accuracy increased for solving the geometry problem. A limitation in this case is that students were not able to identify correspondences between the shells and rocks in the example problem and the angles in the geometry problem. Figure 12.6 summarizes these findings.

You may have noticed that there are some similarities between these initial results on representational transfer and the results on analogical transfer. Spontaneous transfer of either a specific solution or a more general method was poor because of the difficulty of noticing the similarity between two problems that had different physical descriptions, such as the attack-dispersion and radiation problems (Gick & Holyoak, 1983) or the bridges and handshake problems (Novick & Hmelo, 1994). Second, even when people are told to use an analogous problem, transfer of a particular solution depends on how easily people can find correspondences between objects in one problem and objects in the other problem (Gentner, 1983; Reed, 1993). This also limited transfer of the part-whole method from the shells and rocks problem to the geometry problem. A difference between analogical transfer and representational transfer is that successful transfer of a representation does not guarantee greater success in solving the problem if the transferred representation is not an improvement over the representation that is normally used to solve the problem. This is illustrated by the finding that encouraging people to represent the maze as a hierarchy did not result in more correct solutions.

In conclusion, the research on general strategies demonstrates that employing strategies such as subgoal formation, analogy, and construction of diagrams can be useful. However, the challenge is to know when and how to apply each of these strategies. Successful use of the strategies may therefore depend on having some amount of expertise in that problem-solving domain. In particular, many of the problems we encounter in the classroom require knowledge about that topic in order to solve them. Thus, both subject-matter knowledge and general strategies have to be learned if one is to become a proficient problem solver (Glaser, 1984). The next chapter is concerned with acquiring expertise for solving classroom problems and emphasizes the differences between novices and experts.

SUMMARY

Because there are many kinds of problems, constructing a theory of problem solving would be easier if we were able to classify problems according to the skills needed to solve them. One method of classification distinguishes among problems of arrangement, inducing structure, and transformation. Arrangement problems require the problem solver to arrange the elements of a problem in a way that satisfies some criterion. Anagrams are a good example because the letters have to be arranged to spell a word. In problems of inducing structure some elements are given, and the task is to discover how the elements are related. Analogy and series completion problems are examples. Transformation problems consist of an initial state, a goal state, and operations for changing the initial state into the goal state. Many puzzles are of this type, including the missionaries-and-cannibals, Tower of Hanoi, and water-jar problems.

Much of what psychologists know about how people solve problems is the result of the pioneering work of Newell and Simon. Their theory specifies how the basic characteristics of the human information processor, the search space, and different strategies affect problem solving. Performance on a task is influenced by the capacity, storage time, and retrieval time of STM and LTM. It is also influenced by the search space, which determines the number of legal moves available at each point in solving the problem. Newell and Simon have depended on computer simulation models and verbal protocols for testing and developing the many details of their theory.

There are several ways that memory can influence success in solving a problem. Short-term memory is needed to evaluate the alternative choices at each point when searching for a solution. Memory is also needed to store information about previously visited problem states, previously evaluated hypotheses, and previously selected operators. The important role of memory in solving problems is revealed in a simulation model of how people solve the water-jar problem.

Four general strategies for solving problems are means/end analysis, subgoals, analogy, and diagrams. These strategies are called heuristics because, although they are often useful, none guarantees a successful solution. The means/end strategy states that the problem solver should select operators that reduce the difference between the current problem state and the goal state. A table of connections shows which differences can be eliminated by each of the operators. Knowledge of subgoals is valuable because it reduces the size of the search space. A detailed simulation of how people solved the missionaries-and-cannibals problem revealed that a subgoal enabled them to avoid unpromising moves by selecting a better strategy than the one that is frequently used. The use of an analogous solution is often useful, but people may not notice a potential analogy. Diagrams can be beneficial in design tasks, but as is the case for analogy, it is not easy to spontaneously transfer a good representation from one problem to another.

STUDY QUESTIONS

1. Which problems did you find most difficult? Can you pinpoint the source of the difficulty? Which were the easiest for you? Can you say why? As your text asks, try to classify the six problems according to the skills needed to solve them.
2. What do most of the problems in your text have in common with items on standardized intelligence tests?
3. Why did Gestalt psychology tend to deal with problems that are classified as arrangement problems? Where does the "aha!" phenomenon come in?
4. Children (and some adults) are fascinated by Robinson-Crusoe type of adventures. Have you ever found yourself in a situation that required you to overcome functional fixedness? What did you do?
5. What characteristics of analogies place them in the class of induction problems? Make up an analogy of your own to demonstrate your understanding of Sternberg's model. Write out your analogy.
6. Can you think of some real-life problems that are clearly transformation problems. Does knowing the goal state make a problem easier?
7. How did Newell and Simon use the computer in building their theory of human problem solving? What advantages does it confer?
8. Is the problem space determined solely by the given task? How does the person enter into Newell and Simon's theory?
9. What parts do "operators" play in constructing a "table of connections" in the means/end analysis of a transformation problem? How would memory enter into the picture?
10. How good do you think people are at recognizing problem isomorphs? From your understanding of the research on generalized problem-solving strategies, would it do any good to teach such heuristics to all schoolchildren? Why or why not?

KEY TERMS

The page number in parentheses refers to where the term is discussed in the chapter.

algorithm (369)

anagram (356)

analogical transfer (378)

analogy (372)

analogy problem (358)

arrangement problem (356)

functional fixedness (357)

heuristics (369)

inducing-structure problem (358)

insight (356)

means/end analysis (361)

measure of sufficiency (362)

operators (366)

problem isomorphs (376)

problem space (365)

representational transfer (378)

series extrapolation (358)

simulation programs (362)

RECOMMENDED READING

Chapters on thinking by Greeno and Simon (1988) and on problem solving by VanLehn (1989) provide an extensive summary of work on reasoning and problem solving. The classic work on the effect of set on problem solving was conducted by Luchins (1942) in a study using the water-jar problem. The Atwood-Polson model, originally developed for the water-jar problem, was extended by Jeffries, Polson, Razran, and Atwood (1977) to describe performance on the missionaries-and-cannibals problem.

Information-processing models have also been developed to account for performance on Duncker's candle problem (Weisberg & Suls, 1973), on insight problems (Metcalfe, 1986a), and on geometric analogies (Mulholland, Pellegrino, & Glaser, 1980). The books by Vosniadou and Ortony (1989) and Detterman and Sternberg (1993) contain many chapters on the use of analogous solutions. In addition, Reeves and Weisberg (1994) have written a very thorough review of analogical transfer. Ericsson and Simon (1980) critically analyzed the role of verbal reports in constructing theories and argue that verbal reports can be very useful if they are treated like other kinds of data. Simon (1983) discusses the distinction between search and reasoning.

There has been growing interest in the development of information-processing models of how people answer questions on intelligence tests. This interest has been accompanied by the study of individual differences in problem solving. Articles by Hunt and Lansman (1975) and by Pellegrino and Glaser (1979) provide an overview of work in this area. A book edited by Sternberg and Detterman (1979) contains a number of interesting chapters on the growing interaction between intelligence testing and cognitive psychology. Sternberg's (1985) book is particularly recommended.

Expertise and
Creativity

It is strange that we expect students to learn, yet seldom teach them anything about learning. We expect students to solve problems, yet seldom teach them about problem solving. And, similarly, we sometimes require students to remember a considerable body of material, yet seldom teach them the art of memory. It is time we made up for this lack, time that we developed the applied disciplines of learning and problem solving and memory. We need to develop the general principles of how to learn, how to remember, how to solve problems, then to develop applied courses, and then to establish the place of these methods in an academic curriculum.*

DON NORMAN (1980)

---

*From "Cognitive Engineering and Education," by D. A. Norman in *Problem Solving and Education: Issues in Teaching and Research*, edited by D. T. Tuma and F. Reif. Copyright © 1980 by Lawrence Erlbaum Associates, Inc. Reprinted by permission.

O NE DIFFERENCE BETWEEN a puzzle such as the missionaries-and-cannibals problem and a classroom problem such as finding the concentration of a mixture is that we need considerable domain-specific knowledge to solve the latter problem. **Domain-specific knowledge** is knowledge about a particular subject matter. Most people could solve the standard version of the missionaries-and-cannibals problem (three missionaries, three cannibals) without previous experience on this problem, but few people could solve a mixture problem without previous algebra experience. This chapter is concerned with acquiring expertise through learning the domain-specific knowledge that enables us to excel in a particular academic area.

Domain-specific knowl-edge Knowledge about a specific subject, such as chess or physics

A central issue in teaching problem solving is how to balance instruction between teaching the general strategies discussed in the previous chapter and teaching the subject-matter knowledge required to solve classroom problems (Glaser, 1984; Polson & Jeffries, 1985). As Polson and Jeffries argue, good answers to this important practical question will depend on a better theoretical understanding of how people at different skill levels attempt to solve problems.

The opening quote to this chapter is a challenge from Don Norman to put cognitive psychology to use in improving instruction. Norman (1980) recommended four steps:

1. To understand enough about the psychology of learning or problem solving that applied techniques can be developed.
2. To develop applied methods and formal courses in these methods that can aid in the general problem-solving and learning abilities of our students.
3. To use this knowledge in two ways:
   a. To develop courses in methods of learning, memory, and problem solving to provide students with important cognitive tools.
   b. To develop better instructional systems for conventional teaching and make use of new technological developments and new techniques of cognitive science to make interactive, intelligent tutoring systems a reality.
4. To demonstrate the effectiveness of these techniques and to gain sufficient academic and public acceptance that not only will they be taught, they will be sought after.

This chapter discusses how people acquire and use domain knowledge to become good problem solvers in that domain. We look at the effect of prior knowledge on problem solving in the first section. We examine how familiarity influences performance on several reasoning tasks, including evaluating logical statements, estimating answers to mixture problems, and classifying problems according to their mathematical structure. Prior knowledge also influences how people solve more complex transformation problems that require a sequence of steps. The second section discusses the transition from using general search procedures to using more domain-specific procedures as the problem solver acquires expertise. The third section explores the relation between becoming experts at solving fairly routine problems and generating creative solutions. Recent work in cognitive science suggests that a better understanding of expertise will also lead to a better understanding of creativity.

PRIOR KNOWLEDGE OF THE PROBLEM SOLVER

The chapter on text comprehension contained several examples of how the prior knowledge of the reader influenced comprehension. A particularly striking example was the Bransford and Johnson (1973) study in which it was very difficult for readers to comprehend abstract ideas unless they could relate them to familiar experiences such as washing clothes. The same argument applies to reasoning and problem solving. A task that has abstract or unfamiliar content can be very difficult, compared to the same task with familiar content. This point is illustrated by varying the content of a logical reasoning task called the **four-card selection problem**.

Four-card selection problem A reasoning task that requires deciding which of four cards should be turned over in order to evaluate a conditional rule

Prior Knowledge and Logical Reasoning

Imagine that you are shown four cards, each containing a *D*, a *K*, a 3, or a 7 (Figure 13.1). The experimenter tells you that each card has a letter on one side and a number on the other side and then asks which cards you would have to turn over to determine the truth of the sentence *Every card that has a D on one side has a 3 on the other side.* Try to answer this question before reading further.

The experiment, known as the four-card selection problem, has been analyzed by Wason and Johnson-Laird (1972). It is an example of a conditional reasoning task. The correct answer is that you would have to turn over the cards containing a *D* and a 7. The selection of a *D* is fairly obvious—the rule would be false if the other side of the card did not contain a 3. The rule would also be false if you turned over the card containing the 7 and found a *D* on the other side. It is not necessary to turn over the card containing the 3, although this is a common mistake. The rule does not specify what should be on the opposite side of a 3; it only specifies what should be on the opposite side of a *D*. For example, finding a *K* on one side of the card and a 3 on the other side would not make the rule false.

Experiments using this task reveal that the implications of a conditional rule are not very clear to most people. The combined results of four

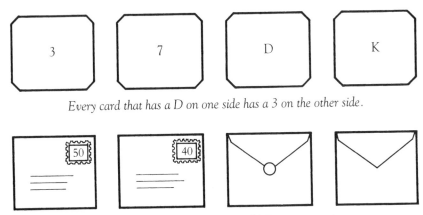

Every card that has a D on one side has a 3 on the other side.

If a letter is sealed, then it has a 50-lira stamp on it.

Figure 13.1   *The four-card selection problem.*

experiments indicated that only 5 of 128 subjects correctly turned over only the two correct cards (Wason & Shapiro, 1971). The most popular choice was to turn over the two cards mentioned in the rule—the letter D and the number 3 for the above example.

Wason and Johnson-Laird (1972) argued that people make mistakes because they seek information that would verify the rule rather than information that would falsify it. Only the latter information is necessary. Turning over the card containing the 3 would verify the rule if a D were found on the other side, but it's not logically necessary to turn over this card since the rule does not specify what should be on the other side. It is necessary to turn over the 7, but people usually overlook this card because they are not seeking ways to disprove the rule.

Wason and Shapiro (1971) hypothesized that the poor performance in this task was due in part to the abstract material. They predicted that using more realistic materials related to everyday knowledge would make the task significantly easier. The realistic rules were of the general form *Every time I go to Manchester I travel by car.* The four cards contained two destinations (Manchester and Leeds) and two modes of transport (car and train). One side of the card specified the destination and the other side the transportation. Of 16 British subjects, 10 selected the two correct cards (Manchester and train) when realistic material was used, compared with only 2 of 16 subjects when abstract material was used.

A problem with even greater appeal as a realistic task is the letter-sorting task used by Johnson-Laird, Legrenzi, and Legrenzi (1972). The subjects were British, and at that time in Britain it cost more to send a sealed letter than an unsealed letter. Subjects in the realistic condition were asked to imagine that they worked at a post office, and their job was to make sure that the letters conformed to each of the following rules: (1) *If a letter is sealed, then it has a 50-lira stamp on it*, and (2) *A letter is sealed only if it has a 50-lira stamp on it.* Two letters were face down, revealing either a sealed or an unsealed envelope, and two letters were face up, revealing either a 40-lira or a 50-lira stamp (see Figure 13.1). Subjects in the symbolic condition were asked to test two abstract rules involving letters with an *A* or a *D* on one side and a 3 or a 5 on the other side. In the realistic condition 17 of the 24 subjects were correct on both rules, compared with none of the 24 subjects in the symbolic condition.

A question raised by these findings is why people improve when they are given realistic information. Do they become better reasoners, or do they recall specific experiences from memory that eliminate the need to reason? Research by Griggs and Cox (1982) initially suggested that the latter explanation is more appropriate. They tested undergraduates at the University of Florida on a variation of the letter task and found that students did as poorly on the realistic task as on the abstract task. Griggs and Cox proposed that the good performance reported by Johnson-Laird and his colleagues could be explained by their British subjects' personal knowledge about the postal rule and its counterexamples. The U.S. subjects, in contrast, lacked personal experience that they could retrieve from memory because U.S. rates are the same for sealed and unsealed letters.

To test the **memory retrieval explanation** for the superiority of realistic materials, Griggs and Cox (1982) gave their subjects a rule that was familiar: *If a person is drinking beer, then the person must be over 19 years of age.* This rule was the law in the state of Florida when the study was conducted. Furthermore, 76% of the subjects later reported that they had personally violated the rule more than once, and 97% of the subjects could remember specific instances of someone other than themselves violating the drinking-age rule. When given the four cards that read DRINKING A BEER, DRINKING A COKE, 16 YEARS OF AGE, and 22 YEARS OF AGE, 29 of 40 subjects made the correct selection for detecting violations of the drinking-age rule (DRINKING A BEER, 16 YEARS OF AGE), whereas none of the 40 subjects did so for the abstract version of the task (*If a card has an A on one side, then it has a 3 on the other side*).

A more recent view, however, is more encouraging about our reasoning abilities than the memory retrieval explanation proposed by Griggs and Cox. According to this view, we posses **pragmatic reasoning schemata** that are general knowledge structures that enable us to reason about a variety of situations that can be interpreted by the schemata (Cheng, Holyoak, Nisbett, & Oliver, 1986). Two examples of pragmatic reasoning schemata are the **permission schema** and the **obligation schema**. The students did well on the drinking-age rule, not only because of their personal familiarity with drinking but because they had a more general understanding of permission. Permission requires that a

Memory retrieval explanation The proposal that people solve reasoning problems about familiar situations by retrieving specific examples from their memory

Pragmatic reasoning schemata Organized knowledge structures used to evaluate practical situations such as seeking permission or fulfilling an obligation

Permission schema Knowledge that taking an action (such as entering a country) requires fulfilling a prerequisite (such as being inoculated)

Obligation schema Knowledge that taking an action (such as paying a pension) is required if a prerequisite (such as retirement) is fulfilled

condition be satisfied (being old enough) before some action (drinking beer) may be taken. According to this hypothesis, people should also do well in evaluating permission statements about situations that are unfamiliar to them. Imagine that you are hired to enforce the rule *If a passenger wishes to enter the country, then he or she must have had an inoculation against cholera.* You are shown the four cards PASSENGER A WISHES TO ENTER THE COUNTRY, PASSENGER B DOES NOT WISH TO ENTER THE COUNTRY, PASSENGER C HAS BEEN INOCULATED, PASSENGER D HAS NOT BEEN INOCULATED. Which cards would you have to turn over to obtain more information in order to enforce the rule?

People should also do well in reasoning about situations that involve obligation, such as *If any urithium miner gets lung cancer, then the company will pay the miner a sickness pension.* An obligation requires that some action (paying a sickness pension) must be taken if some condition (having lung cancer) is satisfied. Research supports the hypothesis that people do much better in evaluating conditional statements about permission and obligation than in evaluating conditional statements about arbitrary relations (Cheng et al., 1986). By the way, the answer to the question in the previous paragraph is that it is necessary to find out more information about passengers A and D by turning over the cards.

Applying Prior Knowledge to Unfamiliar Problems

We would ideally like students to perceive how unfamiliar tasks are related to familiar tasks. They could then apply their prior knowledge to solve unfamiliar problems. Unfortunately, as discussed in the previous chapter, people find it difficult to spontaneously notice an analogy between two problems (Reed, Ernst, & Banerji, 1974; Gick & Holyoak, 1980).

Difficulty in noticing an analogy can occur even when students are very familiar with the analogous problem. One of the experiments on reasoning about the postal regulation was designed to determine if the high level of performance on the postal rule would transfer to the abstract rule (Johnson-Laird et al., 1972). Each subject had two trials with the familiar rule and two trials with the abstract rule. Consistent with the previous results, 22 of the 24 British subjects in this experiment made at least one correct selection with the familiar rule. However, even though they made their selections for the abstract rule immediately afterward, there was no significant transfer from the familiar to the unfamiliar material. Only 7 of the 24 subjects made at least one correct selection for the abstract material.

Johnson-Laird (1989) proposed two reasons for why there was no transfer from the familiar to the unfamiliar task. First, as mentioned in the previous chapter, people often fail to notice analogies because the problems have very different concepts. To notice the analogy between the rules *If a letter is sealed, then it has a 50-lira stamp* and *If a letter has an A on one side, then it has a 2 on the other side*, it is necessary to see the correspondence between *has an A* and *is sealed* and the correspondence between *has a 2* and *has a 50-lira stamp*. Second, even the abstract version of the task may seem easy to people, so they answer quickly without searching for an analogy.

The failure to spontaneously notice a useful analogy is discouraging from an instructional perspective, but research on puzzle problems showed that students were often able to successfully apply an analogy when informed that it was relevant. This research suggests that students might do well on reasoning about complex, unfamiliar problems if the instructor showed how these problems were like more familiar ones. Reed and Evans (1987), in fact, found that students were quite capable of using a familiar analogy to do very well on a complex, unfamiliar task if instructed to use the analogy. The unfamiliar task was to estimate the concentration of an acidic solution formed by mixing together two other acidic solutions. Table 13.1 shows some of the test questions and some principles that were included to help students give accurate estimates. Before reading further, read the principles and then try to answer the test questions.

Table 13.1   *Principles for estimating the concentration of mixtures*

Read the following principles, and then try to answer the test questions.
There are three principles that should help you become a better estimator. Try to follow these principles when you make your estimates. We will illustrate the principles with an example that combines a 25% acid solution with a 45% acid solution to make a 10-pint mixture.

1. If two solutions are mixed together, the concentration of the mixture will be between the concentrations of the two solutions. For example, if a 25% solution is mixed with a 45% solution, the concentration of the mixture will be between 25% and 45%.
2. The concentration of the mixture increases as the proportion of the highest concentration increases. For example, a mixture consisting of 6 pints of the 45% solution and 4 pints of the 25% solution will have a higher concentration than a mixture consisting of 4 pints of the 45% solution and 6 pints of the 25% solution.
3. Identical changes in the proportion of the two solutions produce identical changes in the concentration of the mixture. For example, to make a 10-pint mixture, increasing the 45% solution from 2 pints to 3 pints produces the same increase in the concentration of the mixture as increasing the 45% solution from 7 pints to 8 pints.

Test questions
Estimate the concentration of a mixture when:

1. 1 pint of a 20% concentration is mixed with 9 pints of a 75% concentration
2. 3 pints of a 20% concentration is mixed with 7 pints of a 75% concentration
3. 5 pints of a 20% concentration is mixed with 5 pints of a 75% concentration
4. 7 pints of a 20% concentration is mixed with 3 pints of a 75% concentration
5. 9 pints of a 20% concentration is mixed with 1 pint of a 75% concentration

---

We found that the principles were somewhat helpful, but students' estimates were still not as accurate as we had expected. We therefore tried to use a familiar analogy. We explained the principles by referring to the temperature, rather than the concentration, of the mixture. For instance, the first principle now stated:

1. If two solutions are mixed together, the temperature of the mixture will be between the temperatures of the two solutions. For example, if a 25°C solution is mixed with a 45°C solution, the temperature of the mixture will be between 25°C and 45°C.

We hypothesized that the principles would be much easier to understand in a more familiar situation. Students may not know that the concentration of a mixture is between the concentrations of its two components, but they should know that the temperature of a mixture is between the temperatures of its two components. The results were consistent with our hypothesis. Students gave fairly accurate estimates about the temperature of mixtures before they read the principles and gave very accurate estimates about temperature after reading the principles. They also gave very accurate estimates about the *concentration* of mixtures if we explained the principles in terms of temperature and then told them that the same principles apply to estimating the concentration of mixtures. The more direct approach of explaining the principles in terms of concentration, as shown in Table 13.1, was much less effective in producing accurate estimates of concentration.

Individual Differences in Prior Knowledge

The preceding studies have shown how familiar content enhances people's ability to perform well on a reasoning task. Answers to both logical reasoning problems and mixture problems were more accurate when the problems had familiar content. However, we also saw that it can be difficult to transfer knowledge between two problems that have very different content unless people are explicitly informed that the two problems are solved in the same way. But, as people become better problem solvers and more expert about a particular subject matter, they become more capable of perceiving how problems are related even when they have different content. That is, they become better at classifying problems based on their solutions and are less influenced by the specific story content. A study by Silver (1981) was one of the first to demonstrate this finding.

Silver asked seventh-grade students to form groups of problems that were "mathematically related" and to explain the basis for categorizing them. He used 16 problems that could be represented by a 4×4 matrix.

The four problems in each horizontal row were mathematically related, and the same mathematical procedure could be used to solve each. The four problems in each vertical column described a similar story content but required different procedures to solve them. (The first two problems in Table 13.2 are mathematically related, since the same procedure is used to solve each. The third problem has the same story content as the first but requires a different mathematical procedure.)

Although Silver asked his students to classify mathematically related problems, students who had difficulty perceiving the mathematical structure of the problems might use story content as a basis of classification. Students were asked to solve 12 of the problems after they made their classification in order to determine whether there was any relation between the ability to classify and the ability to solve problems. Silver classified the students as good, average, or poor problem solvers on the basis of the number of problems they solved.

The results indicated that the better problem solvers formed categories on the basis of mathematical structure, and the poorer problem solvers formed categories on the basis of story content. The good problem solvers formed an average of 3.1 categories based on mathematical structure, compared to 1.8 categories for the average problem solvers, and 0.4 category for the poor problem solvers. The opposite trend occurred for story content. The poor problem solvers formed an average of 2.3 categories

Table 13.2   *A word problem and related problems*

Word problem	A farmer is counting the hens and rabbits in his barnyard. He counts a total of 50 heads and 140 feet. How many hens and how many rabbits does the farmer have?
Related structure	Bill has a collection of 20 coins that consists entirely of dimes and quarters. If the collection is worth $4.10, how many of each kind of coin are in the collection?
Related content	A farmer is counting the hens and rabbits in his barnyard. He counts six coops with four hens in each, two coops with three hens in each, five cages with six rabbits in each, and three cages with four rabbits in each. How many hens and how many rabbits does the farmer have?

SOURCE: From "Recall of Mathematical Problem Information: Solving Related Problems," by E. A. Silver, 1981, *Journal for Research in Mathematics Education, 12,* 54–64. Copyright © 1981.

based on story content, compared to 0.6 category for the average problem solvers, and 0.1 category for the good problem solvers.

Similar results were obtained when students were asked to recall information about story problems. Good problem solvers were able to recall information about mathematical structure. Poor problem solvers rarely recalled this information, even when the solutions were discussed prior to their recall. However, they could often remember details about the story content and were sometimes better than the good problem solvers at recalling these details. The results suggest that an important source of individual differences in mathematical problem solving is the ability to categorize problems initially according to the mathematical procedure needed to solve them.

Differences in ability to categorize problems according to their mathematical structure also distinguish novices from experts in more advanced courses. Chi, Glaser, and Rees (1982) asked eight novices and eight experts to sort 24 physics problems into categories based on similarity of solutions. The novices were undergraduates who had recently completed a physics course. The experts were advanced Ph.D. students from the physics department. Each group formed about the same number of categories, but the problems in the categories differed for the two groups. Novices tended to categorize problems on the basis of common objects, such as spring problems and inclined-plane problems. Experts tended to categorize problems on the basis of physics principles that could be applied to solve them, such as the conservation-of-energy law or Newton's second law ($F = MA$). Thus, just as in Silver's (1981) experiment with seventh-graders, the better problem solvers were more sensitive to the formal structure of the problem.

ACQUIRING EXPERTISE

The preceding studies showed how prior knowledge influenced performance on several different kinds of reasoning tasks, including evaluating logical statements, estimating answers to mixture problems, and classifying problems according to their mathematical structure. Prior knowledge also influences how people solve more complex transformation problems, which require constructing a sequence of steps to solve the problem. Early models of problem solving (Newell & Simon, 1972) emphasized general search procedures that used heuristics such as means/end analysis to guide the search. More recent models indicate that, with practice, students can learn specific solutions that replace the less efficient general heuristics (Gick, 1986). This distinction between applying a learned solution and searching for the solution is illustrated in Figure 13.2.

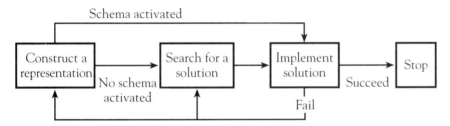

Figure 13.2   *Schematic diagram of the problem-solving process.*
From "Problem-Solving Strategies," by M. L. Gick, 1986, *Educational Psychologist, 21*, 99–120,
Fig. 1. Copyright © 1986 by Lawrence Erlbaum Associates, Inc. Reprinted by permission.

Search versus Implementation

Figure 13.2 shows three major stages in solving a problem (Gick, 1986). The problem solver first attempts to construct a representation of the problem by connecting it to prior knowledge. Certain features of the problem may activate a schema for solving the problem if the problem solver does find a connection with prior knowledge. As we saw in Chapter 9 a *schema* is an organized cluster of knowledge and, in this case it is a cluster of knowledge for a particular problem type. It contains information about the typical problem goals, constraints, and solution procedures for that kind of problem. If schema activation occurs during the construction of a problem representation, the solver can proceed directly to the third stage and implement the solution. There is very little need to search for a solution because the appropriate solution procedures are activated by recognizing the particular problem type.

I have become very proficient at recognizing many types of algebra word problems because I study these problems in my research. When I see an algebra word problem, I usually quickly recognize it as a familiar type and can immediately construct an equation to solve it. But every so often I find an unfamiliar problem that I have to spend some time thinking about before I can solve it. This requires that I search for a solution, which is the second stage in Figure 13.2.

Searching for a solution requires the use of **general strategies** like the ones I discussed in the previous chapter. One strategy is means/end analysis, in which the problem solver attempts to reduce differences between the current problem state and the goal state. A second general strategy is to search for an analogous problem that might provide a useful solution. A third general strategy is planning the solution by breaking down the problem into subgoals.

Gick (1986) emphasizes, however, that general strategies may require some specific knowledge about a problem in order to be successful. For

General strategies
Strategies (heuristics) that apply in many situations but do not always result in a solution

example, planning implies that the problem solver is looking ahead and is not simply taking one step at a time. This, of course, is usually not possible the first time a person encounters a problem. Planning has not been emphasized in much of the research on puzzles because people usually do not have detailed knowledge about how to solve a particular puzzle. Successful models of puzzle solving have therefore been based on general strategies such as means/end analysis (Atwood & Polson, 1976; Simon & Reed, 1976).

A good example of a task that can be accomplished more efficiently through planning is the writing of computer programs (Atwood, Polson, Jeffries, & Ramsey, 1978). The subjects in this experiment were three experienced computer programmers who differed in their knowledge about an assigned task. The task was to write a program that would accept as input the text of a book and would produce as output a list of specified index terms and page numbers on which each term appeared. The results showed that the subjects differed in the extent to which they followed a planning procedure. The protocols of the three subjects showed fairly clear differences in the overall quality, completeness, and organization of their knowledge. The knowledge of one subject was sufficiently developed to allow for the construction of a plan for producing the index. The knowledge of the second subject was less well developed, and, as a result, backtracking was necessary in order to correct deficiencies in the design. The knowledge of the third subject was developed to such an extent that this subject was able to retrieve most of the design directly from memory and therefore required less planning than the other two subjects. These findings suggest that planning is most likely to be carried out by someone who has enough knowledge to approach the task systematically but is unable to retrieve the solution directly from memory.

We can relate these findings to Figure 13.2 by comparing how much each of the three programmers had to rely on a search strategy to solve the problem. The first programmer, who used planning, had partial knowledge about the task. The task activated a schema about designing a book index, but the schema knowledge was not detailed enough to produce a complete solution. Some exploration and search were therefore required in which the partial knowledge guided the search. The second programmer primarily did the task by searching for a solution without the help of a plan. The third programmer could solve the problem by simply implementing the solution from detailed schema knowledge about solving this particular kind of problem.

Learning a Solution

The transition from following a general strategy to applying a specific solution is particularly evident from the study of how people solve physics

---

Table 13.3   *A motion problem*

Problem
A pile driver takes 3.7 sec to fall onto a pile. It hits the pile at 30.4 m/sec. How high was the pile driver raised?

Equations
1. Distance = rate × time
2. Rate = .5 × final rate
3. Final rate = acceleration × time

---

problems. The problems require calculating the value of an unknown variable by using several equations. Table 13.3 shows an example. Before reading further, determine how you would use the equations shown below the problem to calculate the distance the pile driver fell.

Research on how problem solvers solved these problems reveals that novices are more likely to use a general search strategy based on means/end analysis, whereas experts are more likely to **work forward** by referring to the equations in the order that they are actually needed (Larkin, McDermott, Simon, & Simon, 1980). Because the goal is to find the value of the unknown variable, the means/end strategy searches for an equation that contains the unknown variable. The unknown is *distance* in the example problem, so the novice would attempt to use Equation 1 to calculate distance by multiplying rate by time. The value for time (3.7 sec) is stated in the problem, but the value for rate is not stated (30.4 m/sec is the final rate). The novice would then search for an equation that allows calculation of rate. This value is calculated from Equation 2 and then substituted into Equation 1 to solve the problem.

Notice that the novice referred to the equations in the reverse order of how they were actually used. He first referred to Equation 1 because it contained the unknown variable, but he had to calculate a value in Equation 2 before solving Equation 1. In contrast, an expert refers to the equations in the order in which they are needed. An expert would go immediately to Equation 2, calculate rate, and then substitute the value into Equation 1. The expert has learned the correct sequence of steps and doesn't have to search for the solution. Searching for a solution should become more time consuming as the number of equations increases. For instance, if the example problem gave the rate of acceleration rather than the final velocity, it would be necessary to use all three equations.

Research has shown that students switch from a means/end to a working-forward strategy as they become more experienced in solving problems. Sweller, Mawer, and Ward (1983) gave students a series of 25 motion problems like the one in Table 13.3. The average number of solutions

Work forward   Selecting relevant information to solve a problem in the order that it should be used in the solution based on a means/end strategy significantly declined from 3.9 for the first 5 problems to 2.2 for the last 5 problems.

Sweller has argued that, although the means/end strategy is an efficient one for obtaining the goal, it is an inefficient strategy for learning the sequence of steps required to solve the problem. By eliminating differences between the current state and the goal state, the problem solver may rapidly obtain the goal but fail to remember the sequence of steps used. Remembering the steps is difficult because the learner's attention is focused on reducing differences, not on learning steps. Furthermore, reducing differences requires a relatively large amount of cognitive capacity (as we saw in the previous chapter), which is consequently unavailable for learning the solution (Sweller, 1988).

A remedy for encouraging students to learn the correct sequence of steps is to omit the goal by asking them to solve for as many variables as they can, rather than solving for a particular variable. If students were asked to use Equations 1 and 2 in Table 13.3 to solve for as many variables as they could, they would first solve for rate in Equation 2 and then substitute this value into Equation 1 to solve for distance. This approach encourages students to use a working-forward strategy and eliminates the capacity demands of the means/end strategy that make it difficult to learn the correct sequence of steps.

A study of twenty high school students demonstrated the success of this approach (Sweller et al., 1983). Ten of the students were assigned to a goal condition (*Find the distance*), and ten students were assigned to a *nongoal* condition (*Calculate as many variables as you can*). After practicing on solving problems, the students solved two test problems that had a specific goal. Nine of the ten students in the nongoal group solved the test problems by working forward, but only one of the ten students in the goal group solved the problems by working forward. The working-forward strategy helped the nongoal students reduce their search by taking significantly fewer steps in solving the test problems.

Combining Theory and Instruction

We began this chapter with a quote from Don Norman challenging cognitive psychologists to formulate theories that could help people become better learners and problem solvers. Sweller's study demonstrates that psychological theory regarding the capacity demands of the means/end strategy was useful in modifying instruction to improve problem solving. But the most systematic effort to use cognitive theory to improve instruction is the work of John Anderson and his colleagues at Carnegie-Mellon University (Anderson, Boyle, & Reiser, 1985). Their work has focused on the design of intelligent tutoring systems for teaching high school geometry and the LISP programming language. The systems are based on the learning principles of ACT*, a more current version of the ACT theory described in Chapter 9.

ACT* consists of a set of assumptions about both declarative knowledge and procedural knowledge. The assumptions about **declarative knowledge** emphasize the representation and organization of factual information. We looked at this aspect of ACT in Chapter 9 when discussing semantic networks. The assumptions about **procedural knowledge** emphasize how we use this knowledge to carry out various tasks. The procedural assumptions of the theory are particularly relevant for tutoring cognitive skills.

The procedural component of the theory consists of a set of rules (usually called **production rules**) that specify which actions should be performed under a particular set of conditions. A production rule therefore consists of two parts—a condition part and an action part. The action is carried out whenever the condition is satisfied. An example of a production rule is the following:

> IF the goal is to generate the plural of a noun,
> THEN add an *s* to the noun.

Notice that the condition specifies a goal and the action specifies a potential way to achieve the goal.

Production rules provided the basis for constructing a computer tutor that instructs students in how to program in a programming language called LISP. The major theoretical assumptions underlying the construction of the LISP tutor include the following (Anderson, 1990):

1. *Production rules.* A skill like programming can be decomposed into a set of production rules.
2. *Skill complexity.* There are hundreds of production rules that are required to learn a complex skill. This assumption is consistent with the domain-specific view of knowledge.
3. *Hierarchical goal organization.* All productions are organized by a hierarchical goal structure. The condition part of the production therefore specifies a goal, as illustrated above for generating the plural of a noun.
4. *Declarative origins of knowledge.* All knowledge begins in some declarative representation, typically acquired from instruction or example. Before people practice solving problems, they are instructed in how to solve problems.
5. *Compilation of procedural knowledge.* Solving problems requires more than being told about how to solve problems. We have to convert this declarative knowledge into efficient procedures for solving specific problems.

Declarative knowledge Knowledge about factual information

Procedural knowledge Knowledge that relates actions to goals

Production rule A conditional rule that specifies the prerequisite condition for carrying out an action

The LISP tutor consists of 1200 production rules that model student performances on programming problems. It covers all the basic concepts of LISP during a full-semester, self-paced course at Carnegie-Mellon University. It is quite successful. Students who worked on problems with the LISP tutor generally received one letter grade higher on exams than students who had not worked with the tutor.

This success is encouraging, but work continues on improving the theoretical models that can be applied to the construction of effective tutors. One limitation of ACT* as a model of problem solving is that it doesn't provide a good explanation of how people use analogies to solve problems. Anderson and Thompson (1989) report that research on how students construct computer programs and solve mathematical problems revealed that they frequently referred to examples in their textbooks. Anderson and Thompson's goal is therefore to build a theory that uses production systems to represent how people use examples to solve problems. Incorporating these new theoretical ideas about analogy into their instructional programs should further enhance the relation between cognitive theories and computer-assisted instruction.

CREATIVITY

Creativity Creating a novel and useful product or solution

Expertise implies that people are good problem solvers in their area of expertise but doesn't necessarily imply that they are creative. We think of creative problem solvers as being better than simply good problem solvers. **Creativity** implies that the solutions are not simply correct but are both novel and useful. We might even hold a special reverence for creative solutions, believing that they are produced by a mysterious process that requires the ability of a genius to produce them. However, recent work by cognitive scientists suggests that creativity may be less mysterious than we expected. In fact, two recent books even suggest that we can apply what we already know about expertise to explain creativity.

One book, called *Creativity: Beyond the Myth of Genius*, by Weisberg (1993) argues that although the effects of creative ideas are extraordinary, the thought processes that produce them are not:

> Many creative products are indeed extraordinary. They are rare; they are sometimes the result of a lifetime of hard work; they can answer questions that have perplexed people for centuries; they can have far-ranging influence, beyond even the expectations of their creators. It is often assumed that if a creative product has extraordinary effects, it must have come about in extraordinary ways, but that does not necessarily follow. The creative achievement can be extraordinary because of the effect it produces, rather than because of the way in which it was brought about. (p. 10)

Weisberg's "myth of genius" view is based, in part, on his analysis of creative individuals, whose discoveries he felt could be explained by their use of ordinary thought processes. Ordinary thinking goes beyond past achievements, but it does so by slowly accumulating new pieces of information. There are no sudden leaps or unconscious illuminations. Weisberg uses case studies to illustrate that Watson and Crick's discovery of the structure of DNA, the Wright brothers' invention of the airplane, and Picasso's development of a new style of painting occurred through incremental processes that built upon previous work.

I have mixed feelings (elaborated in Box 13.1) about Weisberg's view because of my admiration for highly creative individuals. Perhaps the resolution of the conflict between a great admiration for creative works and the desire to explain their production is contained in the preface to Boden's (1990) book, *The Creative Mind, Myths and Mechanisms*. Boden agrees that creativity is not mysterious and can be explained by the computational concepts of artificial intelligence. But providing explanations,

---

My personal view of creativity

BOX 13.1

I must admit that I have mixed feelings about the view that creativity is often simply good problem solving. As a psychologist whose research has focused on problem solving, I find it gratifying to learn that what we know about problem solving may also help us understand creativity. On the other hand, I have always held such high esteem for creative individuals that I'm not sure that I want to abandon the "myth of genius." When I moved to La Jolla, California, in 1988 I was impressed by the number of creative individuals who had recently lived, or were currently living, in the area. In psychology there was Carl Rogers, the founder of client-centered therapy and the human potential movement. He was awarded both the first Distinguished Professional Award and the Distinguished Scientific Award of the American Psychological Association. I almost heard him speak when I was an undergraduate at the University of Wisconsin. On my way to his lecture, a student asked me if I had heard that President Kennedy had been shot. The lecture was canceled and I never did hear him speak.

In biology there was Jonas Salk, the discoverer of the polio vaccine, who built his Salk Institute in La Jolla. One of its members, Francis Crick, codiscovered the structure of DNA, one of the great discoveries in biology that is often included in biographical accounts of creativity. In business there was Ray Kroc, who built one of the most successful fast-food chains in the world (MacDonald's). But my favorite local resident was Ted Geisel, who is better known by his pen name, Dr. Seuss. I hoped I would get a glimpse of him at some point, and one day found myself driving behind a late-model Cadillac with a personalized license plate that spelled GRINCH. I looked into his car with the same satisfaction as a tourist in Hollywood who had just seen a movie star.

says Boden, should allow us to appreciate the richness of creative thought better than before—even if our sense of mystery is disspelled, our sense of wonder should not be.

Constraining Effects of Examples

Although Weisberg (1993) believes that creative discoveries can often be explained by ordinary thought processes, he admits that highly creative individuals may be exceptional in some respects. Creative individuals are not only experts in their domain but are highly motivated. In contrast to the biographical studies of creativity, laboratory studies have typically studied college students' performance on tasks that do not require much expertise. Although this may limit generalization to the creative thinking of experts, the findings are nonetheless interesting.

The design of these experimental studies are extensions of previous research paradigms in cognitive psychology, modified to emphasize the novelty of the creations. Take the case of using examples. Examples are important in problem solving—they provide the source of analogies in analogical problem solving and are an important source for learning production rules in ACT*. They also can be the source of creative ideas, but there is a subtle difference in how we use examples to solve routine problems and how we use examples to produce creative solutions. When we search for an analogous problem to solve a routine problem, we try to maximize the similarity between the example and test problem in order to minimize the differences in the two solutions. When we use an example to produce something creative, we want to make changes in the example to produce a novel product or solution.

If we are not careful, examples can have a constraining effect on creativity. This is illustrated in a task in which people were given the following instructions:

> Imagine a planet just like Earth existing somewhere in the universe. It is currently uninhabited. Your task is to design new creatures to inhabit the planet. Within the allotted 20 minutes draw as many new and different creatures of your own creative design as you are able. Duplication of creatures now extinct or living on the planet Earth are not permitted. Provide both a side view and front view of each creature. (S. M. Smith, T. B. Ward, & J. S. Schumacher, 1993, p. 839)

One group was then shown the three examples in Figure 13.3 before beginning the task. Their work was compared to that of a control group that received the same instructions without the examples. Would the examples be helpful, as typically found in many studies, or would they stifle creativity by causing the participants to produce "novel" animals that closely resembled the examples? Unfortunately, the examples constrained

Front View   Side View

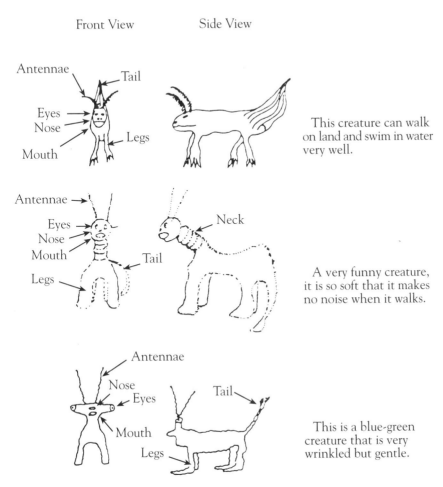

This creature can walk on land and swim in water very well.

A very funny creature, it is so soft that it makes no noise when it walks.

This is a blue-green creature that is very wrinkled but gentle.

Figure 13.3 *Example creatures, along with their labels and descriptions.*
From "Constraining Effects of Examples in a Creative Generation Task," by S. M. Smith, T. B. Ward, and J. S. Schumacher, 1993, *Memory & Cognition, 21*, 837–845. Copyright © 1993 by the Psychonomic Society, Inc. Reprinted by permission.

the productions. The examples group was significantly more likely to draw creatures that had four legs, antennae, and a tail, like those shown in the examples. The same results occurred when participants were instructed to create novel toys. Instructions to create products that differed from the examples had little effect—people were still constrained by the examples.

As I was writing this section I checked the new products section of my local newspaper to see how closely new products resembled old ones.

One product was a small wallet in which credit cards could be kept inside, while dollar bills were clipped on the outside. Because the wallet wasn't folded it was less bulky and could be kept in a shirt or jacket pocket rather than in a pants pocket. This may be enough of a modification to be successful. The other product was motivated by the southern California beach scene in which it is common to see male surfers using a towel wrapped around their waist to change from a wet suit to dry shorts. The new product was actually a new use of an old product, as it was a skirt with an elastic band to replace the towel. In this case the new product too closely resembled the old product. The surfers said they would rather take a chance on the towel slipping than wear a skirt.

Inventing Products through Imagery

Another example of a novel research program on creativity that grew out of previous paradigms in cognitive psychology is the work of Finke (1990). Finke has been one of the main contributors to a theory of visual imagery, and he utilized his expertise in this area to extend imagery paradigms to the study of creativity. Writings by Shepard (1988) and others had indicated that many famous scientific discoveries depended on visual imagery. For instance, Einstein reported that his thought experiments relied on imagery. Imagining the consequences of traveling at the speed of light helped him formulate his special theory of relativity. Faraday claimed to have visualized force lines from electric and magnetic fields, leading to the modern theory of electromagnetic fields. Kekule reported that his discovery of the molecular structure of benzene occurred after he imagined a snake coiled in a circle.

Finke (1990) extended previous studies on the visual synthesis of artificial patterns (such as those by Palmer, 1977) to determine whether people could visually combine basic parts to create useful and novel products. The object parts consisted of such basic forms as a sphere, half sphere, cube, cone, cylinder, rectangular block, wire, tube, bracket, flat square, hook, wheels, ring, and handle (somewhat like the geons in Biederman's [1985] theory of pattern recognition that was discussed in Chapter 2). After either the experimenter or the subject selected three parts, the subjects were instructed to close their eyes and imagine combining the parts to make a practical object or device. They had to use all three parts but could vary their size, position, and orientation. The created object had to belong to one of eight categories: furniture, personal items, transportation, scientific instruments, appliances, tools or utensils, weapons, and toys or games.

Judges then scored the created objects on a 5-point scale for practicality and for originality. Strict criteria were used—the average rating for practicality had to be at least 4.5 to be classified as practical, and the average rating for originality had to be at least 4.0 to be classified as original. In one condition subjects were allowed to select their own parts but were told the category of their invention (such as appliances). In another condition they were allowed to invent an object that belonged to any one of the eight categories, but were told which parts to use (such as half sphere, wheels, and hook). In the most restrictive condition they were told both the parts to use and the category of their invention (use a half sphere, wheels, and a hook to make an appliance). Although the number of inventions scored as practical was approximately the same across the three conditions, the most restrictive condition resulted in the highest number of creative inventions, judged to be both practical and original. The more restrictive the task, the more difficult it was to think of an object that satisfied all the criteria and was like existing objects.

There is, however, an even more restrictive condition than assigning both the parts and category. In another experiment people were again given the parts, but didn't find out about the category until *after* they had assembled their object. Finke (1990) refers to these objects as **preinventive forms** because their use cannot be identified until after the object is constructed. Figure 13.4 shows how a preinventive form that was assembled from a half sphere, bracket, and hook could be used for each of the eight categories. The results demonstrated that this was the most successful condition of all for generating creative inventions.

Preinventive form
Creating an object before determining its use

Figure 13.4   *Multiple interpretations of a single preinventive form (assembled from a half sphere, bracket, and hook). The interpretations are lawn lounger (furniture), earrings (personal items), water weigher (scientific instruments), portable agitator (appliances), water sled (transportation), rotating masher (utensils), ring spinner (toys), and slasher basher (weapons).*

From *Creative Imagery: Discoveries and Inventions in Visualization*, by R. A. Finke, Fig. 7.24. Copyright © 1990 by Lawrence Erlbaum Associates, Inc. Reprinted by permission.

Generation strategy
A strategy for producing preinventive forms

Exploration strategy
A strategy for determining how to use a preinventive form

Even in the less constraining conditions, however, many subjects reported that they preferred to initially use a **generation strategy** in which they imagined interesting combinations of parts, followed by an **exploration strategy** in which they figured out how to use the invented object. Finke, Ward, and Smith (1992) describe these two phases in their Geneplore (generation-exploration) model shown in Figure 13.5.

In the initial phase, the inventor forms preinventive structures that are then explored and interpreted during the second phase. The preinventive structures are the precursors to the final, creative product and would be generated, regenerated, and modified throughout the cycle of invention. Finke, Ward, and Smith (1992) recommend that people should place greater emphasis on generating preinventive structures and then later think of possible uses. Notice that this is contrary to the usual order in which we begin with a particular use in mind—a wallet that fits in a shirt pocket or a garment that allows us to change clothes at the beach—and then try to invent something to accomplish our goal. There is an interesting analogy here between the recommended strategy and the no-goal condition of Sweller, Mawer, and Ward's (1983) research in which people benefited from an initial goal-free exploratory phase. But how successful this approach is in designing creative products remains to be seen.

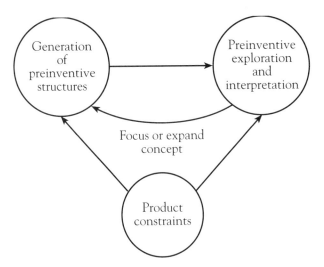

Figure 13.5   *The basic structure of the Geneplore (generation-exploration) model.*

From *Creative Cognition: Theory, Research, and Applications,* by R. A. Finke, T. B. Ward, and S. M. Smith. Copyright © 1992 by MIT Press. Reprinted by permission.

Before concluding, it is worth reflecting again on the differences be-tween the biographical and laboratory approaches to studying creativity. Is there any similarity between how students design a product in a brief psychology experiment and how experts design products in their profes-sion? I think there are some similarities. Let me describe these similarities by considering a product that I admire for both its beauty and function, the Emerald-Shapery Center in San Diego. The design consists of eight six-sided towers combined in clusters to form larger towers (Figure 13.6).

Besides their aesthetic appeal, the hexagonal shapes have advantages for both construction and the quality of the interior spaces. All horizon-tal building faces are the same size, allowing for construction savings from

Figure 13.6   *The Emerald-Shapery Center, San Diego.*
Permission granted by the Pan Pacific Hotel.

the standardization of parts. In addition, there is more window surface area per square foot of floor space than in conventional, rectangular buildings. Every room opens toward the windows, creating a more open, spacious environment than suggested by the physical dimensions.

As has been pointed previously in biographical studies (Weisberg, 1993) and in S. M. Smith, T. B. Ward, and J. S. Schumacher's (1993) research, creative ideas typically build on previous examples. The developers of the Emerald-Shapery Center worked out the basic ideas for the design by following Frank Lloyd Wright's philosophy that good architecture often results from studying nature. In particular, many crystals have a hexagonal structure and this formed the basis for selecting the parts. A hexagonal tower was the starting point but the architects still needed to combine the towers to make an aesthetically pleasing and functional design. Synthesizing objects from their parts, of course, has been the focus of Finke's (1990) research and I suspect that the generative-exploratory phases of the Geneplore model provide a good framework for studying this process.

As I look back at progress in cognitive psychology, I like to identify the major advances in each decade of its short history. For problem solving, the 1970s saw extensive work on how people use general heuristics to search problem spaces. The 1980s witnessed research on how acquisition of domain-specific knowledge is required to become an expert. The 1990s should make up for cognitive psychologists' late start in the study of creativity by contributing new insights about this important topic.

SUMMARY

Our ability to reason and solve problems is influenced by the familiarity of the material. For instance, correctly evaluating the implications of a logical rule depends on whether the semantic content of the rule is abstract (*If a card has a D on one side, then it has a 3 on the other side*) or familiar (*If a person is drinking beer, then the person must be over 19 years of age*). Answers are more accurate for familiar content than for unfamiliar content, and showing students how an unfamiliar task is isomorphic to a familiar task can vastly improve performance on the unfamiliar task. As students acquire expertise, they become better at identifying the formal structure of problems and are less influenced by story content.

Acquiring expertise also results in a change in strategies for how students solve transformation problems. Novices rely on general search strategies such as means/end analysis to search for equations to solve physics problems. In contrast, experts use a working-forward strategy because they have learned the correct order for using equations. Using means/end analysis can interfere with learning a correct sequence of operations because of the cognitive demands of applying a means/end strategy. Requesting that students solve for a variety of unknown variables, rather than for a specific unknown variable, prevents them from using means/end analysis and facilitates learning the correct sequence of operations. However, the most comprehensive program of using cognitive theory to improve instruction involves applying the learning principles of ACT* to assist students in learning to program in LISP and to solve geometry problems.

The early results are now in on a cognitive theory of creativity. They suggest that creativity may not be all that mysterious and that it may simply be good problem solving. A big difference, however, between standard solutions and creative solutions is that creative solutions are novel. This means that our solutions must not be constrained by previous examples. Mental imagery has played an important role in some creative discoveries and is now being analyzed by asking people to create products by mentally synthesizing parts. Limiting the parts that people can use and the categories of their inventions makes the task more difficult, but the product more likely to be novel. The successive generation and exploration phases of developing ideas is captured in the Geneplore model.

STUDY QUESTIONS

1. Where do you stand on the issue of how much time should be allotted to teaching problem solving strategies versus subject-matter instruction? Do you think your academic life would have been more productive if you had had a course in reasoning and problem solving? What's the research on this question?

2. Much of the existing experimental evidence on logical reasoning makes most of us out to be pretty dim bulbs. Is that a fair characterization, or is there some other plausible explanation for the miserable showing?

3. The chapter on Semantic Organization (Chapter 9) listed various characteristics of schemata. Do the permission and obligation schemata proposed by Cheng and her colleagues have these characteristics?

4. Reed and Evans (1987) were successful in teaching students the principles of mixing acid solutions by using the analogy of mixing different quantities of water that also differed in temperature. Think of some unfamiliar domain that you were better able to understand by using an analogy to a familiar domain. Explain your reasoning.

5. Perhaps some members of your class have already completed a course in statistical methods, while others have not. If that is the case, you might compare the two groups' estimates of some simple measures,

such as central tendency and dispersion of class heights. Would you predict a difference in accuracy? Why or why not?

6. Apply Gick's (1986) schematization of the problem-solving process, shown in Figure 13.2, to predict your own performance in these circumstances: choose two specific content domains in which you have widely different degrees of expertise, and make up a test question for each. How would you proceed in your attempt to solve each problem?

7. How does working forward differ from means/end analysis? Which strategy depends on schema activation?

8. From its earliest beginnings U.S. psychological science has exhibited a penchant for studying "the mind in use." Can you make a case for ACT* fitting into this tradition, broadly conceived? Try your hand at the most basic level of application by writing a production rule or two for a grammar to be programmed into a computer tutor for English.

9. Weisberg claims that creativity can be explained by current theories of problem solving. What relation do you see between creativity and theories of problem solving?

10. Why do you think that creativity was stimulated by telling people the functional category of their invented object *after* they had assembled it? Is this result related to the finding that familiar examples can constrain our ability to invent novel examples?

KEY TERMS

The page number in parentheses refers to where the term is discussed in the chapter.

creativity (400)
declarative knowledge (399)
domain-specific knowledge (386)
exploration strategy (406)
four-card selection problem (387)
general strategies (395)
generation strategy (406)
memory retrieval explanation (389)

obligation schema (389)
permission schema (389)
pragmatic reasoning schemata (389)
preinventive forms (405)
procedural knowledge (399)
production rule (399)
work forward (397)

RECOMMENDED READING

Galotti (1989) contrasts formal reasoning with everyday reasoning, and Kuhn (1989) reviews research on scientific reasoning. Holyoak and Spellman (1993) summarize much of the current thinking about thinking. Paige and Simon (1966) and Hinsley, Hayes, and Simon (1977) discuss cognitive processes in solving algebra word problems. The effect of meaningfulness on solving algebraic equations has been studied by Mayer and Greeno (1975) and by Kieras and Greeno (1975). Mayer and Greeno (1972) have also investigated how different instructional procedures influence what people learn about a mathematical formula called the binomial theorem. More recently, the construction of geometry proofs (Lewis & Anderson, 1985) and social science problems (Voss, Greene, Post, & Penner, 1983) have also been studied. The differences between experts and novices continue to be a popular topic of investigation in areas such as physics (Larkin, McDermott, Simon, & Simon, 1980) and computer programming (Adelson, 1984). A two-volume series, *Thinking and Learning Skills* (Segal, Chipman, & Glaser, 1985; Chipman, Segal, & Glaser, 1985), contains many interesting chapters. Books by Roskos-Ewoldsen, Intons-Peterson, & Anderson (1993) and Finke (1990) elaborate on the material presented in the last section of this chapter.

Decision Making

I cannot, for want of sufficient premises, advise you what to determine, but if you please I will tell you how. . . . My way is to divide half a sheet of paper by a line into two columns; writing over one Pro, and over the other Con. Then, doing three or four days' consideration, I put down under the different heads short hints of the different motives, that at different times occur to me for or against the measure. When I have thus got them all together in one view, I endeavor to estimate the respective weights . . . [to] find at length where the balance lies. . . . And, though the weight of reasons cannot be taken with the precision of algebraic quantities, yet, when each is thus considered, separately and comparatively, and the whole matter lies before me, I think I can judge better, and am less liable to make a rash step; and in fact I have found great advantage for this kind of equation, in what may be called moral or prudential algebra.

BENJAMIN FRANKLIN (1772/1887)

*E*VERY DAY WE MAKE many decisions. Most of these are relatively unimportant—what to eat for breakfast, for example. Others—such as selecting a car, a home, or a job—are more important. Making decisions is often difficult because each alternative usually has many aspects, and very seldom does the best alternative excel over all others. One way to simplify the decision process is to emphasize only a single aspect. Box 14.1 illustrates this approach. The Morrisons evaluated many features before buying a house, but they made their final selection on the basis of just one—the quality of the local school. Although this is a very important consideration for parents with school-age children, there was such a small difference in the quality of the schools that the Morrisons really overemphasized this feature.

The first section of this chapter describes models of how people select from a set of alternatives. Examples include selecting a dinner from a menu, a home, or a car. These models do not consider probabilities because they assume that a person knows the values of relevant dimensions, such as price, gas mileage, and optional equipment in the case of buying a car. The following two sections are concerned with examples of risky decision making—those in which the decision maker must consider probabilities. We will first examine how people make probability estimates, including ways they revise their estimates when they receive new information. We will then consider how people use the estimates to make decisions. The study of decision making has been influenced by both normative and descriptive models. **Normative models** specify what a person should do. They often provide a standard for comparing how closely actual decisions match normative decisions. **Descriptive models** seek to describe how people actually arrive at decisions. The relation between normative and descriptive models is a theme that occurs throughout the discussion of risky decision making. The final section of the chapter discusses medical and action-based decision making as examples of complex skills. The discussion illustrates how psychological models can be used to describe each of these skills.

Normative models
Models that describe what people should do

Descriptive models
Models that describe what people actually do

MAKING CHOICES

Compensatory Models

One reason decisions can be difficult is that alternatives usually have many attributes. If one of the attributes is not very attractive, the decision maker must decide whether to eliminate that alternative or continue to consider it because its other attributes may be very attractive. For example, a person may buy a car with low gas mileage because of the

Dream home bypassed for school

KATHY O'TOOLE
EDUCATION WRITER

**BOX
14.1**

Mike and Patty Morrison had hopes this time of getting their dream home—a new one, with carpeting in just the colors they wanted, with a fireplace in the family room and a breakfast area in the kitchen.

The Morrisons, newcomers from southern California with two pre-school children, found their dream home in a new San Ramon subdivision.

But they didn't buy it.

The house lacked one feature. It wasn't near the elementary school whose pupils had the highest test scores in the San Ramon School District.

Instead, the Morrisons bought a more expensive home in Walnut Creek with a floor plan they didn't like, and the carpet a color they didn't like.

They made their decision based on standardized school test score information supplied by a San Ramon Valley real estate agent, Sherry Schiff.

The Morrisons' decision illustrates the relatively small differences parents sometimes consider in deciding what home to buy.

In state reading tests given last May, third-graders at the school near the home the Morrisons bought scored higher than those in 91 percent of the state's schools. The third-graders at the school near the home the Morrisons preferred scored better than those in 84 percent of the schools.

The Morrisons and their real estate agent have played a meaningless statistical game, contend several testing experts for East Bay school districts and the state Department of Education.

The test scores of the two schools compared were so close, say the test experts, that they can't possibly tell parents in which school their child will do better.

SOURCE: From "Dream Home Bypassed for School," by Kathy O'Toole, appearing in the *Oakland Tribune*. Copyright © 1979 by the Oakland Tribune. Reprinted by permission.

---

smooth ride and spaciousness of a large car. Decision-making models that allow attractive attributes to compensate for unattractive ones are called **compensatory models**. The advice by Benjamin Franklin quoted at the beginning of this chapter is consistent with a compensatory model because Franklin combined the pros and cons of each option.

An **additive model** is a kind of compensatory model. An additive model combines the attractive and unattractive attributes to arrive at a total score for each alternative. Consider the case of John Smith. John has lived in a college dormitory for 3 consecutive years. It is now his senior year, and he feels that it is time to enjoy the greater freedom that an apartment can offer. He has found two rather attractive apartments and must select one. John decides to follow Ben Franklin's advice and systematically

Compensatory model
A strategy that allows positive attributes to compensate for negative ones

Additive model   A strategy that adds attribute values to assign a score to each alternative

list the advantages and disadvantages of each. First he lists the attributes that will influence his decision, and then he rates each on a scale that ranges from –3 (a very negative impression) to +3 (a very positive impression). Here are his ratings:

	Apartment A	Apartment B
Rent	+1	+2
Noise level	–2	+3
Distance to campus	+3	–1
Cleanliness	+2	+2
	+4	+6

The sums of the ratings for the various attributes of the two apartments reveal that John's best choice is to select apartment B, which is rated higher.

There are two ways of modifying the summation rule that could change the results. First, the four attributes were equally weighted in the example. If some attributes are more important to John than others, he will want to emphasize these attributes when making his decision. For instance, he might want to emphasize distance from campus if he lives in a cold climate and has to walk to classes. If this variable is twice as important as the others, he could multiply his ratings of distance by 2 to give this dimension greater emphasis. The sum of the ratings would then be +7 for apartment A and +5 for apartment B. Second, adding the ratings of the four attributes does not account for how the attributes might interact. Although apartment A is very noisy, it is so close to campus that the library would be a convenient place to study. The high noise level is therefore not as detrimental as it would be if the apartment were the only convenient place for studying. The low rating for noise level should perhaps be modified to take into account the interaction between that dimension and distance to campus.

Additive-difference model   A strategy that compares two alternatives by adding the difference in their values for each attribute

A model that is very similar to the additive model is called the **additive-difference model.** The latter compares two alternatives by totaling the differences between their values on each attribute. The values on each attribute are shown below. The third column shows the value obtained by subtracting the second column from the first.

	Apartment A	Apartment B	Difference
Rent	+1	+2	–1
Noise level	–2	+3	–5
Distance to campus	+3	–1	+4
Cleanliness	+2	+2	+0
	+4	+6	–2

The sum of the differences is –2, which implies that apartment A is 2 units less attractive than apartment B. The additive model implies the same conclusion—the sum of the ratings for apartment A is 2 less than the sum of the ratings for apartment B. Although the additive and the additive-difference models result in the same conclusion, the search for information is different. The additive model evaluates all attributes of one alternative before considering the next alternative. The additive-difference model compares the two alternatives attribute by attribute. If there are more than two alternatives, a given alternative is compared with the best of the preceding alternatives.

Both the additive and the additive-difference models describe a good procedure for evaluating alternatives. Both evaluate alternatives on all their attributes and allow attractive values to compensate for unattractive values. The models can be used to make realistic decisions, as Box 14.2 illustrates. Box 14.2 describes an additive model in which points are assigned to six attributes depending on how much information each provides. The decision to proceed with further investigation is based on the sum of the points.

Although Ben Franklin's advice is good, we may question how often we follow it. The examples show that the additive model provides a systematic procedure for making decisions, but are we really this systematic in making decisions? How often do we take the time to make the kind of calculations required by the models? Perhaps some other model might better describe how we actually make choices. The alternative to a compensatory model is a **noncompensatory model**, in which unattractive attributes result in eliminating alternatives.

Noncompensatory Models

If we do not calculate, how do we make decisions? A. Tversky (1972) has proposed that we make choices by gradually eliminating less attractive alternatives. His theory is called **elimination by aspects** because it assumes that the elimination is based on the sequential evaluation of the attributes, or aspects, of the alternatives. If the attribute of an alternative does not satisfy some minimum criterion, that alternative is eliminated from the set of choices.

Consider Ms. Green, who is looking for a car. If Ms. Green has only $9,000 to spend, she may first eliminate from her set of possible choices those cars that cost over $9,000. She may also be interested in gas economy and eliminate cars that cannot travel at least 25 miles on a gallon of gas. By continuing to select attributes and rejecting those that do not satisfy some minimum criterion, she will gradually eliminate alternatives until there is only a single car remaining that satisfies all her criteria.

The final choice, based on this procedure, depends on the order in which the attributes are evaluated. If the price of the car is one of the last

Noncompensatory model   A strategy that rejects alternatives that have negative attributes without considering their positive attributes

Elimination by aspects   A strategy that evaluates one attribute at a time and rejects those alternatives whose attribute values fail to satisfy a minimum criterion

Report says police can predict which burglaries can be solved

WASHINGTON (AP)—A new study indicates that police can reliably predict which bur-glaries can be solved and recommends that they stop investigating cases unlikely to lead to an arrest.

The report, released yesterday by the Police Executive Research Forum, said "the characteristics of burglary cases, not follow-up investigations, determine the overall success or failure rate of burglary investigations."

The FBI reported there were 3.1 million burglaries in 1978, but fewer than one in five led to an arrest. It is the most common felony crime in the United States.

The study recommends police departments consider six key elements of pre-liminary burglary reports to decide whether to investigate further.

The forum, a national organization of state and local police executives, used police personnel in 26 cities, including Toledo, to test a rating system first developed in 1972 by the Stanford Research Institute. . . .

The six elements and the numerical value assigned to them were:

Police arrival at scene: Five points for police arrival less than 1 hour after the crime; one point for arrival between 1 and 12 hours after the crime; three-tenths of a point for arrival 12 to 24 hours afterward; no points for arrival more than 24 hours later.
Seven points for a civilian witness report.
One point if a policeman discovered the crime.
Seven points for usable fingerprints of a stranger at the scene.
Nine points for the name or description of a suspect.
One-tenth of a point for a description of a suspicious vehicle at the scene.
No points for all other information.

If the preliminary report had a total value of ten points or less, the study pre-dicted further investigation would not lead to an arrest. It predicted an arrest if the total was more than ten points.

Analyzing the results of 12,001 past burglary investigations, the forum found that its method of weighing the factors was 85% accurate in predicting which cases led to a suspect being arrested, charged, and turned over for prosecution.

Under the screening procedure used by the forum, 86.7% of the burglary cases would not be assigned for further investigation.

SOURCE: From "Report Says Police Can Predict Which Burglaries Can Be Solved," appearing in the *Plain Dealer,* Cleveland, Ohio, January 28, 1980. Copyright © 1980 by Associated Press. Reprinted by permission of Associated Press Newsfeatures.

attributes Ms. Green evaluates, she might have eliminated all cars costing under $9,000 early in her decision process—an undesirable situation if she has only $9,000 to spend. The model therefore proposes that the at-tributes differ in importance, and the probability of selecting an attribute for evaluation depends on its importance. If price is a very important at-tribute, it has a high probability of being selected early in the sequence.

The elimination-by-aspects model has the advantage that it does not require any calculations. The decision maker simply selects an attribute according to some probability that depends on the importance of that attribute. She then determines whether an alternative satisfies a minimum criterion for that attribute and eliminates those alternatives that do not meet the criterion.

The **conjunctive model**—a variant of elimination by aspects—requires that all the attributes of an alternative satisfy minimum criteria before that alternative can be selected. It differs from elimination by aspects by proposing that people finish evaluating one alternative before considering another. The first alternative that satisfies all the minimum criteria is selected. The conjunctive model is an example of what Simon (1957) has called a **satisficing search**. Simon argued that limited capability to evaluate many alternatives often prevents people from selecting the best alternative. Instead, they are willing to settle for a good alternative—that is, one that satisfies all the minimum criteria. Other constraints, such as limits in time or availability, may also influence us to choose a good alternative rather than wait for the best alternative. For example, we may simply become tired of looking at apartments, or an apartment we liked may be rented by the time we return, so we will choose an available alternative rather than continue searching for a better one.

Conjunctive model   A strategy that evaluates one alternative at a time and rejects it if the value of one of its attributes fails to satisfy a minimum criterion

Satisficing search   A strategy that follows the conjunctive model and therefore selects the first alternative that satisfies the minimum criterion for each attribute

Selecting a Strategy

The four models we have looked at differ with respect to how people search for information. Payne (1976) took advantage of this difference in designing a procedure for finding out which strategies people use. He presented information describing the attributes of apartments, such as rent, cleanliness, noise level, and distance from campus. The information describing each apartment was printed on the back of a card, which had to be turned over in order to reveal its value (see Figure 14.1). Subjects were allowed to turn over as many cards as they needed to make their decision. The order in which they turned over the cards should reveal how they

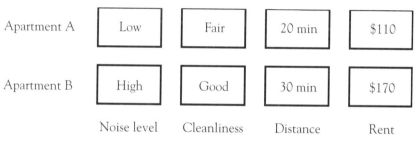

Figure 14.1   *Information search task used by Payne.*

searched for information. Payne gathered additional evidence about how they arrived at a decision by asking them to think aloud as they evaluated the information on the cards.

Payne did not expect that everyone would follow the same strategy in searching for information. His expectations were influenced by work on problem solving that showed how individuals adapted their strategies to the demands of the task. An important characteristic of people's problem-solving strategies is that they attempt to keep the demands of the task within a limited capacity. Payne argued that the heuristics used by decision makers should also be adaptive to the information-processing demands of the task. One implication of this view is that the decision maker might change strategies as the demands of the task change.

Payne's results supported his expectations. Students were given a variety of tasks that differed in both the number of alternatives (2, 4, 8, or 12) and the number of dimensions (4, 8, or 12). The principal finding was that the students changed strategies as the number of alternatives decreased. The search strategies and verbal protocols revealed that, when asked to evaluate many alternatives, the subjects reduced the complexity of the task by using the conjunctive or elimination-by-aspects procedure to eliminate some of the alternatives quickly. When only a few alternatives remained in the choice set, the subjects might then use one of the cognitively demanding procedures—such as the additive or additive-difference strategy—to make the final evaluation and choice.

The following excerpt from a protocol illustrates the use of the elimination-by-aspects model to reduce the number of alternatives:

> I'm going to look at landlord attitude. In H it's fair. In D it's poor. In B it's fair, and in A it's good. In L the attitude is poor. In K it's poor. In J it's good, and in I it's poor. . . . So, that's important to me. . . . So, I'm not going to live any place where it's poor. (Payne, 1976, p. 379)

The subject never again examined alternatives D, I, K, and L.

Contrast that protocol with this excerpt illustrating the use of the additive-difference model to compare two alternatives:

> O.K., we have an A and a B. First look at the rent for both of them. The rent for A is $170 and the rent for B is $140. $170 is a little steep, but it might have a low noise level. So we'll check A's noise level. A's noise level is low. We'll go to B's noise level. It's high. Gee, I can't really very well study with a lot of noise. So I'll ask myself the question, is it worth spending that extra $30 a month for, to be able to study in my apartment. (p. 378)

The two protocols reveal how a low value on a dimension results in elimination of an alternative in the elimination-by-aspects model. However, when the additive-difference model is used, an alternative scoring low on one dimension might still be selected if it scores high on other dimensions; in the example above, the decision requires determining whether a lower rent will compensate for a high noise level.

The additive and additive-difference strategies are cognitively demanding because they require that the decision maker compute values to represent the attractiveness of each alternative. Although they allow for the careful evaluation of each alternative, their greater complexity may result in decisions that are not any better than decisions made by following a simpler strategy, such as elimination by aspects.

One way to compare the effectiveness of the different strategies is to train several groups of people to make decisions by following a particular strategy and then evaluate the quality of their decisions. Paquette and Kida (1988) used this approach to compare the relative effectiveness of the additive, additive-difference, elimination-by-aspects, and mixed strategies. The mixed strategy, based on Payne's finding that people switch strategies, initially used the elimination-by-aspects strategy followed by the additive strategy when the number of alternatives was reduced to three.

The subjects were 48 professionals who had experience at evaluating a firm's financial characteristics. They were given financial data on firms and had to select the one with the highest bond rating by following the strategy taught to them during the training session. The experimenters could then evaluate the accuracy of the selections because they knew the bond rating of each firm. They found no significant differences in the accuracy of the four strategies, but the simpler elimination-by-aspects strategy required significantly less time to make a decision than the more demanding additive and additive-difference strategies. For this particular task the elimination-by-aspects strategy was a highly efficient one.

ESTIMATING PROBABILITIES

We turn now to a somewhat more complex problem: making decisions under conditions of uncertainty. There was some amount of uncertainty in the previous examples. Although the location of an apartment is not likely to change, the noise level can change as the neighbors change. **Uncertainty** is a major factor in the examples discussed in the rest of the chapter and requires that people estimate the probability that a certain event will occur because they do not know which event will occur.

Uncertainty Lacking knowledge about which events will occur

Kahneman and Tversky (1972, 1973; Tversky & Kahneman, 1973) have shown that probability estimates are based on *heuristics* that sometimes yield reasonable estimates but often do not. Two of these heuristics are availability and representativeness. Before reading further, answer the questions in Box 14.3 to determine how you might use these heuristics.

**BOX
14.3**

Questions about subjective probabilities

1. How many cities that begin with the letter *F* do you think you can recall? Give your estimate before you start recalling examples.
2. Are there more words in the English language that start with the letter *K* or that have a *K* as their third letter?
3. Which is the more likely cause of death—breast cancer or diabetes?
4. If a family has three boys (B) and three girls (G), which sequence of births is more likely—B B B G G G or B G G B G B?
5. Are you more likely to find 60 boys in a random sample of 100 children or 600 boys in a random sample of 1000 children?

Availability

Availability heuristic
The ease with which estimating probability by examples can be recalled

The **availability heuristic** proposes that we evaluate the probability of an event by judging the ease with which relevant instances come to mind (A. Tversky & D. Kahneman, 1973). For example, we may assess the divorce rate in a community by recalling divorces among our acquaintances. When availability is highly correlated with actual frequency, estimates should be accurate. But there are other factors besides actual frequency that can influence availability and cause systematic biases.

In the first experiment conducted by Tversky and Kahneman (1973), subjects were shown 9 letters, which were to be used to construct words. They were given 7 sec to estimate the number of words they believed they could produce in 2 min. The average number of words actually constructed varied from 1.3 (for the letters XUZONLCJM) to 22.4 (for TAPCERHOBO). The correlation between the estimates and the number of words produced over 16 problems was .96.

In another experiment subjects were asked to estimate the number of instances they could recall from a category in 2 min. The average number of instances recalled varied from 4.1 (city names beginning with the letter *F*) to 23.7 (four-legged animals). The correlation between estimation and word production was .93 over 16 categories. The high correlation between estimation and production revealed that subjects were quite accurate in estimating the relative availability of instances in the different conditions.

Some instances, however, might be difficult to retrieve from memory even though they occur frequently. The availability hypothesis would predict that frequency should be underestimated in this case. Suppose you sample a word at random from an English text. Is it more likely that the word starts with a *K* or that *K* is its third letter? The availability hypothesis proposes that people try to answer this question by judging how easy it is to think of examples in each category. Since it is easier to think of words that begin with a certain letter, people should be biased toward responding that more words start with the letter *K* than have a *K* in the third position. The median estimated ratio for each of five letters was that there were twice as many words in which that letter was the first letter, rather than the third letter, in the word. The estimates were obtained despite the fact that all five letters are actually more frequent in the third position.

Slovic, Fischhoff, and Lichtenstein (1976) have used the availability hypothesis to account for how people estimated the relative probability of 41 causes of death—including diseases, accidents, homicide, suicide, and natural hazards—that were combined into 106 pairs. A large sample of college students judged which member of the pair was the more likely cause of death; Table 14.1 shows how often they were correct as a function of the relative frequency of the two events. Examination of the events most seriously misjudged provided indirect support for the hypothesis that

Table 14.1   *Judgments of relative frequency for selected pairs of lethal events*

Less Likely	More Likely	True Ratio[a]	Percent of Correct Discrimination
Asthma	Firearm accident	1.20	80
Breast cancer	Diabetes	1.25	23
Lung cancer	Stomach cancer	1.25	25
Leukemia	Emphysema	1.49	47
Stroke	All cancer	1.57	83
All accidents	Stroke	1.85	20
Pregnancy	Appendicitis	2.00	17
Tuberculosis	Fire and flames	2.00	81
Emphysema	All accidents	5.19	88
Polio	Tornado	5.30	71
Drowning	Suicide	9.60	70
All accidents	All diseases	15.50	57
Diabetes	Heart disease	18.90	97
Tornado	Asthma	20.90	42
Syphilis	Homicide	46.00	86
Botulism	Lightening	52.00	37
Flood	Homicide	92.00	91
Syphilis	Diabetes	95.00	64
Botulism	Asthma	920.00	59
Excess cold	All cancer	982.00	95
Botulism	Emphysema	10,600.00	86

SOURCE: From "Cognitive Processes and Societal Risk Taking," by P. Slovic, B. Fischhoff, and S. Lichtenstein, 1976, in *Cognition and Social Behavior*, edited by J. S. Carroll and J. W. Payne. Copyright © 1976 by Lawrence Erlbaum Associates, Inc. Reprinted by permission.
[a]1.20 means 1.20:1, and so on.

availability, particularly as influenced by the media, biases probability esti-mates. The frequencies of accidents, cancer, botulism, and tornadoes—all of which receive heavy media coverage—were greatly overestimated. Asthma and diabetes, which receive less media coverage, were underesti-mated. Similarly, the spectacular event of fire—which often takes many victims and receives much media coverage—was perceived as consider-ably more frequent than the less spectacular event of drowning, even though they are about equally frequent causes of death.

A more selective effect of availability on probability estimates is illus-trated by research on how our mood influences estimates. Emotions can have a substantial impact on the kind of information that people retrieve from LTM. A happy mood makes it more likely that we will recall posi-tive events and a sad mood makes it more likely that we will recall nega-tive events (Blaney, 1986). The greater availability of positive events in memory should increase our estimates that more positive events will oc-cur in the future, and the greater availability of negative events in memory should increase our estimates that negative events will occur.

Wright and Bower (1992) tested these hypotheses by inducing a happy mood or a sad mood in their subjects through hypnosis. The sub-jects then estimated the probability of occurrence of 24 events, some of them positive events (*I will win an important honor or award during the next year*) and some of them negative events (*I will be seriously injured within the next 5 years*). The results were consistent with the prediction of the avail-ability hypothesis. The mean estimate of a positive event occurring was .52 for people in a happy mood and .38 for people in a sad mood. The mean estimate of a negative event occurring was .52 for people in a sad mood and .37 for people in a happy mood. Notice that these results present a challenge for therapists: It may be necessary to change someone's sad mood before convincing them that the future will be brighter.

Representativeness

Representativeness is another heuristic that we use to make probability judgments. You may have used this heuristic to answer Question 4 in Box 14.3. The question asks *If a family has three boys (B) and three girls (G), which sequence of births is more likely—B B B G G G or B G G B G B?* Sub-jects in a study by Kahneman and Tversky (1972) estimated that the se-quence of boy/girl births in the order B G G B G B was significantly more likely than the order B B B G G G, even though the two sequences are equally probable. Three boys followed by three girls appeared too orderly to have been generated by a random process.

The bias toward selecting the unorderly sequence as more probable can be explained by the representativeness heuristic (Kahneman & Tversky, 1972). Questions about probabilities typically have the general form: (1) What is the probability that object A belongs to class B? or (2) What is the probability that process B will generate event A? People frequently answer such questions by evaluating the degree to which A is **representative** of B—that is, the degree to which A resembles B. When A is very similar to B, the probability that A originates from B is judged to be high. When A is not very similar to B, the probability that A originated from B is judged to be low.

> **Representative** The extent to which an event is typical of a larger class of events

We expect that the birth order of boys and girls should form a random pattern. A major characteristic of apparent randomness is the absence of any systematic patterns. The representativeness heuristic therefore predicts that people should judge orderly events as having low probability if they believe the events were generated by a random process. Although there are many sequences of boys and girls that are unorderly, a particular unorderly sequence (such as B G G B G B) is as difficult to obtain as a particular orderly sequence (such as B B B G G G).

One problem with basing decisions solely on representativeness is that the decisions ignore other relevant information, such as *sample size*. For example, finding 600 boys in a sample of 1000 babies was judged as likely as finding 60 boys in a sample of 100 babies, even though the latter event is much more likely. Because the similarity between the obtained proportion (.6) and the expected proportion (.5) is the same in both cases, people do not see any difference between them. However, statisticians tell us that it is easier to obtain a discrepancy for small samples than for large samples.

Another situation in which the representativeness heuristic can cause faulty estimates is when we ignore probabilities entirely by basing our decision only on the similarity between an instance and a concept (Kahneman & Tversky, 1973). Imagine that a team of psychologists has administered personality tests to 30 engineers and 70 lawyers. I then randomly choose the following description from the 100 available descriptions:

> Jack is a 45-year-old man. He is married and has four children. He is generally conservative, careful, and ambitious. He shows no interest in political and social issues and spends most of his free time on his many hobbies, which include home carpentry, sailing, and mathematical puzzles. The probability that Jack is one of the 30 engineers in the sample of 100 is ——%.

Imagine now that you have the same description but were told that 70 of the 100 descriptions came from engineers. *What is the probability that Jack is one of the 70 engineers in the sample of 100?* The average estimate was identical for both questions. People estimated the probability of Jack's being an engineer as .9, which reflected that the personality description matched their concept of an engineer more closely than their concept of a lawyer. But notice that there was a difference between the two cases—in the first case there were 30 engineers in the sample of 100, and in the second case there were 70 engineers in the sample of 100. The probability that Jack is an engineer is influenced both by the number of engineers in the sample (called the **prior probability**) and by the personality description. We should use the personality description to revise the prior probabilities, rather than entirely ignore the prior probabilities.

I mentioned in the chapter on problem solving that heuristics are often useful but do not guarantee success. Similarly, the availability and representativeness heuristics can mislead us if we do not consider relevant information such as how the media may influence the availability heuristic and how prior probabilities and sample size should influence the representativeness heuristic. We can learn to give more accurate estimates if we learn what variables should influence our estimates.

Prior probability The probability that an evident will occur before obtaining additional evidence regarding its occurrence

EXPECTED VALUE

Estimating probabilities accurately is an important decision-making skill, but it is not sufficient for making good decisions. Consider a situation in which U.S. oil interests in the Middle East are threatened. The response to this situation will depend in part on the probability that the threat is a real one. But the response also depends on the perceived consequences of various courses of action that the government might take. For example, one response might be to increase U.S. military forces in the Middle East. This course of action, like other alternative actions, has both advantages and disadvantages. It is therefore necessary to assess both the probability of events and the consequences of various actions when making decisions.

When we considered the different choice models in the first section of this chapter, we assigned values to the different dimensions of each alternative in the choice set. It is also necessary to assign values in risky decision making, but in addition we have to combine the values of the different outcomes with the probabilities that they will occur. A normative procedure for combining probabilities and values is called **expected value**. Like other normative models, expected value provides a standard of reference against which psychologists can compare how people make decisions. Psychologists have usually made this comparison by designing rather simple gambling situations in which they can inform people about probabilities (of winning and losing) and values (amount won or lost). The expected value is the average amount of money people can expect to win or lose each time they decide to gamble. Let us see how it is calculated.

Expected value The average value, as determined by combining the value of events with their probability of occurrence

Calculating Expected Value

Expected value is calculated by multiplying the value of each possible outcome by its probability and adding the products. Its use can be illustrated by a simple game. I'm going to offer you the opportunity to play the game, and you must decide whether it would be to your advantage to play. I'm going to roll a fair die. If a 6 appears, you win $5. If any of the other five numbers appear, you win nothing. It costs $1 every time you play. Should you participate?

Expected value allows you to estimate the average amount of money you can expect to win or lose on every roll of the die. You can calculate this amount if you know the probability of a win, $P(W)$; the amount of a win, $V(W)$; the probability of a loss, $P(L)$; and the amount of a loss, $V(L)$. Substituting these amounts into the equation below yields

$$\text{Expected value} = P(W) \times V(W) \ + \ P(L) \times V(L)$$
$$= \frac{1}{6} \times \$4 \ + \ \frac{5}{6} \times -\$1$$
$$= -\$\frac{1}{6}$$

The probability of a win is 1/6, and the amount of a win is $4 ($5 minus the $1 entry fee). The probability of a loss is 5/6, and the value of a loss is $1. The expected value of this game is –$1/6, implying that you would lose an average of about 17¢ every time you played the game. A decision based on a normative model should be to play the game for a positive expected value and not to play the game for a negative expected value.

A problem with using expected value as a descriptive model is that it does not always predict behavior. Gambling casinos are usually crowded with people playing games that have negative expected values. People also buy insurance in spite of its negative expected value. Since insurance companies pay out less money in claims than they collect in premiums, a purchaser of insurance can expect to lose money. And yet the purchase of insurance can be justified on the basis that it provides protection against a large financial setback.

Subjective Expected Utility

Two changes were made in the concept of expected value in order to make it more descriptive of actual behavior (Payne, 1973). The first change replaced the value of an outcome by its utility. **Utility** is the subjective value of an outcome, or what the outcome is actually worth to an individual. If people enjoy gambling, the act of gambling has utility over

Utility Subjective value as determined by the decision maker

and above the money that is won or lost. If you enjoy winning money and don't mind losing money, then you could formulate a positive expected utility for the game I described earlier. If the utility of a win—$U(W)$—is $6 rather than $4, and the utility of a loss—$U(L)$—remains at $1, the expected utility would be positive rather than negative.

$$\text{Expected utility} = P(W) \times U(W) \ + \ P(L) \times U(L)$$
$$= \frac{1}{6} \times \$6 \ + \ \frac{5}{6} \times -\$1$$
$$= \$\frac{1}{6}$$

The expected-utility model could also explain why people buy insurance if they are more concerned about losing a substantial amount of money at one time than about paying out the much smaller premiums each year.

Another reason why utilities or subjective values are important is that we often do not know what objective value to place on an event. The point is illustrated by Box 14.4, which raises the difficult issue of the

BOX 14.4

Critics want government to put a standard price on human life

K<small>NIGHT</small>-R<small>IDDER</small> N<small>EWS</small> S<small>ERVICE</small>

W<small>ASHINGTON</small>, DC—What's a life worth? In Washington, it all depends on whom you ask.

At the U.S. Consumer Product Safety Commission, a human life is valued at a cool $2 million. But at the Environmental Protection Agency, one of us is worth four times that, while the Nuclear Regulatory Commission splits the difference at $5 million.

The price of a life is the centerpiece of Washington's ultimate numbers game—cost-benefit analysis—a duel of statistics that too often leaves health and safety short-changed, critics say.

Federal officials routinely use such numbers to justify decisions on life and death issues—whether your child rides in a safety seat on an airplane, how polluted the air you breathe is, whether the place you work is safe. The cost of the proposed regulation is weighed against the lives, expressed in dollars, it would save.

Agency economists and other observers defend putting price tags on people as necessary yardsticks in an era of mega-deficits.

"There have to be trade-offs," argues Marvin Fell, a veteran federal economist with the U.S. Coast Guard. "If it costs $50 million to save a man's life, is it worthwhile if you could spend it on AIDS research or vaccinations?"

Even the most vociferous critics of pricing human lives agree that the government must weigh the costs against benefits in making decisions on parceling out finite tax dollars.

monetary value of a human life. To determine whether the benefits of some life-saving device will exceed its cost, it is necessary to estimate how many lives will be saved and how much a life is worth.

A second change in the expected-value model was to make it more descriptive by replacing probabilities with **subjective probabilities**. When decision makers don't know the actual probabilities, they must use subjective probabilities, or what they think the actual probabilities are. As we learned in the previous section, subjective probabilities often differ from actual probabilities. In addition to the possible biases introduced by using the availability and representatives heuristics, the wording or framing of the decision task can influence subjective probabilities. A. Tversky and D. Kahneman (1981) use the term **decision frame** to refer to the decision maker's conception of the acts, outcomes, and contingencies associated with a particular choice.

The following example shows how the formulation of the problem influences the frame adopted by the decision maker (Dunegan, 1993). The subjects were 128 members of an international company that develops high-technology engineering systems. The subjects read a scenario in which a project team was requesting an additional $100,000 for a project

Subjective probabilities Estimated probabilities as determined by the decision maker

Decision frame Decision maker's conception of the decision-making situation

---

But, they argue, any cost-benefit analysis must be based on a standard value for human life—and reflect not just lives lost but catastrophic medical costs for injuries and the less tangible impact on the quality of life.

Cost-benefit analysis, first used to justify dam construction a century ago, sparked hot debates in the 1980s as a chief weapon in Ronald Reagan's campaign for deregulation. Marching to his Executive Order 12291, issued February 17, 1981, all federal agencies began weighing costs against the benefits before writing new regulations.

Under the rule, the benefits must outweigh the costs. Thus, a regulation costing $100 million is acceptable only if it would save 20 lives valued at $5 million each, or 50 lives valued at $2 million.

For example, after 51 construction workers died in 1978 when a scaffold collapsed at a power plant in Willow Island, West Virginia, the Occupational Safety and Health Administration proposed new safety rules the agency said would save on average 23 lives a year and cost industry $27.3 million.

Since OSHA valued a life at $3.5 million, the regulation easily passed the cost-benefit test. But the Office of Management and Budget, the administration's regulatory gatekeeper, stepped in with a new price on a construction worker's life—$1 million, based on its own research—that stalled the rules for years.

SOURCE: From "Critics Want Government to Put a Standard Price on Human Life," appearing in the *San Diego Union,* July 14, 1990. Reprinted by permission of Knight-Ridder Newspapers.

begun several months before. Everyone read the same scenario except for the last sentence. The last sentence for half of the participants read *Of the projects undertaken by this team, 30 of the last 50 have been successful* (a positive frame). The other half read *Of the projects undertaken by this team, 20 of the last 50 have been unsuccessful* (a negative frame). Notice that the probability of successfully completing a project is .6 for both cases, but the positive frame mentions the 60% success rate and the negative frame mentions the 40% failure rate. People given the positive frame allocated significantly more money to the project than people given the negative frame. Such findings indicate that we should be more accurate in predicting people's decisions if we used their subjective probabilities rather than the actual probabilities

Subjective expected utility is calculated the same way as expected value, but the actual probabilities are replaced by subjective probabilities (SP), and the values are replaced by utilities. The subjective probability of each outcome is multiplied by its utility, and the products are added.

Subjective expected utility = $SP(W) \times U(W) + SP(L) \times U(L)$

By replacing probabilities with subjective probabilities and values with utilities, the subjective expected-utility model bases its predictions on subjective information. Therefore it should be more accurate than the expected-value model in predicting people's decisions. Like the expected-value model, however, it assumes that people place an equal emphasis on the four components—$U(W)$, $SP(W)$, $U(L)$, and $SP(L)$. It also implies that people have to calculate since it is necessary to multiply the utility of events by their subjective probabilities.

Information-Processing Models

We learned earlier that decision rules like elimination by aspects or the conjunctive rule simplify decision making by allowing the decision maker to eliminate alternatives without having to calculate. When evaluating the attractiveness of a gamble, people are likely to consider the probability of winning, the amount of a win, the probability of losing, and the amount of a loss. But they may find it difficult to mentally compute expected value or even to place equal emphasis on the four **risk dimensions**, as implied by the model.

Slovic and Lichtenstein (1968) tested the hypothesis that people will be more influenced by some dimensions than others. They had subjects evaluate the attractiveness of gambles, using a special type of gamble illustrated in Figure 14.2. A duplex gamble requires that the subject spin two spinners. The first spinner determines whether he will win money, and the second spinner determines whether he will lose money. There are four possible outcomes for the gamble shown in Figure 14.2: win $1 and lose $4

Subjective expected utility A variation of expected value that uses utilities and subjective probabilities instead of values and probabilities

Risk dimensions The components of a gamble such as the probability of winning and the amount of a loss

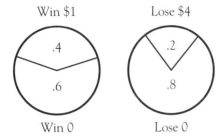

Win $1   Lose $4

.4   .2

.6   .8

Win 0   Lose 0

Figure 14.2   *Example of a duplex gamble where P(W) = .4, V(W) = $1, P(L) = .2, and V(L) = $4.*

From "Relative Importance of Probabilities and Payoffs in Risk Taking," by P. Slovic and S. Lichtenstein, 1968, *Journal of Experimental Psychology Monograph*, 78 (3, Pt. 2). Copyright © 1968 by the American Psychological Association. Reprinted by permission.

(a net loss of $3), win $1 and lose nothing, win nothing and lose nothing, or win nothing and lose $4. Slovic and Lichtenstein used **duplex gambles** in order to change the probability of winning and the probability of losing independently. This is not possible in a standard gamble (represented by only one spinner) because the probability of winning is equal to 1 minus the probability of losing. It is not possible to determine whether people are more influenced by the probability of winning or the probability of losing if the two probabilities cannot be varied independently.

Slovic and Lichtenstein used two methods to evaluate the attractiveness of gambles. One method used a simple rating scale that varied from –5 (strong preference for not playing) to +5 (strong preference for playing). The second method required that subjects indicate the largest amount of money they would be willing to pay the experimenter in order to play the gamble (for attractive gambles) or in order to not have to play the gamble (for unattractive gambles). In both cases Slovic and Lichtenstein correlated the judged attractiveness of the gambles with the four risk dimensions. The correlations should be approximately equal if people were placing an equal emphasis on all four dimensions. The results indicated that there was a large difference in the correlations. A subject's highest correlation was, on the average, twice the size of the lowest correlation. The responses of many subjects were determined by one or two risk dimensions and were unresponsive to changes in the values of the less important dimensions.

The data also revealed that the particular dimension emphasized varied across subjects and that the most important dimension was influenced

Duplex gamble   A gamble in which the probability of winning is assigned independently of the probability of losing

by whether the subject responded with a numerical rating or a monetary response. Table 14.2 shows that, when subjects used a rating scale, the probability of a win was the most important dimension for 50% of the subjects. When subjects responded in terms of the amount of money they would be willing to pay the experimenter (bid), the amount of a loss was the most important dimension for 53% of the subjects. In other words, the response scale influences the way a gamble is evaluated. When responses were expressed in terms of money, subjects attended more to a monetary dimension—$V(L)$—than when the responses were numerical ratings.

Normative models cannot explain either the finding that people place an unequal emphasis on the risk dimensions or the finding that the dimension emphasized is influenced by the response scale. If people are not following normative models, do their ratings of relative attractiveness differ from the relative attractiveness of the gambles as determined by expected value? The average correlation between subjects' ratings and expected value was .79 for numerical ratings and .80 for monetary ratings. The correlations indicate that the expected-value model is a fairly accurate predictor of ratings even though subjects attend more to some dimensions than to others. Although models based on expected value are often useful in predicting responses, results like those obtained by Slovic and Lichtenstein help reveal how people simplify the task and how their decisions depart from expected value.

To summarize, expected-value models are reasonably good, although not perfect, predictors of some decisions. The predictions can often be improved when utilities are substituted for values and subjective probabilities for probabilities. It should also be possible to improve the models' predictions by taking into account the fact that people may emphasize some dimensions of risk more than others.

Table 14.2 *Percent of subjects for whom a given risk dimension was most important*

	Risk Dimension			
	$P(W)$	$V(W)$	$P(L)$	$V(L)$
Rating group	50	9	15	26
Bidding group	18	19	10	53

SOURCE: From "Relative Importance of Probabilities and Payoffs in Risk Taking," by P. Slovic and S. Lichtenstein, 1968, *Journal of Experimental Psychology Monograph, 78* (3, Pt. 2). Copyright © 1968 by the American Psychological Association. Reprinted by permission.

APPLICATIONS

Our emphasis so far has been on examining decision making within simple, but well-controlled laboratory experiments. Cognitive psychologists, of course, hope their theories have some relevance to the real world, and decision making is no exception. In this concluding section, we will look at how some of these ideas are being applied to more complex situations. The first section looks at how physicians arrive at a medical diagnosis. The second section presents current views about what people do in situations in which they must make a series of rapid decisions, without much time for reflection. The third section describes a schema-based model of decision making that I use to integrate some of the research described in this chapter.

Medical Diagnosis

Medical diagnosis is an excellent example of a complex skill that we can relate to many of the issues raised in this chapter. The book *Medical Problem Solving* (Elstein, Shulman, & Sprafka, 1978) summarizes the results of an extensive study of how doctors arrive at a diagnosis. The book is significant not only because of the importance of medical decision making but also because the results are discussed within the context of models of human information processing and normative decision making.

Elstein and colleagues report a series of experiments using various methodologies. Some experiments used actors who played the role of patients; others simply used written descriptions of symptoms. Some allowed the physicians to request whatever information they wanted; others presented information in a fixed order. Some studied what the physicians did; others attempted to train medical students to become better decision makers.

I will summarize the results of one experiment that used high-fidelity simulation that attempted to create a situation closely resembling the actual world of the physician. Actors from the theater department at Michigan State University were carefully trained to simulate patients. The cases were based on actual clinical records and presented problems that a general internist practicing in a community hospital could expect to see. Each physician could decide how much information to collect, including the results of (simulated) laboratory findings. The physicians knew the cases were simulated, but most of the 24 who participated thought the simulations were convincing.

The interactions between physicians and patients were recorded on videotape. The physicians were instructed to think aloud during the interaction and comment on what they had learned or were about to do and why. Additional information was obtained after the session, when an experimenter questioned each physician while both reviewed the videotape.

The simulation experiment presented three cases, all played by college students. The first case was a female student with three main complaints—extreme fatigue and excessive sleeping, poor appetite, and severe headache. Further history showed mild chills and fever with general aching of about 5 days' duration. Information that could be obtained from a physical examination included enlarged tonsils and mild jaundice.

Table 14.3 shows the most frequent hypotheses for this case and the number of physicians who considered each during different stages of the examination. The initial hypotheses are general—infection, for example. One of the major findings across all the simulation experiments was that physicians start to form hypotheses early in the examination, before they have much information. The number of physicians who generated at least one hypothesis during the first 5 min was 20 (of 24) in Simulation 1, 18 in Simulation 2, and 23 in Simulation 3. The process of gathering data can be thought of as a search through a large search space. If the physician simply gathered data unsystematically until a solution emerged, the search space would be so large that a diagnosis could never be reached in

Table 14.3   *Hypotheses considered during various stages of a diagnosis*

Hypothesis[a]	Total at Any Point	At First Hypothesis	At Quarter Mark	At Halfway Mark	At Conclusion
Infection[b]	21	14	15	19	5
Infectious mononucleosis	20	2	9	15	20
Infectious hepatitis	18	5	9	11	5
Hemolytic anemia	17				
Hereditary spherocytic anemia	10				8
Viral illness or viral respiratory infection	8		4	6	1
Meningitis	7		5	4	0
Anemia	6			3	
Influenza	4		3	1	0
Encephalitis	4		2	3	0
Leukemia	4			1	0
Lymphoma	4		0	0	1

SOURCE: From *Medical Problem Solving* by A. S. Elstein, L. S. Shulman, and S. A. Sprakfa, 1978, Cambridge, MA: Harvard University Press. Copyright © 1978 by the President and Fellows of Harvard College. Reprinted by permission of the publishers.
[a]Twelve hypotheses in addition to those listed were each considered by one or two subjects at some point in the problem.
[b]Includes acute febrile illness, viral illness, bacterial infection, and viral respiratory infection.

a reasonable amount of time. Forming hypotheses early in the sequence guides the acquisition of additional data, thus limiting the search by verifying or modifying current hypotheses. Table 14.3 reveals that the number of physicians who considered mononucleosis as a hypothesis increased as additional data were obtained.

The number of hypotheses considered at any one time was very consistent across problems; the means ranged between two and four. On all three simulations the average number of hypotheses considered at any one time remained relatively constant through various stages of the examination, implying that, when a hypothesis was rejected, it was replaced by another or by a reformulation of the rejected hypothesis. It is likely that the hypotheses serve as organizers of data in STM, since the range of two to four is consistent with the number of chunks of complex material that can be retained at once in memory (Simon, 1974).

A central issue in the study was how physicians combine information to form hypotheses. Elstein and colleagues' search for a model that describes what physicians do, rather than what they ought to do, began with the observation that in all the protocols the physicians were consistently able to rank hypotheses but were unable to give more precise estimates of probability.

The physicians did, however, spontaneously classify the cues as positive, negative, or noncontributory for each hypothesis. A simple additive model (in which cues that were interpreted as positive evidence were rated +1, cues that were interpreted as negative evidence were rated −1, and noncontributory cues were rated 0) was fairly successful in predicting which hypotheses would be selected. Note that this procedure is identical to the one suggested by Ben Franklin. Although it is possible to use probabilities in medical diagnosis, physicians apparently use a much simpler procedure to evaluate hypotheses. The simpler procedure avoids the cognitive demands of estimating the initial probabilities of diseases and revising the probabilities on the basis of evidence.

Because of the cognitive demands of complex decision making, people occasionally resort to using **decision aids** to help them make better decisions. For instance, it might be helpful if physicians had the aid of a computer-based system in making diagnoses. An example is described in Box 14.5. Future research should help us decide how human and computer can best work together to make important decisions (see Kleinmuntz [1990] for a recent summary of the effectiveness of decision aids).

Decision aid A tool for helping people make better decisions

Action-based Decision Making

Earlier in this chapter we reviewed some initial research by Payne (1976) that indicated that decision makers adapt their strategies to the demands of the task, selecting a simpler strategy when task complexity increased.

**BOX
14.5**

Personal computers help diagnose illness

WILLIAM HARWOOD
UNITED PRESS INTERNATIONAL

GAINESVILLE—A computer scientist and a physician have joined forces to develop a pioneering system to save time and money by letting doctors double-check their diagnoses on inexpensive personal computers.

Unlike other, more extensive diagnostic systems under development that require costly "main frame" computers, the system being designed at the University of Florida will run on IBM personal computers and compatible machines.

Doctors and hospitals could use the same computer to keep office records and patient information. "One of our aims was to try to develop a system that would be inexpensive that individual physicians would be able to afford," said Douglas Dankel, a University of Florida computer scientist who is working with Julian Russo, a St. Petersburg physician, to develop the system.

Most medical database computer systems are designed to mimic the process a doctor goes through to reach a diagnosis by analyzing all the available data. Using the Florida system, doctors would propose a diagnosis and then answer questions from the computer to confirm it.

Once the program is loaded, the computer asks for the patient's name and an identification number. It then asks the user to enter the patient's weight, height, temperature, race, and sex and if the doctor has a preliminary diagnosis.

"Then the system would go through a series of questions, first off presenting all of the primary criteria that would need to be satisfied for the patient to have that particular disease," Dankel said.

The doctor can answer yes, no, or unknown. He also can ask the computer why it wants the information and an answer is provided.

"If the physician says yes, all of those criteria are satisfied, the system says you have a confirmation of the disease and if a treatment's warranted, it will present a treatment to the physician."

If the doctor answers no to any of the primary criteria, for example, because a lab test has not been conducted yet, the computer will ask more detailed questions.

The program then gives the probability of the patient having the disease and "it specifies any additional laboratory tests that it sees might be required," Dankel said. The final program also will suggest alternate diagnoses.

The continuation of this work was recently summarized in a book called *The Adaptive Decision Maker* (Payne, Bettman, & Johnson, 1993) in which the authors argue that decision makers are guided by the dual goals of maximizing accuracy and minimizing effort, causing them to emphasize different strategies in different situations. The more adaptive decision makers are those who are most efficient in balancing both accuracy and effort. For instance, processing becomes less extensive under time pressure, causing decision makers to simplify their strategies.

The previous example of medical decision making involved a situation in which physicians had the luxury of time. They could carefully examine the patient and wait for the outcome of lab tests before making a diagnosis. But what about those physicians who work in emergency rooms and face emergency cases in which someone is barely clinging to life? Time is no longer a luxury, and decisions have to be made quickly before life slips away.

Here's another scenario that requires a series of rapid decisions (Orasanu & Connolly, 1993). A fire fighting crew arrives at a four-story apartment building, the scene of a reported fire. The commander sends his crew into the first and second stories to extinguish the fire, but they report that the fire has spread beyond the second floor. Observing smoke pouring from the eaves, the commander calls for a second unit. He also orders his crew to stop trying to extinguish the fire and to search the building for people trapped inside.

This scenario comes from the first chapter of a book called *Decision Making in Action: Models and Methods* (Klein, Orasanu, Calderwood, & Zsambok, 1993). The central argument of the book is that the traditional models and methods for studying decision making are not very helpful in explaining what people do in these kinds of emergency situations. The reason is that the traditional approach has focused on only one particular type of decision making—the **decision event**. The decision event consists of a situation in which the decision maker evaluates a fixed set of alternatives according to stable criteria, and differentially weights and combines these criteria to select the best alternative. Most of the tasks that we previously considered, such as selecting the best apartment, are good examples of a decision event.

Decision event Making a single decision, rather than a sequence of decisions, in a changing situation

In contrast, emergency situations have a number of characteristics that distinguish them from the more traditional tasks that we have already considered. For example:

1. Emergency situations typically involve *ill-structured problems* in which the decision maker has to do significant work to generate hypotheses about what is happening. The fire commander knew almost nothing about the extent of the fire when he arrived at the scene.
2. Decision making occurs within an *uncertain, dynamic environment*. Information about what is happening is often incomplete, ambiguous, and/or of poor quality. The environment may also change quickly, as when a small fire suddenly becomes a large fire.
3. There may be *shifting or competing goals*. Goals in the above scenario would include saving the building, the occupants, and the crew.

These goals can shift as the fire grows, from saving the building to saving the occupants to saving the crew.

4. Responses to emergency situations require reacting to a sequence of events rather than to a single event. This creates *action/feedback loops* in which the decision maker has to react to the consequences of each action before determining the next action.

5. There is often considerable *time pressure*. Lack of time will typically produce less complicated reasoning strategies and perhaps high levels of personal stress.

6. There are *high stakes*. One obviously wants to avoid mistakes in life-threatening situations.

7. Often there are *multiple players*. Although there is usually a single person in charge, the leader interacts with others to solve the problem.

8. *Organizational goals* guide the decision making. Unlike the personal life decisions that we all face, medical and fire fighting personnel are guided by rules set by others in the organizations.

Recognition-primed decisions Decisions that are quickly made following recognition of a situation

One of best-known models of how people make decisions in these situations is the **recognition-primed decision (RPD)** model proposed by Klein (1993). The starting premise is that people who make decisions in these situations are typically very experienced. They are therefore capable of responding more quickly than the less experienced subjects tested in laboratory studies. There is, of course, a parallel here to the novice-expert difference that we saw in the previous two chapters on problem solving.

Klein initially formulated the RPD model after interviewing how fire ground commanders made choices. Rather than evaluate many alternatives, they reported that they used their prior experience to immediately generate and modify plans in reaction to the changing situation. The model is called a *recognition-primed* model because of the emphasis it places on situation assessment and recognition of what is occurring. Once the problem is recognized, experienced decision makers can usually identify an acceptable course of action as the first one they consider, rather than having to consider multiple options.

Notice that there are several reasons why this is a plausible strategy in these circumstances. First, expertise allows the decision maker to avoid considering many alternatives that would have a low probability of working. Second, there is not enough time to allow for a thorough consideration of many options. Third, Klein proposes, as did Simon many years earlier, that decision makers usually try to find a *satisfactory* course of action, not the best alternative. This allows them to respond more quickly than if they had to select the best strategy.

I want to conclude by presenting a general schematic framework for decision making that was developed to account for the more traditional (decision event) studies. However, the framework is broad enough that we can use it to contrast different models of decision making, including the RPD model. It was developed to account for how we all make important life decisions, so we will look at that particular application before contrasting it with other applications.

A Schematic Framework

To obtain a more complete picture of how people make major decisions during the course of their lives, we would need to know more about their beliefs and values, their plans and goals, and their evaluations of previously made decisions. This section presents a general, schema-based framework for considering these issues.

We have previously learned how organized knowledge structures in LTM influence our performance on complex tasks such as text comprehension and problem solving. Such clusters of knowledge, or *schema*, also influence how we make decisions. L. R. Beach and T. R. Mitchell (1990; Mitchell & Beach, 1990) describe a theory of decision making that was influenced by Payne's (1976) findings but provides a more general framework for how people make important decisions.

Their theory consists of knowledge structures called *images*. The images are not visual or sensory images but images of one's self and of the goals that one would like to achieve. These images influence how we both make decisions and monitor the progress of our decisions. Beach and Mitchell call the theory **image theory** because of the important role that these images play in influencing our decisions.

Figure 14.3 shows the main components of image theory, including the three kinds of images that guide our decisions. The **value image** consists of an individual's guiding beliefs and basic values. It includes principles that influence the selection of goals and actions to achieve the goals. The goals are part of the **trajectory image**, which consists of a person's future agenda—the landmarks one hopes to achieve along an idealized life course. Goals can be either specific concrete events, such as landing a particular job, or abstract states, such as becoming more self-reliant. The **strategic image** consists of plans that are chosen for achieving the goals. A plan consists of a sequence of actions that are part of a unitary activity such as trying to keep a job, avoid bankruptcy, or be a good parent.

As Figure 14.3 illustrates, the images influence two general kinds of decisions—adoption decisions and progress decisions. **Adoption decisions** involve the selection of a particular course of action. Both the compatibility and the profitability of the alternatives determine which alternative is selected. **Compatibility** measures the extent to which each alternative is consistent with our images. If there are too many violations, the alternative is rejected. The compatibility criterion is noncompensatory—the

Image theory A general framework for modeling decisions by considering a person's values, plans, and future goals

Value image A person's basic beliefs and values

Trajectory image A person's future agenda and life goals

Strategic image Plans for achieving these goals

Adoption decision Initial selection of a course of action

Compatibility Determining whether a course of action is consistent with a person's beliefs and values

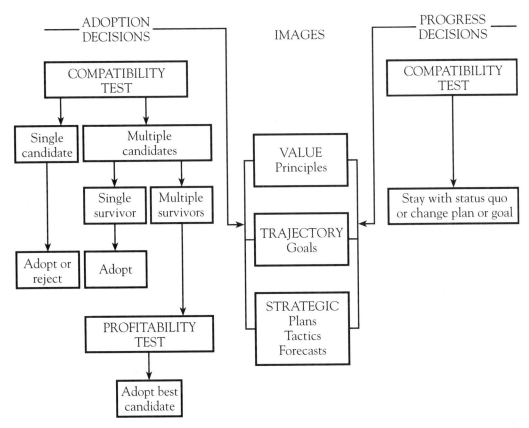

Figure 14.3   *The components of image theory.*

From "Image Theory: A Behavioral Theory of Decision Making in Organizations," by L. R. Beach and T. R. Mitchell, 1990, in *Research in Organizational Behavior, Vol. 12,* 1–41, edited by B. Straw and L. L. Cummings. Copyright © 1990 by JAI Press Inc. Reprinted by permission.

compatible aspects of an alternative do not compensate for the noncompatible aspects. It is therefore similar to the elimination-by-aspects and conjunctive decision rules (described in a previous section).

If more than one alternative is compatible with a person's beliefs and goals, the person tries to select the best alternative by using the profitability criterion. **Profitability** is more difficult to evaluate than compatibility because selecting the best candidate requires multiple judgments about each alternative, a summary of those judgments, retention of the summary, and a comparison of the summary scores. The additive strategy, described in the previous section, is a good example of this kind of decision strategy. In this case the summary score for each alternative is the sum of the scores assigned to each dimension.

Profitability Evaluating compatible alternatives to select the best one

A second type of decision is the **progress decision**. Progress decisions occur whenever we evaluate whether our selected course of action is making satisfactory progress toward achieving our goals. If we anticipate that continuing to follow the selected course of action will result in too many violations of our goals, we replace the existing plan with a new plan of action.

Imagine that, after obtaining your degree, you are fortunate enough to have many job offers. According to image theory, you would first evaluate which of the jobs are compatible with your basic beliefs and values (value image). If you value money, you might reject some offers on the basis of an insufficient starting salary. You might also consider which jobs allow for rapid advancement if one of your goals is to move quickly into a management position (trajectory image). Evaluating the likelihood of a promotion might be easier if you had a specific plan for achieving this goal (strategic image).

Image theory predicts that you would initially use a noncompensatory strategy to determine which job offers were compatible with your values and goals. You would then use a more complex (profitability) strategy to carefully compute the total attractiveness of each remaining offer, selecting the most attractive one. Later you would probably want to make progress decisions regarding whether you were making satisfactory progress toward achieving your goals, such as advancing within the organization. Insufficient progress might cause you to seek other job offers.

I mentioned at the beginning of this section that Beach and Mitchell were influenced by Payne's research, so it is not surprising that there are some consistencies between image theory and Payne's findings. In particular, the emphasis on a noncompensatory strategy (compatibility) followed by a more complex strategy (profitability) is consistent with Payne's findings that subjects used a simpler, noncompensatory strategy to reduce the number of alternatives, followed by a more complex compensatory strategy to make their final selection. But image theory places decision making in a larger schematic framework than had been expressed in most previous theories of decision making. First, guiding principles based on beliefs and values are given an important role. Second, goals and plans become the main focus of decision making. This assumption shows the similarities between decision making and problem solving, wherein goals and plans are also important. Third, image theory allows for the monitoring of our decisions, as well as the retention or replacement of earlier decisions based on their perceived success or failure.

The example of arriving at a medical diagnosis can also be rather easily embedded in this framework. Recall that the number of hypotheses considered by doctors usually ranged from two to four in the Elstein study. We can think of these hypotheses as being the candidates that pass the compatibility test, following the application of a noncompensatory

Progress decision
Reassessment of an initial decision to determine whether the selected course of action should be continued

decision rule. Those promising hypotheses are then evaluated by using the compensatory, additive rule during the profitability test. Progress decisions could be studied by looking at how doctors evaluate the success of their treatment during subsequent visits of the patient. If the patient is not making progress, a new diagnosis and treatment could be required.

We can also try to embed the RPD model in this framework. Note in Figure 14.3 that the compatibility test can result in only a single candidate, which is what occurs in the RPD model. This alternative is either adopted or rejected using a noncompensatory (satisficing) strategy, such as proposed in the conjunctive model. Because the RPD model describes expert decision making, alternative actions are ordered so the first one considered will typically be adopted. The selected action will usually be a good choice, however, because the order is based on the success rate of the alternative actions. Notice that the decision maker does not use compensatory strategies to evaluate multiple candidates in the RPD model. But progress decisions are extremely important in this model because immediate feedback is used to evaluate whether the selected action is working. In contrast, progress decisions are much slower in decision-event situations, such as evaluating whether a purchaser likes her new car or whether a patient is recovering from an illness.

Progress decisions are also much slower in evaluating the success of models and theories in cognitive psychology, and cognitive psychologists will continue to search for the best ones as they obtain feedback from their research. I enjoyed sharing that search with you in this book.

SUMMARY

Making decisions usually requires evaluating at least two alternatives that differ on a number of attributes. Selecting an alternative requires the decision maker to combine this information to form an overall evaluation for each alternative. The study of how people search for information provides evidence about decision strategies.

Four of the more popular decision models can be differentiated by whether people compare the alternatives attribute by attribute or alternative by alternative and whether the decision is a compensatory or noncompensatory one. In the elimination-by-aspects model, alternatives are compared by attributes, and the decision is noncompensatory. The conjunctive model is similar but considers only one alternative at a time; the first alternative that satisfies the minimum criteria for each attribute is selected. The additive and additive-difference models are both compensatory because they allow for positive attributes to compensate for negative attributes. The additive model assigns a numerical score to each attribute and sums the scores to determine the relative attractiveness of each alternative. The additive-difference model compares alternatives attribute by attribute and determines the difference between the scores on each attribute; the sum of the differences determines which alternative is more attractive.

Research on how people select a decision strategy has shown that the choice of a strategy depends on task characteristics. People were likely to use a noncompensatory strategy such as elimination by aspects when there were many alternatives and a compensatory strategy such as the additive model when there were few alternatives. Although compensatory strategies are more thorough than noncompensatory strategies, they are more difficult to use. A study of how effectively professionals could select a firm with the highest bond rating found that elimination by aspects was the most efficient strategy. It produced the same level of accuracy as the additive and additive-difference strategies, but by quicker decisions.

Risky decision making refers to decisions that are concerned with uncertainty—for example, evaluating the potential dangers of a nuclear reactor, buying insurance, and diagnosing medical problems. In order to make good decisions, it is necessary to make accurate estimates of probabilities. Probability estimates are often based on heuristics, which sometimes yield reasonable estimates but often do not. Two heuristics are availability and representativeness. The availability heuristic proposes that we evaluate the probability of an event by judging the ease with which instances can be recalled. The representativeness heuristic states that the probability of an event is estimated by evaluating how similar it is to the essential properties of its population.

Expected value is a normative procedure for making decisions. Expected value is calculated by multiplying the value of events by their probability of occurring and summing the products. Subjective expected utility is a modified version of this procedure in which subjective values (utilities) replace values and subjective probabilities replace probabilities. The expected-value model can be further modified by allowing for the possibility that people may emphasize some components of the model more than others.

Physicians use several heuristics to simplify the task of diagnosing medical problems. They form hypotheses early in the diagnosis to guide their collection of data. They seem to use a simple additive model to combine the data, adding the number of positive cues and subtracting the number of negative cues. This slow, deliberate approach is not possible in emergency situations. In action-based decision making it is necessary to quickly carry out a sequence of actions rather than evaluate a single decision event. The recognition-primed decision (RPD) model proposes that the decision maker quickly assesses the situation, uses his or her expertise to evaluate a single course of action, and evaluates fairly immediate feedback to determine whether that action is working.

A schema theory of decision making provides a broad framework for comparing the RPD model with more traditional models. The theory assumes that people initially use a noncompensatory strategy to eliminate alternatives that are not sufficiently compatible with their values and goals. The remaining alternatives are then evaluated more thoroughly by using a more complex strategy. The theory is called image theory because three images influence decisions: value image (beliefs and basic values), trajectory image (future goals and agenda), and strategic image (plans for achieving goals). Progress decisions evaluate whether previous decisions are resulting in satisfactory progress toward achieving goals. The RPD model differs from previous models by placing greater emphasis on how experts can use a noncompensatory strategy to make a good selection during the initial stage. Rapid feedback then enables progress decisions to evaluate whether the selected actions are working.

STUDY QUESTIONS

1. What is the distinction between normative and descriptive models? What is the utility of each?
2. Try to think of some real-life choices you have made. For example, in choosing which college to attend, did you use a compensatory or noncompensatory model? Did you use the same procedure for all the decisions that you recalled?
3. Assuming that a search for information is involved, Payne devised a rather clever procedure for studying choice making. How did it work, and what did he find?
4. Where is the "risk" in risky decision making—as contrasted with other decision making?
5. If probabilities of events or outcomes of actions are unknown, how do people go about estimating the likelihood of occurrence? Are we very good at doing so?
6. What is the relation between sample size and the accuracy of the estimates of probability of events in the population from which the sample was drawn?
7. Why do you suppose so few people seem to calculate subjective expected utility, let alone expected value? Would lotteries stay in business if they did?
8. Can you think of specific examples of how your mood may have influenced your probability estimates? Think of an experiment that you could design to explore how mood might influence decision making in additional ways.
9. What are some of the differences between making decisions in emergency situations and making decisions when there is no time pressure?

10. Would you like to see your physician use a computer to aid in the diagnosis of your illness? What would be the advantage of programs like the one described in Box 14.5? If you were a doctor, how would you decide whether to buy one?

KEY TERMS

The page number in parentheses refers to where the term is discussed in the chapter.

additive-difference model (416)	normative models (414)
additive model (415)	prior probability (426)
adoption decision (439)	profitability (440)
availability heuristic (422)	progress decision (441)
compatibility (439)	recognition-primed decisions (438)
compensatory model (415)	representative (425)
conjunctive model (419)	risk dimensions (430)
decision aid (435)	satisficing search (419)
decision event (437)	strategic image (439)
decision frame (429)	subjective expected utility (430)
descriptive models (414)	subjective probabilities (429)
duplex gamble (431)	trajectory image (439)
elimination by aspects (417)	uncertainty (421)
expected value (426)	utility (427)
image theory (439)	value image (439)
noncompensatory model (417)	

RECOMMENDED READING

A review article by Payne, Bettman, and Johnson (1992) summarizes recent research on decision making. A statistical model that has influenced many studies of decision making is multiple linear regression. Dawes (1979) evaluated the success of this approach, and Hammond (1971) recommended using the linear model and computer-implemented feedback to improve performance on decision-making tasks. The development of expected value as a psychological model was discussed by Payne (1973). Frish and Clemen (1994) provide a recent critical overview of this approach. B. H. Beach (1975) reviewed studies on the application of Bayesian models to military, business, and medical decisions. Other applications include the study of career (Pitz & Harren, 1980), jury (Penrod & Hastie, 1980), and medical (Fox, 1980) decision making. Work on heuristic biases in risky decision making is described by Kahneman and Tversky (1984) and by Fischhoff and Bar-Hillel (1984). *Decision Making in Action: Models and Methods*, edited by Klein, Orasanu, Calderwood, & Zsambok (1993) contains chapters on making multiple, action-based decisions during a brief time period.

Glossary

Absolute judgment task Identifying stimuli that vary along a single, sensory continuum

Acoustic codes Memory codes based on the sound of the stimulus

Acoustic confusions Errors that sound like the correct answer

Activation rules Rules that determine how inhibitory and excitatory connections combine to determine the total activation of a concept

Additive-difference model A strategy that compares two alternatives by adding the difference in their values for each attribute

Additive model A strategy that adds attribute values to assign a score to each alternative

Adoption decision Initial selection of a course of action

Algorithm A set of rules that will solve a problem if correctly followed

Allocation of capacity When a limited amount of capacity is distributed to various tasks

Ambiguous sentences Sentences that have more than one meaning

Anagram A problem that requires rearranging a string of letters to form a word

Analogical transfer Use of the same solution in solving two problems

Analogy Solving a problem by using a solution to a related problem

Analogy problem A four-term problem that requires finding the answer that completes the relation A is to B as C is to D

Arousal A physiological state that influences the distribution of mental capacity to various tasks

Arrangement problem A problem that requires rearranging its parts to satisfy a specified criterion

Artificial intelligence The study of how to produce computer programs that can perform intellectually demanding tasks

Association value The number of verbal associations generated for a concept

Attention window The attended part of the visual buffer in Kosslyn's model

Attribute learning A concept identification task in which people are told the logical rule (such as conjunctive) but have to discover the relevant attributes

Auditory information store   In Sperling's model this store maintains verbal information in STM through rehearsal

Auditory memory span   Number of items recalled from STM following an auditory presentation of the items

Autobiographical memory   Memory about our personal experiences

Automatic processing   Performing mental operations that require very little mental effort

Availability heuristic   The ease with which estimating probability by examples can be recalled

Average distance rule   A classification strategy that selects the category containing items that have the greatest average similarity to the classified item

Basic-level categories   Intermediate categories in the middle of a hierarchy, such as table, saw, and truck

Beta (ß)   The location of the response criterion in a recognition memory test that determines whether an item is judged as old or new

Biconditional rule   A rule that uses the logical relation *if, then* to relate stimulus attributes in both orders, such as (1) *if small, then square* and (2) *if square, then small*

Bizarre images   Fantastic or unusual images

Bottleneck theories   Theories that attempt to explain how people select information when some information-processing stage becomes overloaded with too much information

Broca's aphasia   A language disorder attributed to damage in the frontal lobe of the brain

Capacity theories   Theories that propose that we have a limited amount of mental effort to distribute across tasks so that there are limitations on the number of tasks we can perform at the same time

Caricature   An exaggeration of distinctive features to make a pattern more distinctive

Category size effect   The finding that members of smaller categories are classified more quickly than members of larger categories

Causal relation   An event that results in the occurrence of another event

Central executive   A component of Baddeley's working memory model that manages the use of working memory

Cerebral blood flow   Measurement of blood flow to localize where cognitive operations occur in the brain

Characteristic features   The features that are usually present in members of that category, but are not necessary

Chunks   Clusters of items that have been stored as a unit in long-term memory

Clustering   Percent of occasions in which a word is followed by its primary associate during the free recall of words

Coding   Semantic elaboration of information to make it easier to remember (Atkinson & Shiffrin model)

Cognitive interview   The use of cognitively based retrieval techniques to improve recall

Cognitive neuroscience   The study of the relation between cognitive processes and brain activities

Cognitive psychology   The study of the mental operations that support people's acquisition and use of knowledge

Cognitive science   The interdisciplinary attempt to study cognition through such fields as psychology, philosophy, artificial intelligence, neuroscience, linguistics, and anthropology

Compatibility   Determining whether a course of action is consistent with a person's beliefs and values

Compensatory model   A strategy that allows positive attributes to compensate for negative ones

Concentration   Investing mental effort in one or more tasks

Concept identification   A task that requires deciding whether an item is an example of a concept, where concepts are typically defined by logical rules

Conceptually driven processes   Processes that are influenced by a person's strategies

Concrete/abstract dimension   Extent to which a concept can be represented by a picture

Conditional rule   A rule that uses the logical relation *if, then* to relate stimulus attributes, such as *if small, then square*

Conjunctive model   A strategy that evaluates one alternative at a time and rejects it if the value of one of its attributes fails to satisfy a minimum criterion

Conjunctive rule A rule that uses the logical relation *and* to relate stimulus attributes, such as *small and square*

Contextual effects The influence of the surrounding context on the recognition of patterns

Continuous dimensions Attributes that can take on any value along a dimension

Control processes Strategies that determine how information is processed

Creativity Creating a novel and useful product or solution

Cued recall Recall that occurs with hints or cues, such as providing the questions asked during the judgment phase of a task

Data-driven processes Processes that are influenced by the stimulus material

Decay theory Proposal that information is spontaneously lost over time, even when there is no interference from other material

Decision aid A tool for helping people make better decisions

Decision event Making a single decision, rather than a sequence of decisions in a changing situation

Decision frame Decision maker's conception of the decision-making situation

Declarative knowledge Knowledge about factual information

Deep structure The underlying meaning of a sentence

Default knowledge Knowledge about the most likely values for the attributes of a schema

Defining features Features that are necessary to be a member of that category

Descriptive models Models that describe what people actually do

Detection paradigm A procedure in which observers have to specify which of two possible target patterns is present in a display

Direct memory tests Tests that ask people to recall or recognize past events

Disjunctive rule A rule that uses the logical relation *or* to relate stimulus attributes, such as *small or square*

Distinctive feature A feature present in one pattern, but absent in another, aiding one's discrimination of the two patterns

Distinctive item An item different in appearance or meaning from other items

Domain-specific knowledge Knowledge about a specific subject, such as chess or physics

d prime (d') A measure of accuracy in a recognition memory test based on the ability to discriminate between old items and new items

Dual-coding theory A theory that memory is improved when items can be represented by both verbal and visual memory codes

Duplex gamble A gamble in which the probability of winning is assigned independently of the probability of losing

Elimination by aspects A strategy that evaluates one attribute at a time and rejects those alternatives whose attribute values fail to satisfy a minimum criterion

Emotional distinctiveness Items that produce an intense emotional reaction

Encoding Creating a visual or verbal code for a test item so it can be compared with the memory codes of items stored in STM (Sternberg's model)

Encoding specificity principle A theory that states that the effectiveness of a retrieval cue depends on how well it relates to the initial encoding of an item

Enduring dispositions Events that automatically influence where people direct their attention

Episodic memory Memory of specific events, including when and where they occurred

Error recovery heuristics Strategies for correcting comprehension errors

Event-related potentials Recording brain waves to measure the timing of cognitive operations

Exchange errors Errors in which two linguistic units are substituted for each other during sentence production

Excitatory connections Reactions to positive evidence for a concept, as when a vertical line provides support for the possibility that a letter is a *K*

Exhaustive search A search that continues until the test item is compared to all items in the memory set

Expected value The average value, as determined by combining the value of events with their probability of occurrence

Explicit memory   Memory evaluated by direct memory tests

Exploration strategy   A strategy for determining how to use a preinventive form in designing a product

External information   Information in the environment, as opposed to **internal information** generated by a person's thoughts

Fact-oriented acquisition   Encoding material in a manner that emphasizes factual knowledge without emphasizing its application

False alarm   When an observer incorrectly reports a signal in a signal detection task or an item that was not previously presented in a recognition memory task

Familiarity   A judgment of how familiar an item is with respect to a particular context

Family resemblance   A measure of how frequently the attributes of a category member are shared by other members of the category

Fan effect   The finding that increasing the number of links to a concept increases the time to verify one of the links

Feature comparison model   A model proposing that items are categorized by matching the item's features to category features

Feature frequency rule   A classification strategy that selects the category that has the most feature matches with the classified item

Feature theories   Theories of pattern recognition that describe patterns in terms of their parts, or features

Filter   That part of attention in which some perceptual information is blocked (filtered) out and not recognized, while other information receives attention and is subsequently recognized

Filter model   The proposition that a bottleneck occurs before pattern recognition and that attention determines what information reaches the pattern recognition stage

Flashbulb memories   Memories of important events that caused an emotional reaction

Four-card selection problem   A reasoning task that requires deciding which of four cards should be turned over in order to evaluate a conditional rule

Frequency theory   A theory that explains the ease of attribute learning by the relative frequency with which the attributes appear in positive and negative examples of the concept

Functional fixedness   The tendency to use an object in a typical way

General strategies   Strategies (heuristics) that apply in many situations but do not always result in a solution

Generation strategy   A strategy for producing preinventive forms in designing a product

Generative   The capability to produce many different messages by combining symbols in different ways

Geons   Different three-dimensional shapes that combine to form three-dimensional patterns

Global coherence   Integration of major ideas that occur throughout a text

Goal-derived categories   Categories whose members are selected to satisfy a specified goal

Grammar   A set of rules for producing correct sentences in a language

Hallucinations   Imagined events or images believed to be real

Heuristics   Strategies that are often, but not always, helpful in solving problems

Hierarchical cluster analysis   An analysis that separates—clusters— patterns into categories of similar patterns by dividing larger categories into smaller and smaller categories

Hierarchically organized   An organizing strategy in which larger categories are partitioned into smaller categories

Hierarchical network model   A model proposing that items are categorized by using the hierarchical relations specified in a semantic network

High-constraint sentences   Sentences that produce a high expectation for a particular word

Human information processing   The psychological approach that attempts to identify what occurs during the various stages (attention, perception, short-term memory) of processing information

Ideals   Attribute values that relate to the goal of a goal-derived category

Imagery potential   Ease with which a concept can be imaged

Image theory   A general framework for modeling decisions by considering a person's values, plans, and future goals

Imaging   Creating visual images to make material easier to remember (Atkinson & Shiffrin model)

Implicit memory   Memory evaluated by indirect memory tests

Imprecise elaboration   Provision or generation of additional material unrelated to remembered material

Incidental learning   Learning that occurs when we do not make a conscious effort to learn

Incidental learning task   A task that requires people to make judgments about stimuli without knowing that they will later be tested on their recall of the stimuli

Indirect memory tests   Tests that do not explicitly ask about past events but are influenced by memory of past events

Inducing-structure problem   A problem that requires finding a pattern among a fixed set of relations

Inference   The use of reasoning to establish relations in a text when the relations are not directly stated

Inhibitory connections   Reactions to negative evidence for a concept, as when the presence of a vertical line provides negative evidence that a letter is a C

Insight   The sudden discovery of a solution following unsuccessful attempts to solve a problem

Interactive activation model   A theory that proposes that both feature knowledge and word knowledge combine to provide information about the identity of letters in a word

Interactive illustration   Illustration in which key concepts interact

Interference theory   Proposal that forgetting occurs because other material interferes with the information in memory

Internal information   Information generated by a person's thoughts, as opposed to **external information** in the environment

Interstimulus interval   The amount of time between the end of a stimulus and the beginning of another stimulus

Keyword   A concrete word that sounds like an abstract word so it can be substituted for the abstract word in an interactive image

Keyword method   A mnemonic strategy using keywords to improve paired-associate learning

Knowledge acquisition   Storage of information in LTM

Language   A collection of symbols, and rules for combining symbols, which can express an infinite variety of messages

Learner-controlled strategy   A strategy in which the learner decides which items to study during learning trials

Levels of processing   A theory that proposes that "deeper" (semantic) levels of processing enhance memory

Lexical alteration   Substituting a word with similar meaning for one of the words in a sentence

Lexical ambiguity   A word that has more than one meaning

Lexical decision task   A task that requires people to decide whether a string of letters is a word

Limited-capacity perceptual channel   The pattern recognition stage of Broadbent's model, which is protected by the filter (attention) from becoming overloaded with too much perceptual information

Links   The format for representing relations in a semantic network

Local coherence   Integration of ideas within an immediate context in a text

Logical rules   Rules based on logical relations, such as conjunctive, disjunctive, conditional, and biconditional rules

Long-term memory   Memory that has no capacity limits and holds information from minutes to an entire lifetime

Low-constraint sentences   Sentences that produce an expectation for a broad range of words

Magnetic resonance imaging   A diagnostic technique that uses magnetic fields and computerized images to locate mental operations in the brain

Maintenance rehearsal   Rehearsal that keeps information active in STM

Means/end analysis   A strategy that can be used to solve transformation problems by eliminating differences between the initial and goal states

Measure of sufficiency   A demonstration that the instructions in a computer program are capable of solving a problem

Memory code   The format (physical, phonemic, semantic) of information encoded into memory

Memory retrieval explanation   The proposal that people solve reasoning problems about familiar situations by retrieving specific examples from their memory

Memory set   A set of items in STM that can be compared against a test item to determine if the test item is stored there

Memory span   The number of correct items that people can immediately recall from a sequence of items

Mental effort   The amount of mental capacity required to perform a task

Mental model   A person's mental representation of a situation

Method of loci   A mnemonic technique for learning the order of objects by imaging them in specific locations

Miss   When an observer fails to report a signal in a signal detection task or a previously presented item in a recognition memory task

Mnemonic techniques   Strategies that improve memory

Momentary intentions   These are conscious decisions to allocate attention to certain tasks or aspects of the environment

Mood dependent memory   Memory that is improved when people are tested under conditions that recreate their mood when they learned the material

Morpheme exchanges   Errors in which two morphemes are substituted for each other during sentence production

Morphemes   The smallest units of meaning in a language

Multimode theory   A theory that proposes that people's intentions and the demands of the task determine the information-processing stage at which information is selected

Naturalistic studies   Studies of the tip-of-the-tongue state in which people record these events as they occur outside the laboratory

Nearest-neighbor rule   A classification strategy that selects the category containing an item that is most similar to the classified item

Neural network model   A theory that uses a neural network as a metaphor in which concepts (nodes) are linked to other concepts through excitatory and inhibitory connections

Nodes   The format for representing concepts in a semantic network

Noncompensatory model   A strategy that rejects alternatives that have negative attributes without considering their positive attributes

Noncued recall   Recall that occurs without hints or cues provided by the experimenter

Noninteractive illustration   Illustration in which key concepts do not interact

Normative models   Models that describe what people should do

Obligation schema   Knowledge that taking an action (such as paying a pension) is required if a prerequisite (such as retirement) is fulfilled

Obstacles   Events that delay or prevent the attainment of a goal

Operators   Actions that are selected to solve problems

Orienting task   Instructions to focus on a particular aspect (physical, phonemic, semantic) of a stimulus

Orthographic distinctiveness   Lowercase words that have an unusual shape

Parallel distributed processing (PDP)   When information is collected simultaneously from different sources and combined to reach a decision

Parallel processing   When we carry out more than one operation at a time, such as looking at an art exhibit and carrying on a conversation

Parallel representation   Representation of knowledge in which more than one item at a time can be processed

Paraphrase   Using different words to express the same ideas in a sentence

Partial-report procedure A task in which observers are cued to report only certain items in a display of items

Path Links in a semantic network that join two concepts

Pattern recognition The stage of perception during which a stimulus is identified

Perceptual confusion A measure of the frequency with which two patterns are mistakenly identified as each other

Permission schema Knowledge that taking an action (such as entering a country) requires fulfilling a prerequisite (such as being inoculated)

Perspective A particular point of view

Phoneme exchanges Errors in which two phonemes are substituted for each other during sentence production

Phonemes The basic sounds of a language that are combined to form speech

Phonemic coding A memory code that emphasizes the pronunciation of the stimulus

Phonological loop A component of Baddeley's working memory model that maintains and manipulates acoustic information

Phrase structure grammar A set of rules for partitioning a sentence into its grammatical units

Plan A temporally ordered sequence of operations for carrying out some task

Plot The sequence of events related to achieving goals in a narrative

Positron emission tomography A diagnostic technique that uses radioactive tracers to study brain activity by measuring the amount of blood flow in different parts of the brain

Pragmatic reasoning schemata Organized knowledge structures used to evaluate practical situations such as seeking permission or fulfilling an obligation

Precise elaboration Provision or generation of additional material closely related to remembered material

Preinventive form Creating an object before determining its use

Primacy effect The better recall of words at the beginning of a list

Primary associates Words that are strongly associated with each other, as typically measured by asking people to provide associations to words

Primary distinctiveness An item distinct from other items in the immediate context

Priming Reduction of time processing a concept caused by prior presentation of related information

Prior probability The probability that an evident will occur before obtaining additional evidence regarding its occurrence

Proactive interference Forgetting that occurs because of interference from material encountered before learning

Problem isomorphs Problems that have different story contents but identical solutions

Problem-oriented acquisition Encoding material in a manner that is helpful for its later use in solving problems

Problem space The set of choices confronted by a problem solver at each step in solving a problem

Procedural knowledge Knowledge that relates actions to goals

Procedural memory Memory for actions, skills, and operations

Processing distinctiveness Creation of a memory code that makes that memory distinct from other memories

Production rule A conditional rule that specifies the prerequisite condition for carrying out an action

Profitability Evaluating compatible alternatives to select the best one

Progress decision Reassessment of an initial decision to determine whether the selected course of action should be continued

Propositional theory A theory that all knowledge, including spatial knowledge, can be expressed in semantic-based propositions

Propositions Meaningful ideas that typically consist of several words

Prototype An item that typifies the members in a category and is used to represent the category

Prototype rule A classification strategy that selects

the category whose prototype is the most similar to the classified item

Readability   The number of recalled propositions divided by reading time

Readability formulas   Formulas that use variables such as word frequency and sentence length to predict the readability of text

Reality monitoring   Discriminating between actual and imagined events

Recency effect   The better recall of words at the end of a list

Recognition memory   Deciding whether an item had previously occurred in a specified context

Recognition-primed decisions   Decisions that are quickly made following recognition of a situation

Rehearsal   Repeating verbal information to keep it active in STM or to transfer it into LTM

Reinstatement search   The search of LTM to place words in STM where they can be used to integrate a text

Relational information   Information specifying how concepts are related

Release from proactive interference   Reducing proactive interference by having information be dissimilar from earlier material

Relevancy   The extent to which an adjective (such as size) is a meaningful modifier of a particular noun

Representational transfer   Use of the same format (such as a matrix) in solving two problems

Representativeness   A measure of how typical an item is as a category member

Resolution   The outcome of events in the plot of a narrative

Response-sensitive strategy   A computer-implemented strategy that uses the learner's previous responses to decide what items to present during learning trials

Retrieval strategies   Strategies for recalling information from LTM

Retroactive interference   Forgetting that occurs because of interference from material encountered after learning

Risk dimensions   The components of a gamble such as the probability of winning and the amount of a loss

Rote learning   Learning by repetition rather than through understanding

Rule learning   A concept identification task in which people are told the relevant attributes (such as *small, square*) but have to discover the logical rule

Satisficing search   A strategy that follows the conjunctive model and therefore selects the first alternative that satisfies the minimum criterion for each attribute

Scan component   The attention component of Sperling's model that determines what is recognized in the visual information store

Scanning   Sequentially comparing a test item with items in STM to determine if there's a match (Sternberg's model)

Schema   A general knowledge structure that provides a framework for organizing clusters of knowledge

Script   Knowledge about what occurs during routine activities

Secondary distinctiveness   An item distinct from items stored in LTM

Selection stage   The stage that follows pattern recognition and determines which information a person will try to remember (Deutsch & Deutsch model)

Selectivity   The selective aspects of attention—we pay attention to some aspects of our environment and ignore other aspects

Self-generation   Generation of items by participants in an experiment, rather than the provision of these items by the experimenter

Self-terminating search   A search that stops as soon as the test item is successfully matched to an item in the memory set

Semantic alteration   Changing the order of words in a sentence to change the meaning of the sentence

Semantic codes   Memory codes based on the meaning of the stimulus

Semantic features   Attributes that represent the meaning of a concept

Semantic memory   Memory of general knowledge not associated with a particular context

Semantic network A theory proposing that semantic information is organized in LTM by linking concepts to related concepts

Sensory store That part of memory that holds unanalyzed sensory information for a fraction of a second, providing an opportunity for additional analysis following the physical termination of a stimulus

Sequential representation Representation of knowledge in which only one item at a time can be processed

Serial learning Learning items in a specified order

Serial position effect The ability to recall words at the beginning and end of a list better than words in the middle of the list

Serial processing When we carry out one operation at a time, such as pronouncing one word at a time

Series extrapolation A problem that requires finding a pattern among a sequence of items in order to continue the sequence in the same pattern

Setting The time and place in which narrative events occur

Shadowing An experimental method that requires people to repeat the message out loud

Short-term memory (STM) The part of memory that has limited capacity and that lasts only about 20 to 30 sec in the absence of attending to its content

Signal detection task A task that requires observers to report whether a signal occurred

Simulation programs Computer programs that attempt to reproduce the operations used by people to carry out various tasks

Situation model Integration of prior knowledge and text information to construct an understanding of the situation described in a text

Slips of the tongue Speech errors

Slope A measure of how much response time changes for each unit of change along the x-axis (memory set size)

Spatial knowledge Knowledge of spatial relations that may be stored as images

Spontaneous retrievals Retrievals that occur without making a conscious effort to recall information

Spreading activation A theoretical construct proposing that activation spreads from a concept in a semantic network to activate related concepts

Spreading activation model A model that accounts for response times by formulating assumptions about how activation spreads in a semantic network

Stereotypes Attribute values believed to be representative of social categories

Stimulus-response (S-R) The approach that emphasizes the association between a stimulus and a response, without identifying the mental operations that produced the response

Strategic image Plans for achieving the goals of decisions

Stroop effect The finding that it takes longer to name the color of the ink a word is printed in when the word is the name of a competing color (for example, the word *red* printed in blue ink)

Structural coding A memory code that emphasizes the physical structure of the stimulus

Structural theories of pattern recognition Theories that specify how the features of a pattern are joined to other features of the pattern

Structured The organization imposed on a language by its grammatical rules

Subgoal A goal that solves part of the problem

Subjective expected utility A variation of expected value that uses utilities and subjective probabilities instead of values and probabilities

Subjective probabilities Estimated probabilities as determined by the decision maker

Subnodes Nodes that link together related ideas in a semantic network

Subordinate categories Small categories at the bottom of a hierarchy, such as lamp table, jigsaw, and pickup truck

Subsidiary task A task that typically measures how quickly people can react to a target stimulus in order to evaluate the capacity demands of the primary task

Subvocalization Silently speaking to oneself

Superordinate categories Large categories at the top of a hierarchy, such as furniture, tools, and vehicles

Suppress   Eliminating inappropriate meanings in a sentence

Suppression task   A task that instructs people not to think specified thoughts, whereas an **expression task** instructs people to think about specified thoughts

Surface ambiguity   Alternative meanings of a sentence that can be differentiated by different phrase structure rules

Surface structure   The structure of a spoken sentence

Symbolic   The use of symbols, such as spoken or written words, to represent ideas

Table of connections   A table that links differences between problem states with operators for eliminating those differences

Tachistoscope   A box that presents visual stimuli at a specified duration and level of illumination

Template   An unanalyzed pattern that is matched against alternative patterns by using the degree of overlap as a measure of similarity

Theme   The main goals of characters in a narrative

Threshold   The minimal amount of activation required to become consciously aware of a stimulus

Tip of the tongue (TOT)   A retrieval state in which a person feels he or she knows the information but cannot immediately retrieve it

Trajectory image   A person's future agenda and life goals

Transfer-appropriate processing   Encoding material in a manner related to how the material will be used later

Transformational grammar   A set of rules for transforming a sentence into a closely related sentence

Transformation problem   A problem that requires changing the initial state through a sequence of operations until it matches the goal state

Typicality   A measure of how well a category member represents that category

Typicality effect   The finding that the more typical members of a category are classified more quickly than the less typical category members

Uncertainty   Lacking knowledge about which events will occur

Underlying ambiguity   Alternative meanings of a sentence that cannot be differentiated by different phrase structure rules

Utility   Subjective value as determined by the decision maker

Value image   A person's basic beliefs and values

Venn diagram   A diagram that shows the set relations (such as overlap) among categories

Verbal knowledge   Knowledge expressed in language

Verbal protocols   Records of verbalized thought processes

Visual buffer   A component of Kosslyn's model in which a generated visual image is maintained in STM

Visual information store (VIS)   This is a sensory store that maintains visual information for approximately a quarter of a second

Visual neglect   Failure to respond to visual simulation on the side of the visual field that is opposite a brain lesion

Visual scanning   A shift of attention across a visual display or image

Visuospatial sketchpad   A component of Baddeley's working memory model that maintains and manipulates visual/spatial information

Wernicke's aphasia   A language disorder attributed to damage in the temporal lobe of the brain

Whole-report procedure   A task that requires observers to report everything they see in a display of items

Word exchanges   Errors in which two words are substituted for each other during sentence production

Word superiority effect   The finding that accuracy in recognizing a letter is higher when the letter is in a word than when it appears alone or is in a nonword

Work forward   Selecting relevant information to solve a problem in the order that it should be used in the solution

Working memory   Use of STM as a temporary store for information needed to accomplish a particular task

Working memory capacity   The amount of information that can be kept active in working memory

References

Adams, L. T., Kasserman, J. E., Yearwood, A. A., Perfetto, G. A., Bransford, J. D., & Franks, J. J. (1988). Memory access: The effects of fact-oriented versus problem-oriented acquisition. *Memory & Cognition, 16,* 167–175.

Adams, M. J. (1979). Models of word recognition. *Cognitive Psychology, 11,* 133–176.

Adamson, R. E. (1952). Functional fixedness as related to problem solving: A repetition of three experiments. *Journal of Experimental Psychology, 44,* 288–291.

Adelson, B. (1984). When novices surpass experts: The difficulty of a task may increase with expertise. *Journal of Experimental Psychology: Learning, Memory, and Cognition, 10,* 483–495.

Alba, J. W., & Hasher, L. (1983). Is memory schematic? *Psychological Bulletin, 93,* 203–231.

Albrecht, J. E., & O'Brien, E. J. (1993). Updating a mental model: Maintaining both local and global coherence. *Journal of Experimental Psychology: Learning, Memory, and Cognition, 19,* 1061–1070.

Anderson, J. R. (1976). *Language, memory, and thought.* Hillsdale, NJ: Erlbaum.

Anderson, J. R. (1978). Arguments concerning representations for mental imagery. *Psychological Review, 85,* 249–277.

Anderson, J. R. (1982). Acquisition of cognitive skill. *Psychological Review, 89,* 369–406.

Anderson, J. R. (1983). *The architecture of cognition.* Cambridge, MA: Harvard University Press.

Anderson, J. R. (1990). Analysis of student performance with the LISP tutor. In N. Frederiksen, R. Glaser, A. Lesgold, & M. Shafto (Eds.), *Diagnostic monitoring of skill and knowledge acquisition* (pp. 27–50). Hillsdale, NJ: Erlbaum.

Anderson, J. R., Boyle, C. F., & Reiser, B. J. (1985). Intelligent tutoring systems. *Science, 228,* 456–462.

Anderson, J. R., & Reder, L. M. (1979). An elaborative processing explanation of depth of processing. In L. S. Cermak & F. I. M. Craik (Eds.), *Levels of processing in human memory.* Hillsdale, NJ: Erlbaum.

Anderson, J. R., & Thompson, R. (1989). Use of analogy in a production-system architecture. In S. Vosniadou & A. Ortony (Eds.), *Similarity and analogical reasoning.* Cambridge, England: Cambridge University Press.

Anderson, R. C., & Pichert, J. W. (1978). Recall of previously unrecallable information following a shift in perspective. *Journal of Verbal Learning and Verbal Behavior, 17,* 1–12.

Anderson, R. E. (1984). Did I do it or did I only imagine doing it? *Journal of Experimental Psychology: General, 113*, 594–613.

Anderson, S. J., & Conway, M. A. (1993). Investigating the structure of autobiographical memories. *Journal of Experimental Psychology: Learning, Memory, and Cognition, 19*, 1178–1196.

Armstrong, S. L., Gleitman, L. R., & Gleitman, H. (1983). What some concepts might not be. *Cognition, 13*, 263–308.

Aronson, E. (1972). *The social animal*. New York: W. H. Freeman.

Atkinson, R. C. (1972a). Ingredients for a theory of instruction. *American Psychologist, 27*, 921–931.

Atkinson, R. C. (1972b). Optimizing the learning of a second-language vocabulary. *Journal of Experimental Psychology, 96*, 124–129.

Atkinson, R. C., & Raugh, M. R. (1975). An application of the mnemonic keyword method to the acquisition of a Russian vocabulary. *Journal of Experimental Psychology: Human Learning and Memory, 104*, 126–133.

Atkinson, R. C., & Shiffrin, R. M. (1968). Human memory: A proposed system and its control processes. In K. W. Spence & J. T. Spence (Eds.), *The psychology of learning and motivation* (Vol. 2) (pp. 89–195). Orlando, FL: Academic Press.

Atkinson, R. C., & Shiffrin, R. M. (1971). The control of short-term memory. *Scientific American, 225*, 82–90.

Atwood, M. E., & Polson, P. G. (1976). A process model for water jar problems. *Cognitive Psychology, 8*, 191–216.

Atwood, M. E., Polson, P. G., Jeffries, R., & Ramsey, H. R. (1978, December). *Planning as a process of synthesis* (Technical Report SAI-78-144-DEN). Englewood, CO: Science Applications.

Baddeley, A. D. (1978). The trouble with "levels": A re-examination of Craik and Lockhart's framework for memory research. *Psychological Review, 85*, 139–152.

Baddeley, A. D. (1982). Domains of recollection. *Psychological Review, 89*, 708–729.

Baddeley, A. D. (1992). Is working memory working? The fifteenth Bartlett lecture. *The Quarterly Journal of Experimental Psychology, 44A*, 1–31.

Baddeley, A. D., & Hitch, G. (1974). Working memory. In G. H. Bower (Ed.), *The psychology of learning and motivation* (Vol. 8, pp. 17–90). Orlando, FL: Academic Press.

Baddeley, A. D., Papagno, C., & Vallar, G. (1988). When long-term learning depends on short-term storage. *Journal of Memory and Language, 27*, 586–595.

Baddeley, A. D., & Warrington, E. K. (1970). Amnesia and the distinction between long- and short-term memory. *Journal of Verbal Learning and Verbal Behavior, 9*, 176–189.

Bahrick, H. P. (1979). Maintenance of knowledge: Questions about memory we forgot to ask. *Journal of Experimental Psychology: General, 108*, 296–308.

Bahrick, H. P., & Boucher, B. (1968). Retention of visual and verbal codes of the same stimuli. *Journal of Experimental Psychology, 78*, 417–422.

Bahrick, H. P., & Hall, L. K. (1991). Lifetime maintenance of high school mathematics content. *Journal of Experimental Psychology: General, 120*, 20–33.

Baron, J. (1978). The word-superiority effect: Perceptual learning from reading. In W. K. Estes (Ed.), *Handbook of learning and cognitive processes*. Hillsdale, NJ: Erlbaum.

Barsalou, L. W. (1985). Ideals, central tendency, and frequency of instantiation as determinants of graded structure in categories. *Journal of Experimental Psychology: Learning, Memory, and Cognition, 11*, 629–654.

Barsalou, L. W. (1991). Deriving categories to achieve goals. In G. H. Bower (Ed.), *The psychology of learning and motivation* (Vol. 27, pp. 1–64). San Diego: Academic Press.

Barsalou, L. W., & Sewell, D. R. (1985). Contrasting the representation of scripts and categories. *Journal of Memory and Language, 24*, 646–665.

Bartlett, F. C. (1932). *Remembering: A study in experimental and social psychology*. New York: Macmillan.

Beach, B. H. (1975). Expert judgment about uncertainty: Bayesian decision making in realistic settings. *Organizational Behavior and Human Performance, 14*, 10–59.

Beach, L. R., & Mitchell, T. R. (1990). Image theory: A behavioral theory of decision making in organizations. In B. Straw & L. L. Cummings (Eds.), *Research in organizational behavior* (Vol. 12, pp. 1–41). Greenwich, CT: JAI Press.

Bellezza, F. S. (1987). Mnemonic devices and memory

schemas. In M. A. McDaniel & M. Pressley (Eds.), *Imagery and related mnemonic processes.* New York: Springer-Verlag.

Bentall, R. P. (1990). The illusion of reality: A review and integration of psychological research on hallucinations. *Psychological Bulletin, 107,* 82–95.

Berkerian, D. A., & Dennett, J. L. (1993). The cognitive interview technique: Reviving the issues. *Applied Cognitive Psyhology, 7,* 275–297.

Biederman, I. (1981). On the semantics of a glance at a scene. In M. Kubovy & J. R. Pomerantz (Eds.), *Perceptual organization.* Hillsdale, NJ: Erlbaum.

Biederman, I. (1985). Human image understanding: Recent research and a theory. *Computer Vision, Graphics, and Image Processing, 32,* 29–73.

Biederman, I., & Cooper, E. E. (1991). Priming contour-deleted images: Evidence for intermediate representations in visual object recognition. *Cognitive Psychology, 23,* 393–419.

Bisiach, E., & Luzzatti, C. (1978). Unilateral neglect of representational space. *Cortex, 14,* 129–133.

Blaney, P. H. (1986). Affect and memory: A review. *Psychological Bulletin, 99,* 229–246.

Blank, M. S., & Foss, D. J. (1978). Semantic facilitation and lexical access during sentence processing. *Memory & Cognition, 6,* 644–652.

Bock, J. K. (1982). Toward a cognitive psychology of syntax: Information processing contributions to sentence formulation. *Psychological Review, 89,* 1–47.

Boden, M. A. (1990). *The creative mind: Myths and mechanisms.* London: Weidenfeld and Nicolson.

Bourne, L. E., Jr. (1970). Knowing and using concepts. *Psychological Review, 77,* 546–556.

Bourne, L. E., Jr., Ekstrand, B. R., Lovallo, W. R., Kellogg, R. T., Hiew, C. C., & Yaroush, R. A. (1976). Frequency analysis of attribute identification. *Journal of Experimental Psychology: General, 105,* 294–312.

Bower, G. H. (1970). Organizational factors in memory. *Cognitive Psychology, 1,* 18–46.

Bower, G. H., Black, J. B., & Turner, T. J. (1979). Scripts in memory for text. *Cognitive Psychology, 11,* 177–220.

Bower, G. H., Clark, M., Winzenz, D., & Lesgold, A. (1969). Hierarchical retrieval schemes in recall of categorized word lists. *Journal of Verbal Learning and Verbal Behavior, 8,* 323–343.

Bower, G. H., & Glass, A. L. (1976). Structural units and the reintegrative power of picture fragments. *Journal of Experimental Psychology, 2,* 456–466.

Bower, G. H., & Winzenz, D. (1970). Comparison of associative learning strategies. *Psychonomic Science, 20,* 119–120.

Brandimonte, M. A., & Gerbino, W. (1993). Mental image reversal and verbal recoding: When ducks become rabbits. *Memory & Cognition, 21,* 23–33.

Bransford, J. D., Barclay, J. R., & Franks, J. J. (1972). Sentence memory: A constructive versus interpretive approach. *Cognitive Psychology, 3,* 193–209.

Bransford, J. D., & Franks, J. J. (1971). The abstraction of linguistic ideas. *Cognitive Psychology, 2,* 331–350.

Bransford, J. D., & Johnson, M. K. (1973). Considerations of some problems of comprehension. In W. G. Chase (Ed.), *Visual information processing.* Orlando, FL: Academic Press.

Brennan, S. E. (1985). The caricature generator. *Leonardo, 18,* 170–178.

Brewer, W. F., & Dupree, D. A. (1983). Use of plan schemata in the recall and recognition of goal-directed actions. *Journal of Experimental Psychology: Learning, Memory, and Cognition, 9,* 117–129.

Brewer, W. F., & Nakamura, G. V. (1984). The nature and function of schemas. In R. S. Wyer & T. K. Srull (Eds.), *Handbook of social cognition.* Hillsdale, NJ: Erlbaum.

Brewer, W. F., & Pani, J. R. (1983). The structure of human memory. In G. H. Bower (Ed.), *The psychology of learning and motivation* (Vol. 17). Orlando, FL: Academic Press.

Britton, B. K., & Gulgoz, S. (1991). Using Kintsch's computational model to improve instructional text: Effects of repairing inference calls on recall and cognitive structures. *Journal of Educational Psychology, 83,* 329–345.

Britton, B. K., Van Dusen, L., Glynn, S. M., & Hemphill, D. (1990). The impact of inferences on instructional text. In A. C. Graesser & G. H. Bower (Eds.), *Inferences and text comprehension.* San Diego: Academic Press.

Broadbent, D. E. (1954). The role of auditory localization in attention and memory span. *Journal of Experimental Psychology, 47,* 191–196.

Broadbent, D. E. (1957). A mechanical model for human attention and immediate memory. *Psychological Review, 64*, 205–215.

Broadbent, D. E. (1958). *Perception and communication.* London: Pergamon Press.

Broadbent, D. E. (1975). The magic number seven after fifteen years. In A. Kennedy & A. Wilkes (Eds.), *Studies in long term memory.* London: Wiley.

Broca, P. (1865). Sur le siege de la faculte du langage articule. *Bulletin de la Societe d'Anthropologie, 6,* 377.

Brooks, L. R. (1968). Spatial and verbal components of the act of recall. *Canadian Journal of Psychology, 22,* 349–368.

Brooks, L. R. (1978). Nonanalytic concept formation and memory for instances. In E. Rosch & B. Lloyd (Eds.), *Cognition and categorization* (pp. 164–211). Hillsdale, NJ: Erlbaum.

Brown, A. S. (1991). A review of the tip-of-the-tongue experience. *Psychological Bulletin, 109,* 204–223.

Brown, E., Deffenbacher, K., & Sturgill, W. (1977). Memory for faces and the circumstances of encounter. *Journal of Applied Psychology, 62,* 311–318.

Brown, J. S., & Burton, R. R. (1978). Diagnostic models for procedural bugs in basic mathematical skills. *Cognitive Science, 2,* 155–192.

Brown, R., & Kulik, J. (1977). Flashbulb memories. *Cognition, 5,* 73–99.

Brown, R., & McNeill, D. (1966). The "tip-of-the-tongue" phenomenon. *Journal of Verbal Learning and Verbal Behavior, 5,* 325–337.

Bruce, V. (1994). Stability from variation: The case of face recognition. *The Quarterly Journal of Experimental Psychology, 47A,* 5–28.

Bruner, J. S., Goodnow, J. J., & Austin, G. A. (1956). *A study of thinking.* New York: Wiley.

Buckhout, R. (1974). Eyewitness testimony. *Scientific American, 231,* 23–31.

Buckhout, R., Eugenio, P., Licitra, T., Oliver, L., & Kramer, T. H. (1981). Memory, hypnosis, and evidence: Research on eyewitnesses. *Social Action and the Law, 7,* 67–72.

Burgess, N., & Hitch, G. J. (1992). Toward a network model of the articulatory loop. *Journal of Memory and Language, 31,* 429–460.

Burke, D. M., & Light, L. L. (1981). Memory and aging: The role of retrieval processes. *Psychological Bulletin, 90,* 513–546.

Cantor, N., & Genero, N. (1986). Psychiatric diagnosis and natural categorization: A close analogy. In T. Milton & G. Klerman (Eds.), *Contemporary directions in psychopathology: Toward the DSM-IV.* New York: Guilford.

Cantor, N., & Mischel, W. (1979). Prototypes in person perception. In L. Berkowitz (Ed.), *Advances in experimental social psychology* (Vol. 12). Orlando, FL: Academic Press.

Cantor, N., Smith, E. E., French, R., & Mezzich, J. (1980). Psychiatric diagnosis as prototype categorization. *Journal of Abnormal Psychology, 89,* 181–193.

Carpenter, P. A., & Daneman, M. (1981). Lexical retrieval and error recovery in reading: A model based on eye fixations. *Journal of Verbal Learning and Verbal Behavior, 20,* 137–160.

Carpenter, P. A., Just, M. A., & Shell, P. (1990). What one intelligence test measures: A theoretical account of the processing in the Raven Progressive Matrices Test. *Psychological Review, 97,* 404–431.

Carroll, D. W. (1986). *Psychology of Language.* Pacific Grove, CA: Brooks/Cole.

Carroll, J. M., Thomas, J. C., & Malhotra, A. (1980). Presentation and representation in design problem solving. *British Journal of Psychology, 71,* 143–153.

Catrambone, R. (1995). Aiding subgoal learning: Effects on transfer. *Journal of Educational Psychology, 87,* 5–17.

Catrambone, R., & Holyoak, K. J. (1989). Overcoming contextual limitations on problem-solving transfer. *Journal of Experimental Psychology: Learning, Memory, and Cognition, 15,* 1147–1156.

Cavanagh, J. P. (1972). Relation between the immediate memory span and the memory search rate. *Psychological Review, 79,* 525–530.

Cermak, L. S., & Craik, F. I. M. (Eds.). (1979). *Levels of processing in human memory.* Hillsdale, NJ: Erlbaum.

Chambers, D., & Reisberg, D. (1985). Can mental images be ambiguous? *Journal of Experimental Psychology: Human Perception and Performance, 11,* 317–328.

Chambers, D., & Reisberg, D. (1992). What an image depicts depends on what an image means. *Cognitive Psychology, 24,* 145–174.

Chang, T. M. (1986). Semantic memory: Facts and models. *Psychological Bulletin, 99,* 199–220.

Chapanis, A. (1965). *Man machine engineering*. Pacific Grove, CA: Brooks/Cole.

Charness, N. (1976). Memory for chess positions: Resistance to interference. *Journal of Experimental Psychology: Human Learning and Memory, 2*, 641–653.

Charrow, R. P., & Charrow, V. R. (1979). Making legal language understandable: A psycholinguistic study of jury instructions. *Columbia Law Review, 79*, 1306–1374.

Chase, W. G., & Ericsson, K. A. (1979, November). A mnemonic system for digit span: One year later. Paper presented at the 20th annual meeting of the Psychonomic Society, Phoenix, AZ.

Chase, W. G., & Simon, H. A. (1973). Perception in chess. *Cognitive Psychology, 4*, 55–81.

Cheng, P. W., Holyoak, K. J., Nisbett, R. E., & Oliver, L. M. (1986). Pragmatic versus syntactic approaches to training deductive reasoning. *Cognitive Psychology, 18*, 293–328.

Cherry, C. (1953). Some experiments on the recognition of speech with one and with two ears. *Journal of the Acoustical Society of America, 25*, 975–979.

Chi, M. T. H., Glaser, R., & Rees, E. (1982). Expertise in problem solving. In R. J. Sternberg (Ed.), *Advances in the psychology of human intelligence* (Vol. 1). Hillsdale, NJ: Erlbaum.

Chiesi, H. L., Spilich, G. J., & Voss, J. F. (1979). Acquisition of domain-related information in relation to high and low domain knowledge. *Journal of Verbal Learning and Verbal Behavior, 18*, 257–273.

Chipman, S. F., Segal, J. W., & Glaser, R. (1985). *Thinking and learning skills* (Vol. 2). Hillsdale, NJ: Erlbaum.

Chomsky, N. (1957). *Syntactic structures*. The Hague: Mouton.

Chomsky, N. (1965). *Aspects of the theory of syntax*. Cambridge, MA: MIT Press.

Clowes, M. (1969). Transformational grammars and the organization of pictures. In A. Graselli (Ed.), *Automatic interpretation and the organization of pictures*. Orlando, FL: Academic Press.

Collins, A. M., & Loftus, E. F. (1975). A spreading activation theory of semantic processing. *Psychological Review, 82*, 407–428.

Collins, A. M., & Quillian, M. R. (1969). Retrieval time from semantic memory. *Journal of Verbal Learning and Verbal Behavior, 8*, 240–248.

Collins, A. M., & Quillian, M. R. (1970). Facilitating retrieval from semantic memory: The effect of repeating part of an inference. *Acta Psychologica, 33*, 304–314.

Conrad, R. (1964). Acoustic confusions in immediate memory. *British Journal of Psychology, 55*, 75–84.

Conrad, R. (1972). Speech and reading. In J. F. Kavanagh & I. G. Mattingly (Eds.), *Language by ear and by eye: The relationships between speech and reading*. Cambridge, MA: MIT Press.

Conway, M.A., Cohen, G., & Stanhope, N. (1991). On the very long-term retention of knowledge acquired through formal education: Twelve years of cognitive psychology. *Journal of Experimental Psychology: General, 120*, 395–409.

Cooper, L. A., & Shepard, R. N. (1973). Chronometric studies of the rotation of mental images. In W. G. Chase (Ed.), *Visual information processing*. Orlando, FL: Academic Press.

Craik, F. I. M. (1979a). Human memory. *Annual Review of Psychology, 30*, 63–102.

Craik, F. I. M. (1979b). Levels of processing: Overview and closing comments. In L. S. Cermak & F. I. M. Craik (Eds.), *Levels of processing in human memory*. Hillsdale, NJ: Erlbaum.

Craik, F. I. M., & Lockhart, R. S. (1972). Levels of processing: A framework for memory research. *Journal of Verbal Learning and Verbal Behavior, 11*, 671–684.

Craik, F. I. M., & Rabinowitz, J. C. (1983). Age differences in the acquisition and use of verbal information: A tutorial review. In H. Bouma & D. G. Bowwhuis (Eds.), *Attention and performance X*. Hillsdale, NJ: Erlbaum.

Craik, F. I. M., & Tulving, E. (1975). Depth of processing and the retention of words in episodic memory. *Journal of Experimental Psychology: General, 104*, 268–294.

Craik, F. I. M., & Watkins, M. J. (1973). The role of rehearsal in short-term memory. *Journal of Verbal Learning and Verbal Behavior, 12*, 599–607.

Crovitz, H. F. (1971). The capacity of memory loci in artificial memory. *Psychonomic Science, 24*, 187–188.

Crowder, R. G. (1976). *Principles of learning and memory*. Hillsdale, NJ: Erlbaum.

Crowder, R. G. (1982). The demise of short-term memory. *Acta Psychologica, 50*, 291–323.

Dawes, R. B. (1979). The robust beauty of improper linear models in decision making. *American Psychologist, 7,* 571–582.

de Groot, A. D. (1965). *Thought and choice in chess.* The Hague: Mouton.

de Groot, A. D. (1966). Perception and memory versus thought: Some old ideas and recent findings. In B. Kleinmuntz (Ed.), *Problem solving: Research, method, and theory.* New York: Wiley.

Dell, G. S. (1986). A spreading activation theory of sentence production. *Psychological Review, 93,* 283–321.

Denes, P. B., & Pinson, E. N. (1963). *The speech chain.* Basking Ridge, NJ: Bell Telephone Laboratories.

DeRosa, D. V., & Tkacz, D. (1976). Memory scanning of organized visual material. *Journal of Experimental Psychology: Human Learning and Memory, 2,* 688–694.

Detterman, D. K., & Ramig, P. (1978, November). The relationship between vocabulary size and memory. Paper presented at the 19th annual meeting of the Psychonomic Society, San Antonio, TX.

Detterman, D. K., & Sternberg, R. J. (Eds.). (1993). *Transfer on trial: Intelligence, cognition, and instruction.* Norwood, NJ: Ablex.

Deutsch, J. A., & Deutsch, D. (1963). Attention: Some theoretical considerations. *Psychological Review, 70,* 80–90.

Deutsch, J. A., Deutsch, D., & Lindsay, P. (1967). Comments on "Selective attention: Stimulus or response." *Quarterly Journal of Experimental Psychology, 19,* 362–367.

Devine, P. G., Hamilton, D. L., & Ostrom, T. M. (1994). *Social cognition: Impact on social psychology.* San Diego: Academic Press.

Dopkins, S., Klin, C., & Myers, J. L. (1993). Accessibility of information about goals during the processing of narrative texts. *Journal of Experimental Psychology: Learning, Memory, and Cognition, 19,* 70–80.

Duncker, K. (1945). On problem solving. *Psychological Monographs, 58* (5, Whole No. 270).

Dunegan, K. J. (1993). Framing, cognitive modes, and image theory: Toward an understanding of a glass half full. *Journal of Applied Psychology, 78,* 491–503.

Dunlosky, J., & Nelson, T. O. (1994). Does the sensitivity of judgments of learning (JOLs) to the ef-

fects of various study activities depend on when the JOLs occur? *Journal of Memory and Language, 33,* 545–565.

D'Ydewalle, G., & Rosselle, H. (1978). Text expectations in text learning. In M. M. Gruneberg, P. E. Morris, & R. N. Sykes (Eds.), *Practical aspects of memory.* Orlando, FL: Academic Press.

Egan, D. E., & Greeno, J. G. (1974). Theory of rule induction: Knowledge acquired in concept learning, serial pattern learning, and problem solving. In L. Gregg (Ed.), *Knowledge and cognition.* Hillsdale, NJ: Erlbaum.

Egan, D. E., & Schwartz, B. J. (1979). Chunking in recall of symbolic drawings. *Memory & Cognition, 7,* 149–158.

Egan, J. P. (1958). Recognition memory and the operating characteristic (Technical Note AFCRTN 58–51). Bloomington: Indiana University Hearing and Communication Laboratory.

Egeland, B. (1975). Effects of errorless training on teaching children to discriminate letters of the alphabet. *Journal of Applied Psychology, 60,* 533–536.

Eich, J. M. (1985). Levels of processing, encoding specificity, and CHARM. *Psychological Review, 92,* 1–38.

Eich, E., Macaulay, D., & Ryan, L. (1994). Mood dependent memory for events of the personal past. *Journal of Experimental Psychology: General, 123,* 201–215.

Elstein, A. S., Shulman, L. S., & Sprafka, S. A. (1978). *Medical problem solving.* Cambridge, MA: Harvard University Press.

Ericsson, K. A. (1985). Memory skill. *Canadian Journal of Psychology, 39,* 188–231.

Ericsson, K. A., & Polson, P. G. (1988). An experimental analysis of the mechanisms of a memory skill. *Journal of Experimental Psychology: Learning, Memory, and Cognition, 14,* 305–316.

Ericsson, K. A., & Simon, H. A. (1980). Verbal reports as data. *Psychological Review, 87,* 215–251.

Ernst, G. W., & Newell, A. (1969). *GPS: A case study in generality and problem solving.* Orlando, FL: Academic Press.

Estes, W. K. (1978a). The information processing approach to cognition: A confluence of metaphors and methods. In W. K. Estes (Ed.), *Handbook of learning and cognitive processes* (Vol. 5). Hillsdale, NJ: Erlbaum.

Estes, W. K. (1978b). Perceptual processing in letter

recognition and reading. In E. C. Carterette & M. P. Friedman (Eds.), *Handbook of perception* (Vol. 9). Orlando, FL: Academic Press.

Estes, W. K., & Taylor, H. A. (1966). Visual detection in relation to display size and redundancy of critical elements. *Perception & Psychophysics, 1,* 9–16.

Eysenck, M. W. (1978). Levels of processing: A critique. *British Journal of Psychology, 69,* 157–169.

Eysenck, M. W. (1979). Depth, elaboration, and distinctiveness. In L. S. Cermak & F. I. M. Craik (Eds.), *Levels of processing in human memory.* Hillsdale, NJ: Erlbaum.

Eysenck, M. W., & Keane, M. T. (1990). *Cognitive psychology: A student's handbook.* Hove, England: Erlbaum.

Farah, M. J. (1988). Is visual imagery really visual? Overlooked evidence from neuropsychology. *Psychological Review, 95,* 307–317.

Farah, M. J., & McClelland, J. L. (1991). A computational model of semantic memory impairment: Modality specificity and emergent catagory specificity. *Journal of Experimental Psychology: General, 120,* 339–357.

Finke, R. A. (1980). Levels of equivalence in imagery and perception. *Psychological Review, 87,* 113–132.

Finke, R. A. (1985). Theories relating mental imagery to perception. *Psychological Bulletin, 98,* 236–259.

Finke, R. A. (1990). *Creative imagery: Discoveries and inventions in visualization.* Hillsdale, NJ: Erlbaum.

Finke, R. A., Ward, T. B., & Smith, S. M. (1992). *Creative cognition. Theory, research, and applications.* Cambridge, MA: MIT Press.

Fischhoff, B., & Bar-Hillel, M. (1984). Focusing techniques: A shortcut to improving probability judgments? *Organizational Behavior and Human Performance, 34,* 175–194.

Fischler, I., Rundus, D., & Atkinson, R. C. (1970). Effects of overt rehearsal processes on free recall. *Psychonomic Science, 19,* 249–250.

Fisher, K. M., Faletti, J., Patterson, H., Thornton, R., Lipson, J., & Spring, C. (1990). Computer-based concept mapping. *Journal of College Science Teaching, 19,* 347–352.

Fisher, R. P., & Craik, F. I. M. (1977). Interaction between encoding and retrieval operations in cued recall. *Journal of Experimental Psychology: Human Learning and Memory, 3,* 701–711.

Fisher, R. P., Geiselman, R. E., & Amador, M. (1989). Field test of the cognitive interview: Enhancing

the recollection of actual victims and witnesses of crime. *Journal of Applied Psychology, 74,* 722–727.

Fletcher, C. R. (1986). Strategies for the allocation of short-term memory during comprehension. *Journal of Memory and Language, 25,* 43–58.

Foss, D. J. (1988). Experimental psycholinguistics. *Annual Review of Psychology, 39,* 301–348.

Fox, J. (1980). Making decisions under the influence of memory. *Psychological Review, 87,* 190–211.

Franklin, B. (1887). *Complete works* (Vol. 4, J. Bigelow, Ed.). New York: Putnam.

Frazier, L., Taft, L., Roeper, T., Clifton, C., & Ehrlich, K. (1984). Parallel structure: A source of facilitation in sentence comprehension. *Memory & Cognition, 12,* 421–430.

Frish, D., & Clemen, R. T. (1994). Beyond expected utility: Rethinking decision research. *Psychological Bulletin, 116,* 46–54.

Gagne, E. (1985). *The cognitive psychology of school learning.* Boston: Little, Brown.

Galambos, J. A., & Rips, L. J. (1982). Memory for routines. *Journal of Verbal Learning and Verbal Behavior, 21,* 260–281.

Galotti, K. (1989). Approaches to studying formal and everyday reasoning. *Psychological Bulletin, 105,* 331–351.

Gardner, H. (1985). *The mind's new science: A history of the cognitive revolution.* New York: Basic Books.

Garner, W. R. (1974). *The processing of information and structure.* Hillsdale, NJ: Erlbaum.

Garner, W. R. (1979). Letter discrimination and identification. In A. D. Pick (Ed.), *Perception and its development: A tribute to Eleanor J. Gibson.* Hillsdale, NJ: Erlbaum.

Gegenfurtner, K. R., & Sperling, G. (1993). Information transfer in iconic memory experiments. *Journal of Experimental Psychology: Human Perception and Performance, 19,* 845–866.

Geiselman, R. E., Fisher, R. P., MacKinnon, D. P., & Holland, H. L. (1985). Eyewitness memory enhancement in the police interview: Cognitive retrieval mnemonics versus hypnosis. *Journal of Applied Psychology, 70,* 401–412.

Gentner, D. (1983). Structure-mapping: A theoretical framework for analogy. *Cognitive Science, 7,* 155–170.

Gernsbacher, M. A. (1993). Less skilled readers have less efficient suppression mechanisms. *Psychological Science, 4,* 294–298.

Gernsbacher, M. A., & Faust, M. E. (1991). The mechanism of suppression: A component of general comprehension skill. *Journal of Experimental Psychology: Learning, Memory and Cognition, 17,* 245–262.

Geyer, L. H., & De Wald, C. G. (1973). Feature lists and confusion matrices. *Perception & Psychophysics, 14,* 479–482.

Gibson, E. J. (1969). *Principles of perceptual learning and development.* Englewood Cliffs, NJ: Prentice-Hall.

Gibson, E. J., Osser, H., Schiff, W., & Smith, J. (1963). An analysis of critical features of letters, tested by a confusion matrix. In *A basic research program on reading (Cooperative Research Project No. 639).* Washington, DC: U.S. Office of Education.

Gibson, E. J., Schapiro, R., & Yonas, A. (1968). Confusion matrices for graphic patterns obtained with a latency measure. In *The analysis of reading skill: A program of basic and applied research (Final Report, Project No. 5–1213).* Ithaca, NY: Cornell University and U.S. Office of Education.

Gick, M. L. (1986). Problem-solving strategies. *Educational Psychologist, 21,* 99–120.

Gick, M. L., & Holyoak, K. J. (1980). Analogical problem solving. *Cognitive Psychology, 12,* 306–355.

Gick, M. L., & Holyoak, K. J. (1983). Schema induction and analogical transfer. *Cognitive Psychology, 15,* 1–38.

Gilhooly, R. H., Logie, R. H., Wetherick, N. E., & Wynn, V. (1993). Working memory and strategies in syllogistic-reasoning tasks. *Memory & Cognition, 21,* 115–124.

Glaser, R. (1984). Education and thinking: The role of knowledge. *American Psychologist, 39,* 93–104.

Glenberg, A. M., Meyer, M., & Lindem, K. (1987). Mental models contribute to foregrounding during text comprehension. *Journal of Memory and Language, 26,* 69–83.

Glucksberg, S., & McCloskey, M. (1981). Decisions about ignorance: Knowing that you don't know. *Journal of Experimental Psychology: Human Learning and Memory, 7,* 311–325.

Goldberg, L. R. (1986). The validity of ratings procedures to index the hierarchical level of categories. *Journal of Memory and Language, 25,* 323–347.

Goldenberg, G., Podreka, I., Steiner, M., & Willmes, K. (1987). Patterns of regional cerebral blood flow related to memorizing of high and low imagery words: An emission computer tomography study. *Neuropsychologia, 25,* 473–486.

Goldstein, A. G. (1977). The fallibility of the eyewitness: Psychological evidence. In B. D. Sales (Ed.), *Psychology in the legal process.* New York: Spectrum.

Goodglass, H., & Geschwind, N. (1976). Language disorders (aphasia). In E. C. Carterete & M. P. Friedman (Eds.), *Handbook of Perception: Vol. 7, Languange and speech* (pp. 389–428). San Diego: Academic Press.

Gopher, D., & Kahneman, D. (1971). Individual differences in attention and the prediction of flight criteria. *Perceptual and Motor Skills, 33,* 1335–1342.

Graesser, A. C., & Bower, G. H. (Eds.). (1990). *Inferences and text comprehension.* San Diego: Academic Press.

Graesser, A. C., & Nakamura, G. V. (1982). The impact of a schema on comprehension and memory. In G. H. Bower (Ed.), *The psychology of learning and motivation* (Vol. 16). Orlando, FL: Academic Press.

Graesser, A. C., Singer, M., & Trabasso, T. (1994). Constructing inferences during narrative text comprehension. *Psychological Review, 101,* 371–395.

Greene, R. L. (1986). Sources of recency effects in free recall. *Psychological Bulletin, 99,* 221–228.

Greeno, J. G. (1978). Natures of problem solving abilities. In W. K. Estes (Ed.), *Handbook of learning and cognitive processes* (Vol. 5). Hillsdale, NJ: Erlbaum.

Greeno, J. G., & Simon, H. A. (1988). Problem solving and reasoning. In R. C. Atkinson, R. J. Herrnstein, G. Lindzey, & R. D. Luce (Eds.), *Stevens' handbook of experimental psychology* (pp. 589–672). New York: Wiley.

Griggs, R. A., & Cox, J. R. (1982). The elusive thematic-materials effect in Wason's selection task. *British Journal of Psychology, 73,* 407–420.

Grossberg, S., & Stone, G. (1986). Neural dynamics of word recognition and recall: Attentional priming, learning, and resonance. *Psychological Review, 93,* 46–74.

Gruneberg, M. M., Morris, P. E., & Sykes, R. N. (Eds.). (1978). *Practical aspects of memory.* Orlando, FL: Academic Press.

Gunter, B., Clifford, B. R., & Berry, C. (1980). Release from proactive interference with television news items: Evidence for encoding dimensions within televised news. *Journal of Experimental Psychology: Human Learning and Memory, 6,* 216–223.

Guttentag, R. E. (1985). Memory and aging: Implications for theories of memory development during childhood. *Developmental Review, 5,* 56–82.

Haber, R. N. (1969). Introduction. In R. N. Haber (Ed.), *Information-processing approaches to visual perception.* New York: Holt, Rinehart & Winston.

Haberlandt, K. F., & Graesser, A. C. (1985). Component processes in text comprehension and some of their interactions. *Journal of Experimental Psychology: General, 114,* 357–374.

Hammond, K. R. (1971). Computer graphics as an aid to learning. *Science, 172,* 903–908.

Hardyck, C. D., & Petrinovich, L. F. (1970). Subvocal speech and comprehension levels as a function of the difficulty level of reading materials. *Journal of Verbal Learning and Verbal Behavior, 9,* 647–652.

Harris, R. J. (1977). Comprehension of pragmatic implications in advertising. *Journal of Applied Psychology, 62,* 603–608.

Harris, R. J. (1978). The effect of jury size and judge's instructions on memory for pragmatic implications from courtroom testimony. *Bulletin of the Psychonomic Society, 11,* 129–132.

Hasher, L., & Zacks, R. T. (1979). Automatic and effortful processes in memory. *Journal of Experimental Psychology: General, 108,* 356–388.

Hasher, L., & Zacks, R. T. (1984). Automatic processing of fundamental information: The case of frequency of occurrence. *American Psychologist, 39,* 1372–1388.

Haviland, S. E., & Clark, H. H. (1974). What's new? Acquiring new information as a process of comprehension. *Journal of Verbal Learning and Verbal Behavior, 13,* 512–521.

Hayes, J. R. (1952). Memory span for several vocabularies as a function of vocabulary size. *Quarterly Progress Report, Acoustics Laboratory, Massachusetts Institute of Technology.*

Hayes, J. R. (1966). Memory, goals, and problem solving. In B. Kleinmuntz (Ed.), *Problem solving: Research, method, and theory.* New York: Wiley.

Hayes, J. R., & Simon, H. A. (1977). Psychological differences among problem isomorphs. In N. J. Castellan, D. B. Pisoni, & G. R. Potts (Eds.), *Cognitive theory* (Vol. 2). Hillsdale, NJ: Erlbaum.

Hayes-Roth, B., & Hayes-Roth, F. (1977). Concept learning and the recognition and classification of examples. *Journal of Verbal Learning and Verbal Behavior, 16,* 321–338.

Haygood, R. C., & Bourne, L. E., Jr. (1965). Attribute and rule learning aspects of conceptual behavior. *Psychological Review, 72,* 175–195.

Healy, A. F. (1980). Proofreading errors on the word "The": New evidence on reading units. *Journal of Experimental Psychology: Human Perception and Performance, 6,* 45–57.

Hegarty, M. (1992). Mental animation: Inferring motion from static displays of mechanical systems. *Journal of Experimental Psychology: Learning, Memory, and Cognition, 18,* 1084–1102.

Heidbreder, E. (1961). *Seven psychologies.* New York: Appleton-Century-Crofts.

Hellige, J. B. (1990). Hemispheric asymmetry. *Annual Review of Psychology, 41,* 55–80.

Herrmann, D. J., & Neisser, U. (1978). An inventory of everyday memory experiences. In M. M. Gruneberg, P. E. Morris, & R. N. Sykes (Eds.), *Practical aspects of memory.* Orlando, FL: Academic Press.

Hertel, P. T., Anooshian, L. J., & Ashbrook, P. (1986). The accuracy of beliefs about retrieval cues. *Memory & Cognition, 14,* 265–269.

Hinsley, D. A., Hayes, J. R., & Simon, H. A. (1977). From words to equations: Meaning and representation in algebra word problems. In P. A. Carpenter & M. A. Just (Eds.), *Cognitive processes in comprehension.* Hillsdale, NJ: Erlbaum.

Hintzman, D. L. (1990). Human learning and memory: Connections and dissociations. *Annual Review of Psychology, 41,* 109–139.

Hirst, W., Spelke, E. S., Reaves, C. C., Caharack, G., & Neisser, U. (1980). Dividing attention without alternation or automaticity. *Journal of Experimental Psychology: General, 109,* 98–117.

Hitch, G. J., & Baddeley, A. D. (1976). Verbal reasoning and working memory. *Quarterly Journal of Experimental Psychology, 23,* 603–621.

Hock, H. S., & Tromley, C. L. (1978). Mental rotation and perceptual uprightness. *Perception & Psychophysics, 24,* 529–533.

Hoffman, R. R., & Deffenbacher, K. A. (1992). A brief

history of applied cognitive psychology. *Applied Cognitive Psychology, 6*, 1–48.

Holbrook, M. B. (1975). A comparison of methods for measuring the interletter similarity between capital letters. *Perception & Psychophysics, 17*, 532–536.

Holley, C. D., & Dansereau, D. F. (1984). Networking: The technique and the empirical evidence. In C. D. Holley & D. F. Dansereau (Eds.), *Spatial learning strategies*. New York: Academic Press.

Holley, C. D., Dansereau, D. F., McDonald, B. A., Garland, J. C., & Collins, K. W. (1979). Evaluation of a hierarchical mapping technique as an aid to prose processing. *Contemporary Educational Psychology, 4*, 227–237.

Holst, V. F., & Pezdek, K. (1992). Scripts for typical crimes and their effects on memory for eyewitness testimony. *Applied Cognitive Psychology, 6*, 573–587.

Holyoak, K. J., & Spellman, B. A. (1993). Thinking. *Annual Review of Psychology, 44*, 263–315.

Holyoak, K. J., & Thagard, P. (1989). Analogical mapping by constraint satisfaction. *Cognitive Science, 13*, 295–355.

Homa, D. (1984). On the nature of categories. In G. H. Bower (Ed.), *The psychology of learning and motivation* (Vol. 18). Orlando, FL: Academic Press.

Howe, J. A. M. (1978). Artificial intelligence and computer-assisted learning: Ten years on. *Programmed Learning and Educational Technology, 15*, 114–125.

Hubel, D. H., & Wiesel, T. N. (1962). Receptive fields, binocular interaction, and functional architecture in the cat's visual cortex. *Journal of Physiology, 160*, 106–154.

Hubel, D. H., & Wiesel, T. N. (1963). Receptive fields of cells in the striate cortex of very young visually inexperienced kittens. *Journal of Neurophysiology, 26*, 994–1002.

Humphreys, M. S., & Bain, J. D. (1983). Recognition memory: A cue and information analysis. *Memory & Cognition, 11*, 583–600.

Humphreys, M. S., Bain, J. D., & Pike, R. (1989). Different ways to cue a coherent memory system: A theory for episodic, semantic, and procedural tasks. *Psychological Review, 96*, 208–233.

Hunt, E. (1989). Cognitive science: Definition, status, and questions. *Annual Review of Psychology, 40*, 603–629.

Hunt, E., & Lansman, M. (1975). Cognitive theory applied to individual differences. In W. K. Estes (Ed.), *Handbook of learning and cognitive processes* (Vol. 1). Hillsdale, NJ: Erlbaum.

Hunt, E., Pellegrino, J. W., & Yee, P. L. (1989). Individual differences in attention. In G. H. Bower (Ed.), *The psychology of learning and motivation* (Vol. 24, pp. 285–310). Orlando, FL: Academic Press.

Hunt, R. R., & Elliott, J. M. (1980). The role of nonsemantic information in memory: Orthographic distinctiveness effects on retention. *Journal of Experimental Psychology: General, 109*, 49–74.

Hyde, T. S., & Jenkins, J. J. (1969). The differential effects of incidental tasks on the organization of recall of a list of highly associated words. *Journal of Experimental Psychology, 82*, 472–481.

Intons-Peterson, M. J. (1983). Imagery paradigms: How vulnerable are they to experimenter's expectations? *Journal of Experimental Psychology: Human Perception and Performance, 9*, 394–412.

Jackson, S. L., & Griggs, R. A. (1990). The elusive pragmatic reasoning schemas effect. *Quarterly Journal of Experimental Psychology, 42A*, 353–373.

Jacoby, L. L., & Brooks, L. R. (1984). Nonanalytic cognition: Memory, perception, and concept learning. In G. H. Bower (Ed.), *The psychology of learning and motivation* (Vol. 18). Orlando, FL: Academic Press.

Jacoby, L. L., & Dallas, M. (1981). On the relationship between autobiographical memory and perceptual learning. *Journal of Experimental Psychology: General, 110*, 306–340.

James, W. (1890). *The principles of psychology* (2 vols.). New York: Holt.

Jarvella, R. J. (1979). Immediate memory and discourse processing. In G. H. Bower (Ed.), *The psychology of learning and motivation* (Vol. 13). Orlando, FL: Academic Press.

Jeffries, R., Polson, P. G., Razran, L., & Atwood, M. E. (1977). A process model for missionaries-cannibals and other river-crossing problems. *Cognitive Psychology, 9*, 412–440.

Jenkins, J. J. (1969). The acquisition of language. In D. A. Goslin (Ed.), *Handbook of socialization theory and research*. Skokie, IL: Rand McNally.

Johnson, M. K. (1983). A multiple-entry, modular memory system. In G. H. Bower (Ed.), *The psychology of learning and motivation* (Vol. 17). Orlando, FL: Academic Press.

Johnson, M. K., & Hasher, L. (1987). Human learning and memory. *Annual Review of Psychology, 38,* 631–668.

Johnson, M. K., Hashtroudi, S., & Lindsay, D. H. (1993). Source monitoring. *Psychological Bulletin, 114,* 3–28.

Johnson, M. K., & Raye, C. L. (1981). Reality monitoring. *Psychological Review, 88,* 67–85.

Johnson, M. K., Raye, C. L., Wang, A. Y., & Taylor, T. T. (1979). Fact and fantasy: The roles of accuracy and variability in confusing imaginations with perceptual experiences. *Journal of Experimental Psychology: Human Learning and Memory, 5,* 229–240.

Johnson, S. (1967). Hierarchical clustering schemes. *Psychometrika, 32,* 241–254.

Johnson-Laird, P. N. (1989). Analogy and the exercise of creativity. In S. Vosniadou & A. Ortony (Eds.), *Similarity and analogical reasoning.* Cambridge, England: Cambridge University Press.

Johnson-Laird, P. N., Legrenzi, P., & Legrenzi, M. S. (1972). Reasoning and a sense of reality. *British Journal of Psychology, 63,* 395–400.

Johnston, W. A., & Dark, V. J. (1986). Selective attention. *Annual Review of Psychology, 37,* 43–75.

Johnston, W. A., & Heinz, S. P. (1978). Flexibility and capacity demands of attention. *Journal of Experimental Psychology: General, 107,* 420–435.

Just, M. A., & Carpenter, P. A. (1980). A theory of reading: From eye fixations to comprehension. *Psychological Review, 87,* 329–354.

Just, M. A., & Carpenter, P. A. (1987). *The psychology of reading and language comprehension.* Newton, MA: Allyn & Bacon.

Kahneman, D. (1973). *Attention and effort.* Englewood Cliffs, NJ: Prentice-Hall.

Kahneman, D., Ben-Ishai, R., & Lotan, M. (1973). Relation of a test of attention to road accidents. *Journal of Applied Psychology, 58,* 113–115.

Kahneman, D., & Tversky, A. (1972). Subjective probability: A judgment of representativeness. *Cognitive Psychology, 3,* 430–454.

Kahneman, D., & Tversky, A. (1973). On the psychology of prediction. *Psychological Review, 80,* 237–251.

Kahneman, D., & Tversky, A. (1984). Choices, values, and frames. *American Psychologist, 39,* 341–350.

Keenan, J. M., Baillet, S. D., & Brown, P. (1984). The effects of causal cohesion on comprehension and memory. *Journal of Verbal Learning and Verbal Behavior, 23,* 115–126.

Keenan, J. M., MacWhinney, B., & Mayhew, D. (1977). Pragmatics in memory: A study of natural conversation. *Journal of Verbal Learning and Verbal Behavior, 16,* 549–560.

Keil, F. C., & Batterman, N. (1984). A characteristic-to-defining shift in the development of word meaning. *Journal of Verbal Learning and Verbal Behavior, 23,* 221–226.

Kemler-Nelson, D. G. K. (1984). The effect of intention on what concepts are acquired. *Journal of Verbal Learning and Verbal Behavior, 23,* 734–759.

Keppel, G., & Underwood, B. (1962). Proactive inhibition in short-term retention of single items. *Journal of Verbal Learning and Verbal Behavior, 1,* 153–161.

Kieras, D. E. (1978). Good and bad structure in simple paragraphs: Effects on apparent theme, reading time, and recall. *Journal of Verbal Learning and Verbal Behavior, 17,* 13–28.

Kieras, D. E. (1983). A simulation model for the comprehension of technical prose. In G. H. Bower (Ed.), *Psychology of learning and motivation* (Vol. 17). Orlando, FL: Academic Press.

Kieras, D. E., & Greeno, J. G. (1975). Effect of meaningfulness on judgments of computability. *Memory & Cognition, 3,* 349–355.

Kintsch, W. (1979). On modeling comprehension. *Educational Psychologist, 14,* 3–14.

Kintsch, W. (1988). The use of knowledge in discourse processing: A construction-integration model. *Psychological Review, 95,* 163–182.

Kintsch, W. (1994). Text comprehension, memory, and learning. *American Psychologist, 49,* 294–303.

Kintsch, W., & Bates, E. (1977). Recognition memory for statements from a classroom lecture. *Journal of Experimental Psychology: Human Learning and Memory, 3,* 150–159.

Kintsch, W., & Van Dijk, T. A. (1978). Toward a model of text comprehension and production. *Psychological Review, 85,* 363–394.

Kintsch, W., & Vipond, D. (1979). Reading comprehension and readability in educational practice and psychological theory. In L. G. Nilsson (Ed.), *Perspectives on memory research*. Hillsdale, NJ: Erlbaum.

Klapp, S. T., Marshburn, E. A., & Lester, P. T. (1983). Short-term memory does not involve the "working memory" of information processing: The demise of a common assumption. *Journal of Experimental Psychology: General, 112*, 204–264.

Klatzky, R. L. (1984). *Memory and awareness*. New York: W. H. Freeman.

Kleiman, G. M. (1975). Speech recoding in reading. *Journal of Verbal Learning and Verbal Behavior, 14*, 323–339.

Klein, G. A. (1993). A recognition-primed (RPD) model of rapid decision making. In G. A. Klein, J. Orasanu, R. Calderwood, & C. E. Zsambok (Eds.), *Decision making in action: Models and methods*. Norwood, NJ: Ablex.

Klein, G. A. , Orasanu, J., Calderwood, R., & Zsambok, C. E. (Eds.). (1993). *Decision making in action: Models and methods*. Norwood, NJ: Ablex.

Kleinmuntz, B. (1990). Why we still use our heads instead of formulas: Toward an integrative approach. *Psychological Bulletin, 107*, 296–310.

Kohler, W. (1925). *The mentality of apes*. New York: Harcourt.

Kolers, P. A. (1983). Perception and representation. *Annual Review of Psychology, 34*, 129–166.

Komatsu, L. K. (1992). Recent views of conceptual structure. *Psychological Bulletin, 112*, 500–526.

Kosslyn, S. M. (1975). Information representation in visual images. *Cognitive Psychology, 7*, 341–370.

Kosslyn, S. M. (1981). The medium and the message in mental imagery: A theory. *Psychological Review, 88*, 46–66.

Kosslyn, S. M. (1983). *Ghosts in the mind's machine: Creating and using images in the brain*. New York: Norton.

Kosslyn, S. M. (1987). Seeing and imagining in the cerebral hemispheres: A computational approach. *Psychological Review, 94*, 148–175.

Kosslyn, S. M. (1991). A cognitive neuroscience of visual cognition: Further developments. In R. H. Logie and M. Demis (Eds.), *Mental images in human cognition* (pp. 351–381). Amsterdam: Elsevier.

Kosslyn, S. M., Ball, T. M., & Reiser, B. J. (1978). Visual images preserve metric spatial information:

Evidence from studies of image scanning. *Journal of Experimental Psychology: Human Perception and Performance, 4*, 47–60.

Kosslyn, S. M., & Pomerantz, J. R. (1977). Imagery, propositions, and the form of internal representations. *Cognitive Psychology, 9*, 52–76.

Kounios, J., & Holcomb, P. J. (1994). Concreteness effects in semantic processing: ERP evidence supporing dual-coding theory. *Journal of Experimental Psychology: Learning, Memory, and Cognition, 20*, 804–823.

Kroll, N. E. A., & Parks, T. E. (1978). Interference with short-term visual memory produced by concurrent central processing. *Journal of Experimental Psychology: Human Learning and Memory, 4*, 111–120.

Kroll, N. E. A., Schepeler, E. M., & Angin, K. T. (1986). Bizarre imagery: The misremembered mnemonic. *Journal of Experimental Psychology: Learning, Memory, and Cognition, 12*, 42–53.

Kuhl, P. K. (1991). Human adults and human infants show a "perceptual magnet effect" for the prototypes of speech categories, monkeys do not. *Perception & Psychophysics, 50*, 93–107.

Kuhl, P. K. (1993). Infant speech perception: A window on psycholinguistic development. *International Journal of Psycholinguistics, 9*, 33–56.

Kuhl, P. K., Williams, K. A., Lacerda, F., Stevens, K. N., & Lindblom, B. (1992). Linguistic experience alters phonetic perception in infants by 6 months of age. *Science, 225*, 606–608.

Kuhn, D. (1989). Children and adults as intuitive scientists. *Psychological Review, 96*, 674–689.

LaBerge, D. L. (1990). Attention. *Psychological Science, 1*, 156–162.

LaBerge, D. L., & Samuels, S. J. (1974). Toward a theory of automatic information processing in reading. *Cognitive Psychology, 6*, 292–323.

Lachman, R., Lachman, J. L., & Butterfield, E. C. (1979). *Cognitive psychology and information processing: An introduction*. Hillsdale, NJ: Erlbaum.

Lambiotte, J. G., Dansereau, D. F., Cross, D. R., & Reynolds, S. B. (1989). Multirelational semantic maps. *Educational Psychology Review, 1*, 331–367.

Larkin, J. H. (1980). Teaching problem solving in physics: The psychological laboratory and the practical classroom. In D. T. Tuma & F. Reif

(Eds.), *Problem solving and education: Issues in teaching and research*. Hillsdale, NJ: Erlbaum.

Larkin, J. H., McDermott, J., Simon, D. P., & Simon, H. A. (1980). Expert and novice performance in solving physics problems. *Science, 208,* 1335–1342.

Laughery, K. R. (1969). Computer simulation of short-term memory: A component decay model. In G. H. Bower & J. T. Spence (Eds.), *The psychology of learning and motivation* (Vol. 3). Orlando, FL: Academic Press.

Lesgold, A. M., Roth, S. F., & Curtis, M. E. (1979). Foregrounding effects in discourse comprehension. *Journal of Verbal Learning and Verbal Behavior, 18,* 291–308.

Levine, D. N., Warach, J., & Farah, M. J. (1985). Two visual systems in mental imagery: Dissociation of "what" and "where" in imagery disorders due to bilateral posterior cerebral lesions. *Neurology, 35,* 1010–1018.

Levine, M. (1966). Hypothesis behavior by humans during discrimination learning. *Journal of Experimental Psychology, 71,* 331–338.

Levy, B. A. (1978). Speech processing during reading. In A. M. Lesgold, J. W. Pellegrino, S. D. Fokkema, & R. Glaser (Eds.), *Cognitive psychology and instruction*. New York: Plenum.

Lewis, M. W., & Anderson, J. R. (1985). Discrimination of operator schemata in problem solving: Learning from examples. *Cognitive Psychology, 17,* 26–65.

Light, L. L., & Carter-Sobell, L. (1970). Effects of changed semantic context on recognition memory. *Journal of Verbal Learning and Verbal Behavior, 9,* 1–11.

Lindsay, D. S., & Read, J. D. (1994). Psychotherapy and memories of childhood sexual abuse: A cognitive perspective. *Applied Cognitive Psychology, 8,* 281–338.

Lockhead, G. R., & Crist, W. B. (1980). Making letters distinctive. *Journal of Educational Psychology, 72,* 483–493.

Loftus, E. F. (1975). Leading questions and the eyewitness report. *Cognitive Psychology, 7,* 560–572.

Loftus, E. F. (1993). The reality of repressed memories. *American Psychologist, 48,* 518–537.

Loftus, G. R., Shimamura, A. P., & Johnson, C. A. (1985). How much is an icon worth? *Journal of Experimental Psychology: Human Perception and Performance, 11,* 1–13.

Logan, G. D. (1988). Toward an instance theory of automatization. *Psychological Review, 95,* 492–527.

Long, G. M. (1980). Iconic memory: A review and critique of the study of short-term visual storage. *Psychological Bulletin, 88,* 785–820.

Lorayne, H., & Lucas, J. (1974). *The memory book.* New York: Ballantine.

Luchins, A. S. (1942). Mechanization in problem solving. *Psychological Monographs, 54* (Whole No. 248).

Lundeberg, M. A., & Fox, P. W. (1991). Do laboratory findings on test expectancy generalize to classroom outcomes? *Review of Educational Research, 61,* 94–106.

Lutz, K. A., & Lutz, R. J. (1977). Effects of interactive imagery on learning: Applications to advertising. *Journal of Applied Psychology, 62,* 493–498.

Lyons, J. (1970). *Chomsky.* London: Collins.

MacKay, D. G. (1966). To end ambiguous sentences. *Perception & Psychophysics, 1,* 426–435.

MacLeod, C. M., Hunt, E. B., & Mathews, N. N. (1978). Individual differences in the verification of sentence-picture relationships. *Journal of Verbal Learning and Verbal Behavior, 17,* 493–507.

Malpass, R. S., & Devine, P. G. (1981). Guided memory in eyewitness identification. *Journal of Applied Psychology, 66,* 343–350.

Malt, B. C. (1990). Features and beliefs in the mental representation of categories. *Journal of Memory and Language, 29,* 289–315.

Mandler, G. (1967). Organization and memory. In K. W. Spence & J. T. Spence (Eds.), *The psychology of learning and motivation* (Vol. 1). Orlando, FL: Academic Press.

Mandler, G. (1980). Recognizing: The judgment of previous occurrence. *Psychological Review, 87,* 252–271.

Mandler, J. M., & Bauer, P. J. (1988). The cradle of categorization: Is the basic level basic? *Cognitive Development, 3,* 247–264.

Marcel, A. J. (1983). Conscious and unconscious perception: An approach to the relations between phenomenal experience and perceptual processes. *Cognitive Psychology, 15,* 238–300.

Marr, D., & Nishihara, H. K. (1978). Representation and recognition of three dimensional shapes.

Proceedings of the Royal Society of London (Series B), 200, 269–294.

Marschark, M., & Hunt, R. R. (1989). A reexamination of the role of imagery in learning and memory. Journal of Experimental Psychology: Learning, Memory, and Cognition, 15, 710–720.

Marslen-Wilson, M. D., & Welsh, A. (1978). Processing interactions and lexical access during word recognition in continuous speech. Cognitive Psychology, 10, 29–63.

Martin, R. C., & Caramazza, A. (1980). Classification in well-defined and ill-defined categories: Evidence for common processing strategies. Journal of Experimental Psychology: General, 109, 320–353.

Martindale, C. (1991). Cognitive psychology: A neural-network approach. Belmont, CA: Wadsworth.

Massaro, D. W. (1989). Testing between the TRACE model and the fuzzy logical model of speech perception. Cognitive Psychology, 21, 398–421.

Massaro, D. W., & Cohen, M. M. (1991). Integration versus interactive activation: The joint influence of stimulus and context in perception. Cognitive Psychology, 23, 558–614.

Massaro, D. W., & Cowan, N. (1993). Information processing models: Microscopes of the mind. Annual Review of Psychology, 44, 383–425.

Mauro, R., & Kubovy, M. (1992). Caricature and face recognition. Memory & Cognition, 20, 433–440.

Mayer, R. E. (1987). Educational psychology: A cognitive approach. Boston: Little, Brown.

Mayer, R. E., & Greeno, J. G. (1972). Structural differences between learning outcomes produced by different instructional methods. Journal of Experimental Psychology, 63, 165–173.

Mayer, R. E., & Greeno, J. G. (1975). Effects of meaningfulness and organization on problem solving and computability judgments. Memory & Cognition, 3, 356–362.

McCarty, D. L. (1980). Investigation of a visual imagery mnemonic device for acquiring face-name associations. Journal of Experimental Psychology: Human Learning and Memory, 6, 145–155.

McClelland, J. L., & Rumelhart, D. E. (1981). An interactive-activation model of context effects in letter perception: Part 1. An account of basic findings. Psychological Review, 88, 375–407.

McClelland, J. L., Rumelhart, D. E., & The PDP Research Group. (1986). Parallel Distributed Processing: Explorations in the microstructure of cognition. Cambridge, MA: MIT Press.

McCloskey, M. (1991). Networks and theories: The place of connectionism in cognitive science. Psychological Science, 2, 287–295.

McCloskey, M., & Glucksberg, S. (1979). Decision processes in verifying category membership statements: Implications for models of semantic memory. Cognitive Psychology, 11, 1–37.

McDaniel, M. A., & Einstein, G. O. (1986). Bizarre imagery as an effective memory aid: The importance of distinctiveness. Journal of Experimental Psychology: Learning, Memory, and Cognition, 12, 54–65.

McKoon, G., & Ratcliff, R. (1990). Dimensions of inference. In A. C. Graesser & G. H. Bower (Eds.), Inferences and text comprehension. San Diego: Academic Press.

McKoon, G., Ratcliff, R., & Dell, G. S. (1986). A critical evaluation of the semantic-episodic distinction. Journal of Experimental Psychology: Learning, Memory, and Cognition, 12, 295–306.

McNamara, T. P. (1992). Priming and constraints it places on theories of memory and retrieval. Psychological Review, 99, 650–662.

McNamara, T. P., & Miller, D. L. (1989). Attributes of theories of meaning. Psychological Bulletin, 106, 355–376.

Medin, D. L. (1989). Concepts and conceptual structure. American Psychologist, 44, 1469–1481.

Medin, D. L., Altom, M. W., Edelson, S. M., & Freko, D. (1982). Correlated symptoms and simulated medical classification. Journal of Experimental Psychology: Learning, Memory, and Cognition, 8, 37–50.

Medin, D. L., & Ross, B. H. (1989). The specific character of abstract thought: Categorization, problem-solving, and induction. In R. J. Sternberg (Ed.), Advances in the psychology of human intelligence (Vol. 5). Hillsdale, NJ: Erlbaum.

Medin, D. L., & Schaffer, M. M. (1978). Context theory of classification learning. Psychological Review, 85, 207–238.

Medin, D. L., & Smith, E. E. (1984). Concepts and concept formation. Annual Review of Psychology, 35, 113–138.

Mervis, C. B., & Rosch, E. (1981). Categorization of natural objects. Annual Review of Psychology, 32, 89–115.

Metcalfe, J. (1986a). Feeling of knowing in memory and problem solving. *Journal of Experimental Psychology: Human Perception and Performance, 6*, 58–66.

Metcalfe, J. (1986b). Premonitions of insight predict impending error. *Journal of Experimental Psychology: Learning, Memory, and Cognition, 12*, 623–634.

Meyer, D. E., & Schvaneveldt, R. W. (1976). Meaning, memory structure, and mental processes. *Science, 192*, 27–33.

Mihal, W. L., & Barett, G. V. (1976). Individual differences in perceptual information processing and their relation to automobile accident involvement. *Journal of Applied Psychology, 61*, 229–233.

Milgram, S. (1970). The experience of living in cities. *Science, 167*, 1461–1468.

Miller, G. A. (1956). The magical number seven, plus or minus two: Some limits on our capacity for processing information. *Psychological Review, 63*, 81–97.

Miller, G. A., Galanter, E., & Pribram, K. (1960). *Plans and the structure of behavior.* New York: Holt, Rinehart & Winston.

Miller, J. R., & Kintsch, W. (1980). Readability and recall of short prose passages: A theoretical analysis. *Journal of Experimental Psychology: Human Learning and Memory, 6*, 335–354.

Minsky, M. (1975). A framework for the representation of knowledge. In P. Winston (Ed.), *The psychology of computer vision.* New York: McGraw-Hill.

Mitchell, D. B., & Richman, C. L. (1980). Confirmed reservations: Mental travel. *Journal of Experimental Psychology: Human Perception and Performance, 6*, 58–66.

Mitchell, T. R., & Beach, L. R. (1990). ". . . Do I love thee? Let me count . . ." Toward an understanding of intuitive and automatic decision making. *Organizational Behavior and Human Decision Processes, 47*, 1–20.

Miyake, A., Just, M. A., & Carpenter, P. A. (1994). Working memory constraints on the resolution of lexical ambiguity: Maintaining multiple interpretations in neutral contexts. *Journal of Memory and Language, 33*, 175–202.

Moray, N. (1959). Attention in dichotic listening: Affective cues and the influence of instructions. *Quarterly Journal of Experimental Psychology, 11*, 56–60.

Morris, C. D., Bransford, J. D., & Franks, J. J. (1977). Levels of processing versus transfer appropriate processing. *Journal of Verbal Learning and Verbal Behavior, 16*, 519–533.

Morris, P. E., Jones, S., & Hampson, P. (1978). An imagery mnemonic for the learning of people's names. *British Journal of Psychology, 69*, 335–336.

Moscovitch, M., & Craik, F. I. M. (1976). Depth of processing, retrieval cues, and uniqueness of encoding as factors in recall. *Journal of Verbal Learning and Verbal Behavior, 15*, 447–458.

Mulholland, T. M., Pellegrino, J. W., & Glaser, R. (1980). Components of geometric analogy solution. *Cognitive Psychology, 12*, 252–284.

Murphy, G. L. (1990). Noun phrase interpretation and conceptual combination. *Journal of Memory and Language, 29*, 259–288.

Murphy, G. L., & Medin, D. L. (1985). The role of theories in conceptual coherence. *Psychological Review, 92*, 289–316.

Myers, J. L., O'Brien, E. J., Balota, D. A., & Toyofuku, M. L. (1984). Memory search without interference: The role of integration. *Cognitive Psychology, 16*, 217–242.

Naveh-Benjamin, M. (1988). Recognition memory of spatial location information: Another failure to support automaticity. *Memory & Cognition, 16*, 437–445.

Navon, D., & Gopher, D. (1979). On the economy of the human-processing system. *Psychological Review, 86*, 214–255.

Neely, J. H., & Keefe, D. E. (1989). Semantic context effects on visual word processing: A hybrid prospective-retrospective processing theory. In G. H. Bower (Ed.), *The psychology of learning and motivation* (Vol. 24). Orlando, FL: Academic Press.

Neisser, U. (1967). *Cognitive psychology.* New York: Appleton-Century-Crofts.

Neisser, U., & Becklen, R. (1975). Selective looking: Attending to visually specified events. *Cognitive Psychology, 7*, 480–494.

Nelson, T. O. (1977). Repetition and depth of processing. *Journal of Verbal Learning and Verbal Behavior, 16*, 151–171.

Nelson, T. O., Dunlosky, J., Graf, A., & Narens, L. (1994). Utilization of metacognitive judgments in the allocation of study during multitrial learning. *Psychological Science, 5,* 207–213.

Nelson, T. O., & Narens, L. (1990). Metamemory: A theoretical framework and some new findings. In G. H. Bower (Ed.), *The psychology of learning and motivation* (Vol. 25). Orlando, FL: Academic Press.

Nelson, T. O., & Smith, E. E. (1972). Acquisition and forgetting of hierarchically organized information in long-term memory. *Journal of Experimental Psychology, 95,* 388–396.

Neumann, P. G. (1974). An attribute frequency model for the abstraction of prototypes. *Memory & Cognition, 2,* 241–248.

Newell, A., Shaw, J. C., & Simon, H. A. (1958a). Chess-playing problems and the problem of complexity. *IBM Journal of Research and Development, 2,* 320–335.

Newell, A., Shaw, J. C., & Simon, H. A. (1958b). Elements of a theory of human problem solving. *Psychological Review, 65,* 151–166.

Newell, A., & Simon, H. A. (1972). *Human problem solving.* Englewood Cliffs, NJ: Prentice-Hall.

Nickerson, R. S., & Adams, M. J. (1979). Long-term memory for a common object. *Cognitive Psychology, 11,* 287–307.

Nielsen, G. D., & Smith, E. E. (1973). Imaginal and verbal representations in short-term recognition of visual forms. *Journal of Experimental Psychology, 101,* 375–378.

Noice, H. (1991). The role of explanations and plan recognition in the learning of theatrical scripts. *Cognitive Science, 15,* 425–460.

Norman, D. A. (1968). Toward a theory of memory and attention. *Psychological Review, 75,* 522–536.

Norman, D. A. (1980). Cognitive engineering and education. In D. T. Tuma & F. Reif (Eds.), *Problem solving and education: Issues in teaching and research.* Hillsdale, NJ: Erlbaum.

Nosofsky, R. M. (1991). Tests of an exemplar model for relating perceptual classification and recognition memory. *Journal of Experimental Psychology: Human Perception and Performance, 17,* 3–27.

Novick, L. R. (1990). Representational transfer in problem solving. *Psychological Science, 1,* 128–132.

Novick, L. R., & Hmelo, C. E. (1994). Transferring symbolic representations across nonisomorphic problems. *Journal of Experimental Psychology: Learning, Memory, and Cognition, 20,* 1296–1321.

Orasanu, J., & Connolly, T. (1993). The reinvention of decision making. In G. A. Klein, J. Orasanu, R. Calderwood, & C. E. Zsambok (Eds.), *Decision making in action: Models and methods* (pp. 3–20). Norwood, NJ: Ablex.

Paap, K. R., Newsome, S. L., McDonald, J. E., & Schvaneveldt, R. W. (1982). An activation-verification model for letter and word recognition: The word superiority effect. *Psychological Review, 89,* 573–594.

Paige, J. M., & Simon, H. A. (1966). Cognitive processes in solving algebra word problems. In B. Kleinmuntz (Ed.), *Problem solving: Research, method, and theory.* New York: Wiley.

Paivio, A. (1969). Mental imagery in associative learning and memory. *Psychological Review, 76,* 241–263.

Paivio, A. (1971). *Imagery and verbal processes.* New York: Holt, Rinehart & Winston.

Paivio, A. (1975). Coding distinctions and repetition effects in memory. In G. H. Bower (Ed.), *Psychology of learning and motivation* (Vol. 9). Orlando, FL: Academic Press.

Paivio, A., Smythe, P. E., & Yuille, J. C. (1968). Imagery versus meaningfulness of nouns in paired-associate learning. *Canadian Journal of Psychology, 22,* 427–441.

Palmer, S. E. (1977). Hierarchical structure in perceptual representation. *Cognitive Psychology, 9,* 441–474.

Paquette, L., & Kida, T. (1988). Effect of decision strategy and task complexity on decision performance. *Organizational Behavior and Human Decision Processes, 41,* 128–142.

Payne, J. W. (1973). Alternative approaches to decision making under risk. *Psychological Bulletin, 80,* 439–453.

Payne, J. W. (1976). Task complexity and contingent processing in decision making: An information search and protocol analysis. *Organizational Behavior and Human Performance, 16,* 366–387.

Payne, J. W., Bettman, J. R., & Johnson, E. J. (1992). Behavioral decision research: A constructive processing perspective. *Annual Review of Psychology, 43,* 87–131.

Payne, J. W., Bettman, J. R., & Johnson, E. J. (1993). *The adaptive decision maker.* Cambridge, England: Cambridge University Press.

Pellegrino, J. W., & Glaser, R. (1979). Cognitive correlates and components in the analysis of individual differences. *Intelligence*, 3, 187–216.

Penrod, S., & Hastie, R. (1980). A computer simulation of jury decision making. *Psychological Review*, 87, 133–159.

Perfetti, C. A., Beverly, S., Bell, L., Rodgers, K., & Faux, R. (1987). Comprehending newspaper headlines. *Journal of Memory and Language*, 26, 692–713.

Perfetto, G. A., Bransford, J. D., & Franks, J. J. (1983). Constraints on access in a problem solving context. *Memory & Cognition*, 11, 24–31.

Peterson, L. R., & Peterson, M. J. (1959). Short-term retention of individual verbal items. *Journal of Experimental Psychology*, 58, 193–198.

Phillips, W. A. (1974). On the distinction between sensory storage and short-term visual memory. *Perception & Psychophysics*, 16, 283–290.

Pintrich, P. R., Cross, D. R., Kozma, R. B., & Mckeachie, W. J. (1986). Instructional psychology. *Annual Review of Psychology*, 37, 611–651.

Pittenger, J. B., & Shaw, R. E. (1975). Aging faces as viscal-elastic events: Implications for a theory of nonrigid shape perception. *Journal of Experimental Psychology: Human Perception and Performance*, 1, 374–383.

Pitz, G. F., & Harren, V. A. (1980). An analysis of career decision making from the point of view of information processing and decision theory. *Journal of Vocational Behavior*, 16, 320–346.

Pitz, G. F., & Sachs, N. J. (1984). Judgment and decision: Theory and application. *Annual Review of Psychology*, 35, 139–163.

Pollatsek, A., & Rayner, K. (1989). Reading. In M. I. Posner (Ed.), *Foundations of cognitive science*. Cambridge, MA: MIT Press.

Polson, P. G., & Jeffries, R. (1985). Instruction in general problem-solving skills: An analysis of four approaches. In J. W. Segal, S. F. Chipman, & R. Glaser (Eds.), *Thinking and learning skills* (Vol. 1). Hillsdale, NJ: Erlbaum.

Polya, G. (1962). *Mathematical discovery* (Vol. 1). New York: Wiley.

Posner, M. I. (Ed.). (1989). *Foundations of cognitive science*. Cambridge, MA: MIT Press.

Posner, M. I., Boies, S. J., Eichelman, W. H., & Taylor, R. L. (1969). Retention of visual and name codes of single letters. *Journal of Experimental Psychology Monograph*, 79, 1–13.

Posner, M. I., Goldsmith, R., & Welton, K. E. (1967). Perceived distance and the classification of distorted patterns. *Journal of Experimental Psychology*, 73, 28–38.

Posner, M. I., & Keele, S. W. (1968). On the genesis of abstract ideas. *Journal of Experimental Psychology*, 77, 353–363.

Posner, M. I., & Rothbart, M. K. (1994). Constructing neuronal theories of the mind. In C. Koch & J. Davis (Eds.), *Large scale neuronal theories of the brain* (pp.183–199). Cambridge, MA: MIT Press.

Posner, M. I., & Snyder, C. R. R. (1975). Attention and cognitive control. In R. L. Solso (Ed.), *Information processing and cognition: The Loyola Symposium* (pp. 58–85). Hillsdale, NJ: Erlbaum.

Postman, L., & Phillips, L. W. (1965). Short term temporal changes in free recall. *Quarterly Journal of Experimental Psychology*, 17, 132–138.

Potter, M. C., & Faulconer, B. A. (1979). Understanding noun phrases. *Journal of Verbal Learning and Verbal Behavior*, 18, 509–521.

Pressley, M., Levin, J. R., Hall, J. W., Miller, G. E., & Berry, J. K. (1980). The key word method and foreign word acquisition. *Journal of Experimental Psychology: Human Learning and Memory*, 6, 163–173.

Pylyshyn, Z. W. (1973). What the mind's eye tells the mind's brain: A critique of mental imagery. *Psychological Bulletin*, 80, 1–24.

Pylyshyn, Z. W. (1981). The imagery debate: Analogue media versus tacit knowledge. *Psychological Review*, 88, 16–45.

Radransky, G. A., & Zacks, R. T. (1991). Mental models and fact retrieval. *Journal of Experimental Psychology: Learning, Memory, and Cognition*, 17, 940–953.

Ratcliff, R., & McKoon, G. (1988). A retrieval theory of priming in memory. *Psychological Review*, 95, 385–408.

Raven, J. C. (1962). *Advanced progressive matrices, Set II*. London: H. K. Lewis. (Distributed in the United States by the Psychological Corporation, San Antonio, TX.)

Read, J. D., & Bruce, D. (1982). Longitudinal tracking of difficult memory retrievals. *Cognitive Psychology*, 14, 280–300.

Reder, L. M. (1980). The role of elaboration in the comprehension and retention of prose. *Review of Educational Research*, 50, 5–53.

Reder, L. M., & Anderson, J. R. (1980). Partial resolution of the paradox of interference: The role of integrating knowledge. *Cognitive Psychology, 12,* 447–472.

Reder, L. M., & Ross, B. H. (1983). Integrated knowledge in different tasks: The role of retrieval strategy on fan effects. *Journal of Experimental Psychology: Learning, Memory, and Cognition, 9,* 55–72.

Reed, S. K. (1972). Pattern recognition and categorization. *Cognitive Psychology, 3,* 382–407.

Reed, S. K. (1993). A schema-based theory of transfer. In D. K. Detterman & R. J. Sternberg (Eds.), *Transfer on trial: Intelligence, cognition and instruction.* Norwood, NJ: Ablex.

Reed, S. K., Ernst, G. W., & Banerji, R. (1974). The role of analogy in transfer between similar problem states. *Cognitive Psychology, 6,* 436–450.

Reed, S. K., & Evans, A. C. (1987). Learning functional relations: A theoretical and instructional analysis. *Journal of Experimental Psychology: General, 116,* 106–118.

Reed, S. K., & Friedman, M. P. (1973). Perceptual vs. conceptual categorization. *Memory & Cognition, 1,* 157–163.

Reed, S. K., Hock, H., & Lockhead, G. R. (1983). Tacit knowledge and the effect of pattern configuration on mental scanning. *Memory & Cognition, 11,* 137–143.

Reed, S. K., & Johnsen, J. A. (1975). Detection of parts in patterns and images. *Memory & Cognition, 3,* 569–575.

Reeves, L. M., & Weisberg, R. W. (1994). The role of content and abstract information in analogical transfer. *Psychological Bulletin, 115,* 381–400.

Reicher, G. M. (1969). Perceptual recognition as a function of meaningfulness of stimulus material. *Journal of Experimental Psychology, 81,* 275–280.

Reitman, J. S. (1974). Without surreptitious rehearsal, information in short-term memory decays. *Journal of Verbal Learning and Verbal Behavior, 13,* 365–377.

Reitman, J. S., & Bower, G. H. (1973). Storage and later recognition of exemplars of concepts. *Cognitive Psychology, 4,* 194–206.

Rhodes, G., Brennan, S., & Carey, S. (1987). Identification and ratings of caricatures: Implications for mental representations of faces. *Cognitive Psychology, 19,* 473–497.

Richardson-Klavehn, A., & Bjork, R. A. (1988). Measures of memory. *Annual Review of Psychology, 39,* 475–543.

Richman, H. B., & Simon, H. A. (1989). Context effects in letter perception: Comparison of two theories. *Psychological Review, 96,* 417–432.

Roediger, H. L. (1980). Memory metaphors in cognitive psychology. *Memory & Cognition, 8,* 231–246.

Roediger, H. L. (1990). Implicit memory: Retention without remembering. *American Psychologist, 45,* 1043–1056.

Roland, P. E., & Friberg, L. (1985). Localization of cortical areas activated by thinking. *Journal of Neurophysiology, 53,* 1219–1243.

Rosch, E. (1973). Natural categories. *Cognitive Psychology, 4,* 328–350.

Rosch, E. (1975). Cognitive representations of semantic categories. *Journal of Experimental Psychology: General, 3,* 192–233.

Rosch, E., & Mervis, C. B. (1975). Family resemblances: Studies in the internal structure of categories. *Cognitive Psychology, 7,* 573–605.

Rosch, E., Mervis, C. B., Gray, W. D., Johnsen, D. M., & Boyes-Braem, P. (1976). Basic objects in natural categories. *Cognitive Psychology, 8,* 382–440.

Roskos-Ewoldsen, B., Intons-Peterson, M. J., & Anderson, R. E. (1993). *Imagery, creativity, and discovery.* Amsterdam: North Holland.

Ross, B. H. (1984). Remindings and their effects in learning a cognitive skill. *Cognitive Psychology, 16,* 371–416.

Ross, B. H., & Kennedy, P. T. (1990). Generalizing from the use of earlier examples in problem solving. *Journal of Experimental Psychology: Learning, Memory, and Cognition, 16,* 42–55.

Rumelhart, D. E. (1970). A multicomponent theory of perception of briefly exposed stimulus displays. *Journal of Mathematical Psychology, 7,* 191–218.

Rumelhart, D. E. (1977). Toward an interactive model of reading. In S. Dornic (Ed.), *Attention and performance* (Vol. 6). Hillsdale, NJ: Erlbaum.

Rumelhart, D. E. (1980). Schemata: The building blocks of cognition. In R. Spiro, B. Bruce, & W. Brewer (Eds.), *Theoretical issues in reading comprehension.* Hillsdale, NJ: Erlbaum.

Rumelhart, D. E. (1989). The architecture of mind: A connectionist approach. In M. I. Posner (Ed.),

Foundations of cognitive science. Cambridge, MA: MIT Press.

Rumelhart, D. E., Hinton, G. E. & McClelland, J. L. (1986). A general framework for parallel distributed processing. In D. E. Rumelhart, J. L. McClelland, & the PDP Research Group (Eds.), *Parallel distributed processing: Explorations in the microstructure of cognition* (Vol. 1). Cambridge, MA: Bradford.

Rumelhart, D. E., & McClelland, J. L. (1982). An interactive-activation model of context effects in letter perception: Part 2. The contextual enhancement and some tests and extensions of the model. *Psychological Review, 89,* 60–94.

Rundus, D. (1971). Analysis of rehearsal processes in free recall. *Journal of Experimental Psychology, 89,* 63–77.

Rushmer, R. F. (1970). *Cardiovascular dynamics.* Philadelphia: Saunders.

Saariluoma, P. (1992). Visuospatial and articulatory interference in chess players' information intake. *Applied Cognitive Psychology, 6,* 77–89.

Sachs, J. S. (1967). Recognition memory for syntactic and semantic aspects of connected discourse. *Perception & Psychophysics, 2,* 437–442.

Salasoo, A., & Pisoni, D. B. (1985). Interaction of knowledge sources in spoken word identification. *Journal of Memory and Language, 24,* 210–231.

Sanders, A. F., & Schroots, J. J. F. (1969). Cognitive categories and memory span: III. Effects of similarity on recall. *Quarterly Journal of Experimental Psychology, 21,* 21–28.

Schacter, D. L. (1987). Implicit memory: History and current status. *Journal of Experimental Psychology: Learning, Memory, and Cognition, 13,* 501–518.

Schacter, D. L. (1989). Memory. In M. I. Posner (Ed.), *Foundations of cognitive science* (pp. 683–725). Cambridge, MA: MIT Press.

Schank, R., & Abelson, R. (1977). *Scripts, goals, and understanding.* Hillsdale, NJ: Erlbaum.

Schmidt, S. R. (1991). Can we have a distinctive theory of memory? *Memory & Cognition, 19,* 523–542.

Schneider, V. I., Healy, A. F., & Gesi, A. T. (1991). The role of phonetic processes in letter detection: A reevaluation. *Journal of Memory and Language, 30,* 294–318.

Schneider, W., & Graham, D. J. (1992). Introduction to connectionist modeling in education. *Educational Psychologist, 27,* 513–530.

Schneider, W., & Shiffrin, R. M. (1977). Controlled and automatic human information processing: I. Detection, search, and attention. *Psychological Review, 84,* 1–66.

Schoenfeld, A. H. (1979). Explicit heuristic training as a variable in problem-solving performances. *Journal for Research in Mathematics Education, 10,* 173–187.

Schvaneveldt, R. W., Meyer, D. E., & Becker, C. A. (1976). Lexical ambiguity, semantic context, and visual word recognition. *Journal of Experimental Psychology: Human Perception and Performance, 2,* 243–256.

Schwanenflugel, P. J., & Shoben, E. J. (1985). The influence of sentence constraint on the scope of facilitation for upcoming words. *Journal of Memory and Language, 24,* 232–252.

Schweickert, R., Guentert, L., & Hersberger, L. (1990). Phonological similarity, pronunciation rate, and memory span. *Psychological Science, 1,* 74–77.

Segal, J. W., Chipman, S. F., & Glaser, R. (1985). *Thinking and learning skills* (Vol. 1). Hillsdale, NJ: Erlbaum.

Seidenberg, M. S. (1993). Connectionist models and cognitive theory. *Psychological Science, 4,* 228–235.

Seidenberg, M. S., Waters, G. S., Sanders, M., & Langer, P. (1984). Pre- and postlexical loci of contextual effects on word recognition. *Memory & Cognition, 12,* 315–328.

Sejnowski, T. J., & Rosenberg, C. R. (1987). Parallel networks that learn to pronounce English text. *Complex Systems, 1,* 145–168.

Semb, G. B., & Ellis, J. A. (1994). Knowledge taught in school: What is remembered? *Review of Educational Research, 64,* 253–286.

Sharkey, N. E., & Mitchell, D. C. (1985). Word recognition in a functional context: The use of scripts in reading. *Journal of Memory and Language, 24,* 253–270.

Shaughnessy, J. J. (1981). Memory monitoring accuracy and modification of rehearsal strategies. *Journal of Verbal Learning and Verbal Behavior, 20,* 216–230.

Sheikh, A. A. (Ed.). (1983). *Imagery: Current theory, research, and application.* New York: Wiley.

Shepard, R. N. (1967). Recognition memory for words, sentences, and pictures. *Journal of Verbal Learning and Verbal Behavior, 6*, 156–163.

Shepard, R. N. (1988). The imagination of the scientist. In K. Egan & D. Nadaner (Eds.), *Imagination and education* (pp. 153–185). New York: Teachers College Press.

Shepard, R. N., & Metzler, J. (1971). Mental rotation of three-dimensional objects. *Science, 171*, 701–703.

Shepard, R. N., & Podgorny, P. (1978). Cognitive processes that resemble perceptual processes. In W. K. Estes (Ed.), *Handbook of learning and cognitive processes* (Vol. 5). Hillsdale, NJ: Erlbaum.

Shiffrin, R. M. (1988). Attention. In R. C. Atkinson, R. J. Hernstein, G. Lindzey, & R. D. Luce (Eds.), *Stevens' handbook of experimental psychology* (pp. 731–811). New York: Wiley.

Shiffrin, R. M., & Schneider, W. (1977). Controlled and automatic human information processing: II. Perceptual learning, automatic attending, and a general theory. *Psychological Review, 84*, 127–190.

Shulman, H. G. (1971). Similarity effects in short-term memory. *Psychological Bulletin, 75*, 399–415.

Silver, E. A. (1981). Recall of mathematical problem information: Solving related problems. *Journal for Research in Mathematics Education, 12*, 54–64.

Simon, H. A. (1957). *Models of man*. New York: Wiley.

Simon, H. A. (1974). How big is a chunk? *Science, 183*, 482–488.

Simon, H. A. (1983). Search and reasoning in problem solving. *Artificial Intelligence, 21*, 7–29.

Simon, H. A., & Gilmartin, K. (1973). A simulation of memory for chess positions. *Cognitive Psychology, 5*, 29–46.

Simon, H. A., & Kaplan, C. A. (1989). Foundations of cognitive science. In M. I. Posner (Ed.), *Foundations of cognitive science*. Cambridge, MA: MIT Press.

Simon, H. A., & Newell, A. (1971). Human problem solving: The state of the theory in 1970. *American Psychologist, 26*, 145–159.

Simon, H. A., & Reed, S. K. (1976). Modeling strategy shifts in a problem-solving task. *Cognitive Psychology, 8*, 86–97.

Singer, J. L. (Ed.). (1990). *Repression and dissociation: Implications for personality theory, psychopathology, and health*. Chicago: University of Chicago Press.

Slovic, P., Fischhoff, B., & Lichtenstein, S. (1976). Cognitive processes and societal risk taking. In J. S. Carroll & J. W. Payne (Eds.), *Cognition and social behavior*. Hillsdale, NJ: Erlbaum.

Slovic, P., & Lichtenstein, S. (1968). Relative importance of probabilities and payoffs in risk taking. *Journal of Experimental Psychology Monograph, 78* (3, Pt. 2).

Slowiaczek, M. L., & Clifton, C. (1980). Subvocalization and reading for meaning. *Journal of Verbal Learning and Verbal Behavior, 19*, 573–582.

Smith, E. E. (1978). Theories of semantic memory. In W. K. Estes (Ed.), *Handbook of learning and cognitive processes* (Vol. 6). Hillsdale, NJ: Erlbaum.

Smith, E. E., Adams, N., & Schorr, D. (1978). Fact retrieval and the paradox of interference. *Cognitive Psychology, 10*, 438–464.

Smith, E. E., & Nielsen, G. D. (1970). Representation and retrieval processes in short-term memory: Recognition and recall of faces. *Journal of Experimental Psychology, 85*, 397–405.

Smith, E. E., Shoben, E. J., & Rips, L. J. (1974). Structure and process in semantic memory: A featural model for semantic decision. *Psychological Review, 81*, 214–241.

Smith, M. E. (1983). Hypnotic memory enhancement of witnesses: Does it work? *Psychological Bulletin, 94*, 387–407.

Smith, S. M., Ward, T. B., & Schumacher, J. S. (1993). Constraining effects of examples in a creative generation task. *Memory & Cognition, 21*, 837–845.

Smyth, M. M., & Scholey, K. A. (1994). Interference in immediate spatial memory. *Memory & Cognition, 22*, 1–13.

Snyder, A. Z., Abdullaev, Y. G., Posner, M. I., & Raichle, M. E. (1995). Scalp electrical potentials reflect regional cerebral blood flow responses during processing of written words. *Proceedings of the National Academy of Sciences USA, 92*, 1689–1693.

Sperling, G. (1960). The information available in brief visual presentations. *Psychological Monographs, 74* (11, Whole No. 498).

Sperling, G. (1963). A model for visual memory tasks. *Human Factors, 5*, 19–31.

Sperling, G. (1967). Successive approximations to a model for short-term memory. *Acta Psychologica, 27*, 285–292.

Spilich, G. J., Vesonder, G. T., Chiesi, H. L., & Voss, J. F. (1979). Text processing of domain-related information for individuals with high and low domain knowledge. *Journal of Verbal Learning and Verbal Behavior, 18,* 275–290.

Squire, L. R., Knowlton, B., & Musen, G. (1993). The structure and organization of memory. *Annual Review of Psychology, 44,* 453–495.

Standing, L. (1973). Learning 10,000 pictures. *Quarterly Journal of Experimental Psychology, 25,* 207–222.

Stanovich, K. E. (1990). Concepts in developmental theories of reading skill: Cognitive resources, automaticity, and modularity. *Developmental Review, 10,* 72–100.

Stanovich, K. E., & West, R. F. (1983). On priming by a sentence context. *Journal of Experimental Psychology: General, 112,* 1–36.

Stein, B. S., & Bransford, J. D. (1979). Constraints on effective elaboration: Effects of precision and subject generation. *Journal of Verbal Learning and Verbal Behavior, 18,* 769–777.

Stein, N. L., & Trabasso, T. (1982). What's in a story: An approach to comprehension and instruction. In R. Glaser (Ed.), *Advances in instructional psychology* (Vol. 2). Hillsdale, NJ: Erlbaum.

Sternberg, R. J. (1977). Component processes in analogical reasoning. *Psychological Review, 84,* 353–378.

Sternberg, R. J. (1985). *Beyond IQ: A theory of human intelligence.* Cambridge, England: Cambridge University Press.

Sternberg, R. J., & Detterman, D. K. (Eds.). (1979). *Human intelligence: Perspectives on its theory and measurement.* Norwood, NJ: Ablex.

Sternberg, R. J., & Gardner, M. K. (1983). Unities in inductive reasoning. *Journal of Experimental Psychology: General, 112,* 80–116.

Sternberg, S. (1966). High-speed scanning in human memory. *Science, 153,* 652–654.

Sternberg, S. (1967a). Retrieval of contextual information from memory. *Psychonomic Science, 8,* 55–56.

Sternberg, S. (1967b). Two operations in character recognition: Some evidence from reaction time measurements. *Perception & Psychophysics, 2,* 45–53.

Stevens, A., & Coupe, P. (1978). Distortions in judged spatial relations. *Cognitive Psychology, 10,* 411–437.

Strauss, M. S. (1979). Abstraction of prototypical information by adults and 10-month-old infants. *Journal of Experimental Psychology: Human Learning and Memory, 5,* 618–632.

Stroop, J. R. (1935). Studies of interferences in serial verbal reactions. *Journal of Experimental Psychology, 18,* 643–662.

Suinn, R. M. (1983). Imagery and sports. In A. A. Sheikh (Ed.), *Imagery: Current theory, research, and application.* New York: Wiley.

Sulin, R. A., & Dooling, D. J. (1974). Intrusion of a thematic idea in retention of prose. *Journal of Experimental Psychology, 103,* 255–262.

Sutherland, N. S. (1968). Outlines of a theory of visual pattern recognition in animals and man. *Proceedings of the Royal Society, 171,* 297–317.

Sweller, J. (1988). Cognitive load during problem solving: Effects on learning. *Cognitive Science, 12,* 257–285.

Sweller, J., Mawer, R. F., & Ward, M. R. (1983). Development of expertise in mathematical problem solving. *Journal of Experimental Psychology: General, 112,* 639–661.

Swinney, D. A. (1979). Lexical access during sentence comprehension: Reconsideration of some context effects. *Journal of Verbal Learning and Verbal Behavior, 18,* 645–659.

Swinney, D. A., & Hakes, D. T. (1976). Effects of prior context upon lexical access during sentence comprehension. *Journal of Verbal Learning and Verbal Behavior, 15,* 681–689.

Swinney, D. A., & Osterhout, L. (1990). Inference generation during auditory language comprehension. In A. C. Graesser & G. H. Bower (Eds.), *Inferences and text comprehension.* San Diego: Academic Press.

Tanaka, J. W., & Taylor, M. (1991). Object categories and expertise: Is the basic level in the eye of the beholder? *Cognitive Psychology, 23,* 457–482.

Taylor, S. E., & Crocker, J. (1981). Schematic bases of social information processing. In E. T. Higgens, C. P. Herman, & M. P. Zanna (Eds.), *Social cognition: The Ontario Symposium* (Vol. 1). Hillsdale, NJ: Erlbaum.

Thomson, D. M., & Tulving, E. (1970). Associative encoding and retrieval: Weak and strong cues. *Journal of Experimental Psychology, 86,* 255–262.

Thorndyke, P. W. (1977). Cognitive structures in comprehension and memory of narrative discourse. *Cognitive Psychology, 9,* 77–110.

Thorndyke, P. W. (1984). Applications of schema theory in cognitive research. In J. R. Anderson & S. M. Kosslyn (Eds.), *Tutorials in learning and memory.* San Francisco: W. H. Freeman.

Thorndyke, P. W., & Stasz, C. (1980). Individual differences in procedures for knowledge acquisition from maps. *Cognitive Psychology, 12,* 137–175.

Toth, J. P., Reingold, E. M., & Jacoby, L. L. (1994). Toward a redefinition of implicit memory: Process dissociations following elaborative processing and self-generation. *Journal of Experimental Psychology: Learning, Memory, and Cognition, 20,* 290–303.

Townsend, J. T. (1971). Theoretical analysis of an alphabetic confusion matrix. *Perception & Psychophysics, 9,* 40–50.

Townsend, J. T., & Ashby, F. G. (1982). Experimental test of contemporary mathematical models of visual letter recognition. *Journal of Experimental Psychology: Human Perception and Performance, 6,* 834–864.

Townsend, J. T., Hu, G. G., & Evans, R. J. (1984). Modeling feature perception in brief displays with evidence for positive interdependencies. *Perception & Psychophysics, 36,* 35–49.

Trabasso, T., & Sperry, L. L. (1985). The causal basis for deciding importance of story events. *Journal of Memory and Language, 24,* 595–611.

Trabasso, T., & van den Broek, P. (1985). Causal thinking and the representation of narrative events. *Journal of Memory and Language, 24,* 612–630.

Treisman, A. M. (1960). Contextual cues in encoding listening. *Quarterly Journal of Experimental Psychology, 12,* 242–248.

Treisman, A. M., & Geffen, G. (1967). Selective attention and cerebral dominance in responding to speech messages. *Quarterly Journal of Experimental Psychology, 19,* 1–17.

Treisman, A. M., & Gelade, G. (1980). A feature-integration theory of attention. *Cognitive Psychology, 12,* 97–136.

Treisman, A. M., & Schmidt, H. (1982). Illusory conjunctions in the perception of objects. *Cognitive Psychology, 14,* 107–141.

Tulving, E. (1972). Episodic and semantic memory. In E. Tulving & W. Donaldson (Eds.), *Organization of memory* (pp. 381–403). New York: Academic Press.

Tulving, E. (1985). How many memory systems are there? *American Psychologist, 40,* 385–398.

Tulving, E., & Thomson, D. M. (1973). Encoding specificity and retrieval processes in episodic memory. *Psychological Review, 80,* 352–373.

Tversky, A. (1972). Elimination by aspects: A theory of choice. *Psychological Review, 79,* 281–299.

Tversky, A., & Kahneman, D. (1973). Availability: A heuristic for judging frequency and probability. *Cognitive Psychology, 5,* 207–232.

Tversky, A., & Kahneman, D. (1981). The framing of decisions and the psychology of choice. *Science, 211,* 453–458.

Tversky, B. (1981). Distortions in memory for maps. *Cognitive Psychology, 13,* 407–433.

Uhr, L. (1966). *Pattern recognition.* New York: Wiley.

Van Dijk, T. A., & Kintsch, W. (1983). *Strategies of discourse comprehension.* Orlando, FL: Academic Press.

vanLehn, K. (1989). Problem solving and cognitive skill acquisition. In M. I. Posner (Ed.), *Foundations of cognitive science.* Cambridge, MA: MIT Press.

Vipond, D. (1980). Micro- and macroprocesses in text comprehension. *Journal of Verbal Learning and Verbal Behavior, 19,* 276–296.

Vosniadou, S., & Ortony, A. (1989). *Similarity and analogical reasoning.* Cambridge, England: Cambridge University Press.

Voss, J. F., Greene, T. R., Post, T. A., & Penner, B. C. (1983). Problem-solving skill in the social sciences. In G. H. Bower (Ed.), *The psychology of learning and motivation* (Vol. 17). Orlando, FL: Academic Press.

Walker, C. H., & Yekovich, F. R. (1987). Activation and use of script-based antecedents in anaphoric reference. *Journal of Memory and Language, 26,* 673–691.

Warrington, E. K., & Shallice, T. (1984). Category specific semantic impairments. *Brain, 110,* 1273–1296.

Warrington, E. K., & Weiskrantz, L. (1968). New method of testing long-term retention with special reference to amnesic patients. *Nature, 217,* 972–974.

Warrington, E. K., & Weiskrantz, L. (1970). Amnesic syndrome: Consolidation or retrieval? *Nature, 228,* 628–630.

Wason, P. C., & Johnson-Laird, P. N. (1972). *Psychology of reasoning: Structure and content.* Cambridge, MA: Harvard University Press.

Wason, P. C., & Shapiro, D. (1971). Natural and contrived experience in a reasoning problem. *Quarterly Journal of Experimental Psychology, 23,* 63–71.

Watson, J. B. (1924). *Behaviorism.* New York: Norton.

Waugh, N. C., & Norman, D. A. (1965). Primary memory. *Psychological Review, 72,* 89–104.

Weber, R. M. (1970). First-graders' use of grammatical context in reading. In H. Levin & J. T. Williams (Eds.), *Basic studies in reading.* New York: Basic Books.

Wegner, D. M., & Schneider, D. J. (1989). Mental control: The war of the ghosts in the machine. In J. S. Uleman & J. A. Bargh (Eds.), *Unintended thought.* New York: Guilford.

Wegner, D. M., Schneider, D. J., Carter, S. R., & White, T. L. (1987). Paradoxical effects of thought suppression. *Journal of Personality and Social Pychology, 53,* 5–13.

Weisberg, R. W. (1993). *Creativity: Beyond the myth of genius.* New York: W. H. Freeman.

Weisberg, R. W., & Suls, J. M. (1973). An information-processing model of Duncker's candle problem. *Cognitive Psychology, 4,* 255–276.

Wernicke, C. (1874). *Der aphasische symptomencomplex.* Breslau, Germany: Franck U. Weigart.

Wickelgren, W. A. (1964). Size of rehearsal group and short-term memory. *Journal of Experimental Psychology, 68,* 413–419.

Wickelgren, W. A. (1965). Acoustic similarity and intrusion errors in short-term memory. *Journal of Experimental Psychology, 70,* 102–108.

Wickelgren, W. A. (1974). *How to solve problems.* New York: W. H. Freeman.

Wickens, C. D., & Kramer, A. (1985). Engineering psychology. *Annual Review of Psychology, 36,* 307–348.

Wickens, D. D. (1972). Characteristics of word encoding. In A. W. Melton & E. Martin (Eds.), *Coding processes in human memory.* Washington, DC: Winston.

Wickens, D. D., Born, D. G., & Allen, C. K. (1963). Proactive inhibition and item similarity in short-term memory. *Journal of Verbal Learning and Verbal Behavior, 2,* 440–445.

Widiger, T. A., & Trull, T. J. (1991). Diagnosis and clinical assessment. *Annual Review of Psychology, 42,* 109–133.

Winograd, E., & Neisser, U. (1992). *Affect and accuracy in recall: Studies of "flashbulb" memories.* New York: Cambridge University Press.

Wittgenstein, L. (1953). *Philosophical investigations.* (G. E. M. Anscombe, trans.). Oxford, England: Blackwell.

Wright, W. F., & Bower, G. H. (1992). Mood effects on subjective probability assessment. *Organizational Behavior and Human Decision Processes, 52,* 276–291.

Yarmey, A. D. (1979). *The psychology of eyewitness testimony.* New York: Free Press.

Yates, F. A. (1966). *The art of memory.* London: Routledge & Kegan Paul.

Yerkes, R. M., & Dodson, J. D. (1908). The relation of strength of stimulus to rapidity of habit-formation. *Journal of Comparative Neurology and Psychology, 18,* 459–482.

Zurif, E. B., Caramazza, A., Meyerson, R., & Galvin, J. (1974). Semantic feature representation for normal and aphasic language. *Brain and Language, 1,* 167–187.

Name Index

Subject Index

TO THE OWNER OF THIS BOOK:

We hope that you have found *Cognition: Theory and Applications,* 4th Edition, useful. So that this book can be improved in a future edition, would you take the time to complete this sheet and return it? Thank you.

School and address: _____

Department: _____

Instructor's name: _____

1. What I like most about this book is: _____

_____

_____

2. What I like least about this book is: _____

_____

_____

3. My general reaction to this book is: _____

_____

4. The name of the course in which I used this book is: _____

_____

5. Were all of the chapters of the book assigned for you to read? _____

   If not, which ones weren't? _____

6. In the space below, or on a separate sheet of paper, please write specific suggestions for improving this book and anything else you'd care to share about your experience in using the book.

_____

_____

_____

_____

_____

Optional:

Your name: _____ Date: _____

May Brooks/Cole quote you, either in promotion for *Cognition: Theory and Application,* 4th Edition, or in future publishing ventures?

Yes: _____ No: _____

Sincerely,

Stephen K. Reed

FOLD HERE

- -

BUSINESS REPLY MAIL

FIRST CLASS   PERMIT NO. 358   PACIFIC GROVE, CA

POSTAGE WILL BE PAID BY ADDRESSEE

ATT: *Stephen K. Reed*

Brooks/Cole Publishing Company
511 Forest Lodge Road
Pacific Grove, California 93950-9968

FOLD HERE